Histories of Anthropology

Gabriella D'Agostino • Vincenzo Matera
Editors

Histories of Anthropology

palgrave
macmillan

Editors
Gabriella D'Agostino
Department of Cultures and Societies
University of Palermo
Palermo, Italy

Vincenzo Matera
Department of Languages, Literatures,
Cultures and Mediations
University of Milano
Milan, Italy

ISBN 978-3-031-21257-4   ISBN 978-3-031-21258-1   (eBook)
https://doi.org/10.1007/978-3-031-21258-1

© The Editor(s) (if applicable) and The Author(s), under exclusive licence to Springer Nature Switzerland AG 2023
This work is subject to copyright. All rights are solely and exclusively licensed by the Publisher, whether the whole or part of the material is concerned, specifically the rights of translation, reprinting, reuse of illustrations, recitation, broadcasting, reproduction on microfilms or in any other physical way, and transmission or information storage and retrieval, electronic adaptation, computer software, or by similar or dissimilar methodology now known or hereafter developed.
The use of general descriptive names, registered names, trademarks, service marks, etc. in this publication does not imply, even in the absence of a specific statement, that such names are exempt from the relevant protective laws and regulations and therefore free for general use.
The publisher, the authors, and the editors are safe to assume that the advice and information in this book are believed to be true and accurate at the date of publication. Neither the publisher nor the authors or the editors give a warranty, expressed or implied, with respect to the material contained herein or for any errors or omissions that may have been made. The publisher remains neutral with regard to jurisdictional claims in published maps and institutional affiliations.

This Palgrave Macmillan imprint is published by the registered company Springer Nature Switzerland AG.
The registered company address is: Gewerbestrasse 11, 6330 Cham, Switzerland

CONTENTS

1 **Introduction: For a History of Anthropology in the Plural**   1
Gabriella D'Agostino and Vincenzo Matera

2 **People and Ideas from Elsewhere: Notes on Social Anthropology in the UK**   47
Luca Rimoldi and Marco Gardini

3 **French Anthropology, Ethnology of France and the Contemporary Turn**   75
Matteo Aria

4 **From Herder to Strecker: Birth and Developments of the Anthropological Notion of Culture in Germany**   127
Marco Bassi

5 **Cultural Anthropology in Italy in the Twentieth Century**   157
Fabio Dei

6 **Chronology of a Discipline: Social and Cultural Anthropology in Spain**   181
María Rubio Gómez, F. Javier García Castaño, and Gloria Calabresi

v

vi CONTENTS

7 From the Regime Ethnologists to the Democratic
Generation: Histories of Portuguese Anthropology 225
Giacomo Pozzi and Chiara Pussetti

8 Anthropology in Russia: From Nineteenth-Century
Ethnography to the New Post-Soviet Anthropology 251
Pietro Scarduelli

9 Indigenous Ethnologists, National Anthropologists,
Post-colonial Intellectuals: The Trajectory of
Anthropology in French-Speaking West and Equatorial
Africa 271
Alice Bellagamba

10 A Nerve Centre of the Discipline on the Periphery
of the Empire: South Africa and Anthropology in the
Twentieth Century 299
Stefano Allovio

11 American Anthropology: Some Distinctive Features 319
Angela Biscaldi

12 From Hegemony to Fragmentation: North American
Cultural Anthropology Over the Past Fifty Years 333
Berardino Palumbo

13 Trajectories and Subjects of Brazilian Anthropology 387
Valeria Ribeiro Corossacz

14 From the Study of Indigenous Cultures to the Critics
of Modernity: On Anthropology *made in* Colombia 403
Alessandro Mancuso

15 History of Anthropology in Mexico: From Nation
Building to the Recognition of Diversity 439
Rodrigo Llanes Salazar

CONTENTS vii

16 Social Anthropology in India: Studying the Self in the
   Other   469
   Sara Roncaglia

17 The Diverse Accounts of Anthropology in Viet Nam   517
   Elena Bougleux

18 Australian Anthropology in Its Colonial Context   549
   Dario Di Rosa

19 Five Paths for a History of the Pacific Islands   569
   Adriano Favole

20 Chinese Perspectives on Anthropology and Ethnology   593
   Roberto Malighetti

21 The Birth and Development of Anthropology in Arab
   Countries: A still Controversial and Marginalised
   Knowledge?   619
   Irene Maffi

Index   657

Notes on Contributors

Stefano Allovio is Full Professor of Social Anthropology and Cultural Anthropology. He has conducted ethnographic research in Italy (Western Alps) and in sub-Saharan Africa (Burundi, Democratic Republic of the Congo, South Africa). Among his works include *Pigmei, Europei e altri selvaggi* (Roma-Bari, 2010) and *Riti di iniziazione. Antropologi, stoici e finti immortali* (Milano 2014).

Matteo Aria is Associate Professor of Economic Anthropology, Popular Culture and Oceanian Culture at Sapienza University of Rome, where he also chairs the anthropology curriculum on the PhD programme in history, anthropology and religion. He conducted research work in Ghana on fishery and heritage-making processes, in French Polynesia on memory, land, heritage and the *passeurs culturels*, in New Caledonia on the *objets ambassadeurs* and the cultural policies of the Centre Culturel Tjibaou, and in Italy on blood donation, material culture and domestic objects. His most recent publications include *I doni di Mauss. Percorsi di antropologia economica* (Pisa, 2016); *Nuovi fermenti dell'antropologia oceanistica italiana* (eds. M. Aria, A. Favole, A. Paini), *L'Uomo*, n. 2, (Roma, 2018); *Occulto, segreto, indicibile* (ed. M. Aria), *Rivista di antropologia contemporanea*, n. 2 (Bologna, 2020); *Economie umane, economie intime: né per Dio né per denaro* (ed. M. Aria), *Lares*, LXXXVI, 2 (Roma); and *Ermenautica. Dai mari condivisi il segreto della convivenza* (ed. M. Aria, Milano, 2021).

Marco Bassi is Associate Professor of Anthropology. He is President of the Italian Association for Applied Anthropology (SIAA) and Councillor for Southern Europe and the Mediterranean of the ICCA Consortium.

He has experience in research and teaching at European, American and African universities, including Addis Ababa University, Alma Mater Studiorum University of Bologna, Johns Hopkins University, the University of Oxford and the University of Trento. He implemented his doctoral research among the Oromo-Borana and maintained interest in Oromo Studies (in Ethiopia). For this activity he received the Distinguished Scholarship Award of the Oromo Studies Association in 2011. He also engaged in applied and interactive research and in advocacy, networking and collaborating with the World Conservation Union (IUCN) and several other international organizations in rural development, biodiversity conservation, pastoralism, higher education and minority rights. Among his publications are the ethnographic book *Decisions in the Shade* (2005), the article "On the Borana Calendrical System: A Preliminary Field Report", published on *Current Anthropology* (1988, n. 4), and the chapter "Prophecy and Apocalypse Among the Oromo-Borana: The Power of chiasmus", in *Anthropology as Homage. Festschrift for Ivo Strecker* (2018).

Alice Bellagamba is Full Professor of Political Anthropology and African Cultures and Societies at the University of Milano-Bicocca, where she coordinates the PhD in Cultural and Social Anthropology. She was Alexander Von Humboldt Fellow at the University of Bayreuth in 2004–2005, Marie Sklodowska Curie–Eurias Fellow at the Institute for Advanced Studies in Berlin in 2011–2012 and Principal Investigator of the ERC grant "Shadows of Slavery in West Africa and Beyond: A Historical Anthropology" (2013–2018). With a long experience in ethnographic and historical research in West African contexts, she is the author of *L'Africa e la stregoneria. Saggio di antropologia storica* (Roma-Bari, 2008). With Sandra E. Greene and Martin A. Klein she edited *African Voices on Slavery and the Slave Trade, Vol. 1: The Sources* (2013) and *African Voices on Slavery and the Slave Trade, Vol. 2: Essays on Sources and Methods* (2016). She is the Principal Investigator of the research project Genealogies of African Freedoms (PRIN-2017, 2020–2023).

Angela Biscaldi is Associate Professor. Her research focuses on ethnography of communication, with particular interest in the performative, agentive and indexical aspects of everyday educational practices. She is co-author, with Vincenzo Matera, of the book *Ethnography. A Theoretically Oriented Practice* (Palgrave, 2021).

Elena Bougleux is Associate Professor of Cultural Anthropology, Anthropology of Asian areas and Anthropology of Intercultural Processes. She is the coordinator of the "Cultures and Knowledge" curriculum for the PhD in Humanistic Transcultural Studies at the University of Bergamo. Her research interests focus on the development of scientific thought from a constructivist and multicultural perspective and on the epistemological and social implications of knowledge construction processes. She has carried out extensive ethnographic research in Germany, India and Thailand. Since 2014 she collaborates with the Anthropocene Curriculum Project (Max Planck Institute for the History of Science and Haus der Kulturen der Welt, Berlin). Among her most recent publications include the following: "Complesso non controverso", in Risk Elaboration, Integrated Strategies for Resilience (www.riskelaboration.it, Vol. 2, n.1, 2021) and "La de / construzione dell'Antropocene". *Contaminazioni. Un approccio interdisciplinare* (Bergamo, 2021).

Gloria Calabresi teaches Sociology of Education, Methodology and Technique of Social Research. She is also a researcher at the Institute for Migration Research (University of Granada) and in the CEMYRI (Centre for the Study of Migration and Intercultural Relationships, Universidad de Almería). Her research is focused on the analysis of identities recognition processes and ethnic recognition movements in educational contexts and ethnic tourism with indigenous and Afro-descendants' communities (Brazil, Argentina and Colombia). Some of her recent publications are "Ethnicity and Religion in the Archipelago of San Andrés, Providencia and Santa Catalina (Colombia)", in *Bulletin of Latin American Research*, 35(4), 2016: 481–495; and "Les représentations identitaires dans l'éducation: une étude des élèves raizal de l'archipel de San Andrés, Providencia et Santa Catalina", in N. Le Vourch, F. Rodriguez (eds), *Pérennité ou changement: identités et représentations dans les aires culturelles caraïbes*, CRBC, Brest 2016.

F. Javier García Castaño is Full Professor (senior academic staff) of Social Anthropology. His research interest focuses on the anthropological analysis of educational processes as a process of transmission and construction of culture in contexts of cultural diversity (Andalucía, Spain). Since its creation, he was the coordinator of the research group Laboratorio de Estudios Interculturales at the Universidad de Granada. In 2009, he was designated director of the Institute for Migration Research, and from 2013, he is a supervisor of the inter-university doctoral programme in

xii   NOTES ON CONTRIBUTORS

migration studies (Universidad de Granada, University of Jaén and University of Pablo de Olavide). Some of his recent publications are "The Media Representation of Refugee Women in Spain: The Humanitarian Crisis of the First Female Refugees in the Press" (with A. Castillo Fernández, and A. Granados Martínez), in I. M. Gómez Barreto (ed.), *Handbook of Research on Promoting Social Justice for Immigrants and Refugees Through Active Citizenship and Intercultural Education* (2021); "La trampa de la diversidad: (des)igualdades en la escuela" (with M. Rubio Gómez), in Á. Solanes Corella (ed.) *Discriminación, racismo y relaciones interculturales* (2019, Aranzadi Thomson Reuters).

Valeria Ribeiro Corossacz is Associate Professor of Anthropology. She holds a doctorate degree in Social Anthropology from the EHESS of Paris and the University of Siena (2003). Since 1996 she has been conducting fieldwork in Brazil on racism, sexism and their intersection, focusing her interests on racial classification in day-to-day life and health documents, reproductive health, racism and white privilege, and the intersection of racism and sexism in paid domestic work. In Italy, she has carried out research on immigration and racism among industrial workers and on the intersection of racism and sexism in male violence against women. Among her last publications include the following: *White Middle-Class Men in Rio de Janeiro. The Making of a Dominant Subject* (2018) and the special issue "Brasil dividido. Os efeitos da eleição e do governo de Bolsonaro", *Confluenze. Rivista di Studi Iberoamericani*, 2021, organized with Filippo Lenzi Grillini.

Gabriella D'Agostino is Full Professor of Cultural Anthropology at University of Palermo. She is vice-president of the Italian Society of Cultural Anthropology (SIAC), editor-in-chief of the journal of human sciences *Archivio Antropologico Mediterraneo* https://journals.openedition.org/aam/ and scientific director of the international documentary film festival Sole Luna Doc Film Festival. Among her latest works is the book *Sous le traces. Anthropologie et contemporanéité* (Paris, 2018).

Fabio Dei is Associate Professor of Cultural Anthropology. His research focuses mainly on the forms of popular and mass culture in Italy and the anthropology of violence. He directs the scientific journals *Lares* (Olschki) and *Rivista di Antropologia Contemporanea* (Il Mulino). Among his most recent publications include *Cultura popolare in Italia. Da Gramsci all'UNESCO* (Bologna, 2018) and *James G. Frazer e la cultura del Novecento. Antropologia, psicoanalisi, letteratura* (Roma, 2021).

Dario Di Rosa after receiving his BA (University of Palermo) and MA (Ca' Foscari University of Venice), was awarded a PhD in Pacific History at the Australian National University (Canberra). Thanks to a generous Wenner-Gren Foundation grant, he conducted 15 months of ethnographic fieldwork with Kerewo speakers of the Kikori region of Papua New Guinea, complementing his extensive archival research on the colonial past of the region. After a period of precariat, he joined The University of South Pacific (Fiji) where is a lecturer at the School of Law and Social Science.

Adriano Favole Full Professor of Cultural Anthropology, is co-director of the "Luigi Bobbio" Centre for Public and Applied Social Research in Turin. He founded and directs the "Arcipelago Europa" Laboratory. An expert on Pacific Islands, he carries out field research in various areas and societies of Overseas Europe (Futuna and Wallis, New Caledonia, La Réunion, French Guiana) and has been a visiting professor at the Université de la Nouvelle-Calédonie and the Université de La Réunion. His main thematic interests are political anthropology, anthropology of the body and anthropology of the environment. He also boasts a significant commitment to the dissemination of scientific and anthropological knowledge, collaborating with various national newspapers and participating in festivals and radio and television broadcasts. His latest works include *Il mondo che avrete* (with M. Aime and F. Remotti) (Torino, 2020), as well as the editing of *L'Europa d'Oltremare* (Milano, 2020).

Marco Gardini is senior researcher (Rtd-B) in Cultural and Social Anthropology at the Department of Political and Social Sciences of the University of Pavia. He conducted research in Togo from 2006 to 2012, dealing with land conflicts and accusations of witchcraft. Since 2013 he has been conducting research in Madagascar on the legacy of slavery and contemporary forms of labour exploitation. He is the author of *La terra contesa. Conflitti fondiari e lavoro agricolo in Togo* (Milano, 2017) and of numerous articles in national and international journals, including *American Ethnologist, Social Anthropology, Politique Africaine, Ethnos, L'Uomo: società, tradizione e sviluppo* and *Africa. Rivista Semestrale di studi e ricerche*.

xiv NOTES ON CONTRIBUTORS

María Rubio Gómez works as junior research (assistant professor) in the Social Anthropology Department (Universidad de Granada) since 2017. She is a tutor in the doctoral programme in migration studies and coordinator of the bachelor's degree in social and cultural anthropology at the same university. The construction of otherness and diversity management in the school linked to the migration phenomenon and the intercultural education are their priority research lines. Some of her recent publications are: "Formación universitaria, migraciones e interculturalidad en España: Una revisión de la oferta educativa de los estudios de Grado de Educación Infantil, Educación Primaria, Pedagogía y Educación Social", *RASE. Revista de Sociología de la Educación*, 12 (2), (2019): 337–350; "Between Linguistic Sovereignty and Protected Migration: Language as Safe-Conduct in Migration from the Philippines to Italy" (with M. Cama, and F. J. García Castaño), *Deusto Journal of Human Rights*, n. 6, 2020: 43–68.

Irene Maffi is Professor of Cultural and Social Anthropology. A specialist on the Arab world, her research focuses on the emergence of post-colonial states in relation to cultural heritage–building processes and on women's sexual and reproductive health and rights and state health-care policies. Her most recent publications include *Women, Health and the State in the Middle East: The Politics and Culture of Childbirth* in *Jordan* (2012) and *Abortion in Post-revolutionary Tunisia: Politics, Medicine and Morality* (2020).

Roberto Malighetti is Full Professor of Cultural Anthropology at the University of Milano-Bicocca, where he inaugurated the first Italian chair of Anthropology of China and teaches a course on research methods in anthropology. After more than 20 years of ethnographic work in Brazil, mainly dedicated to the study of Afro-Brazilian cultures, he moved his research to China, focusing on Chinese anthropology and on the study of scientific, religious and ethnic complex articulations. Since 2013 he is visiting professor at Minzu University of China. His publications in several languages for national and international publishers deal with the above-mentioned topics.

Alessandro Mancuso is Associate Professor of Anthropology of Development and Anthropology of Environment at the University of Palermo. Doctor in Ethno-anthropological Sciences (University of Rome "La Sapienza"), he was awarded a post-doc research grant from the

Wenner-Gren Foundation and he has been "Maître de Conférences associé" au Collège de France (Chair of Anthropologie de la Nature). He has carried out a long field research in Colombia among the Wayùu of the Guajira peninsula and continues even today to have professional and research relationships with Colombian academic institutions. He is the author of several publications on Wayùu social organization and cosmology, on the ethnology of the indigenous peoples of South America, on the issues of indigenous rights and movements, on different aspects of the history of anthropology and on the "ontological turn" in anthropology. He is writing a book on the history of the ethnography of Yanomami. Among his works include *Altre persone. Antropologia, visioni del mondo e ontologie indigene* (Milano, 2018).

Vincenzo Matera is Full Professor of Cultural Anthropology at the University of Milan. He also teaches Social History of Culture at USI (Università della Svizzera Italiana). Latest publications include *Antropologia contemporanea* (Roma-Bari, 2017), *Antropologia dei social media* (with A. Biscaldi, Roma, 2019) and *Ethnography. A Theoretically Oriented Practice* (with A. Biscaldi, Palgrave Macmillan, 2021).

Berardino Palumbo teaches at the University of Messina where he is Full Professor of Social Anthropology. He has been a visiting professor at École pratique des hautes études (EPHE) in Paris and the University of Lausanne. He has carried out ethnographic research in Ghana (Western Region), North America (USA and Canada) and Italy (Campania, Sicily and Puglia). His most recent interests include processes of cultural heritage construction and their relationship with neoliberal governance, relationship between the Mafia and festive rituals, the anthropology of institutions and the nation state, and the links between religion and politics. In addition to numerous monographs (the most recent of which include: *Lo strabismo della DEA. Antropologia, accademia e società in Italia*, Palermo, 2018; *Piegare i santi. Inchini rituali e pratiche mafiose*, 2020; *Lo sguardo inquieto. L'etnografia tra scienza e narrazione*, Bologna, 2020), he has also published in international journals (*Comparative Studies in Society and History, Journal of Modern Italian Studies, Ethnology, Terrain, Anthropological Quarterly*, and *History and Anthropology*) and major national journals.

Giacomo Pozzi is a researcher in Cultural Anthropology. Between 2018 and 2020 he was a research fellow at the University of Milano-Bicocca. In 2018 he obtained the title of PhD in Cultural and Social Anthropology at the University of Milano-Bicocca in cotutorship with the PhD in Urban Studies of ISCTE-IUL and Universidade Nova de Lisboa. Since 2013, he has been conducting research in the areas of urban and contemporary anthropology on the topics of housing vulnerability, marginality and public policies between Portugal, Italy and Cape Verde. He is author of national and international articles and of the monograph *Fuori Casa. Antropologia degli sfratti a Milano* (Milano, 2020). He is also editor, together with Luca Rimoldi, of the volume *Pensare un'antropologia del welfare. Etnografie dello stato sociale in Italia* (Milano, 2022) and, together with Roberto Malighetti, of the volume *Antropologie giuridiche. Sguardi trasversali sulla contemporaneità* (Brescia, 2022).

Chiara Pussetti has lectured at graduate and post-graduate levels in Italy, Portugal and Brazil and has published extensively about migration, healthcare, body and emotions, social inequality, suffering and well-being. Chiara is an associate researcher at the Institute of Social Sciences of the University of Lisbon, PI of the ICS-UL team of the H2020 project ROCK (rockproject.eu) and of the project EXCEL (excelproject.eu). Her most recent publications include: Jarrín, A., Pussetti, C. (eds) 2021, *Remaking the Human*; Pussetti, C., Rohden, F., Roca, A. (eds) 2021, *Biotecnologias, transformações corporais e subjetivas*, ABA, UFRGS Edições; Pussetti, C., Barbosa, M. (eds) 2021, *Super-humanos* (Lisboa).

Luca Rimoldi is senior researcher (Rtd-B) in Cultural Anthropology at the "Riccardo Massa" Department of Human Sciences for Education (University of Milano-Bicocca). Between 2019 and 2021 he was junior researcher (Rtd-A) at the Department of Political and Social Sciences of the University of Catania. He is the author of national and international articles and of the monograph *Lavorare alla Pirelli-Bicocca. Antropologia delle memorie operaie* (Bologna, 2017). Since 2008 he has been carrying out ethnographic research in Italy and Senegal, focusing on social memory, work, urban smartization policies and waste management.

Sara Roncaglia has developed extended researches in the framework of anthropology of India, focusing on the anthropology of work and on the anthropology of food. She has published *Nutrire la città. I dabbawala di Mumbai nella diversità delle culture alimentari urbane* (Milano, 2010), *Feeding the City. Work and Food Culture of the Mumbai* (2013) and *Canti urbani. Trasformazioni del lavoro e degli spazi di vita a Mumbai* (Milano, 2019).

NOTES ON CONTRIBUTORS   xvii

Rodrigo Llanes Salazar is a Doctor in Anthropological Sciences (Metropolitan Autonomous University of Mexico). He is a full-time researcher at the National Autonomous University of Mexico, where he coordinates the undergraduate degree programme in intercultural development and management and teaches courses. His research has focused on the history of anthropology in Mexico, ethnicity, indigenous movements and anthropology of human rights. He was president of the Colegio de Antropólogos de Yucatán (Yucatecan Anthropological Association) between 2015 and 2019. His publications include the book *De la reforma multicultural a los megaproyectos: los derechos humanos del pueblo maya de Yucatán* (in press).

Pietro Scarduelli professor (retired) at the University of Piemonte Orientale, held seminars and courses at the University of Milan, University of Turin and University of Milano-Bicocca. His first fields of interest were the human sacrifice among the Aztecs and the mythology of the Siberian societies. After a fieldwork in 1980 among the Batangi of the Mbao district, in Kivu (Congo), he carried out researches for two decades in Indonesia, in the island of Nias, Alor and among the Toraja of Sulawesi, focusing on different issues as the traditional political organization (precolonial chiefdoms), "feasts of merit", headhunting, tourism and dynamics of cultural change. His last researches concern the feast of Indra Jatra in the Kathmandu Valley (Nepal) and the symbolic organization of the territory in Bhutan. He has published dozens of papers in scientific journals and 17 books on several issues such as ethnography of Indonesia, the symbolic organization of the space, religion, rite and power, ethnicity, nationalism and cultural globalization. His most recent books are *Per un'antropologia del XXI secolo* (2005), *Sciamani, stregoni, sacerdoti* (2007), *Culture dell'Indonesia* (2009), *L'Europa disunita. Etnografia di un Continente* (2013), *I riti del potere* (2014) and *Antropologia del nazionalismo. Stati Uniti, Unione europea, Russia* (2017).

CHAPTER 1

Introduction: For a History of Anthropology in the Plural

Gabriella D'Agostino and Vincenzo Matera

PAST REASONS, PRESENT PATHS

What are the reasons behind the "scientific" positioning that anthropology had adopted since its origins up to a few decades ago? They were certainly cognitive reasons, but they were intertwined with political concerns, ideological frameworks and cultural references. The urge to gain academic legitimacy, reliance on "Western-centric" perspectives and the aspiration to build broad, universal knowledge all played a role. Another significant role was played by its involvement in the project and the projection of colonial supremacy. These are all implicit factors that started to take on an increasingly deliberate problematic form and finally culminated in the "crisis of representation", falling into the wide-open sea of post-modernism, in an effort to "give a voice" to those who, despite

---

G. D'Agostino (✉)
University of Palermo, Palermo, Italy
e-mail: gabriella.dagostino@unipa.it

V. Matera
University of Milan, Milan, Italy
e-mail: vincenzo.matera@unimi.it

© The Author(s), under exclusive license to Springer Nature Switzerland AG 2023
G. D'Agostino, V. Matera (eds.), *Histories of Anthropology*,
https://doi.org/10.1007/978-3-031-21258-1_1

everything, still did not have one.[1] The structure of anthropology, which was a Western projection and, inside the West, a projection of modernity on the domestic "pockets" of backwardness, was forced to change because it was challenged by the increasingly strong quests for pluralism and the consequent requirement to rethink its very organisation. This change involved the standard perspective (from above) from which external and internal others were observed, and a rethinking of the overall epistemology that guided its action (theoretically and in the field). In the most recent debates, these changes were expressed and condensed into a few lines of reflection; for example, the notion of post-colony (Mbembe, 2021), the pressing quests for restitution (of the artefacts subtracted by European colonialism) and the notion of ontological turn (rethinking/ overcoming the nature-culture dualism, as well as many other central traits in Western intellectual history) (Colajanni, 2020; Descola, 2005; Mancuso, 2018, 2020). Such a trajectory marks not only the relationship between anthropology and its traditional objects of study, in the past as well as in the present, but also the relationship within the discipline, between centres and peripheries, between international and local trends (and influences), and between those who write in English and those who write in their national languages (Hannerz, 2010).

Let us take a step back. Anthropology is the attempt to produce knowledge and representations of other people. With regard to geographical spaces and historical times in which worldviews, systems of values and everyday dimensions of experience took on a form inscribed "in the behaviour and memory of living men" (Malinowski, 1978, p. 3), anthropology created tools, theoretical frameworks and methods in order to constitute differential discursive fields for focusing on these conceptions, values and experiences, with an ethical effort to change the very strong attitude of perceiving certain contexts—with reference to either the exotic other or the internal other, both of which are marginal, backward and, at best,

---

[1] As part of the post-modern turn, discussions were about, among other things, the idea that anthropological knowledge could be constituted by other voices and other points of view than those of researchers, to the extent of asking who, between the anthropologist and the natives, was really the author of the field notes and then of the ethnographic monograph (cf. Clifford, 1988), thus bringing the identity of the discipline, and at the same time its crisis, to the centre of attention. Among the relevant bibliographical references, see Said, 1978; Butler, 2002; Harvey, 1989; Rosaldo, 1993; Clifford, 1988, 1997; Spiro, 1996; Clifford & Marcus, 1986.

1 INTRODUCTION: FOR A HISTORY OF ANTHROPOLOGY IN THE PLURAL

traditional—as imperfect forms in comparison to ourselves. This inclination is so strong and deep-rooted that it still persists today.

Pushed, at least initially, by the risk of the disappearance of a huge number of cultural worlds, a richness for the whole of humanity—both in the wake of an improper biological metaphor and due to contact with the West, which would have ended up imposing its own way of life on those cultural worlds—the discipline has progressively developed full awareness of the mechanisms of construction of otherness that, at first sight, appeared to have been taken for granted.[2]

An anthropologist's work still focuses on a studied/constructed otherness, which is implicitly defined according to a tacit standard, that of Malinowski, the scholar with the colonial helmet of Euro-American origin and features, a white male, who lived alone amidst the natives for a year (Barley, 1986; Rabinow, 1977) and carried out asymmetric, top-down research (Hannerz, 2010; Nader, 1969), an ethnographic archetype (Clifford, 1988) that has still not been completely challenged (Fillitz, 2013). It is well known that anthropologists—especially those from the first part of the twentieth century—attempted to describe people whom they studied in the field not in their actual condition of contemporaneity with respect to the researcher, but placing aside the changes, the Westernisations and the modernisations, sometimes without hiding a certain annoyance or disappointment for the excessive "modernity" shown by the natives (external but also internal) in order to be able to reconstruct the original and authentic institutions and customs (Matera, 2017). This attempt constitutes the specificity of the discipline identified in its ability to produce "out-of-date knowledge" (Remotti, 2014). The British anthropologist Sally Falk Moore, in her history of Africanist anthropology, skilfully reconstructs the change in theoretical perspective that marked anthropology in the second half of the twentieth century. She identifies, alongside the main line of research, part of A. R. Radcliffe-Brown's comparative project of social anthropology, a second, scientifically marginal line of research. The first was aimed at the "pure" description of specific ways of life, as they probably were "before", as a result of the atemporal abstraction clearly deconstructed by Fabian (1983), but before when? Before the colonial period, of course, when indigenous life took place in full autonomy and with no contaminations. In addition, the second line was aimed at grasping ongoing changes in African communities because of

---

[2] Cf. Beattie, 1964; Kilani, 1994; Fabian, 2000.

migration or because of the influence of colonial institutions; it was a way of reporting that focused on the historical moment of fieldwork, but it did not have full academic recognition.

> Only the first approach fitted into Radcliffe-Brown's comparative project, however, and consequently only the first was treated as theoretically worthy and potentially productive of social laws and theoretical inference (Falk Moore, 1994, p. 39).

The colonial situation of almost all peoples studied by social anthropologists (or, in any case, the status of formal subaltern minority encapsulated within a hegemonic national state, as was the case for the American Indians) undoubtedly contributed towards enhancing "ahistorical" and essentialist stances.

In British colonial service roles, for example, the position of the civil servant anthropologist existed, who was both a researcher and a government consultant (Colajanni, 2012). On the other hand, the persistence of an "applied" approach in ex-colonial contexts is not a coincidence, as some of the chapters in this book will underline, as well as the perception of anthropology as a discipline "of the past", thus unfit to provide the requirements of modernity that several local universities were expected to support from their governments, as other chapters in the present volume will point out. Thus, the history of anthropology, the history of the gaze on cultural diversity that, from a certain point onwards, emerged in Western society, reveals, on the one hand, an undeniable "cognitive" dimension that moves and stimulates study, reflection and research; on the other hand, however, it reveals the cultural-historical and political components that opacify the former—today with strong evidence. From a certain period onwards, moreover, deconstruction invaded the field of the discipline and profoundly modified its frames of reference, possibly even weakening them.

According to Jean-Loup Amselle (2001, p. 45), it is a sort of contradiction to modify the idea of anthropology in a pluralist way. Indeed:

> a multiculturalist view of anthropology ignores the fact that this discipline has as its ultimate foundation the philosophy of the Enlightenment of the 18th century, that is, a universalist understanding of human knowledge [...]. The very idea of an anthropological pluralism—beyond the presence

1 INTRODUCTION: FOR A HISTORY OF ANTHROPOLOGY IN THE PLURAL

of different schools—therefore appears inconsistent with regard to the historical phenomenon that represents, in the history of the West, the emergence of a scientific comparative perspective.

This is where we believe that the conceptual framework from which this volume, *Histories of Anthropology*, originates becomes explicit. It is a framework in which several reflections converge. The awareness that cultural anthropology is made of the same material it studies brings the explicit understanding that although the connection with the universalism of the "philosophy of Enlightenment" is (or is supposed to be) clearly recognisable in other fields of knowledge, it is only partially so in anthropology. As Comaroff and Comaroff pointed out:

> Western enlightenment thought has, from the first, posited itself as the wellspring of universal learning, of Science and Philosophy, uppercase; concomitantly, it has regarded the non-West—variously known as the ancient world, the orient, the primitive world, the third world, the underdeveloped world, the developing world, and now the global south—primarily as a place of parochial wisdom, of antiquarian traditions, of exotic ways and means. Above all, of unprocessed data. These other worlds, in short, are treated less as sources of refined knowledge than as reservoirs of raw facts: of the historical, natural, and ethnographic minutiae from which Euromodernity might fashion its testable theories and transcendent truths, its axioms and certitudes, its premises, postulates, and principles. Just as it has capitalized on non-Western "raw materials"—materials at once human and physical, moral and medical, mineral and man-made, cultural and agricultural—by ostensible adding value and refinement to them. (2012, p. 1)

This essay does not intend to undertake a detailed survey of all the periods in the history of anthropology when the paradigm or comparative project dominated, as well as the scientific aspiration: the fact is that cultural and social anthropology has often been defined as "a comparative science of societies and cultures". Moreover, there have been many authoritative and influential voices of anthropologists who have followed the "universalist" line in their reflections and contributions to the discipline, faithful to the conception of Western science that tends to overcome historical and cultural diversity and variation, reducing them to a logical unity and invariance.[3] A few significant references will suffice here: Claude Lévi-Strauss, who defined the anthropologist's analytical task as a "path to abstraction", from the historical and empirical level of ethnography to the logical and abstract level of social anthropology (1953); Ernesto de Martino, in the name of "critical ethnocentrism"[4]: an effort to enlarge one's cultural consciousness in the face of every "other" culture, a critical awareness of the limits of one's own cultural, social and political history; tension underlying the "ethnographic humanness" that involves the historical understanding of oneself and of one's own culture, and even self-criticism, but without denying the primacy of Western civilisation, the most advanced model of scientific knowledge, of technology, of cultural development that cannot abdicate to other models and world visions. On the contrary, all of these, even though we must study, understand and legitimise them, have only one possible perspective for their future: the Western one.

The theoretical and methodological proposals of anthropologists like Dell Hymes (1974), who was aware of ethical and political issues, distinguishing between ethical and emic perspectives, or Clifford Geertz (1983), who presented the distinction between close to experience and far from experience concepts, can be considered along these epistemological lines. The quest for universalism, in short, penetrates even the most extreme relativism, such as that of interpretative anthropology, and rests on a basic discontinuity between "us" and the "others", which assumed many guises, for example, that between science and ethnosciences:

> We know that the natural world exists, some of us even make the study and knowledge of this or that aspect of it the object of their professional activity; and, of course, to be able to do this they have to avoid metaphysical and potentially paralysing doubts about the true existence of these worlds. Botany and zoology study forms that have tangible, analysable representations; [...]. The same classifications that one uses to collocate plants and animals in the larger schema that seems to underlie natural expressions are called scientific in order to convey the fact that, although they are created by men, they avoid variability and variation and instead provide an unfailing framework to which different forms can be anchored. [...] We westerners,

---

[3] With regard to the comparative character of anthropology and the main considerations on this matter, we merely refer here to Fabietti, 2001, 189-226 (chapter VI "Comparing") and the references cited there.

[4] See: Lanternari, 1977, 1990; Signorelli, 2015; Satta, 2018.

1 INTRODUCTION: FOR A HISTORY OF ANTHROPOLOGY IN THE PLURAL   7

however, are accustomed to reserving the name "science" for a particular way of knowing, with specific requirements of universality, verifiability, coherence and objectivity. [...]. Nevertheless, each culture has its own worldviews, moulded by specific cognitive needs, which are not necessarily valid for other cultures. At their very heart, these visions display constitutive principles, and regularities, and empirical verifiability: they are fully entitled sciences; but, in order to comply with their local and non-ecumenical character, we might call them ethnosciences. (Cardona, 1986, pp. 10-11)

Giorgio Cardona tacitly claims the supremacy of Western science with its logics, its models, its criteria of categorisation, its comparative analyses from which and thanks to which we are able to study ethnosciences; nonetheless, there is a strong interest in the ways of thinking and classification of other peoples, people who live according to their ontologies and think according to their epistemologies, as we would say today.[5]

These few references clearly demonstrate the conceptual gap that marks the history of the discipline: as a scientific comparative perspective, anthropology cannot abdicate its own universe of recognition, even though it dedicates itself—but we could even say *in order to dedicate* itself—to the study and understanding of different universes of recognition (Augé, 1994). The knowledge-oriented approach that moves anthropologists (Fabietti, 1998) is not present in other epistemologies, which do not derive from the philosophy of Enlightenment and cannot thus be at the foundation of any universal knowledge. This strain—which is always present and experienced by anthropologists to different extents—is at the very core of the so-called ontological turn, which dominates the debate today and appears as the pluralistic "revolution" capable of rebalancing the discipline's placement. We will return to this point later.

The anthropological stance, therefore, however one regards it, appears to be hierarchical. "We" have supremacy (political, cultural, scientific) and from such supremacy we look to "others". However, despite many efforts, the movement leading to the constitution of a scientific discipline (progressive definition of paradigms—objects, terms, theories, common goals) in anthropology remains incomplete. Indeed, it provoked deconstructions, self-criticisms and many turns. More generally, it provoked the crisis of representation. The discipline struggles to emerge from this crisis, at

---

[5] Furthermore, if Western science is a procedure that provides "order" to the world, its paradigms are also part of a "cosmology" (Herzfeld, 2001).

least with regard to the theory of culture, notwithstanding the great diffusion and, to some extent, the strengthening that it has had in recent years. Yet Edward Said made it very clear that only a change in power relations between the imperialist West and its anthropological "other" would lead to a way out of the crisis (Said, 1978). Such a marked sense of self-criticism has had and still has consequences on the entire cognitive project undertaken by anthropology.

This is another reason why we decided to write a partial, but still significant, history of anthropology in the plural; in other words, we asked ourselves whether the categories anthropologists used throughout the twentieth century were indeed the same; whether we can really say, without a doubt, that "we" anthropologists share a common body of knowledge. If not, as many of the essays in this book make clear, it follows specifically from the perspective of a plural history of the discipline that perhaps anthropologists should have done more to create a community (an academic community).

Many of the core categories of the discipline—"culture", "identity", "diversity", "people and folk", "magic", "religion", "ritual" and "ethnography"—reveal similarities, but on closer analysis these similarities appear to be merely superficial, and substantial differences emerge. Are these differences just "differences of schools"? Or are they more significant? And when "native" anthropologists appeared on the disciplinary scene, did they not increase their divergences? It is well known that "native" anthropologists have in some cases developed very different perspectives and contributions, sometimes even contrasting with those of their Western colleagues, who are internationally acknowledged (in the centres), though extraneous to the culture they studied. For example, as Adriano Favole points out in his contribution to this volume, many local anthropologists in the Pacific Island area:

> would choose *fiction* (novellas, poems, novels, theatre) as their format for anthropological dissemination. For these authors, it is non-fiction, with its "cold", abstract and detached language, with its theories far removed from the experience of the natives, that conveys the colonial legacy of anthropological studies. The decolonisation of knowledge in the Pacific passed through this literary turning point [...] (*infra*).

Anthropology in its academic form—says Favole—is a kind of knowledge that, as one would say in the Polynesian language of Futuna, is *mei*

1 INTRODUCTION: FOR A HISTORY OF ANTHROPOLOGY IN THE PLURAL   9

tai, from "overseas", originating in those European and Western countries such as the United Kingdom, France and the United States, which were the protagonists of the colonisation of the Pacific.

Alice Bellagamba in her chapter argues a similar point:

> African anthropologists [...] found themselves at a dead end. The more they practised the discipline according to European and North American academic standards, the more their governments considered them worthless; the more they focused on objectives that made sense with regard to the transformation processes going on, the more their scientific production was diminished by their European and North American colleagues (*infra*).

Pluralism, then, stimulates the discipline from different directions, triggers radical upheavals and invites it to deal with a broad demand for a methodological and epistemological decolonisation of the way of thinking (Mbembe, 2021). *Out of the Dark Night*, the title of an important book by Achille Mbembe, a leading figure in the post-colony debate, means breaking the epistemological hegemony that the West—Europe, France and the United States—in the name of "technical thought" represented as neutral, has imposed and still strives to impose today. Anthropology, in particular "scientific" anthropology (but it is not the only type, since many deconstructions do not remove the primacy of the West), is involved.

Let us take Franz Fanon's thought as a starting point for a reflection that could lead to reversing the current idea of decolonisation as a historical process that started around the 1950s and ended thirty years later with the progressive declaration of the sovereignty of previously colonised territories and peoples (cf. Geertz, 2004). Without much friction, the colonial countries found very little contradiction between their proclaimed liberality—the self-determination of peoples and other "sacred" principles—and the brutalities of their colonialism. The technical connotation wraps up and delimits a political process, whose consequences and extent would be very much wider. It would be enough, for example, to consider potential research hypotheses in the history of ideas with regard to decolonisation to fully comprehend its scope:

> Another possibility is to start looking for key areas in the history of ideas, for the intellectual challenges that fostered the end of colonial empires and that, in turn, were raised by decolonization. This allows us to capture voices both in the formerly colonized world and in the ex-metropoles, as well as to do

justice to the overlap between intellectual and practical-political questions. At least four such challenges may be discerned: the "discovery" of decolonization as a normal historical path; the different ways of thinking about postcolonial sovereignty; the interpretation of colonialism as a historically finite situation; finally, the "invention" of the Third World as a new concept for world order. (Jansen & Osterhammel, 2017, pp. 158-59)

According to Fanon (1961), and later Mbembe (2021), post-decolonisation African elites, instead of embracing the idea that Western modernity was imperfect, incomplete and partial, followed the European models of capitalist development, popular sovereignty and self-determination. According to Fanon, decolonisation would be a chance to culturally provincialise Europe and its claims to represent Universal History and Reason, and to constitute something new, a "new humanism" (Fanon, 1961) that would overcome nationalism, capitalism, racism, indiscriminate exploitation and environmental devastation. Things went differently. The technical approach based on a Western positivist perspective—which was objective and neutral—imposed itself almost everywhere, from politics to economics, from administration to education, health, culture and art. Half a century later, what do we have? As Mbembe points out:

As Fukuyama wrote his epitaph to history, Africa was in the midst of a spectacular collision. While Apartheid and white minority rule were coming to a formal end in South Africa, a genocide of cataclysmic proportions was unfolding in Rwanda. The apotheosis of long years of struggle on the one hand, self-destruction on the other. Declining per capita incomes and production, low levels of savings and investment, slow growth in agricultural production, failing export earnings, strangled imports and unserviceable foreign debt burdens—all plagued most of sub-Saharan Africa. [...]. Disease, overpopulation, unprovoked crime, scarcity of resources, refugee migrations, the increasing erosion of nation-states and international borders, and the empowerment of private armies, security firms, and international drug cartels are now most tellingly demonstrated through a West African prism". (Mbembe, 2021, pp. 8-9)

Developments in Africa and its experiments in neoliberal deregulation are nothing but the future of global capitalism itself. This, in Mbembe's view, is a bleak future, characterised by a growing crisis of reproduction in which human lives are increasingly devalued and worthless. The destructive action of an economic morality (or moral economy) that revalues

1 INTRODUCTION: FOR A HISTORY OF ANTHROPOLOGY IN THE PLURAL   11

human beings as commodities, and in so doing reformulates the self as a market device, is particularly evident.[6] Africa—as well as many other areas of the world—demonstrates that capitalism in its neoliberal form is increasingly incompatible with democracy. Indeed, Mbembe does not disregard the fact that Africa has become an experimental playground for the global rise of power and influence of China, a "power without idea" (2021, p. 65).[7] Mbembe identifies a way out of hegemony and catastrophe in what he calls *Afropolitanism*. Its basic components are, on the one hand, the post-colonial literature by African intellectuals such as Ahmadou Kourouma and Yambo Ouologuem in the 1970s, together with the reflections of scholars such as Paul Gilroy, Stuart Hall, Felwine Sarr, Saidiya Hartman, Hazel Carby and Eduoard Glissant; on the other, a renewal of mobility, migrations and new African diasporas. *Afropolitanism* amplifies the idea held by Edouard Glissant of the valorisation of "strangeness" and of relational identities (Glissant, 1996). For Mbembe, the act of acknowledging the truth and undertaking reparatory actions would be crucial historical and cultural actions and would promote new connections and relationships. Since then, however, the events of history took a different direction.[8] In other words, post-colonial theory, which was a cornerstone

---

[6] A device that has already been identified at the root of global organ trafficking (Scheper-Hughes, 2000): the act of selling a kidney, of selling an eye, by placing a blood print on a sheet of paper, are choices (so to say) that reflect the grip of technical perspectives (economics, biomedical practices, social relations, or hierarchies) in a (re)definition of the relationship between subjectivity and corporeality.

[7] As Comaroff and Comaroff observed: "What if we posit that, in the present moment, it is the global south that affords privileged insight into the workings of the world at large? [...] That, in probing what is at stake in it, we might move beyond the north-south binary, to lay bare the larger dialectical processes that have produced and sustain it" (Comaroff & Comaroff, 2012, pp. 1-2). And then: "these frontiers fostered conjunctures of Western and non-Western values, desires, conventions, and practices, fusions that fueled the destructive, innovative urges of Euromodernity, but with little of the ethical restraint that reined them in 'back home'" (Comaroff & Comaroff, 2012, p. 5).

[8] Recurrent waves of xenophobia, racism and violence; the assault by right-wingers against critical race theory and post-colonial theory, in the United States, United Kingdom, France and many other European countries. Riots in the Parisian banlieues reveal France's failure in thinking post-colonial, according to Mbembe (2021), a failure that is catastrophic in its consequences on how France faces its persistent problems of racism and discrimination against minorities, whether they are African, Arab, Asian or Caribbean. This failure not only is a mark of France, as is quite evident, but causes a Western downfall (or return) to inhumanity. In all of this, it is extremely difficult to think that Westerners will ever be able to stop approaching others without the attitude that only their own reality matters.

of Western intellectual and cultural discourse throughout the 1980s and 1990s, did not have any effect; on the contrary, it is now being rejected, which is perhaps a sign of a crisis among Western intellectual elites in the face of globalisation, making historical self-praise and claims to represent humanism and universalism increasingly outdated. The trend noted by Clifford Geertz (2000) towards the "cultural centrality of the self" is thus affirmed.

The discussion about the restitution of objects and artefacts subtracted from native peoples during European colonialism, a regular discussion connected with decolonising movements in Africa, Australia and other parts of the world and Europe, is significant in this regard.[9] There are several arguments against restitution. One such argument is legalism: since the original owners of the artefacts in European museums are not always known, they cannot be legally returned. Or, according to others, the "universal" rights of access by the majority, as well as the rights of the institutions in charge of "studying" these objects, prevail over the rights of the local communities reclaiming them.[10] Another such argument is paternalism: in Africa and elsewhere there are not institutions, knowledge or resources to preserve artefacts. We do not have space here to discuss all of the aspects that the issue of restitution presents, but the one that involves the curatorship (related to museums, curators, archaeologists, anthropologists and indigenous communities) of the artefacts deserves a mention (Harrison, 2013; Isaac, 2009). To a large extent, the indigenous critique of museum practices concerns the categorisation, management and preservation of artefacts according to procedures that are not only extraneous to indigenous ontologies, but also potentially offensive, or even dangerous (Henry, 2004; Sully, 2007) in relation to a perspective that perceives artefacts as people-objects. This leads us to the second theme that was previously mentioned: the ontological turn. Limiting ourselves to the essential questions for the purposes of this text, in the wake of the early work of Bruno Latour (1991, 1999), Philippe Descola (2005) and Viveiros de Castro (2012), we shall condense the last turn (after the interpretative, linguistic and moral ones),[11] towards perspectivism and indigenous "ontologies" as seriously taking in all its consequences a minimal common trait that consists in an enlargement of human beings' (subjects') own

[9] Cfr. Fforde *et al.* 2002; Kramer, 2006.
[10] Harrison, 2013; Paini & Aria, 2017.
[11] Cfr. Fassin, 2012, 2013; Faubion, 2011.

1 INTRODUCTION: FOR A HISTORY OF ANTHROPOLOGY IN THE PLURAL 13

agentivity to a large realm of non-humans. Perhaps the most relevant of all these consequences in the present theoretical and historical framework might be the dissolution of the very foundations of anthropology itself: in addition to the nature/culture dichotomy, gift, structure, kinship, identity, body, ethnography, reflexivity, participant observation and so on, in an overall dissolving of Science (Latour, 1991). Dell Hymes (1974), within the framework of linguistic anthropology (Matera, 2005), however, already stressed that no phenomenon can be considered in advance as non-communicative,[12] quoting a scholar who has been remembered (see Mancuso, 2018) as a precursor of the ontological turn:

> An informant told me that many years before he was sitting in a tent one summer afternoon during a storm together with an old man and his wife. There was one clap of thunder after another. Suddenly the old man turned to his wife and asked, "did you hear what was said?" "No", she replied, "I didn't catch it". My informant, an acculturated Indian, told me he did not at first know what the old man and his wife referred to. It was, of course, the thunder. The old man thought that one of the Thunder Birds had said something to him. He was reacting to this sound in the same way as he would respond to a human being, whose words he did not understand. The casualness of the remark and even the trivial character of the anecdote demonstrate the psychological depth of the "social relations" with other-than-human beings that becomes explicit in the behavior of the Ojibwa as a consequence of the cognitive "set" induced by their culture. (Hallowell, 1960, p. 33)

Among the Ojibwa, as Hallowell (1960, p. 56) reports, stones are conceived as potentially animate and are, in fact, classified in their grammar as an animate gender.

Additional interesting contributions come from the studies of hunter-gatherer groups in the subarctic area.[13] Many others can be added to this data; for example, the more recent ones presented by Elizabeth Povinelli (1994a, 1994b, 2002), which nonetheless predate the "ontological turn", concerning the disputes for lands between Aborigines and non-Aborigines in Australian courts. The Aboriginal conception of rocks and other objects as beings that were capable of hearing, feeling, smelling and so on was incomprehensible to the officials of the Lands Commission who did not

---

[12] Nevertheless, the structuralist and semiotic lessons do not say anything different.
[13] Ridington, 1988; Rushefort, 1986; Scollon & Scollon, 1979.

belong to local communities. They could only qualify Dream narratives as native beliefs, whereas for Aboriginal people they were evidence of the authenticity of their claims. As Povinelli argues, they are more than just native "beliefs": they are indications of a set of relationships with nature and a set of practices with and within the natural environment in opposition to the capitalist notion of "work". Moreover, the UNESCO paradigm itself was forced to revise its claims to universality in the wake of the requests made by those who could not make reference to the notion of heritage according to the standards of the International Organisation, with the Conventions of 2003 and 2005.[14]

Towards World Anthropologies

The issues discussed in the previous pages pertain to the epistemological sphere; they are accompanied by a reflection on the historical events and trajectories of the discipline. Unlike works concerning the history of anthropology in the singular, as a unique discipline with respect to a range of different traditions, this volume intends to offer a perspective on the *histories* of anthropology. In addition to what is widely known, this approach embraces some disciplinary traditions that are still mostly unknown to non-specialists. The aim is to present a privileged insight as to how the main traditions have been accepted, adapted and adjusted in different cultural and historical-geographical contexts, as well as to define the current role of the anthropological approach in such contexts.

Indeed, the volume introduces the histories of anthropology including not only the best-known European and American traditions but also the minor traditions in Europe and beyond, with a specific focus on the outcomes of these traditions in the present. With an eye on the schematic, yet useful partition introduced by Stocking (1982) and later resumed by Hannerz (2010), between "nation-building" anthropology and "empire-building" anthropology, the forms and paths of the discipline are investigated. Special attention will be paid to former colonial contexts, so as to underline how dominant anthropologies have been accepted and then organised, which theoretical and methodological perspectives have been privileged by different institutions and academies, how the anthropological approach has been shaped up and adapted to the quest for

---

[14] The Convention for the Safeguarding of the Intangible Heritage and the Convention on the Protection and Promotion of the Diversity of Cultural Expressions respectively.

1 INTRODUCTION: FOR A HISTORY OF ANTHROPOLOGY IN THE PLURAL 15

knowledge related to specific territorial configuration, and which schools have been consolidated. In brief, chapters are "cultural stories" pinpointing the historical and geo-political contexts that have influenced and produced every single disciplinary tradition; and such stories also draw attention to the local contributions, the influential role of centres towards peripheries or, vice versa, how peripheries have "learnt from centres" so as to reprocess significant, recognisable disciplinary lines with special attention to current research.

It is also a way to think about "locality in the schemes about global cultural flows" (Appadurai, 1996, p. 178), and it has something to do with how a nation-state is established through its past and preserved thanks to its vision for the future. Academic communities are "neighbourhoods", namely tangible, real, even different social forms that potentially allow self-replication within a "locality" depending on mutual power relations too. We found this to be the highest spatial and scalar dimension that can be singled out as the origin of disciplinary stories. The neighbourhoods and localities underlying such stories can be put down to colonisation (historically verified or not), and we will look to bringing out the modalities and (any possible) forms of decolonisation. In this volume we intend to put into action a project that has been with us for a long time, that is, the plural declension of the history of the discipline in a double sense: pluralism in traditions that, to some extent, are connected to Western-European centres of knowledge production, with interesting known paths and possible future scenarios, as well as pluralism of possible narratives in relation to each detected area.

We are aware we might be giving a partial and partisan account of how that knowledge has shaped up over time. Partial because in nearly all cases the authors of the chapters do not belong in those contexts, despite their wealth of direct experience in fieldwork and/or as members of collaborative networks. We are also aware of the fact that some areas of the world still haven't managed to make their voice heard. In some cases, we were not able to identify any available representatives; at other times, despite trying to bring them in the project, we had to give up as they didn't show their unwillingness until it was "past the deadline", which made it difficult to replace them. In the end, it was too late when we realised that we hadn't taken Ulf Hannerz's precious advice to heart when it comes to editorial work as a concrete intellectual and organizational exercise. [...] you have to come up with a basic idea, and polish it, delimit it [...], and you have to identify your desired contributors (and also those who, having acquired notoriety for not delivering, should be avoided), recruit them, and then manage them. (2010, pp. 13-14)

A partisan project? Yes, because it is certainly an Italian point of view about the stories of anthropology. We are well aware of all the risks and limitations, yet we intended to make a contribution to anthropological narratives on behalf of an academic context that is not given much widespread visibility in spite of its international exchanges. However, all historical reconstructions are subject to the risk of partiality that might only be reduced with multiplied viewpoints on the same context, but we are not certain how fruitful this would be. Needless to say, all perspectives are contingent on the observer's position, their space and time, and this will inevitably have an impact on the selection process as well as the product of historical narration. Not to mention that any form of historical narration runs the risk of being an "inverted filiation", an arbitrary choice of prior events starting from the present and its queries for those questioning the past (D'Agostino, 2020, p. 120).

If such initiatives have not been taken in the Italian publishing system, other areas have already come up with some aspects to reflect on, so we would like to call attention to some directions.[15] Beforehand, interest in the history of the discipline as an autonomous "sub-field" of study had articulately arisen in the 1960s. In 1977, Regna Darnell[16] authored a

---

[15] However, a recent work edited by Matera and Biscaldi (2021) follows a disciplinary historical reconstruction, although it has a different configuration. Amongst the *histories* that have been circulating, Barth, Gingrich, Parkin, Silverman's work (Barth et al., 2005) has certainly held a prominent place, although it is limited to the British, German, French and American patterns, as seen in its subheading. More recently, in 2018, as discussed later, *The International Encyclopedia of Anthropology* published by Wiley offers a more deliberate openness to disciplinary national and regional histories.

[16] A well-known academic in the field of history of anthropology; other than her works about anthropological linguistics, among her scholarly output concerning our topic of interest, we mention *And Along Came Boas: Continuity and Revolution in Americanist Anthropology* (John Benjamins Publishing Company, 1988); *Theorizing the Americanist Tradition* (University of Toronto Press, 1999); *Invisible Genealogies: A History of American Anthropology* (University of Nebraska Press, 2001). She is the credited author of the annual series "Histories of Anthropology" (HOAA), co-editor Frederic W. Gleach, published by the University of Nebraska Press.

1 INTRODUCTION: FOR A HISTORY OF ANTHROPOLOGY IN THE PLURAL   17

significant article about the history of anthropology in "historical perspective" ("History of Anthropology in Historical Perspective"), where she pinpointed 1962 as the year when such interest and approach first emerged in the conference endorsed by *Social Science Research Council* in New York. When reviewing the conference, Dell Hymes pointed out that its interest didn't lie in the "intrinsic value of an occurrence [...] as much as the fact that it *did* occur":

> The occurrence of a formal conference on the history of anthropology marks a definite shift that affects the interests and fortunes of all anthropologists. (Hymes, 1962, p. 25)

Since it was a conference about the history of social sciences, Hymes expressed his appreciation for the fact that the conference participants were also anthropologists but wondered about whether historians or anthropologists would write the disciplinary history, or whether only historians or anthropologists would take part in it.[17] Hymes encouraged training initiatives for professionals who required both historical and anthropological education. He briefly focused on three distinctive features: whether such professionalisation was already in effect; the importance of disciplinary history compared to theory; and how the disciplinary historical and anthropological perspectives could be made to converge (Hymes, 1962, p. 26). And, as an example of real history of professional anthropology, he mentioned Stocking's conference paper.[18] This account is interesting, however brief, because it provides us with an undefined epistemological picture that will then become clear and more mature with the following outcomes.[19] In addition to that, taking Stocking's

---

[17] See also Rubio Gómez, García Castaño, and Calabresi's essay in this volume.

[18] "Matthew Arnold, E.B. Tylor, and the Uses of Invention", published the following year (Stocking Jr., 1963).

[19] When noticing that only few conference participants could be called professional historians, Hymes identified some qualifying common traits in their approach: the use of unusual unpublished sources, such as letters; attention to textual datum, to the relation between ideas and their verbal incorporation; attention to meanings while keeping track of their use in the past and not as mere semantics; the ability to refer to an author in the horizontal dimension of his contemporaneity rather than following a vertical dimension as a linear sequence through time; acute awareness of the historical context and its issues in order to avoid articulating a priori anachronistic analyses to favour evaluations emerging from historical relativism instead, which could keep ethnocentrism under control (Hymes, 1962, p. 26).

18   G. D'AGOSTINO AND V. MATERA

conference papers as an instructive example of the history of anthropology is a clear indicator of the direction being taken.

Nevertheless, in the above-mentioned article, Darnell commented on Stocking's role as follows:

> His own credentials as a historian gave him the dubious honour of becoming the methodological mentor of the emerging subfield of history of anthropology. (Darnell, 1977, p. 400)[20]

In the few final pages on national traditions, the scholar underlined how in reference literature about the history of anthropology, the discipline was considered uniquely as a product of Western civilisation and remarked that "the question of how many anthropologies there might be within that western tradition remains obscure" (Darnell, 1977, p. 412). The production in the Anglophone area mainly looked at the American and British traditions, with brief references to the French and German traditions. So, she added:

> The specific relationship of anthropology in other parts of the world to these major developments is not explored in comparative terms. The literature which does exist is widely scattered and tends to present dates, names, and facts in the restricted context of a single country. (*ibidem*)

In 1973, thanks to a Stocking's initiative, *History of Anthropology Newsletter* (HAN) was implemented as a publishing project with the aim of providing different perspectives in the global context. The Editorial Board included Robert Berkhofer (University of Wisconsin), Dell Hymes (University of Pennsylvania), Robert Bieder (Newberry Library), Judith Modell (University of Minnesota), Regna Darnell (University of Alberta), George Stocking (University of Chicago) and Timothy Thoresen (University of Texas). In the opening typewritten page, Stocking (remembering how a decade after the Conference of Social Science Research Council had taken place, interests in the perspective on history of anthropology had increased) introduced the goals of such an initiative:

---

[20] With regard to this, Darnell makes reference to Stocking's reflection on "historicism" and "presentism", which launched a mature focalisation of the matters involved in history writing. The essay was published both in the first issue of *Journal of the History of the Behavioral Sciences* (1965), and in Stocking Jr. (1968).

1 INTRODUCTION: FOR A HISTORY OF ANTHROPOLOGY IN THE PLURAL 19

As in any developing field of historical inquiry, the prospects are inviting, but the problems are many. It is nice to have all that unobstructed acreage, but it would be nice also to have a few more landmarks to guide one through it: information as to archival holdings, bibliographic aids, research in progress, recent publications, and so forth. It is to meet such needs that a group of us decided to try to put out a semi-annual newsletter. We figure we can sustain one or two issues on our own resources and enthusiasm. After that, it will probably take a good deal of audience participation. We encourage you all to join in. (1973)[21]

As for the later productions, it is interesting to mention some works about an articulate and almost complete recognition of contemporary national anthropologies. Among these is *The Shaping of National Anthropologies*, a special issue of "Ethnos" journal in 1982. Project editors Tomas Gerholm and Ulf Hannerz stated its purposes as follows:

our concern is metaanthropology; an anthropology of anthropology. Or actually of anthropolog*ies*. For we are inquiring into the bases of unity and diversity of international social and cultural anthropology. (1982, p. 5)[22]

They introduced anthropology as practised in six different countries— India, Poland, Sudan, Canada, Brazil, Sweden—and entrusted the analysis

---

[21] A reference point for decades, in 2016, HAN's issue n. 40 was put online on open access. HAN stopped printing in 2013 due to Henrika "Riki" Kuklick's death (she took up the reins from Stocking in 2004). The editorial contains a short reminder of the history of the journal, while its goals and purposes are herein reaffirmed and renewed in view of its new digital format. In 2019 its name was changed to *History of Anthropological Review* (HAR). In 2016 HOAN, "History of Anthropological Network", was relaunched during the 14th EASA biennial conference in Milan, and it came after HEAN, "History of the European Anthropology Network", born at the 2nd EASA conference in Prague in 1992. HOAN's Advisory Board is made up of 14 members belonging to institutions from Austria, Brazil, Czech Republic, France, Germany, Great Britain (2 members), Poland, Portugal, Slovenia, Sweden, United States (3 members). Its "Circle of Correspondents" includes scholars from Austria, Brazil, Canada, Croatia, France, Germany, Great Britain, Greece, Hungary, Italy, Lithuania, New Zealand, the Netherlands, Norway, Poland, Portugal, Romania, Russia, Serbia, Spain, Turkey, the United States and an expert from the Arctic and Siberian areas. The Italian correspondent is Filippo Zerilli, from the University of Cagliari.

On the HOAN website—History of Anthropology Network (HOAN) (easaonline.org)— additional references to other editorial projects on the history of the discipline are also available for anyone who is interested.

[22] For a summary of this issue cf. Hannerz, 2010, pp. 14-18.

20   G. D'AGOSTINO AND V. MATERA

to six experts, along with Hannerz, who saw to the chapter about Sweden[23] and George W. Stocking, who penned the afterword. Although some works looked further on the situations underlying the chosen paths and styles in their respective contexts, a wider question arose: "The world order of anthropology" (*ibid.*, p. 6). And even though the editors were subscribing the content of Maurice Freedman's epigraph—"it could be argued as an absorbing paradox that internationalism and transcultural nature of anthropology lie precisely in its plurality of national viewpoints"—they noticed how those traditions didn't carry the same relevance and, with the exception of nineteenth-century Germany,[24] Great Britain, France and the United States undoubtedly played a prominent role:

> the map of the discipline shows a prosperous mainland of British, American, and French anthropologies, and outside it an archipelago of large and small islands—some of them connected to the mainland by sturdy bridges or frequent ferry traffic, others rather isolated. (*ibid.*)

Here, in his comments on the special issue, Stocking kept his focus on the Euro-American tradition and could identify "nation-building" and "empire-building" anthropologies, those revolving around *Volkskunde* and *Völkerskund*, as well as internal otherness in the nation state building process and external otherness as the bedrock and driving force of overseas empires (1982, p. 172). Therefore, the scholar brought up the issue of

---

[23] The table of contents is listed as follows: "Uncertain Transplants: Anthropology and Sociology in India", by Satish Saberwal (Jawaharlal Nehru University, New Delhi); "Polish Ethnography after World War II", by Józef Burszta (University of Poznań, Poland) and Bronislawa Kopczyńska-Jaworska (University of Lódź, Poland); "The State of Anthropology in the Sudan", by Abdel Ghaffar M. Ahmed (University of Khartoum, the Sudan); "In Bed with The Elephant: Anthropology in Anglophone Canada", by Gordon Inglis (Memorial University of Newfoundland, Canada); "After the Quiet Revolution: Quebec Anthropology and the Study of Quebec", by Gerald L. Gold (York University, Toronto, Canada) and Marc-Adélard Tremblay (Université Laval, Quebec, Canada); "Through Althusserian Spectacles: Recent Social Anthropology in Brazil, by Otávio Guilherme Velho (Universidade Federal do Rio de Janeiro, Brazil); "Twenty Years of Swedish Social Anthropology: 1960-1980", by Ulf Hannerz (University of Stockholm, Sweden). The afterword, "Afterword: A View from the Center", is by George W. Stocking jr.

[24] See Bassi's essay in this volume.

1 INTRODUCTION: FOR A HISTORY OF ANTHROPOLOGY IN THE PLURAL

centre-periphery relations and of the meaningfulness of an international anthropology both as a "multinational" post-colonial anthropology and as an ideal to be pursued, bridging the gap between centre Euro-American anthropologies and the peripheral post-colonial ones.

It is worth recalling here how he keyed in on what he believed were the dominant "hegemonic national traditions" in anthropology, such as Great Britain, France, Germany, the United States and former Soviet Union. The latter not for its hegemonic anthropology, but rather for its acknowledged Marxist perspective. In the journal, the featured traditions (India, Poland, Sudan, Canada, Brazil, Sweden) are all influenced by hegemonic traditions that gave rise to some "types" of anthropological traditions: "secondary metropolitan anthropologies" (Sweden and Poland), "anthropology of white supremacy" (Anglophone Canada, Quebec, Brazil), "post-colonial anthropologies" (India, Sudan). Clearly, the meaning of such categorisations cannot make up for the complexity of each national tradition. However, according to Stocking, they are useful to detect their different ways of relating to otherness and emulating hegemonic anthropologies, they all share the use of English apart from their national language, and Anglo-American anthropology is dominant over the peripheral traditions. Therefore, Stocking states:

> Indeed, on the basis of what is presented here, anthropology at the periphery seems neither so nationally varied nor so sharply divergent from that of the center as the conception of "the shaping of national anthropologies" might have implied. While the accounts of intellectual influence, institutional development, and substantive concerns differ of course in specific detail, there is little that qualifies as reinvented or radically alternative anthropology, and not too much specifically national uniqueness. (1982, pp. 180-181)

Since Stocking's consideration, as many years have gone by, there have been tensions and second thoughts, scholars have moved towards and away from Euro-American hegemonic anthropology, they have tried to find alternative solutions in both content and form, they have shown a certain willingness to explore new perspectives, methodological and theoretical considerations in order to develop the status of the discipline in light of political, historical dynamics and current orders in former colonial contexts.[25] Some essays contained in this volume detect this dimension very well. Indeed, this must also be taken into account in the trajectory reconstruction through which the anthropological centre-periphery relationship has become widespread and long established. This framework also includes some experiences that have mainly focused on their outcomes and the opportunity to rethink world anthropologies, starting from historical investigation. The creation of some collaboration networks has prompted the development of an articulated vision of the discipline that will factor into both the development trajectories within the different traditions and the current research pathways, with a close plural perspective aware of systems of power. The turning point comes with the implementation of *Red de Antropologías del Mundo* (RAM), also known as *World Anthropologies Network* (WAN). In 2002 the Network participated in numerous meetings in the United States, and in 2003, they organised a conference in Pordenone (Italy) with the support of the Wenner-Gren Foundation for Anthropological Research together with founders Gustavo Luis Ribeiro and Arturo Escobar, aiming to spread wider knowledge of anthropological production from outside the North Atlantic area. Researchers from Australia, Brazil, England, India, Japan, Canada, Cameroon, Mexico, Norway, Russia, Spain and the United States gave life to a transnational community (in which Italy is conspicuous by its absence both as a research field and as a tradition) and became involved in different subjects. Not only do they have a mind to emphasise a significant

---

[25] However, according to Palumbo, nowadays both hegemonic and subaltern anthropologies tend towards a higher "residual position" compared to other fields of knowledge. They "dispel the illusion of organicity to take up a critical-deconstructive position: a solid social science [...] that since its very beginnings one century earlier, had essentially taken a step back from modern, rational, reformist imagination [...] it is therefore clear that the contrast between *empire building* and *nation-state building anthropologies* is eventually toned down on a political-intellectual level [...]. If the verbiage of those representations [...] is to be retained, we might then argue that, regardless of "hegemonic" and "subaltern" traditions, this field of study seems to be currently closer to a "critical" analysis of "local" rearrangement/adjustment processes in certain national states and supranational dynamics (*nation-state deconstructing anthropologies*) and modulation/articulation processes of a new global empire (*global empire (de)structuring anthropologies*)" (Palumbo, 2018, p. 195).

1 INTRODUCTION: FOR A HISTORY OF ANTHROPOLOGY IN THE PLURAL   23

distinction of practices, but they are also aware of the need to disseminate their research results through technology.[26]

Remarkably, one of the outcomes of the Conference is *World Anthropologies: Disciplinary Transformations Within Systems of Power*, a volume edited by Ribeiro and Escobar (2006).[27] Importantly, the volume gets a mention because some of the questions we touched on earlier in this

---

[26] ram-wan—Red de Antropologías del Mundo—World Anthropologies Network. The Conference programme in Pordenone, introduced by Ribeiro and Escobar, was structured as follows: Part I: "Transnationalism and State Power", speeches: *Reshaping Anthropology: A View from Japan*, Shinji Yamashita; *Transformations in Siberian Anthropology: An Insider's Perspective*, Nikolai Vakhtin; *In Search of Anthropology in China: A Discipline Caught in the Web of Nation Building Agenda, Socialist Capitalism, and Globalization*, Josephine Smart; *Mexican Anthropology's Ongoing Search for Identity*, Esteban Krotz. Part II: "Power and Hegemony in World Anthropologies", speeches: *How many 'centers' and 'peripheries' in anthropology? A critical view on France*, Eduardo Archetti; *The Production of Knowledge and the Production of Hegemony: Anthropological Theory and Political Struggles in Spain*, Susana Narotsky; *Anthropology in a Post-Colonial Africa: the Survival Debate*, Paul Nchoji Nkwi. Part III: "Epistemological, Sociological and Disciplinary Predicaments", speeches: *Generating Non-Trivial Knowledge in Awkward Situations: Anthropology in the UK*, Eeva Berglund; *The Production of Other Knowledges and its Tensions: From Andeanist Anthropology to Interculturalidad?*, Marisol De la Cadena; *A Time and Place Beyond and of the Center: Australian Anthropologies on the Process of Becoming*, Sandy Toussaint; *Official Hegemony and Contesting Pluralisms*, Shiv Visvanathan; Part IV: "From Anthropology today to World Anthropologies", speeches: *The Pictographics of Tristesse: An Anthropology of Nation-Building in the Tropics and its Aftermath*, Otávio Velho; *"World Anthropologies": Questions*, Johannes Fabian.

[27] The Spanish edition of the volume, *Antropologías del mundo. Transformaciones disciplinarias dentro de sistemas de poder*, published in 2008, is available on the Network's website. The translation of the opening chapter of the book was published on ANUAC, vol. 7, n. 1, June 2018. Also included in the general project, WCAA, The World Council of Anthropological Associations, was founded by Gustavo Lins Ribeiro, in 2004, in Recife (Brazil), with the aim of establishing a global community in dialogue. For this reason, representatives of associations in different areas of the world have served as presidents (Brazil, Japan, Australia, Poland, Ireland), up to Isaac Nyamongo from Pan-African Anthropological Association, who is currently in office. Likewise, Gustavo Lins Ribeiro started "Déjà Lu" journal, where selected articles from major specialised peer-reviewed journals are republished in order to spread research worldwide.

A recent monographic issue of "Horizontes Antropológicos" (y. 28, n. 62, 2022), *História das Antropologias do Mundo*, a Portuguese journal edited by Patrícia Ferraz de Matos, Frederico Delgado Rosa and Eduardo Dullo follow this striving towards world anthropologies. Significantly, the editors' opening text is called: "Caminhos para uma história inclusiva das antropologias do mundo" (https://www.scielo.br/j/ha/i/2022.v28n62/). We want to thank Valeria Ribeiro Corossacz for suggesting the journal in time so that it could be mentioned in this introduction.

24   G. D'AGOSTINO AND V. MATERA

introduction are included in the book. Additionally, it must be noted that in relation to our main theme, such connections need to be considered before writing a new chapter of *Histories* of anthropology in the near future.

Going back to where we started, we feel it is appropriate to recall the editors' remarks in regard to Stocking's partition:

> in modern times, behind empire building there has always been a nation-state. Indeed, anthropologies of empire building are also anthropologies of nation building, although the converse is not necessarily true. Moreover, there are cases in which "national anthropologies" became internationalized without becoming empire-building anthropologies, such as the Australian, Brazilian, Canadian, and Mexican cases. (Ribeiro & Escobar, 2006, p. 12)

As for Brazilian anthropology, they also cited João de Pina-Cabral, who detected "a fifth tradition" "that identifies itself with none of the imperial projects that have historically moved scientific development" (Pina Cabral, 2004, p. 263, cit. in Ribeiro & Escobar, 2006, p. 12).[28] Moreover, as Eduardo Archetti argues in their volume, a hegemonic anthropology can occasionally move towards both nation-building and empire-building processes, as is the case with France,[29] or even a certain tradition can take or privilege an imperial attitude based on the circumstances, as happened with Japanese anthropology (*ibid.*).

Conversely, Ribeiro and Escobar put forward a perspective that causes tension within the two key elements of hegemonic and peripheral traditions: "metropolitan provincialism" and "provincial cosmopolitanism". The former goes over "the ignorance that anthropologists in hegemonic centers have of the knowledge production of practitioners in nonhegemonic sites", as previously noted by Gupta and Ferguson (1997); the latter, on the other hand, refers "to the often exhaustive knowledge that people in nonhegemonic sites have of the production of hegemonic

[28] See Pozzi and Pussetti's essay in this volume.
[29] See Aria's contribution to this volume.

1 INTRODUCTION: FOR A HISTORY OF ANTHROPOLOGY IN THE PLURAL   25

centres (Ribeiro & Escobar, 2006, p. 13).[30] As further proof of "this asymmetrical ignorance" they mention how the history of hegemonic traditions in peripheral contexts is the subject matter of scholarly research, but the opposite hardly ever occurs. Furthermore, peripheral traditions do not often investigate their own disciplinary history along with hegemonic history, whereas the common opinion is that foreign anthropologists produce "classics" that are considered worth reading (ibid., p. 13).

Such questions, as is common knowledge, have something to do with English monolingualism in scientific communication, which means that hegemonic traditions are not generally liable to provide translations. With their project of "world anthropologies", they, as editors of that volume, seek to rebalance the unequal power relations as an expression of this linguistic hegemony. The control over scientific publishing is then connected to linguistic hegemony. Among the others,[31] Takami Kuwayama, quoted by Ribeiro and Escobar observed:

> the world system of anthropology defines the politics involved in the production, dissemination, and consumption of knowledge about other peoples and cultures. Influential scholars in the core countries are in a position to decide what kinds of knowledge should be given authority and merit attention. The peer-review system at prestigious journals reinforces this structure. Thus, knowledge produced in the periphery, however significant

---

[30] Interestingly for this purpose, young researchers from peripheral traditions striving for international recognition by hegemonic traditions tend to avoid considering some consistent "peripheral" bibliographical references in their scientific production to focus exclusively on hegemonic traditions. Likewise, what further underlines the centre/periphery relationships is the fact that some of the young scholars occasionally conducting research within the institutions of "hegemonic" centres and aiming to secure permanent positions in "peripheral" centres fail to take account of potential reference sources, and this speaks well for "metropolitan provincialism" in their centres.

[31] See at least Hannerz (2010), Ch. VI on linguistic anthropology.

and valuable, is destined to be buried locally unless it meets the standards and expectations of the core.[32] (cit. *ibid.*, p. 3)

In the wake of this new opening, in 2018 *The International Encyclopedia of Anthropology* was launched. Hilary Callan (2018, p. i) introduces the birth of this project as follows[33]:

> In recent years, anthropologists have become increasingly aware of the need to recognize multivocality across the discipline and the existence of distinctive anthropologies, together with the traffic occurring between them, as opposed to one or a few exclusive paradigms. This shift of vision brings with it a parallel recognition of the need for global anthropology to reach outward beyond its traditional academic boundaries and to connect both with neighboring disciplines in the human and social sciences and with broader spheres of civil society.

In relation to the "tension" between anthropology and its declination in the plural, it should be noted that:

---

[32] These are sensitive questions that, on the one hand, are linked to an increasingly shared sense of intolerance towards these "neoliberal" procedures, which has little to do with evaluation and exchanges, but affects the increasingly standardised procedures; on the other hand, these procedures have an impact on the involved individuals when it comes to starting their academic career advancement path or living their ordinary life. And this very impact determines how deliberate avoidance of this can be difficult, complicated and even dangerous. Over the last few years, our experience as members of comparative assessment panels (public exams) as well as the National Scientific Habilitation process, namely a necessary requirement to apply for permanent positions in Italian universities, has prompted the candidates to strategically build up their curricula as far as scientific publications are concerned. Generally, after conducting extensive research as part of their doctoral studies, all applicants (including candidates with long-standing experience) will eventually publish their results as monographs. Later, the monograph is broken down into single journal essays that will be published nationally and, more often, internationally in English and French without any significant and substantial changes from the original draft. If anything, sometimes the monograph is not even included in the current bibliographical references, or the monograph is preceded by journal essays or chapters in miscellaneous volumes that are later left unchanged and put together in the monograph with no explicit reference to the previous publisher. Those are important clues to understand how the Italian evaluation system has become more focused on reaching "thresholds" and fulfilling formal quantitative criteria at the expense of quality, freedom and originality, as well as the development and interpretive phases of research.

[33] Introduction-1615327025.pdf (wiley.com) (last reference 20th February 2022).

1 INTRODUCTION: FOR A HISTORY OF ANTHROPOLOGY IN THE PLURAL   27

The placing of "World Anthropologies" as a theme at the heart of the project was a fundamental decision of principle, albeit one that creates an immediate dilemma. Across the discipline, the shared sense that there are core organizing concepts that characterize the anthropological style—such as holism, deep local understanding, and comparison—coexists with a diversity of perspectives across the environments in which anthropology is practiced and taught. Anthropologies across the globe are deeply situated in their several histories, environments, and contexts of practice. At the same time, these same world anthropologies also *converse* with one another in multiple ways. Such conferring across anthropologies occurs on many levels and scales; is dialectical in character; and often reflects imbalances of power between so-called central and peripheral locations. (Callan, 2018, p. iii)

Hence, the connection with the past is fundamental, not just as a mere research topic, but rather as a dimension that must be clearly included among these entries to let *histories* emerge alongside history.[34] Eduardo Restrepo is the author of the "World Anthropologies" entry, where he provides a useful summary of some of the stages that have led up to this opening. The Colombian anthropologist goes on to expose a shared feeling of discomfort that grew in the early 2000s in relation to "certain disciplinary practices [that] made invisible diverse traditions, authors, and forms of doing anthropology worldwide" (Restrepo, 2018, p. 1), and singles out the most significant contribution to the "word anthropologies" debate in a collective conceptualisation of the way in which visibilisation and silencing mechanisms operate both in the transnational field of anthropology and within national anthropological establishments. He puts some anthropologists and their considerations before this perspective, such as Brazilian anthropologist Roberto Cardoso de Oliveira (1999–2000) with his reflection on "metropolitan and peripheral anthropologies" and Mexican anthropologist Esteban Krotz (1997), who

---

[34] It is interesting to remark how the question about the language chosen for the contributions is brought up. The use of English as a *lingua franca* is a clear advantage, albeit the apparent prejudice and opposition from the academy due to the fact that it is still the dominant language of scientific publications. Two entries examine this phenomenon: "Anthropological Knowledge and Styles of Publications", by Gordon Mathew, and "Academic Literacies, Ethnographic Perspectives on", by Anna Robinson-Pant. If Mathew hopes for the use of universal English among non-native speakers for global anthropology, English is still the main language for the Encyclopedia, although the "editorial effort" to encourage and favour non-Anglophones in all the editing phases must be pointed out (Callan, 2018, pp. v-vi).

introduced "anthropologies of the South", as the result of power relations between world anthropologies and the way "histories and trajectories are silenced and made invisible", so much so that they come across as "anthropologies without history".[35] This inclination towards a plural vision "aims at decentering the idea of one genealogy, or of a series of trajectories united in a single and happily coherent disciplinary project" (Restrepo, 2018, p. 3).[36] Therefore, Restrepo's entry is connected to 45 terms concerning national and regional traditions: Argentina, Australia, Austria, Brazil, Chile, Colombia, Denmark, Ethiopia, France, Germany, Great Britain, India, Indonesia, Israel, Japan, Mexico, Norway, the Netherlands, Poland, Portugal, Russia, Siberia, Spain, South Africa, Sub-Saharan Africa, Sudan, Sweden, Turkey, the United States, as well as a couple of entries on spatial linguistic research and a few others on cross-cutting topics.[37] And again, Italy is notably absent from this editorial initiative. Furthermore, *Coleción Memorias* from *Biblioteca Digital Latinoamericana del Antropologías del Sur* must certainly be remembered among the initiatives revolving around the need for dialogue and exchange within a culturally "homogeneous" area perceived as the "global south". It was launched in Venezuela in 2015 to "prompt integration and visibility of anthropologies in Latin America and the Caribbean area [...] aiming to include other regions of the global 'South'". So it reads on page 12 in the introduction of the opening volume *Antropologías del Sur. Cinco miradas*, published in 2017, whose contributions from Venezuelan, Colombian, Mexican anthropologists—Jacquelin Clarac de Briceño, Esteban Krotz, Esteban Emilio Mosonyi, Nelly García Gavidia, Eduardo Restrepo—pave the way for some considerations on the "state of the art" of anthropologies in their regions and an open confrontation on different needs.

---

[35] See "Anthropologies of the South" dossier, published on the first issue of the Network's e-journal (June 2005), and available for download on www.ram-wan.net. Restrepo found some additional key elements at the bottom of the debate on world anthropologies: considerations on both "indigenous anthropologies" (Fahim & Helmer, 1980) and "native anthropologies" (Jones, 1988; Narayan, 1993), Hymes' considerations (1974) as mentioned earlier, the "anthropologies with an accent" notion by Teresa Caldeira (2000), Haitian anthropologist Michel-Ralph Trouillot's contribution (1991) (also cf. 2003) as well as the active involvement of South African Archie Mafeje (2001).

[36] Available for download here. \lround\wbiea2119.dvi (ram-wan.net)

[37] *Anthropological Knowledge and Styles of Publications; Globalization; Glocalisation; Interculturality; Interethnic Frictions; Postcolonialism; Postsocialist Europe; World Music.*

Palumbo (2018), in his original recognition on anthropological research in Italy and its relations with the international context, underlined some questions that had arisen along with the world anthropologies project. As he observes:

> Even though I agree on the ethical ambitions and most critical considerations of the scholars within the network [...], I feel that, other than the actual possibility/ability/willingness to disrupt the sedimented intellectual hegemonies, the idea of creating a new, different scientific area may somehow bring about some paradoxical effects. Among the risks, [...] righteous criticism of a certain model of social and political organisation in the field of international anthropology may eventually turn into a request to envision and build up a "game" that is structurally different from that of social science as we understand it today, thus finally producing results that are in line with the desired outcomes of those centres of power that, in fact, keep practitioners of "other" anthropologies out of "real" science. (Palumbo, 2018, p. 191)

He goes on to report some possible actions to be taken, which ought to take into account the actual research status in "peripheral" contexts as well (*ibid.*, p. 192). He believes that it would be useful to:

> bring the dispute to the heart of hegemony [...] work in order to remark how the amnesia, omissions and superficiality that we sometimes perceive while reading what they "write" about "us" [...] might undermine the cognitive plausibility of what is produced, from the inside and inside the same "dominant" scientific rules. Therefore, behind such limitations, we will not only find the general political-intellectual asymmetry of the global scenario in contemporary anthropology. As I see it, these can cause some non-generalisable inherent attitudes leading a large amount of scholars to neglect the products, as well as the contexts and the production process of "other" anthropological knowledge. Such lack of ethnographic knowledge in the political-intellectual field that inevitably comes with the territory when conducting research in certain "national" areas, has an effect on the anthropologists belonging to "hegemonic" areas and their qualitative ethnographic work. (*ibid.*, p. 193)

However, not only can reading *history* through *histories* help to understand certain moments of the discipline, but it can also facilitate comprehension of connections and disconnections throughout the decades. Plus, it makes it possible to change the paths that were sometimes thought to be following a sequence and put them into parallel positions to make genealogical lines and breaking points clearly visible. It may also be an incentive to prompt other "minority" traditions to make their contribution so as to change their position in relation to the dominant narrative. To this end, it is no coincidence that this initiative came from Italy, one of the world's Souths, whose "peripheral, yet [...] perhaps worthy" tradition (Cirese, 1976, p. 122) has undoubtedly had to face the language barrier[38] that has been partially resolved in recent years, as well as limited colonial experience and its finalisation that, unlike other European experiences, failed to nurture relationships between former colonies and their "motherland", except for empty and futile self-referential" rhetoric, to an extent that afterthoughts and critical considerations of such a cross section of national history notably made a late start: if, in the field of historiography, reflection has grown and matured, the process of rethinking and critical awareness in the field of anthropology has not yet completed. Repeated attempts to try to fathom the causes of such poor visibility of anthropology in Italy may turn out to be worthless, but the *reasons of history* might still teach us something.

In conclusion, some remarks. The fact that anthropology has developed some sophisticated instruments to illuminate both the mechanisms through which reality is constructed and the influence of power in shaping hegemonies has not prevented the discipline from falling into the same 'ideological' traps it aimed to reveal and which, at least internally, it could and should have escaped. Actually, the hegemony of the Euro-American tradition refers only to a portion of the cultural space it seems to be referring to. Nowadays, it has to be faced with other traditions homing in on a different "world order". This is a more inclusive project that all the same comes across as an "uneven" comparison due to its inclination towards the dominant traditions of Great Britain and the United States for their institutional visibility and prominence, financial resources, international relations, vehicular language, namely "knowledge production, dissemination and utilisation policies". The process has already begun, and the outcomes

---

[38] The language question is obviously only one of the reasons of this condition for Italian anthropology. For this purpose, Giovanni Pizza recently wrote an essay on this topic in relation to "hermeneutic frontiers" and "hegemonic dialectics among 'several intellectual traditions'", to inquire into "mutual receptions/omissions among global anthropologies" (Pizza, 2017, pp. 198-199), with a special focus on Ernesto de Martino. For further considerations on de Martino in international anthropological literature, see Palumbo, 2018, Ch. 5 and *passim*. Cf. see also Dei's contribution to this volume.

1 INTRODUCTION: FOR A HISTORY OF ANTHROPOLOGY IN THE PLURAL   31

are still not quite predictable, but something has changed. Now, the task of gaining greater awareness of what is at stake falls to younger anthropologists, who will have to ensure a better balance among the direct and indirect participants to this worldwide comparison.

This book contains twenty chapters. The first, by **Marco Gardini** and **Luca Rimoldi**, is about British social anthropology, a cornerstone of mainstream anthropology, which is both an expression and a symbol of colonial politics. What emerges in the essay, as the title suggests, is the importance of connections, which are not always hierarchical but productive nonetheless, between hegemonic and peripheral anthropology (see below India, South Africa and Australia): the circulation of ideas and the exchanges become part of the local academic *milieu* and promote a specific declination of the discipline. In this framework, it is interesting to note the role that "marginal scholars" played on the very foundation of British anthropology. These scholars were able to introduce and enhance different perspectives, carrying meanings "other" than those that were typical of the "British" cultural and academic context.

Matteo Aria presents French anthropology, focusing on the most recent outcomes of theoretical and methodological perspectives that distinguished French ethnology, anthropology and ethnography throughout most of the twentieth century. The author identifies continuities and discontinuities in the genealogical lines of these main narratives, analysing academic situations and public spaces of the discipline, which in France are directly linked to the main museological institutions and to heritage issues. Furthermore, much attention is devoted to the relationships between anthropology and sociology, history, psychology, linguistics as well as some areas of natural sciences and neuroscience; in addition, the ongoing loss of "classical" fields of study, concerning both external otherness with regard to former colonies and internal otherness with regard to rural contexts, emerges as a relevant topic of recent French Anthropology.

The chapter written by **Marco Bassi**, on the anthropological tradition in the German area, focuses on the discipline's most important concept that is at its very foundations, marking its fortunes and its crises, its influences on other disciplinary fields and its distinctiveness: the concept of culture. The history of Germany, Nazism, racism and genocide shaped the history of the entire world and also fractured the potential of German thought—with its strong philosophical tradition—to influence, via the circulation of ideas, such a crucial process for the cultural and political rise of a discipline, the theoretical events of international anthropology regarding the concept of culture. Had Boas remained in Germany, in other words, he would not have encountered the American Indians, so important for his proposals, and perhaps the American "culturalist" hegemony would not have been established. The events in Germany perfectly illustrate the inextricable intertwining—if not through an accurate work of historical deconstruction, such that conducted in the text—between "politics" and "culture", the former understood as the process of constructing a sense of belonging, of cohesion, of nationalism, that draws on the latter understood as authenticity, essence and spirit of peoples. We are at the very heart of the "nation-building" anthropology, which totalitarian regimes use in a very effective way, and which profoundly marks the discipline, to such an extent that Germany only started emerging a few decades ago from the theoretical dead end that it was stuck in.

The chapter by **Fabio Dei** presents Italian anthropology, whose distinctive feature is the opposition between Culture with a capital "C", that of Benedetto Croce's philosophy, and various attempts, not always facilitated by politics (and definitely not by fascism, for example) to leave room for culture with a lower case "c", that of Ernesto de Martino, Antonio Gramsci and Alberto Mario Cirese. "Does a national tradition exist?" the author wonders in the title, and in his account this question remains unanswered. The discipline in Italy remained largely marginal, due above all to the linguistic problem, a conflict that inevitably arises when a prestigious literary tradition weighs down on a language such as Italian, hardly functional to the needs of international scholarly communication, and moreover unspoken outside the national borders. The strong interest in oral tradition and folklore since the end of the nineteenth century, which has led to the elaboration of refined theoretical paradigms, has been ignored outside Italy and, from a certain point onwards, has been neglected in many cases by the same Italian anthropologists, who frequently followed traditions of international standing or internal traditions "returned" from other hegemonic traditions.

The next chapter, by **María Rubio Gómez, Javier García Castaño** and **Gloria Calabresi** is about the history of anthropology in Spain. The chapter opens with a question that we have already faced with respect to the debate raised in connection with the origin of the disciplinary subsector of the history of anthropology (see above): "who should write a history of anthropology?", an anthropologist, because of his/her "internal" position, or a historian, because the task is a specific one that requires specialists? After a critical presentation of some alternative perspectives (presentism, historicism, "expired" and extended history, internalist and externalist history, continuist and discontinuist history), the authors state their intention to formulate a disciplinary (local) history that does not involve celebratory intentions. The "journey" through Spanish anthropology is divided into four stages: the first is the foundation of the first museums and associations, based on a generalist vision of human beings and folklore; the second is the academic institutionalisation of social anthropology (after 1960); the third is the period after the 1980s, marked by the end of the dictatorship, when the discipline began to become visible in Spain, due to its strong social roots and was therefore able to solve the most relevant and pressing questions with its own tools such as those posed by the growing regional claims within the framework of European transnational integration process; the fourth and last stage is distinguished by an increasingly clear professionalisation of anthropology, its openness outside the academic world and public recognition of the contribution anthropology can provide (e.g. against the resurgence of racist, nationalist, supreme and imperialist practices and rhetoric).

A transition from dictatorship to democracy also marks anthropology in Portugal, as underlined by **Giacomo Pozzi** and **Chiara Pussetti** in their chapter. The authors articulate a route that links Lusophone anthropology more markedly than in other cases to geographical, cultural, historical and political characteristics of the country. Portugal, at the tail end of Europe, over the centuries preferred to sail the waves rather than look to other European countries, an Atlantic inclination that was at the root both of the construction of a real "empire" and of a sort of "isolation". The latter fostered, in a negative way, the establishment of a long dictatorship, which also influenced anthropology until the 1970s. In such a marginality, the authors explain the propulsive role that Portugal played, giving rise to EASA, because of anthropologists who had trained in an anglophone context and then returned to their homeland. Portuguese anthropology, therefore, developed between two poles, the national and the imperial: for almost a century, reflection turned around binomial "popular culture-national identity", a binomial that also involved colonies. After the fall of Salazar, everything changed to such an extent that a "New Country" seems to have been created: independence of colonies joined a revolutionary phase, which also involved anthropology, the focus of a social, cultural, democratic renewal.

34   G. D'AGOSTINO AND V. MATERA

Pietro Scarduelli opens his chapter by pointing out a similarity between the origin of nineteenth-century ethnography in Russia and the origin of cultural anthropology in the United States: the former originated from the studies of indigenous communities in Siberia, which were later encompassed within the Tzarist Empire; the latter, similarly, studied American Indians who had been forced into reserves because of their strenuous resistance to the expansion of settlers. Unlike the latter, Siberian natives were basically left in peace to continue their customs and way of life. Another interesting point concerns contributions that dissidents who were dispatched to Siberia by the Tsarist regime gave to anthropology in Russia: isolated from the world, they committed themselves to the study of local customs and traditions. After the revolution in 1917, Soviet ethnography changed course, with an institutionalisation of studies concerning local minorities and a focus on ethnic nationalism, a potential threat to the internationalist ideology, purged within a theoretical framework of Marxist inspiration. This remained a hallmark of Soviet anthropology for many decades. An exception to this canvas was Propp's formalist studies, remembered in Scarduelli's essay as the only international projection during this period. With the fall of the Soviet Union, the catastrophe also overtook Academia. A profound loss of references invested ethnographic research, which had previously been centred on ethnos, a topic that was no longer relevant as it lacked the minimum bases towards international research and was profoundly constrained from a linguistic, ideological and cultural point of view; this made the path of Russian anthropology very rough, with a few interesting exceptions such as the attempts to deconstruct stereotypes that surround the Western perception of *Homo Sovieticus*.

Alice Bellagamba's chapter enters deeply into the roots of anthropology in Francophone Africa whose development, just as in British Empire areas, appears to be inextricably linked to both colonial expansion and colonial legitimisation. French domination drove an action of "coverage", so to speak, of purely and brutally military actions of conquest, through "cultural" efforts, geographical knowledge, competence on local societies, and languages and cultures; this knowledge ultimately constituted the "colonial library", an ensemble of texts produced by the West on Africa and Africans to which ethnographers-missionaries contributed in a decisive way. This knowledge stands alongside administrative knowledge, and in their convergence, we can identify the origins of anthropology in this area. The chapter accurately traces some of the most significant passages of the early period and points out how the leading role exerted by colonial

1 INTRODUCTION: FOR A HISTORY OF ANTHROPOLOGY IN THE PLURAL

power later provoked, after independence, a marginalisation of compromised knowledge, or at least perceived as such, in favour of the more prospective and neutral sociology: it was prospective because it was able to serve the demands of modernity of the new states, and neutral because it was not generated by colonialism. By the late 1980s, African anthropology was destined for subalternity: an erudite interlocutor to Western anthropology.

Stefano Allovio's contribution is dedicated to an area of great interest to our discipline. South African anthropology, in fact, despite being geographically peripheral, gave remarkable contributions to anthropology, first and foremost because of its double and solid link with British anthropology, both academic and political. The convergence of these two dimensions reinforced a pressure that already existed in Great Britain in the early twentieth century to study local customs and traditions of colonised peoples, which led to the institution of a teaching of social anthropology at the University of Cape Town that was taught by A. R. Radcliffe-Brown, directly from Oxford. This is the starting point of the critical reconstruction of the events of South African anthropology that Allovio presents, which aims to show the superficiality of reconstructions that too hastily identify the politics/anthropology nexus with regard to African contexts. South African anthropology arose out of a political decision, of course, but scholars who contributed to its consolidation were not at all subjected to politics, especially not to colonial politics, starting from Radcliffe-Brown and on to his students, some of whom were able to maintain a difficult balance between the teaching of a discipline like social anthropology and a context like South Africa, which was certainly not marked with an openness to diversity. It was only with the promulgation of the apartheid regime that South African anthropologists surrendered, moving elsewhere, to the United Kingdom or the United States. Hence, perhaps, the main reasons for the striking contributions from South Africa to social anthropology in the motherland, which were very innovative in terms of research themes and theoretical innovations.

Some distinctive traits of US anthropology are the benchmark for an orientation in the first period of North American anthropology, which was very complex in terms of its articulation and its influence on the overall structure of world anthropology. **Angela Biscaldi**'s chapter highlights three emblematic elements of North American anthropology from its origins: empiricism, relativism and the inclination to become "applied". The first trait, linked above all to the question of "internal" otherness, was characterised by its immediacy, because in the United States there was not the dense philosophical and literary imaginary to mediate and orient relationships with diversity as in European countries. It played a role at once determinant and ambiguous with regard to its internal identity and its projection to the outside world. The second trait, which is not independent from the first one, is well known and, despite many misunderstandings, characterised world anthropology, as well as rooting itself in an occasionally excessive way in American anthropology. It concerns Boasian relativism, which became an essential ingredient of theoretical reflection and field research, providing foundations to break down core concepts of a ferocious and discriminatory ideology, those of "race", "gender", "sexuality" and "disability" and outlining the very basis for that cultural critique that is still today the cornerstone of the intellectual style of our discipline. And finally it presents the practical repercussions of knowledge that Boas and his students emphasise, thus declining questions of ethics and responsibility, as well as politics, which are inseparable from research, especially when it interrelates with the very diverse spaces of the human condition.

The contribution by **Berardino Palumbo** on contemporary North American anthropology constitutes an incisive synthesis of a complex body of work, in terms of theoretical perspectives, themes and methods, which, on the one hand and for some aspects, have deeply affected European anthropologies and, on the other hand, have incorporated theoretical perspectives from outside the "American tradition" that gave rise to internal debates and, by a sort of "cross-reference", were captured in some "minor" traditions. The author unfolds this route by articulating it through four phases, from the early 1970s to the present. With regard to each step, he shows the articulation of the most institutional placements and alternatives that developed in parallel, providing timely examples of the most representative works in relation to an internal arena and an external hegemony. Some topics addressed in this chapter are about how to represent research findings, power and forms of resistance, relationships between global history and local histories, economic and material dimensions and cultural dimensions, globalisation and processes of de-territorialisation and re-territorialisation, and the centrality of the ethnographic approach as a critical practice and as the "specific trait of anthropology". It characterises North American anthropology, yet with a "remote glance", and allows us to perceive continuities, as well as interruptions, within theories, practices and poetics of research that exerted and still continue to exert a hegemony in the global anthropological landscape.

1 INTRODUCTION: FOR A HISTORY OF ANTHROPOLOGY IN THE PLURAL   37

In some Latin American contexts, as we saw, new reflections and new questions to the discipline matured, together with original research directions, thanks to some anthropologists who were able to dialogue internationally and to wonder how much room anthropology might have in the future because of its leading role in public policy and because of its representativeness. In the chapter devoted to anthropology in Brazil, **Valeria Ribeiro Corossacz**, through an ethically and politically committed placement, outlines a problematic picture of a historical, social and political story, aimed to construct a renewed project of nationhood; Brazilian anthropology provided adequate tools to interpret it. Brazilian anthropologists, furthermore, played a very active role with regard to racial issues and hierarchies of skin colour, which even include "whiteness". It is an important contribution not only to the internal debate, but also with respect to a wider epistemological dimension. Far from being a neutral category, "whiteness" is a crucial key to understanding and deconstructing racism and other forms of discrimination.

The chapter by **Rodrigo Llanes Salazar**, on the history of Anthropology in Mexico, highlights how Mexican anthropology counts very specific traits according to its relationship with the building of the Mexican national state in the twentieth century. State and nationalism are specific issues that, merged with a marked applied vocation, contributed to the "mestizo" identity of Mexico as a solution to the "indigenous problem", the integration of indigenous cultures into the Mexican nation. The chapter also explores how Mexican cultural anthropology has changed in recent years, since new generations of anthropologists questioned the privileged relationship between anthropology and the Mexican state, claiming a more marked commitment of the discipline with indigenous struggles. This critical review coincided with a process of the "academisation" of Mexican anthropology, that is, a greater presence and visibility of the discipline in university spaces and research institutions, with a consequent theoretical and thematic diversification of the research carried out by Mexican anthropologists. Over the last three decades, the growing socioeconomic inequality, the increase in the levels of violence in the country as well as the Covid-19 pandemic have inspired new proposals to practise the profession with a public commitment to the recognition of diversity.

The history of anthropology in Colombia, presented by **Alessandro Mancuso**, highlights a complex story in a context that is still characterised by the highest inequality indexes in the world and further complexified by an "undeclared civil war" and "internal armed conflict" linked to drug trafficking. Anthropological training here also had to provide tools for analysing the country's social problems with a strong vocation for the applied dimension. A strong Marxist commitment was also directed to the development of programmes for the recognition of indigenous people's rights as well as for collaborative research experiences. The 1991 Constitution is significant of the route outlined thanks to the commitment of anthropologists to overcome assimilationist policies and become open to cultural pluralism. Colombian anthropology is aware of international debate and able to give significant contributions to "readjusting" relationships between anthropologies of the global North and South, despite being damaged, as is true elsewhere, by forms of precariousness and increasing adherence "to the logics of governmentality and market", with the consequent equally progressive limitation of ethical-political tension that characterised it in the phase of so-called anthropology of modernity.

Sara Roncaglia's chapter is on anthropology in India and outlines not only the colonial perspective of the disciplinary approach, but more importantly its specificity in a context that for nearly seventy years was studied by native anthropologists who did not conduct research elsewhere. From "village" to "tribal" studies, after Independence, anthropological research in India took on an applied perspective towards a sort of collaboration with political projects aimed at social equality. Such a perspective consolidated itself starting from the 1970s by a growing focus on issues related to gender relations, forms of exclusion, marginalisation and discrimination, issues to which Subaltern studies also made a significant contribution from the point of view of a renewal of theoretical and epistemological paradigms that became part of the entire Indian historical story.

Elena Bougleux's chapter is devoted to the context of Vietnam, where a number of different narratives and historical reconstructions of the discipline intersect, independently of each other, reflecting the complexity of the country and also the role played by international actors who were involved in designing its institutional and academic structure. Like other former colonial contexts, the influence of the anthropological tradition of the colonising countries is also evident in the history of anthropology in Vietnam; here, however, divergences emerge, opposing political visions contrast vigorously, often with the explicit intention of erasing previous thinking and replacing one tradition with another. These contrasts gave rise to a theoretically fragmented, but very rich and original scenario. The essay, as the author states, does not seek a coherent history of the discipline; it seeks to restore that fragmentation in the process of an

1 INTRODUCTION: FOR A HISTORY OF ANTHROPOLOGY IN THE PLURAL   39

introduction of anthropology in Vietnam by making use of heterogeneous sources and with the awareness that no body of sources is ever complete. The applied vocation of anthropology in colonial contexts emerges once again in the reconstruction that **Dario Di Rosa** makes in his chapter on Australia. Aboriginal communities were an important research area for a number of issues that were central not only to anthropology in the late nineteenth and early twentieth centuries, but also because they represented a challenge to the discipline and to colonial and post-colonial administrations. Melanesia and Papua New Guinea constituted a ground for the elaboration of new models and theoretical perspectives as well as for displaying early systematic interest in the area's disciplinary history. The closeness to British academic centres, which was not free of tension, determined the institutionalisation of anthropology in these territories. It is intertwined with important political, social and religious historical periods that have strongly shaped the profile of the relationship between indigenous and non-indigenous people until recent times.

Adriano Favole offers an interesting key for entering anthropology in insular Oceania using a five-step route. The chapter highlights its peculiarities and traits of originality with respect to the landscape of mainstream anthropologies. In this area, the presence of an "anthropology at work" since the origins of its population is identified by the author as one of the possible reasons why an eccentric position was assigned to insider anthropologists compared to those in other places around the world, as well the early founding of some institutions that determined the consolidation of an anthropology in the Pacific. Compared to the dominant research model of the two main hegemonic English and French traditions involved in the area, anthropology in Oceania has, for example, taken a stand against the standard mode of ethnographic reporting of the monographic genre, pursuing an open approach that questions the "classical" model of research, fieldwork, the status of "informants" and the relationship between the theory and practice of ethnographic inquiry.

The chapter on anthropology in China takes us to a context that is still little studied by the academic community, even though Malinowski already appreciated it and wrote the preface to the book by Fei Xiaotong, who obtained his doctorate at the London School of Economics in the 1930s. **Roberto Malighetti** takes us through a reconstruction of the formation of an anthropological school and its articulations, illustrating how "this process [overcomes] the rigid dualism between internal and external influences and the idea of so-called *indigenous anthropologies*, encapsulated

40 G. D'AGOSTINO AND V. MATERA

within unlikely forms of authenticity and purity", and reconstructing the dialogue that Chinese anthropology had with the Soviet Union, with hegemonic traditions and with Japan, shaping "a complicated dialogue, creative and critical". Indeed, the analysis Malighetti devotes to contemporaneity shows great vivacity and ability to decline conceptual tools elaborated elsewhere for an original reading of a layered and complex context that interrogates anthropology far beyond issues related to multiculturalism and pluralism.

Irene Maffi's contribution on anthropology in Arabic-speaking countries closes this book. A difficult context, so to speak, both with respect to the acquisition of distinctly critical and deconstructive perspectives, such as those of cultural and social anthropology, and with respect to the problematic possibility of acquiring useful sources to trace their route, which are very little indicated and traceable. The author exposes the difficulties she encountered, and the solutions adopted to obtain enough elements to (partially) complete the task of outlining a history of the discipline in the Arab countries. What emerges is how difficult it is to establish disciplinary roots in Maghreb, Mashreq and the Arabian Peninsula of knowledge that is still perceived, in some respects, as an expression of colonial power, a fact that delays academic institutionalisation and circulation in terms of an internal dialogue in Arabic. In fact, attempts to give visibility to reconstructions of local anthropology in Arabic by Arab anthropologists are rare, and English and French mostly monopolise local anthropological studies, also because they are often aimed at interacting with the NGOs involved there. The concept of "disconnection" appears as an emblematic trait of anthropological production (and of social sciences in general) in the area: a disconnection of Arab societies from their colonial past, a disconnection of local research from the knowledge produced by the global North, contested and rejected as an expression not only of colonial logic but also of economic and political dependencies. It provides a *radical* perspective that does not fail to emphasise some local discursive fields in a critical and therefore interesting way.[39]

---

[39] We would like to thank Charlotte Buckmaster for her competent and professional approach in reviewing the English language.

1 INTRODUCTION: FOR A HISTORY OF ANTHROPOLOGY IN THE PLURAL   41

REFERENCES

Abu-Lughod, L. (1991). Writing Against Culture. In R. G. Fox (Ed.), *Recapturing Anthropology* (pp. 466–479). School of American Research Press.

Affergan, F. (1987). *Exotisme et alterité. Essai sur les fondements d'une critique de l'anthropologie*. PUF.

Amselle, J.-L. (2001). *Branchements, Anthropologie de l'universalité des cultures*. Flammarion.

Appadurai, A. (1996). *Modernity at Large*. University of Minnesota Press.

Augé, M. (1994). *Pour une anthropologie des mondes contemporains*. Aubier.

Barley, N. (1986). *The Innocent Anthropologist: Notes from a Mud Hut*. Penguin.

Barth, F., Gingrich, A., Parkin, R., & Silverman, S. (Eds.). (2005). *One discipline, four ways: British, German, French, and American Anthropology*. Chicago University Press.

Beattie, J. H. M. (1964). *Other Cultures. Aims, Methods and Achievements in Social Anthropology*. Routledge & Kegan Paul.

Butler, C. (2002). *A Very Short Introduction to Postmodernism*. Oxford University Press.

Caldeira, T. (2000). *City of Walls: Crime, Segregation, and Citizenship in São Paulo*. University of California Press.

Callan, H. (2018). Introduction. In H. Callan (Ed.), *The International Encyclopedia of Anthropology*. John Wiley & Sons.

Cardona, G. R. (1986). *I sei lati del mondo*. Laterza.

Cardoso de Oliveira, R. (1999-2000). Peripheral Anthropologies 'versus' Central Anthropologies. In *Journal of Latin American Anthropology*, 4 (2)—5 (1), pp. 10-30.

Cirese, A. M. (1976). *Intellettuali, folklore, istinto di classe. Note su Verga, Deledda, Scotellaro, Gramsci*. Einaudi.

Clifford, J. (1988). *The Predicament of Culture: Twentieth-Century Ethnography, Literature and Art*. Harvard University Press.

Clifford, J. (1997). *Routes: Travel and translation in the late twentieth century*. Harvard University Press.

Clifford, J., & Marcus, G. (1986). *Writing Culture. The Poetics and Politics of Ethnography*. University of California Press.

Colajanni, A. (2012). *Gli usignoli dell'imperatore*. CISU.

Colajanni, A. (2020). Il 'prospettivismo' e le 'ontologie' indigene amerindiane. Una ricostruzione storico-critica del dibattito degli ultimi decenni. *Rac—Rivista di antropologia contemporanea*, 1, 9–54.

Comaroff, J., & Comaroff, J. L. (2012). *Theory from the South. Or, How Euro-America is Evolving Toward Africa*. Routledge.

D'Agostino, G. (2020). Questioni storiografiche e didattica universitaria della demologia in Italia. *Voci, XVII*, 120–144.

42 G. D'AGOSTINO AND V. MATERA

Darnell, R. (1977). History of Anthropology in Historical Perspective. *Annual Review of Anthropology*, 6, 399–417. http://www.jstor.org/stable/2949338.

Descola, P. (2005). *Par-delà nature et culture*. Gallimard.

Fabian, J. (1983). *Time and the Other: How Anthropology Makes Its Object*. Columbia University Press.

Fabian, J. (2000). The Other Revisited: Critical Afterthoughts. *Anthropological Theory*, 6(2), 139–152.

Fabietti, U. (Ed.). (1998). *Antropologi e informatori*. Carocci.

Fabietti, U. (2001). *Antropologia culturale. L'esperienza e l'interpretazione*. Laterza.

Fabietti, U., Malighetti, R., & Matera, V. (2020). *Dal tribale al globale*. Pearson.

Fahim, H., & Helmer, K. (1980). Indigenous Anthropology in Non-Western Countries: A Further Elaboration. *Journal of Latin American Anthropology*, 21(5), 644–663.

Falk Moore, S. (1994). *Anthropology and Africa: Changing Perspectives on a Changing Scene*. University of Virginia Press.

Fanon, F. (1961). *Les damnés de la terre*. François Maspero.

Fassin, D. (2012). Toward a Critical Moral Anthropology. In D. Fassin (Ed.), *A Companion to Moral Anthropology* (pp. 1–17). Wiley-Blackwell.

Fassin, D. (2013). The Moral Question in Anthropology. In D. Fassin & S. Lézé (Eds.), *Moral Anthropology: A Critical Reader* (pp. 1–12). Routledge.

Faubion, J. (2011). *An Anthropology of Ethics*. Cambridge University Press.

Fillitz, T. (2013). Spatialising the Field: Conceptualising Fields and Interconnections in the Context of Contemporary Art of Africa. In V. Matera (Ed.), *De-constructing the Field. Archivio Antropologico Mediterraneo*, XVI, 15, 2, 19–28.

Fischer, M. (2007). Culture and Cultural Analysis as Experimental Systems. *Cultural Anthropology*, 22, 1–65.

Forde, C., Hubert, J., & Turnbul, I. P. (Eds.). (2002). *The Dead and Their Possessions: Repatriation in Principle, Policy and Practice*. Routledge.

Geertz, C. (1983). From the Native Point of View, on the Nature of Anthropological Understanding. In C. Geertz (Ed.), *Local Knowledge, Further Essays in Interpretative Anthropology*. Basic Books.

Geertz, C. (2000). *Available Light. Anthropological Reflections on Philosophical Topics*. Princeton University Press.

Geertz, C. (2004). What Is a State If It Is Not a Sovereign?: Reflections on Politics in Complicated Places. *Current Anthropology*, 45(5), 577–593. 10.1086/423972.

Gerholm, T., & Hannerz, U. (Eds.). (1982). The Shaping of National Anthropologies. *Ethnos: Journal of Anthropology*, 47, 1–2.

Glissant, E. (1996). *Introduction à une poétique du diverse*. Gallimard.

Gupta, A., & Ferguson, J. (1997). Discipline and Practice: The 'Field' as Site, Method, and Location in Anthropology. In A. Gupta & J. Ferguson (Eds.),

1 INTRODUCTION: FOR A HISTORY OF ANTHROPOLOGY IN THE PLURAL   43

Anthropological Locations: Boundaries and Grounds of a Field Science (pp. 1–47). University of California Press.

Hallowell, I. (1960). Ojibwa Ontology, Behavior & World View. In S. Diamond (Ed.), *Culture & History* (pp. 19–52). Columbia University Press.

Hannerz, U. (1996). *Transnational Connections. Culture, People, Places.* Routledge.

Hannerz, U. (2010). *Anthropology's World. Life in a Twenty-First-Century Discipline.* Pluto Press.

Harrison, R. (2013). *Heritage. Critical Approach.* Routledge.

Harvey, D. (1989). *The Condition of Postmodernity: An Enquiry into the Origins of Cultural Change.* Basil Blackwell.

Henry, J. P. (2004). Challenges in Managing Culturally Sensitive Collections at the National Museum of the American Indian. In L. E. Sullivan & A. Edwards (Eds.), *Stewards of the Sacred* (pp. 105–112). American Association of Museums.

Herzfeld, M. (2001). *Anthropology: Theoretical Practice in Culture and Society.* Blackwell.

Hymes, D. H. (1962). On Studying the History of Anthropology. *ITEMS, 16*(3), 25–27.

Hymes, D. H. (Ed.). (1969). *Reinventing Anthropology.* Vintage Books.

Hymes, D. H. (1974). *Foundations in Sociolinguistics. An Ethnographic Approach.* Pennsylvania University Press.

Ingold, T. (1993). The Art of Translation in a Continuous World. In G. Pálsson (Ed.), *Beyond Boundaries: Understanding, Translation and Anthropological Discourse* (pp. 210–230). Berg.

Ingold, T. (2004). Culture in the Ground. *Journal of Material Culture, 9*(3), 315–340.

Ingold, T. (2007). *Anthropology is not Ethnography.* Radcliffe-Brown Lecture to the British Academy.

Isaac, G. (2009). Responsibilities Towards Knowledge: The Zuni Museum and the Reconciling of Different Knowledge Systems. In S. Sleeper-Smith (Ed.), *Contesting Knowledge: Museums and Indigenous Perspectives* (pp. 303–321). University of Nebraska Press.

Jansen, J. C., & Osterhammel, J. (2017). *Decolonization: A Short History.* Princeton University Press.

Jones, D. (1988; ed. or. 1970). *Towards a Native Anthropology.* In J.B. Cole (Ed.), *Anthropology of the Nineties: introductory readings*, London: Collier Macmillan, New York: Free Press, pp. 30–41.

Keesing, R. (1994). Theories of Culture Revisited. In R. Borowsky (Ed.), *Assessing Cultural Anthropology* (pp. 301–312). McGraw Hill.

Kilani, M. (1994). *L'invention de l'autre. Essais sur le discours anthropologique.* Payot.

Kramer, J. (2006). *Switchbacks: Art, Ownership, and Nuxalk National Identity.* University of British Columbia Press.

44 G. D'AGOSTINO AND V. MATERA

Krotz, E. (1997). Anthropologie of the South: Their Rise, Their Silencing, Their Characteristics. *Critique of Anthropology*, *17*(3), 237–251.

Kuclick, H. (Ed.). (2008). *A New History of Anthropology*. Blackwell.

Lanternari, V. (1977). Ernesto de Martino etnologo meridionalista: Vent'anni dopo. *L'Uomo Società Tradizione Sviluppo*, *1*(1), 29–56.

Lanternari, V. (1990). *"L'incivilimento dei barbari"*. *Problemi di etnocentrismo e d'identità*. Dedalo.

Latour, B. (1991). *Nous n'avons jamais été modernes. Essai d'anthropologie symétrique*. La Découverte.

Latour, B. (1999). *Politiques de la nature. Comment faire entrer les sciences en démocratie*. La Découverte.

Lévi-Strauss, C. (1953). *Anthropologie structurale*. Librairie Plon.

Mafeje, A. (2001). Anthropology in Post-independence Africa: End of an Era and the Problem of Self-Redefinition. In *African Social Scientists' Reflections, Part 1*, Nairobi: Heinrich Böll Foundation, pp. 28-74.

Malinowski, B. (1922 [1978]). *Argonauts of the Western Pacific*. Routledge and Kegan Paul.

Mancuso, A. (2018). *Altre persone. Antropologia, visioni del mondo e ontologie indigene*. Mimesis.

Mancuso, A. (2020). La 'svolta ontologica' e le questioni epistemologiche in antropologia. *Rac—Rivista di antropologia contemporanea*, *1*, 55–89.

Matera, V. (2005). *Antropologia culturale e linguistica*. Unicopli.

Matera, V. (2017). *Antropologia contemporanea. La diversità culturale in un mondo globale*. Laterza.

Matera, V., & Biscaldi, A. (Eds.). (2021). *Ethnography. A Theoretically Oriented Practice*. Palgrave Macmillan.

Mbembe, A. (2021). *Out of the Dark Night. Essays on Decolonization*. Columbia University Press.

Nader, L. (1969). Up the Anthropologist—Perspectives Gained from Studying Up. In D. H. Hymes (Ed.), *Reinventing Anthropology* (pp. 284–311). Pantheon.

Narayan, K. (1993). How Native is a 'Native' Anthropologist? *American Anthropologist*, *95*(3), 671–682.

Obeyesekere, G. (1997). *The Apotheosis of Captain Cook. European Mythmaking in the Pacific*. Princeton University Press.

Paini, A., & Aria, M. (Eds.). (2017). *La densità delle cose. Oggetti ambasciatori tra Oceania e Europa*. Pacini.

Palumbo, B. (2018). *Lo strabismo della dea. Antropologia, accademia e società in Italia*. Edizioni Museo Pasqualino.

Pina Cabral, J. de (2004). Uma história de sucesso: A antropologia brasileira vista de longe. In W. Trajano Filho & G. Lins Ribeiro (Eds.), *O campo da antropologia no Brasil* (pp. 249–265). Contracapa/ABA.

1 INTRODUCTION: FOR A HISTORY OF ANTHROPOLOGY IN THE PLURAL   45

Pizza, G. (2017). Ernesto de Martino fuori di sé. Dal Nordamerica alla Francia. *nostos*, *2*(dicembre), 193–236.

Povinelli, E. A. (1994a). Do Rocks Listen? The Cultural Politics of Apprehending Australian Aboriginal Labor. *American Anthropologist, 97*(3), 505–518.

Povinelli, E. A. (1994b). *Labor's Lot: The Power, History, and Culture of Aboriginal Action*. University of Chicago Press.

Povinelli, E. A. (2002). *The Cunning of Recognition: Indigenous Alterities and the Making of Australian Multiculturalism*. Duke University Press.

Rabinow, P. (1977). *Reflections on Fieldwork in Morocco*. University of California Press.

Remotti, F. (2014). *Per un'antropologia inattuale*. Eléuthera.

Restrepo, E. (2018). World Anthropologies. In H. Callan (Ed.), *The International Encyclopedia of Anthropology*. John Wiley & Sons, s.v.

Ribeiro, G. L., & Escobar, A. (Eds.). (2006). *World Anthropologies: Disciplinary Transformations within Systems of Power*. Berg Publishers.

Ridington, R. (1988). Knowledge, Power and the Individual in Subarctic Hunting Societies. *American Anthropologist, 1*(90), 127–144.

Rosaldo, R. (1993). *Culture and Truth. The Remaking of Cultural Analysis*. Beacon & Press.

Rushefort, S. (1986). The Bear Lake Indians. In Morrison & Wilson (Ed.), *The Canadian Experience*. McClelland & Stewart.

Sahlins, M. (1981). *Storie d'altri*. Guida.

Said, E. (1978). *Orientalism*. Pantheon.

Satta, G. (2018). L'etnocentrismo critico e le alterne fortune dell'umanesimo etnografico demartiniano. In A. Fanelli (Ed.), Una "difficile alleanza": il carteggio tra Alberto Mario Cirese e Ernesto de Martino. In *Lares. Quadrimestrale di studi demoetnoantropologici*, anno LXXXIV, n. 3, 521–532.

Scheper-Hughes, N. (2000). The Global Traffic in Human Organs. *Current Anthropology, 41*(2), 191–224. 10.1086/300123.

Scollon, R., & Scollon, S. (1979). *Linguistic convergence: An Ethnography of Speaking at Fort Chipewyan*. Academic Press.

Signorelli, A. (2015). *Ernesto de Martino. Teoria antropologica e metodologia della ricerca*. L'Asino d'Oro.

Spiro, M. E. (1996). Postmodernist Anthropology, Subjectivity, and Science: A Modernist Critique. *Comparative Studies in Society and History, 38*(1), 759–780.

Stocking, G. W., Jr. (1963). Matthew Arnold, E.B. Tylor, and the Uses of Invention. *American Anthropologist, 65*, 783–799.

Stocking, G. W., Jr. (1968). *Race, Culture, and Evolution. Essays in the History of Anthropology*. The University of Chicago Press.

Stocking, G. W., Jr. (1973). Prospects and Problems. *History of Anthropology Newsletter, 1*(1), 2.

Stocking, G. W., Jr. (1982). Afterword: A View from the Center. *Ethnos: Journal of Anthropology, 47*(1–2), 172–186.
Sully, D. (Ed.). (2007). *Decolonising Conservation: Caring for Maori Meeting Houses outside New Zealand*. Left Coast Press.
Trouillot, M.-R. (1991). Anthropology and the Savage Slot: The Poetics and Politics of Otherness. In R. Fox (Ed.), *Recapturing Anthropology: Working in the Present* (pp. 18–44). School of American Research Press.
Trouillot, M.-R. (2003). *Global Transformations: Anthropology and the Modern Word*. Palgrave Macmillan.
Viveiros de Castro, E. B. (2012). *Cosmological perspectivism in Amazonia and elsewhere. Four lectures given in the Department of Social Anthropology, Cambridge University, February-March 1998*. HAU Books.
Wagner, R. (1980). *The Invention of Culture*. Chicago University Press.

CHAPTER 2

People and Ideas from Elsewhere: Notes on Social Anthropology in the UK

Luca Rimoldi and Marco Gardini

Introduction[1]

With a few key exceptions (including Gaillard, 1997 and Vermeulen & Roldàn, 1995), until at least the early twenty-first century, accounts of the history of anthropology concentrated almost exclusively on the disciplinary traditions developed by the main victors of the two World Wars: Great Britain, France, and the United States. There are multiple reasons for this tendency: as scholars have shown, the development of anthropology in other colonial or former colonial Western countries (such as Italy or

---

[1] Although the authors worked together to draft the entire text, Sects. 2, 3 and 4 can be attributed to Luca Rimoldi and the Introduction, Sect. 1 and Conclusions to Marco Gardini.

L. Rimoldi (✉)
"Riccardo Massa" Department of Human Sciences for Education, University of Milano-Bicocca, Milan, Italy
e-mail: luca.rimoldi@unimib.it

M. Gardini
Department of Political and Social Sciences, University of Pavia, Pavia, Italy
e-mail: marco.gardini@unipv.it

© The Author(s), under exclusive license to Springer Nature Switzerland AG 2023
G. D'Agostino, V. Matera (eds.), *Histories of Anthropology*,
https://doi.org/10.1007/978-3-031-21258-1_2

47

Germany) was often hindered by the emergence of totalitarian regimes and did not find fertile grounds for revival until the 1950s or later. In newly independent countries, given the strongly colonial connotations that the discipline had assumed, it was not until decolonisation, and sometimes even later, that university chairs in anthropology were established. Furthermore, there were significant linguistic barriers: few British or French anthropologists were able to read texts in Spanish, Portuguese, German, Italian or Russian, and there was a long delay before the major anthropological texts written in those languages were translated (e.g. De Martino's work).

Thanks to increasing interest in the role of anthropology in other national scholarly traditions, we are now able not only to reflect more broadly on the development of the discipline, but also to critically rethink its relative status in the more "hegemonic" national traditions. The resulting insight is that the development of anthropology cannot be reconstructed on a national basis without also underlining its extreme interconnectedness with an intellectual landscape that was, in itself, profoundly transnational, a landscape composed of dialogue, exchange and the circulation of ideas and people.

The tradition of British social anthropology is certainly a case in point. While it might appear hegemonic when viewed from the standpoint of non-English-speaking countries, as many observers have pointed out (Barth, 2005; Kuklick, 2008a, 2008b), it was founded and developed by thinkers whose positions were eccentric or marginal in relation to British academic institutions (religious minorities, non-aristocrats, migrants, and women). It was able to take root as one of the most significant anthropological traditions in the world not only thanks to the vastness of British colonial possessions and dominions, but also because the heart of the Empire operated as both a destination and space of transit or departure for anthropologists from the imperial peripheries or other contexts. These "external" contributions had a considerable influence on the birth and development of the "local" disciplinary tradition (Firth, 1951). As Kuklick (2008, p. 77) argued:

> Of course, British anthropology has distinctive features, if only because it is practised within distinctive institutional structures. At every level, from the departmental to the national, there are idiosyncratic characteristics. But it is fair to say that British anthropology today is at least as international as it was in the late nineteenth century. And the range of subjects that interest its practitioners is at least as broad as it was then.

2 PEOPLE AND IDEAS FROM ELSEWHERE: NOTES ON SOCIAL... 49

Rather than summarising a story that has already been extensively recounted (Barth, 2005; Bernard, 2000; Bohannan & Glazer, 1988; Schippers, 1995; Deliège, 2006; Mcgee & Warms, 2013; Fabietti, 2020; Kuper, 1983, 2015; Urry, 1993; Moore, 2009; Kuklick, 2008a), our aim in this chapter is to describe how British social anthropology has managed to elaborate, collect and fruitfully employ perspectives from "elsewhere". We do not wish to downplay the important role of complex institutional dynamics (the foundation of a department, e.g.) and political ones (see Mills, 2018) in shaping the history of this discipline. Nor do we set out to recapitulate such a complex trajectory in this brief account. Nonetheless, the chapter sets off from questions such as: "Is British social anthropology still typically 'British'? Or, to pose the question in a different way, it is still distinctly 'social'?" (Spencer, 2000, p. 1). We take this tack on the belief that the trajectory of British social anthropology, like that of any other national anthropological tradition, can be interpreted as a series of intense, often conflict-ridden exchanges and dialogues that transcend geographical, social and political boundaries. It is perhaps no coincidence that many of the authors who have tried their hand at encapsulating this history, such as Fredrik Barth (Norwegian), Adam Kuper (South African), Paul Bohannan or Henrika Kucklick (both American), and Talal Asad (Saudi Arabian), hailed from elsewhere whilst also participating in UK anthropology at various stages of their respective careers.

To this end, after briefly discussing the degree of internationalisation of British anthropology from its inception to the end of the twentieth century, we concentrate on the "dialogues" between this current of scholarship and American anthropology, the former colonies and the rest of Europe. As space limitations prevent us from aiming at a detailed reconstruction of these multifaceted inflows and outflows, we instead focus on several figures who both formed an integral part of a history of British social anthropology and acted as the bridges the discipline succeeded in extending beyond national borders.

DIALOGUES FROM ELSEWHERE: BRITISH SOCIAL ANTHROPOLOGY

On various occasions, Meyer Fortes (1953, 1969) suggested that anthropology comprises at least two distinct lineages: the first can be traced back through the work of Alfred R. Radcliffe-Brown, Robert Lowie and William HR Rivers to Lewis H. Morgan and Henry JS Maine, while the latter ranges from Alfred Kroeber, Bronislaw Malinowski and James G. Frazer to Edward B. Tylor and Franz Boas. "I see the first line – wrote Fortes (1969, p. 14) – as the source of our structural concepts and theories, the second as the source of our specialty in the study of the facts of custom, or culture". USA cultural anthropology and British social anthropology could thus be seen as having exchanged "their founding ancestors". Indeed, the first anthropological definition of culture was formulated by Tylor,[2] a British Quaker who was appointed as the first professor of anthropology in the United Kingdom (at Oxford) in 1896; this definition then became the central concept of American anthropology from Boas onwards. Meanwhile, the foundations for kinship studies, a topic widely investigated in early twentieth-century British social anthropology, were laid in mid-nineteenth century by Morgan, an American anthropologist. However, as George W. Stocking (1996, p. 13) and Thomas H. Eriksen and Finn S. Nielsen (2001, p. 31) have noted, this interpretation remains partial in many respects. Both Tylor's definition of culture and Boas' historical particularism and cultural relativism had their respective roots in the broader intellectual arena of nineteenth century German anthropology, an intellectual milieu in which an insistence on the importance of *Kultur* represented the romantic antithesis to Enlightenment-style universalism (see Remotti, 2011).

The concepts of culture and the "psychic unity of mankind" (as theorised by Adolf Bastian, 1860 and adopted in an evolutionary framework by Tylor) were not the only elements Germany exported. German diffusionist theories also influenced a component of emerging anthropological thought and provided a prompt—albeit less widely embraced—counterargument to the prevailing evolutionist paradigm that characterized British anthropology at the time (Eriksen & Nielsen, 2001). The debates between these two perspectives were short-lived, however. The limits of the kind of "armchair anthropology" characterising both evolutionism and diffusionism became more and more evident in the face of the need to collect firsthand ethnographic data. The Torres Strait expedition, organised in 1898 by Alfred C. Haddon and involving Charles George Seligman and William H. Rivers among others, was emblematic of this new need for data

---

[2] "Culture or civilization, taken in its wide ethnographic sense, is that complex whole which includes knowledge, belief, art, morals, law, custom, and any other capabilities and habits acquired by man as a member of society" (Tylor, 1871, p. 1).

2 PEOPLE AND IDEAS FROM ELSEWHERE: NOTES ON SOCIAL... 51

collection and in many ways mirrored the kind of ethnographic surveying North American anthropologists were carrying out among Native Americans.

It was the centrality of field research that paved the way for the establishment of Malinowski's functionalist and Radcliffe-Brown's structural-functionalist perspectives in the 1920s and 1930s. With some internal variation, these theoretical frameworks became the epistemological scaffolding of British social anthropology in the first half of the twentieth century, and they, too, were developed thanks to thinkers and theories from elsewhere. Malinowski was a Polish immigrant who, struck by James Frazer's Golden Bough, decided to study anthropology under Seligman and the Finnish sociologist Edward Westermarck. As a non-British citizen living in Australia at the outbreak of World War I, Malinowski was automatically classified as an internal enemy, but the Australian government allowed him to continue his research. Given these circumstances, Malinowski was able to develop a long-term, solo (so to speak) model of field research centred on a solid understanding of native languages and "participant observation", the very methodology that went on to constitute the foundations of anthropology as a whole (D'Agostino, 2021). Many consider his monograph on the Trobriand Islanders (Malinowski, 1922) to be the first "modern" anthropological text. Hired as a reader in 1923 at the London School of Economics (LSE) where Seligman and Westermarck already taught, Malinowski was given the school's first chair in social anthropology in 1927. From 1924 onwards, his seminars came to represent one of the most important educational moments in British anthropology, attended by many of the most authoritative anthropologists of subsequent generations including Edward E. Evans-Pritchard, Ashley Montagu, Raymond Firth, Edmund Leach, Hortense Powdermaker, Isaac Schapera, Siegfried Nadel, Audrey Richards, Jack H. Driberg and Lucy Mair. Many of these figures, such as Evans-Pritchard or Mair, could "boast of solid British origins"; others, however, came from very different backgrounds: Powdermaker was a student from the USA, Nadel was born in Vienna and trained in Germany, Schapera was originally from South Africa and Firth was from New Zealand.

The London School of Economics was also a training ground for the first generation of female anthropologists who ended up contributing deeply to the internationalisation of British social anthropology. Most of the female professional anthropologists working in the 1920s and 1930s had been Malinowski's students: in addition to the aforementioned Audrey

Richards, Hortense Powdermaker and Lucy Mair, there was also Monica Hunter (Wilson), Hilda Beemer (Kuper), Edith Clarke, Rosemary Firth and Elizabeth Brown. Audrey Richards began studying at LSE in 1927 alongside Evans-Pritchard, Firth and Schapera under the supervision of Malinowski. She was the first female anthropologist to conduct fieldwork research in Northern Rhodesia between 1930 and 1933. In 1932 she earned her doctorate based on research with the Bemba, a population she continued to study until 1934. After teaching at LSE (1937) and Johannesburg (1938), Richards was hired as secretary of the Colonial Office's Colonial Council for Scientific Research (1941). From 1944 to 1950 she taught at Witwatersrand before becoming director of the Institute of Research into Eastern Africa, where she remained until 1955. In 1956, she returned to England to teach at Cambridge and, that same year, published one of her most well-known works, *Chisinau: A Girl's Initiation Ceremony among the Bemba in Northern Rhodesia* (Richards, 1982). This book recounted a young woman's perspective on an initiation ritual for the first time in the history of the discipline, and Richards outlined the relationship between these rites and the local society's broader social structure and values.

Phyllis Kaberry provides another example of this internationalisation. Born in California to English parents, Kaberry spent most of her youth in Australia after her father, an architect, moved to Sydney. It was there that she became interested in anthropology, taking courses by Raymond Firth and Ian Hogbin before moving to London (1936), where she—together with Audrey Richards—became one of Malinowski's assistants and earned a doctorate (1939). She carried out field research in Australia, New Guinea, Nigeria and Cameroon, always paying particular attention to the role of women and thereby helping to broaden the perspective of the discipline.

As Edmund Leach (1984) and Fredrik Barth (2005) have noted, the London School of Economics was the real driving force behind British social anthropology in the 1920s and 1930s. At Oxford, which had hosted Tylor, and Cambridge, where Rivers and Haddon had taught, anthropological studies languished at that time. The discipline's position at Oxford remained marginal until at least 1937 when Radcliffe-Brown assumed the chair in anthropology. At Cambridge, Malinowski's *Sex and Repression in Savage Society* (Malinowski, 1927) was considered scandalous and students were not permitted to read it without faculty permission (Leach, 1984). However, renewed impetus arrived in 1949 when Meyer Fortes, a

2 PEOPLE AND IDEAS FROM ELSEWHERE: NOTES ON SOCIAL... 53

South African-born student of Radcliffe-Brown (and in some ways the one who carried forward his teacher's structural functionalist legacy), was recruited to the faculty. He was soon joined by Edmund Leach, a student of Malinowski and Firth who instead represented a critical voice in relation to the disciplinary tradition founded by Radcliffe-Brown.

Unlike Malinowski, Radcliffe-Brown was a British citizen by birth, albeit from a modest background. However, he was profoundly influenced by Durkheim's work and embraced the sociologist's idea of concentrating on the notion of social structure. Radcliffe-Brown was also friends with the exiled Russian anarchist Kropotkin, an association that earned him the nickname "Anarchy Brown" in his youth. It was likely these influences that led him to develop a curiosity for so-called stateless societies (destined to become a pivotal theme in British anthropology) and rendered him eccentric, in many respects, vis-à-vis the academic norms of the time.

While Malinowski has been acknowledged in historical accounts as the founder of a new way of doing ethnography, Radcliffe-Brown was recognised as having an unquestionable aptitude for theorising, laying the foundations for wide-ranging comparative investigation, and establishing the line of inquiry considered to constitute British social anthropology until at least the 1950s. Moreover, Radcliffe-Brown followed an extremely international academic trajectory as a scholar. Not only did he conduct multiple field trips (Andaman Islands, Australia), but for many years he held teaching positions well outside the United Kingdom: in South Africa (1920–1925) where he trained prominent anthropologists such as Schapera and collaborated with Winifred Tucker Hoernlé, in Australia (1925-1931) where he helped younger colleagues such as Gregory Bateson, Margaret Mead and Raymond Firth, and in the United States (1931–1937). His return home in 1937 to take the Oxford anthropology chair coincided with Malinowski's departure for the United States, where the latter died five years later. Under the aegis of Radcliffe-Brown and his students and collaborators (such as Meyer Fortes and Evans-Pritchard, who inherited Radcliffe-Brown's chair in 1946), Oxford and subsequently Cambridge soon became key competitors for the leading position held by the London School of Economics, where Raymond Firth succeeded Malinowski in 1944.

They were not alone. In 1949, Max Gluckman became head of the department in Manchester and gathered around him many anthropologists who, driven by their interest in the dynamics of social change and conflict in colonial Africa, gradually moved away from the relatively static structural-functionalist approaches. Gluckman, who was born in South Africa and trained with Hoernlé and Schapera, soon became part of the circle of Africanists gathered around Radcliffe-Brown, thanks to the research he conducted among the Zulus. He also contributed to the ambitious collective, comparative volume *African Political System* (1940). Gluckman joined the Rhodes-Livingstone Institute in 1938 and took over as its director after Wilson's resignation in 1941. Over the course of the following years, he worked together with his collaborators and students to analyse both labour migration to the colonial mines and the processes of de/re-tribalisation triggered by these migratory flows and the multiple conflicts cutting across colonial societies (Gardini & Rimoldi, 2021; Gordon, 2018).

Gluckman's arrival in Manchester testified to the high degree of interconnection between the colonies and metropolises characterising British anthropology. As Kuper argues (Kuper, 1999b, p. 83—see also Kuper, 1999a):

> Not only were funds, jobs, even careers sometimes on offer to metropolitan anthropologists from colonial or dominion governments: there was also a two-way traffic in ideas. Indeed, it could be argued that the institutional and intellectual origins of British social anthropology should be traced to Australia and South Africa.

In Manchester, Gluckman assembled a circle of anthropologists whose research agenda featured significant thematic similarities to those developed in the same period in France by George Balandier and his students: on both sides of the channel, the study of colonial contexts, conflicts, migration, urbanisation and social change processes led to a profound rethinking of the static and ahistorical theoretical models that had been formulated up to that point and opened the doors of anthropology to implicitly or explicitly Marxist perspectives. Many members of this group likewise came from "elsewhere": J. Clyde Mitchell, director of the Rhodes-Livingstone Institute after Gluckman the then-professor of urban anthropology, first at Manchester and later at Oxford, was South African, as were Hilda and Adam Kuper. Abner Cohen, later a professor at School of Oriental and African Studies (SOAS), was born and raised in Baghdad before going to work in Tehran and Israel, Elizabeth Bott was Canadian, and John A. Barnes was Australian.

These contributions from elsewhere were not limited to Manchester, however. There are many possible examples: Christoph von Fürer-Haimendorf, a student of Malinowski who secured the chair at SOAS in 1951 and went on to help render it an important centre of anthropological study, was born and trained in Austria. Jean La Fontaine, professor at LSE between 1978 and 1983, was born in Kenya; Mary Douglas, who studied under Malinowski and contributed, together with Leach and Needham, to maintaining a lively dialogue with French anthropological thought (cf. Fardon, 1999), was born in San Remo, studied at the Sorbonne and was the first British anthropologist to conduct research in a French-speaking African country (the Belgian Congo). Ernest Gellner carried out his first fieldwork among the Berbers after drawing inspiration from Evans-Pritchard's work on segmentation and went on to become one of the most important scholars of nationalism; he was born into a Jewish Czech family that took refuge in London in 1939.

After undergoing a lengthy process of academic consolidation, thanks in part to these contributions, British anthropology enjoyed a period of considerable expansion between the 1950s and the 1970s both numerically and in terms of its plurality of theoretical approaches. Even while it grew, however, key figures such as Meyer Fortes, Evans-Pritchard, Firth and Gluckman continued to exert intense control over the discipline as a whole via their respective departments. According to Barth (2005), these were the golden years of British social anthropology in which a heterogeneous array of research foci was accompanied by a marked capacity for synthesis and common grounds for discussion (see also Foreman, 2013).

When Fortes, Evans-Pritchard, Firth and Gluckman retired in the late 1960s and early 1970s, the field opened up to the arrival of a younger generation that ferried British social anthropology towards new topics and theoretical perspectives. At Cambridge, Meyer Fortes was replaced by Jack Goody, followed by Ernest Gellner in 1984 and Marilyn Strathern in 1993 (later succeeded by Henrietta Moore and James Laidlaw). At Oxford, Evans-Pritchard was followed by Maurice Freedman and then Rodney Needham, while the Gluckman chair at Manchester passed first to Emrys Peters and then to Marilyn Strathern, Tim Ingold and John Gledhill. In terms of theoretical frameworks, new approaches contributed to calling into question both structural functionalism and structuralism and to opening up fissures in an academic field that up to that point had succeeded in remaining, if not homogeneous, at least engaged in close dialogue. Examples of these fissures include the growing influence of Marxist perspectives in the 1970s, the feminist approaches and anthropology of gender developed by Shirley Ardener, Strathern and Moore, the renewed dialogue with history characterising the work of Jack Goody or Alan Macfarlane, and the growth of post-colonial stances as introduced by Talal Asad or linked to the growing influence of French authors such as Foucault, Bourdieu and Derrida.

One of the factors behind this pluralisation was undoubtedly the considerable increase in the number of anthropologists, university centres establishing new anthropology professorships (Sussex, Aberdeen, and Edinburgh, to name a few) and research settings: while at the end of the 1940s, British universities hosted only 30 anthropologists, by 1963 the number had increased to 50 before rising to 120 in 1983 and 220 in 1999 (Spencer, 2000). By 2021, the Association of Social Anthropologists (ASA) had grown to represent 600 members, approximately 90% of whom were based in the United Kingdom (https://www.theasa.org/history.html). African societies had traditionally represented the main research field of structural functionalism between the 1930s and 1950s, and scholars continued to focus on the continent (e.g. Edwin Ardener, Henrietta Moore, Pat Caplan and James Fairhead). However, the discipline also became more varied, thanks to emerging interest in studying Eastern and Western Europe (fuelled in part by the work of Gellner and Frankenberg), and a considerable increase in research on the Indian subcontinent (e.g. David Mosse, Helen Lambert, James Laidlaw), South East Asia (e.g. Roy Ellen, Janet Carsten), Central Asia (e.g. Caroline Humphrey), the Middle East (e.g. Dawn Chatty), Madagascar (e.g. Maurice Bloch and Rita Astuti), the Arctic (e.g. Tim Ingold) and Pacific Island societies (e.g. Harvey Whitehouse).

Another aspect worth underlining is the way women fought to achieve key roles in the history of British social anthropology, interweaving broader political battles with the theoretical tools offered by feminist anthropology. The resulting achievements have been significant: as Spencer (2000: 10) reminds us, while female anthropologists in teaching positions in the 1970s accounted for about 15%, by 1999 the percentage had reached 41%. Considering only the post-1989 generation of entering faculty, the ratio shifted to 43% men and 57% women. Beginning in the 1970s, the influence of feminism (in close dialogue with developments in the rest of Europe and the United States) began to cause marked changes in the British anthropological perspective geared towards making the condition of women in different societies central to ethnographic and theoretical analyses. Over time, this stance gave way to a perspective framing gender as a social process of constructing the masculine and feminine and a system of relationships between men and women. The gender perspective thus became a methodology for thinking and rethinking power relations more broadly. Shirley Ardener was among those spearheading this shift through the establishment of the Centre for Cross-Cultural Research on Women (now the International Gender Studies Centre) at Oxford University. Her husband, Edwin Ardener, was one of the scholars (along with Rodney Needham) who took over from Evans-Pritchard at Oxford. In this position, he pursued his interests in the relationship between anthropology and linguistics, a topic that was decidedly outside the canons of British social anthropology. As Henrietta Moore (1988) notes, Edwin Ardener was among the first to recognise that dominant groups often generate and control the expressive modes of dominated groups and to argue that "male bias" has also played a crucial role in the development of anthropology's own explanatory models (Ardener, 1985). This insight represented a fundamental turning point paving the way for the shift from an anthropology of women to a feminist anthropology that challenged gendered power dynamics. Beginning in the 1980s, the critique launched by Henrietta Louise Moore (1988) found that male anthropologists' work tended to reproduce patriarchal prejudices. Critical voices called for broadening the horizons of anthropological research and paying more attention to reflexivity and anthropologists' positioning in the field. Feminist anthropology pushing in these directions has made a fundamental contribution to the methodological development of the discipline as a whole (Strathern, 1987).

As many accounts have emphasised, this increasing pluralisation of theories, methods and fields as well as the increasing number of both male and female anthropologists makes it extremely challenging to synthesise developments in British anthropology between the end of the twentieth and the beginning of the twenty-first century. In their attempts to discuss this trajectory, both Barth (2005, p. 56) and Kuper (1983) have acknowledged that British anthropology succeeded in retaining high-quality standards and a diversity of research foci despite the numerous cuts to social science research funding during the Thatcher era. At the same time, however, both have bemoaned the progressive waning of the field's distinctiveness and weight as compared to other national traditions since the 1970s/80s. Regardless of whether this is in fact the case, the dialogue British anthropology has continued to cultivate with anthropology from

58   L. RIMOLDI AND M. GARDINI

"elsewhere" remains central to the field. Such dialogue can clearly be seen in the biographical and scientific trajectories of many of its scholars, both those who have transited in either direction between Great Britain and the United States and those who have continued to forge links between the UK and former colonies or between the UK and the rest of Europe.

North Atlantic Dialogues

The channels of exchange we can term North Atlantic dialogues have certainly been quite multifaceted and intense. As mentioned above, such exchanges have characterised the discipline since its earliest development, albeit unfolding in different directions depending on the historical period. As Barth (2005, pp. 56–57) argues when observing the main trend over the last few decades of the twentieth century:

> While ideas have flowed in, personnel have been leaking out. For more than thirty years there has been a distinct brain drain from Britain to the United States. This reverses the previous trend, most visible in the 1950s, when many important North American scholars [...] chose to work for extended periods in England. Since then, the significant movement in the other direction has inevitably reduced the vitality and authority of British anthropology departments.

It is worth recalling that the policies of Britain's Conservative party in the 1970s and 1980s led to the suppression of the Social Science Research Council and caused the Royal Anthropological Institute to give up its offices in Bedford Square and sell off its library to the Museum of Mankind. Many anthropologists in that period transferred into sociology departments—even though, as Mills (2018, p. 111) notes, this was perceived as tantamount to abandoning the discipline—while others moved from the UK to the USA[3].

In this section, we have chosen to briefly consider the biographical and professional trajectories of several scholars who illustrate this transatlantic dialogue. The work by Paul and Laura Bohannan, Victor Turner and David Graeber, the development of their ideas and their contributions to the history of anthropology have been shaped in part by dialogue, contact

---

[3] Examples of the former are Peter Worsley, Max Marwick and Ronald Frankenberg, while the latter included English anthropologists or those passing through the UK such as Mary Douglas, Stanley Jeyaraja Tambiah and Talal Asad.

2 PEOPLE AND IDEAS FROM ELSEWHERE: NOTES ON SOCIAL...

and exchanges between British social anthropology and American cultural anthropology.

Paul and Laura Bohannan met at the University of Arizona in 1943 and married the following year. The outbreak of World War II interrupted their studies; they both ended up graduating in 1947. Shortly after, they moved to the United Kingdom and Paul enrolled in Queen's College at Oxford University where he earned a degree in anthropology (1949). Both scholars completed doctorates in anthropology in 1951, having come into contact with the influential thought of anthropologists such as Evans-Pritchard, Fortes and Gluckman. It was in that period (1949–1953) that the Bohannan husband-wife team carried out their most important research in Africa, focusing first on the legal aspects of the Tiv in Nigeria and then developing a specific interest in the economy of this itinerant farming-based society in the years immediately preceding Nigerian state independence (1960). This fieldwork gave rise to publications including the co-written volumes *The Tiv of Central Nigeria* (Bohannan & Bohannan, 1953) and *Tiv Economy* (Bohannan & Bohannan, 1960) as well as *Justice and Judgment Among the Tiv* (Bohannan, 1957), a classic work of legal anthropology that broke with Gluckman's approach to instead underline the specificity of local juridical categories and their non-equivalence with Western ones.

It was this research among the Tiv that generated Laura's most famous article, "Shakespeare in the Bush" (Bohannan, 1966), in which the anthropologist describes Tiv elders' reactions to hearing Hamlet's story and their comments on family ties and work relationships, interactions between the world of the dead and that of the living and, of course, the construction of power relations between youth and the elderly. Writing under the pseudonym Elenore Smith Bowen, Laura Bohannan also published the novel *Return to Laughter: An Anthropological Novel*, first released in 1954. In this novel the author, the only non-fictional character, uses a first-person narrative to describe events that really happened but attributes them to fictional characters. In so doing she underlines how relationships between anthropologists and informants are constructed in a colonised and deeply hierarchical and stratified world (Cfr. Di Leonardo, 1998).

From 1951 to 1956 Paul taught at Oxford, taking the position vacated by Mary Douglas, before returning to the United States to teach first at Princeton (1956-1959), then at Northwestern (1959–1976) and finally at the University of California, Santa Barbara (1975–1982). In 1982, he was appointed director of the Department of Social Sciences and Communications at Southern California University, and he remained there until his retirement (1987). Laura, on the other hand, worked at the University of Chicago for several years before becoming a lecturer at the University of Illinois.

In the wake of work by Karl Polanyi and the substantivist school, Paul Bohannan's research interests led him to investigate how the development of the market economy in Africa had been shaped by the constraints imposed by colonial authorities. His notion of "spheres of exchange" (Bohannan, 1954, 1957), in particular, went on to become one of the central concepts of economic anthropology, and the insights he developed in the book *Markets in Africa*, edited together with Dalton, proved equally influential. Beginning in the 1960s, his research trajectories revisited issues central to economic anthropology and the anthropology of kinship, ethnographically investigating divorce, relationships between couples and their in-laws, and the lives of divorcees in the San Francisco and San Diego areas. In the book *All the Happy Families: Exploring the Varieties of Family Life* (Bohannan, 1985), Paul Bohannan argued that the rise of the divorce industry—comprising judges, lawyers, detectives, consultants and other figures dealing directly with divorce cases—represented one of the main characteristics of American society at the time (Paul and Laura Bohannan had divorced in 1975). Overall, the topics Paul and Laura Bohannan addressed in their work reflect the tension between the British social anthropology in which they were trained and the American anthropology they helped to develop.

Like the Bohannans, Victor Turner also completed his degree in the United Kingdom and then pursued a career as an anthropologist in the United States, contributing to the development of anthropological studies on religion and the performative aspects of local cultures. Turner was born in Glasgow in 1920 to an actress mother and electrical engineer father. He studied in London (UCL) and Manchester and in 1943 married Edith Lucy Brocklesby Davis. They had six children between 1944 and 1963. From 1950 to 1954, Turner worked as a Researcher at the Rhodes-Livingstone Institute in Lusaka (Zambia). It was during that time that, together with his wife Edie, he conducted his famous ethnographic research among the Ndembu of Northern Rhodesia, first investigating demography, social structure, economics and politics and then shifting his focus to the study of ritual and the interpretation of its associated symbols. His doctoral thesis, defended in Manchester in 1955 and published a few

2 PEOPLE AND IDEAS FROM ELSEWHERE: NOTES ON SOCIAL...

years later, was significantly titled *Schism and Continuity in an African Society* (1957). Here, Turner introduced the concept of "social drama" to indicate the endemic conflicts running through Ndembu society while also framing such conflicts as part of the social "mechanisms" that operate to foster group unity.

This interest in the procedural and conflictual aspects of social interaction signalled a progressive break with functionalism; at the same time, Turner's interest in the meanings that rites have for their participants and the symbols connected to such rituals prefigured the symbolic anthropology approach he went on to formulate, especially in the United States. While from 1954 to 1963 Turner worked as an assistant professor and lecturer at the University of Manchester, in 1961 he moved to Palo Alto to teach at Stanford University's Center for Advanced Study in the Behavioral Sciences (1961–1962) and then Cornell University (1963). He stayed at Cornell until 1968, serving as a professor of Anthropology and chair of the university's committee on African studies. He was on the faculty of the University of Chicago in the Department of Anthropology until 1977 when he moved to the University of Virginia, remaining there until the early 1980s. During his years at Cornell and Chicago, Turner developed and subsequently reformulated the concept of "liminality" through the paper "Betwixt and Between" presented at the 1964 conference of the American Ethnological Society (Turner, 1964) and the publication of one of his most famous works, *The Forest of Symbols* (Turner, 1967). According to Turner, by analysing rituals—and rites of passage in particular—anthropologists can grasp aspects of a group's social structure because such rituals contain and activate certain symbols that relates to group's conceptions of the world and ways of representing the principles and values underlying their social life (De Matteis, 1995). The symbolic anthropology approach introduced by Turner during his time in Chicago, together with theoretical perspectives developed first at Chicago and later at Princeton, played a decisive role in the genesis of Clifford Geertz's interpretative anthropology. Furthermore, Turner's interests in theatre, cultural performance and the "liminoid" phenomena of complex post-industrial societies converged during the period he taught at the University of Virginia to produce the 1979 volume *Process, Performance, and Pilgrimage: A Study in Comparative Symbology* (Turner, 1979). His receiving the Rivers Memorial Medal from the Royal Anthropological Institute (1965), being invited to give a Lewis Henry Morgan Lecture at the University of Rochester (1966) and occupying the William R. Kenan professorship at the University of Virginia attest to the influence and resonance his ideas enjoyed across the Atlantic.

While Turner's move from Great Britain to the United States is symptomatic of the beginning of the brain drain denounced by Barth, the opposite trajectory of the recently deceased American anthropologist David Graeber constitutes a (much more recent) counterexample, perhaps testifying to a resurgence in the appeal of British anthropology. Indeed, we are convinced that Graeber's work represents the contemporary continuation of the same North Atlantic dialogues that had developed in the early years of the discipline. Graeber, a native of New York and pupil of Marshall Sahlins at the University of Chicago, found his position as a professor at Yale being cut in 2005 (apparently for reasons related to his political activism) and thus moved to England. He obtained a readership at Goldsmiths College, working there from 2008 to 2013, and then a professorship at LSE in 2013. Combining field research (Madagascar, bureaucratic systems in Western societies) and broader theoretical and historical reflections (on debt, the state, theories of value and forms of monarchical sovereignty) with anarchist-oriented political activism (his active, enthusiastic participation in the Occupy Wall Street and Extinction Rebellion movements are well-known), Graeber has contributed to revitalising and synthesising an anthropological tradition developing from Polanyi to Sahlins, Marcel Mauss to Pierre Clastres and Edmund Leach to Maurice Bloch, a testament to the degree of exchange between distinct yet continuously dialoguing national academic traditions.

Post-Colonial Dialogues

As the centre of history's most far-reaching empire and then the British Commonwealth, over the course of the twentieth century, Great Britain both powerfully attracted intellectuals born in its "peripheries" and co-opted their work. At the same time, as Talal Asad critically asserted early on (1973) and the aforementioned Kuper (1999b) also noted, many of these peripheries were central to the birth of British social anthropology not only as grounds for research but also in terms of institutional and intellectual activity. Of the many biographical trajectories building bridges between the Empire's margins and its centre, those of Mysore Narasimhachar Srinivas, Abner Cohen, Talal Asad and Adam Kuper are particularly interesting; they are also quite varied in their foci, research contexts and contributions to the wider historical-methodological development of the discipline.

Mysore Narasimhachar Srinivas was born in 1916 to a Brahmin family in the town of Mysore in southeastern India. He studied social philosophy at the local university and then continued his studies in sociology in Bombay under the supervision of Govind Sadashiv Ghurye, one of the most important Indian sociologists at the time. Ghurye is known for his work on Indian castes, incorporating ideas by Rivers and Haddon into his doctoral dissertation, and being the second sociologist to chair a sociology department in India. As early as his degree thesis *Marriage and Family in Mysore* (published in 1942), Srinivas set himself up against the supposed immobility of the caste system by coining the concept of "Sanskritisation" to indicate attempts by lower-caste individuals to raise their status by adopting the rituals and practices of higher castes. As Ghurye's assistant, he had the opportunity to conduct ethnographic research with the Coorg people in the forests of Karnataka. Like his teacher, Srinivas moved to the United Kingdom after graduation and remained there until 1951. Working at the University of Oxford under the guidance of Radcliffe-Brown and Evans-Pritchard, he reworked his ethnographic materials to produce the thesis "The Social Function of Religion in a South Asia Community" in 1947, published under the title *Religion and Society among the Coorgs of South India* a few years later (Srinivas, 1952a). Srinivas returned to India in 1951, and the research post he had occupied had been taken over by Louis Dumont before the latter moved back to France in 1955. As a professor at Baroda University in Gujarat, Srinivas posed a profound critique of contemporary Indian anthropology, accusing it of not granting enough importance to fieldwork and failing to clarify its theoretical frameworks (Srinivas, 1952b). In 1959, he was entrusted with the task of founding and directing the Department of Sociology at the Delhi School of Economics.[4] Between 1969 and 1970, he worked at the Stanford University Behavioral Science Center and from 1972 until 1979 he lived once again in his home region, serving as director of the Institute of Social and Economic Change in Karnataka and, subsequently, the National Institute for Advanced Studies in Bangalore. Srinivas is undoubtedly recognised for having investigated local Hindu traditions with careful attention to the practices and transformations of Indian society, reasserting the

---

[4] One figure who stands out among the many scholars who have attended the Delhi School of Economics is the anthropologist Veena Das, who earned her doctorate there in 1970.

fluidity of the caste system with his concepts "vertical (inter-caste)" and "horizontal (intra-caste) solidarity".

Careful attention to social change processes also characterised the work of Abner Cohen, one of the most brilliant students of the Manchester School. Cohen was born and raised in Baghdad and completed a university degree there in Philosophy and Psychology. After graduation, he found work first as a clerk in the railway system and then as a freelance journalist. In 1947, he moved to Iran where he worked as a teacher; a few years later, he moved to Jerusalem and secured a job there as a school inspector. In Israel, he came into contact with anthropology and especially the work of Max Gluckman, and indeed he went to study under Gluckman at Manchester, beginning in 1956. It was there that he met his future wife, Gaynor Jones, who was also an anthropologist. Thanks to a research grant, at the beginning of the 1960s Cohen enrolled at the School of Oriental and African Studies (SOAS) and continued his career there to the point of becoming a faculty member in 1972. He stayed at SOAS until he retired in 1985. It is telling that, during his academic career, Cohen spent several periods of time in the United States as a visiting professor at Cornell University, the State University of New York in Binghamton and the Center for Advanced Study in the Behavioral Sciences, the same research lab where Victor Turner had worked a few years earlier.

Although Gluckman often discouraged his students from trying their hand at studying "complex societies" (Mills, 2018, p. 143), Cohen conducted research in both Israel and the United Kingdom as well as West Africa. In his book *Arab Border-Villages in Israel* (Cohen, 1965), Cohen put Gluckman's teachings into practice by applying the extended-case method. He described processes of social change and outlined interactions both between individuals and society and between specific events and the larger social forces impacting locals' life trajectories in several Palestinian villages relegated to the margins of the newborn state of Israel after the 1948 Arab-Israeli war that had resumed a set of social dynamics involving competition between traditional patrilineal groups (called *hamula*). Cohen insightfully recognised that these "revived" social roles assigned to "old" kinship obligations and rules constituted a source of economic and political security and support that was indispensable for these villagers in a time of radical change, such as when facing land confiscation or the division of family groups.

At the end of the 1960s, Cohen became interested in a topic that was drawing the attention of many researchers at the time, especially at

Manchester: the relationship between social change and urbanisation processes in relation to ethnic groups. This was the focus of texts such as *Custom and Politics in Urban Africa* (Cohen, 1969) and the edited volume *Urban Ethnicity* (Cohen, 1974a): the first presented a study of trade and ethnicity showing how the Hausa merchants of northern Nigeria monopolised cattle trading by employing networks based on kinship, ethnicity and religion, while the preface to the second—as well as the book *Two-Dimensional Man* (Cohen, 1974b)—built on Victor Turner, Max Gluckman and J. Clyde Mitchell's insights to look at the emotional and political significance of symbols and the way they are flexibly deployed to secure loyalty and consent. In the United Kingdom, Cohen investigated the Notting Hill Carnival, highlighting how it was adapted depending on the groups that organised it and their respective political agendas. Furthermore, he argued that the carnival was not only a vehicle for asserting claims but also the object of conflict or, in other words, that it represented not only a way of expressing differences but also the means through which those differences were socially constructed (Cohen, 1993). This approach framed the ritual as an engine of social change rather than a way of evoking tradition. By including both social structures and rituals in the same analytical gaze, he was able to frame traditional practices not as mere representations of social structures but rather as elements shaping the structures themselves.

While Srinivas certainly contributed to strengthening and innovating the Indian socio-anthropological tradition, and Cohen played the same role in the Manchester School, Talal Asad and Adam Kuper, among others, can be credited with giving shape to important, critical works dealing with the history of anthropology. Talal Asad is a distinguished professor at New York University's Graduate Center. Born in Saudi Arabia and raised partly in India and partly in Pakistan, he trained at the Universities of Edinburgh and Oxford between the 1960s and 70s. He worked in Sudan—the field of his original doctoral ethnographic research—and the United Kingdom (at Hull University). As Asad himself explained in a 2011 interview (Watson, 2011), the Oxford Institute of Anthropology had special arrangements with the Department of Anthropology at the University of Khartoum that involved recruiting professors from among Oxford graduates who had yet to complete their PhDs. While the agreement with the University of Khartoum was in effect, Asad—together with his wife—conducted fieldwork with a nomadic group in north-west Sudan with funding from the Ford Foundation. This population, the Kababish, turned out to be particularly interesting in part because they had been constituted as a "tribe" under British colonial rule in the first half of the twentieth century. At the end of the 1980s, Asad moved to the United States, and in the course of his career, he taught not only at prestigious American universities—the New School for Social Research and Johns Hopkins University—but also as a visiting professor in Egypt, Saudi Arabia, California and France. Although Asad made significant contributions to the study of religion (1993) and secularism (2003), for our purposes here it is important to mention his analysis of relations between British social anthropology and colonialism (1973). These observations preceded Edward Said's famous book *Orientalism* (Said, 1978), underlining the profoundly colonial character of Western ways of constructing the Orient.

Lastly, Adam Kuper, born in Johannesburg in 1941, studied history at the University of the Witwatersrand and received his doctorate from Cambridge in 1966. Between 1967 and 1976 he taught in Uganda and then he returned to Europe (UCL, Leiden, Gothenburg, Brunel). Between 1985 and 1994 he served as editor-in-chief of Current Anthropology. It was his aunt—Hilda Kuper, a student of Malinowski—who trained him in fieldwork during periods spent in Swaziland. Kuper's ethnographic work in Jamaica and South Africa continues to represent a fundamental contribution to the discipline, but his best-known and most cited works are about the history of British anthropology. His publications constitute indispensable sources of insight for anyone seeking to understand the history of the discipline (see also Fausto & Neiburg, 2002).

DIALOGUES ACROSS THE CHANNEL

A shared language undoubtedly facilitated the flow of people and ideas between Britain and the United States or other former colonies. However, the language barriers separating Britain from other European countries were not a terribly difficult obstacle to overcome. As discussed at the beginning of this chapter, British social anthropology was established and developed in part on the basis of contributions from other parts of Europe. The biographical trajectories of some of the most important European anthropologists bear witness to these two-way exchanges. Prominent examples include Fredrik Barth, Bernardo Bernardi, Jack Goody and Maurice Bloch, among others.

Born in Leipzig in 1928 and raised in Norway, Barth began his university education in Chicago before moving first to the London School of Economics and then to Cambridge. It was at Cambridge that he completed his doctorate in 1959 under Leach's supervision, presenting a PhD thesis titled "Political Leadership among Swat Pathans". Two years later, he was invited by the University of Bergen to set up a department of anthropology there. This provided Barth with the opportunity to import the current social anthropology into Norway. After his time in Bergen, Barth taught for many years in Oslo before moving to the United States (Emory University and Boston University). Over the course of his lengthy career, he conducted research in Pakistan, Iran, Norway, New Guinea, Bali and Bhutan. He favoured the theoretical perspectives of British anthropology that focused on studying processes rather than the static analysis of social structures (Firth and Leach rather than Radcliffe-Brown or Meyer Fortes) and emphasised individual agency as the driving force behind social action. As such, his work followed the currents of action theory that many Manchester School scholars were developing at the same time and sided with the formalist approach in economic anthropology debates. His most cited work, *Ethnic Groups and Boundaries: The Social Organization of Culture Difference*, continues to represent a landmark in the analysis of the political and social processes that feed into the creation and maintenance of ethnic distinctions. It also took the lead in suggesting many of the paradigms developed in following years to deconstruct reified and reifying representations of ethnicity.

Another scholar who helped "export" British social anthropology was unquestionably Bernardo Bernardi, one of the founding fathers of Italy's African studies tradition. After graduating from Rome's La Sapienza University in 1946, Bernardi was awarded a scholarship from the International African Institute in London to conduct research in South Africa. There, he earned his doctorate in social anthropology under the supervision of Isaac Schapera. He went on to conduct research in Kenya on the role of the Mugwe and, in 1970, was assigned the Cultural Anthropology chair at the University of Bologna. In this position he invited Jack Goody, Ioan M. Lewis and Jan Vansina to Bologna to give noteworthy seminars. From 1982 until his retirement, Bernardi taught at La Sapienza. His ongoing dialogue with British anthropology can be seen in both his numerous visits to the departments of UK universities such as Manchester and Cambridge and the fact that his monograph on the Magwe was published in Italian 30 years after it first appeared in English

68 L. RIMOLDI AND M. GARDINI

(1953). One of his most famous texts, *I sistemi delle classi d'età* (Bernardi, 1984; translated as *Age Class Systems: Social Institutions and Polities Based on Age*), revisited and synthesised a field of study that was a classic in British social anthropology; it was published nearly simultaneously in Italian (1984, Loescher) and English (1985, Cambridge University Press). This connection with the United Kingdom has continued to imbue the training, research and careers of many Italian anthropologists both Africanist and non, including Vanessa Maher, Cesare Poppi, Filippo Osella, Pier Paolo Viazzo, Bruno Riccio, Francesca Declich, and Marco Bassi, to name a few.

Whereas Barth and Bernardi can be considered key "exporters" of British social anthropology into Europe, Jack Goody might instead be considered a great "critical importer" of ideas. In continuous and close dialogue with both Marxist perspectives and the work of "continental" historians such as Norbert Elias, Fernand Braudel and the Annales school, Goody's work reinforced the relationship between British social anthropology and French and German currents of historical research, building on their ideas and often denouncing their implicit or explicit Eurocentrism. After studying under Fortes and serving as his assistant, Goody replaced Fortes as professor of social anthropology at Oxford in 1973. During the early stages of his career, he conducted research in northern Ghana, focusing on well-established anthropological subjects such as kinship, forms of inheritance and the developmental cycles of domestic groups. In the 1970s, instead, he began to pursue a wide-ranging and historically profound comparative analysis of European, Asian and African societies. The goal of this project was to challenge the alleged exceptionality of European development and look to settings far from Europe to identify the economic, social, technological, and environmental factors that have given rise to examples of the kinds of political and economic organisation and cultural values historians so often characterise as exclusively Western. Goody's work has been a source of inspiration not only for British anthropologists seeking to break with the a-historicity of functionalism, but also for all those European anthropologists seeking to oppose more culturalist tendencies from the USA.

Maurice Bloch was another scholar who helped nurture and synthesise the fruitful dialogue between British anthropology and French Marxist anthropology (Currie & Rey, 1985). Born in France in 1939, he lost his father during World War II. His mother was the daughter of a cousin of Marcel Mauss and the great-granddaughter of Durkheim and, after

2 PEOPLE AND IDEAS FROM ELSEWHERE: NOTES ON SOCIAL... 69

remarrying an English biologist, she moved to Great Britain. Bloch continued his university studies in England, first at the London School of Economics and then at Cambridge where he earned his doctorate in 1967. The entirety of Bloch's academic career unfolded at LSE and he became one of its leading exponents: he secured a position as lecturer in 1969 (the year after Firth's retirement), followed by a full professorship in 1983. On the ethnographic front, one of the significant "imports" Bloc introduced into British social anthropology was his pioneering role as the first British anthropologist to carry out fieldwork in Madagascar, a research context that, at the time, had been explored exclusively by French anthropologists; on the theoretical front, Bloch was the main importer (sometimes with a critical gaze) of French Marxist anthropology. In a 1988 interview (Houtman, 1988), he pointed out that:

> The one significant thing coming from France now are studies showing a remarkably high level of scholarship. This is so especially amongst Africanists such as Terray and Izard. This is the kind of work few of us in British universities can do because we don't have the facilities for spending so much time on research. [...] Marxists tend to be honest about the political significance of what they are saying or doing. This is not to say that the Marxist approach is always sufficient in my view. [...] There are questions which Marxism can't deal with. Marxism is heavily ethnocentric, though less so than most other theories employed in the social sciences [...]. (p. 19)

In the same interview, he also stressed how important it was for British anthropology to maintain the high degree of internationalisation that had always distinguished it:

> The present LSE Department is marked by a continuing link with the Cambridge anthropology department and also the close link with members of departments in such places as France and above all the USA. It is a very varied department. [...] I have been going around Europe a lot recently, especially last year. And you do find a lot of anthropology departments growing up all over the place. The growth of anthropology in Europe in places where anthropology was weak is quite extraordinary. In Italy there are some young departments. In Catalonia there are four departments, and we are a little isolated from all these people. I could quite happily do without an ASA and have a European association instead, about the size of the AAA with branches. (pp. 18-21)

The following year, the European Association of Social Anthropologists (EASA) was founded with Adam Kuper heading its steering committee.

Thanks in part to EASA, between the end of the twentieth and the beginning of the twenty-first century, the flow of mutual exchange between the United Kingdom and the rest of Europe became even more evident, particularly if we consider examples of shared approaches, topics and research settings spanning the two sides of the English Channel. Although a profound degree of Anglocentrism does continue to permeate many anthropological discussions (Erickson & Murphy, 2016), British theoretical approaches have fully incorporated authors such as Foucault, Bourdieu and, more recently, Gramsci just as they had previously done with Durkheim (via Radcliffe-Brown), Lévi Strauss (via Leach) and French Marxism (via Bloch). Many of the issues at the top of the agenda of contemporary English research, such as the anthropology of social media (e.g. Daniel Miller) and migration (e.g. Pnina Werbner), are extensively studied in the anthropology departments of all other European countries, and there is a constant intellectual exchange between these centres. One illustrative example is the recent development of environmental anthropology, discussions around the notion of Anthropocene and efforts to radically redefine the culturally and socially constructed dichotomy between nature and culture. Among scholars grappling with these issues, it is common to seek to bring together the work of French scholars such as Philippe Descola and Bruno Latour with the insights of British anthropologists such as Strathern, Ingold and Laura Rival.

CONCLUSION

Since its foundation, British anthropology has proven capable of embracing, synthesising and catalysing theoretical perspectives and currents of thought that transcend both its national borders and the class and gender affiliations characterising the UK academic sphere. In this sense British anthropology has long been less "British" than is commonly thought. While Fredrik Barth has a point when arguing that, until the 1970s, anthropology in the United Kingdom was in many ways "an internal conversation among a handful of professional colleagues in the Oxford-Cambridge-London-Manchester circuit" (Barth, 2005, p. 56), the fact remains that this "intimate conversation" was carried on by people—and supported by ideas—whose social origins and backgrounds often diverged markedly from those of the intellectual elite populating many British departments at the time. These contributions from elsewhere have been interwoven and held together by a deep-rooted seminar culture which, as Spencer (2000) argues, has characterised British anthropology since Malinowski.

Some observers have suggested that this force of attraction was a function of the imperial role the United Kingdom played in the global panorama until at least the decolonial shift (Asad, 1973); others have pointed out that the history of the development of anthropology in Great Britain tended to foster the careers of scholars who strayed from the academic norm in multiple ways. As Barth (2005, p. 52) has argued: "It is ironic that the Polish freethinker Malinowski and his ragtag band of radical, largely non-establishment, even foreign disciples should be faulted for serving and aligning with the empire".

The intellectual biographies we have outlined in this chapter with their specific traits support both of these explanations and account for both the appeal/co-optation drive of British anthropology and the dialogues it has woven with the anthropological traditions of other countries. Such internationalisation has become even more marked in recent decades as UK anthropology has seen a proliferation of research centres and theoretical frameworks, an increase in the number of anthropologists and research fields, and an intensification of academic exchanges across the globe—as well as employment precarity in academic positions. Obviously, the future of "British" anthropology after Brexit is a story yet to be written.

REFERENCES

Ardener, S. (1985). The Social Anthropology of Women and Feminist Anthropology. *Anthropology Today, 1*(5), 24–26.

Asad, T. (Ed.). (1973). *Anthropology and the Colonial Encounter*. Ithaca Press e Humanities Press.

Barth, F. (2005). Britain and the Commonwealth. In F. Barth et al. (Eds.), *One Discipline, Four Ways British, German, French, and American Anthropology* (pp. 3–57). Chicago University Press.

Bastian, A. (1860). *Der Mensch in der Geschichte: zur Begründung einer Psychologischen Weltanschauung*. O. Wigand.

Bernard, A. (2000). *History and Theory in Anthropology*. Cambridge University Press.

Bernardi, B. (1984). *I sistemi delle classi d'età: ordinamenti sociali e politici fondati sull'età*. Loescher.

Bohannan, L. [Smith Bowen, E.] (1954). *Return to Laughter. An Anthropological Novel.* Victor Gollancz Ltd.

Bohannan, P. (1957). *Justice and Judgment Among the Tiv.* Oxford University Press.

Bohannan, L. (1966). Shakespeare in the Bush. An American anthropologist set out to study the Tiv of West Africa and was taught the true meaning of Hamlet. *Natural History, 75,* 28–33.

Bohannan, P. (1985). *All the Happy Families: Exploring the Varieties of Family Life.* McGraw-Hill.

Bohannan, P., & Bohannan, L. (1953). *The Tiv of Central Nigeria.* International African Institute.

Bohannan, P., & Bohannan, L. (1960). *Tiv Economy.* Northwestern University Press.

Bohannan, P., & Glazer, M. (1988). *High Points in Anthropology.* Knopf.

Cohen, A. (1965). *Arab Border- Villages in Israel: A Study of Continuity and Change in Social Organization.* Manchester University Press.

Cohen, A. (1969). *Custom and Politics in Urban Africa. A Study of Hausa Migrants in Yoruba Towns.* Routledge.

Cohen, A. (Ed.). (1974a). *Urban Ethnicity.* Tavistock Publications.

Cohen, A. (1974b). *Two-Dimensional Man. An Essay on the Anthropology of Power and Symbolism in Complex Society.* Routledge.

Cohen, A. (1993). *Masquerade Politics Explorations in the Structure of Urban Cultural Movements.* University of California Press.

Currie, K., & Rey, L. (1985). Recent Trends in Contemporary British Anthropology: Innovations and Revivals. *Dialectical Anthropology, 9,* 209–216.

D'Agostino, G. (2021). Participant Observation: The Personal Commitment in Native Life-A Problematic Methodological *Topos.* In Matera, V. & Biscaldi, A. (Eds.), *Ethnography. A Theoretically Oriented Practice* (pp. 313–340). Palgrave Macmillan.

De Matteis, S. (1995). *Echi lontani, incerte presenze. Victor Turner e le questioni dell'antropologia contemporanea.* Ed. Montefeltro.

Deliège, R. (2006). *Une histoire de l'anthropologie. Ecoles, auteurs, théories.* Seuil.

Di Leonardo, M. (1998). *Exotics at Home: Anthropologies, Others, and American Modernity.* Chicago University Press.

Erickson, P. A., & Murphy, L. D. (2016). *A History of Anthropological Theory, Fifth Edition.* Toronto University Press.

Eriksen, T. H., & Nielsen, F. S. (2001). *A History of Anthropology.* Pluto Press.

Fabietti, U. (2020). *Storia dell'Antropologia.* Zanichelli.

Fardon, R. (1999). *Mary Douglas: An Intellectual Biography.* Routledge.

Fausto, C., & Neiburg, F. (2002). An Interview with Adam Kuper. *Current Anthropology, 43*(2), 305–313.

Firth, R. (1951). Contemporary British Social Anthropology. *American Anthropologist, 53*(4), 474–489.

Foreman, G. P. (2013). *Horizons of Modernity: British Anthropology and the End of Empire*, PhD. Thesis, University of California, Berkeley, shorturl.at/nrzSX (last access 25 September 2021).

Fortes, M. (1953). *Social Anthropology at Cambridge Since 1900: An Inaugural Lecture*. Cambridge University Press.

Fortes, M. (1969). *Kinship and the Social Order: the Legacy of Lewis Henry Morgan*. Routledge and Kegan Paul.

Gaillard, G. (1997). *Dictionnaire des ethnologues et des anthropologues*. A. Colin.

Gardini, M., & Rimoldi, L. (2021). The Bridge and the Dance: Situational Analysis in Anthropology. In V. Matera & A. Biscaldi (Eds.), *Ethnography. A Theoretically Oriented Practice* (pp. 159–179). Palgrave.

Gordon, R. J. (2018). *The Enigma of Max Gluckman. The Ethnographic Life of a "Luckyman" in Africa*. University of Nebraska Press.

Houtman, G. (1988). Interview with Maurice Bloch. *Anthropology Today*, 4(1), 18–21.

Kuklick, H. (Ed.). (2008a). *A New History of Anthropology*. Blackwell.

Kuklick, H. (2008b). The British Tradition. In H. Kuklick (Ed.), *A New History of Anthropology* (pp. 52–78). Blackwell.

Kuper, A. (1983). *Anthropology and Anthropologists. The Modern British School*. Routledge and Kegan Paul.

Kuper, A. (1999a). *Among Anthropologists. History and Context in Anthropology*. Athlone.

Kuper, A. (1999b). South African Anthropology, An inside Job. *Paideuma: Mitteilungen zur Kulturkunde*, 45, 83–101.

Kuper, A. (2015). *Anthropology and Anthropologists. The British School in the Twentieth Century*. Routledge.

Leach, E. (1984). Glimpses of the Unmentionable in the History of British Social Anthropology. *Annual Review of Anthropology*, 13, 1–24.

Malinowski, B. (1922). *Argonauts of the Western Pacific: An Account of Native Enterprise and Adventure in the Archipelagoes of Melanesian New Guinea*. G. Routledge & Sons.

Malinowski, B. (1927). *Sex and Repression in Savage Society*. Kegan Paul, Trench, Trubner & Co.

Mcgee, R. J., & Warms, R. L. (2013). *Theory in Social and Cultural Anthropology: An Encyclopedia*. Sage.

Mills, D. (2018). *Difficult Folk? A Political History of Social Anthropology*. Berghahn.

Moore, H. L. (1988). *Feminism and Anthropology*. University of Minnesota Press.

Moore, J. D. (2009). *Visions of Culture. An Introduction to Anthropological Theories and Theorists*. AltaMira Press.

Remotti, F. (2011). *Cultura. Dalla complessità all'impoverimento*. Laterza.

Richards, A. [1982 (1956)]. *Chisinau: A Girl's Initiation Ceremony among the Bemba in Northern Rhodesia*. Routledge.

Said, E. W. (1978). *Orientalism.* Pantheon Books.

Schippers, T. K. (1995). A History of Paradoxes: Anthropologies of Europe. In H. F. Vermeulen & A. A. Roldàn (Eds.), *Fieldwork and Footnotes. Studies in History of European Anthropology* (pp. 234–246). Routledge.

Spencer, J. (2000). British Social Anthropology: A Retrospective. *Annual Review of Anthropology, 29,* 1–24.

Srinivas, M. N. (1952a). *Religion and Society among the Coorgs of South India.* Clarendon Press.

Srinivas, M. N. (1952b). Social Anthropology and Sociology. *Sociological Bulletin, 1*(1), 28–37.

Stocking, G. W. (Ed.). (1996). *Volkgeist as Method and Ethic: Essays on Boasian Ethnography and the German Anthropological Tradition.* University of Wisconsin Press.

Strathern, M. (1987). An Awkward Relationship: The Case of Feminism and Anthropology. *Signs, 12*(2), 276–292.

Turner, V. (1964). Betwixt and Between: The Liminal Period in Rites de Passage, *The Proceedings of the American Ethnological Society (1964). Symposium on New Approaches to the Study of Religion,* 4–20.

Turner, V. (1967). *The Forest of Symbols: Aspects of Ndembu Ritual.* Cornell University Press.

Turner, V. (1979). *Process, Performance, and Pilgrimage: A Study in Comparative Symbology.* Concept Publishing Company.

Tylor, E. B. (1871). *Primitive Culture: Researches into the Development of Mythology, Philosophy, Religion, Language, Art and Custom.* John Murray.

Urry, J. (1993). *Before Social Anthropology: Essays on the History of British Anthropology.* Routledge.

Watson, J. (2011). Modernizing Middle Eastern Studies, Historicizing Religion, Particularizing Human Rights: An Interview with Talal Asad. *The Minnesota Review, 1*(77), 87–100.

CHAPTER 3

French Anthropology, Ethnology of France and the Contemporary Turn

Matteo Aria

INTRODUCTION

The present chapter aims to chart some of the primary epistemological developments and lines of research in the current panorama of French anthropology, taking into account the key role played by the three master narratives that marked the discipline's horizons throughout the twentieth century: the sociology school founded by Émile Durkheim and furthered by Marcel Mauss; Lévi-Straussian structuralism and the Marxist perspectives pursued by Georges Balandier and taken up by Pierre Bourdieu, Maurice Godelier and Claude Meillassoux.[1] We will focus on the ways in which these theoretical perspectives were reinterpreted between the 1980s and 1990s by new generations of researchers, such as Françoise Héritier,

[1] An in-depth discussion of classic disciplinary approaches and their history lies outside the remit of this study. These are, however, generally well known in the anthropological debate, as attested by a vast bibliography. By way of example, a comprehensive treatment of Francophone anthropology was given by Parkin (2010).

M. Aria (✉)
Sapienza University of Rome, Rome, Italy
e-mail: matteo.aria@uniroma1.it

© The Author(s), under exclusive license to Springer Nature Switzerland AG 2023
G. D'Agostino, V. Matera (eds.), *Histories of Anthropology*,
https://doi.org/10.1007/978-3-031-21258-1_3

75

Marc Augé, Philippe Descola, Jean-Loup Amselle as well as by exponents of the *anthropologie/ethnologie du présent*, Gérard Althabe, Christian Bromberger, Daniel Fabre and Gérard Lenclud, who for their part became reference points for the so-called contemporary turn in French anthropology. In view of this, we will address the various modes of a remarkable propensity to build thick descriptions for interpreting and reducing the complexity of the real or for highlighting objective economic and political configurations which can engender inequalities and violence.

At the same time, the chapter will attend specifically to the changed scenarios that characterize field research to examine what remains of that "exemplary tension" (Clifford, Clifford, 1988) between an enthusiastic trust in the circumstantial—and later initiatory—method of Marcel Griaule and the troubled uncertainty and endless autobiography of Michel Leiris.

To conclude, we will deal with the unremitting influence of a division inherited from colonial times between modern societies, based on high social differentiation, and traditional societies, envisioned as homogeneous and resistant to change (Chevalier, 2017; Hottin, 2016; Barbichon, 2009; Macdonald, 2008; Rogers, 2002). Such division reflects a separation and a difference in prestige and academic status between anthropologists who carry out intense *fieldwork* in distant worlds and those who instead "limit themselves" to investigating what is close at hand. As we shall see, while many theoretical proposals and field research programmes have disputed such assumptions, the enduring fascination of *le grand partage* is testified by the history of major institutions, museums and research centres. The very field of study newly set up to explore contemporary dynamics has reworked classic disciplinary notions to apply them to an understanding of contexts increasingly marked by globalization (Chevalier, 2015).

Our analysis will only tangentially touch upon major anthropological and ethnographic contributions linked to the so-called area specialisms (Oceanists, Africanists, Americanists), which are addressed elsewhere in this volume. On the one hand, we intend to account for general features (institutional framework, relations with other social sciences, concepts, theories, research methods and new fields of investigation) which trace the state of the discipline in France over the last three decades. On the other, we wish to look in some detail at the proposals put forth by the nascent ethnology of the present.

To cope with this complex disciplinary tangle, it may be profitable to plot some institutional developments, starting with the 2008 foundation of a new federation of anthropologists—*Association française d'ethnologie et d'anthropologie* (AFEA)—until then tied to two distinct associations: the AFA (*Association française des anthropologues*) and APRAS (*Association pour la recherche en anthropologie sociale*).[2] This event marks the final outcome of a process set in motion with the 2007 conference, *Les Assises de l'ethnologie et de l'anthropologie en France*, held in Paris. On that occasion, most French anthropologists debated one another for the first time in thirty years[3] over the general state of the discipline: they tackled issues related to teaching, research and the public use of knowledge in the face of the challenges posed by recent transformations. Discussion around epistemological issues intertwined with the need to establish a compact and unitary body for facing reforms and the general overhaul of the human sciences sector (which includes anthropology), announced in stages by the scientific direction of the *Centre National de la Recherche Scientifique* (CNRS). Over the years, the intense debate held at the time generated a wide array of publications which include charts, detailed breakdowns and assessments. Data thus collected makes it more readily feasible to outline the distinctive features of current French anthropology.

Contemporary French Anthropology

The Institutional Framework: Academic Weakness and Public Resonance

The works of Chevalier and Lallament (2015) and Chevalier (2017) underline how, despite its irrefutable fame worldwide, French anthropology appears weak on national academia, especially when set aside other

---

[2] Macdonald (2008) argues that AFA, founded in 1979, is a more open and mainstream association, because it is largely composed of young university researchers, yet untenured. The topics covered by AFA's reference magazine seem to confirm his view. On the contrary, APRAS—which Chevalier (2017) labelled as more elitist, anchored to the CNRS and involved in the realization of the *Musée du Quai Branly*—is the result of an internal split that occurred in 1989. The rift began to heal following the retirement of professors whose influence had marked previous decades. Further advances, set in motion via a forum of anthropological associations held at Aix-en-Provence in 2008, led to the creation of a research group tasked with setting up a new association. Hence the *Association Française d'Ethnologie et d'Anthropologie* (AFEA), which merged AFA and APRAS.

[3] In 1977 an international colloquium was held in Paris under the tile *L'Anthropologie en France: situation actuelle et* avenir. That gave rise to the first society of anthropologists named AFA and established in 1979.

78 M. ARIA

related social sciences. Out of the total number of tenured teachers, in itself seen by many as rather insubstantial figure (Roger, 2002; Chevalier, 2017), half is tied to universities [4] with most positions held at the *École des Hautes Études en Sciences Sociales* (EHESS)—and nearly half at *Centre National de la Recherche Scientifique* (CNRS). [5] Although there have been steady calls for delocalized centres across the country, most of the teaching, research institutes and museums continue to be based in Paris. Anthropology departments and specific degree courses are few and far between, while ethnologists in large numbers are scattered inside departments ruled by other disciplines. This state of affairs seriously affects study paths for students, who are forced to train in non-anthropological subjects first and can turn to their chosen field of knowledge only at an advanced stage of their academic career. At least until the 1970s, philosophy was one of the prevalent formative pathways. It is no coincidence that many of the leading anthropologists in contemporary France from Maurice Godelier to Philippe Descola to Marc Abélès should have started precisely in that field of study. It was only later, with the expansion of the university system and of curricula, that the social sciences, and in particular sociology, gained increasing relevance. To be sure, limited presence inside universities makes anthropology vulnerable to abrupt changes: to the risk of seeing research positions suppressed or redeployed to other sectors. Such institutional precariousness should alert us to the way in which anthropology's lively debates over disciplinary identity, coherence or relation to other fields are stirred not solely by concern of method or epistemology but also by highly pragmatic interests of an institutional nature. At the same time, we may want to connect this state of affairs to the fact that, starting with the Second World War, French ethnology developed less as an academic

---

[4] Other employment opportunities for anthropologists may include *The National Institut de la Santé et de la Recherche médicale* (INSERM) or the IRD (*Institut de Recherche pour le Développement*). The latter was set up in 1998 as an extension of ORSTOM (*Office de la Recherche Scientifique et Technique d'Outre-Mer*). Its aims were (1) to kick-start scientific and technical research—based on agreements undersigned by France and a few countries of the so-called global South, and—as outlined on the official website—(2) to promote an innovative model of fair scientific partnership between Southern countries and an interdisciplinary science committed to sustainable development.

[5] There is a difference in France between academic teachers ("enseignants-chercheurs") linked to a university and "researchers" belonging to the CNRS, who are not required to teach courses but are urged to set up "workshops" (research units) related to university departments to obtain the resources needed for projects.

discipline than as a research activity,[6] akin to what Marcel Mauss and Lucien Lévy-Bruhl had already envisioned when they founded the *Institut d'ethnologie* back in 1925.[7] While anthropologists are generally more or less bound to carry out regular teaching activities, their basic institutional affiliations and duties lie elsewhere. The dominant model is the one set out by CNRS:[8] recruited by a national commission of peer anthropologists, most French ethnologists are grouped inside research laboratories which may at times be transdisciplinary but are more often defined by geographical area or by subjects to be investigated. Roger (2002) and Chevalier (2017) unanimously note that, while it is undoubtedly a mark of distinction for every scholar to belong to such centres, tight affiliations reduce the chance of establishing fruitful exchanges with colleagues from other research groups. In fact, even though cooperation among the various CNRS centres is substantial, it rarely goes beyond the scheduling of periodic seminars or the occasional publishing of collective volumes. In the absence of widely shared analytical frameworks, laboratories tend to promote individual creativity and excellence, rather than the achievement of common objectives. The system ultimately promotes a broad range of study programmes, which is rather surprising when seen against the limited size of the scientific community.

These specific bodies partake of an institutional and administrative framework in which both higher education and scientific research are the responsibility of the State. The university system and the CNRS fall under the jurisdiction of the Ministry of Higher Education and the Ministry of Research, which supervise appointments or resources and thus may seriously affect the academic paths of scholars. Conversely, teachers and

---

[6] On the historical rift between professors who "theorize ex cathedra" and researchers engaged in fieldwork, see among others Guolo (2021).

[7] The Institute was in fact supposed to be generally relieved of all the red tape involved in teaching. Emphasis was placed on practice rather than on teaching, following Mauss's appeal to abandon the land of ideas for the terrain of facts: to cultivate the descriptive side of social sciences (Guolo, 2021, p. 3).

[8] Research laboratories named *labo* (an abbreviation for 'laboratory' borrowed from experimental science) refer to the CNRS and to universities. The best-known anthropology *labo* is undoubtedly the Laboratoire d'anthropologie sociale (LAS) (founded by Lévi-Strauss) which has a generalizing thrust, while most similar facilities maintain an area-based orientation. So, for instance, we have Centre de Recherche et de Documentation sur l'Océanie (CREDO) for studies on the Pacific, Centre d'études nord-américaines (CENA) for North America, Institut de recherches asiatiques (IRASIA) for Southeast Asia and Institut des mondes africains (IMAF) for Africa.

80   M. ARIA

researchers enjoy considerable public visibility. Newspapers, for example, regularly feature comments and interviews by anthropologists, whose books are often extensively promoted and disseminated to audiences far outside the select remit of professionals. Sector journals sell regularly in bookshops across major cities. Thus, even though academia gives it short shrift and little space, ethnology in France manages to take on much greater resonance in the public debate than in other countries.

Museum Revolutions: From the Ethnological to the Aesthetic

A similar dialectic may be found in the recent transformations of the two most prominent French museums, which have contributed to give greater visibility to a discipline whose representation in universities remains scarce. Between 2005 and 2006, the *Musée de l'Homme*, inaugurated in 1937 by Paul Rivet also as a site of resistance under the Vichy regime, and the *Musée National des Arts et Traditions Populaires* (MNATP), founded by Henri Rivière in the same year under the impulse of the Popular Front, were stripped of their roles as "laboratory museums" (de L'Estoile, 2015) and of their collections. Most of their tangible heritage was in fact made to converge, in the first case, into the *Musée du Quai Branly* in Paris[9] and, in the second, in the *Musée des civilizations de l'Europe et de la Méditerranée* (Mucem) of Marseille. The new facilities, defined by de L'Estoile (2015) *as* "Post ethnographic museums", are devised as cultural centres in which the architecture of buildings and spaces and the aesthetics of displays take precedence over the collections themselves. Such mutations mark a momentous paradigm shift in "post museum" anthropology. "Founding museums", which were less keen on exhibits than on research, embodied a naturalistic model whereby artefacts had to be studied as means to gain a firmer understanding of the societies that had produced them. Unlike these, the "carrefours culturels" of Paris and Marseille respond to an aesthetic/artistic model in which objects are to be admired solely within a "scenography of wonders".

[9] The collections of the *Musée du Quai Branly* consist of the 280,000 Ethnology department pieces from the former *Musée de l'Homme* and of the 30,000 works from the former *Musée des Arts d'Afrique et d'Océanie*, to which were added recent acquisitions, gifts and legations. As Lorenzo Brutti (2009) argues, we are dealing here with a crucial issue: for the *Musée du Quai Branly* is no longer, in fact, a new museum in the strict sense of the term. Rather, the *Musée* receives the heritage and integrates the collections of two institutions which wrote a large portion of the history of French museography and anthropology.

What however persists and recurs is the division between Us and the Others, as evidenced by both the redistribution of objects between the two centres (which perpetuates the dichotomy *Musée de l'Homme/ MNATP*) and the engagement of senior officials, exhibition curators, architects and set designers, who strive to infuse classic geography divisions dating back to colonial times with new vigour and fresh legitimacy. In the heated debates following new and contested creations, several French anthropologists in fact highlighted the resurgence of views and practices centred on an exotic fascination with the primitive, which had long prevailed in the Western imagination and is now being tapped to entice the general public. In such contexts, exhibits of a romanticized otherness prevail and reinforce the stereotype of a discipline lost in "sad tropics" and in a nostalgia for lost authenticities. In particular, the *Musée du Quai Branly* has become the poster boy of a new French cosmopolitan universalism built around its distinctive ability to value the arts and cultures of distant human groups. [10] A similar vision has taken shape thanks to the shift from the ethnological to the aesthetic, whereby new imposing museums are no longer imagined as centres of knowledge production but as places of mass culture and the leisure industry (de L'Estoile, 2015). In this sense within both the *Musée du Quai Branly* and the Mucem, increasing space has been given to design, communication and artistic management experts, with a view to streamlining cultural dissemination, a phenomenon no longer seen as the prerogative of a small elite and no longer controlled by anthropologists. The latter have been relegated to a marginal position and forced to measure up with a markedly ethnocentric, aesthetic/artistic type of universalism (Brutti, 2009).[11]

[10] Strongly pursued by President Jacques Chirac—a collector and expert of non-Western art, assisted and advised in his choices, among other things, by gallery owner Jacques Kerchache—the *Musée du Quai Branly* appears as an attempt to make two irreducibly incompatible entities coexist: the universalist approach of the primitive art expert and the specialist approach of the ethnologist, who reads material production as evidence of social organization.

[11] In the harsh critiques levelled at the establishment of the *Musée du Quai Branly*, many scholars and intellectuals inveighed against what they saw as a coterie of twenty first-century European art dealers and historians not only concluding that art is universal and exists among non-Western peoples but also defining which material productions of the Other ought to be called "artistic" and which ones ought not (Brutti, 2009). In this sense, the new facility would appear as a large, culture-less art gallery or, as Pietro Clemente writes (2014, p. 289), "a playroom of Western aesthetics [...] tombstone of an anthropological gaze towards other worlds".

As Chevalier (2017) points out, however, it is true that over the years such institutions have become bona fide research centres. They have started funding projects for doctoral and post-doc students; promoting courses, seminars and conferences; and setting up temporary exhibitions to display the results of long ethnographic studies. And it is under the pressure of such intense organizing impulse that the *Musée du Quai Branly* was made to take on a leading role in laying out anthropological practice (Chevalier, 2017). Similar tensions also concern the Mucem which, in line with Sarkozy's pro-European policies, acquired a Mediterranean connotation—away from the exclusive celebration of a "traditional" French rural world—along the classic canons of salvage anthropology, championed for a long time by the MNATP.

Within such an aesthetics-based horizon, ethical-political issues were left in the background. And what went missing was namely a reflection on historical and colonial heritages and on how to deal with them in the current postcolonial context. It is no coincidence that the collections on display, the result of bristling colonial and postcolonial relations between Europe and the peoples of other continents, should often be presented as French heritage. Such "predatory narrative" was eventually ripped apart by those anthropologists who, in recent decades, have turned museums into a rewarding and dynamic object of study (Blanckaert, 1997; de L'Estoile, 2007; Debary & Roustan, 2012). To these we should add the unprecedented policies carried out by the new editor (2020) of *Quai Branly*, Emmanuel Kasarhérou, and inspired by the idea of "objets ambassadeurs" of Kanak culture: of a shared history traversed by bundles of relationships. These ideas were raised in the late 1990s by Kasarhérou himself as curator of the *Centre Cultural Tjibaou* in New Caledonia.[12]

Ambivalent Relationship to Other Social Sciences: Contiguity and Fractures

An equally distinctive trait of contemporary French anthropology has to do with the fractious relationship with some of the other disciplines. The foremost and somewhat more complex relationship involves sociology, whose firmer status within academia often confines ethnologists to the margins. Entanglements between the two disciplines, which were historically joined by Durkheim's and Mauss's social theory, remain

[12] On the notion of "objets ambassadeurs", see Paini and Aria (2014).

institutionally dense to this day. Many anthropologists nominally belong to sociology departments, and throughout their careers and along their intellectual paths scholars often move between these two sectors. Consider for instance leading current authors such as Didier Fassin, Bruno Latour or Serge Latouche or, even before them, key figures such as Bourdieu and obviously Mauss himself. Their paths reflect the Mauss's project for a science of the social, in which there exists no epistemological difference between sociology and anthropology.

Other ethnologists, on the other hand, advocate the need to preserve an identity and a space for action that should be quite distinct from an academically stronger discipline. For the latter will compete for access to resources and is known to be rather prone to recurrent theoretical and methodological field invasions (think for instance of how the ethnographic method was appropriated). To researchers of exotic otherness, such divide signalled an undisputed foundational feature, since Claude Lévi-Strauss sanctioned a clear-cut separation between sociology "which studies our societies and anthropology which is dedicated to the societies of others" (1958, p. 371). Already in 1950, as he made Mauss's work known with the publication of *Sociologie et anthropologie* (Lévi-Strauss, 1950), the author of *The Elementary Structures of Kinship* had accomplished the alchemical feat of bringing together and at once setting apart the two realms of anthropology and sociology. His proposal enabled meaningful connections with the models of structural linguistics and the mathematization of data. Such forays were able to stir up the theoretical ambitions of philosophical anthropology, which had partly marked Durkheim's project, to the detriment of empirical description and factual knowledge claimed by Mauss's approach. A detailed study of the complex relationship between concepts advanced respectively by Durkheim, Mauss and Lévi-Strauss is presented in the first part of Tcherkézoff (2016), devoted to the history of the French school.

Lévi-Strauss's distancing from sociology, in favour of an anthropology capable of pinpointing the basic objectifying layers of reality, went hand in hand with a resolute rejection of modernity. It aimed at reclaiming the central role of traditions and at discrediting emerging studies on French rural worlds carried out by the MNATP and its journal, *Ethnologie Française*. This double aversion (to the sociology and ethnology of France) has had an enduring influence. It has contributed to the discipline's delay in facing the critical questions raised by postmodernity. Indeed, it was only in the 1980s that an interest in cities, industrial life, migrants, sports, social organizations and gender issues emerged.

Across these oppositions and closures, the attempts of Bourdieu and his students (in particular Alban Bensa and Florence Weber) to merge structuralism and Marxism and to propose a socio-anthropology theory of "what is here" as well as elsewhere have failed to set the tone of discussion. As Weber (2012) argues, an entire generation faded away in a vain attempt to combine Lévi-Strauss and Bourdieu (Bourdieu, Lamaison 1985) or to champion an anthropology built on an intense exchange with history, sociology and political science (Karnoouh, 1973; Lenclud, 1987).[13] Over this rubble, the theories of Bruno Latour (among others) were to prevail. Like Bourdieu but unlike Lévi-Strauss, Latour is read both by anthropologists and by sociologists, both in France and abroad. His epistemologies, which are partly antithetical to Bourdieu and Lévi-Strauss, call for the heirs of both to endow the sociology and anthropologies of both Western and exotic societies with equal dignity, via a radical critique of the major rifts brought in by Lévi-Strauss. Even more recently, Didier Fassin, via heterogeneous methods and subjects, from medical anthropology (1996, 2008) to the logic of humanism (2010), from the social and political construction of the body to an ethnography of suburbs and law enforcement agencies (2011, 2017), made it possible to take a further leap to deconstruct disciplinary boundaries and the fractures that mark and divide them.

The socio-anthropology of development, inspired by the visions of another great master like Balandier and rooted in a close exchange with Marxist history and analysis, falls within this critical space. And this space aims to establish links between "philosophy's two younger sisters" (Guolo, 2021) and to open up to the complex layering of modernity.

This new perspective, strongly supported by IRD (and earlier by ORSTOM), took shape in the early 1980s thanks to the appeals of some well-known Africanist researchers such as Marc Augé, Jean Pierre

---

[13] When he entered the *Collège de France*, Bourdieu was hailed as a great sociologist rather than as a great anthropologist. In France, and even more so probably at the *Collège de France*, social anthropology at the time was embodied by Lévi-Strauss. Today, Bourdieu's work is taught in anthropology courses and translated by ethnologists from various parts of the world. Bourdieu's research on the Kabyle population and his theory of practice, where he lays out the key concepts of habitus, social fields and symbolic capital, have also represented, in France as elsewhere, an unavoidable reference point for many ethnographers affected by the reflexive turn. Despite his markedly anthropological approach, Bourdieu is readily defined by many as a sociologist.

Chavenau, Jean-Loup Amselle, Jean Copans, Jean Pierre Dozon and Jean-Pierre Olivier de Sardan.[14] Their reflections weave together dynamist political anthropology, attentive to colonial "situation" and social change, and Marxist economic anthropology, which in turn attends to the transformations of societies under the influence of an ever-expanding capitalist system. These converging goals have given substance to an empirical notion of development (Copans, 2009), quite distinct from the "discursive" and deconstructionist approach supported more or less in the same years by authors such as James Ferguson (1994) or Arturo Escobar (1994). As they claimed the impossibility of separating sociology and anthropology and firmly distanced themselves from Lévi-Strauss's theories, exponents of this new approach carried out multidisciplinary research programmes on development. Their aim was to highlight the relevance of both a historical analysis of the failures of colonial and state policies, and "deviation" and "selection" strategies pursued by local societies.[15]

Although focused originally on analysing the interaction between the practices and representations of local actors (target communities) and those of developers (development configuration), this socio-anthropology of social change has over recent decades extended its fields of action and theoretical reflection. It has given ever-more space to the study of African public and collective administrations and services (Olivier de Sardan, 1995), national administrations (Bierschenk & Olivier de Sardan, 2014) and global social engineering (Bierschenk, 2014), thereby outlining an anthropology of public action in the context of aid programmes (Lavigne Delville, 2016; Fresia & Lavigne Delville, 2018) and globalization (Copans, 2009, 2016). This set of themes has increasingly interfaced with relevant contributions from the anthropology of institutions (Abélès, 2000, 2001, 2008), from studies on *governance*, on bureaucracy and

[14] In 1991, Olivier de Sardan, together with Chauveau himself and Thomas Bierschenk, established APAD (*Association euro-africaine pour l'anthropologie du changement social et du développement*).

[15] In particular, Chauveau was among the first to propose a historical sociology of development. He revisited Augé's postulate (1972) whereby "the only possible sociological object of the study of a so-called developmental action is action itself and its modalities: the complex ensemble made up of 'developers' and of the 'developed'". While insisting on the diversity of these two categories, Chauveau put forth a definition which has since become canonical: "Logically, there is development where there are developers, where specialized actors who claim to be in charge of development have the authority to act on communities" (Chauveau, 1982, pp. 16–17). Similar perspectives were then reworked and expanded in the several works by Olivier de Sardan (see especially 1995).

corruption (Bayart, 1989),[16] which all favoured a shift from political anthropology to the anthropology of the political and of the contemporary. These new, specialized lines of research have emphasized the study of the State, of public institutions and of international organizations in Western societies and elsewhere. By doing so, they have reasserted the central role of ethnographic investigation, precisely since "institutions themselves must be conceived as an ongoing process", "fully connected to the daily lives of those who conduct it" (Abèlés, 2001, p. 31).

More generally, the different approaches outlined so far underline the two main ways of reading anthropology today: either as a social science or, on the contrary, as a science of humanity. The fact is that, in the contemporary French scenario, the question of ethnology's positioning with respect to other disciplines remains partially unsolved. It remains to be established whether ethnology should be placed side by side with political sciences, demography, sociology and the sciences of communication and education, or whether it should instead be grouped with archaeology, prehistory, history, art history and biological anthropology.[17] And institutional bodies themselves, such as the National Council of the University (CUN), never cease to bring forth new sectoral definitions and divisions (de L'Estoile, 2012).

As he interrogates these phenomena, Charles MacDonald (2008) identifies a further "double movement" running through anthropology. On the one hand, we witness a confluence of concepts and methods from sibling disciplines, such as sociology, political science and history, which call into question old disciplinary barriers, and advocate an "all-encompassing anthropology". On the other, there exists a divergent current which leans towards cognitive approaches: psychology, linguistics and the constructs of Neo-Darwinist evolutionary theories, close to biology

---

[16] See among others Blundo (2000); Blundo and Le Meur (2009); Blundo and Olivier de Sardan (2006, 2007).

[17] These divergent perspectives emerged in 2010 when the French Ministry of Higher Education and Research championed a new nomenclature for the Sciences of Man and Society by grouping under a broad umbrella named "SHS 2 *Human and Social Sciences*" law, political science, sociology, anthropology, ethnology and demography. Several scholars questioned this reconfiguration of knowledge because it threatens anthropology's status as an independent disciplinary field in French universities. They issued a counterproposal in which social and cultural anthropology and ethnology are placed side by side to archaeology, prehistory, history, art history and biological anthropology, in a sector renamed "Ancient and contemporary worlds, society, cultures, heritage" (de L'Estoile, 2012).

and the natural sciences, especially ethology, as well as to neuroscience. For MacDonald, the stakes of this second position, aimed at recovering original philosophical leanings, seem to be much higher, because it hopes for a readmission of anthropology into the cradle of the natural sciences, thereby inaugurating, as de L'Estoile (2012) noted with a tinge of criticism, a "new era" dominated by the return of a naturalistic paradigm.[18] The latter positions[19] may find inspiration in Descola's own mission (2005) to enhance philosophical anthropology, that is, to support an anthropology whose purpose is no longer the study of diverse cultures against the background of a universally homogeneous nature, but the discovery of models, of structures for objectifying reality, of which the nature/culture opposition would be but one possible realization (Kelly, 2014).

Anthropology, Ethnology, Ethnography

The controversies described so far intercept the terminological dispute between "anthropology"—nowadays a favourite term in models most sensitive to theory and philosophy along the suggestions of Durkheim and Lévi-Strauss—and "ethnology"—prevalent among scholars who inherited the notions developed by *L'Institut d'ethnologie* and found in Rivet's work at the *Musée de l'Homme*.

As is known, with the creation of the famous *Laboratoire d'Anthropologie sociale* of the *Collège de France* in 1960, Lévi-Strauss demanded that the term "anthropology" be used instead of "ethnology" which had held sway until then. At the same time, he set up a tripartition between the various phases of the knowledge process: ethnography, which collects data at the source; ethnology, which provides an initial synthesis on a regional or historical basis; and anthropology, which collates and theorizes (Lévi-Strauss, 1958, pp. 386–388).[20] Not only does this tripartition establish which disciplinary field is the most prestigious, that is, which is better detached from the long-term field experience and aims to yield general explanations

---

[18] In this regard, de L'Estoile (2007) and Zerilli (1998) pointed out how, as we analyse the history and status of French anthropology, we tend to forget ethnology's naturalist rooting and to overestimate Durkheim's influence instead.

[19] Along these lines we ought to place recent developments in ethnobiology and ecological anthropology, which were granted a new lease of life by the rise of environmental issues and of the Anthropocene, as well as by the development of Descola's thought.

[20] This chart was taken up by the authors of *Dictionnaire de l'ethnologie et de l'anthropologie* (Bonte & Izard, 2002, pp. VI–VII).

on human societies. It also strengthens compartmentalization into separate cultural sectors and sub-sectors whose exclusive experts will be Oceanist ethnologists, Africanists, Americanists and so on, often out of touch with one another and generally reluctant to venture beyond the confines of their local skills across the "perilous savannah of theories" (Macdonald, 2008, p. 620).

As Macdonald candidly states, "[P]rofessionally, it is easier to be recognized as a specialist in the Siberian Great North or the Andes than in general anthropology. In France, in any case, one might ask whether anthropologists, for example of the Asian South-East, would be better inclined to exchange views with other specialists of the region, geographers or political scientists, rather than with Africanist ethnologists" (Macdonald, 2008, p. 621). Sharp separation between experts from different geographical sector has in fact worn off over recent decades, along with a colonial legacy that long contributed to directing and incentivizing research exclusively towards French-speaking territories. As a result, in the current landscape, Oceanists and Africanists have increasingly undertaken studies of social phenomena not subjected to the direct or indirect influence of Paris, while researchers in Asia have turned their interest to China and India. Along similar lines, Americanists have broadened their scope from indigenous communities to include also metropolitan clusters.

This softening of strict area specialism is linked to ethnologists' proclivity to attend multiple areas, simultaneously and over time, and to practice multi-site ethnographies. And the emergence of this type of investigation, no longer focused on a single context but on a set of places and groups that may differ in language and culture, is in turn tied to recent shifts in methodology in the anthropological paradigm and to changes in the contemporary world. As he traces such intertwinings, Macdonald (2008) argues that French ethnography today depends less on localized realities than on wider issues. As a result, the very notion of "terrain" has been thoroughly rethought. Although conventional research fields (the study of a given population) are still prevalent, French researchers now frequently travel to regions that are very distant from each other and often for shorter periods of time. To the extent that it lowers the level of vernacular linguistic competence and decreases the density usually produced by long-term field stays, multi-site versions of *fieldwork* may be found lacking. However, Macdonald concludes (2008, p. 261) that what seems lost in terms of depth may in fact open up to possible expansions enabled by a new comparative gaze.

As Chevalier (2017) states, in this ever-changing scenario, field research in France continues to be seen as a crucial feature of anthropological knowledge, even though it is widely claimed as a distinctive trait by other social sciences, namely those which have recently experienced rapid and successful dissemination (such as sociology). These combined factors have contributed not only to enhance and reaffirm the structural characteristics of field research, such as long-term immersion and the density of informal relationship spaces, but also to drastically reduce the divide between anthropological theory (which compares in order to determine universals and differences) and ethnographic practice (which observes and collects). And that poses a serious challenge to Lévi-Strauss's model.

Theory After the Demise of Grand Narratives

The world that gave birth to ethnology as a self-contained discipline centred on the primitive or the exotic has, for the most part, disappeared. Contemporary French anthropology has lost its two traditional objects of study: on the one hand, peoples without a history today produce postcolonial theories and undergo changes in the face of rampant urbanization, and partially re-inhabited by new heterogeneous flows. These political and economic phenomena are entwined with the demise of the grand narratives of Marxism and structuralism, yet to be replaced in recent decades by equally momentous paradigms.[21] Lévi-Strauss's own pupils no longer define themselves as structuralists, as shown by the paths undertaken by his two foremost intellectual and institutional heirs: Françoise Héritier and Philippe Descola.[22] In this regard Désveaux (2015) believes that, as they alternated in the direction of the LAS and at *Collège de France*, both Héritier and Descola acted ambivalently towards their mentor, at once claiming his legacy and contesting it. For Désveaux, this is obvious in Descola (2005) who first questioned the nature/culture dichotomy, and then reinterpreted it and reconnected with Lévi-Strauss's thought. Héritier seems to have taken an inverse path: after introducing himself as the main inheritor (1981) of kinship theory, he voiced major criticism of Lévi-

---

[21] In the mid-1980s, Lévi-Strauss and the research group he had set up were still active; however, powerful theoretical options that had swayed French anthropology in previous decades lost their central role and were never replaced by equally influential intellectual projects.

[22] Both succeeded Lévi-Strauss at the *Collège de France*: Héritier in 1983 and Descola in 2000.

Strauss's views by proposing the notion of "second-type incest", which, based as it is on the notion of substance, effectively reintroduces biology as an explanatory factor for kinship. Héritier's and Descola's positions reflect a general tendency in post-Lévi-Strauss's anthropology, which for Désveaux relies on "reiterated rejection of one's master's thought" (Désveaux, 2015, p. 44).

At the same time, it is precisely with the waning of structuralist ascendancy since the 1990s that we have witnessed the rediscovery of some great classics, such as Durkheim, Maurice Merleau-Ponty and, above all, Mauss. Mauss's theories, especially his theory of the gift, have been taken up, far beyond national borders, by many scholars who have felt the need to free them from Lévi-Strauss's influence. Treated with reverential awe but at the same time gravely underestimated, Mauss's gift has also given rise to a wide spectrum of positions in France, only partially outlined here.[23] Godelier (1996) saw in the gift the universal role of inalienable possessions which provide foundation to human societies. For their part, Jean Starobinski (1994), Luc Boltanski (1990) and Jacques Derrida (1991), who were influenced by George Bataille's readings of humans' propensity to unproductive *dépense* against the principles of economic science, have sensed a chance to free the gift from reciprocation and the expectation of return, thereby transcending mere utility in favour of gratuitousness. Finally, Jacques T. Godbout (1992), Alain Caillé (1989) and other exponents of the *Revue du Mauss* have brought the idea of the gift back to centre stage. They see the gift as a hybrid between interest and disinterest and between obligation and freedom, as a constitutive aspect of relation building in Western societies themselves, an alternative to the State and the market.

Beyond these significant re-propositions, the solid theoretical models underpinning the thought of social sciences have mostly been replaced by a vast and diversified array of more limited and fragmented analyses, carried out over disparate issues and analytical frameworks but united by a commitment to pay close heed to shared meanings, modes of social cohesion and perceptions of difference. According to Chevalier (2017), three prevailing, coexisting orientations may be said to emerge from this scenario: the first aiming to understand the distinctive cultural features of groups by focusing on the articulations between individual actions and collective norms; the second leaving behind the quest for underlying social

---

[23] For a more in-depth analysis, see Aria (2016) and Tcherkézoff (2016).

structures in favour of analysing the practices that actors share. The third direction may be found in the so-called ontological turn and in some studies on material culture which, inspired by the works of Descola (2005) or Latour, devote ever-greater attention to the relationship between humans and non-humans, causing the former to lose their exclusive political status.

The one common feature of these three approaches is a progressive shift of analytical gaze from rural and traditional contexts to spaces marked by major economic, political and epistemological changes over the last thirty years. As Michel Agier points out, the "contemporary turn" of French anthropology, which began especially under the impulse of Augé and Gérard Althabe, and, even earlier, of Balandier and his Marxist students, favoured the assertion of a pragmatic approach, interested in the meanings and practices implemented by subjects in the "here and now" (Agier, 2015). This radical change of perspective has highlighted the need to interrogate the culture of anthropologists themselves and of their complex societies. What emerges is an altogether different interpretation of distant worlds once considered silent objects of study, relegated out of history and now caught up instead in the profound changes and the forceful political claims of the nascent native anthropology.

As is well known, similar changes have affected the discipline as a whole, placing new emphasis on field work, reflexivity and critical positioning, with a view to better understanding the effects of relentless globalization, which tends to blend identities and differences in unprecedented manners. In the French context, all this has meant opening up new fields of investigation, concentrated above all in urban areas, and promoting new research topics related to development, migration, health, work, the environment and new technologies. Renewed interest for worlds in the making has gone hand in hand with a radical rethinking of key concepts such as "tradition", "ethnicity", "identity", "culture" and their essentializations, in favour of views aimed to unpack the dynamics whereby these terms are constructed, as attested most notably in Amselle's work (1990, 2001).

At the same time, the study of kinship, religion, economics and politics has been injected into global contexts and made to face indigenous movements, new religions and discrimination against minorities, which in turn has granted ever-more space to creativity, to artistic, emotional and political activism. In this sense, as Chevalier (2017) notes, French anthropology lags slightly behind current trends in anthropology, having however also lost the international recognition enjoyed at least until the 1980s by leading French anthropologists; a phenomenon which is interestingly at

92   M. ARIA

variance with the contemporary rise of *French theory* in the Anglophone world. The expansion of postcolonial studies in the United States seems in fact to have resulted from the encounter between Foucault's and Derrida's French post-structuralism and the rediscovery of prominent scholars actively involved in the anti-colonial struggle in the Francophone sphere, such as Aimé Césaire and Frantz Fanon (Zecchini & Lorre, 2011, p. 69). These perspectives became first entrenched in literary criticism departments and later spread to the human and social sciences, where they were woven into a re-reading of Geertzian and post-Geertzian American anthropology, aimed at deconstructing the idea and practice of *fieldwork* and at zeroing in on the knowledge/power binary. On the contrary, the legacy of Lévi-Strauss and, to a different extent, of the Africanist Marxist school itself[24] in France at the time worked as a powerful antidote against postcolonial theory and partially also against Foucault and interpretative anthropology. It was the tightening of a policy on the part of French anthropology to safeguard "its territories and its traditional themes (kinship, symbolism, rite, etc.)" (Abélès, 2008, pp. 113–114).[25]

ETHNOLOGY OF FRANCE AND IN FRANCE

It is within the scenario described so far that the ethnology of France has taken shape, weaving complex tangles of power and diverse threads of interaction both with the so-called exotic anthropology and, once again, with cognate sciences such as sociology and history.

As they fell back on themes of classic anthropology, emerging late twentieth-century ethnographies on the Paris metro (Augé, 1986) and its

[24] Within the most critical fringes of Marxist anthropology, postcolonial studies have been labelled as an "academic carnival" (Bayart, 2010, p. 66) and as an "ideological" perspective influenced by "Eurocentric philosophers" (Amselle, 2008). Criticism was accordingly levelled not only at issues of epistemology, theory or politics, but also against the identity of researchers themselves, dismissed as "a relatively small group of Western-style and Western-trained writers and thinkers who perform the function of intermediaries in the trade of cultural products between global capitalism and its periphery" (Bayart, 2010, p. 7). A recurrent motif in the critiques by these Africanist researchers, long involved in the study of ethnicity and the "colonial situation", may be summed up in the idea of a "déjà vu" or, perhaps, as Bayart quips, "been there already" (2010, p. 20).

[25] As Julien Debonneville (2017) pointed out, defensiveness against postcolonial studies, which tend to blur disciplinary boundaries, marks the specific élan of French academia, resolutely rooted in clear-cut divisions, to the point that some have spoken of "disciplinarisme nationaliste français" (Bourcier, 2006).

suburbs (Pétonnet, 1979), on football stadiums in Marseille (Bromberger, 1995), on witchcraft in Bocage (Favret Saada, 1977), on kinship (Late, 1998) or on time and history (Zonabend, 1980), it signalled a decisive questioning of "the grand partage" between "chez soi" anthropology and exotic anthropology. In the same years *Writing Culture* was issued in the United States, in France an ethnology of the present was thus affirmed. Its aim was to overcome the sharp distinction between "us" and "others", relentlessly bringing attention back to the fraught relationship with the most theoretically and academically prestigious research on "distant" societies. This novel thrust came to define itself within a self-contained space. It set up its own original status with respect to other fields of knowledge and positioned itself in the wake of the extensive critical overhaul sweeping across the discipline. It is precisely along the fault-lines opened up both by the crisis of grand epistemological paradigms and by the rapid surge in globalization and decolonization that the chance for a "homecoming" for French ethnology may be seen, along a trajectory that is markedly similar to the one followed by British and American schools of thought. However, unlike Great Britain or the United States, where such evolution was conceptualized in spatial terms (the study of "Western" societies), changes in France were conceptualized in temporal terms, with a distinct accent on "contemporary worlds" or on the "present". At the same time, French ethnologists focused almost exclusively on research within their own country, along the models of history and sociology, while Anglo-Saxon anthropologists also worked on other European contexts, establishing lasting ties with the field of *cultural studies*, based on literary criticism.

From Folklore to an Ethnology of the Present

Such peculiarities are better understood if placed inside the specific national history of the discipline, on which we will now dwell briefly.

It has been pointed out by many that his new field of study seems largely to have derived from "parents who are separated or belong to different social classes" (Rogers, 2002): on the one hand twentieth-century ethnology, conventionally defined via a genealogy of intellect that goes from Durkheim to Mauss and from the latter to Lévi-Strauss; on the other, folklore—generally associated with less prestigious ancestors—headed by Arnold Van Gennep, André Varagnac and Georges-Henri Rivière (Chiva, 1987; Segalen, 1989a; Cuisenier & Segalen, 1993; Bromberger, 1987). In Durkheim's well-known project, ethnology took part in establishing a

94   M. ARIA

broad and universal science of society, centred on the primitive forms of human communities and aimed at analysing the basic structures of social life. Folklore, on the other hand, was to turn to the study of the practices and beliefs of the European countryside considered as survivors of a pre-industrial past (Belmont, 1986; Cuisenier & Segalen, 1993).[26] Heavily discredited, folklore in France never achieved the academic status reached elsewhere in Europe and is still mainly associated with museums and local environs. It also lacked the political weight in building national identity which folklore instead had in other countries.[27] Nonetheless, during the 1970s and 1980s, some scholars set out to reclaim the full legitimacy of the discipline and to have it reinstated. To this end, they radically reviewed the intellectual legacy of French folklore and its relation to ethnography, showing the surreptitiousness of fine distinctions between the two as well as their mutual permeability (Cuisenier & Segalen, 1993; Chiva, 1987).[28] Anchored to the rural environment and devoted almost exclusively to

[26] At the same time, for Durkheim and his intellectual heirs, ethnology was all the more distant from folklore, insofar as the scientific rigour of the former clashed with the antiquarian futility of the latter (Barthélémy and Weber, 1989, p. 27).

[27] For many, this phenomenon is largely due to the fact that the customs of rural people, perceived as potentially reactionary subjects, were of little use to celebrate the nation's rational or revolutionary roots (Belmont, 1986; Bromberger, 1995). Also, political support extended to folklore in the Second World War by the Vichy regime led to stall the discipline's progress, tarnishing its reputation for years to come (Fabre, 1998; Weber, 2000).

[28] Cuisenier, Segalen (1993) and Chiva (1987) have thus highlighted intertwinings and connections, with special focus on the institutional origins of the two disciplines. In turn, studies by Belmont (1974), Chiva (1985) and Desvallées (1987) have revalued the scientific rigour in research by key figures such as Georges-Henri Rivière or Arnold Van Gennep and have underlined their adherence to analytical frameworks and empirical models of ethnology, as indeed attested by the scholars' professional trajectories. Van Gennep's publications prior to 1924 were all based on ethnographic material relating to primitive societies (Belmont, 1974), while Rivière started his career as an anthropologist in an ethnography museum. Along different lines, Louis Dumont's early works were devoted to the study of a popular festival in Southern France (Dumont, 1987) and Lucien Bernot, a specialist of Southeast Asia, inaugurated his career with a monograph on a French village (Bernot & Blancard, 1953). The *Musée d'Ethnographie du Trocadéro* itself, established in 1878, was rethought as representing a shared history precisely because it included, alongside objects collected in primitive or exotic societies, a *Salle de France*, intended for the exhibition of regional collections. Only in 1937, under the auspices of the Front Populaire, did a separation take place between the *Musée de l'Homme* (mainly dedicated to the collections of non-European societies) and the *Musée des Arts et Traditions Populaires* (reserved for French popular culture), led by Georges-Henri Rivière, who came from Trocadéro and had been strongly influenced not only by Paul Rivet, the future director of the *Musée de l'Homme*, but also by Mauss.

reconstruct traditional ways of life, the newly established French ethnology sought vestiges of traditions, beliefs, rites, material culture and techniques still present in local peasant societies. At the same time, field research conformed to ethnology's conventions: relying both on temporal distance—with the archaic replacing the primitive—and on spatial distance—with rural contexts acting as exotic lands—researchers from France dedicated themselves to "lukewarm" (rather than cold) and relatively simple societies. Results took the form of monographs, which attest to the relevance of classic anthropology subjects—kinship, rituals, witchcraft, collective and private property, concepts of time and space and social cohesion processes—and of the analytical tools essential for understanding them.[29] This partial transformation of folklore into "regional" ethnology falls within the historical-political setup of the time and partakes of the cultural and heritage initiatives undertaken by state institutions in France. New installations[30] at the *Musée National des Arts et Traditions Populaires* (aimed at collecting and archiving objects) were deployed to sustain this line of research, along with the active assistance of two laboratories: the *Centre d'Ethnologie Française*, aimed at furthering research and national ethnology heritage conservation in France, and the *Laboratoire d'Anthropologie Sociale*, whose goal was instead to promote opportunities for "actual anthropologists" to exercise their skills also on the national scene. This large institutional framework also includes the *Societé de l'Ethologie Française*, which founded the *Ethnologie Française* journal in 1973.

At the same time, as outlined above, the nascent discipline came to terms with the other human sciences involved in the study of France. History, for example, dominated at the time by the *École des annales* and by a social analysis of pre-revolutionary peasant environments, turned out to be a powerful ally. On the contrary, a propensity for the local, for deep structures and for the still perceptible traces of a relatively stable past marked ethnology's sharp rift from rural sociology. At the time, the latter was engaged in an investigation of the major upheavals and changes taking place in the countryside.

---

[29] Besides the works mentioned above by Favret-Saada (1977) and Zonabend (1980), see also Verdier (1979), Karnoouh (1980), Assier-Andrieu (1981), Claverie, and Lamaison (1982) and Segalen (1985).

[30] Inauguration of the new buildings in 1972 marks this new phase, which brought into play new toolsets and new cultural policies (Segalen, 2005).

96   M. ARIA

By the end of the 1980s, the scenario we have described so far was already witnessing dramatic changes: folklore suddenly became a largely outdated topic, while interest in rural contexts was partially replaced by a strengthening of the "ethnology of the present" and of an anthropology of contemporary worlds. A *liaison* with history was no longer on the agenda and differences between sociological and anthropological approaches became blurred. There followed a new phase, characterized by debates on disciplinary cohesion and on legitimate objects of anthropological research.[31]

Over the past thirty years, this turn has been sustained by the *Mission du Patrimoine ethnologique*, set up in 1980 under the Management of the Heritage of the French Ministry of Culture by Isac Chiva and endorsed by several researchers. At the time, Chivan, a partner of Lévi-Strauss's and director of the *Laboratoire d'Anthropologie Sociale*, had already collaborated with Georges-Henri Rivière to the *Musée des Arts et Traditions Populaires* (Chiva, 1990; Langlois, 1999; Fabre, 2000). Officially independent from research laboratories or universities, the Mission pursued the building of ethnological heritage via specific surveys on France. It channelled considerable resources to fund research projects on contemporary social practices, issuing the *Terrain* magazine in 1983[32] and ensuring the publication of several books. In this new configuration, the Republic's political agenda for disseminating a specific notion of national identity and citizenship was thus intertwined with a novel understanding of heritage, defined not solely in terms of objects but also in terms of practices and representations. And that paved the way to an assessment of the immaterial aspect of heritage. At the same time, as Chevalier (2017) points out,

---

[31] The issues and tensions that converged into this turn were brilliantly condensed in a 1986 special issue of *L'Homme* magazine meant to take stock of the state of the discipline. The monographic volume was intended to celebrate the 25th anniversary of the magazine, founded by Lévi-Strauss two years after being elected at the *Collège de France* in 1959 and having set up the *Laboratoire d'Anthropologie social*. Faced with the need to overcome the great divide between exotic anthropology and an ethnology of France, which once made it possible to define the discipline as an analysis of specific places or societies, scholars found it necessary and urgent to reflect on what their objects of study should be and to reassess their relationships with other human sciences (Pouillon, 1986, pp. 21–22).

[32] Each issue—two are published yearly—focuses on one subject and features field research essays intended both for the professional community and for a wider audience. While over the years the number of articles on research carried out elsewhere in Europe or in more "exotic" fields has increased, the journal is still primarily focused on France.

the MNATP nevertheless continued to encourage studies on rural France, also in light of transformations brought about by administrative decentralization policies in 1982–1983, which for the first time granted power to local authorities over Paris. That opened fruitful spaces for establishing and supporting new regional, departmental and municipal collective affiliations. A similar propensity towards a celebration of the past and of traditions hitherto "unseen" also took place via the institution of local exhibitions and museums and a direct involvement of ethnologists themselves.

Eventually this setup underwent further modifications, as a heritage paradigm emerged within the framework of universal cultural heritage policies laid out by UNESCO and by the strategies put in place by scholars who were directly called upon to address this reconfiguration. As Hottin (2016) noted, since the mid-1990s a large number of ethnologists working for the Ministry of Culture and Communication progressively moved away from the project of shaping a national ethnological heritage via research on France's ethnology. They joined LAICH[33] instead to develop a reflexive and critical perspective which considers heritage institutions themselves as objects of study. Enforcement of the UNESCO Convention for the Safeguarding of Intangible Cultural Heritage in 2006 and the policies that ensued generated a wide range of dispositions within the national ethnological community, from bitter rejection to rapturous support via a whole series of intermediate attitudes. The Ministry's ever-increasing pressure on ethnologists to take on French cultural heritage as their object of study forced some researchers into an awkward balancing act, between developing their proper fields of scientific investigation and actively engaging in creating a national inventory and devising appropriate actions for its promotion and conservation.

A few—including Christian Bromberger (2014)—have levelled scathing criticism at this predicament and attacked the very notion of "immaterial" for implying an artificial distinction between tangible and intangible and for the political leveraging this possibly entails. Many ethnologists have also highlighted the risk of fossilizing cultures by way of formal UNESCO recognitions,[34] and at the same time exposing the dubious

---

[33] LAICH is a mixed research unit of CNRS and the Ministry of Culture and Communication, set up in 2001 on the initiative of Daniel Fabre.

[34] See in this regard Bortolotto (2011).

98   M. ARIA

intellectual merit of works or analyses issued by UNESCO itself.[35] Finally, several critics have shown how protection policies promoted by the heritage paradigm apply to non-distinctive communities, which have neither conflicts nor social or class differences, and cohere around the issue of safeguarding cultural traits. Such discursive practices crush internal differences into a blurry idea of immaterial or intangible. They end up flattening the poetics found in giving voice to people from the lower ranks of history, a practice cherished by ethnologists intent on investigating "poaching" or "semantic guerrilla" (de Certeau, 1980; Bourdieu, 1979) as exercised by the lower classes.

Alongside this "heritage vogue", over recent years we have witnessed a mutual seep-through between "exotic" and domestic themes or fields, as well as an ever-deeper intermingling of researchers of the here and of the elsewhere. In a sense, this has involved a weakening of claims for ethnology of France as an autonomous field (Chevalier, 2015). At the same time, it is also true that in more or less explicit terms the distinction between Oceanists, Africanists, Americanists—other experts of distant otherness (with their own methods and traditions of ethnographic writing)—and scholars anchored within national borders persists. There also persists a structural lack of opportunities for dialogue and shared tools for scientific dissemination (journals, conferences, associations).

The Search for the Symbolic and the Primacy of the Subject

Having outlined the crucial passages of a "homecoming" for ethnology, we may move on to focus on theoretical and methodological features and on key research subjects. A cursory look at titles in the thematic issues of journals like the *Ethnologie française* and *Terrain* shows that it is hard to condense the vast range of themes and perspectives that have emerged in the last twenty years thanks to the work of many scholars, at times also

---

[35] Along a somewhat different path, between 2008 and 2011 Noël Barbe, Marina Chauliac and Jean-Louis Tornatore carried out a participatory democracy project focused on intangible cultural heritage in the Northern Vosges Regional Nature Park. In this Alsatian enclave of the Lorena region, scholars called upon locals to lend objects they deemed representative of their intangible heritage in order to install an exhibition. While only modestly successful, the collection enabled scholars to shed light on a notion of heritage seen through the eyes of local inhabitants rather than via categories established by experts (Barbe et al., 2015).

affiliated with other laboratories established only recently.[36] We may none-theless chart prevailing trends, including the significant space accorded both to the ideal and emotional aspects of actions and to the acting subject and his individuality, so much so that, as Barbichon (2009, p. 238) notes, individualism is now often evoked as an all-encompassing social fact. This orientation is matched by an equally solid predilection for the "manufac-turing" involved in representations (of the landscape, or of nature), in images (of the body, of the woman or of the farmer) and in those that Clifford Geertz (1973) would define as the universes of meaning wherein subjects operate. It is a historical trend well attested, among others, in the works of Alain Corbin (1990, 1995) on the invention of the sea and free time as well as in Michel de Certeau's (1980) analysis on the invention of the daily newspaper.

The primacy reserved to the ideal is also matched by a commitment to unveil the constructed character of many cultural phenomena, which ties into the well-known reflections on the invention of tradition—understood in its multiple symbolic aspects (myths, emblems, celebrations, party rites etc.)—and on the imaginative ability to engender new senses of identitar-ian belonging for territorial entities or homelands of various sizes.[37] In the nascent ethnology of France, above all thanks to Lenclud's (1987) revalu-ation of work by Pouillon (1975), a new way of understanding tradition has gained ground. That is no longer seen as a product of the past, but as a "retro-projection", a choice, a selection in the present acted out by vari-ous subjects on another time or, again, an interpretation of "yesterday" conducted according to rigorously contemporary criteria. Rather, this sys-tem deploys an alternative pattern of filiation: it is no longer fathers who generate their children but children who generate their own fathers; that is, it is no longer the past that produces the present, but the present that shapes its own past.

---

[36] See, for example, the *Laboratoire d'anthropologie des institutions et des organizations sociales* (LAIOS), the *Centre d'anthropologie des mondes contemporains* (CAMC), the *Laboratoire d'anthropologie urbaine*, or the *Centre d'anthropologie de Toulouse* and *L'Institut d'ethnologie méditerranéenne et comparative* based in Aix-en-Provence.

[37] On identity constructions linked to specific regions or new small homelands, see in par-ticular Bertho-Lavenir (1980) on Brittany. As for Provence, in addition to works by Duret and Gueusquin mentioned earlier, see also Bertrand and Fournier (2014). For a more gen-eral approach on "elective homelands", see Thiesse (1997).

Access to this prolific symbolic exchange is obtained via a scrupulous observation of the materialized expressions given in painting, novels or films, as well as through an exploration and decoding of the signs featured in stories, in the language constructs of children and adolescents, in collective musical practices and productions, in the semiology of fashion or in the political claims of specific territorial groups. These approaches are also attentive to *discourse analysis* and to unveiling and deconstructing strategies, which aim as much to warn against narratives that seek final objective data, facts or structures, as to critique the essentializing, reifying and substantialist tendencies that have long ruled the discipline. As Daniel Fabre writes (1992) in the introduction to one of the pivotal works which characterize this turn, the issue of interpretation takes pride of place. That is because explanatory models based on pinpointing objective causal links in phenomena fail to account for human activities that are involved in the production of meaning. What we are dealing with is ultimately an ever-shifting contemporary terrain, where the discipline is forced into a close dialogue with other powerful hermeneutics, including, as Giordana Charuty (1992) reminds us, psychoanalysis.[38]

As evidenced by the 1994 issue of *Terrain* (Ermisse, 1994), the push towards the interpretation of subjectivity and individuals' inner life has lent ample space to issues of affection and emotion, as well as to the many ways of relating to one's body: a sense of decency, sport, physical violence, trance, risk behaviour and self-mutilation. At the same time, this push has called into question ethnologists themselves, their intimate involvement in research, their relation to local actors, in ways that remind one of what took place in anthropology as a whole with the so-called reflexive turn and with the shift from participating observation to participation observation (Tedlock, 1991). As Chiva and Jeggle (1987), Segalen (1989b) and, more recently, Barbichon (2009)—among others—have shown, by joining such broad critical turn, French society opened to two alternative ways of doing research, which may be defined in terms of an *ethnologie du proche différent* and an *ethnologie en miroir*. In the first case, ethnologists have lingered on the interpretation of otherness at "home"—that is, the otherness of marginal groups, of suburban or immigrant cultures—based on methodologies not dissimilar to the classic strategies used in exotic lands. That is how *close-by-stranger* analysis began to take shape, ever careful to

---

[38] Consider also developments in ethnopsychiatry (Fassin, 2000b) and the resumption of studies on Devereux which was championed, among others, by Nathan (2000).

minimize the risk of projecting one's own ethnocentric categories, which is always entailed in material proximity. In the second case, instead, an ethnology of the self and the similar which applies to the culture of the observer himself is implemented. In this context, a thrust towards self-analysis and introspective confinement is offset by comparative projects, in which the distant and the exotic endow the familiar self with meaning—as for instance in cases when an ethnologist analyses and tries to understand a new rite of passage, or a new sociability norm, by comparing them with ceremonies or rules from other places or other times.[39]

Between Holism and Particularism

The prevalence of the emotional and of the symbolic, and of a narrative-like, dialogic and reflexive ethnography, which qualifies many a research programme within the confines of France, is nevertheless accompanied by a broad propensity to "continuity", that is, towards models aimed at overcoming the radical dichotomies which recur in most classic theories, such as the binaries between meaning and matter (Warnier 1999), between people and things (Latour, 1991) or, again, between gift and merchandise.

Think for instance of the works of de La Pradelle[40] on markets as social, cultural and economic spaces at the same time, or to the contributions of Chevalier, Monjaret (1998), which are partially at variance with the markedly discontinuist literature issued by the *Revue du Mauss*. Equally signifi-

---

[39] If ethnologies of contemporary societies, entangled as they are in a dialectic of the Self and the similar, may seem perilously debilitating, in the case of an ethnology practiced in France by the French, another road has opened, which consists in associating and comparing the analyses of external and internal ethnologists. Yet Rogers (2002) has convincingly argued that French scholars involved in the development of an anthropology of "contemporary societies" have "resisted" the autobiographical tensions which arose within Anglo-American "postmodern" anthropology. Brief personal accounts of field experiences occasionally enrich ethnographic monographs. Nonetheless, systematic introspection never became a French genre. Whether conducted "at home" or far away, ethnological investigation is not considered as research on the individual self.

[40] In her work, Michelle de La Pradelle (1996) identifies three markets: the fair market in the old town, the huge and cold fruit and vegetable market of the station and the small and discreet truffle market. In doing so, she formulates the hypothesis that "insofar as it temporarily brings together equivalent partners in the same game" the exchange "underlies in these three cases the setting up of a specific space detached from ordinary social life and from the relationships of inequality that govern it, albeit in three distinct ways" (1996, p. 35).

cant is the interest granted to transitional spaces: borders and thresholds, as evidenced by research on natural environments (coasts and marshes) or those on areas of cultural intersection and on the role of mediation actors, a topic discussed in other contexts by Gruzinski and Bénat-Tachot (2001) on their work on *passeurs culturels*. As we shall see, the growing esteem granted to the hybrid status of family and kinship systems now undergoing major changes falls within the same ideal line of investigation.

At the same time, it should be noted that, since it endeavours to build its own specific sector and to legitimize itself with respect to exotic anthropology and social sciences such as sociology, the sizable body of ethnological research carried out in France in recent decades also incurs a tension between a universalist and a particularist vocation. On the one hand, borrowing and tweaking conceptual and analytical toolsets developed in "exotic" fields, scholars have endeavoured to understand the collective phenomena whereby individuals gather or break out into cohesive groups. On the other, they have at times perpetuated an antiquated "division of labor", retreating to those corners of French society left unexplored by researchers of other disciplines. In both cases there remains an underlying conviction that the social processes observable today throughout the country are fundamentally similar to those present elsewhere and that ethnologists may present themselves as experts in the knowledge of symbolic devices and of hidden dimensions undetected by other specialists. The risk is that, by focusing exclusively on the French scene, these same experts may end up generalizing the specific traits of their own national context, hence losing sight of the comparative perspective which defines and distinguishes the discipline (Rogers, 2002). That brings up the issue of holism and the call to establish whether or not to concentrate on "total" social facts, which may shed light on a given society as a whole, as suggested by conventional anthropology. Although research projects have occasionally been launched with the intent to provide an overall ethnological analysis of France, more often than not research has dealt with particular segments, either socially or territorially defined. These do not cover the whole national territory and often leave to history, sociology or political science the task of drawing intriguing frescoes of "French society" and its specifics. Rogers (2002) and Chevalier (2015) believe that this state of affairs marks the persistence of the "great fracture" with classic anthropology of the exotic societies. Certain cultures would seem well-suited to anthropology's holistic approach. Others, arguably more complex or less distant, might

3 FRENCH ANTHROPOLOGY, ETHNOLOGY OF FRANCE... 103

lend themselves better to a study of limited features or parts.[41] Rogers (2002) claims that the same issue cropped up in studies on kinship, which until the early 1990s were hailed as one of the most fertile grounds in opening ethnology to French contemporaneity. Between the 1970s and 1980s, driven by the same need to find integration and obtain recognition within the discipline, some researchers immersed in rural universes investigated kinship systems, thus appropriating one of the most prestigious notions of French anthropology. However, as ethnologists opted to move away from the archaic countryside and towards modern urban clusters, such analyses have lost their relevance. Most publications on these issues that appeared in those years focused primarily on the world of peasants and paid little heed to new contexts in the making (Lamaison, 1987; Zonabend, 1987; Salitot et al., 1989; Segalen, 1992). That attests to the difficulty of applying conceptual tools developed in kinship-centred societies to contexts marked by other forms of social relations. In later years, a prevalence of kinship studies based on a stricter sociological approach (Singly, 1991) concurred to a sharp decrease in the use of classical anthropology categories, except for works of historical anthropology on fictitious kinship or ritual (Cadoret, 1995; Fine, 1994, 1998) or for the intriguing suggestions of Zonabend (1994), Weber (2000, 2013) and Martial (2003, 2009).[42] This weakening in status was also reflected, for example, in the fact that in public debates around PACS and cohabitation, journalists and legislators sought the expertise of family sociologists and exotic society anthropologists but did not consult France ethnologists (Borrillo et al., 1999). At the same time, the special issue of *L'Homme* magazine commemorating the 50th anniversary of Lévi-Strauss's *The Elementary Structures of Kinship* features only two articles on France, one on genealogical memory across rural areas (Zonabend, 2000) and the other penned by a peculiar anthropologist like Fassin (2000a). Such exclusion may be read as a symptom of the stubborn resistance on the part of the discipline to acknowledge contemporary France as a legitimate ground for ethnological research or as an adequate context for testing complex scenarios and grand theories.

---

[41] Faced with this state of affairs, some researchers have pulled the discipline into the opposite direction, denouncing as mere illusion anthropologists' hope to grasp the whole of a society, either in exotic lands or in France (see, e.g., de La Pradelle, 2000).

[42] See also Porqueres (2009).

To paraphrase David Graeber (Graeber & Houtman, 2012) this field of study seems ultimately bound to the imperative of small-scale thinking.

Some notable exceptions exist, however. For instance, in Bromberger's attempt to transcend the local roots of his research on football matches and delve into the nature of social relations across the contemporary world.[43] Or even more so, in ethnography studies on the functioning of local politics and on the rituals tied to public institutions, as in Abélès's (1990, 1992, 2001). In his analyses of the French State apparatus, charged with constituting a cohesive society, Abélès captures the logic underlying the integrated model of the French territorial layout, as well as some of the key features of national identity.

Somewhat analogous views may also be found in the so-called anthropology of contemporary worlds advocated by Augé, which is sensitive to shifts in local anchorages (Augé, 1992) and in otherness (Augé, 1994a) as well as to the formation of new social and cultural "worlds" (Augé, 1994b). The same orientation has also fuelled the project of a general, multidisciplinary anthropology to be found partially both in those ethnologies on French rural contexts, which maintain a close exchange with social historians, and in studies on the cultures of the aristocracy, the bourgeoisie and the working class.

In the 1980s, the "first" ethnologists of contemporary France rehabilitated diachrony and the study of the past in order to underline continuities to trace constants in the ever-changing production of new forms across peasant worlds. These must face relentless globalization and are also made to cope with changes caused by administrative decentralization, as discussed earlier.[44] Their commitment was thus intertwined with the needs of local authorities (regional, departmental, municipal) invested with unexpected power and resonance to give substance to new collective frames of belonging via a revaluation "of the continuity of the past in the present"

---

[43] Studying football matches, Bromberger (1995) zeroed in on well-defined spaces, in which sociologically diverse individuals are led to take part in a show, somewhat similar to the classic Durkheimian ritual of social integration and collective identity but also revelatory of distinctive features of social relations across the modern world.

[44] At the time, a comparative and multidisciplinary thrust gained prominence among ethnologists, who continued to take an interest in rural contexts with a view to delineating cultural areas wider than small village communities or self-sufficient units, as evidenced in research by Chiva and Goy (1981) on *Les Baronnies des Pyrénées*, or by Bonnin, Perrot and de la Soudière (1983) on *La Margeride*. The latter works were preceded by Burguière's investigations (1975) on the Bretons of Plozévet and their external networks.

3 FRENCH ANTHROPOLOGY, ETHNOLOGY OF FRANCE...   105

(Althabe, 1992). A proclivity to chart steady trends (rather than report or lament their disappearance) may be found especially in the studies on hunting rites and practices (Bozon et al., 1982; Hell, 1985; Testart, 1987; Vincent, 1987),[45] and on the ways of ensuring the knowledge and patrimonial transmission in rural societies (Augustins, 1989; Lamaison, 1987).[46] With regard to chariot races in Provence, subsequent works by Duret (1993) and Gueusquin (2000) pointed rather to a reworking and re-signification of given structural elements. In turn, de La Paradelle's ethnography (1996) on the Carpentras market clearly shows how the staging of a new ecology cult may fit within solid lines of continuity. Daniel Fabre (1987) famously remarked at the time that just as vast ritualistic frameworks seem on the wane, others continue or take their place within new institutions and via new sets of knowledge.[47] Finally, recent developments (which we will address shortly) have investigated the occurrence of totally new rituals. Hence an overall inclination to probe the functional structures of a specific social formation via a thick observation of local changes introduced to cope with or to remake features imposed from the outside. It is a new outlook aimed at glimpsing the appearance and disappearance of specific, time-bound cultural setups, along with the conjunctural determinants that might have originated them (Barbichon, 2009).

Popular, Bourgeois and Urban Universes

Yet another feature that arguably characterizes this field of study is a perspective shift that turns both to the ruling classes and towards urban proletarian groups, hitherto excluded in favour of peasant societies.[48] On the one hand, a sizable strand of contemporary ethnology followed and problematized Bourdieu's (1979) claims on distinction strategies deployed via cultural and mass consumption in contemporary France. The trend, closely tied up with sociological issues, has embraced an analysis of the

---

[45] See Études *rurales* (1982).

[46] See also Barthelemy de Saizieu (2004).

[47] See, for example, Verdier's (1979) reflections on girls' embroidery of entire alphabets (*marquette*); Fabre's remarks on children, learning and the language of birds (1986); and Fabre-Vassas (1985) and Charuty (1987) on the new rites of passage for role differentiation between the sexes.

[48] At the time, a comparative and multidisciplinary thrust gained prominence among ethnologists who continued to take an interest in rural contexts with a view to delineating cultural areas wider than small village communities or self-sufficient units.

106   M. ARIA

norms, institutions and "likes and dislikes" of the bourgeoisie and of old and new aristocratic dynasties,[49] advocating an ethnography of elites and of hegemonic forces. Yet, as remarked earlier in the wake of the pioneering works of Althabe et al. (1985) and Verret (1988), there emerged a resolute and keen interest in rethinking and complexifying the concept of popular culture,[50] making the working class itself an object of anthropological study; a study that may bring to the fore opportunities for emancipation and action for subordinate worlds. Claude Grignon and Jean-Claude Passeron (1989), in particular, distinguished themselves in their appeal for such agency and such connections. By doing so, they also exposed the limits in the theory of symbolic domination outlined by Bourdieu (1979), guilty of "forcing" subordinates into a position of radical inertia. Criticism of the passive role imposed on dominated subjects also drew inspiration from the well-known reflections of de Certeau (1980), on the invention of everyday life, on consumption practices or on walking in the city. These reinterpreted hegemony/subordination relations in terms of tactical moves "from below", which are a fragmentary and contingent, and aim to make habitable those goods (tangible and intangible) produced from above and on a "strategic" level by the hegemonic culture.

A prolific field of research on the popular and the contemporary bourgeois developed along these lines. The demise of countryside, the anchoring to the present time and the blurring of boundaries with sociology eventually blended with a firm trust in the analytical tools of classical ethnology, all the more enlightening because finally unmoored from the terrains of the archaic, the exotic: the land of exclusion (Althabe et al., 1985). In this hybrid and innovative landscape, multiple research paths opened up, such as those of Florence Weber (1989) on the daily life of the working class in a small industrial town in rural eastern France; Sabine Chalvon-Demersay (1998) on the way in which social distinctions are both ostentatious and concealed in a Parisian neighbourhood undergoing gentrification; Béatrix Le Wita (1988) on the mechanisms whereby the capital's bourgeoisie mimic the idiosyncrasies of their own culture while denying them; Irène Bellier (1993) on social dynamics within the prestigious *École Nationale d'Administration*; or finally Jean-Pierre Hassoun (2000) on Paris Stock Exchange traders.

[49] Think of the works we mentioned by Le Wita (1988) or the abundant production of Pinçon, Pinçon-Charlot (1996, 1998, 2013 and 2021).
[50] See also Gérome (1990).

Similar features—that is, affinity or distance from sociology's approaches, valorisation of conceptual classical categories and methodologies of "distant societies" anthropology and at the same time openness to new objects of investigation undergoing deep transformations—are to be found also in the genesis of urban anthropology, which occurred in the same period and focused on analogous subjects. It is an area of study that took shape starting from Pétonnet's (1979) pioneering work on marginal and excluded subjects from Parisian *banlieues* (be they poor or impoverished French people, Jews and Arabs of either ancient or recent migration) (1979)[51]; from Althabe's contributions (1977) on forms of popular inhabiting in Nantes[52]; and in further essays collected and edited by Gutwirth & Pétonnet (1987).[53] To these must be added, subsequently, the reflections of Martine Segalen (1990) on French families in their transition from rural to urban life in Nanterre, those of Schwartz (1990) on the forms of family life of the working class in a mining region of Northern France and work by Patrick Gaboriau and Daniel Terrolle (2003) on the homeless in Paris.

In the move from small village communities to urban universes, we may still find a propensity for small, restricted, compact and clearly definable units. It is no coincidence that early works should have focused on suburbs populated by restricted communities of "Others" or "alternative subjects" and on forms of social marginality such as that of inhabitants of suburban residential clusters (Pétonnet, 1982; Lepoutre, 1997), Parisian homeless people (Gaboriau, 1993), gypsies (Williams, 1993) or ethnic minorities (Hassoun, 1997; Raulin, 2000).[54]

What is also relevant is that, in the decades to follow, anthropologists *dans la ville* (de La Pradelle, 2000), *de la ville* (Milliot, 1997) and/or *d'une ville* (Raulin, 1997; Monjaret, 2012) approaching sociological and historical perspectives centred on the specific outlines, the genesis and the metamorphosis of cities, have often continued to dwell on easily identifiable collectives, such as diasporic groups across the national territory or communities that share interests and practices such as bowls and chess players, art collectors, the public at football or rugby matches, professional

---

[51] Influenced by the perspectives of Roger Bastide and the Chicago school, Pétonnet founded the Urban Anthropology Laboratory (LAU) with Gutwirth in 1984.

[52] See also the 1982 issue of *L'Homme* and the 1984 issue of *Ethnologie française*.

[53] See also Terrolle (1983).

[54] See also Lepoutre (1997) and Bouillon (2009).

108   M. ARIA

bodies and disabled families. At the same time, they zeroed in on micro "territoriality" inhabitants, such as subjects on ships and boats (Dufoulon, 1998; Dufoulon et al., 1998; Duval, 1995, 1998; Brulé-Josso, 2012), nuclear power plants (Fournier, 2012), hospitals (Arborio, 2012), penitentiaries (Le Caisne, 2000, 2008; Bessin & Lechien, 2002) or schools.[55] Such placements are aligned with the aforementioned focus on subjects,[56] their actual universe and their existential intimacy, and thus less attuned to a quest for general theories or all-encompassing social facts. If anything, real actors, also investigated as active members within a wider social system and its transformations, become examples of broader scenarios and become vital cultural junctures.

New Studies on Material Culture

Urban anthropology and the renewed literature on workers' and popular cultures described so far also intersect with the successful rise of studies on material culture over the last twenty years. The continuist inclination mentioned above is a distinctive feature of this research field which—thanks in particular to the contributions of Warnier (1999), Segalen and Bromberger (1996), Bromberger and Chevallier (1999), Bonnot (2002) and Dassié (2010), as well as the remarkable influence of Latour (1991)—exposed the groundless separation between matter and the symbolic, and invalidated the tenuous distinction between a material culture and an immaterial culture. Along this line, and in a close exchange with Douglas and Isherwood (1980), Appadurai (1986) and Kopytoff (1986), scholars have developed the notions of a "career" and a "biography" of objects and of the "social life of things". All this was upheld by an ever-increasing interest in technical action, that is in the analysis of the steps involved in the

[55] As Roger (2002) argues, ethnological lines of research generally disclaim the mainstream interpretation of marginal groups as isolated clusters trapped inside a static culture. Rather, they aim to explore the strategies whereby subjects construct a social universe that is both internally coherent and actively located within the French context. Using criteria of ethnological inquiry to analyse social relations, how they are expressed, for example, in ritual practices, in the modes of exchange, in the uses of language and names and in the meaning of everyday objects, new urban anthropology studies set themselves apart from sociological investigations, which instead address social exclusion and disorder experienced by marginal groups as signalling a failure of the policies supported by French institutions. For a view that takes into account the most recent developments of such approaches, see among others Teissonnières, Terrolle (2012).

[56] See also Yvonne Verdier (1979).

manufacturing of objects. Preference for sociotechnical devices signals, however, a distance from the economic anthropology approach endorsed in the Anglo-American context and centred on the use of objects and on the consumption space of the mass culture industry (Miller, 1987 in particular). As attested in compendia by Jean Pierre Warnier (1999) and Marie-Pierre Julien and Céline Rosselin (2005), while new themes seem to have been adopted en masse, most authors do maintain strong ties with Marcel Mauss's work on the gift and the techniques of the body, as well as with subsequent research by André Leroi-Gourhan. The specifically French context stands in sharp contrast to other study traditions, such as the English or North American school, where the foregrounding of material culture entailed a clean break with self-contained or theoretically weak research traditions linked to collection, collation and cataloguing and still bound to positivistic methodologies and an exclusive interest in authentic or traditional objects. While in an Anglophone context such break with the past was pushed through under the pressure of *cultural studies* and the work of Raymond Williams and Stuart Hall, something quite different happened in France. In the 1960s and 1970s, Leroi-Gourhan's (1964–1965) proposal "of coming to terms with matter" as the core of an anthropological view of culture gained ascendancy. This led researchers to turn to technical and productive processes rather than the dynamics of consumption. This legacy, along with the systematic rediscovery of Mauss's thought, thus guided French ethnologists through the complex universe of objects and of relationships with subjects, in everyday life as much as in domestic spaces.[57] In these spaces, things "are no longer just the expression of a culture, of something external to individuals, but acquire meaning through a process of signification" (Chevalier, 2010, p. 147). What is also foregrounded in this field of research is intimacy; people's ability to elude the hopeless traps of cultural domination and their resourcefulness to continue operating in the world via tactics that once again recall de Certeau's brilliant suggestions.

Gender and Generations

The urge to make sense of current social and cultural dynamics also translates in openness to unprecedented fields of investigation, especially

---

[57] On domestic spaces and furnishings, in addition to the many works by Chevalier (and in particular Chevalier 1996) see also, among others, Bonnin & Perrot (1989).

notable in the contemporary French landscape. As attested in two monographs of *Ethnologie française*, *Vieillir en Europe* (2018) and *Genre; crise politiques et révolutions* (2019), *generation* and gender—already core issues in Africanist Marxist anthropology of the 1960s and 1970s—re-emerge as new vital modes of thinking about kinship and its recent changes. Female and male researchers have gradually begun to explore age groups—that is, those strata of society usually neglected in favour of a vertical ranking of economic classes—with a view to uncovering strategies of subjugation. Studies on childhood cultures observed in school and domestic spaces and through games, rituals and imaginaries have begun to spread accordingly. In parallel, as Claudine Attias-Donfute and Martine Segalen (2007) have pointed out, there has been a growing interest in those "old age" cultures engendered by global changes in politics and economics and by a reworking of family models.[58]

And the emergence of an anthropology of youth sports practices, championed in particular by Saouter (2000) and Bromberger (1995),[59] sheds light on a more general tendency to reassess practices once dismissed as deviant in the new terms of youth subcultures pliable enough to bring about meaningful regeneration (Raineau, 2006). Along similar lines, ethnography in France and on France focuses on spaces of individual expression which are independent of family, school or work and are experienced in playful, festive and artistic scenarios (dance, music, theatre). The "Intimité de la jeunesse" project (Raineau, 2006) falls within the broader investigation of collective aggregation modes, which often entail body-inscribed language (tattoos, piercing, burns). For Le Breton (2005, 2012, 2018), these may be vestiges of rites of passage or initiation related to pain.[60]

This fervent debate about generations is mirrored by widespread political sensitivity to gender issues, now reinterpreted beyond the exclusively vertical terms of unilateral power, inequality or violence. More recent theoretical works such as those of Théry (2007) and Théry, Bonnemère (2008)—which aim to transcend Héritier's critique of Lévi-Strauss in order to embrace the perspectives of the "relational person" model

[58] Among the most recent studies, see also Marec, Reguer (2013); Leider, Moulaert (2014); Amiotte-Suchet & Anchisi, (2017).

[59] For an anthropology of sporting practices, see also Callède (1987) and Chantelat et al. (1996). One could add the works by Niko Besnier, a part-French anthropologist who publishes regularly in French (Besnier et al., 2020).

[60] See also: Jeffrey et al. (2016); Ducournau et al. (2010).

proposed by Marilyn Strathern—tend not to limit themselves to denouncing female dependency or male domination, preferring rather to dwell on complex intra- and inter-gender relations, particularly in the anthropology of Oceania (Bonnemère, 2015; Tcherkézoff, 2022).

The Return of Ritual

So far, we have insisted on the central role of representations, of affects and of subjects' intimacy in the urban or domestic spaces of current France. As we have already mentioned in passing, however, this orientation was accompanied by a broader interest in ritual actions and by a rehabilitation of theories connected to them, which highlights their innovative dynamics (rituals as melting pots and workshops for new forms). Such rediscovery partakes of the wider questioning of Weber's model of modernity and of the so-called disenchantment of the world (as keenly observed by Latour, 1991), so much so that postmodernity's resumption of rituality may be read as a general inversion of secularization.

According to Guy Barbichon (2009), various male and female ethnologists, reworking the classic anthropology approaches of Durkheim, Mauss and Van Gennep with the new contributions of Bourdieu, Erving Goffman or Victor Turner, have shifted goal from cults and religious practices towards profane rites, in which a change of state is either determined or confirmed via symbolic operations. The large repertoire identified and described by Segalen (1998) shows that even though they may directly pertain to a religious or magic dimension, many ceremonial actions arouse emotional impulses, spin imaginary visions and build up reference frameworks that can strengthen social bonds and create a sense of community. And they are upheld in this also by the resonance of mass media.

The researchers' gaze has thus turned both to ritual practices that persist, return or are newly set up inside sects, brotherhoods or restricted associations, and to those which instead take shape in the interstices of institutional bodies, such as the army, the judiciary or large state bodies, or in public performances of consecration and investiture held by authorities or established bodies. In any case, these are actions in which symbolic efficacy, albeit partial, remains crucial and oath-taking comes to confirm and substantiate an unprecedented implication of the sacred (Barbichon, 2009). Over recent decades, present-day investigation of the nature of these acts has become a constitutive feature of a historical anthropology focused on power-related rites. This has spun a plethora of published work on collective and cultural memory and on the ways in which given social groups forge representations of the past to support present values or opportunities. Similar perspectives, close to the well-known study project of the places of memory proposed by Pierre Nora (1984), look at the "social dramas" and the political uses of public spaces that imply a strict discipline of bodies and movements, a sense of community and emotional elation.[61] Such acts disrupt the daily course of life and may at times rework space and time in extraordinary and meaningful manners. Scholars in this line of research have attended to expressive features, liturgies and grammars (the lyricism of gestures and words which try to capture or imprison the senses) in election campaigns, civic holidays, commemorations and inaugurations, political manifestations, republican folklore (Agulhon, 1995) and the installation of authorities and constituent bodies. Attention to public events also interfaces with abundant literature on enhancement strategies for cultural heritage sites (monuments, tangible and intangible assets, museums, archives) and on the "heritage" communities which deploy them, use them or appropriate them (Fabre & Iuso, 2010). A recent critical and reflexive thread of research along the lines of heritage ethnology is now directed by LAHIC and relies on a prolific exchange between historians, ethnologists and archaeologists. Such collaborative project has preceded and oriented subsequent debates on intangible cultural heritage and on UNESCO policies and languages, opening up, among other things, a new field of study on "heritage emotions" (Tornatore & Barbe, 2011; Fabre, 2013).

Following the requests of Fabre (1987), Cuisenier (1998), Rivière (1996) and Segalen herself (1998), ample space has been given to those old and new ceremonies which mark the private life of individuals and groups, which are often linked to new living conditions brought about by social change. The same thrust is seen in research on the new "rites" performed on children's birthdays (Sirota, 1998), on teenagers' successful driving tests, to mark Saint Catherine Day in couture workshops (Monjaret, 1997), or in special funeral events, such as cremations, funeral services for violence or AIDS victims (Broqua et al., 1998).

---

[61] Think also of the works edited by Christophe Traini (2009) on the key role of emotions in contemporary social mobilizations: from victim empathy to anger against tyrants, from hero worship to impassioned grassroots action.

CONCLUSIONS

The considerable body of ethnological research assembled in recent decades testifies to an intense commitment to reposition the discipline in relation to global dynamics. Development has been largely driven by the powerful institutional support and substantial material resources that the Ministry of Culture's Ethnological Heritage Mission has made available.

At the same time, decolonization has upset the "division of labor" between sociology and anthropology, inherited from the colonial era and very much alive in both academia and museums. Hence anthropology's homecoming. The current landscape is nonetheless still traversed by a sharp fault line between "actual" anthropologists, most often defined by the spatial distance of their (exotic) field of study, and ethnologists who conduct research on France, often characterized by the temporal proximity of their research object (the present).

A paradox comes to us by way of conclusion: as we have seen, ethnology in France on France pays close heed to the symbolic, to subjects, to meanings, to ritual dimensions and, therefore, to representations and interpretations of cultural features. That probably takes place, however, at the expense of political commitment and the denunciation of inequalities and subjugation. Such perspectives seem very distant, if not altogether antithetical, to the orientations of Anglophone critical anthropology, which advocates a strong theory of society and power and aims to deconstruct the very concept of culture—as an ideological construct masking the mechanisms of exploitation—precisely through the suggestions of those French *maîtres à penser* (from Foucault to Fanon) who now seem instead to keep a weaker hold in the contemporary landscape of transalpine anthropology.

REFERENCES

Abélès, M. (1990). *Anthropologie de l'État*. Arman Colin.
Abélès, M. (1992). *La Vie quotidienne au Parlement européen*. Hachette.
Abélès, M. (2000). *An ethnologue à l'Assemblée*. Éditions Odile Jacob.
Abélès, M. (2001). *Politica, gioco di spazi*. Meltemi.
Abélès, M. (2008). *Anthropologie de la globalisation*. Payot.
Agier, M. (2015). The contemporary turn of anthropology. In S. Chevalier (Ed.), *Anthropology at the crossroads: The view from France* (pp. 50–68). Royal Anthropological Institute.
Agulhon, M. (Ed.). (1995). *Cultures et folklores républicains*. CTHS.

114 M. ARIA

Althabe, G. (1977). Le quotidien en procès, (entretien avec Marc Abélès). *Dialectiques, 21*, 67–77.

Althabe, G. (1992). Vers un ethnologie du présent. In G. Althabe, D. Fabre, & G. Lencloud (Eds.), *Vers un ethnologie du présent* (pp. 247–257). Maison des Sciences de l'Homme.

Althabe, G., Marcadet, C. P., & de La Selim, M. (1985). *Urbanisation et enjeux quotidiens.* Anthropos.

Amiotte-Suchet, L., & Anchisi, A., eds. (2017). *Vieillir en institution, vieillesses institutionnalisées.* Nouvelles populations, nouveaux lieux, nouvelles pratiques, ethnographiques.org. http://www.ethnographiques.org/2017/ Amiotte-Suchet_Anchisi

Amselle, J. L. (1990). *Logiques métisses, Anthropologie de l'identité en Afrique et ailleurs.* Payot.

Amselle, J. L. (2001). *Branchements. Anthropologie de l'universalité des cultures.* Flammarion.

Amselle, J. L. (2008). *L'Occident décroché: enquête sur les post colonialismes.* Stock.

Appadurai, A. (1986). Introduction: Commodities and the politics of value. In A. Appadurai (Ed.), *The social life of the things: Commodities in cultural perspective* (pp. 3–63). Cambridge University Press.

Arborio, A. M. (2012). *Un personnel invisible. Les aides-soignantes à l'hôpital.* Économica.

Aria, M. (2016). *I doni di Mauss. Percorsi di antropologia economica.* CISU.

Assier-Andrieu, L. (1981). *Coutumes et rapports sociaux. Étude anthropologique des communautés paysannes du Capcir.* Éditions du CNRS.

Attias-Donfute, C., & Segalen, M. (2007). *Grands-Parents. La famille à travers les générations.* Odile Jacob.

Augé, M. (1972). Sous-développement et développement: terrain d'étude et objets d'action en Afrique francophone. *Africa, 42*(3), 205–216.

Augé, M. (1986). *An ethnologue dans le métro.* Hachette.

Augé, M. (1992). *Non-lieux. Introduction à une anthropologie de la surmodernité.* Seuil.

Augé, M. (1994a). *Pour une anthropologie des mondes contemporains.* Aubier.

Augé, M. (1994b). *Le sens des autres. Actualité de l'anthropologie.* Fayard.

Augustins, G. (1989). *Comment se perpétuer? Devenir des lignées et destins des patrimoines dans les paysanneries européennes.* Université de Nanterre.

Barbe, N. Chauliac, M., & Tornatore, J. L. (2015). Intangible cultural heritage exposed to public deliberation: A participatory experience in a regional park. In N. Adell-Gombert, R. Bendix, C. Bortolotto, & M. Tauschek (Eds.), *Between imagined communities and communities of practice. Participation, territory and the making of heritage.* Göttingen Studies in Cultural Property (Vol. 8, pp. 201–218). Göttingen University Press.

Barbichon, G. (2009). Ethnologie en France, ethnologie de la France. Champs nouveaux, manières neuves. *Anthropologie et Sociétés, 33*(2), 237–254.

Barthelemy de Saizieu, T. (2004). Introduction. L'héritage contre la famille? De l'anthropologie a l'économie, des approches plurielles. *Sociétés contemporaines, 56*(4), 5–18.

Barthélémy de Saizieu, T., & Weber, F. (1989). *Les campagnes à livre ouvert. Regards sur la France rurale des années trente.* Presses de l'ENS-éditions de l'EHESS.

Bayart, J. F. (1989). *L'État en Afrique. La politique du ventre.* Fayard.

Bayart, J. F. (2010). *Les Études postcoloniales, une carnaval académique.* Karthala.

Bellier, I. (1993). *L'ENA comme si vous y étiez.* Le Seuil.

Belmont, N. (1974). *Arnold Van Gennep, le créateur de l'ethnographie française.* Payot.

Belmont, N. (1986). Le folklore refoulé ou les séductions de l'Archaïsme. *L'Homme, 26*(97–98), 259–268.

Bernot, L., & Blancard, R. (1953). *Nouville, un village française.* Institut d'ethnologie.

Bertho-Lavenir, C. (1980). L'invention de la Bretagne: genèse social d'un stéréotype. *Actes de la recherche en sciences sociales, 35,* 45–62.

Bertrand, R., & Fournier, L. S. (Eds.). (2014). *Les fêtes en Provence autrefois et aujourd'hui.* Presses Universitaires de Provence.

Besnier, N., Brownell, S., & Carter, T. F. (2020). *L'anthropologie du sport: Corps, nations, migrations dans le monde contemporain.* Éditions de la rue d'Ulm.

Bessin, M., & Lechien, M. H. (2002). Hommes détenus et femmes soignants: l'inimité des soins en prison. *Ethnologie française, 32*(1), 69–80.

Bierschenk, T. (2014). From the anthropology of development to the anthropology of global social engineering. *Zeitschrift für Ethnologie, 139*(1), 73–97.

Bierschenk, T., & Olivier de Sardan, J. P. (Eds.). (2014). *States at work. Dynamics of African bureaucracies.* Brill.

Blanckaert, C. (1997). *Le muséum au premier siècle de son histoire.* Éditions du Muséum National d'Histoire Naturelle.

Blundo, G. (Ed.). (2000). *Monnayer les pouvoirs: espaces, mécanismes et représentations de la corruption.* PUF.

Blundo, G., & Le Meur, P. Y. (Eds.). (2009). *The governance of daily life in Africa: Explorations of public and collective services.* Brill.

Blundo, G., & Olivier de Sardan, J. P. (Eds.). (2006). *Everyday corruption and the state. Citizens and public officials in Africa.* Zed Books.

Blundo, G., & Olivier de Sardan, J. P. (Eds.). (2007). *État et corruption en Afrique: une anthropologie comparative des relations entre fonctionnaires et usagers (Benin, Niger, Sénégal).* Karthala.

Boltanski, L. (1990). *L'amour et la justice comme compétences. Trois essais de sociologie de l'action.* Métailié.

Bonnemère, P. (2015). *Agir pour un autre. La construction de la personne masculine en Papouasie-Nouvelle-Guinée*. Presses Universitaires de Provence.

Bonnin, P., Perrot, M., & de La Soudière, M. (1983). *L'Ostal en Margeride*. Publications de la Sorbonne.

Bonnin, P., & Perrot, M. (1989). Le décor domestique en Margeride. *Terrain, 12*, 40–53.

Bonnot, T. (2002). *La vie des objets. D'ustensiles banals à objets de collection*. Éditions de la Maison des Sciences de l'Homme.

Bonte, P., & Izard, M. (Eds.). (2002). *Dictionnaire de l'ethnologie et de l'anthropologie*. PUF / Quadrige.

Borrillo, D., Fassin, E., & Lacub, M. (Eds.). (1999). *Au-delà du Pacs. L'expertise familial à l'épreuve de l'homosexualité*. PUF.

Bortolotto, C. (2011). Le trouble du patrimoine culturel immatériel. In C. Bortolotto, A. Arnaud, & S. Grenet (Eds.), *Le patrimoine culturel immatériel. Enjeux d'une nouvelle catégorie* (pp. 21–42). Éditions de la Maison des sciences de l'Homme.

Bouillon, F. (2009). *Les mondes du squat, anthropologie d'un habitat précaire*. PUF.

Bourcier, M. H. (2006). Études culturelles et minorités indisciplinées dans la France métropolitaine. *Médias et informations, 24–25*, 87–99.

Bourdieu, P. (1979). *La distinction: critique sociale du jugement*. Les Éditions de Minuit.

Bourdieu, P., & Lamaison, P. (1985). De la règle aux stratégies: Entretien avec Pierre Bourdieu. *Terrain, 4*, 93–100.

Bozon, M., Chamboredon, J. C., & Fabiani, J. L. (Eds.). (1982). Chasse et la cueillette aujourd'hui. *Études rurales*, 87–88.

Bromberger, C. (1987). Du grand au petit. Variations des échelles et des objets d'analyse dans l'histoire récente de l'ethnologie de la France. In G. Althabe, D. Fabre, & G. Lencloud (Eds.), *Ethnologies en miroir. La France et les pays de langue allemande* (pp. 67–94). Maison des Sciences de l'Homme.

Bromberger, C. (1995). *Le match de football. Ethnologie d'une passion partisane à Marseille, Naples and Turin*. Maison des Sciences de l'Homme.

Bromberger, C. (2014). "Le patrimoine immatériel" entre ambiguïtés et overdose. *L'Homme, 209*(1), 143–151.

Bromberger, C., & Chevallier, D. (Eds.). (1999). *Carrières d'objets, innovations et relances*. Maison des Sciences de l'Homme.

Broqua, C., Loux, F., & Prado, P. (1998). Sida: deuil, mémoire, nouveaux rituels. *Ethnologie française, 28*(1), 5–9.

Brulé-Josso, S. (2012). Les plaisanciers et le vrai marin. *Ethnologie française, 42*(4), 733–745.

Brutti, L. (2009). L'antropologia cannibalizzata dall'arte "primitiva". Una lettura etnografica del Musée du Quai Branly a partire da oggetti melanesiani. In

E. Gnecchi-Ruscone & A. Paini (Eds.), *Antropologia dell'Oceania* (pp. 315–338). Pacini.

Burguière, A. (1975). *Bretons de Plozevet*. Flammarion.

Cadoret, A. (1995). *Parenté plurielle. Anthropologie du placement familial.* L'Harmattan.

Caillé, A. (1989). *Critique de la raison utilitaire.* La Découverte.

Callède, P. (1987). *L'Esprit sportif: essai sur le development associatif de la culture sportive.* Presses Universitaires de Bordeaux.

Chalvon-Demersay, S. (1998). *Le triangle du XIVe. Des nouveaux habitants dans un vieux quartier de Paris.* Maison des Sciences de l'Homme.

Chantelat, P., Fodimbi, M., & Camy, J. (1996). *Sports de la cité: anthropologie de la jeunesse sportive.* L'Harmattan.

Charuty, G. (1987). Le mal d'amour. *L'Homme, 27*(3), 43–72.

Charuty, G. (1992). Anthropologie et Psychanalyse. Le dialogue inachevé. In G. Althabe, D. Fabre, & G. Lenclud (Eds.), *Vers une ethnologie du présent* (pp. 75–115). Maison des Sciences de l'Homme.

Chauveau, J. P. (1982). *Pour une sociologie historique du développement.* ORSTOM.

Chevalier, S. (1996). Transmettre son mobilier? Le cas contrasté de la France et de l'Angleterre. *Ethnologie française, 26*(1), 115–128.

Chevalier, S. (2010). *Costruire il proprio universo. Una comparazione franco-britannica.* In S. Bernardi, F. Dei, & P. Meloni (Eds.), *La materia del quotidiano. Per un antropologia degli oggetti ordinari* (pp. 145–158). Pacini.

Chevalier, S. (Ed.). (2015). *Anthropology at the crossroads. The view from France.* Sean Kingston Publishing.

Chevalier, S. (2017). *The trajectory of French anthropology seen through a recent transformative episode.* In A. Barrera-Gonzalez, M. Heinz, & A. Horolets (Eds.), *European anthropologies* (pp. 128–148). Berghahn.

Chevalier, S., & Lallament, E. (2015). Anthropology in France today: A view from inside. In S. Chevalier (Ed.), *Anthropology at the crossroads: The view from France* (pp. 1–25). Canon Pyon.

Chevalier, S., & Monjaret, A., (Eds.). (1998). Les cadeaux à quel prix?. *Ethnologie française, 28* (4).

Chiva, I. (1985). Georges-Henri Rivière. A demisiècle d'ethnologie de la France. *Terrain, 5,* 76–83.

Chiva, I. (1987). Entre livre et musée. Emergence d'une ethnologie de la France. In I. Chiva & U. Jeggle (Eds.), *Ethnologies en miroir. La France et les pays de langue allemande* (pp. 9–33). Maison des Sciences de l'Homme.

Chiva, I. (1990). Le patrimoine ethnologique L'exemple de la France. *Encyclopædia Universalis, 24,* 229–241.

Chiva, I., & Goy, J. (Eds.). (1981). *Les Baronnies des Pyrénées. Anthropologie et histoire, permanences et changements, vol. 1, Maisons, mode de vie, société.* Éditions de l'Ehess.

118 M. ARIA

Chiva, I., & Jeggle, U. (Eds.). (1987). *Ethnologies en miroir. La France et les pays de languishes allemande*. Maison des Sciences de l'Homme.

Claverie, E., & Lamaison, P. (1982). *L'impossible mariage. Violence et parenté en Gévaudan, xviie-xviiie-xixe siècles*. Hachette.

Clemente, P. (2014). Prigioneri e ambasciatori. In Paini, M. Aria (eds.), *La densità delle cose. Oggetti ambasciatori tra Oceania e Europa* (pp. 285–297). Pacini.

Clifford, J. (1988). *The predicament of cultures: Twentieth-century ethnography, literature and art*. Harvard University Press.

Copans, J. (2009). Un développement sans acteurs mais non sans politique. La difficile empiricité d'un engagement anti-impérialiste. *Journal des anthropologues, 118–119*, 65–88.

Copans, J. (2016). L'Afrique noire a-t-elle besoin du développement (de l'anthropologie) ou au contraire d'une anthropologie (du développement)? In M. Lafay, F. Le Guennec-Coppens, & E. Coulibaly (Eds.), *Regards scientifiques sur l'Afrique depuis les indépendances* (pp. 377–396). Karthala.

Corbin, A. (1990). *L'Occident et le désir du rivage, 1740-1840*. Flammarion.

Corbin, A. (Ed.). (1995). *L'avènement des loisirs, 1850-1960*. Aubier.

Cuisenier, J. (1998). Cérémonial ou rituel? *Ethnologie française, 1*, 10–19.

Cuisenier, J., & Segalen, M. (1993). *Ethnologie de la France*. Presses Universitaires de France.

Dassié, V. (2010). *Objets d'affection. Une ethnologie de intimate*. Éditions du CTHS.

de Certeau, M. (1980). *L'Invention du quotidien, vol. 1, Arts de faire*. Union générale d'éditions.

de L'Estoile, B. (2007). Le Musée de l'Homme, laboratoire de l'ethnologie française, 1938-2003. In C. Jacob (Ed.), *Les lieux de savoir* (pp. 737–760). Albin Michel.

de L'Estoile, B. (2012). Anthropologie et sociologie: croisements et bifurcations. *Genèses, 89*(4), 2–9.

de L'Estoile, B. (2015). Can French anthropology outlive its museums? Notes on a Changing landscape. In S. Chevalier (Ed.), *Anthropology at the crossroads: The view from France* (pp. 81–94). Canon Pyon.

de La Pradelle, M. (1996). *Les Vendredis de Carpentras, faire son marché en Provence ou ailleurs*. Fayard.

de La Pradelle, M. (2000). La ville des anthropolougues. In T. Paquot, M. Lusseal, & S. Body-Gendrot (Eds.), *La ville et l'urbain. L'état des savoirs* (pp. 45–52). La Découvert.

Debary, O., & Roustan, M. (2012). *Voyage au musée du quai Branly. Anthropologie de la visits du plateau des collections*. La Documentation française.

Debonneville, J. (2017). (Re) connaissances anthropologiques du postcolonial. Circulations, résistances et institutionnalisations. *Revue d'anthropologie des connaissances, 11*(3), 283–302.

Derrida, J. (1991). *Donner le temps*. Galilée.

Descola, P. (2005). *Par-delà nature et culture*. Gallimard.

Desvallées, A. (1987). Les musées de l'homme, du temps, de l'Espace. *Ethnologie française, 17*(1), 59–60.

Désveaux, E. (2015). Lévi-Strauss and his Heirs. In S. Chevalier (Ed.), *Anthropology at the crossroad, the view from France* (pp. 30–49). Sean Kingston Publishing.

Douglas, M., & Isherwood, B. (1980). *The world of goods. Towards an anthropology of consumption*. Penguin.

Ducournau, N., Lachance, J., Mathiot, L., & Sellami, M. (Eds.). (2010). *La recherche d'extase chez les jeunes*. Presses de l'Université Laval.

Dufoulon, S. (1998). *Les Gars de la marine, ethnographie d'un navire de guerre*. Anne-Marie Métailié.

Dufoulon, S. Saglio, J., & Trompette, P. (1998). *La Différence perdue. La féminisation de l'équipage du Montcalm*, rapport pour le Center d'études en sciences sociales de la Défense (C2SD).

Dumont, L. (1987). *La Tarasque. Essai de description d'un fait local d'un point de vue ethnographique*. Gallimard.

Duret, E. (1993). Les charrettes festives en Provence rhodanienne. Variations d'un rite et de son espace de référence du XVIII au XX siècle. *Le Monde alpin et rhodanien. Revue régionale d'ethnologie, 1–2*, 35–61.

Duval, M. (1995). Sous la protection de Neptune. Le rite d'initiation des élèves de la marine. *Terrain, 24*, 133–144.

Duval, M. (1998). *Ni morts, ni vivants: marins! Pour une ethnologie du huit clos*. PUF.

Ermisse, G. (Ed.). (1994). Les émotions. *Terrain, 22*.

Escobar, A. (1994). *Encountering development: The making and unmaking of the third world*. Princeton University Press.

Fabre, D. (1986). La voie des oiseaux sur quelques récit d'apprentissage. *L'Homme, 26*(99), 7–40.

Fabre, D. (1987). Le rite et ses raisons. *Terrain, 8*, 3–7.

Fabre, D. (1992). Introduction. In G. Althabe, D. Fabre, & G. Lenclud (Eds.), *Vers une ethnologie du present* (pp. 1–5). Maison des Sciences de l'Homme.

Fabre, D. (1998). L'ethnologie française à la croisée des engagements (1940–1945). In J.-Y. Boursier (ed.), *Résistants et résistance* (pp. 319–400). L'Harmattan.

Fabre, D. (2000). L'ethnologie devant le monument historique. In D. Fabre (Ed.), *Domestiquer l'histoire. Ethnologie des monuments historiques* (pp. 1–29). Maison des Sciences de l'Homme.

Fabre, D. (Ed.). (2013). *Patrimonial Emotinons*. Maison des Sciences de l'Homme.

Fabre, D., & Iuso, A. (Eds.). (2010). *Les monuments sont habités*. Maison des Sciences de l'Homme.

Fabre-Vassas, C. (1985). La cure de l'hernie. In *Le corps, nature, culture et surnaturel*. Actes du 110° Congrès National des Sociétés Savantes (pp. 277–288). CTHS.

Fassin, D. (1996). *Espace politique de la santé. Essai de généalogie.* Presses Universitaires de France.

Fassin, D. (2000b). Les politiques de l'ethnopsychiatrie. La psyché africaine, des colonies africaines aux banlieues parisiennes. *L'Homme, 153,* 231–250.

Fassin, D. (2008). *Faire de la santé publique.* Éditions de l'École des Hautes Études en Santé Publique.

Fassin, D. (2010). *La raison humanitaire. Une histoire morale du temps present.* Gallimard-Seuil.

Fassin, D. (2011). *La force de l'ordre. Une anthropologie de la police des quartiers.* Seuil.

Fassin, D. (2017). *Punir. Une passion contemporaine.* Seuil.

Fassin, E. (2000a). Usages de la science et science des usages. A propos des familles homoparentales. *L'Homme, 154*(5), 391–408.

Favret-Saada, J. (1977). *Les Mots, la mort, les sorts. La sorcellerie dans le Bocage.* Gallimard.

Ferguson, J. (1994). *The anti-politics machine: Development, depoliticization, and bureaucratic power in Lesotho.* University of Minnesota Press.

Fine, A. (1994). *Parrains, marraines. Parenté spirituelle en Europe.* Fayard.

Fine, A. (Ed.). (1998). *Adoptions. Ethnologie des parentés choisies.* Maison des Sciences de l'Homme.

Fournier, P. (2012). *Travailler dans le nucléaire. Enquête au cœur d'un site à risques.* Armand Colin.

Fresia, M., & Lavigne Delville, P. (Eds.). (2018). *Au cœur des mondes de l'Aide internationale. Regards et postures ethnographiques.* Karthala.

Gaboriau, P. (1993). *Clochard.* Julliard.

Gaboriau, P., & Terrolle, D. (Eds.). (2003). *L'Ethnologie des sans-logis.* L'Harmattan.

Geertz, C. (1973). *Interpretation on cultures.* Basic Books.

Gérome, N. (1990). L'ethnologie, la "culture de masse" et les ouvriers: fragments d'une perspective. *Le Mouvement Social, 152*(2), 49–60.

Godbout, J. T. (1992). *L'esprit du don.* La Découverte.

Godelier, M. (1996). *L'énigme du don.* Fayard.

Graeber, D., & Houtman, G. (2012). The Occupy Movement and Debt. An Interview with David Graeber. *Anthropology Today, 28* (5), 17–18.

Grignon, C., & Passeron, J. P. (1989). *Le savant et le populaire. Misérabilisme et populisme en sociologie et en literature.* Gallimard-Seuil.

Gruzinski, S., & Bénat-Tachot, L. (2001). *Passeurs Culturels. Mécanismes De Métissage.* Maison des Sciences de L'Homme.

Gueusquin, M. F. (2000). *La Provence arlésienne, traditions et avatars.* Actes Sud/ Réunion des Musées nationaux.

Guolo, R. (2021). *I ferventi. Gli etnologi francesi tra esperienza interiore e storia.* Mondadori.

Gutwirth, J., & Pétonnet, C. (1987). *Les chemins de la ville: enquêtes ethnologiques.* Les Éditions du CHTS.

Hassoun, J. P. (1997). *Hmong du Laos en France. Changement social, initiatives et adaptations.* Presses Universitaires de France.

Hassoun, J. P. (2000). Le surnom et ses usages sur les marchés à la criée du MATIF. Contrôle social, fluidité relationnelle et représentations collectives. *Genèse, 41,* 5–40.

Hell, B. (1985). *Entre chien et loup. Faits et dits de la chasse dans la France de l'Est.* Maison de Sciences de l'Homme.

Hottin, C. (2016). L'ethnologie, un métier du patrimoine ? Réflexions autour de la question du patrimoine culturel immatériel. http://journals.openedition.org/insitu/13633

Jeffrey, D., Le Lachance, J., & Breton, D. (Eds.). (2016). *Penser l'adolescence.* Presses Universitaires de France.

Julien, M. P., & Rosselin, C. (2005). *La culture matérielle.* Découverte.

Karnoouh, C. (1973). L'impossible démocratie. Parenté et politique dans un village lorrain. *Études rurales, 52,* 24–56.

Karnoouh, C. (1980). Le pouvoir et la parenté. In H. Lamarche, C. Kamoouh, & S. C. Rogers (Eds.), *Paysans, femmes et citoyens. Luttes pour le pouvoir dans un village lorrain* (pp. 141–210). Actes Sud.

Kelly, J. D. (2014). Introduction: The ontological turn in French philosophical anthropology. *Hau: Journal of Ethnographic Theory, 4*(1), 259–269.

Kopytoff, I. (1986). The cultural biography of things: Commoditization as process. In A. Appadurai (Ed.), *The social life of things. Commodities in cultural perspective* (pp. 64–91). Cambridge University Press.

Lamaison, P. (1987). Parenté 2: filiation et alliance. In I. Chiva & U. Jeggle (Eds.), *Ethnologies en miroir. La France et les pays de langue allemande* (pp. 109–121). Maison des Sciences de l'Homme.

Langlois, C. (1999). Recent developments in French anthropology of France and the role of the mission du Patrimoine Ethnologique. *Cultural Anthropology, 14,* 409–416.

Latour, B. (1991). *Nous n'avons jamais été modernes. Essai d'anthropologie symétrique.* La Découverte.

Lavigne Delville, P. (2016). Pour une socio-anthropologie de l'action publique dans les pays 'sous régime d'aide'. *Anthropologie & développement, 45,* 33–64.

Le Breton, D. (2005). Le corps, la limite: signes d'identité à l'adolescence. In C. Bromberger et al. (Eds.), *Un corps pour soi* (pp. 89–114). PUF.

Le Breton, D. (2012). *Anthropologie de la douleur.* Métailié.

Le Breton, D. (2018). *La sociologie du corps.* Presses Universitaires de France.

Le Caisne, L. (2000). *Prison. Une ethnologue en centrale.* Odile Jacob.

Le Caisne, L. (2008). *Avoir 16 ans à Fleury. Ethnographie d'un centre de jeunes détenus.* Seuil.

122 M. ARIA

Le Wita, B. (1988). *Ni vue ni connue: approche ethnographique de la culture bourgeoise*. Éditions de la Maison des Sciences de l'Homme.

Leider, B., & Moulaert, T. (2014). Résistance (s) et vieillissement (s). *Émulations*, 13, http://www.revue-emulations.net/archives/n13-vieillissement

Lenclud, G. (1987). La tradition n'est plus ce qu'elle était. Sur les notions de tradition et de société traditionnelle en ethnologie. *Terrain, 9*, 110–123.

Lepoutre, D. (1997). *Cœur de banlieue. Codes, rites et langages*. Odile Jacob.

Leroi-Gourhan, A. (1964–1965). *Le geste et la parole*. Albin Michel.

Lévi-Strauss, C. (1950). Introduction à l'œuvre de Marcel Mauss. In M. Mauss (Ed.), *Sociologies and anthropologies* (pp. ix–lii). PUF.

Lévi-Strauss, C. (1958). *Anthropologie structural*. Plon.

Macdonald, C. (2008). L'anthropologie sociale en France, dans quel état? *Ethnologie française, 38*(4), 617–625.

Marec, Y., & Reguer, D. (Eds.). (2013). *De l'hospice au domicile collectif. La vieillesse et ses prises en charge de la fin du XVIIIe siècle à nos jours*. Publications des Universités de Rouen et du Havre (PURH).

Martial, A. (2003). *S'apparenter: Ethnologie des liens de familles recomposes*. Maison des Sciences de l'Homme.

Martial, A. (Ed.). (2009). *La valeur des liens: Hommes, femmes et transactions familiales*. Éditions Presses Universitaires du Mirail.

Miller, D. (1987). *Material culture and mass consumption*. Blackwell.

Milliot, V. (1997). Ethnographie d'une mauvaise vague. Une question de regard. In J. Métral (Ed.), *Les aléas du lien social. Constructions identitaires et culturelles dans la ville* (pp. 15–29). Ministère de la Culture et de la Communication.

Monjaret, A. (1997). *La Sainte-Catherine. Culture festive dans l'entreprise*. CTHS.

Monjaret, A. (Ed.). (2012). Le Paris des ethnologues, des lieux, des hommes. *Ethnologie française, 42*, 3.

Nathan, T. (2000). L'héritage du rebelle. Le rôle de Georges Devereux dans la naisance de l'ethnopsychiatrie clinique en France. *Ethonopsy. Les mondes contemporains de la guérison, 1*, 197–226.

Nora, P. (1984). *Les Lieux de mémoire*. Gallimard.

Olivier de Sardan, J. P. (1995). *Anthropologie et développement: essai en socio-anthropologie du changement social*. Karthala.

Paini, A., & Aria, A. (Eds.). (2014). *La densità delle cose. Oggetti ambasciatori tra l'Oceania e l'Europa*. Pacini.

Parkin, R. (2010). I paesi francofoni. In F. Barth, A. Gingrich, R. Parkin, & S. Silverman (Eds.), *Storie dell'antropologia. Percorsi britannici, tedeschi, francesi e americani* (pp. 103–170). SEID.

Pétonnet, C. (1979). *On est tous dans le brouillard. Ethnologie des banlieues*. Galilée.

Pétonnet, C. (1982). *Espaces habités. Ethnologie des banlieues*. Galilée.

Pinçon, M., & Pinçon-Charlot, M. (1996). *Grandes fortunes, dynasties familiales et formes de richesse en France*. Payot - Collection "Documents".

Pinçon, M., & Pinçon-Charlot, M. (1998). *Les Rothschild, une famille bien ordonnée*. La Dispute - Collection "Instants".

Pinçon, M., & Pinçon-Charlot, M. (2013). *La violence des riches. Chronique d'une immense casse social*. La Découverte.

Pinçon, M., & Pinçon-Charlot, M. (2021). *Notre vie chez les riches. Mémoires d'un couple de sociologues*. La Découverte.

Porqueres, E. (2009). *Défis contemporains de la parenté*. EHESS.

Pouillon, J. (1975). *Fétiches sans fétichisme*. Maspero.

Pouillon, J. (1986). Introduction. De Chacun à tout autre, et réciproquement. *L' Homme, 26*(97–98), 27–35.

Raineau, C. (2006). Du rite de passage au souci de soi: vers une anthropologie de la jeunesse? *Siècles, 24*, 25–37.

Raulin, A. (1997). *Manhattan ou la mémoire insulaire, Mémoires de l'Institut d'Ethnologie*. Muséum National d'Histoire naturelle.

Raulin, A. (2000). *L'ethnique est quotidien. Diasporas, marchés et cultures métropolitaines*. L'Harmattan.

Rivière, C. (1996). Pour une théorie du quotidien ritualisé. *Ethnologie française, 26*(2), 229–239.

Roger, S. C. (2002). L'anthropologie en France. *Terrain, 39*, 141–162.

Salitot, M., Segalen, M., & Zonabend, F. (1989). Anthropologie de la parenté et sociétés contemporaines. In M. Segalen (Ed.), *L'autre et le semblable. Regards sur l'ethnologie des sociétés contemporaines* (pp. 79–88). Presses du CNRS.

Saouter, A. (2000). *Être Rugby: Jeux du masculin et du féminin*. Maison des Sciences de l'Homme.

Schwartz, O. (1990). *Le monde privé des ouvriers. Hommes et femmes du Nord*. PUF.

Segalen, M. (1985). *Quinze générations de Bas-Bretons. Parenté et société dans le pays bigouden Sud, 1720–1980*. Presses Universitaires de France.

Segalen, M. (Ed.). (1989a). *L'autre et le semblable. Regards sur l'ethnologie des sociétés contemporaines*. Presses du CNRS.

Segalen, M. (1989b). Introduction. In M. Segalen (Ed.), *L'autre et le semblable. Regards sur l'ethnologie des sociétés contemporaines* (pp. 7–14). Presses du CNRS.

Segalen, M. (1990). *Nanterriens, les familles dans la ville*. Presses universitaires du Mirail.

Segalen, M. (1992). La parenté. Des sociétés "exotiques" aux sociétés modernes. In G. Althabe, D. Fabre, & G. Lenclud (Eds.), *Vers une ethnologie du present* (pp. 175–193). Maison des Sciences de l'Homme.

Segalen, M. (1998). *Rites et rituels contemporains*. Nathan.

Segalen, M. (2005). *Vie d'un musée. 1937–2005*. Stock.

Segalen, M., & Bromberger, C. (1996). L'objet moderne: de la production sérielle à la diversité des usages. *Ethnologie française, 26*, 5–16.

Singly, F. de (éd.). (1991). *La famille, l'état des savoirs*. La Decouverte.

124 M. ARIA

Sirota, R. (1998). Les copains d'abord. Les anniversaires de l'enfance, donner et recevoir. *Ethnologie française, 28*(4), 457–471.

Starobinski, J. (1994). *Largesse.* Réunion des Musées Nationaux.

Tcherkézoff, S. (2016). *Mauss à Samoa. Le holisme méthodologique et l'esprit du don polynésien.* Pacific-Credo publications.

Tcherkézoff, S. (2022). *Vous avez dit « troisième sexe » ? Les transgenres polynésiens et le mythe occidental de l'homosexualité.* Au Vent des Îles.

Tedlock, B. (1991). From participant observation to the observation of participation: The emergence of narrative ethnography. *Journal of Anthropological Research, 47*(1), 69–94.

Teissonnières, G., & Terrolle, D. (Eds.). (2012). *A la croisée des chemins. Contributions and reflections épistémologiques en anthropologie urbaine.* Éditions du Croquant.

Terrolle, D. (1983). *Travaux d'ethnographie urbaine.* PUV.

Testart, A. (1987). De la chasse en France, du sang, et de bien d'autres choses encore. (A propos de Bertrand Hell, entre chien et loup …). *L'Homme, 27*(102), 151–167.

Théry, I. (2007). *La distinction de sexe, une nouvelle approche de l'égalité.* Odile Jacob.

Théry, I., & Bonnemère, P. (Eds.). (2008). *Ce que le genre fait aux personnes.* EHESS.

Thiesse, A. (1997). *Ils apprenaient la France. L'exaltation des régions dans le discours patriotique.* Maison des Sciences de l'Homme.

Tornatore, J. L., & Barbe, N. (Eds.). (2011). *Les Formats d'une cause patrimoniale. Émotions et actions autour du château de Lunéville.* Lahic-ministère de la Culture et de la Communication.

Traïni, C. (Ed.). (2009). *Émotions… mobilisation! Mobilisation!* Les Presses de Sciences Po.

Verdier, Y. (1979). *Façons de dire, façons de faire. La laveuse, la couturière, la cuisinière.* Gallimard.

Verret, M. (1988). *La culture ouvrière.* ACL.

Vincent, O. (1987). Chasse et rituel. *Terrain, 8,* 63–70.

Warnier, J. P. (1999). *Construire la culture matérielle. L'homme qui pensit avec ses doigts.* PUF.

Weber, F. (1989). *Le travail à-côté. Étude d'ethnographie ouvrière.* EHESS. Paris.

Weber, F. (2000). Le folklore, l'histoire et l'état en France (1937-1945). *Revue de synthèse, 121*(3–4), 453–467.

Weber, F. (2012). De l'ethnologie de la France à l'ethnographie réflexive. *Genèses, 89*(4), 44–60.

Weber, F. (2013). *Penser la parenté aujourd'hui.* Rue d'Ulm.

Williams, P. (1993). *"Nous, on n'en parle pas". Les vivants et les morts chez les Manouches.* Maison des Sciences de l'Homme.

Zecchini, C., & Lorre, L. (2011). Le Postcolonial dans ses allers-retours transatlantiques: glissements, malentendus, reinvention. *Revue française d'études américaines, 126*(4), 66–81.

Zerilli, F. (1998). *Il lato oscuro dell'etnologia. Il contributo dell'antropologia naturalista al processo di istituzionalizzazione degli studi etnologici in Francia.* CISU.

Zonabend, F. (1980). *La mémoire longue, temps et histoire au village.* PUF.

Zonabend, F. (1987). La parenté I. Origines et méthodes de la recherche et usages sociaux de la parenté. In I. Chiva & U. Jeggle (Eds.), *Ethnologies en miroir. La France et les pays de langue allemande* (pp. 95–107). Maison des Sciences de l'Homme.

Zonabend, F. (1994). Laboratoire d'anthropologie sociale. Équipe d'anthropologie de la parenté. *Terrain, 23,* 178–180.

Zonabend, F. (2000). Les maîtres de parenté. Une femme de mémoire in Basse-Normandie. *L'Homme, 154–155,* 505–523.

CHAPTER 4

From Herder to Strecker: Birth and Developments of the Anthropological Notion of Culture in Germany

Marco Bassi

During the eighteenth and the first half of the nineteenth centuries, the classification of human groups did not clearly differentiate between biological and cultural factors. Different theoretical propositions and articulations could combine, overlap or confound both aspects and were at times object of public disquiet. Retrospectively we can identify two key issues. The first refers to the opposed theories of polygenesis and monogenesis. To assert the separate origin of the various human groups, whether in terms of different species, or, with theological perspective, of separate creation, meant establishing an unyielding difference with respect to European Whites, the group which, by an obvious ethnocentric move, was identified with the most perfect representation of civilised humanity. From the mid-nineteenth century, Darwinian evolutionism gave impetus to the monogenesis theory, but it did not free the field from theories and classifications based on biological notions of race. It is referring to this notion that the

M. Bassi (✉)
University of Palermo, Palermo, Italy
e-mail: marco.bassi@unipa.it

© The Author(s), under exclusive license to Springer Nature Switzerland AG 2023
G. D'Agostino, V. Matera (eds.), *Histories of Anthropology*,
https://doi.org/10.1007/978-3-031-21258-1_4

second issue takes form, meaning whether and how many differences were linked to biological differences. On the one hand, we find those who explained the differences between what we now call 'cultures' in biological terms—this is the typical racist position, exemplified by Nazi ideology. On the other hand, we find those who asserted the substantial equality of all peoples and who explained the reason for difference with historical and geographical factors. This difference could be bridged by means of the 'civilising' action of enlightened colonialism. It is within this latter position, markedly humanistic, that—for socio-political factors—the French-German distinction between the concepts of civilisation and culture took shape. We are talking about the tension that moved German intellectuals to define *Kultur* (culture) in the particularistic and relativistic terms, that, through the influence of Edward Tylor in the United Kingdom and Franz Boas in the Americas, caused culture to become the key concept of anthropology till this day.

THE CIVILISATION AND CULTURE JUXTAPOSITION

The concept of culture was for a long time linked to the classic idea of individual education acquired through the effort to adapt to an ideal model of humanity (Rossi, 1975, p. 1143; Cuche, 1996; Remotti, 2014, p. 13). The Enlightenment contributions went on to better define the universalistic dimension of the concept, with reference to a 'culture'—always in the singular—stored and handed down over time, referred to whole humanity and to distinguish it from the state of 'nature'. In the French context, the concept of culture was assimilated to the emerging one of *civilisation* ('civilization' or 'civility'). This passed quickly from the original meaning of 'refinement of custom' to the rationally enriched significance of reforming process in the institutional, legislative and educational fields, in the context of the optimistic expectation of a positive change that interests the whole society and all peoples, based on reason. To illustrate this progress, the 'Illuminists' used the description of phases related to the various subsistence forms of Earth peoples. While 'civilisation' referred to the idea of common progress of humankind—'culture', rather, continued to refer to an individual's achievements, becoming, in France, more and more marginal respect to the centrality of the civilisation concept (Cuche, 1996).

Norbert Elias (1939) is often mentioned for underlining the different destinies of the term *Kultur* in the German sphere, in a political

4 FROM HERDER TO STRECKER: BIRTH AND DEVELOPMENTS... 129

environment marked by division until 1867. At that point, for the Prussian action of King William I and Prime Minister Otto von Bismarck, Prussia was able to establish, in a hegemonic position and in opposition to Austria, the North German Confederation in a real Federal State. Then in 1871, Prussia was able to realise, through the French-Prussian War, the unification with the southern states in the German Empire (*Deutsches Reich*), also known as the Second Reich. Until the unification period, the German states had been characterised by the presence of an aristocratic class, inspired by manners and styles of the French court and resistant to the pressure of an increasingly influential middle class that continued to remain excluded from the exercise of political power. The *intelligentsia* expressed criticism of the aristocracy by proposing two value systems, one based on the real practice of science, art, philosophy and religion, and the other based on the formal and superficial exercise of civilised manners. *Kultur* took the function of expressing the first sphere, the authenticity, referred firstly to the German authenticity, whose definition and enhancement were developing as a specific mission of the *intelligentsia* connected with the academic world. As such, the domain of *Kultur* was opposed to 'civilisation' to express, in these early phases, a class dichotomy within the German context. The Prussian defeat against the Napoleonic armies (Jena, 1806) inflamed the nationalistic reaction, a sentiment officially ridden and promoted by Prussia after the riots of 1848, in the period when this State established national unification, keeping its hegemony. Andre Gingrich characterised the intellectual environment of this period through the metaphor of the 'double introspection', the first regarding the German themes, the second towards the discovery and celebration of the 'spirit' and the 'soul' of peoples, rather than practices and facts (Gingrich, 2005, pp. 72–3). According to Elias, in this context the concept of civilisation, referred mainly to the technical-scientific human achievements, was more and more identified with the French and Western intellectual world, hostile towards a Germany in search of national unity, while *Kultur* became functional to express the German nationalist demands. With the romantic, essentialist and primordialist turn, *Kultur* went on to configure, in the wake of Hegelian influence, the soul, or the spirit (*Geist*) of a people obtained once and forever and the basis of national unity. Especially from the beginning of the twentieth century and then in the Nazi period, the emphasis of nationalism—meant no longer as a legitimate aspiration to political autonomy, but as an affirmation of superiority—led to *Kultur* assuming celebratory tones. These evoked the idea of a specific mission of

130   M. BASSI

German people in regard to humanity and the re-emergence of racial suggestions.

THE HERDERIAN CONCEPT OF CULTURE

We owe the systematic elaboration of the semantic passage of 'culture' towards its anthropological meaning to Johann Gottfried Herder. Herder was an eclectic researcher, who in his youth was a pupil and friend of Immanuel Kant (Zammito, 2002). In the pamphlet *Auch eine Philosophie der Geschichte zur Bildung der Menschheit* (1774), he explicitly attacked some recurring ideas of the enlighteners' scripts, earning the acknowledgement of a forerunner of romantic historicism (Rossi, 1975, p. 1144). He criticised the Enlightenment for the abstractness of its universalising attempts to reduce the diversity of peoples to a single scheme, which reflected the practice of comparing every single human expression with European civilisation, considered the quintessence of humankind. To this theoretic process, Herder counterposed the reality given by the 'applied capabilities' and the practical experience of different human groups, in specific historical and geographical formations (Denby, 2005, pp. 57–58; Remotti, 2014). Herder never gave his definition of the concept of culture, but in *Ideen zur Philosophie der Geschichte der Menschheit* (1784–1791) the use he made of it is complex, articulated and historicised, explicable through a series of related concepts. The first key concept is the one of *Humanität* (literally 'humanity', 'human condition'), a quality that is not related to a moral attitude or to a feeling, but rather to an essence that characterises all human groups and distinguishes their sociality, politicisation and their cognitive, artistic and scientific achievements (Barnard, 1965, p. 97). It is a potential that occurs differently among different peoples, through two related processes, *Bildung* and *Tradition* (Denby, 2005, p. 66). *Bildung*—in the common language 'education', 'formation'—is here understood in its philosophical meaning of active processing, or new configuration of elements that lead to the harmonisation of the individual with the collectivity. Herder gives the concept a collective dimension, related to the active process of interaction and mutual construction of values and knowledge, that is at the foundation of social community (Barnard, 1969, p. 388). This effort starts from a wealth of knowledge—*Tradition*, or from cognitive elements acquired through diffusion processes—and refines through experience and evaluation. With the term *Tradition*, Herder brings the focus to the inter-generational transmission

4 FROM HERDER TO STRECKER: BIRTH AND DEVELOPMENTS... 131

process, conceived not in the sense of conservative behaviours, but rather emphasising the continuous process of merging old and new elements. Frederick Mechner Barnard, one of the most profound connoisseurs of Herder's work, noted that while *Bildung* punctuates the attention on the internalisation process of cultural models and the construction of mutual models of social behaviour, *Tradition* shifts the emphasis to the social context of communication and socialisation through which *Bildung* can take shape and the models become institutionalised (Barnard, 1969, p. 389). Culture therefore emerges as a dynamic entity, constantly shaped by the two processes in specific historic, geographic and linguistic contexts. It is Barnard again who gives us what we can consider a definition of the Herderian concept of culture:

> Culture [...] is presented as the relational attribute of a social group, indeed as the very hallmark of its existence as a group, in that it is the distinctive quality which is at once the product and the source of its shared activities, ideas, values, artifacts and process, in short, its shared way of life over an inter-generational period of time. (Barnard, 1969, p. 390)

We are, clearly, already in the context of a fully particularistic idea of the concept, whereby for every people or community, but also certain employment subgroups in the environment of a wider society, a specific cultural configuration is determined (Barnard, 1969, p. 386). Compared to the characteristics of such a configuration, Herder firstly discards the idea, prevalent at that time, to differentiate among material and spiritual expressions, recognising their interdependence within a cultural community (Barnard, 1969, p. 386). He equally paid attention in proposing a model that took account of different facets and functions of cultural phenomenon, avoiding reductive, homogenising or reifying definitions. As recalled by Barnard, the emphasis is on the relational and procedural dimension of culture, where different elements are interacting in a composite and dynamic configuration. The interaction among factors causes effects within different fields of human activities that cannot simply be reduced to the elements themselves (Barnard, 1969, pp. 385–6). We are therefore also inside a properly holistic idea of culture.

The Relativism Issue and the Hermeneutic Approach

Herder's relativism is more controversial. Barnard frames it in his anti-Enlightenment and anti-colonialist polemic, based, itself, on his critique of the progress theory that considers European culture as the universal condition of our species, on which to measure the stage of progress reached by the different peoples (Herder, cit. in Barnard, 1969, p. 382). Herder counterposed a vision to the universal model of progress, referred to the human species as a whole and based on theories related to the process of *Bildung*, according to which improvement and betterment would always take place in specific contexts, subject to various forms of influences and obstacles that may possibly block its development. It is, therefore, a particularised vision of progress, as it refers to specific human communities rather than to humankind as a whole in general. Consequently, progress requires a historicised analysis. In this direction, Herder strongly criticised the practice of bringing together and then comparing different earth peoples along the few categories outlined by the general theory of progress stages, pointing out the deep differences encountered even within the categories of peoples that base their subsistence on hunting-harvesting, on pastoralism or on agriculture (Barnard, 1996, p. 386). In this regard, he came to discuss the impossibility of comparing or grouping communities without even making the effort to enter into the spirit of their thought and actions, or into the different ways to perceive satisfaction (Barnard, 1969, p. 382). These are elements—read together with the insistence on the cultural capacity of all human groups in antithesis to the polygenic and racist theories of the time—that strongly recall the descriptive and moral relativism of Boas. Probably this strong analogy led Barnard to point out the fact that Herder conceived the presence of 'culture'—in the plural—rather than culture in general (Barnard, 1969, pp. 382, 386; 2003, p. 143). However, this is a point that David Denby considers a real forcing (2005, p. 67, 69). Denby's critique fits in an operation of reinterpretation of Herder's contribution, leading him back in the context of the late Enlightenment. Some of the rigid counterpoints, which over time became a cliché in Herder's representation, were reconsidered, among which the counterpoint between a relativistic Herder and a universalistic Kant and between universalism and particularism (Zammito, 2002). Denby recalls the influence of some relatively recent anthropological tendencies—including cultural hermeneutic, communitarianism, feminism and post-modernism—that would bring to a selective emphasis of Herder's anti-Enlightenment elements (Denby, 2005, pp. 56, 62). For Gingrich it was the nineteenth- and twentieth-century romantic and nationalistic turn that induced some German ideologists of the time to extrapolate and emphasise only certain aspects of Herder's work. Both researchers therefore propose a reinterpretation of Herder's contribution, whereby the consideration of specificities and historicisation does not hinder the simultaneous conceptualisation of a universal dimension, both of culture and of progress, and, with them, the possibility to examine processes and to formulate ethical judgements of transcultural nature (Denby, 2005, p. 71; Gingrich, 2005, pp. 72–5).

The debate over Herder's relativism requires a closer consideration of his contribution about the relationship between culture and language. Herder is actually also considered a precursor of linguistics, or, more interestingly here, of linguistic and cognitive anthropology, thanks to some innovative theories within the field of philosophy of language, of interpretation (or hermeneutic) and of translation.[1] He supported the dependence of thought and significance of language, insofar as one can think if he has a language, and he can think only what he can linguistically express. Consequently, meanings or concepts are not objectionable in independent way from language but are rather the expression of particular uses of words. In relation to hermeneutics, Herder pointed out the profound difference in concepts, beliefs and values among peoples of different areas and different cultures, and therefore the necessity, but also the great difficulty, of the operation of interpretation: it is necessary to avoid reducing, or assimilating, the thought of others by minimising it to the interpreter's categories. Given the correlation between language and thought, the methodological emphasis has to be put on the linguistic evidence (Stanford Encyclopedia of Philosophy, 2017; Taylor, 2017). Thought is therefore conditioned by the specific language of a community, and language is "the medium through which man becomes conscious of his inner self and the key to the understanding of his outer relationships, of the world in which he lives (Barnard, 1969, p. 391). In the same way, the perception of the natural world is mediated by particular mythological representations and the cosmogony that each human group inherits, determining specific

---

[1] The relevant arguments are presented in scattered writing, mainly *Über den Fleiss in mehreren gelehrten Sprachen* (*On Diligence in Several Learned Languages*) (1764), *Über die neuere deutsche Literatur: Fragmente* (*Fragments on Recent German Literature*) (1767–1768), *Abhandlung über den Ursprung der Sprache* (*Treatise on the Origin of Language*) (1772).

world views, a Herderian representation that Denby himself qualifies in terms of 'interiority' of culture (Denby, 2005, pp. 58–59). The Linguistic and cognitive specificity of different cultural groups comes into play also in determining progress, since the experience and evaluation related to the process of *Bildung* are attributable to environmental factors in which every community acts. But these are perceived, due to linguistic faculties, not in purely naturalistic terms, but through sets of ideas that refer to specific linguistic and social groups (Barnard, 1969, p. 388; Taylor, 2017).

We see, therefore, how much Herder's relativism is pushed towards the cognitive side, perhaps more than the moral one, with a focus on the linguistic issues that we also can find in Boas. Certainly, we cannot qualify Herderian relativism in the epistemological terms, typical of the hermeneutic and post-modern turn of the second twentieth century. Barnard himself recognised that Herder's relativism could not be pushed to the extreme of completely rejecting comparison and generalisations (Barnard, 1969, p. 383).

Linguistic Studies

Andre Gingrich is among the critics of the too sharp contrast defined by Norbert Elias between a French context, centred on a rationalist, Universalist and enlightened idea of civilisation, and a German context, filled with a romantic, relativistic and nationalistic notion of culture. He thus regains a number of German researchers with an enlightened approach, who nonetheless gave a contribution to the development of international anthropology, but who, because of the failed realisation of political unity, did not have a great following in Germany (Gingrich, 2005, pp. 64–66). Among these, the contribution of the non-European philological studies, active since the seventeenth century, was fundamental. From the latter half of the eighteenth century these studies were influenced by Herder's ideas in the linguistic field (Forster, 2010, 2011). It is a strongly empirical approach, conducted by travelling researchers with deep knowledge of specific extra-European languages. The term 'ethnography' was introduced for the first time in the 1770s by the Gottingen School in this study realm. The term was used as a synonym of *Völkerkunde* (ethnology), to indicate "the science of the world's cultures, languages and peoples" (Gingrich, 2005, p. 71). Gingrich attributes to Johann Christoph Adelung (1732–1806) more than to Herder the systematic use of the term *Kulturen*, in the plural, together with the introduction of the concept of *Kulturgeschichte* ('cultural history') (Gingrich, 2005, p. 69). Among these researchers, there persisted a tendency to praise the German language and the European languages, flanked however by a profound respect for the languages with writing, counterposed throughout to the languages of primitive and illiterate peoples. This originated a strong opposition between *Naturvölker* (people of nature) and *Kulturvölker* (people of culture), a distinction also used by Herder (Gingrich, 2005, pp. 69–70), but tempered by him through the expressed acknowledgement that every human group living together develops culture.[2] Adelung's hierarchical linguistic relativism was further developed by Wilhelm von Humboldt (1767–1835), who argued that any specific language, determining the human thought, represents a 'cosmovision' (*Weltansicht*) and that therefore it would be unavoidable "to assume a general hierarchy of cognitive potentialities among languages". For Gingrich it was this interpretation of the Herderian thought, without the universalistic dimension, that, from the 1830s, led to attributing to Herder himself a vision which was much more relativistic and internalistic than it actually was (Gingrich, 2005, pp. 71–2).

FOLKLORE STUDIES AND PRE-EVOLUTIONISM

Gingrich defines the development of folklore studies of the German-speaking countries along two lines. In the territory corresponding to Germany, nationalism and romanticism encouraged the emergence of a renewed interest in the German rural world, pursued inside and outside the academy, often connected with museographic projects. This led up to the birth of the *Volkskunde* (folklore) as a field of study devoted to popular traditions, detached from the *Völkerkunde*, which in the meantime became a term for describing ethnology and ethnography. In connection with the museographic projects, folklore studies concerned material culture, but also documentation of popular music and literature, involving various academic fields. With the consolidation of German historicism as a dominant approach of Human Sciences (*Geisteswissenschaften*), folklore studies increasingly became a branch of historic studies, until the early twentieth century.

---

[2] "Wherever men have lived together as a group over a period of time there is a culture. To be sure, there are differences, but these are differences of degree, not of kind" (Herder cit. in Barnard, 1969, p. 382).

The second line concerned mainly, but not exclusively, German-speaking areas of Switzerland and the Habsburg Empire, where linguistic and cultural difference was a fact. In these contexts, nationalism was not officially backed. It was rather seen as an antagonist and secessionist force. These are desk-researchers, belonging to other scientific areas and devoid of a nationalistic approach, known, already by the acknowledgement given to them by Robert Lowie (1937), for the elaboration that brought to the academic definition of the discipline and in particular as forerunners of evolutionism. These researchers maintained a specific focus on peoples of ethnological interest, in a framework conditioned by new ideas generated by the concept of culture but were still interested in a historic approach characterised by a broad comparative vision and connected to the enlightenment theme of the development stages of humanity (Gingrich, 2005, pp. 76–80).

The Swiss jurist Johann Jakob Bachofen with his famous text *Das Mutterrecht* (Bachofen, 1861) introduced the theme of matriarchy, which was then picked up in the United States by Morgan and long debated in the international evolutionary sphere. Bachofen's theory postulated an initial 'promiscuous' stage, where human society did not include any sexual or social organisation. Children stayed physically bounded to their mother. In this context, agriculture started on the initiative of women, who became land owners, thus consolidating stable families around themselves, including their husband. In this phase, land was sacralised and became the object of a cult centred on the female figure. The condition of female supremacy and the transmission of maternal descent and inheritance constitute matriarchy, a stage that would later be overcome by patriarchy, characterised by male dominance and descent (Bernardi, 1995, pp. 157–158).

Already in the years 1843–1852, with *Allgemeine Kulturgeschichte der Menschheit,* the librarian and collector Gustav Klemm fully assimilated the particularistic and holistic concept of *Kultur* and made it the central object of a general project of culture-history of which all human groups are part. Klemm defined a unified transition process from the 'Stage of Savagery', corresponding to hunting and gathering, to the 'Stage of Tameness', corresponding to animal domestication and breeding, and finally to the 'Stage of Freedom', corresponding to agriculture (Gingrich, 2005, p. 79). Klemm's thought remained ambiguously linked to the idea of the influence of racial differences, an element that was completely overcome by Theodor Waitz, professor of psychology and philosophy at the Marburg

University. In the first volume of the work *Anthropologie der Naturvölker* (1858–1872) (Anthropology of nature peoples), he argued explicitly in favour of the monogenetic theory of humankind and against the racial theories of his contemporaries Gobineau and Agassiz, at that time very influential. He did not reject the idea of the existence of different human races but linked the physical differences to external elements due to environmental factors, to food and living conditions, pointing out, as Boas did later in the United States, the fact that physical characteristics can change rapidly in relation to those factors. In psychological terms, he underlined that race diversity cannot affect intellectual attitudes and that, anyway, these are not empirically determinable. The great differences in social and productive forms that one can find among the various groups therefore had to be attributed to differences in opportunities linked to climatic, geographical, environmental factors—note here the continuity with Herder's arguments—and, above all, to historic events, also admitting the role of migration and diffusion processes. He therefore suggested the use of linguistic rather than racial criteria to classify various human groups (Heine-Geldern, 1964, pp. 407–410).

The Academic Institutionalisation and Franz Boas

The academic anthropological institutionalisation occurred at a time when interest in *Völkerkunde* was favoured by the colonialist aims of the emerging German empire (Zitelmann, 1999). The institutional traction favoured the establishment of ethnological and anthropological societies, with a strong development of museums in the main cities of the German-speaking area (Gingrich, 2005, pp. 54–5). The first academic habilitation in *Völkerkunde* went in 1869 to Adolf Bastian, a museography enthusiast who had travelled for a long time as a ship's doctor and who had posed the problem of similarities and differences between all peoples of the earth. In 1873, he was appointed the first director of the *Königliches Museum für Völkerkunde* in Berlin. He keenly promoted field research and created a strong group of students around himself. The subtitle of his main work— *Der Mensch in der Geschichte. Begründung einer psychologischen Weltanschauung* (Bastian, 1860)—fully reveals his interest in psychology, developed through knowledge of Wilhelm Wundt's work. Bastian expressed the idea of psychological and attitudinal similarity of all people through the notion of *Elementargedanken* ('elementary ideas')—ideas and thoughts common to all people but more clearly identifiable among nature

138   M. BASSI

peoples—which assume different forms due to climatic, environmental, geographical and historical factors. For this second component, which causes variability in the observable cultural manifestations, he used the notion, for many not sufficiently clear, of *Völkergedanke* ('people's thought', 'folk ideas'). Klaus-Peter Köpping (1984) tried to make the concepts expressed in the notoriously incomprehensible style of Bastian more intelligible. He identified Herder and Humboldt as his inspirers, and he attempted, in an unconvincing way according to Stocking (1985), to delineate the international influence on Boas, on Levi-Straussian structuralism, on German diffusionism and on evolutionism.

Beyond his influence, Bastian is credited with having kept *Völkerkunde* (ethnology, including both ethnography and the theoretical reflection) clearly separate on an academic level from *Anthropologie*, physical anthropology. One of the most authoritative exponents of the latter in those years was Rudolf Virchow—a doctor who was sensitive to the growing anti-Semitic and racist suggestions (Gingrich, 2005, pp. 86–7). Bastian collaborated with Rudolf Virchow for the Berliner Society for Anthropology, Ethnology and Prehistory, sharing his monogenetic theory. Once the behavioural and cultural relevance of physical difference had been dismissed, in his main work he could deal directly with what we a posteriori can qualify in terms of psychic unity, or universal cultural, of humankind (Heine-Geldern, 1964). It is an atmosphere and a debate, which certainly had a great impact on the young Boas. Boas had a scientific education that ended in 1881 at the University of Kiel with a doctoral dissertation in physics, titled *Beiträge zur Erkenntnis der Farbe des Wassers* (Contributions to the Perception of the Colour of Water) (Lewis, 2008, p. 192). Immediately after that, he developed an interest in Geography, which he had already studied in his university courses, at a time when the typical German theme of the relationship between environment and culture was much debated among geographers.[3] The desire to study the colour perception of water in a real environment and in extreme Artic conditions led him to make the self-funded research journey to Baffin Island in 1883. This experience led him to profoundly interact with the Inuit people and their way of life for 15 months (Boas, 1969). As underlined in the necrology written by Ruth Benedict, Boas himself later commented that he started out on that journey with an overwhelming confidence in the importance of the geographical factors, but he returned

---

[3] See, for instance, Ratzel's contribution (Ratzel, 1882)

4 FROM HERDER TO STRECKER: BIRTH AND DEVELOPMENTS... 139

with the full conviction that, to understand human behaviour, it was necessary to know the object that is seen as much as the eye that looks at it. The eye is not simply an organ, but an instrument of perception, conditioned by traditions with which its holder has grown up (Benedict, 1943, p. 60). On his return from the voyage, Boas got closer to the *Völkerkunde*. He collaborated with Bastian at the Ethnography Museum of Berlin, probably through the mediation of Virchow, with whom Boas had interacted during the preparation of his journey. In 1886, the year in which he started the periods of research in British Columbia, Boas obtained his habilitation in Geography with a dissertation on Baffin's Land, systematised two years later in the ethnography dedicated to the central Eskimo (Inuit). In 1887, he moved definitively to the United States, where he founded, in opposition to evolutionism and to racist physical anthropology, the formidable American school of cultural anthropology.

THE CULTURE-HISTORY SCHOOL

Despite the education of a certain number of scholars oriented to field research, Bastian's approach did not overcome the irruption of a new paradigm. It was based on the emphasis given to diffusion in the territory of cultural elements, called 'traits'. This approach stands in opposition both to the international evolutionary theory, by which peoples autonomously reach the same achievements, and, in Germany, to Bastian's idea, by which similarities could be explained in terms of psychic unity of humankind. Diffusionism was a transnational approach, but it is in the German-speaking environment that convincing conceptual and methodological instruments were developed at the turn of the century. The Austro-German diffusionism fully entered the great national anthropological schools that characterised the first half of twentieth century, a classic reference of the basic manuals of anthropology. It survived in Germany until the 1970s, and although today there are no more research projects with such an approach, many anthropologists have internalised this kind of reasoning and are using it, at least in part, in their analysis. We owe the first contribution to Friedrich Ratzel, zoologist and geography professor in Leipzig with a strong interest in ethnology.[4] Differently from Bastian, Ratzel started from the assumption that humanity was not creative at all; therefore, cultural achievements must come from processes of cultural

[4] He named his approach 'anthropo-geography' (Ratzel, 1882, 1891, 1899).

140   M. BASSI

diffusion. According to his theory, single objects were liable to diffusion, but the actual development had to be attributed to collective migration or conquest processes, a condition that allowed the diffusion of 'culture complexes', or of cultural traits connected to each other. He then established the 'quality criterion' to evaluate if a historical contact between two peoples, even distant, was conceivable on the basis of analogies among objects which were found near them (Ratzel, 1893). The best-known example is the comparison between the Melanesian longbow and the West African one. Ratzel found various similarities—flat shape of the bow, type of knot, shape of arrows—that cannot be due to the functional needs of a longbow, such as to produce, for practical needs, a merging process in the two contexts. They can rather be explained only by the hypothesis of a common origin of the object, which assumes some historical contact between the two peoples (Ratzel, 1891). Leo Frobenius, an explorer of Africa and museum ethnologist with an autodidact personality, first coined the concept of *Kulturkreis* ('culture circle') (Frobenius, 1897). In the effort to reconstruct the origin of the African cultures, Frobenius noted that the analogies between Melanesia and West Africa were not limited to the bow and arrow but were also related to a number of other cultural traits, among which are masks, drums, clothes, architectural lines and shields. Thus, he assumed the existence of a Melanesian-African culture circle, a very strong cultural influence that from Indonesia reached the eastern coast of Africa and from there spread to West Africa, only then disappearing from East Africa because of the subsequent Hamitic and Bantu migrations (Frobenius, 1898). In that way, he introduced the 'quantity criterion' of shared cultural traits, to evaluate the processes of contact and cultural diffusion. Soon after, Frobenius also tried to delineate a temporal sequence of cultures for Oceania, based on the geographical distribution of cultural traits (Frobenius, 1900). However, it was an approach that was institutionalised by others. In 1904, the historians Fritz Graebner and Bernhard Ankermann presented two coordinated reports on the cultural cycles respectively in Oceania and Africa at the conference of the *Berliner Gesellschaft für Anthropologie, Ethnologie und Urgeschichte* (Berlin Society for Anthropology, Ethnology, and Prehistory (Graebner, 1905; Ankermann, 1905)). Graebner matched the quality and quantity criteria to assess the contact possibilities among peoples, even those who were geographically very distant, and defined the *Kulturkreise* as culture complexes, made of cultural traits related in a given historical moment and place. For Oceania, he identified the Tasmanian circle, that of the Australian

4 FROM HERDER TO STRECKER: BIRTH AND DEVELOPMENTS... 141

boomerang, the Melanesian bow and the Polynesian patrilineality. Chronologically these clusters became *Kulturschichten* (cultural layers), with the indication of the sequence with which the different *Kulturkreise* were presumably diffused in Oceania. Ankermann applied the same model to Africa. The temporal attribute added the characterisation of 'cultural cycle' to *Kulturkreis*. As pointed out by Robert Heine-Geldern (1964, pp. 412–3), Graebner then pushed the approach too far, as in the case of the theorisation and discussion of the 'Melanesian bow culture', observed in five continents in connection with the recurrence of single elements of the same original culture complex (Graebner, 1909). However, the author himself in his methodological manual (Graebner, 1911) and in his advanced reflection (Graebner, 1923) later reconsidered this formulation.

The culture-historical approach had an enormous development in Austria, thanks to Father Wilhelm Schmidt's contribution. He was a German linguist who lived for a long time in Australia before attending the catholic missionary school of the Society of the Divine Word near Wien. In 1906, he founded the magazine *Anthropos* and in 1936 the institute *Anthropos*. Schmidt seemed not to be aware of the historical-cultural approach until the publication of Graebner's methodological book in 1911 (Schmidt, 1911). The Wien School engaged in the systematic identification of the world's *Kulturkreise*, but applied the concept in rigid dogmatic form, and referred to the global scale as Graebner did before (Heine-Geldern, 1964, pp. 413–14). A second theme interwove with this contribution, announced in an article by Schmidt about the origin of the idea of God (Schmidt, 1908). He developed it throughout his life, in the 12 volume-work *Der Ursprung der Gottesidee* (1926–1955).[5] In contrast with prevailing evolutionary interpretations, he considered that hunter-gatherers, in virtue of their higher antiquity and nearness to God the creator, were characterised by an original culture, *Urkultur*, and a primeval monotheism, *Urmonotheismus*, an idea that would then degenerate with the progress of technique.[6]

---

[5] The first edition of the first volume, inspired by Andrew Lang, had already been published in 1912 (Bernardi, 1995, p. 167).

[6] Bernardi notices how in the sixth volume Schmidt manifests the fact that he really believed in a divine revelation of correct religious ideas to humankind (Bernardi, 1995, p. 168).

The Cultural Morphology School

The culture-history school, particularly in the interpretation of Frobenius, Ratzel and Graebner, embraced a positivist approach, whereby the researcher, using objective assessment's criteria, reconstructed cultural processes along geographical and temporal axes. Culture assumed a life of its own and was considered as an object of study, reified in definable traits, even if interwoven, but fundamentally separated from peoples and human groups, which acted only as non-protagonist 'bearer'. Evidently, both Herderian and romantic cultural concepts, intimately linked to the notion of people, were lost. During his career, Frobenius deeply reviewed his approach. He criticised the 'statistic method' by which Graebner and Ankermann correlated heterogeneous cultural traits to define a circle and traced its expansion on a disproportionate scale, as, by his own admission, he had also wrongly done (Frobenius, 1921, pp. 3–4, cit. in Heine-Geldern, 1964, p. 414). He alternatively suggested focusing on organically integrated cultures, identifying what he called *Paideuma* (in Greek 'education', 'what is taught', 'the content of learning', 'the teachers and those that are taught'), which corresponds to the romantic concept of *Volksgeist* (spirit, soul of a people), but referred to culture itself, such as it appears in a specific cultural context (*Kulturkreis*). Frobenius conceived culture as a separate entity. It is not produced by men, but lives through them (Frobenius, 1921), influencing both society and the particular world view. It emerges from a particular context and is subject, like organisms, to get through a life cycle corresponding to birth, maturity and senility. *Paideuma* corresponds to a principle, an undefinable internal logic, investigable through an intuitive and empathic approach, which moves the phases of a culture and therefore conditions every given configuration of cultural traits (Frobenius, 1921; Sylvain, 1996, pp. 490–1). In his studies on Africa, he outlined two basic configurations, Ethiopic and Hamitic, articulated on their part in more specific configurations. He examined them as stratifications of culture complexes to investigate by comparing extrapolated elements through ethnographic research. This complex of ideas, which restored Herder's organic vision of culture and the romantic suggestions in combination with a fundamentally diffusionist methodological approach (Sylvain, 1996; Gingrich, 2005, pp. 96, 108), went on to constitute the cultural morphology (*Kulturmorphologie*) school. Frobenius's research was connected to the German colonial interests in Africa (Sylvain, 1996; Zitelmann, 1999). In 1898, in Berlin he had established the *Afrika Archiv*, which moved to Munich after the First World War and in 1920 became the *Forschungsinstitut für Kulturmorphologie*. Frobenius was appointed to Frankfurt to teach at the Johann Wolfgang Goethe University. In 1925, he transferred the institute and affiliated it to the same university. The institute promoted a large number of research projects, especially in Africa, but also in other continents and in Italy. After Frobenius's death it was renamed *Frobenius-Insitut*. Together with the magazine *Paideuma,* which was founded in 1938, it has continued to be one of the most important centres of German ethnology up to today.

The strength of the cultural morphology school consists in the rigour of the field research and in the application of a defined but not mechanistic method, so as to permit the understandings of the specificities of local cultures. The theme of the age classes is a case in point. It had already been brought to international attention by the culture-historian Heinrich Schurtz (1902). Frobenius perceived its significance. He acknowledged that his own theory about the organicity of culture and its phases had been inspired by the African age-class systems (Frobenius, 1921, p. 57, cit. in Sylvain, 1996, p. 492). However, it was his successor to the Institute direction, Adolf Jensen, who understood the cultural centrality of the *gadaa* system of generational classes for the Darassa (Oromo-speaking group), acknowledged as the basis of their 'constitution'. He investigated its organisational and ceremonial aspects and, in the classic culture-historical style, expanded the research and comparison to neighbouring groups, among which the Gujji (other Oromo group) and the Konso (Jensen et al., 1936).[7]

It was the fourth director of the Institute, Eike Haberland, also one of Frobenius's scholars, who extended the research about the *gadaa* to the whole Oromo area and related this institution to other Oromo institutions and to the calendar (Haberland, 1963). Haberland's argumentation shows a diffusionist approach, also applied to the transcontinental scale. These two studies are impressive for the lucidity with which they delineated the pan-Oromo relevance of the *gadaa* system, despite local variants, at a time

---

[7] Among the discoveries that are still very topical today, is the acknowledgement of institutional components reserved for women, relevant at the contemporary political level with regard to the issue of customary institutions and human rights, and the practice of mummifying some leaders, relevant, even today, in a diffusionist fashion, for the debate of the connection of Oromo culture with ancient Egypt or the Nubian State.

when all other anthropological research, in the wake of British functional-structuralist approach, fragmented the ethnographic reality into territorial subgroups. These are the two ethnographic works that anticipated political developments, which have been deeply marking Ethiopian politics since the 1970s: a progressive growth of pan-Oromo self-consciousness, based on the recovery of *gadaa* as a symbol of political democratic identity, on the revival of the institution and its recognition as intangible heritage of the UNESCO (Bassi, 2020). Given the use of the German language for the two volumes, which have never been translated, it is difficult to think of a direct influence on the Oromo intellectuals; rather, it suggested that both ethnologists emphatically perceived in the *gadaa* a deep identity and educational motive—*Paideuma*—independently recovered by the Oromo nationalists to get out of the trap of domestic colonialism.

THE NAZI BREAK AND THE DIFFICULT RECONSTRUCTION

The reflection on the responsibilities of anthropology for the development of the racist theories of the Nazi phase and on the involvement of anthropologists in the extermination is a burning issue, which has only been considered in depth since the 1990s. On this topic we can again rely on Gingrich's reflections (2005, pp. 11–36).[8] He clarified that the premises of twentieth-century racist anthropology should be sought not so much in Herder's legacy, but in some of his contemporaries who were openly more anti-Kantian and who can be classified in the physical anthropology category. Later, writings by a physical anthropologist of the late nineteenth century may have provided academic legitimacy to the racism of the early twentieth century and to growing anti-Semitism within the society, up to the openly racist positions of anthropologists such as Eugen Fisher, Egon von Eickstedt and Otto Reche. There was an emblematic letter signed by various influential German anthropologists in 1933—among whom Fritz Cruise, Reche, Fischer and even the culture-history ethnologist Ankermann—which proposed the fusion of ethnology with physic anthropology to sustain Hitler's ideas on racial superiority. The scenarios that Gingrich presents us on the Nazi period are detailed. In a general atmosphere of little opposition from the academic class to the rise of the Third

---

[8] In addition to several in-depth analyses on specific situations and personalities, Gingrich considers some wide-ranging critical contributions to the topic (Streck, 2000; Byer, 1999; Linimayr, 1994; Zimmermann, 2001).

4 FROM HERDER TO STRECKER: BIRTH AND DEVELOPMENTS...   145

Reich, there were schools and research projects openly obstructed or persecuted, researchers who left the land even before the takeover—including Franz Boas, Siegfried Nadel, Eric Wolf and Heine-Geldern—researchers who simply tried to survive together with their institutions, some who sought advantages for themselves and their school by reformulating the discipline parameters in response to the public and ideological demands of the regime, others who were directly involved in the crimes. Although the most famous cases and the criminal convictions regarded physics anthropologists, the fusion of physical anthropology with the *Völkerkunde* and the more or less serious involvement by scholars of the latter do not allow ethnology itself to be absolved from general critique. The post-war phase saw an attempt to reset pre-Nazi conditions. Some important anthropologists, who were forced to exile or marginalised, came back to their key positions, including Father Schmidt in Wien. The cultural morphology school under the conduction of Haberland regained its old impetus. After the disastrous fusion effects, the *Völkerkunde* was again clearly separated from physical anthropology. Due to the very negative sense that the term *Volk* (people) had acquired, in the academic field *Völkerkunde* was renamed *Ethnologie*, in line with international tendencies. Only those who were accused of direct responsibility for Nazi crimes were imprisoned or emigrated. The others were downgraded to less prestigious academic positions, or dismissed for a while and then, once distanced from their past, reintegrated into academic life. This substantial continuity, however, did not bring German ethnology to the leading role it had played on an international level. Gingrich points out that the decline cannot be explained only by the loss of prestige of the German language and the rise of English as a global language. German ethnology had lost prestige because of its involvements in the Nazi affair, to which the weakening due to the division of the two Germanies was added. Funding for ethnological research was greatly reduced. Crippled by the very serious brain drain that had characterised the previous period, German anthropology was not able to renovate itself any longer. The three great schools formed by diffusionism, functionalism and cultural morphology continued to prevail in Germany, Austria and Switzerland until the late 1970s (Gingrich, 2005, pp. 139–40). Only in the 1980s was there a substantial generation renewal, which delineated two main new branches. The historical anthropology approach can be traced back to domestic tradition. Once again, it was the activity of museums that gave impetus to an ethno-historical research renewed in methods, empirically oriented, based on extensive archival research

146   M. BASSI

projects and on a strong linguistic competence, which could be found within the various departments of the German-speaking area that had reaped the enlightenment heritage of philological studies. The second branch, at that time generically grouped into the name of *Ethnosoziologie*, or social anthropology, emerged instead from the acceptance of new international paradigms, including new orientations of British anthropology, applied anthropology and development anthropology (Gingrich, 2005, pp. 151–152).

THE POST-REUNIFICATION RENAISSANCE

In general, the 1980s laid the premises for the strong impetus that German anthropology acquired after the reunification. The opening in 1999 in Halle-Saale of an Institute of the *Max Planck Society* for sociocultural anthropology is emblematic. It happened, as Ulf Hannerz reminds us (2010), in conjunction with the preparation of the volume *One Discipline, Four Ways: British, German, French and American Anthropology* (Barth et al., 2005), with which the anthropology of the German-speaking area, illustrated by the Austrian researcher Gingrich often recalled in these pages, is fully recognised among the great national traditions. The *Max Planck Institute for Social Anthropology* started with two departments headed by Chris Hann on the theme of Resilience and Transformation in Eurasia and by Günther Schlee on Integration and Conflict.[9] Soon they were flanked by the department dedicated to legal anthropology, and then by that of anthropology of economic experimentation and, very recently, by the Department of Politics and Governance Anthropology. The Institute has established numerous study groups and promoted publications on various topics of contemporary and practical interest, in the field of development, migration, policy, environment and law, with an approach based on solid field research and attention to the production of theory of social change. Like other institutes of the *Max Planck Society*, it has proved to be a key institution in providing support, in partnerships with universities, to doctoral research and in the post-doctoral phase, which is critical for the professional and academic integration of researchers. It has also supported many non-European researchers.[10]

[9] This department closed in 2020.
[10] The institute is probably the European centre that gathers the largest number of anthropologists, a primacy disputed with the Anthropology Department of the University of Durham.

4 FROM HERDER TO STRECKER: BIRTH AND DEVELOPMENTS... 147

Another paradigmatic example is the *Rhetoric Culture* project, promoted by Ivo Strecker and his school. Strecker's anthropological work is strongly rooted in field experience among the Hamar of southern Ethiopia, with whom he engaged, along with his wife Jean Lydall, in long-lasting ethnographic work, set in dialogic and visual perspective. The field style of the couple is based on strong interactivity with the local population, from which great competence in the local language follows. Thanks to their foundation of the *South Omo Research Centre*, the two researchers have facilitated the fieldwork of many young anthropologists of various nationalities. While teaching at the Institute of Anthropology and African Studies at the Johannes Gutenberg University, Mainz, Strecker thought of combining the renewed academic interest in rhetoric with anthropology. Along with Stephen Tyler of Rice University (Houston, Texas) and his students Christian Meyer and Felix Girke, between 2002 and 2005, he began a series of four international conferences held in Mainz.[11] The project was soon supported by other anthropologists and researchers of other disciplines of great international prestige, including the American economic anthropologist, Stephen Gudeman. Gudeman is also known for his epistemological relativist critique of neoclassic economy (Gudeman, 1986). Then there were other symposia and seminars, mainly organised independently at the Universities of Evanston, Boulder, Durham, Cape Town and Hannover. Many of the contributions are collected in the series *Studies in Rhetoric and Culture* of Berghahn Books, starting with the founding volume *Culture and Rhetoric* (Strecker & Tyler, 2009). Because of the markedly interdisciplinary character and the inevitably open theoretic grid of the initiative, it is difficult to reduce the project content to a few strokes, but it is certainly possible to identify in culture, anthropologically understood, the focus of attention. The project originated in the attempt to reformulate the understandings of 'culture' when, within anthropology, this notion came under attack towards the end of the twentieth century (Hariman et al., 2022).[12] It built on the new, post-modern and cognitive oriented 'rhetorical turn' in anthropological studies (Mokrzan, 2014), merging it with a growing tradition of ethnographic studies based on accounts and analysis of recorded texts (Hariman et al., 2022). Tyler and Strecker came up with the proposition of studying

[11] The online *Oxford Bibliographies* carries a rich, annotated bibliography of the project (Meyer et al., 2016).
[12] I thank Ivo Strecker for sharing the draft.

the various ways culture and rhetoric are interlinked. As indicated by Strecker himself "as rhetoric is grounded in culture, culture is grounded in rhetoric" (Strecker, 2016, p. 23). Therefore, the investigation is into how cultural forms may influence rhetoric constructions in specific ethnographic contexts (or in particular literary genres), but also into how rhetoric instruments, tropes and figuration are at the base of intersubjective communication and, within a dialogic conception of culture (Tedlock & Mannheim, 1995), of the construction of shared cultural meanings (Paul & Wiseman, 2014, p. 3; Meyer & Girke, 2011). It is not difficult to find here the Herderian themes,[13] starting from the attention paid to linguistic and cognitive issues, up to the consciousness of a cultural particularism based on the universal faculties of humankind, in this case the rhetoric capacity, and with it the explicit attempt to build an approach allowing transcultural understanding (Oesterreich, 2009; Pelkey, 2016). While Herder was mostly elaborating on the emotional elements and feelings that cannot be translated into sounds, and consequently on the polysemic and elusive (for non-native speakers) meaning of words within specific cultural contexts (Herder, 1772), the rhetoric culture approach explores the multiple possibilities to bridge meanings and to produce emotions through specific figurations.

The International Influence of German Anthropology

The German contribution to international anthropology clearly revolves around the idea of culture, declined under several hermeneutical, positivistic, relativist and universalist declinations, with the correlated methodological instruments. Two lines of direct international influence should be delineated, which, beginning from Herder, led to two different elaborations that together converged in making culture the central notion of global anthropology. The first line is based on the Herderian particularistic and holistic concept of culture, though filtered through the enlightened and historically oriented sensibility of the pre-evolutionist German-speaking researchers. It concerns the elaboration of what is popularised as the first anthropological definition of culture, provided in 1871 by the British evolutionist Edward Burnett Tylor in *Primitive culture*. Tylor was

[13] On a phone call made early in January 2022, Strecker confirmed that he has direct knowledge of classic writings of Herder and Humboldt.

well acquainted with German contributions. In an 1865 publication he mentioned and appreciated Klemm's contribution (Gingrich, 2005, p. 79; Kluckhohn & Kroeber, 1952, cit. in Remotti, 2014, p. 13). Nevertheless, it was only after the *London Anthropological Society* award to Waitz's first volume and its translation in 1863 that Tylor fully embraced an approach that had finally completely been freed of the correlation between culture and racial difference (Gingrich, 2005, pp. 79–80). Although it cannot be sustained that Tylor was directly acquainted with Herder's work, there is no doubt that the Herderian idea of specific articulation of culture in relation to a particular group or people, along with his broad definition, is the foundation of Klemm and Waitz's proposals (Rossi, 1975, p. 1143; Remotti, 2014, p. 13–15). In the early twentieth century, with the irruption of the structural-functionalist paradigm in the United Kingdom, culture and its evolution would cease to be the centre of analysis, but the particularist and holistic concept would remain rooted in the consciousness of young generations of social anthropologists and in studies of identity. For example, for the holistic aspect of culture, fully attributed to the British functionalist Bronisław Malinowski, Clifford Geertz (2000) recalls the transition between the generic characterisation of culture to the configurational one due to Herder and Humboldt. During the twentieth century, the stimuli on the anthropological concept of culture continued to reach European anthropologists even from overseas, where the second line of international influence gave life to cultural anthropology. This second line is obviously referred to Boas's contribution. This influence developed slightly later, but is more direct, given Boas's formation in Germany. It is different from the previous one for its strong relativism and the anti-evolutionistic approach. Underlining Boas's role in the elaboration of the concept of specific culture of a human group as an entity of its own—and therefore conceiving the existence of 'cultures', in the plural—George Stocking (1968) identifies a direct line, which goes from Herder to Lazarus and Steinthal. For linguistic and cognitive aspects, there is no evidence that the young Boas had direct knowledge of Herder, but his biographer Douglas Cole reports that he read Humboldt with reverence (Cole, 1999, p. 124). Therefore, as also pointed out by George Steiner, it can be said that Herder came to Boas through the elaboration of Humboldt and Steinthal, to finally generate the Sapir-Whorf hypothesis (Steiner, 1978, pp. 138–43; Gingrich, 2005, p. 72), one of the matrices of linguistic and cognitive anthropology (Duranti, 1996; Matera, 2005; Matera, 2006; Biscaldi & Matera, 2016).

150   M. BASSI

Lowie (1937, pp. 16–18), Streck (2001) and Gingrich (2005, p. 80) have noted the continuity of moral relativism of Boas and his students in the United States with Waitz, for his positions on monogenesis and the strong relativisation of the racial factors compared to the cultural element, firmly taken up by Boas in the United States. After all, Waitz had directly inspired both Bastian and Virchow, teachers of Boas.

The culture-history and cultural morphology schools continued to influence global anthropology until the 1960s. Europe was strongly influenced by the later elaboration of the Wien school, also through the catholic network.[14] In the United States, there was rather a strong influence of the previous German culture-history and cultural morphology schools through the Boasian students' generation. The migration wave led by growing racism in the early twentieth century, which became unsustainable in the 1930s with Nazism, brought a significant number of intellectuals to the United States, who were able to read the contributions that continued to be published in the German language. Alfred Kroeber, Robert Lowie, Edward Sapir, Clyde Kluckhohn and Abraham Kardiner are among the scholars of German origin or German native speakers. The first three transplanted the concept of *Kulturkreis*, applied in terms of 'cultural area', an analytic instrument that was fundamental for the collection and theoretic organisation of ethnographic data related to American natives. Among others, Clark Wissler adopted a proper diffusionistic approach, explicitly recognising the debt to the cultural morphology school (Heine-Geldern, 1964, p. 415). The concept of *Kulturkreis* was also borrowed in the sense of culture complex, as in the 'cattle complex' theorised by Melville Herskovits, an ensemble of related traits that characterise the pastoral societies of eastern Africa. Again, Alan Barnard points out how Frobenius's concept of *Paideuma* and his studies on Africa contributed to the definition of the concept of 'world view' (*Weltanschauung*), widely applied by American relativist anthropologists (Barnard, 2000).

With the arrival of Nazism, as seen above, German anthropology entered a phase of crisis and stagnation. After more than five decades, German ethnology is now regaining a clear international reprieve. It has managed this through a strong process of contamination and

---

[14] For example, there was a strong influence on Vinigi Grottanelli and on the formative period of Bernardo Bernardi, the two teachers who followed one another at the first Ethnology Chair at the University La Sapienza of Rome (Grottanelli et al., 1977, p. 565; Bernardi, 1990, p. 7; Pavanello, 2020, pp. 17–18, 21; Bassi, 2020, pp. 292–5).

4 FROM HERDER TO STRECKER: BIRTH AND DEVELOPMENTS... 151

hybridisation—in a period in which it is no longer so easy to identify specific schools—but always with the awareness of its roots. It has made use of the traditional integration of universities with research centres and museums, and of an approach empirically founded and solidly grounded in ethnography and field research. An example of this is the fusion, which happened in the project *rhetoric culture*, with which post-modern anthropology seems to have been able to recuperate concreteness and ethnographic competence that belong to the German cultural tradition. On the other hand, thanks to inputs of cognitive anthropology, post-modernism and literary criticism, with this project it seems that American anthropology is reciprocating part of the theoretic debt accumulated towards German anthropology.

REFERENCES

Ankermann, B. (1905). Kulturkreise und Kulturschichten in Afrika. *Zeitschrift für Ethnologie, 37*, 54–86.

Bachofen, J. J. (1861). *Das Mutterrecht. Eine Untersuchung über die Gynäkokratie der alten Welt nach ihrer religiösen und rechtlichen Natur*. Krais & Hoffmann.

Barnard, F. M. (1965). *Herder's Social and Political Thought*. Clarendon Press.

Barnard, F. M. (1969). Culture and Political Development: Herder's Suggestive Insights. *The American Political Science Review, 63*(2), 379–397.

Barnard, A. (2000). *History and Theory in Anthropology*. Cambridge University Press.

Barnard, F. M. (2003). *Herder on Nationality, Humanity and History*. McGill-Queen's University Press.

Barth, F., Gingrich, A., Parkin, R., & Silverman, S. (2005). *One Discipline, Four Ways: British, German, French and American Anthropology*. University of Chicago Press.

Bassi, M. (2020). I sistemi delle classi d'età. Il contributo teorico di Bernardo Bernardi e la loro riscoperta contemporanea in chiave identitaria e patrimoniale. In M. Geraci & A. Ndreca (Eds.), *Insigni Maestri: Tra storia, etnologia e religione* (pp. 283–312). Urbaniana University Press.

Bastian, A. (1860). *Der Mensch in der Geschichte: Zur Begründung einer psychologischen Weltanschauung* (Vol. 3 vols). Verlag Otto Wigand.

Benedict, R. (1943). Franz Boas. *Science, 97*(2507), 60–62.

Bernardi, B. (1990). An Anthropological Odyssey. *Annual Review of Anthropology, 19*, 1–15.

Bernardi, B. (1995). *Uomo Cultura Società: Introduzione agli studi demo-etno-antropologici*. Franco Angeli.

Biscaldi, A., & Matera, V. (2016). *Antropologia della comunicazione*. Carocci.

152   M. BASSI

Boas, F. (1969). *The Ethnography of Franz Boas: Letters and Diaries of Franz Boas Written on the Northwest Coast from 1886 to 1931*. (Edited by R. P. Rohner), Chicago University Press.

Byer, D. (1999). *Der Fall Hugo Bernatzik. Ein Leben zwischen Ethnologie und Öffentlichkeit 1897–1953*. Böhlau.

Cole, D. (1999). *Franz Boas: The Early Years, 1858–1906*. University of Washington.

Cuche, D. (1996). *La notion de culturedans lessciences sociales*. Éditions La Découverte.

Denby, D. (2005). Herder: Culture, Anthropology and the Enlightenment. *History of the Human Sciences, 18*(1), 55–76.

Duranti, A. (1996). *Antropologia del linguaggio*. Meltemi.

Elias, N. (1939). Über den Prozeß der Zivilisation. In *Soziogenetische und psychogenetische Untersuchungen*, 2 vols, Verlag Haus zum Falken.

Forster, M. N. (2010). *After Herder: Philosophy of Language in the German Tradition*. Oxford University Press.

Forster, M. (2011). *German Philosophy of Language: From Schlegel to Hegel and Beyond*. Oxford University Press.

Frobenius, L. (1897). Der westafrikanische Kulturkreis. *Petermanns Geographische Mitteilungen, 43*, 225.

Frobenius, L. (1898). Der Ursprung der afrikanischen Kulturen. Verlag Gebriider Borntraeger.

Frobenius, L. (1900). Die Kulturformen Ozeaniens. *Peternanns Mitteilungen, 46*, 204–15, 234–38, 262–71.

Frobenius, L. (1921). *Paideuma: Umrisse einer Kultur und Seelenlehre*. C. H. Beck'sche Verlagsbuchhandlung.

Geertz, C. (2000). *The World in Pieces: Culture and Politics at the End of the Century, in Available Light: Anthropological Reflections on Philosophical Topics*. Princeton University Press.

Gingrich, A. (2005). The German-Speaking Countries. In F. Barth, A. Gingrich, R. Parkin, & S. Silverman (Eds.), *One Discipline, Four Ways: British, German, French, and American Anthropology* (pp. 59–153). The University of Chicago Press.

Graebner, F. (1905). Kulturkreise und Kulturschichten in Ozeanien. *Zeitschrift fur Ethnologie, 37*, 28–53.

Graebner, F. (1909). Die melanesische Bogenkultur und ihre Verwandten. *Anthropos, 4*(726-80), 998–1032.

Graebner, F. (1911). *Methode der Ethnologie*. Carl Winter's Universitäts-Buchhandlung.

Graebner, F. (1923). Ethnologie. In G. Schwalbe & E. Fischer (Eds.), *Anthropologie* (pp. 435–587). Verlag B. G. Teubner.

4 FROM HERDER TO STRECKER: BIRTH AND DEVELOPMENTS... 153

Grottanelli, V., et al. (1977). Ethnology and/or Cultural Anthropology in Italy: Traditions and Developments. *Current Anthropology, 18*(4), 593–614.

Gudeman, S. (1986). *Economics as Culture: Models and Metaphors of Livelihood.* Routledge & Kegan Paul.

Haberland, E. (1963). *Galla Süd-Äthiopien.* W. Kohlhammer Verlag.

Hannerz, U. (2010). *Anthropology's World: Life in a Twenty-first Century Discipline.* Pluto Press.

Hariman, R., LaTosky, S., Mokrzan, M. Pelkey, J., and Strecker, I. (2022). Rhetoric culture theory. In *Oxford Research Encyclopedia of Anthropology,* Online. https://doi.org/10.1093/acrefore/9780190854584.013.588

Heine-Geldern, R. (1964). One Hundred Years of Ethnological Theory in the German-Speaking Countries: Some Milestones. *Current Anthropology, 5*(5), 407–418.

Herder, J. (1767–1768). *Ueber die neuere Deutsche Literatur: Fragmente.* 3 voll. Riga: Hartknoch. (Eng. transl. *Fragments on Recent German Literature* (Excerpts on Language), in *Herder: Philosophical Writings,* M. Forster (Ed.), *Cambridge Texts in the History of Philosophy,* Cambridge University Press, pp. 33–64, 2002).

Herder, J. (1772). *Abhandlung über den Ursprung der Sprache.* Berlin Auf Befehl der Academie herausgegebe. (Eng. transl. *Treatise on the Origin of Language,* in J. Herder, *Philosophical Writings,* transl. & ed. by M. N. Forster, Cambridge University Press, 2002, pp. 65–164).

Herder, J. (1774). *Auch eine Philosophie der Geschichte zur Bildung der Menschheit. Beytrag zu vielen Beyträgen des Jahrhunderts,* in *Sämtliche Werke* (1st ed.). Riga Hartknoch.

Herder, J. (1784–1791). *Ideen zur Philosophie der Geschichte der Menschheit.* In B. Sufan (Ed.), *Sämtliche Werke,* voll. XIII–XIV, 1887–1909.

Herder, J. (1764). *Über den Fleiss in mehreren gelehrten Sprachen.* Riga. Republished in *Herders sämmtliche Werke: Band 1.,* Adamant Media Corporation, 2001 (Engl. transl. On Diligence in Several Learned Languages, in E. Menze, A. K. Menges, & M. Palma (Eds.), *Johann Gottfried Herder: Selected Early Works, 1764–7,* Pennsylvania State University Press, 1992)

Jensen, A., et al. (1936). *Im Lande des Gada: Wanderungen zwischen Volkstrümmern Südabessinien.* Strecker und Schröder.

Klemm, G. (1843–1852). *Allgemeine Kultur-geschichte der Menschheit.* 10 vols. Leipzig.

Kluckhohn, C., & Kroeber, A. L. (1952). *Culture. A Critical Review of Concepts and Definitions.* Harvard University Press.

Köpping, K. P. (1984). *Adolf Bastian and the Psychic Unity of Mankind. The Foundations of Anthropology in Nineteenth-Century Germany.* University of Queensland Press.

154   M. BASSI

Lewis, H. S. (2008). Franz Boas: Boon or Bane? *Reviews in Anthropology, 37*(2–3), 169–200.

Linimayr, P. (1994). *Wiener Völkerkunde im Nationalsozialismus. Ansätze zu einer NS-Wissenschaft*. P. Lang.

Lowie, R. H. (1937). *The History of Ethnological Theory*. Holt, Rinehart.

Matera, V. (2005). *Antropologia culturale e linguistica*. Unicopli.

Matera, V. (2006). Antropologia cognitiva. In *Enciclopedia Italiana*, VII Appendice,   Online.   https://www.treccani.it/enciclopedia/antropologia-cognitiva_%28Enciclopedia-Italiana%29/

Meyer, C., & Girke, F. (Eds.). (2011). *The Rhetorical Emergence of Culture*. NED-New Edition, 1. Berghahn Books.

Meyer, K., Girke, F., & Mokrzan, M. (2016). Rhetoric Culture Theory. In *Oxford Bibliographies*, Online. https://doi.org/10.1093/OBO/9780199766567-0157

Michel, U. (1995). Neue ethnologische Forschungsansätze im Nationalsozialismus? Aus der Biographie von Wilhelm Emil Mühlmann (1904–1988). In T. Hauschild (Ed.), *Lebenslust und Fremdenfeindlichkeit: Ethnologie im Nationalsozialismus*. Suhrkamp.

Mokrzan, M. (2014). The Rhetorical Turn in Anthropology. *ČESKÝ LID, 101*(1), 1–18.

Oesterreich, P. L. (2009). Homo Rhetoricus. In I. Strecker & S. Tyler (Eds.), *Culture and Rhetoric* (pp. 49–58). Berghahn Books.

Paul, A., & Wiseman, B. (2014). Introduction. In *Chiasmus and Culture* (pp. 1–16). Berghahn Books.

Pavanello, M. (2020). L'etnologia africanista italiana negli studi di Vinigi L. Grottanell e Bernardo Bernardi. In M. Geraci & A. Ndreca (Eds.), *Insigni Maestri: Tra storia, etnologia e religione* (pp. 11–30). Urbaniana University Press.

Pelkey, J. (2016). Symbiotic Modelling. Linguistic Anthropology and the Promise of Chiasmus. *Reviews in Anthropology, 45*(1), 22–50.

Ratzel, F. (1882). *Anthropo-Geographic oder Grundzeuge der Anwendung der Erdkunde auf die Geschichte*. Engelhorn.

Ratzel, F. (1891). *Die afrikanischen Bögen, ihre Vernietung und Verwandtschaften, Nebst Einem Anhang Über die Bögen Neu-Guineas, der Veddah und der Negritos: Eine Anthropogeographische Studie*. Hirzel.

Ratzel, F. (1893). *Beiträge zur Kenntnis der Verbreitung des Bogens und des Speeres im indoafrikanischen Völkerkreis*. Verhandlungen der K. Sächs.

Ratzel, F. (1894–1895). *Völkerkunde*. 2 voll. Bibliographisches Institut.

Ratzel, F. (1899). *Anthropogeographie*. Engelhorn.

Remotti, F. (2014 [2011]). *Cultura, dalla complessità all'impoverimento*. Gius, Laterza, Bari, dig ed., www.laterza.it

Rossi, P. (1975). Cultura. In *Enciclopedia del Novecento*. Istituto della Enciclopedia Italiana fondata da Giovanni Treccani, vol. 1, 1143–1157.

Schmidt, W. (1908). L'origine de l'idée de Dieu. *Anthropos*, 3, 125–62, 336–68, 559–611, 801–36, 1081–1120.

4 FROM HERDER TO STRECKER: BIRTH AND DEVELOPMENTS... 155

Schmidt, W. (1911). Die kulturhistorische Methode in der Ethnologie. *Anthropos*, 6, 1010–1036.

Schmidt, W. (1926–1955). *Der Ursprung der Gottesidee: eine historisch-kritische und positive Studie*. 12 vols, Aschendorffsche Verlagsbuchhandlun.

Schurtz, H. (1902). *Altersklassen und Männerbünde*. Georg Reimer.

Stanford Encyclopedia of Philosophy. (2017). (1st ed. 2001), Johann Gottfried von Herder. Retrieved September 12, 2021, from https://plato.stanford.edu/entries/herder/

Steiner, G. (1978). *On Difficulty and Other Essays*. Oxford University Press.

Stocking, G. W. (1968). Franz Boas and the Culture Concept. In *Race, Culture and Evolution: Essay in the History of Anthropology* (pp. 195–233). Free Press and Collier Macmillan.

Stocking, G. W. (1985). *Klaus-Peter Koepping, Adolf Bastian and the Psychic Unity of Mankind. The Foundations of Anthropology in Nineteenth-Century Germany, St. Lucia*. University of Queensland Press, 1984. Medical History, 29 (3), 338–339.

Streck, B. (2000). *Ethnologie und Nationalsozialismus*. Escher.

Streck, B. (2001). Theodor Waitz. In W. Marshall (Ed.), *Hauptwerke der Ethnologie* (pp. 503–508). Kroner.

Strecker, I. (2016). From Hamar Ethnography to Rhetoric Culture Theory. In E. Ficqet, A. H. Omer, & T. Osmond (Eds.), *Movements in Ethiopia, Ethiopia in Movement: Proceedings of the 18th International Conference of Ethiopian Studies* (pp. 23–32). Tsehai Publishers.

Strecker, I., & Tyler, S. (Eds.) (2009). *Culture and Rhetoric*. NED-New Edition, 1. Berghahn Books.

Sylvain, R. (1996). Leo Frobenius. From 'Kulturkreis to Kulturmorphologie'. *Anthropos*, 91(4-6), 483–494.

Taylor, C. (2017). Philosophy as Philosophical Anthropology (Interview). In A. Waldow & N. DeSouza (Eds.), *Herder: Philosophy and Anthropology* (pp. 13–29). Oxford University Press.

Tedlock, D., & Mannheim, B. (Eds.). (1995). *The Dialogic Emergence of Culture*. University of Illinois.

Tylor, E. B. (1871). *Primitive Culture*. John Murray.

Waitz, T. (1858–1872). *Anthropologie der Naturvölker*. 6 vols. Friedrich Fleischer.

Zammito, J. H. (2002). *Kant, Herder, and the Birth of Anthropology*. University of Chicago Press.

Zimmermann, A. (2001). *Anthropology and Antihumanism in Imperial Germany*. University of Chicago Press.

Zitelmann, T. (1999). *Des Teufels Lustgarten. Themen und Tabus der politischen Anthropologie Nordostafrikas*. Habilitationsschrift (Post-Doctoral Thesis), Institut für Ethnologie, Fachbereich Politik und Sozialwissenschaften, Freie Universität Frobenius, Berlin.

CHAPTER 5

Cultural Anthropology in Italy in the Twentieth Century

Fabio Dei

LINGUISTIC INVISIBILITY

A specifically 'Italian' anthropology might as well not exist, and never have existed, from the point of view of current international debates. Of course, national schools have become largely irrelevant due to globalised frameworks of research that are dominated by the English language and by partially deterritorialised training. Yet the invisibility of Italian anthropology is particularly striking. The main reason is—I believe—fundamentally related to language. Italian anthropologists, ethnologists and folklorists, and intellectuals in the humanities more generally, wrote predominantly in their native language. Only reluctantly are they now abandoning the great Italian literary tradition in favour of what they perceived to be more neutral and weaker codes of international communication. This worked in favour of the quality of their output, but at the same time marginalised it from English and French specialised publications (see D'Agostino, 2020, pp. 97–8). On the other hand, there have been only a few late translations

F. Dei (✉)
University of Pisa, Pisa, Italy
e-mail: fabio.dei@unipi.it

© The Author(s), under exclusive license to Springer Nature
Switzerland AG 2023
G. D'Agostino, V. Matera (eds.), *Histories of Anthropology*,
https://doi.org/10.1007/978-3-031-21258-1_5

157

158 F. DEI

of Italian works into other languages. Thus, accounts of the history of anthropology did not take notice of a distinctive Italian 'canon' or 'research style'. In comparison, other 'minor' traditions received more attention, thanks to their reliance on the English language (see Alvarez Roldan & Vermeulen, 1995). Only recently, through European research projects and co-tutored doctoral programmes, younger generations of Italian scholars have become more organically embedded in international frameworks of research. English has become their language of choice in publishing, along with, to a lesser extent, French. These are, however, largely personal and piecemeal strategies. The result is a discontinuity with previous Italian anthropological schools. The existence of a specifically Italian anthropology today is thus even more difficult to discern, despite the much bigger number of practitioners of the discipline. It is perhaps inevitable, in line with the radically cosmopolitan outlook of contemporary Humanities and Social Sciences. Accordingly, nineteenth and twentieth-century 'national traditions' are deemed but embarrassing relics, if not irremediably implicated with the current upsurge of nationalism. The flip side to this is increased subordination to anglophone intellectual trends or cultural fashions. So-called postcolonial studies are a case in point: rooted as they are in political conflicts within the American academia of the 1980s and 1990s, rather than—as some claim—in Third Worldism and the Algerian and Cuban liberation struggles, they have now spread by virtue of linguistic hegemony into Europe. Their acritical application to the study of phenomena such as transnational migration flows or gender relations has thus led to evident distortions.

In sum, a wealth of Italian anthropological scholarship runs the risk of being consigned to oblivion or irrelevance. Despite its lack of international recognition, this research tradition has been theoretically significant and sophisticated, at least in some of its moments. In this chapter, I will outline some peculiarities and issues of this history, focusing on anthropological, ethnological and folkloric (or demological) studies in the second half of the twentieth century.

HISTORICAL BACKGROUND

I will first provide a concise historical background of the disciplines that, in Italy, are grouped under the acronym DEA, that is, D(emology)-E(thnology)-A(nthropology). In his historical periodisation, Pier Paolo Viazzo (2017) describes the century between 1869 and 1968 as a period of 'slow and antagonistic development'. Like others (e.g. Alliegro, 2010; Grottanelli, 1977; Saunders, 1984), Viazzo singles out the establishment in Florence, in 1869, of the first university professorship of anthropology, entrusted to Paolo Mantegazza, as the birth of Italian anthropology. A year later the same Mantegazza would also establish the *Società Italiana di Antropologia e Etnologia*. At the time, positivistic approaches to the study of man had become popular in Italian academia, despite the latter's strong humanist, artistic and literary tradition. Mantegazza was a physician and his programme revolved around physical anthropology. But central for him was also the gathering of ethnographic data on the behaviour and customs of 'peoples' and 'races'. In the last decades of the nineteenth century, ethnography developed, on the one hand, through the work of explorers like Carlo Piaggia, Giovanni Miani, Elio Modigliani and Guido Boggiani (Puccini, 1999). On the other hand, through folklore research, it initially focused on the philological analysis of oral literature; later, Giuseppe Pitrè adopted an idea of culture that included material artefacts. Lamberto Loria can be identified as the intermediary figure between these two fields. After his scientifically productive expeditions to Asia, Oceania and Africa (Dimpflmeier, 2020; Dimpflmeier & Puccini, 2018), Loria 'converted' to domestic cultural diversity, and established the first Italian regional ethnographic museum, as well as the *Società Italiana di Etnografia* and the journal *Lares* (Puccini, 2005).

This intense positivistic phase for Italian anthropology and ethnography ended with the Great War. The interwar period, in Europe, saw broad developments in the human and social sciences, and in anthropology itself. The Italian landscape, however, was stagnant. We can identify two main reasons: first, aversion to the very notion of a social 'science', in accordance with the then prevailing historicist trends, represented by Benedetto Croce; second, the autarchic policies of the fascist regime, which fostered closure towards anglophone and francophone cultural influences. Indeed, fascism endeavoured to exploit folklore for its propaganda machine, to gain political consensus among the popular masses. To this end, it took direct control of journals and research institutions (Cavazza, 2003; Coppola, 2021). At the same time, it led to the adoption of racial theories by physical and cultural anthropology, to furnish ideological support to colonial policies. Of course, folklore had never been politically neutral: in nineteenth-century Europe it was closely entangled with nationalism, but folkloric research still enjoyed institutional autonomy, and its relationship with political power was complex and open. Quite another thing was such straightforward subservience to fascism, not unlike *Volksdkunde* in Nazi Germany. Scholars such as Paolo Toschi and Raffaele Corso tried to exploit the situation to further the standing of folklore (grotesquely renamed *popolaresca* in the 1930s in deference to 'linguistic autarchy'), without compromising methodological rigour: this was in vain, since several scholars lent themselves and their writings to ideological support for the imperialist thrusts and racist policies of Mussolini's government. Until a few years ago, Italian anthropology had been reluctant to acknowledge this phase of its history and the racism of many of its exponents. Suffice it to say that the most widely adopted manual for several decades, *Cultura egemonica e cultura subalterna* (Hegemonic culture and subaltern cultures), by Alberto M. Cirese (1973, p. 190 ff.), barely mentions fascism. Only recently has a critical and historiographical appraisal begun to take place (see Dimpflmeier, 2021 for an extensive review).

After World War II, Italian anthropology entered a new phase, which can be summarised in the following points:

a) Italian culture became more receptive to international debates in the human sciences (in anthropology and ethnology, as well as sociology, psychoanalysis and history of religions), thanks to successful publishing initiatives such as the book series *Collana Viola*, by publisher Einaudi (de Martino & Pavese, 1991), which gradually entered university curricula.

b) Anglophone cultural anthropology, especially from North America, grew its influence and brought an emphasis on cultural relativism, fieldwork research methodologies and social inquiry. Tullio Tentori, a student of historian of religions Raffaele Pettazzoni, was the main promoter of these lines of inquiry in Italy. After a training period in the United States (studying, in particular, with Robert Redfield), he introduced Boasian theoretical and methodological principles into Italian academia—not without encountering some opposition from the prevailing historicist trends.

c) Folklore and popular culture studies underwent a radical transformation under the influence of the thought of Antonio Gramsci, and the work of Ernesto de Martino. No longer considered picturesque curiosity, folklore was then seen as a manifestation of the living conditions and social consciousness of the lower classes, and thus studied and appreciated (in museums and through musical and theatrical revival) as crucial to theory and even political struggle.

This became, for decades, the peculiarity of Italian DEA studies, in their prevalent Marxist declination. We shall return to this point in due course.

In the 1950s and 1960s, interest in anthropological-cultural matters grew, but these remained underrepresented in university teaching and research. There were few chairs of *Letteratura e Storia delle Tradizioni Popolari* (Literature and History of Popular Traditions, established in 1949), Ethnology (established in 1967) or Cultural Anthropology (established in 1971, see: Alliegro, 2010, pp. 364, 435, 507). Lack of public funding for ethnographic research led Vinigi L. Grottanelli, professor of Ethnology in Rome, to say that research in this field was only suitable to 'high-born' people. For this reason, Viazzo writes of 'slow' and 'antagonistic' development, with the latter adjective describing splits along thematic, research and theoretical positions that make it difficult to see the DEA field as a unitary one.

FROM THE 1970S UNTIL TODAY: INSTITUTIONAL SHIFTS

A transformation took place at the end of the 1960s. A series of reforms eased access to higher education for social strata that had been hitherto excluded. Increase in university enrolment was accompanied by the creation of new curricula, and the partial overcoming of long-established hierarchies of knowledge that ranked the social sciences lower than more classical humanistic disciplines (history, philosophy, philology). In the 1970s, anthropology curricula multiplied and were established in most Italian universities. Yet, they were split across more traditional departments, thus hindering the creation of authentic research centres. Since the 1980s, the number of anthropologists in Italian universities, at different ranks (full and associate professor, and researcher), has been around 200 (Saunders, 1984, p. 448; Viazzo, 2017, p. 7; Palumbo, 2018, p. 29 ff.). The number is higher if we include temporary research staff, such as PhD students, research fellows and non-tenured researchers who contribute to research and teaching. Such roles have gained increased importance since the establishment, in 1980 and more consistently in 1998, of the position of *professore a contratto* (professor with a temporary appointment). Concurrently, the work of non-academic anthropologists has also gained in importance. For example, those working in the cultural heritage sector, ethnographic museography, intercultural mediation (in the fields of

162   F. DEI

education, healthcare, civic activities, etc.) and international cooperation[1]. Enough, then, for the constitution of a small scientific community with its associations, conferences and an ever-increasing number of journals and other publishing initiatives (mostly in Italian, although English is becoming more widespread, in the name of 'internationalisation'). Moreover, a unitary community, since in 1979 its three subfields, Ethnology, Cultural Anthropology and History of Popular Traditions were merged into a single scientific disciplinary sector. According to Enzo V. Alliegro (2010), this marked the end of the classical phase of Italian anthropology. Deep divisions, disagreements and competition indubitably remained, yet they no longer pertained to the three disciplinary subfields. Further, the fraught relationship between cultural and physical anthropology was resolved at the institutional level, with the former assigned to humanities departments and the latter to scientific-naturalistic ones. Lack of conflict, however, might signal that conversation and exchange are equally absent: only recently do physical and cultural anthropologists seem to have found common ground, albeit with residual diffidence, for instance around the problem of racism in contemporary societies (Destro Bisol et al., 2018).

A result of these developments has been the founding of new scientific societies. The first was *Italian Association for the Ethno-Anthropological Sciences* (AISEA), in 1991, with a membership made up of university scholars and professional anthropologists operating outside academia. In 2006, it was joined by *National University Association of Cultural Anthropologists* (ANUAC). In 2017, the two would eventually merged into *Italian Society of Cultural Anthropology* (SIAC). Alongside these generalist associations, others are more sectorial, in terms of specific research fields, or 'mission'. Examples of the former are SIAM (*Italian Society of Medical Anthropology*, founded by Tullio Seppilli in 1998) and SIMBDEA (*Italian Society for Demo-Ethno-Anthropological Museography and Heritage*, founded in 2001), and of the latter, SIAA (*Italian Society of Applied Anthropology*, 2013) and ANPIA (Italian Professional Association of Anthropologists, founded in 2016). Plenty of other, more informal networks of scholars have also been active around issues such as migration and racism, historical anthropology, visual, literary and urban

[1] For a thorough reflection on the 'profession of anthropologists' in Italy, see Clemente, 1991.

anthropology. Such intellectual liveliness is reflected in the number of publications that have emerged in recent decades, which have typically been of low circulation, self-produced or printed by minor publishers, and often with a precarious, short lifespan. Yet they indicate the pervasive exchange of ideas and debate. According to the Italian National Agency for the Evaluation of the University and Research Systems (ANVUR), 20 demoethnoanthropological journals (scientific sector 11 /A5) are today rated as 'class A'.

The number of 'professional' anthropologists has therefore increased (despite the transient decline, in the 2000s, of university professors, due to cuts in education budget and an ongoing decline of university staff turnover). All this was the result of major changes in opportunities offered, in terms of academic career trajectories and training. First, the institution of doctoral programmes in anthropology, in 1986, meant the creation of around 15 to 20 positions for young doctoral researchers every year. Nevertheless, few, even after accessing postdoctoral research grants, seem to find stable, permanent academic employment. Of relevance to anthropology was the university reform of 1999, which introduced the '3 + 2' system, that is a 3-year degree, corresponding to a bachelor's, plus a 2-year, master's type, or 'specialist' degree. Thanks to the diversification of the education offer distinctly anthropological courses were established, whereas previously DEA curricula or courses existed within more general, humanistic ones. In theory, the new DEA courses were meant to train students for specific professional opportunities in three broad areas: museums and cultural heritage, intercultural mediation and international cooperation. However, the distinction between vocational and research-oriented training was not successful. The availability of jobs in these sectors was conditional on the allocation of significant spending in culture and welfare, which did not materialise due to a lack of political will and the protracted economic crisis. In 2017, a reform of high school teacher recruitment introduced the prerequisite of a cultural anthropology exam. New anthropology courses have thus been created. However, these have been run primarily on precarious work contracts and, as a result, the DEA sector has not gained academic strength. It remains underrepresented in comparison with traditional humanities, but also with other social sciences: the number of sociologists in Italian universities, for instance, is at least five times higher (Viazzo, 2017, p. 122; D'Agostino, 2020).

Antonio Gramsci, Ernesto de Martino and the Popular Culture Paradigm

In order to describe the current state of anthropological teaching and research in Italy, it is necessary to step back and consider the last 50 years of scientific production. I mentioned how, after World War II and at least into the 1980s, the rethinking of folklore along Gramscian lines had been the most defining feature of Italian anthropology as well as the best known abroad. Gramsci's *Prison Notebooks*, a collection of writings widely known in social theory, had great influence on British Cultural Studies, Indian Subaltern Studies and other critical and neo-Marxist approaches. The reason might be found in Gramsci's ability to articulate, in comparison to other Marxist theorists, a sophisticated and conscious understanding of the relationship between the 'substructure' of economic and material interests and the 'superstructure' of culture. Moving from a radical repudiation of positivist determinism, this relationship was revisited in the light of the concept of hegemony. The power held by the ruling classes was not understood to be derived mechanically from a particular mode of production, nor simply interpreted as an imposition: rather, it was exercised through politico-cultural strategies, aimed at the lower classes and mediated by institutions and communication technologies (e.g. schools, newspapers and literature) as well as by intellectuals. In theories centred on ideology, culture creates false consciousness in somehow passive subjects. The concept of hegemony implies instead a domain of social struggle among fully agentive subjects. Ethnography, thereby, offers a way to study how social groups utilise certain cultural elements by shaping and modifying their meanings.

The *Notebooks* were first published in 1948, on the initiative of the Italian Communist Party. For decades, their influence, however great, was largely limited to Italy. Gramsci's treatment of folklore does not posit an inert accumulation of picturesque 'survivals' waiting to be collected and classified. Folklore is made for him of 'conceptions of the world and life' of the dominated, or subaltern, classes (Gramsci, 1975). The very existence of folklore points to the partial failure of imposing a hegemonic moral system by the dominant class. When Gramsci writes of 'conceptions of the world and of life' and 'moral systems', he does not imply a quasi-anthropological concept of culture (Crehan, 2002; Pizza, 2020). Yet anthropologists and folklorists apply this perspective to their material. Popular culture repertoires are therefore reclassified as evidence of class

5 CULTURAL ANTHROPOLOGY IN ITALY IN THE TWENTIETH CENTURY 165

differences: on the one hand proof of subordination (due to their being fragmentary and chaotic), on the other hand expression of a quest for emancipation. They can even fulfil a 'progressive' political role. Indeed, a tension between folklore as a kind of 'backward' culture, that should be overcome, and the progressive means of 'struggle', is already in the *Notebooks* (Boninelli, 2007; Cirese, 1976; Dei, 2018). At any rate, it greatly influenced folklore studies, which thus far had been regarded as subsidiary to philology and were practised (with few exceptions) as the second choice of literary scholars. As Gramsci remarked, their purpose had been documentary collection. Now 'popular traditions' could do away with the overtones of picturesque curiosity that had been associated with them. They gained a position at the very centre of a broader social theory of Marxist slant. Or, at least, of a historicist and anti-deterministic Marxism, typical of Gramsci and even of certain manifestations of political militancy.

Ernesto de Martino was indisputably the main interpreter of Gramsci's thought in anthropology, a field of inquiry which he preferred to be described as ethnological and historical-religious. In this way he drew a distinction with American applied anthropology, which was taking root in Italy. A student of Benedetto Croce, de Martino's intent was to rid the discipline of its naturalistic aporias in favour of a historicist approach. His *Il mondo magico* (*The World of Magic*, 1948) decries the inability of the existing anthropological schools, burdened as they were with naturalistic prejudice, to understand magical thought. Dogmatic assumptions are at work in relation to the knowing subject and 'reality' itself, to the extent that comprehension of magic thought is precluded. For de Martino, the latter should rather be seen as evidence of the struggle of humanity and culture to stabilise a subjectivity (de Martino used the expression *presenza*, 'presence'), and a reality, which are not given once and for all (de Martino, 1948). His interests evolved around this evocative philosophical nucleus, even after the shift, affected by the discovery of Gramsci, in the 1950s. It is no longer an ethnology of 'primitive' culture, but an ethnography of magical-religious peasant practices in Southern Italy, to which he accompanied political commitment to their emancipation. In this context, he supported the agrarian reforms championed by trade unions. On the one hand, this led him to initiate a lively 'debate on folklore' with Crocian and Marxist intellectuals. The matters of contention were the autonomy of popular culture and Italy's 'southern question', that is, its alleged economic and cultural 'backwardness', or 'underdevelopment', and possible solutions (Clemente et al., 1976; Pasquinelli, 1977; Rauty, 2015 [or. ed.

1976]). On the other hand, de Martino's Gramscian disposition drove him to undertake 'ethnographic expeditions' in the Southern Italian regions of Lucania and Apulia. Three monographs followed, his undisputed masterpieces, dedicated respectively to mourning ritual lament, ceremonial magic and tarantism (a culturally conditioned syndrome and its corresponding therapeutic ritual, typical of the Salento area of Apulia). In these books, perhaps the only 'classics' of Italian anthropology, de Martino (1958, 1959, 1961) looks at southern magical-religious forms as cultural devices, means for existential protection, inextricably connected with the material condition of rural populace. He recognises their value yet anticipates their extinction. Their protective purpose, based on a 'dehistorification of becoming', cannot but come into conflict with historical emancipatory projects.

When he died in 1965, at the age of 57, de Martino was developing an anthropology of contemporary society, which was left unfinished. He was also establishing closer connections with international research. His heirs' appeal to a socially and politically engaged approach to the culture of the lower classes was equally strong. They believed that folklore could be reinterpreted in this light. To underline the theoretical discontinuity, they renamed folklore as 'Demology' (the 'D' in the acronym DEA, followed by Ethnology and Anthropology). Scholars in this line of inquiry are Luigi M. Lombardi Satriani, Alfonso M. Di Nola, Annabella Rossi and all those who—from the 1960s to the 1980s—investigated the facets of Southern magical-religious culture, grounding their interpretations on de Martino's hypothesis of its protective-therapeutic function. Folklore thus acquires, implicitly, an antagonistic or even oppositive character with regard to the dominant culture (Lombardi Satriani, 1980).[2] Similar positions were held by Gianni Bosio and the members of the *Istituto Ernesto de Martino* (founded in 1966), enthusiastic oral historians of the peasant and working classes of the North of Italy. Working in the context of post-1968 student movements, these authors attributed militant characteristics to folk music and saw anthropological research itself as an instrument of social struggle. Others, while still heavily influenced by de Martino, moved from slightly different theoretical perspectives. Vittorio Lanternari, for example, counted himself among de Martino's 'followers' (Lanternari, 1997). His research on religious and charismatic movements, however, took him outside Europe, in settings of decolonisation (Lanternari, 1963). The only

---

[2] See Ricci (2019) for an overview of this period.

true follower of de Martino, however, was Clara Gallini. In her rather original intellectual trajectory, she turned to the study of magical-religious phenomena through the lens of historical anthropology. For instance, she explored hegemony and subalternity through the study of mesmerism and nineteenth-century Marian apparitions at Lourdes (Gallini, 1983, 1988). The married couple Elsa Guggino and Antonino Buttitta brought about major transformations to the 'school of Palermo', which dated back to Giuseppe Pitrè (1841–1916) and Giuseppe Cocchiara (1904–1965). While remaining close to de Martino's themes (AA.VV., 1979), they drew from French influences as well, chiefly through their interest in semiotics and structuralism (Buttitta, 1979; Guggino, 1978). They also trained scholars in a wide range of theoretical directions, for example Silvana Miceli (1990) and Salvatore D'Onofrio (2005), among others.

Finally, we should mention Alberto M. Cirese, the main champion of the transition from folklore to demology (Cirese, 1973). After an initial historicist period, Cirese turned to structuralism. He developed an innovative anthropological project combining cultural invariabilities, and logical and cybernetic languages for their representation. He and his students, such as Pietro Clemente, Pier Giorgio Solinas and Giulio Angioni, did not follow the 'trend' of magical-religious phenomena, but focused instead on labour, economy and family structures of the peasant world, such as Tuscan sharecropping and Sardinian sheep farming (Angioni, 2011; Clemente, 2013; Solinas, 2010).

THE CRISIS OF DEMOLOGY

Despite individual differences, Italian anthropology in the period between the end of the 1970s and the beginning of the 1980s can be broadly characterised by its adherence to Marxism and prevalent interest in magical-religious phenomena. This is the conclusion, for example, of George R. Saunders (1984, p. 449), one of the few international scholars who paid attention to Italian anthropology at the time. The expansion of mass university education had brought to academia a generation of scholars trained in the 1960s of the student movements. Indeed, Marxism was now pervasive not only among anthropologists. Leftist culture, often of a rather radical sort, was dominant above all in humanities and social science faculties. Various Marxist schools of thought were current. In fact, these could be seldom described as 'Gramscian'. They were 'scientific' and anti-historicist and connected with so-called *operaismo* (workerism). There was thus very little room left for 'culture': 'ideology' was instead the category utilised to account for all the superstructural facets of social life. The implications of applying categories like 'class' and 'mode of production' in anthropology are not trivial, given that they might not be relevant in traditional, small-scale societies. In the same years, in France, an attempt was underway to lay the foundations of a 'primitive' political economy and harmonise Marxism and structuralism. In Italy, a critique of imperialism and its underlying structural and political inequalities was prevalent, together with interpretations of popular culture as an expression and instrument of class struggle.

Demology and—to a large extent—cultural anthropology were therefore decidedly Marxist. In the 1958 essay 'L'antropologia culturale nelle scienze dell'uomo. Appunti per un memorandum' (Cultural anthropology in the human sciences. Notes for a memorandum), a group of scholars, including the abovementioned Tullio Tentori, Tullio Seppilli and Amalia Signorelli, promoted the study of contemporary societies through economics, sociology and cultural anthropology, social sciences that shared an overall Marxist viewpoint. They would deal, respectively, with economic substructures, socio-political superstructures and 'forms of social consciousness', with the latter analogous to anthropological 'culture' (see Tentori et al., 1958). Significantly, the most compelling representations of the discipline in the 1970s and 1980s could be found in two issues of the political periodical *Problemi del socialismo*: one on 'Marxist orientations and Italian anthropology', the other on 'Italian anthropology and class relations'. During this period, reliance on Marxist theoretical jargon sometimes had the effect of stifling empirical research. The field of popular culture studies, for example, treated mass consumption or transformations in the forms of labour and political participation only as targets of criticism rather than topics of investigation and documentation (see Signorelli, 1983). Indeed, the demological approach faced a contradiction. Its Gramscian roots would have suggested an appraisal of the relationship between hegemonic and subaltern domains of culture in the contemporary context: industrialisation, the passage from self-subsistence to market economies, from widespread illiteracy to the democratisation of education, transformations in the media, and so on. Traditional subject matters for folklore, such as popular music, oral fairy tales, rural festivals, indicate "subalternity" in particular historical-social contexts. The implication is that the peasant world is partially isolated from urban and bourgeois life, and from the centres of production and dissemination of culture.

Modernisation, however, has transformed how class relations shape cultural difference. Subalternity is not the same studied by nineteenth-century folklorists: we should rather look at mass culture, albeit with the new tools employed by British Cultural Studies and scholars like Hermann Bausinger, in Germany, and Orvar Löfgren, in Sweden. Yet, Italian demology was not ready for this. Due to the influence exerted by Marxism and the Frankfurt School, market and mass culture were seen as mere tools of capitalism, vehicles of ideology and false consciousness. They were disregarded because not 'authentically' popular, as opposed to the old repertoire of rural traditions, which was seen as the only genuine alternative to cultural domination and colonisation. This repertoire, however, belongs to the past and comes back only in the form of nostalgic revival which, paradoxically, can be characterised as socially elitist.[3] In the meantime, the lower social sectors are consumers of the cheapest and kitschiest products of the cultural industry.

These contradictions caused a jamming in the theoretical apparatus of Italian demology, and ultimately its decline in the 1990s. Marxist language and theory entered a crisis as well, in connection with the collapse of real socialism in Eastern Europe, coinciding—in Italy—with the end of the so-called First Republic—the end, also, of the wave of protest movements and radical political transformations. It is paradoxical that the popularity of Italian Marxism, and Gramsci's thought, started increasing internationally at the very time when they were being abandoned in Italy. A noticeable example is that of Stuart Hall and the Birmingham School of Cultural Studies, whose analysis of cultural consumption in the context of Thatcherism was based on Gramsci, rather than Adorno or Althusser (Hall, 1988). From India to Latin America, postcolonial and decolonial movements—as they were starting to be called—took Gramsci's analysis of Italy's Southern Question as a model. The concept of subalternity became central to analyses of social inequalities that transcended the notion of 'class', albeit in some cases in ways that betrayed Gramsci's intentions. Bizarrely, the new generations who, in the 2000s, adopted these approaches in Italy saw them as a 'trend' from overseas, without even a sense of *déjà vu*. They had forgotten their theoretical sources. In the last decade of the twentieth century, Italian anthropology attempted to recover from what could be seen as the smothering embrace of Marxism

---

[3] See Plastino (2016) and Fanelli (2017) for an exhaustive analysis of the debate on folk and revival music.

and went beyond the 'domestic' gaze of demology, without however acquiring a distinct, coherent identity. To some extent, postmodernist themes imparted a sceptical attitude towards 'grand narratives'. Along with Marxism, for example, the heavily analytical style of structuralism was hastily abandoned as well. At first, it was Clifford Geertz's interpretive anthropology, widely translated into Italian, which gained currency. Then, although somewhat belatedly, it was the turn of rhetorical analysis of ethnographies and reflexive accounts of the relationship between anthropology and literature, which sprang from the publication of *Writing Culture* (Matera, 1991, 2015; Sobrero, 1999, 2009). At any rate, in Italy, 'postmodernism' has meant, above all, abandoning a 'national tradition', in favour of radical theoretical eclecticism and the fragmentation of research subjects and approaches.

Towards the 2000s

In such a diverse context, we can still identify certain research lines that show continuity and coherence. I will sketch out four:

a) Extra-European ethnology. As mentioned earlier, starting in the 1970s, ethnology could no longer be differentiated, academically, from cultural anthropology and demology. However, distinct traditions of research on extra-European geographic areas and cultures continued to exist, in the wake of scholars such as Vinigi L. Grottanelli, Ernesta Cerulli, Bernardo Bernardi, Vittorio Maconi and Italo Signorini. With the demological-Marxist nucleus in crisis, many believed that Italian anthropology had to catch up with other international traditions in terms of fieldwork in 'distant' places. Francesco Remotti, for example, had already taken the demologists to task in the 1970s for their 'autarchic' closure (theoretically as well as in the choice of their subject of study). He proceeded to start a solid tradition of ethnography in Turin, with an Africanist focus, which over time established its research presence in Equatorial and Sub-Saharan Africa (under the direction, respectively, of Cecilia Pennacini and Roberto Beneduce). Ugo Fabietti followed suit at the University of Milan-Bicocca, where the geographical focus of research widened from the Middle East to other areas. In Rome, the Ethnological Missions in Ghana and Mexico were founded respectively by Vinigi Grottanelli and Italo Signorini (the latter is currently directed by Alessandro Lupo; also grounded in Rome are the

Italian Ethnological Mission in Ethiopia-Tigray, directed by Pino Schirripa, and the Argentinian mission, directed by Alessandro Simonicca). Brazil and the Amazon, Oceania, the French overseas territories, India and China are other areas where Italian anthropology has focused its efforts. The Missions, supported by the Italian Ministry of Foreign Affairs, have guaranteed access to funding. They also allow young scholars to train, carry out fieldwork research and join international networks and debates. Furthermore, research is typically concomitant with cooperation projects: applied anthropology becomes, implicitly, indistinguishable from the 'purely academic' one (Malighetti, 2020).

b) Theoretical debates. The paramount role of theoretical and epistemological concerns with respect to empirical research has been a defying feature of Italian anthropology, compared to other European schools. We observed how the work of the principal Italian reformer of the discipline after World War II, de Martino, had moved from a historicist philosophical background, which remained central to its conception of ethnology. The cultural anthropology approach, besides the North American borrowings, gained considerable ground in Italy through philosophical circles already alert to the theme of cultural relativism. Philosophers such as Remo Cantoni and Enzo Paci, in Milan, and Nicola Abbagnano and Pietro Rossi, in Turin, saw anthropology as the most coherent development of the critiques of Eurocentrism and of Hegel's and Croce's idea of history as progress of the spirit. Cantoni, for example, was among the main organisers, in 1962, of the first conference of cultural anthropology in Italy, in Milan. Rossi was the author and editor of the first systematic works on the concept of culture in the Italian language (Rossi, 1970, 1983). In the 1960s, he taught Cultural Anthropology in Turin, succeeded by Francesco Remotti. The latter's philosophical background has remained central in his work, even with the experience of African ethnography. To this extent, his book *Noi, primitivi* (Remotti, 1990) remains to this day the most systematic treatment of the anthropological implications of the history of philosophy. Ugo Fabietti's work is likewise built on solid epistemological foundations. He is the author of widely adopted manuals, and his work remains informed by philosophical preoccupations, also through a lengthy collaboration with epistemologist Silvana Borutti and anthropologists like Vincenzo Matera and Roberto Malighetti (Fabietti, 1993, 1999; Fabietti et al., 2002; Fabietti & Matera, 1997). There are numerous examples of academic careers that move across anthropology, social theory and philosophy. This is likely the result of the less sectoral basic training offered in Italian anthropological curricula, in comparison with English-speaking ones. Is it an advantage? Not according to Viazzo, who maintains that it perpetuates the discipline in academia without advancing a 'pedagogy of practical skills'—the only one that could engender anthropological expertise outside universities (Viazzo, 2017, p. 124-25). I am less categorical. Anthropology is not, by itself, 'practical' knowledge. It is not made up of skills that can be learned 'neutrally', without problematising how data are generated, for example, or how models of understanding of social practices developed, and so on. In other words, anthropologists can never simply be 'technicians': their approach is inherently critical; it feeds constantly on epistemological self-reflexivity and wider relationships with the whole humanities field. Instead, we should worry about the recent signs of a dwindling theoretical vocation: for instance, strained relations with philosophy within academia, and the fragmentation of knowledge caused by reforms of university teaching and research evaluation. The latter, in particular, deters multidisciplinarity as well as forms of dissemination of research results and participation in public debate that are broader and not strictly specialised.

c) The sub-disciplines. Overcoming the threefold division of anthropology, ethnology and demology has unified the discipline, but has simultaneously opened the way to sectorial specialisations. These are, on the one hand, geographical (Africanists, Americanists, Oceanists), on the other hand thematic, or pertaining to research methodologies. I have already mentioned medical anthropology, museum and heritage anthropology and applied anthropology, which have their own scientific societies, journals, publishing series and websites. Medical anthropology follows de Martino's research on 'culturally conditioned syndromes' and magical-religious therapeutic practices in Southern Italy, as well as studies on folk medicine dating back to the nineteenth century. Tullio Seppilli, a long-time Professor of Anthropology at the University of Perugia, consolidated these historical strands in line with the broader international directions of Medical Anthropology. He gathered around himself a network of scholars who focus on anthropological mediation in hospitals, healthcare of migrants, gender, ethnopsychiatry, medical cooperation in developing countries, research on

5 CULTURAL ANTHROPOLOGY IN ITALY IN THE TWENTIETH CENTURY   173

folk, alternative and complementary medicine (Cozzi, 2012)[4]. As for museum and heritage anthropology, they are the main successors to demology, or 'history of popular tradition'. Due to the dwindling of the concept of 'popular culture', the very process of the patrimonialisation of 'intangible cultural heritage' has taken its place as a subject of inquiry. Hence, on the one hand, growing interest in museographic strategies and support for the inscription of particular heritage items on UNESCO lists of the Intangible Cultural Heritage (ICH). On the other hand, critical appraisals of the very processes of patrimonialisation, with their political-institutional and identity implications (Palumbo, 2003). Applied anthropology, originally concerned primarily with international cooperation projects, has now widened its remit to the entire domain of public uses of the discipline. Other important sub-disciplines, with a wide following, are visual anthropology, associated with major ethnographic film festivals such as *Festival dei popoli* (in Florence), *MAV - Materiali di Antropologia Visiva* (Rome) and IsReal, formerly Sardinia International Ethnographic Film Festival (Nuoro); anthropology of education, which has addressed, for instance, intercultural teaching and school ethnography (Bonetti, 2019; Callari Galli, 1994; Simonicca, 2011; Dei, 2021); and political anthropology, which investigates state institutions as well as social movements (AAM, 2015; Koensler & Rossi, 2012).

d) Anthropology of the contemporary. One of the most noteworthy aspects of the last 20 years of Italian anthropology is its growing concern with contemporary mass culture. In de Martino's days, anthropology seemed to be confined to fringe issues (the 'underdeveloped' South, residual forms of magical-religious and peasant culture, etc.). Today, it has decidedly turned its gaze onto innovation and cultural change. I am referring, first, to immigration, which until the 2000s had received little attention. If anything, there had been lines of research on Italian emigration abroad (Bianco, 1974). It is now one of the most popular topics for doctoral research and publishing. The ethical-political commitment of anthropologists, especially in the younger generations, is without doubt prompted by humanitarian and political concerns associated with immigration. The focus of what had been de Martino's commitment seems to have shifted from poor Southern

---

[4] Seppilli, 1983, 2008; see also the journal *AM - Antropologia Medica* for an overview of the anthropological output of Tullio Seppilli's students.

174   F. DEI

peasants, the 'last' in 1950s Italy, to migrants with experiences of suffering, displacement and extreme poverty, lacking basic rights and living in intolerable conditions; hence a broad range of research that draws on the life histories of asylum seekers, labour exploitation, housing conditions, gender, but also on the wider structural patterns of diasporic and transnational flows.[5] Italian anthropology's research agenda encompasses other aspects of contemporaneity as well. A vigorous line of urban and environmental anthropology has developed, for example, from the works of Amalia Signorelli (1999) and Alberto Sobrero (1992). It is concerned with processes of gentrification, recovery of degraded areas, and more generally bottom-up production of 'sense of place' (Fava, 2016; Giglia, 1997; Scarpelli, 2021; Signorelli, 1989). We should also mention anthropological research on tourism (Aime & Papotti, 2012; Barberani, 2006; Canestrini, 2001; Simonicca, 2000), sport (Barba, 2021; Giorgis & Sanga, 2009), material culture and mass consumption (Meloni, 2018), new communication technologies and social media (Biscaldi & Matera, 2019), and mass violence and conflicts around memory (Clemente & Dei, 2005; D'Orsi, 2020; Di Pasquale, 2010; Jourdan, 2010).

Conclusion: Today's Issues

Anthropology in Italy is a very lively but overly fragmented discipline. It receives widespread attention, as testified by the wealth of publishing initiatives, despite a crisis-stricken publishing market. The number of students it continues to attract is also a sign of liveliness. Its weight in academia, however, remains inadequate when compared to the traditional humanities and other social sciences. The capacity to disseminate research outside Italy has also been affected (see Jahrbuch, 2010; Loux & Papa, 1994; Matera & Biscaldi, 2021; Papa & Favole, 2016). Another problem is the lack of recognition for professions that rely on anthropological skills. These are, in a nutshell, the defining features of DEA disciplines in Italy, today. If we now turn to the opening question: Can we speak of an Italian 'school' or scientific community? The answer seems to be in the negative, if we compare the current situation to that of the last century. Two factors help explain this: the availability of scholarship online and the almost

[5] See among the many contributions Riccio (2014, 2019); Bachis and Pusceddu (2013); Capello et al. (2014); Sorgoni (2011).

complete lack of research funding. Students, PhD students and scholars can access immense repertoires of books and journals, in English, something that previously involved the availability of specialised libraries or travel abroad. Paradoxically, it is more difficult to access Italian books and journals, as these are frequently distributed by small publishers, covered by traditional copyright and available in paper format only. National 'schools' are therefore no longer necessary intermediaries, to be able to take part in international debates and lines of research. Young scholars pursue their own paths, and identify cultural landmarks, in the unfathomable vastness of what is available online. The role universities occupy as intellectually aggregative research centres has likewise been weakened. Moreover, universities can only provide resources for research to a very limited degree: the only significant funding organisation is the European Research Council (ERC), whose criteria and standards are at odds with the Italian research tradition. Moreover, the system of research evaluation and publications selection promotes standardisation along linguistic, methodological and stylistic lines. The peer-to-peer review system, for example, although advantageous, ends up endorsing a style of writing in the light of which most of the canonical texts of Italian anthropology, with their richness, would not be acceptable. Nonetheless, at least for now, an anthropological scientific community continues to exist: it is made up of individuals and groups who collaborate and debate, of lines of research that are coherent and continuous over time, and theoretical and stylistics legacies to engage with (de Martino's, e.g. has grown over time). Let us hope that the increasing opening up of Italian anthropology to the international scientific community, as inevitable and desirable as it is, will not lead to the dissipation of this intellectual legacy but rather make its distinctiveness emerge.

REFERENCES

AA.VV. (1979). *La magia: segno e conflitto.* Flaccovio.
AAM. (2015). Etnografia dei movimenti sociali. *Archivio Antropologico Mediterraneo,* dossier monografico, XVIII(1), 5-58.
Aime, M., & Papotti, D. (2012). *L'altro e l'altrove. Antropologia, geografia e turismo.* Einaudi.
Alliegro, V. E. (2010). *Antropologia italiana. Storia e storiografia, 1869-1975.* SEID.
Alvarez Roldan, A., & Vermeulen, H. (Eds.). (1995). *Fieldwork and footnotes. Studies in the History of "European Anthropology".* Routledge.

176 F. DEI

Angioni, G. (2011). *Dire, fare, sentire. L'identico e il diverso nelle culture.* Il Maestrale.

Bachis, F., & Pusceddu, A. M. (Eds.). (2013). *Storie di questo mondo. Percorsi di etnografia delle migrazioni.* CISU.

Barba, B. (2021). *Il corpo, il rito, il mito, Antropologia dello sport.* Einaudi.

Barberani, S. (2006). *Antropologia e turismo. Scambi e complicità culturali nell'area mediterranea.* Guerini.

Bianco, C. (1974). *The Two Rosetos.* Indiana University Press.

Biscaldi, A., & Matera, V. (2019). *Antropologia dei social media. Comunicare nel mondo globale.* Carocci.

Bonetti, R. (2019). *Etnografie in bottiglia. Apprendere per relazioni nei contesti educativi.* Meltemi.

Boninelli, G. M. (2007). *Frammenti indigesti. Temi folclorici negli scritti di Antonio Gramsci.* Carocci.

Buttitta, A. (1979). *Semiotica e antropologia.* Sellerio.

Callari Galli, M. (1994). *Antropologia e processi educativi.* La Nuova Italia.

Canestrini, D. (2001). *Trofei di viaggio: per un'antropologia dei souvenir.* Bollati Boringhieri.

Capello, C., Cingolani, P., & Vietti, F. (2014). *Etnografia delle migrazioni. Temi e metodi di ricerca.* Carocci.

Cavazza, S. (2003). *Piccole patrie. Feste popolari tra regione e nazione durante il fascismo.* Il Mulino.

Cirese, A. M. (1973). *Cultura egemonica e culture subalterne.* Palumbo.

Cirese, A. M. (1976). *Intellettuali, folklore, istinto di classe.* Einaudi.

Clemente, P. (2013). *Le parole degli altri. Gli antropologi e le storie della vita.* Pacini.

Clemente, P., Meoni, M. L., & Squillacciotti, M. (1976). *Il dibattito sul folklore in Italia.* Edizioni di Cultura Popolare.

Clemente, P. (Ed.). (1991). Professione antropologo. *La ricerca folklorica,* monographic issue, 23.

Clemente, P., & Dei, F. (Eds.). (2005). *Poetiche e politiche del ricordo. Memoria pubblica delle stragi nazifasciste in Toscana.* Carocci.

Coppola, M. (2021). *Construire l'italianité. Traditions Populaires et identité nationale (1800-1932).* L'Harmattan.

Cozzi, D. (Ed.). (2012). *Le parole dell'antropologia medica. Piccolo dizionario.* Morlacchi.

Crehan, K. (2002). *Gramsci, Culture and Anthropology.* Pluto Press.

D'Agostino, G. (2020). Questioni storiografiche e didattica universitaria della demologia in Italia. *Voci. Annuale di scienze umane.* Anno XVII, 120–144.

de Martino, E. (1948). *Il mondo magico. Prolegomeni a una storia del magismo.* Einaudi.

de Martino, E. (1958). *Morte e pianto rituale nel mondo antico.* Einaudi.

de Martino, E. (1959). *Sud e magia.* Feltrinelli.

5 CULTURAL ANTHROPOLOGY IN ITALY IN THE TWENTIETH CENTURY 177

de Martino, E. (1961). *La terra del rimorso*. Il Saggiatore.

de Martino, E., & Pavese, C. (1991). *La collana viola. Lettere 1945–50*, P. Angelini (ed.). Bollati Boringhieri. (New ed. 2021).

Dei, F. (2018). *Cultura popolare in Italia. Da Gramsci all'Unesco*. Il Mulino.

Dei, F. (2021). *La scuola multiculturale: una critica antropologica*. Movimento di Cooperazione Educativa.

D'Onofrio, S. (2005). *Gli oggetti simbolici*. Sellerio.

D'Orsi, L. (2020). *Oltraggi della memoria. Generazioni, nostalgie e violenza politica nella sinistra in Turchia*. Meltemi.

Destro Bisol, G., et al. (2018). *Manifesto per l'Unità e le Diversità Umana. Società, discriminazione e nuovi saperi ottant'anni dopo le leggi razziali*. Istituto italiano di Antropologia. https://sites.google.com/uniRome1.it/ilmanifesto/

Dimpflmeier, F. (2020). *Il giro lungo di Lamberto Loria. Le origini papuane dell'etnografia italiana*. CISU.

Dimpflmeier, F., & Puccini, S. (2018). *Nelle mille patrie insulari. Etnografia di Lamberto Loria nella Nuova Guinea britannica*. CISU.

Dimpflmeier, F. (Ed.). (2021). *L'antropologia italiana e il fascismo, Lares*. Anno LXXXVII (2-3).

Di Pasquale, C. (2010). *Il ricordo dopo l'oblio. Sant'Anna di Stazzema, la strage, la memoria*. Donzelli.

Fabietti, U. (1999). *Antropologia culturale. L'esperienza e l'interpretazione*. Laterza.

Fabietti, U. (Ed.). (1993). *Il sapere dell'antropologia. Pensare, comprendere, descrivere l'altro*. Mursia.

Fabietti, U., & Matera, V. (1997). *Etnografia. Scritture e rappresentazioni dell'antropologia*. Carocci.

Fabietti, U., Malighetti, R., & Matera, V. (2002). *Dal tribale al globale. Introduzione all'antropologia*. Bruno Mondadori.

Fanelli, A. (2017). *Controcanto. Le culture della protesta dal canto sociale al rap*. Donzelli.

Fava, F. (2016). *Lo zen di Palermo. Antropologia dell'esclusione*. Franco Angeli.

Gallini, C. (1983). *La sonnambula meravigliosa. Magnetismo e ipnotismo nell'Ottocento italiano*. Feltrinelli.

Gallini, C. (1988). *Il miracolo e la sua prova. Un etnologo a Lourdes*. Liguori.

Giglia, A. (1997). *Crisi e ricostruzione di uno spazio urbano dopo il bradisismo a Pozzuoli*. Guerini.

Giorgis, E., & Sanga G., eds. (2009). Antropologia dello sport. *La ricerca folklorica*, monographic issue, 60.

Gramsci, A. (1975). Osservazioni sul folclore, in *Quaderni del carcere*, edizione critica a cura di V. Gerratana. Einaudi, vol. III: 2309–2317.

Grottanelli, V. (1977). Ethnology and/or Cultural Anthropology in Italy: Traditions and Developments. *Current Anthropology, 18*(4), 593–614.

Guggino, E. (1978). *La magia in Sicilia*. Sellerio.

178 F. DEI

Hall, S. (1988). The Toad in the Garden: Thatcherism Among the Theorists. In C. Nelson & L. Grossberg (Eds.), *Marxism and the Interpretation of Culture*. London/Urbana.

Jahrbuch. (2010). Italien. *Jahrbuch für Europäische Ethnologie*, monographic issue, 5.

Jourdan, L. (2010). *Generazione Kalashnikov. Un antropologo dentro la guerra in Congo*. Laterza.

Koensler, A., & Rossi, A. (2012). *Comprendere il dissenso. Etnografia e antropologia dei movimenti sociali*. Morlacchi.

Lanternari, V. (1963). *The Religion of the Oppressed: A Study of Modern Messianic Cults*. A. Knopf.

Lanternari, V. (1997). *La mia alleanza con Ernesto De Martino*. Liguori.

Lombardi Satriani, L. M. (1980). *Antropologia culturale e analisi della cultura subalterna*. Rizzoli.

Loux, F., & Papa, C., eds. (1994). Italia. Regards d'anthropologues italiens. *Ethnologie Francaise*, monographic issue, 24 (3).

Malighetti, R. (2020). *Antropologia applicata. Problemi e prospettive*. Scholé.

Meloni, P. (2018). *Antropologia del consumo. Doni, merci, simboli*. Carocci.

Matera, V. (1991). *La scrittura etnografica*. Il Bagatto.

Matera, V. (2015). *La scrittura etnografica. Esperienza e rappresentazione nella produzione di conoscenze antropogiche*. Eleuthera.

Matera, V., & Biscaldi, A. (Eds.). (2021). *Ethnography. A Theoretically Oriented Practice*. Palgrave Macmillan.

Miceli, S. (1990). *Orizzonti incrociati. Il problema epistemologico in antropologia*. Sellerio.

Palumbo, B. (2003). *L'Unesco e il campanile. Antropologia, politica e beni culturali nella Sicilia orientale*. Meltemi.

Palumbo, B. (2018). *Lo strabismo della DEA. Antropologia, accademia e società in Italia*. Edizioni Museo Pasqualino.

Papa, C., & Favole, A., eds. (2016). Italie. Trouble dans la famille. *Ethnologie francaise*, monographic issue, 46 (2).

Pasquinelli, C. (1977). *Antropologia culturale e questione meridionale*. La Nuova Italia.

Pizza, G. (2020). *L'antropologia di Gramsci. Corpo, natura, mutazione*. Carocci.

Plastino, G. (Ed.). (2016). *La musica folk. Storie, protagonisti e documenti del revival in Italia*. Il Saggiatore.

Puccini, S. (1999). *Andare lontano. Viaggi ed etnografia nel secondo Ottocento*. Carocci.

Puccini, S. (2005). *L'itala gente dalle molte vite. Lamberto Loria e la Mostra di etnografia italiana del 1911*. Meltemi.

Rauty, R., ed. (2015). *Quando c'erano gli intellettuali. Rileggendo 'Cultura popolare e marxismo'*. Milan: Mimesis [new edition of Id. (1976). *Cultura popolare e marxismo*. Rome: Editori Riuniti].

Remotti, F. (1990). *Noi, primitivi. Lo specchio dell'antropologia.* Bollati Boringhieri.

Ricci, A. (Ed.). (2019). *L'eredità rivisitata. Storie di un'antropologia in stile italiano.* CISU.

Riccio, B. (Ed.). (2014). *Antropologia e migrazioni.* CISU.

Riccio, B. (Ed.). (2019). *Mobilità. Incursioni etnografiche.* Mondadori.

Rossi, P. (1983). *Cultura e antropologia.* Einaudi.

Rossi, P. (Ed.). (1970). *Il concetto di cultura. I fondamenti teorici della scienza antropologica.* Einaudi.

Saunders, G. E. (1984). Contemporary Italian Cultural Anthropology. *Annual Review of Anthropology, 13,* 447–466.

Scarpelli, F. (2021). *Centro storico, senso dei luoghi, gentrification. Antropologia dei rioni di Roma.* CISU.

Seppilli, T. (2008). *Scritti di antropologia culturale,* voll. I e II, M. Minnelli e C. Papa eds. Florence: Olschki.

Seppilli, T. (Ed.). (1983). La medicina popolare in Italia. *La ricerca folklorica,* monographic issue, 8.

Signorelli, A. (1999). *Antropologia urbana. Introduzione alla ricerca in Italia.* Guerini.

Signorelli, A. (Ed.). (1983). Cultura popolare e cultura di massa, *La ricerca folklorica,* monographic issue, 7.

Signorelli, A. (Ed.). (1989). Antropologia urbana. Progettare e abitare: le contraddizioni dell'*urban planning. La ricerca folklorica,* monographic issue, 20.

Simonicca, A. (2000). *Antropologia del turismo. Strategie di ricerca e contesti etnografici.* Carocci.

Simonicca, A. (Ed.). (2011). *Antropologia dei mondi della scuola. Questioni di metodo ed esperienze etnografiche.* CISU.

Sobrero, A. M. (1992). *Antropologia della città.* Carocci.

Sobrero, A. M. (1999). *L'antropologia dopo l'antropologia.* Meltemi.

Sobrero, A. M. (2009). *Il cristallo e la fiamma. Antropologia fra scienza e letteratura.* Carocci.

Solinas, P. G. (2010). *La famiglia. Un'antropologia delle relazioni primarie.* Carocci.

Sorgoni, B. (Ed.). (2011). Chiedere asilo in Europa. Confini, margini e soggettività, *Lares.* Anno LXXVII (1).

Tentori, T., et al. (1958). *L'antropologia culturale nel quadro delle scienze dell'uomo. Appunti per un memorandum, in Atti del Primo Congresso Nazionale di Scienze Sociali* (Vol. I, pp. 235–253). il Mulino.

Viazzo, P. (2017). Anthropology and Ethnology in Italy. Historical Development, Current Orientations, and Problems of Recognition. In A. Barrera Gonzales, M. Heintz, & A. Horolets (Eds.), *European Anthropologies* (pp. 110–127). Berghahn.

CHAPTER 6

Chronology of a Discipline: Social and Cultural Anthropology in Spain

María Rubio Gómez, F. Javier García Castaño, and Gloria Calabresi

When we were presented with the opportunity to write a text on the "history of Anthropology in Spain" for an international audience, as professionals located in the academic area of Social and Cultural Anthropology in the twenty-first century, we were both excited and concerned about embarking on a project of such magnitude. Our concerns ranged from the mere logic of the story that we could tell and that, without overlooking the constitutive background upon which our discipline was built, would offer a sufficiently broad overview to understand the complex process of academic institutionalisation and the varied disciplinary development, from institutionalised centres and not-so-sacred peripheries within the

---

M. Rubio Gómez (✉) • F. J. García Castaño
Institute for Migration Research, Universidad de Granada, Granada, Spain
e-mail: mariarubio@ugr.es; fjgarcia@ugr.es

G. Calabresi
Universidad de Almería, Almería, Spain
e-mail: igloria@ual.es

© The Author(s), under exclusive license to Springer Nature Switzerland AG 2023
G. D'Agostino, V. Matera (eds.), *Histories of Anthropology*,
https://doi.org/10.1007/978-3-031-21258-1_6

181

academic sphere. Being in a position to generate a narrative, partly lived, the most recurrent reflection is linked to the scope of our "historiographic" ability. Using this approach to create a history (not the only one) of Anthropology in Spain has led us to resituate ourselves in questions and debates that the discipline from various European and (North) American latitudes faced in the seventies, regarding who can (or cannot) make a "history" of Anthropology or where the beginning of the discipline should in fact be located.

We will address these questions with reference to the case of Spain, but not without first stating that our position as members of the scientific tribe of Anthropology enables us to offer our own vision in which, despite having tried to be exhaustive, we may have left out figures, events or spaces that some readers may deem essential in their own narratives on the discipline. We recognise that from this moment, our intention is to offer the reader—unaware of the reality of the discipline in Spain—a general overview of the constitutive background, academic institutionalisation and development of the discipline, backed by reference works within our context that have addressed such issues (Ortiz García & Sánchez Gómez, 1994; Aguilar Criado, 1996; Sánchez Gómez, 1997; Prat, 1999; Gómez Pellón, 2017; etc.). We therefore state that any potential absences are not intentional.

Following these initial reflections, we will present "a history" of the development of the discipline of Anthropology within the state of Spain, with a chronological description of the events that have been considered and that we deem to be the most significant within said discipline from the last century, until today. Although it may appear that we are starting from not very remote origins, the following sections will clarify where we situate this question of origins in the case of Anthropology in Spain. As part of this chronological development, we invite the reader to discover several milestones that have been considered by various authors as being of importance to the development of Anthropology in Spain. We refer to issues such as ethnographic museums that, in the early years, concentrated much of the anthropological activities, scientific journals that drove the development of Anthropology itself, or the conferences and associations that, from the beginning, and especially in recent years, have come to form the support necessary in order to back the discipline in Spain.

To Whom Do We Entrust the History of Anthropology?

We cannot deny that we have always had stories that have described significant events in a way that is more or less precise, and have marked the journey of Anthropology as a scientific discipline. It is common for them to be accompanied by biographies of "heroes" and "heroines", although less so the latter. However, many of these "traditional" stories had a wide range of issues. Their main objective was to classify scientists of the past in a Manichean way, in terms of "good" and "bad", according to whether or not they anticipated the current state of the discipline (Llobera, 1976). It is the type of stories that have been referred to as presentist by some of the individuals who have dedicated themselves to these tasks in a more critical way. Fermín del Pino, one of the most distinguished historians in the history of Anthropology in Spain, offers us a clear definition of this type of history:

> Presentism is a historiographic attitude that refers to the past in order to legitimise the present, only selecting figures who supposedly founded the current scientific trends: this tends to wane into a heroic and purely apologetic history- or, by opposition, a purely disavowing one, as in the case of Marvin Harris. The worst aspect is the global attitude, however neutral it may seem, whereby the past matters only insofar as it precedes and leads to the present, not in itself. On the contrary, the historicist proposes the study of the past independently of the present, as a matter that has its own logic and even its own language. (Del Pino Díaz, 1994a, p. 570)

The distinction is well known among those who make history from Anthropology, promoted by George Stocking (1968), who opposed historicism to presentism. For his part, Bachelard (1951) distinguishes between *sanctioned history* (thoughts that have been confirmed by contemporary science) and outdated history (thoughts that do not make sense from the current state of scientific rationality). Josep Ramón Llobera (1976) makes a further distinction between the types of history of Anthropology. He speaks of an *internalist* history (which focuses exclusively on scientific work, thus placing science "outside society") versus an *externalist* history that also considers other influences such as technological, socioeconomic, institutional, political and ideological factors. He also speaks of a *continuist* history (progress and historical change take place

184 M. RUBIO GÓMEZ ET AL.

step by step) or *discontinuist* (in which science is seen as an epistemological eruption that arises in a specific historical period).[1]

We are particularly interested in presenting a history of Anthropology located within the context of the Spanish State that does not serve for the greater glory of those who write it. We are, however, aware that our position is limited in this and many other aspects, as we lack a historiographical specialty that we consider to be not at all negligible in these tasks of historical constructions. This already announces a certain position on our part as to who should write the history of Anthropology. In other scientific disciplines, where a distinction is made between the theoretical and the experimental, the history is written by specialists in historical disciplines. In Anthropology, it has been different until relatively recently. Note, as Llobera (1976) describes, the moment of dedication to the history of Anthropology by professionals within this discipline as opposed to those other disciplines we mentioned:

> The case of anthropology is completely different. At best, the practitioner of our discipline is conceived as a sort of late Renaissance. In the good old days, she or he, during their active years, would have to account for the entire culture of a people (or even several peoples). Later, they would be in a position to theorise (or perhaps we should say, compare). Lastly, in the twilight years, if they felt like it there would be time to write a history of the discipline. (Llobera, 1976, p. 17)

As Stolcke (2008, p. 13) reminds us, it is in recent times that the profession of Anthropology has ceased to be reluctant to "reflect on its own scientific work". The aforementioned Llobera offers an explanation:

> It is often said, in line with A. N. Whitehead (1925), that a science that does not forget its founders is lost. This is undoubtedly the reason used by many anthropologists to downplay the importance of the history of the discipline. (Llobera, 1976, p. 19)

Examples of this absence of interest in the history of Anthropology can be identified elsewhere. As Fermín del Pino reminds us:

---

[1] This last distinction is important insofar as the former looks closely at the question of the precursors of the discipline, as opposed to discontinuist history, which rejects such an idea.

6 CHRONOLOGY OF A DISCIPLINE: SOCIAL AND CULTURAL... 185

There is no professional historiography of Anthropology neither in England nor in France. Perhaps as a result of this, Adam Kuper is obliged to defend the position that states that the history of Anthropology should be undertaken by the anthropologists themselves. (Del Pino Díaz, 1994a, p. 565)

Despite this lack of interest, it has not impeded some anthropologists from venturing into the construction of histories of Anthropology. Some have positioned themselves on what should be a task of Anthropology, as Ubaldo Martínez Veiga reminds us in his voluminous work (written from Spain), consisting of two volumes on the history of Anthropology, but with clear global reference to anthropological theories.[2] It is perhaps the only work of historical character with these pretensions of critical meeting of theories that has been written in Spain. Martínez Veiga himself (2010), without wishing to go into the background of the discussion regarding whether historians or anthropologists should undertake the task of demonstrating the history of the discipline, reminds us of the title of a 1965 article by Irving Hallowell ("A History of Anthropology as an Anthropological Problem" 1974), which amply justifies the interesting position of professionals in the discipline to dedicate themselves to the task of historicising it.[3]

In the case of the Spanish State, a part of the history of Anthropology on Spain has been written by people who have dedicated monographically, or almost monographically, their work to this area. It has not prevented the existence of many other historical approximations by professionals within Anthropology in Spain, who "in the twilight years", as mentioned by Llobera, undertook "personalist" of local history in the discipline.

---

[2] Perhaps influenced by his teacher at Columbia University, Marvin Harris, whose work in this same area is well known.

[3] In the same vein, Llobera reminds us that perhaps the practice of Anthropology itself, with its ethnographic method, can be a good guide for the practice of historicising the discipline. The way the historian of Anthropology acts is no different from the anthropologist in the field. "Both collect genealogies and both know that these genealogies cannot be taken at face value. As ideologies, these genealogies are not intended to explain history but to justify the structure of the present" (Llobera, 1976, p. 24).

186 M. RUBIO GÓMEZ ET AL.

Among those who have converted the history of Anthropology into their professional endeavour within the discipline in recent years,[4] we can highlight Encarnación Aguilar Criado (University of Seville), Luis Calvo de (Consejo Superior de Investigaciones Científicas), Fermín Del Pino Díaz (Consejo Superior de Investigaciones Científicas), Waltraud Müllauer-Seichter (National University of Distance Education), Carmen Ortiz García (Consejo Superior de Investigaciones Científicas), Joan Prat i Carós (Universitat Rovir Virgili), Luis Ángel Sánchez Gómez (Complutense University of Madrid) and the late Fernando Estévez González (University of La Laguna).[5]

On the other hand, there are those who have undertaken a one-off approach to the history of Anthropology. Here, the list is significantly longer, but it should be understood that in this case the orientations have been, although not always the case, significantly much more presentist. We refer to historical approaches to specific periods, some of which are very recent, such as the works of Anta Félez (2005), Jiménez de Madariaga

---

[4] We should not miss the opportunity to include here young researchers who seem to be orienting their careers in the field of Anthropology towards historicising the discipline. This is the case of Miguel Ángel Carvajal Contreras (trained at the University of Granada) and Ignacio de Domínguez Gregorio (2018), with his recent thesis on *Historia de la antropología americanista española* read at the Complutense University of Madrid.

[5] For all readers interested in delving deeper into the history of Anthropology in Spain, we recommend consulting the reference works of the authors cited above. Specifically on the origins and development of Andalusian Anthropology, the works of Aguilar Criado (1989, 1992 and 1993) stand out. To investigate Catalan Anthropology, the works of Prat (Prat et al. 1992) and Calvo Calvo are of reference, an author who devotes part of his work to analysing the impact on the development of Spanish Anthropology of reference publications such as *Revista de Dialectología y Tradiciones Populares and Éthnica* (2022). In his case, Joan Prat is one of the relevant figures for understanding the history of Anthropology in Spain, with a special focus on the second half of the twentieth century (Prat, 1983, 1991 and 1999). Similarly, a critical review of anthropological production and disciplinary development during the nineteenth century is provided by Sánchez Gómez (1986), an author who pays special attention to the living ethnological exhibitions that took place at the beginning of the twentieth century and to whom we owe one of the reference works, the *Diccionario histórico de la Antropología Española* (Ortiz García & Sánchez Gómez, 1994). The co-editor of this work, Carmen Ortiz, has made enormous contributions to the history of the discipline, particularly her work on Luis de Hoyos Saiz (Ortiz, 1984 and Ortiz, 1987)and Julio Caro Baroja (1996) and her precise look at the development of the anthropological discipline in the last three decades of the twentieth century (2003). A more global vision, of essential references for those who want to know the themes, authors and keys to the development of the discipline in Spain during the twentieth century, is provided by the work edited by Müllauer-Seichter (2016) with an excellent introductory chapter.

and Checa Olmos (2012), Gómez García (2000) or Gómez-Pellón (2017). Other works analyse more distant periods or focus on the study of anthropological societies of the time, journals of the past or the contributions of museums to the history of the discipline: Bustamante (2005), Bouza Vila (2001), Calvo Calvo (1997), Galera Gómez et al. (1984), Garralda Benajes (2010), González Montero de Espinosa (1996), Pujol and Sanmartín (1999), Rodríguez Becerra and Medina San Román (2002), Sánchez Montañés and Iglesias Ponce de León (2022).

This list of contributions to the history of Anthropology in Spain must not exclude those of some of the professionals who in homages or in recognition of figures considered more or less relevant, have been able to contribute with a one-off piece of writing that could be considered a contribution to the history of the discipline. Here, the list would be endless, and its location would be easier if we refer to the recognition and tributes to those personalities we are referring to: tributes to Luis Hoyos Saiz (Ortiz García, 1984), Julio Caro Baroja (Carreira Vérez et al., 1978), Carmelo Lisón Tolosana (Velasco Maíllo, 2020), Claudio Esteva Fabregat (Prat & Martínez, 1996; Moreno Navarro, 2019; Roigé Ventura, 2019) or José Alcina Franch (Cabello, 2004).[6]

Lastly, a special mention in this collection of histories of Anthropology produced from within Spain and often for Spain, should be given to the aforementioned work by Martínez Veiga (2010), in two volumes devoted to socioeconomic formations and anthropological praxis, theory and ideologies, in addition to theories, praxis and places of study. Additionally, an article by Josep Ramón Llobera dedicated to problematising different issues of the history of Anthropology (1976), and along a similar line, but with other positions, the work of Verena Stolcke (2008), which stands out for its reflection and critical view of the historical construction of the discipline itself.

---

[6] One should not fail to consult more recent tributes dedicated to anthropologists of more recent times who have either passed away or retired from their work in academia. These tribute texts are often a place where people look back and the texts are filled with references to the past. We recommend consulting the following tributes: Agudo and Catón (2016), Cátedra and Devillard (2014), Contreras et al. (2012), Couceiro and Gómez (2012), Del Pino Díaz (2013), Devillard (2020), Fernández and Díaz (2020), Ferrándiz et al. (2015), González and Molina (2002), Henríquez Sánchez & Clavijo Redondo (2015), Mármol et al. (2016), Medeiros (2019), Palenzuela Chamorro (2017), Prat (2012), Tomé et al. (2021) or Vila (2019).

In Search of the Origin: Protohistory of the "Spanish" Anthropology

In this text, we have aimed to problematise regarding who should create the history of Anthropology and to locate this question within the case of Spain. However, this subject does not resolve those key points that should be addressed prior to undertaking a historical account of the discipline, similar to that which we aim to develop from hereon. Llobera proposes three questions upon which we should reflect in order to construct a history of Anthropology, namely, a delimitation of the epistemic status of Anthropology,[7] a declaration regarding its origins and, lastly, a reflection of what he refers to as "scientific externalism",[8] which does not differ from

---

[7] Verena Stolcke tells us that "it should be obvious, although it is not always so, that a history of any discipline requires first of all a definition of that discipline as a precondition for being able to delimit its field of research, to fix the starting point of this history and to decide on its periodisation" (2008, p. 11). In doing so, she also reminds us of the dilemma that this entails, for in order to delimit the disciplinary field, it is necessary to make a history of it. She resolves the dilemma by avoiding a formalist definition of the discipline and structures her proposal "around a constitutive tension which has never been overcome and which has been inherent in anthropological reflections, namely that between the unitary idea of the human species and the reality of its manifest socio-cultural multiplicity" (Stolcke, 2008, p. 131). For his part, Llobera (1976, pp. 30–31) resolves this issue as follows: "A provisional way out of the question of the epistemic status of anthropology that I advocate is to consider anthropology as a science in formation, whose foundations were laid by the Enlightenment, but which was never consolidated as a science due to a series of epistemological and ideological obstacles that arose around the discipline in the nineteenth century and have persisted into the twentieth century. This epistemological obstacle is the result of uncritically accepting the natural scientific model. Among the epistemological obstacles that I have been able to study are the effects of inductivism, empiricism, mechanical materialism and fixist evolutionism. They are the result, enshrined by Comte and Stuart Mill among others, of a misreading of natural scientific practice and the denial of the specificity of the social sciences. I will come back to this issue later on when dealing with the problems of theoretical externalism. Ideological obstacles are the result of the class character of the society that produced and developed the social sciences. The effect of these obstacles is to drag the social sciences from the purely cognitive to the more practical-social level, where they can be used, directly or indirectly, by the ideology and interests of the ruling class".

[8] "With the concept of theoretical externalism, I have tried to point out, in a rather schematic way, the situation of scientific dependence in which the social sciences have found themselves and still find themselves today. This situation is not without important consequences. If it is true, as I believe to be the case and have briefly shown, social scientists have systematically misrepresented scientific practice and have not normally taken into account the specificity of the social sciences" (Llobera, 1976, p. 37).

6 CHRONOLOGY OF A DISCIPLINE: SOCIAL AND CULTURAL... 189

the dependency of models from other disciplines in the construction of anthropological science. It is beyond the scope of this chapter to develop, in detail, each and every one of these points, and they are not always of significant relevance for a history of Anthropology in Spain. The second question would constitute a separate issue. The determination of the origin of Anthropology in Spain can clearly contribute to the history of the discipline at this time.

Llobera clearly establishes what he proposes to be considered as the beginnings of Anthropology:

> There are several reasons for which I consider that we must focus on The Enlightenment as the period in which the basis for a science of man and society was established: 1. The attempt to formulate laws of man and society. These laws were considered in terms of cause and effect. 2. The idea that there were invariable laws of human nature and changing laws of society. 3. The formulation of the idea that history can be best explained as a succession of modes of production. The evolution from one stage to another is triggered by changes taking place at an economic level. (1976, p. 35)

On his part, Claude Levi-Strauss has mentioned the following factors in several of his works: the cultural shock of geographical discoveries, colonialism, the French Revolution and Darwinian evolutionism (1970); Marvin Harris (1979) refers to Scientific Revolution as a crucial factor, and Gouldner (1973) speaks of the influence of romanticism on nineteenth century Anthropology. In this sense, Lowie, in the History of Ethnology (1937), opts to start the history with German thinkers Meiners and Klemm, as, in his opinion, the first who had a relatively clear idea of culture as a key concept of ethnology.

But we must pay attention to what Verena Stolcke tells us:

> All these anthropologists, historians of their own discipline, indeed, in choosing their ancestors, creating myths of origin and inventing honourable traditions expurgated from unconfessed affinities and at the same time conforming to contemporary criteria of theoretical efficacy and professional respectability, did not behave very differently from the peoples (primitive or otherwise) they sought to describe. (2008, p. 20)

And a few lines later, she indicates that

190   M. RUBIO GÓMEZ ET AL.

until the seventies, for as long as the anthropologists have been interested in the past of their discipline, they have tended to interpret it from a conceptual and theoretical perspective that orientated their own anthropological activities. (2008, p. 21)

in order to later critically conclude with the following statement:

The shortcomings of these genealogical evolutionary histories lie, however, not only in the fact that they tend to be idiosyncratic, that they fail to explain the historical circumstances and ways of conceiving the differentiations in humankind that gave rise to the concepts and paradigms that their authors claim as anthropological heritage: but in that they also exclude from history ways of approaching and interpreting human diversity in the past that are at odds with current fashions and/or are politically uncomfortable for them. (Icke, 2008, pp. 21–22)

For their part, and also from Anthropology developed in Spain, Bestard and Contreras (1987) defend, following Godelier, that

anthropology as a discipline developed with the expansion of capitalism and its colonial domination over non-capitalist societies (on this point, we have already approached the content of some chapters of this book), constituting its field from its own practice. It was born with the discovery of the "non-Western" world by Europe and with the development of the different forms of colonial domination of the world. Gradually, a field of study was delimited, populated by all the non-Western societies that the West discovered in its global expansion. Historians left them to anthropologists, as their study could not rely on written documents to date the monuments and material traces of the past. Moreover, the study of these societies required direct observation and oral enquiry. (Bestard & Contreras, 1987, p. 3)

And although it may seem that in the case of Spain this question of origins is a minor issue, we have come to argue that it is not. And this is so, if we consider the possibility, defended by an important part of the profession, that the work carried out by some of the missionaries sent to America after the so-called Conquest should be considered anthropological. We have already mentioned how Fermín Del Pino, one of the historians of the discipline in Spain, championed such consideration and sought

6 CHRONOLOGY OF A DISCIPLINE: SOCIAL AND CULTURAL... 191

recognition for this first Anthropology; what he calls the "proto-anthropology" of the sixteenth century.[9]

In the first instance, he turned to none other than one of the greatest authorities in the history of Anthropology for such recognition:

> Stocking himself acknowledged in 1968 (p. IX of the preface) that the structure of his ultimately miscellaneous book originally formed "a grandiose edifice of four large sections, arranged in time from about 1500 to the present". (Del Pino Díaz, 1994a, p. 567)

He wonders why this recognition, clear for American Anthropology, has no correspondence in English Anthropology:

> Evans-Pritchard, the same leader at Oxford, stated it pallidly in an article in Man (1950, n. 198), and in a series of BBC lectures of the same year, later translated: "There is a limit beyond which it is of no great interest to specify the origins. This limit period for the evolution of social anthropology is the 18th century" (1967, pp. 36–37). (Del Pino Díaz, 1994a, p. 567)

But to reinforce his arguments, he then turns to other authorities also from the history profession:

> Professor Pagden has argued since 1982 that the school of Salamanca, led by Francisco de Vitoria, made an important contribution to this culturalist approach (which Pagden sometimes considers to be psychological), by using the Aristotelian philosophy of the barbarian not so much in its naturalistic sense—barbarians are born to be slaves—but in a more pedagogical and historical one: barbarians are born as slaves, but they can be brought to political freedom through education, like children. (Del Pino Díaz, 1994a, p. 572)

Alongside these arguments, Fermín Del Pino (1975) looks to general anthropologies and histories of Anthropology in defence of his arguments:

> We are not the first to deal with the matter, because there have already been Spaniards who have preceded us, both from the Anthropology and History

---

[9] Fermín del Pino himself acknowledges that his first interest in the history of Anthropology had for him a presentist and nationalist character "since he wanted to understand why the Spanish chronicles of the Indies were considered properly 'anthropological' in the North American manuals, and not in the European ones" (Del Pino Díaz, 1994b, p. 565).

192   M. RUBIO GÓMEZ ET AL.

guilds, and both residing in Spain and abroad (Lisón, Palerm, Esteve Barba, Nicolau d'Olwer, Ballesteros or Pérez de Tudela, to mention only the closest ones). On the other hand, we are well accompanied by a good cohort of colleagues, especially North Americans, who have begun to rethink a previously dogmatic position in anthropological histories (Irving Hauowell, 1960; Margaret Hodgen, 1964, and John H. Rowe, 1964), apart from the English historian J. H. Elliot (1970 and 1972). (Del Pino Díaz, 1975, p. 108)

To this end, he continues to investigate reference works by authors such as Tylor, Morgan and Schimdt, in whose works Del Pino locates a considerable number of references to the contributions of the so-called Chroniclers of the Indies. This support enables him to continue denouncing the disappearance of such references from some histories of modern Anthropology. The above quotation continues with the following lament: "This I believe can seriously correct the absolute ignorance, or the deficiency of treatment, that the most famous histories of our science (Haddon, Penniman, Lowie, Mercier, Poirier, Kroeber, etc.) make of the subject" (Del Pino Díaz, 1975, p. 108).

But it is not our intention to place this debate about certain absences in the histories of the origin of the discipline at the centre. Although we were keen to mention it, we understand that it is not an issue that we can take up at this point. We are thus in line with Ortiz and Sánchez, who consider that "addressing this field would imply the need for a different kind of reflection on the particular social, political and scientific contexts surrounding the vision and interpretation of human groups other than one's own" (Ortiz García & Sánchez Gómez, 1994, p. 8).

CHRONOLOGY OF ANTHROPOLOGY IN SPAIN

After demonstrating possible past anchors, our work now proceeds to focus on offering various coordinates to readers unfamiliar with the development of the anthropological discipline in Spain. Following in the footsteps of such reference works as those of Prat and Martínez (1996), Joan Prat (1983), Carmen Ortiz (1996, 2001, 2004), María Cátedra (1991), Encarnación Aguilar (1993, and Aguilar, Feixa y Melis, 2000), Del Pino Díaz (1994b) or Fernández de Rota (1996), we therefore propose four reference phases for this "journey".

The first phase, which we date between the end of the nineteenth century and the middle of the twentieth century, was characterised by the generalist look at the human being, by the precursor studies of folklore, the constant threat of political instability[10] and the emergency of museums and key associative movements for the understanding of the development of Social and Cultural Anthropology today. A second phase dates back to the 1960s and 1980s, in which Anthropology studies were progressively introduced in universities, creating chairs and specialised studies that accompanied the change in the sociopolitical model and the territorial organisation of the state (with the creation of the autonomous state). We will then introduce a third phase, from 1980 to 2010, consisting of thirty years in which the academic institutionalisation of the discipline itself will be consolidated by the democratic system, uniting in a way of "doing anthropology" that will "exoticise" local minorities by putting the issue of "identities" at the heart of research agendas, by way of dependence on the autonomous states for research and hence the formation of research groups throughout the territory, consisting of different approaches and theoretical objects of study that will make visible a plural panorama at a time of openness to new areas of professionalisation outside the academic world. Finally, it is with this last argument in mind that we will make a brief allusion to the last decade, which is crucial to our understanding of the current evolution of the discipline itself. From 2010, when the Bologna Process was implemented and Anthropology studies in Spain became undergraduate studies, we will see that the need for professionalisation and location of the discipline outside academic boundaries is increasingly pronounced.

MUSEUMS, FOLKLORE, ASSOCIATIONS, MONARCHIES, REPUBLICS AND DICTATORSHIPS

This narrative commences in the context of Spain at the end of the nineteenth century. We find ourselves at a time of reflection across Europe, on the liminal position of Anthropology among Social Sciences and Natural Sciences, and on the evolutionist ideas of the period. These questions, which entered the Spanish context by way of publications such as *Revista*

---

[10] During the nineteenth century, political instability was constant and it continued until the twentieth century. This kept the country in continuous political changes since the Bourbon Restoration (1875), the dictatorship of Primo de Rivera (1923–1930), the Second Republic (1931–1939) followed by the Civil War (1936–1939) and the Franco dictatorship (1939–1975). These historical events directly affected the development of research and teaching, in many cases frustrating the consolidation of social disciplines such as Anthropology.

194 M. RUBIO GÓMEZ ET AL.

Europea (1874–1880) and which had been addressed from multidisciplinary perspectives in spaces of debate such as the *Ateneo Científico Literario y Artístico de Madrid* (created in 1835), were concretised in the conception of a notion of Anthropology that was intrinsically linked to evolutionist and diffusionist paradigms (Aguilar Criado, Feixa & Melis, 2000). Thus, priority was given to the study of popular culture and traditional practices; that is, folklore studies began to develop hand in hand with the rise of nationalist movements determined to find the "soul of the people" and the cultural "roots" that would support their political claims. Thus, these studies, more descriptive than interpretative, began to be promoted with greater enthusiasm in the Basque country (by the journalist Vicente de Arana, creator of the *Sociedad de Folklore Vasco Navarro* in 1884), in Galicia (with the leadership of historian and precursor of Galician nationalism, Manuel Murguía) or in Catalonia (with the creation in 1876 of the *Asociación Catalana D'Excursionistas científicos* by the hand of Ramón Arabía and Solanas). These studies did achieve a "scientific" status as a result of their political charge (Prat, 1991), and arose in parallel to another orientation that Anthropology was taking in Central and Southern Spain. The Darwinian debate and its translation into the social sphere was deeply rooted in Spanish anthropological thought of that time, and it was at this time that the *Sociedad Antropológica Española* (1865) was created by Pedro González Velasco in Madrid as a channel for said debates. At that time, the liberal and Krausist ideas established by intellectuals such as Antonio Machado and Nuñez, or his son, Antonio Machado Álvarez— better known as Demófilo—from Andalusia (Southern Spain), crystallised in the *Sociedad Antropológica de Sevilla* (1971–1874), of which they were members from its creation. Tylor's evolutionist works on survival and the explanatory bases of his theory had an impact on the way of coming to understand uses, customs and beliefs in the "anthropological" works of that time which, although they could be works on folklore, were timidly building theoretical bodies on Spanish cultural diversity.[11]

---

[11] At this time, several leading publications included Anthropology-related topics in their pages: the *Revista de España* (1868–1894), the *Revista Mensual de Filosofía, Literatura y Ciencias* (1869–1874), from which Krausist and Darwinist ideas were disseminated; the publication *Anales de la Sociedad Española de Historia Natural* (1872–1902), which included the minutes of the society's meetings and research reports of its members (among whom Manuel Antón Ferrándiz, Francisco de las Barras de Aragón and Telesforo Aranzadi stood out); or the *Revista de Antropología* published by the *Sociedad Antropológica Española* in which Darwinist and evolutionist theories found a space for dissemination in our context, not without criticism and internal debate (Galera et al., 1984).

6 CHRONOLOGY OF A DISCIPLINE: SOCIAL AND CULTURAL... 195

With the repeal of the first Republic in 1875 and the establishment of the monarchy—which led to a clear, conservative thought linked to the Catholic church—the expectations of Anthropology in terms of consolidating itself as a scientific discipline in its own right were lessened, but did not disappear, as it was at this time that the *Sociedad de "Folk-Lore Español"* (1881) and the *Museo de Antropología* (1875) were founded by Antonio Machado Álvarez, with a clear focus on physical Anthropology. The latter had been created by the aforementioned Pedro González Velasco who had originally called it the *Museo Anatómico*. Thus, during these years, several regionalist organisations were created, from which work was undertaken in order to highlight the customs, traditions and studies linked to these territories (such as the *Sociedad del Museo Canario, the Sociedad de Folklore Andaluz, la Sociedad Demológica Asturiana* or the *Sociedad de Folklore Extremeño,* among others). It was also the time of the creation of the ambitious secular pedagogical project of the *Institución Libre de Enseñanza* (1886–1936), supported by intellectuals of the time, namely Nicolás Salmerón or Francisco Giner de los Ríos. The intention of this alternative space to the state structures (of traditional and dogmatic cut) was to bring both culture and science closer to the Spanish people from a Krausist and positivist orientation in which, as it could not be otherwise, anthropological studies (mostly linked to physical Anthropology) were present.

This would be the trend of anthropological thought observed in early twentieth century Spain, an amalgam of evolutionary approaches closely linked to positivism, prehistoric studies and physical Anthropology (with a particular interest in the "knowledge of racial characterisation and peninsular ethnogenesis") (Tomas Cardoso, 2012, p. 127), and prehistoric studies, while addressing folklore from a position that was clearly influenced by German Anthropology and its notable diffusionist approaches.

At this time, and from the creation of the first university chair at the Central University of Madrid (1892) occupied by Manuel Antón and Ferrándiz, who refounded the *Sociedad Antropológica Española* in 1921, calling it *"Sociedad Española de Antropología, Etnografía y Prehistoria"*,[12] making visible the generalist nature of the discipline itself—the first gen-

---

[12] The text by Luis Sánchez Gómez (1990) can be consulted for further information on the history of this society and its work linked to physical Anthropology and prehistory, as well as the complex relations of this organisation with the Bernardino Sahagún Institute of Anthropology and Ethnology of the CSIC in the service of the dictatorship, which ended up dissolving the former.

196 M. RUBIO GÓMEZ ET AL.

eration of Spanish anthropologists was recognised academically, among whom we highlight Luis de Hoyos Sainz[13] and Telesforo de Aranzadi, both of whom were creators of the first manual of ethnography called "Ethography: Its bases, methods and application in Spain" (Aranzadi & Hoyos, 1917). Robust work networks were established at that time with the Catalan prehistorical Pedro Bosch Gimpera of the *Associació Catalana d'Antropología, Etnología y Prehistoria* in Barcelona (1922), or with the Basque priest and ethnographer José Miguel de Barandiarán, the founder of the Sociedad de Eusko Folklore (1921). All of them and their works are essential to an understanding of the formulation of the main academic and scientific institutions from which Anthropology would then take shape in Spain in the first quarter of the twentieth century.

We can observe that although at the end of the nineteenth century Madrid and Seville concentrated a significant part of the "seed" activity of present-day Anthropology, at the beginning of the century the Basque Country and Catalonia emerged strongly through associations (such as those mentioned previously and others of relevance, such as the *Associació Catalana d'Antropologia, Etnologia i Prehistoria*), the organisation of congresses such as the *I Congreso Internacional de Lengua Catalana* (1906) or the *I Congreso de Estudios Vascos* (1918); or the edition of periodical publications such as the *International Journal of Basque Studies* (1907), which is still alive today, the *Estudis I Materials* (1916–1918) journal or the journal *Arxiu de Tradicons Populars* (1938–1935). In addition to this creative effervescence, there were other notable regional initiatives, such as the creation of the *Seminario de Estudos Galegos* (1923), the *Centro de Estudios Extremeños* (1927) or the *Instituto de Estudios Canarios* (1932), all of which have publications and spaces for debate.

However, the Civil War cut short the potential future development of the anthropological discipline. Many of the aforementioned names were forced to go into exile and there was no room for ideas contrary to those which were established by the Franco regime, imposed from 1939

---

[13] To learn more about the figure of this author, we recommend the text by Carmen Ortiz (1987), who makes an exhaustive approach to the contributions and anthropological work of Luis de Hoyos Saiz.

onwards.[14] The only figure who remained in a discreet place undertaking ethnological work, especially in the Basque context, and who turned out to be the sole connection of Spanish Anthropology with what was being done outside our borders, was Julio Caro Baroja, a student of the afore-mentioned Aranzadi.[15] Far from the university spaces, Caro Bajora is, even today, an unavoidable reference in terms of discussions of Anthropology in Spain,[16] since his works on social history, material culture, myths, beliefs, festivals and "cultural identities" (Aguilar Criado & Carles Feixa, 2000) drew a favourable panorama to think of both a social and cultural orientation of anthropological studies located closer to the functionalist approaches that were on the rise throughout Europe.

His admiration for the work of Evans-Pritchard led to his friendship with Julian Pitt Rivers, who as part of his interest in investigating Spanish society, relied on Caro Baroja to undertake key work in the history of Anthropology in Spain.[17] *The People of the Sierra* (1954) is therefore a work that is considered crucial (Prat, 1999) in the history of modern

---

[14] This period was not a period devoid of anthropological initiatives. In fact, in the 1940s important institutions were founded, such as the Bernardino de Sahagún Institute of Anthropology and Ethnology (CSIC), directed by J. Pérez de Barradas (for further information, see the work of Sánchez, 1992); the Centre for Peninsular Ethnology Studies; the Institute of Pyrenean Studies (1942–1983) or the Spanish Institute of Musicology, Folklore Section (1943–1985), currently the Department of Ethnomusicology at the Autonomous University of Barcelona. All these institutions had associated journals and periodicals (Ikuska, Anuario Musical, Munibé, etc.), which did not free them from the censorship of the time, but allowed a certain expression of the research and work that was carried out (closer to the interests of the regime than to the enhancement of the diversity of the Spanish State itself).

[15] For more in-depth knowledge of Caro Baroja's work, see the works of Velasco (2014) Ortiz (1996) and Velasco and Lisón (1995).

[16] Co-founder of the first national journal specialising in ethnography and what we know today as Social and Cultural Anthropology in Spain: *Revista de Dialectología y Tradiciones Populares* (1944). Published by the Consejo Superior de Investigaciones Científicas (CSIC-Madrid) which, in 2019, changed its name to *Disparidades. Revista de Antropología*. For more details on this journal, see Ortiz García (1994), Casado (1991) and Calvo (2002).

[17] We can see part of this friendship in Velasco and Caro (2015), where we can find personal letters between Julio Caro Baroja and Julian Pitt-Rivers. We can also find it in a chapter written by George M. Foster, North American anthropologist from University of California, Berkeley. But the fact that his work *The People of the Sierra* was dedicated to Julio Caro Baroja was irrefutable evidence of this.

198   M. RUBIO GÓMEZ ET AL.

Spanish Anthropology.[18] It is a moment of rupture with the previous logics and in which Spain is dimensioned as a privileged space of research for Anthropology thought from outside our borders. It was to be the moment in which we would see the birth of "an anthropology of Spain, without Spanish anthropologists" (Aguilar Criado & Carles Feixa, 2000, p. 106).

1960–1980: TOWARDS THE ACADEMIC INSTITUTIONALISATION OF ANTHROPOLOGY: FROM THE STUDY OF "THE PRIMITIVE OTHER" TO THE STUDY OF THE "FOLKLORIC US"

This was a period of development for Social Anthropology with works whose "object of study" would be the Spanish territory, its rural life, migratory processes, poverty, grace or shame (Peristiany, 1965; Peristiany & Pitt-Rivers, 2005 [1968]; or Gilmore, 1982, among others). From foreign and exoticising perspectives, Spanish society at the time was constructed as part of an idea of a "Mediterranean cultural area" formed by countries such as Italy, Greece and Spain. It would seem that the focus that Anglo-Saxon anthropologists had hitherto with a focus on colonised spaces was now placed on territories that were more accessible, in the broad sense of the term, due to their geographical location and their lack of connection with direct colonial processes. Identified as "backward" in relation to the rest of Europe, these territories were highlighted for their emphasis on tradition or their rural character (thus accentuating that which was deemed more simple or curious, as opposed to the complexity of any context or processes that at the time were taking place in relation to growing urbanisation or the impact of state policies). In addition to the harsh criticisms of this limiting and epistemologically dubious notion of "the Mediterranean" (Llobera, 1990), the 1970s saw an important debate within the ranks of Spanish Anthropology, now increasingly present in the academic world, which was visibly uncomfortable with said foreign approaches. Thus, the colonialist viewpoint of the aforementioned works (Moreno, 1972, 1975) was criticised, and the idea of the validity of studies on Spanish territory by non-Spanish anthropologists was raised. A debate

---

[18] In spite of the importance of Pitt-Rivers work, critics were abundant. In this way, we can see Moreno's works (1972, 1975). But we can also find a positive interpretation of Pitt-Rivers works in Honorio Velasco (1989). Pitt-Rivers work crosses the line of the Anthropology in Spain and has a large tradition of both presenters and critics.

which, on the other hand, crossed the discipline at an international level and which emphasised the "decolonisation" of Anthropology (Stavenhagen, 1971) and the importance of "native anthropology" and its theoretical contributions to the discipline (Jones, 1971; Hsu, 1973), which was beginning to make itself felt in Latin America and the United States" (Narotzky, 2011, p. 27). This would consequently give rise to the need for a local view of the phenomena occurring on our borders from the logic of a "new-born" disciplinary knowledge that sought to claim an exclusive place of enunciation. This position, however, had a certain trap, as the lack of a state research policy to promote work outside Spain, and the dependence on associations and museums to undertake anthropological research, meant that local proposals monopolised ethnographic work at that time.

However, times were changing, and between the 1960s and the 1980s, parallel to these discussions, Anthropology was being introduced to Spanish universities as a field of study separate from Geography, Archaeology, History or Prehistory. Curiously enough, during this process it was mostly Spaniards, trained abroad, who "disciplined" Anthropology in the universities.[19]

The establishment of introductory courses in Anthropology at various universities created a new market of potential readers, and a publishing development began to take place, giving rise to the publication of translations of Anthropology classics, manuals and introductory books, by both foreign and Spanish authors. Works appeared that introduced new theoretical orientations (cultural ecology, French structuralism and Marxism) which gradually replaced the hegemonic structural-functionalist discourse of the previous period, in addition to works that reflected the progressive delimitation of the thematic fields that was taking place at the time: Culture and Personality, Industrial Anthropology, Anthropology and Education, Applied Anthropology, Culture and Language, and so on.

In an exercise of both focus and selection, we will centre on offering a very brief biography on two of the masters of reference for understanding

---

[19] In this way, it is important to highlight the work of Spanish Americanist anthropologists such as Manuel Ballesteros Gaibrois, linked to the Franco regime and promoter of the *Seminar of Americanist Studies* (1951), teacher of José Alcina Franch, also an Americanist anthropologist, who founded the Department of Anthropology and Ethnology of America at the *University of Seville* in 1959. Coming back to Madrid, Alcina and Ballesteros created the Department of Anthropology and Ethnology of America at the Faculty of Geography and History of the Complutense University of Madrid (1967).

the development of Anthropology in Spain[20]: Claudio Esteva Fabregat and Carmelo Lisón Tolosana. The former trained in Mexico in the American culturalist tradition of "Boasian orientation" (Calvo Calvo, 2002), and the latter trained in the British school, specifically in Oxford under the guidance of Evans-Pritchard (supervisor of his doctoral thesis). Both contributed to the renewal of university anthropological studies in Spain, thus contributing new ideas regarding how to approach fieldwork and sharing theoretical approaches hitherto unworked in the Spanish academy (Capel, 2009).

In 1965, Claudio Esteva Fábregat, with the support of José Alcina Franch and Manuel Ballesteros Gaibrois, created the "School of Anthropological Studies" in Madrid within the *Museo Nacional de Etnología* (directed by Esteva after Caro Baroja). A complex commitment to postgraduate studies inspired by the logic of North American Anthropology, in which Social and Cultural Anthropology was combined with "other disciplines such as archaeology and linguistics, which in the European tradition did not form part of social Anthropology, in addition to the social sciences as auxiliary disciplines, such as statistics, history or psychology" (Rodríguez, 2018, p. 159). This academic structure, in which a large part of the current teaching staff of Anthropology in Spain were trained, was a milestone in the academic institutionalisation of Social and Cultural Anthropology.[21] At the end of the 1960s, Esteva moved to Barcelona and obtained a teaching post in the Department of Prehistory, but linking his work to ethnology (Gómez-Pellón, 2017). It was in 1972 that the first chair of Cultural Anthropology in Spain was created—which he occupied—and the Department of Cultural Anthropology at the

[20] We recognise the difficulty involved in the selection of references and we cannot fail to mention people whose promotion of Anthropology in their respective universities is part of the history of the discipline, such as Alberto Galván (University of La Laguna), José Antonio Fernández de Rota (Santiago de Compostela), María Cátedra, Ricardo Sanmartín, Teresa San Román or Isidoro Moreno (a key reference in Andalusian Anthropology). An approach to their work and contributions is masterfully presented in the work of José Luís Anta (2007).

[21] The debate on whether to call the anthropological discipline social or cultural in its process of institutionalisation in Spain has its origins in these moments when disputes over university spaces and fields of knowledge were recognised. Thus, Carmelo Lisón, from the Complutense University of Madrid, placed himself in "Social Anthropology" close to sociology in order to develop his work, while Claudio Esteva, already in Barcelona, defended "the cultural" as a priority area of study for Anthropology. For more on this "identity of Anthropology as a negotiated problem" (Esteva in Brufau et al., 2011), see Lisón (1975), Frigolé (1975) and Moreno (1975).

6 CHRONOLOGY OF A DISCIPLINE: SOCIAL AND CULTURAL...   201

Autonomous University of Barcelona (of which he was director until 1986). At the same time, from Madrid, Carmelo Lisón, already a tenured professor at the Complutense University, created a speciality in Social Anthropology within the Sociology degree studies, creating the chair of the same name in the Faculty of Sociology and Political Science at the Complutense University of Madrid. With the creation of the Department of Social Anthropology (of which he was director until 1990) and the transformation of the syllabus, Lisón created the first PhD syllabus in Social Anthropology[22] (Sanmartín, 2020).

While all these changes were being undertaken behind the doors of Spanish universities, outside, the death of the dictator Franco (1975) and the end of the dictatorship would give rise to a process of social opening that had never been seen before in Spain.[23] The gradual democratisation of Spanish society, together with the expansion of Higher Education (the creation of new universities and departments) and the creation of the State of Autonomies (from 1979 onwards)[24] would form the perfect scenario for the discipline to transform itself and its new objects of study: the processes of identification, ethnicity and nationalism.

[22] We are aware that the history of a discipline in a given historical period is not made by just two people, despite the fact that they are very important and decisive figures for the anthropological discipline. For this reason, we do not want to forget to underline the fact that Esteva Fabregat and Lisón Tolosana were surrounded by an environment and people that allowed the academic flourishing of the discipline, as well as the development of specialisations in the discipline and in research. Another important nucleus was formed at the University of Seville and at the University of Oviedo: at the former, under the influence of J. Alcina Franch (who was followed by Isidoro Moreno), the Seminar of American Anthropology was founded (where Americanist and Andalusian studies were carried out, under a methodology and theoretical orientation inspired by the trend of the cultural areas of American Anthropology), while at the latter anthropological knowledge was built around R. Valdés, who later moved to the Autonomous University of Barcelona.

[23] Franco's dictatorship was from 1939 till 1975. For the Spaniards citizenship and for the academics background, that means a large period of obscurantism, academic tardiness and freedom limitations. To know the influence of dictatorship in Spain, see Otero Carvajal works (2014, 2017).

[24] The process of autonomous regions started in 1978 and it ended in 1995. It signifies the conformation of seventeen autonomous territories and two autonomous cities (in the north of Africa); three territories were recognised directly through the so-called rapid way (Catalonia, Basque Country and Galicia), thanks to an autonomous statute approved during the Second Republic (1931–1936). The rest of the territories went through different processes more or less quickly.

During the political transition in the second half of the 1970s, the Departments of Culture of the new autonomous governments began to take an interest in regional folklore and "popular culture". This interest, with eminently political aims, later resulted in the proliferation of centres created and financed by the autonomous administrations, generating in turn an avalanche of congresses, conferences and seminars on ethnography, folklore, or traditional and popular culture. To this end, anthropological journals emerged and proliferated, both with markedly international themes, in addition to journals specialising in folkloric and regionalist issues of the autonomous communities and others devoted to an attempt to combine national/regional themes with international themes and issues.[25]

One example of these publications is *Ethnica Revista de Antropología*,[26] which was founded in Barcelona (1971) by Esteva, together with the group *Centro de Etnología Peninsular del Consejo Superior de Investigaciones Científicas* "with the desire to provide a space within which to present a specific way of doing and understanding anthropology as a science, a configuration that had holism and interdisciplinarity as central aspects" (Calvo, 2002, p. 77). This journal, which originated as a response to the postcolonial shift that took place in the discipline at an international level in those years, had a short life (its trajectory was cut short in 1985), due to various issues including scarce funding, insufficient human resources, or uncertain continuity and periodicity. The precariousness that characterised its existence is a common denominator of the publications at that time, a fact that "one might wonder, for example, about the level of co-responsibility and support that the anthropological community itself has given to the editorial projects born within it" (Calvo, 2002, p. 4), and one of the key questions to explain the discontinuity of the publications themselves was the fact that the funding did not come directly from the univer-

---

[25] Between the 1960s and 1980s was the period of the greatest proliferation of anthropological journals in Spain; however, as Calvo (2002) points out, this is a paradigmatic issue during the institutionalisation of the discipline "given that, being one of the most outstanding academic instruments, anthropological journals in Spain have certainly had an eventful and difficult life during these three decades of institutionalisation" (Calvo 2002, pp. 6–7).

[26] For further details on this journal, see Alcañiz (1994) and Calvo Alaniz (2002). The initial article written by Esteva Fabregat himself (1969) and the one at the end of the period, when it ceased publication (Esteva Fabregat, 1984a) are also very enlightening.

sities, but rather from associations, museums, and so on, despite the fact that the publications were fundamentally fed by the work of academics. These problems are also to be found in most of the publishing projects and periodicals that emerged or were renewed and/or taken up again during this period, which were quite numerous, although they had different fates and fortunes. Only the *Revista de Dialectología y Tradiciones Populares* exceeded the margin of time and continuity truly comparable to that of other reference publications in other countries.

Congresses were another key space at the time of institutionalisation of the anthropological discipline: Specifically, the I Congreso Español de Antropología (Barcelona, 28th March to 2nd April 1977) and *Etnología y Tradiciones Populares*. I Congreso Nacional de Artes y Costumbres Populares (Zaragoza, 1968). This joint effort to disseminate the discipline in order to institutionalise it among academia, publications, congresses, associations and museums was not undertaken with the forcefulness required in Spain, as a result of the anachronism of museums and associations with respect to journals, research and academic studies. The associations with more international, more external themes and issues remained anchored closely to Darwinist ideas of the discipline, slave to a colonialist approach; while the associations that are characterised by their dedication to more internal themes, more of "our own", produced research that would act as the basis for the construction of regionalist, autonomous identifications of Spain.

For their part, museums, which should be centres for the promotion, dissemination and training of the anthropological discipline to the public and which, in the words of Romero Tejada, could be a "highly effective means for the general public to discover what anthropology truly is and not limit it to the study of the physical form of man, as has been the case until now in Spain, in non-specialised environments" (1975, p. 346), did not live up to expectations. The two most important museums in Spain dedicated to the discipline, the *Museo del Pueblo Español* and the *Museo de Etnología*, did not follow the current of renewal and innovative spirit that took off in other fields of the discipline at that time, so that Spanish museology remained tied to an old notion of Anthropology, linked to Archaeology or History, as an exhibition of a series of elements of material culture, not all understood as living.

Three Decades for Anthropology in Spain: The Founding Period, Local Perspectives, Associations, Congresses, Journals and Progressive Specialisation(s) (1980–2010)

The contradictions of Spanish society at the beginning of the 1980s cannot be ignored with regards to explaining the subsequent development of Anthropology in Spain. One of them is linked to the process of opening up (culturally, economically and socially) to the European space, which was accompanied by identity claims throughout a large part of the Spanish territory. These were claims that even went beyond the nascent state of the autonomous regions. This complex "socio-historical-political" context determined the evolution of anthropological studies at the time.[27] The focus from here was, on the one hand, on "ethnic minorities" (which replaced those "exotic others" of classical Anthropology and whose interest lay, not infrequently, in their positions of exclusion and marginality) and, on the other hand, on "collective identities" (interpreted either as cultural facts, as ethnicity from a processual and dynamic perspective—inspired by the work of Barth (1969)—or from the nationalist and legitimising prism of their own "signs of identity").

The interest in these moments of consolidation of the autonomous governments in arguing for their own differential identifications undoubtedly contributed to the increase in research work financed by universities and emerging research groups within them, which focused on traditions, on the search for "roots"—in the style of the first folklorists, but now with more anthropological arguments, in some cases—through the study of festivals, rites, and so on. This was to be an institutional moment for

---

[27] It is not our intention to give a detailed analysis of this stage here; we simply want to offer the foreign reader some coordinates to understand the development of the discipline today, but we cannot fail to recommend reading the text by Anta (2005) in which the development of Spanish Anthropology in the 1980s is presented in detail and with a critical orientation. Similarly, we would like to highlight the importance of the so-called Americanists, of the links with the Latin American context that have remained a central part of the development of Spanish Anthropology, especially from the Catalan and Andalusian schools (in both cases Anthropology studies were located in university centres in the field of History) from which links and networks were built, solidly anchored and instituted around exiled anthropologists such as Ángel Palerm or Carmen Viqueira who maintained their professional work in these territories (Aguilar Criado & Carles Feixa, 2000; Pujadas, 2017).

6 CHRONOLOGY OF A DISCIPLINE: SOCIAL AND CULTURAL...   205

Anthropology in which, as Anta points out, anthropologists came to the fore:

> The contradictions of a structuralist anthropology came to the fore and where, without blushing, the most classical Marxism, regionalist studies based on thematic views of community studies, the search for jobs within the university and the creation of a certain map of power distribution were unashamedly in evidence. (2005, p. 10)

A distribution of power that, in a way, was marked by regional/territorial boundaries, which also determined the scope of the associative movement of Anthropology professionals[28] (almost all of whom were linked to a large extent to university academia). Just before the beginning of the 1980s (1978), the Institut Català d'Antropologia (ICA) was established. At the beginning of that decade, three associations were founded in as many territories, all in line with the new political-territorial entities we have mentioned: the autonomous communities. These were, in chronological order of creation, the *Asociación Canaria de Antropología* (ACA) in 1981, the *Asociación Andaluza de Antropología* (ASANA) in 1984 and the Asociación de Antropología de Castilla y León "Michael Kenny" (ACYLMK) in 1989. In the 1990s, two more associations with similar characteristics joined the previous list: in 1993 the Asociación Galega de Antropoloxía Social e Cultural (AGANTRO) and in 1994 Ankulegi, Asociación Vasca de Antropología. At the beginning of the twenty-first century, two new anthropological associations were created: in 2004 the *Asociació Valenciana d'Antropología* (AVA) and in 2009 the Instituto Madrileño de Antropología (IMA). In the 2010s, this "autonomous" map of Anthropology associations was completed: in 2010 the *Asociación Castellano Manchega de Antropología* (ACMA) was created, in 2014 the Asociación Asturiana de Antropología y Patrimonio Etnológico (ASAPE) and in 2017 the Institut d'Antropologia de les Illes (IAI).

It is, however, fair to say that associations were not only created with links to the territories of the autonomous communities. In 1982, a group of anthropologists linked to the University of Granada and other educational centres created the *Asociación Granadina de Antropología*. Also with university links, the Institut Tarragonès d'Antropologia (ITA) was created in 1984, in 2010 the *Associació Catalana de Professionals de*

---

[28] For more information about each association, you can visit their websites.

l'Antropologia (ACPA), in 2011 the *Sociedade Antropolóxica Galega* (SAGA) and recently, in 2018, the *Asociación de Antropología de Toledo* (ASANTO) was created. In all cases, these are Anthropology associations located in territories that already had associative structures intended to cover an entire autonomous community.

A somewhat special and different case from many of the previous associations is that of the AIBR Association (Antropólogos Iberoamericanos en Red). It was legally established in 2002, but is the result of the creation of "El Portal del Antropólogo" (The Anthropologist's Portal) in 1996. It is an association in Spain, but with a clear "Americanist" vocation and, moreover, not exclusively linked to the university sphere.

The complex building of associative structures in Anthropology in Spain has a certain explanation located in the need to structure the discipline in Spain as a whole. Thus, at the *II Congreso de Antropología* held in Madrid in 1981—a time when most of the aforementioned associations did not exist—the need to articulate the actions of the Anthropology associations that existed in Spain at that time and to create formal associative structures in the autonomous communities in which they were lacking, was raised.[29] It was time to become visible in society as an autonomous discipline (and not auxiliary to sociology or history), "a social science capable of responding to numerous questions and problems of our time" (*Asociación de Antropología del Estado Español,* ASAEE). From this "feeling" and after many discussions, finally in 1987, during the *IV Congreso de Antropología* organised in Alicante, the statutes of the FAAEE (Federation of Anthropology Associations of the Spanish State) were approved, thus establishing an organisational structure in which all the local and regional associations converged.[30] From this Federation (from 2017 transformed into the current Association of Anthropology of the Spanish State—ASAEE, with an explicit character more open and less limited to territorial logics) the biannual state meetings, known as *Congresos de Antropología* (Anthropology Congresses), were promoted.

This mention of the so-called Congresos de Antropología is of great significance for the recent history of Anthropology in Spain. Although

---

[29] Despite the previous list of territorial anthropological associations in 1981, the reference year for this II *Congreso* does not include many of them; it is true that they already existed, but without legal recognition. What we have offered here is the year of legal creation of each association.

[30] Prior to this IV *Congreso*, these statutes had been discussed at the II *Congreso de Antropología* held in San Sebastian in 1984.

6 CHRONOLOGY OF A DISCIPLINE: SOCIAL AND CULTURAL... 207

they are also clearly linked to the university world, they were, and still are, the most significant meeting place for the profession. Not only as builders of processes of identification of the profession and the discipline, but also as a means by which to monitor its progress. Let us make a fair mention of the twenty that have already taken place with some significant data[31]:

- *I Congreso Español de Antropología* took place at the Universitat de Barcelona in 1977. It was organised by the Department of Cultural Anthropology at the Universitat de Barcelona, and consists of six symposiums (one of which was dedicated to the history of Anthropology). The proceedings of the papers presented at this congress are collected in two volumes (AA.VV., 1980a, 1980b).
- *II Congreso Español de Antropología* took place at the Autonomous University of Madrid in 1981. It was organised by the *Asociación Madrileña de Antropología*. It was organised in three large subject areas: the situation of Anthropology in Spain, Anthropological theory in Spain and Ethnicity: nations, regions and towns. There is a book of the proceedings of this congress published by the Ministry of Culture (AA.VV., 1985).
- *Antropologiaren III Batzarrea*. III Spanish Congress of Anthropology held at the University of the Basque Country/Euskal Herriko Unibertsitatea in Donostia/San Sebastian in 1984. It is organised by the Department of Anthropology of the Faculty of Philosophy and Educational Sciences of the University of the Basque Country/ Euskal Herriko Unibertsitatea. It has already held ten symposia and we highlight two of them because of their importance for the development of the discipline and the profession: the current situation of Anthropology and the professional status of Anthropology in Spain.

---

[31] Before this long list of congresses that we have summarised, scientific meetings were held in Spain that attempted to bring together the bulk of the (mainly academic) Anthropology of the time. We should mention at least two antecedents: the First Meeting of Spanish Anthropologists held in Seville in 1973 (Jiménez Núñez, 1975) and organised by the University of Seville, and a year later, the Second Meeting of Spanish Anthropologists in Segovia organised by the Complutense University of Madrid (Rivera Dorado, 1977, 1978). It is worth mentioning these two meetings because they marked the delimitation of two anthropologies in Spain: on the one hand, the more historicist one linked to the so-called Americanist Anthropology and, on the other hand, the more social one linked to British Anthropology.

- *IV Congreso de Antropología* held at the University of Alicante (Alicante) in 1987. It is organised by the Humanities Anthropology Section of the Universitat d'Alacant and the *Federación de Asociaciones del Estado Español* (FAAEE). It now has fourteen symposia and once again, one of them is dedicated to the history of Anthropology. Oliver Narbona (1987) published a book with the invited lectures presented at this congress, the abstracts of the papers and the programme.
- *V Congreso de Antropología* held at the University of Granada in 1990. It was organised by the *Asociación Andaluza de Antropología* (ASANA) and the *Federación de Asociaciones del Estado Español* (FAAEE). It has ten symposia (one of them dedicated to the history of Anthropology).
- *VI Congreso de Antropología* held at the University of La Laguna, Tenerife, in 1993. It is organised by the Asociación Canaria de Antropología (ACA) and the *Federación de Asociaciones del Estado Español* (FAAEE). It has eight symposia and three working groups.
- *VII Congreso de Antropología* held in Zaragoza in 1996. It is organised by the *Instituto Aragonés de Antropología* (IAA) and the *Federación de Asociaciones del Estado Español* (FAAEE). It has eight symposia (one of them dedicated to the history of Anthropology) and nine discussion groups.
- *VIII Congreso de Antropología* held in Santiago de Compostela in 1999. It was organised by the *Asociación Galega de Antropoloxía* (AGANTRO) and the *Federación de Asociaciones del Estado Español* (FAAEE). It has eight symposia (one of them dedicated to Anthropology outside the academy) and a working group.
- *IX Congrés d'Antropologia* held at the Universitat de Barcelona (Barcelona) in 2002. It is organised by the *Institut Català d'Antropologia* (ICA) and the *Federación de Asociaciones del Estado Español* (FAAEE). It has eleven symposia and four working groups (one of them dedicated to the professional practice of Anthropology).
- *X Congreso de Antropología* held in Seville in 2006. It is again organised by the *Asociación Andaluza de Antropología* (ASANA) and the *Federación de Asociaciones del Estado Español* (FAAEE). It has twelve symposia and four working groups.
- *XI Antropologia Kongresua* held in Donostia/San Sebastián in 2008. It is organised by the Ankulegi, *Asociación Vasca de Antropología* and the *Federación de Asociaciones del Estado Español* (FAAEE). It has

twelve symposia (one dedicated to public-oriented Anthropology) and three working groups.

- *XII Congreso de Antropología* held in León in 2011. It is organised by the *Asociación de Antropología de Castilla y León "Michael Kenny"* (ACyLMK) and the *Federación de Asociaciones del Estado Español* (FAAEE). It has twelve symposia (one dedicated to the meaning of Anthropology today) and twelve working tables (one dedicated to the history of Iberian Anthropology).
- *XIII Congrés d'Antropologia.* Held at the Universitat Rovira i Virgili, Tarragona, in 2014. Organised by the *Institut Tarragonès d'Antropologia* (ITA) and the *Federación de Asociaciones del Estado Español* (FAAEE). It has twenty-one symposia (two of them dedicated to the professionalisation of Anthropology). A volume with part of the work presented at this congress was edit by Andreu et al. (2014).
- *XIV Congreso de Antropología/XIV Congrés d'Antropologia* is held at the Universitat de València (Valencia) in 2017. It is organised by the *Asociació Valenciana d'Antropología* (AVA) and the *Federación de Asociaciones del Estado Español* (FAAEE). It features twenty-four symposia. Vicente Rabanaque et al. (2017) edited a book with some of the work presented at this congress.
- *XIV Congreso Internacional de Antropología*[32] It is convened by *Asociación de Antropología del Estado Español* (ASAEE) and organised by the *Instituto Madrileño de Antropología* (IMA), the departments of Social Anthropology of the Autonomous University of Madrid, the Complutense University of Madrid, the National University of Distance Education (UNED) and the Higher Centre for Scientific Research (CSIC). As a result of the COVID-19 global pandemic, it was held virtually in 2021. It has twenty-six symposia (one of them dedicated to the professionalisation of Anthropology).

As can be observed, in each congress we have alluded to the symposia dedicated to the history of Anthropology and its professionalisation. In the first case, it alludes to the interests of this text, and we refer to these congresses to extend this brief chronology of Anthropology in Spain. The first five congresses had space for these themes, and this has to do with the process of "construction" of Anthropology in Spain and with a more than

---

[32] Observe how it came to be referred to as "international".

possible presentist history. Afterwards, only the VII and XII congresses had symposia dedicated to the history of the discipline. In the second case, it refers to the attempts to extend the professional practice of Anthropology beyond the academy. In this case, the attempts are repeated in different congresses with different formulas. Our interest here has to do with the fact that this issue marks and will mark the future of Anthropology in Spain. In addition to these issues, each of these congresses diversifies in a remarkable way the specialisation of Anthropology in Spain and they are therefore a good resource for learning about the development of the discipline. A list of the topics dealt with in these conferences, which is certainly incomplete, but which represents a good part of the globality of the specialisations of Anthropology in Spain, can be summarised with the following titles: Anthropology of Food, Anthropology of Education, Anthropology of Religion, Anthropology of Health, Anthropology of Migration, Anthropology of Gender, Anthropology of Kinship, Digital and Media Anthropology, Urban Anthropology, Anthropology and Cultural Heritage or Ethnicity and Processes of Identification, among others.

As one might expect, these are not the only anthropological scientific meetings held in Spain. The list of other congresses, seminars and conferences would be endless: from "regional" associations that periodically hold their congresses, to areas of thematic specialisation that follow the same path. But it is worth mentioning the appearance of an annual congress organised by the above-mentioned *Asociación Antropólogos Iberoamericanos en Red* (AIBR). Since 2015, this association has been organising what it calls the AIBR International Congress.[33] It is worth highlighting its clear "Americanist" link and its clear commitment to internationalisation by trying to hold each edition in a country of America, Central, South, Caribbean or the Iberian Peninsula and, for the time being, its continuity on an annual basis.

In parallel to the associative activity and the holding of the aforementioned scientific meetings, the specialised journals experienced an enormous boom in this period, first on paper, then in electronic versions, with more than thirty titles that, thanks to research groups, associations,

---

[33] This first one was in Madrid and then followed in Barcelona (2016), Puerto Vallarta (2017), Granada (2018), Madrid (2019), online edition (2020) and Vila Real (2021). For more information about each edition, you can visit the AIBR website. The programme of every edition is available.

museums and university departments, have had different "lives" and periodicities.[34] The following is a list of the journals which have appeared in this new era, constituting true organs for the dissemination of Anthropology, in many cases with the disciplinary and academic organisation itself in mind, but which clearly show its growth as an incipient professional field in Spain[35]:

- *Anales del Museo Nacional de Antropología*[36] started in 1994 but is heir to the journal *Anales del Museo del Pueblo Español*[37] (founded in 1935 and with a second period in 1988). It is the journal of the *Museo Nacional de Antropología* that integrates the *Museo del Pueblo Español* and the *Museo Nacional de Antropología*, the journal taking on the name of the latter.
- *Gazeta de Antropología*[38] was founded in 1980 by a group of anthropologists (some of whom were academic, some were not) who formed the *Asociación Granadina de Antropología*. Due to its antiquity, it is already the doyenne of the journals in the discipline. The same year saw the appearance of *Quaderns de l'Institut Català d'Antropologia*,[39] which ceased publication in 1987 and resumed publication in 1994.
- *Arxiu d'Etnografia de Catalunya*[40] was founded in 1982 and is the organ of expression of a group of professionals and enthusiasts—as stated in its first issue—of Cultural Anthropology. It also clarifies that

---

[34] Throughout this chapter we have listed some of the most important journals in the discipline, but to learn more about periodical publications in the field of Social and Cultural Anthropology in the Spanish context, the work of Celeste Jiménez and Francisco Checa (2012) published in *Gazeta de Antropología* is a compulsory reference. There is also a monographic issue of the *Revista de Dialectología y Tradiciones Populares* which describes in each article the details of a good part of the "living" Anthropology journals in Spain. It was published in 2002 (volume XVII, number 1) and coordinated by Luis Calvo Chica.

[35] It should be pointed out that in the period we are now chronicling, in addition to the birth of a significant number of journals, some journals that had been published in previous periods also disappeared. This is the case of the aforementioned *Ethnica. Revista de Antropología*, which disappeared in 1984.

[36] A brief history of the journal can also be found in Carretero Pérez (2002).

[37] A description of the journal also appears in the above-mentioned text by Carretero Pérez (2002) and, previously, in Carretero Pérez (1994).

[38] A history of the journal also appears in Solana Ruiz (2002).

[39] A brief history of the journal can be found in Quaderns Editorial Board (Consejo de Redacción de Quaderns, 2002).

[40] A retrospective of the journal can be found in Bodoque Puerta (2002).

it is the effort made by the *Departament d'Antropologia Cultural de la Facultat de Lletres de Tarragona* to disseminate anthropological knowledge, which would end up being the driving force behind the *Institut Català d'Antropologia*. A year after this journal appeared (1983), *Temas de Antropología Aragonesa*[41] was founded, which ceased publication in 2013. In the 1990s, the journal *Historia y Fuentes Orales* appeared, which in 1995 took on a new title to identify its dedication to the discipline: *Historia, Antropología y Fuentes Orales*.[42]

- In the 1990s, the emergence of Anthropology journals continued. In 1991, it was the *Revista de Antropología Social*,[43] founded by Carmelo Lisón and promoted by the Department of Social Anthropology of the Complutense University of Madrid. In 1992, *Fundamentos de Antropología*,[44] promoted by the *Centro Ángel Ganivet* of the *Diputación Provincial de Granada*, but which disappeared in 2001. A journal closely linked to Anthropology was *Trans, Revista Transcultural de Música*, with a clear ethnomusicological content, which appeared in 1995. And *Ankulegi*, published by the Basque Association of Anthropology in 1997, is the last of the list of magazines published in this decade.

- Finally, this century saw the appearance of academic journals clearly dedicated to Anthropology. In 2001 *Antropología Experimental*, an electronic journal was published by the University of Jaén. In 2003, *Pasos. Revista de Turismo y Patrimonio Cultural* was published by the University of La Laguna. In 2004 *Perifèria. Revista de Recerca i Formació en Antropologia* appeared, which was promoted by the people who carry out research in the doctoral programme in Anthropology at the *Universitat Autònoma de Barcelona*. The journal *(Con)textos: Revista d'Antropologia i Investigació Social* had a similar origin, but in this case the promoter was the University of Barcelona. In 2004, the journal *AIBR* appeared, with the same name as the association that promotes it, *Antropólogos Iberoamericanos en Red*. It is a journal that was created in Spain, with a clear interna-

---

[41] In some cases (the first ten issues), the full text of each article is available. Sánchez Sanz and Gari Lacruz (2002) also made an assessment of the journal shortly before the twentieth anniversary of its first issue.

[42] A history of the journal is also available in Úbeda (2002).

[43] There is a short text on the history of the journal: Sanmartín Arce (2002).

[44] A description of the journal can be found in González Alcantud (2002).

6 CHRONOLOGY OF A DISCIPLINE: SOCIAL AND CULTURAL... 213

tional vocation, by a group of professionals with degrees in Anthropology and not always with academic links. Lastly, in 2011 the *Revista Andaluza de Antropología* was founded, an organ of expression of the *Asociación Andaluza de Antropología* (ASANA).

As can be seen, the development of the discipline in the academic world has run parallel to the appearance of a large number of journals dedicated to Anthropology, and it can be affirmed that these contributed to that development.[45] The simple fact of having such a wide network for the exhibition and dissemination of anthropological work was a step forward for the recognition and enhancement of the discipline (and of what it could be and do) in different spheres. From the 1990s onwards, and returning to the thematic orientations, research into the processes of identification, which was so popular in the 1980s, began to take on a new dimension and new specialisations emerged in the heat of new times, interests and social concerns.

We have since witnessed an unprecedented diversification of fields of study, contexts, units of analysis, research techniques and diverse epistemological and methodological orientations within the discipline.[46] All this internal diversity began to gain strength in 1991, with the reform of the curricula and the creation of the Master's degree in Social and Cultural Anthropology (two years of training). This Master's could be accessed from undergraduate studies with a clear professional orientation such as teaching, nursing or social work, among others.

From this point onwards, the considerable increase in the number of Anthropology graduates was not reflected in the construction of employment niches beyond the academic and research spheres. This, together with the threat of only being placed at the Postgraduate level in the plans

---

[45] We have not included in the list other journals close to the field of Anthropology, but with content clearly dedicated to the study of popular traditions and folklore, which were published on similar dates. These would be *Revista de Folklore*, 1980, *Kalathos. Revista del Seminario de Arqueología y Etnología Turolense*, 1981, and *Aixa. Revista anual la Gabella. Revista biannual del Museu Etnològic del Montseny*, 1987.

[46] Studies on gender, migratory processes, work, heritage, health, development, racism, education, inter-ethnic relations, religion, ecology, food, sexuality, tourism, music, family, drugs, housing, sport, and so on generate specialisations that have become consolidated as "sub-disciplines" or "fields" of reference, present in all study programmes, such as the Anthropology of Gender, Urban Anthropology, the Anthropology of Education or the Anthropology of Health (among others) that share academic space with traditional economic, kinship or political anthropologies.

for university adaptation to the European Higher Education Area, meant that in 2003 several professionals from universities where the Bachelor's degree was already established, organised themselves to work for their own degree model and to demand the consideration of Anthropology as part of the undergraduate degrees in Spain, in addition to working for the professionalisation and visibility of the discipline outside the academy. For this reason, the State Commission of the Degree in Anthropology (CEGA) was created in 2004 as a working group which, among other issues, drew up the proposal for the syllabus for the Degree in Social and Cultural Anthropology[47] which, finally and after an arduous struggle, was included among the university degrees implemented under the so-called Bologna Plan or European Higher Education Area in 2010.[48] Thus, Social and Cultural Anthropology can now be studied in eleven public universities in Spain.[49]

THE WAY FORWARD: THE NECESSARY PROFESSIONALISATION OF ANTHROPOLOGY IN SPAIN

The presence of a university degree programme across a significant part of the country has not resolved the necessary visibility that Anthropology requires in Spanish society. Nor have the studies of Anthropology at the University solved the issue of the professionalisation of the people who study this university degree. In 2007, the Commission for the Professionalisation of Anthropology (CPA) was created in conjunction with the CEGA, with the long-term objective of promoting the creation of a Professional Association of Anthropologists. For various reasons that do not fit into this space, this initiative came to a standstill and the ASAEE is currently promoting this issue. A new working group has been set up to prepare a diagnosis of the profession with experts from different fields of

---

[47] Currently, training in Social and Cultural Anthropology in Spain consists of 240 ECTS Bachelor's degrees (equivalent in 2400 hours), 60, 90 or 120 ECTS Master's degrees and specialised doctoral studies (equivalent in 600, 900 or 1200 hours).

[48] The famous process, popularly known as the *Bologna Process* in Europe, gives rise to the European Higher Education Area.

[49] *Universidad Autónoma de Madrid, Universidad Complutense de Madrid, Universidad de Granada, Universidad de La Laguna, Universidad de Salamanca, Universidad de Sevilla, Universidad de Valladolid, Universidad del País Vasco, Universidad Nacional de Educación a Distancia, Universitat Autònoma de Barcelona, Universitat de Barcelona* and *Universitat Rovira y Virgili.*

Anthropology (companies, universities, research organisations, etc.). The idea is to rethink strategies to make the discipline more visible in society and in the workplace. All this is due to the possibilities of the moment, as the discipline in Spain is situated in a context of unprecedented opportunities.

The stability of associative networks, public investment in research (which can always be improved, but in which Anthropology has a place) and the presence of undergraduate and postgraduate studies with a considerable demand in Spain, is already a fact. The skills acquired by graduates in these studies are of great value for work in social fields related to the management of cultural diversity (in educational centres, neighbourhoods, associations, etc.), cultural heritage and museums, territorial development, development cooperation, teaching and research, consultancy work, human resources, advertising, health, finance, and so on. Today, more than ever, with the production of information and data at unprecedented levels, constant geopolitical tensions and the development of new ways of relating and communicating, society requires the holistic and transcultural view that the anthropological discipline provides.

We must ensure that all the above is made evident to society as a whole. From within the academic spheres, we must commit ourselves to the renovation of university curricula, orienting them towards these new workplaces in order to make effective this insertion and connection of Anthropology with emerging social phenomena. The already existing subjects that advocate a look towards applied Anthropology and the professionalisation of the discipline (Gregorio, 2021), as well as the inclusion of curricular practices in the syllabus (Soto, 2021), are currently specific experiences that, in our opinion, should be replicated in all universities in Spain that offer a degree in Social and Cultural Anthropology.

Linking the necessary connection with the labour spheres from the training logic itself, and even committing to a corporate strategy—from which we can claim consolidated employment spaces, guarantees minimum ethical standards in our practices, and so on,—such as the creation and consolidation of a professional association, could clear horizons for the discipline at this time. This is a struggle taking place both internally (as there are still colleagues in the profession who do not clearly perceive the applicability of the discipline) and externally (where we are still confused with other disciplines such as Archaeology or Sociology, where we do not have a clearly defined and identified professional niche, and where, often, not even the public administrations themselves take into account the profiles of Anthropology when offering public jobs).

Those of us who dedicate ourselves professionally to Anthropology are fully aware of how complex our task is. However, on the basis that "the strength of any disciplinary field depends fundamentally on the contribution it can make to the society in which it finds itself" (Moya, 2021, p. 221), we wish to end this chapter by inviting colleagues of all origins to continue working to make Anthropology more socially visible, to increase its presence in the media, in virtual spaces, in different social and political scenarios which can show the value that Anthropology contributes to societies, so that the (re)knowledge of our profession becomes a fact. We propose, along the lines of the European Association of Social Anthropologists (EASA) applied Anthropology network, that we should commit ourselves to multiplying actions to ensure visibility of Anthropology and enhancement of its value. These should be strategic lines of action for university departments, research groups and different workplaces, because the world does need anthropological knowledge.

REFERENCES

AA.VV (Ed.). (1980a). *Actas del I Congreso Español de Antropología. Volumen I*. Universidad de Barcelona.

AA.VV (Ed.). (1980b). *Actas del I Congreso Español de Antropología. Volumen II*. Universidad de Barcelona.

AA.VV (Ed.). (1985). *Actas del 2º Congreso de Antropología*. Ministerio de Cultura.

Agudo Sanchíz, A., & Cantón Delgado, M. (2016). *Perspectivas antropológicas transculturales: Latinoamérica y Andalucía. Ensayos en homenaje a Pilar Sanchíz Ochoa*. Dharana.

Aguilar Criado, E. (1989). Los primeros estudios sobre la cultura popular en Andalucía. *Revista de Estudios Andaluces, 13*, 21–44.

Aguilar Criado, E. (1992).Treinta años de antropología andaluza (1960–1990). *Anales de la Fundación Joaquín Costa, 9*, 83–100.

Aguilar Criado, E. (1993). Del folklore a la antropología en Andalucía: 1881–1993. Balance de un siglo de continuidades y discontinuidades. *El Folklore Andaluz, 10*, 91–118.

Aguilar Criado, E. (Ed.). (1996). *De la construcción de la historia a la práctica de la Antropología en España. Actas del I Simposio del VII Congreso de Antropología Social*. Instituto Aragonés de Antropología y Federación de Asociaciones de Antropología del Estado Español.

6 CHRONOLOGY OF A DISCIPLINE: SOCIAL AND CULTURAL... 217

Aguilar Criado, E., Feixa, C., & Melis, A. (2000). Tradiciones y escenarios actuales de la antropología en España. *Nueva Antropología. Revista de Ciencias Sociales, 58*, 101–112.

Alcañiz, B. (1994). Ethnica. Revista de Antropología. In C. O. García & L. Á. S. Gómez (Eds.), *Diccionario histórico de la Antropología española* (pp. 281–283). CSIC.

Andreu Tomás, A., Bodoque Puertas, Y., Comas d'Argemir, D., Pujadas Muñoz, J., Roca Girona, J., & Soronelles Masdeu, M. (2014). *Periferias, fronteras y diálogos. Una lectura antropológica de los retos de la sociedad actual. Actas del XIII Congreso de la FAAEE.* Universitat Rovira i Virgili.

Anta Félez, J. L. (2005). La Antropología Social española en los 80 como paradigma tardomoderno. *Revista de Dialectología y Tradiciones Populares, 60*(2), 5–27.

Aranzadi, T. de, & de Hoyos, L. (1917). *Etnografía: Sus bases, sus métodos y su aplicación en España.* Biblioteca Corona.

Bachelard, G. (1951). *L'actualité de l'histoire des sciences.* Ed. Du Palais de la Descouverte.

Barth, F. (1969). *Ethnic Groups and Boundaries: The Social Organization of Culture Difference.* Little Brown & Co.

Bestard, J., & Contreras, J. (1987). *Bárbaros, paganos, salvajes y primitivos: Una introducción a la Antropología.* Barcanova.

Bodoque Puerta, Y. (2002). La revista Arxiu d'Etnografia de Catalunya: una retrospectiva. *Revista de Dialectología y Tradiciones Populares, LVII*(1), 139–152.

Bouza Vila, J. (2001). Bibliografía para una historia de la Antropología en Cataluña. *Biblio 3W. Revista Bibliográfica de Geografía y Ciencias Sociales, VI*(321). https://www.ub.edu/geocrit/b3w-321.htm

Brufau, J., Permanyer, M., & Zulet, X. (2011). El trabajo de un antropólogo termina en el momento en que este es como el otro. Entrevista a Claudi Esteva Fabregat. Perifèria. *Revista de Recerca i Investigació en Antropologia, 14*, 1–32.

Bustamante, J. (2005). La institucionalización de las ciencias antropológicas en las nuevas naciones y el papel de los museos. *Revista de Indias, LXV*(234), 303–318.

Cabello Carro, P. (2004). José Alcina Franch. Esbozo Biográfico de Un Americanista. *Anales Del Museo de América, 12*, 309–324.

Calvo Calvo, L. (1997). África y la Antropología española: La aportación del Instituto de Estudios Africanos. *Revista de Dialectología y Tradiciones Populares, 52*(2), 169–185.

Calvo Calvo, L. (2002). Éthnica. Revista de Antropología y su significación histórica para la Antropología en España. *Revista de Dialectología y Tradiciones Populares, 57*(1), 71–81.

Calvo Calvo, L. (2012). La Antropología y la construcción del "área cultural mediterránea". In J. Contreras, J. J. Pujadas, & J. Roca (Eds.), *Pels camins de l'etnografia: Un homenatge a Joan Prat* (pp. 141–149). Editorial Universitat Rovira i Virgili.

218 M. RUBIO GÓMEZ ET AL.

Capel, H. (2009). La antropología española y el magisterio de Claudio Esteva Fabregat. Estrategias institucionales y desarrollo intelectual en las disciplinas científicas. *Scripta Nova. Revista Electrónica de Geografía y Ciencias sociales, XIII* (287). https://www.ub.edu/geocrit/sn/sn-287.htm

Carrera Vérez, A., Cid Martínez, J. A., Gutiérrez Esteve, M., & Rubio Hernández, R. (Eds.). (1978). *Homenaje a Julio Caro Baroja*. Centro de Investigaciones Sociológicas.

Carretero Pérez, A. (1994). Anales del Museo del Pueblo Español. In C. O. García & L. Á. S. Gómez (Eds.), *Diccionario histórico de la Antropología española* (pp. 281–283). CSIC.

Casado, C. (1991). La Revista de Dialectología y Tradiciones Populares. In C. Amiel, J. P. Piniès, & R. Piniès (Eds.), *Au miroir des revues. Ethnologie de L'Europe du Sud* (pp. 103–107). Garae-Hesiode.

Cátedra, M. (1991). *Los españoles vistos por los antropólogos*. Júcar.

Cátedra, M., & Devillard, M. J. (Eds.). (2014). *Saberes culturales. Homenaje a José Luis García García*. Bellaterra.

Comelles, J. M., & Prat, J. (1992). El estado de las antropologías. Antropologías, folclores y nacionalismos en el Estado español. *Antropología. Revista de Pensamiento Antropológico y Estudios Etnográficos, 3*, 35–61.

Consejo de Redacción de Quaderns. (2002). Reflexiones en torno a la Revista Quaderns del Institut Cátala d'Antropología. *Revista de Dialectología y Tradiciones Populares, LVII*(1), 109–120.

Contreras Hernández, J., Pujadas Muñoz, J., & Roca Girona, J. (Eds.). (2012). *Pels camins de l'etnografia: un homenatge a Joan Prat*. Editorial Universitat Rovira i Virgili.

Couceiro Domínguez, E., & Gómez Pellón, E. (2012). *Sitios de la Antropología: patrimonio, lenguaje y etnicidad. Textos en homenaje a José Antonio Fernández de Rota*. Universidade da Coruña.

De Madariaga, C., & Checa Olmos, F. (2012). Treinta años de antropología en España. Memoria desde la Gazeta. *Gazeta de Antropología, 28*(3).

Del Pino Díaz, F. (1975). Los cronistas de las culturas indígenas de América: su valor antropológico. In A. J. Núñez (Ed.), *Primera reunión de antropólogos españoles* (pp. 107–125). Universidad de Sevilla.

Del Pino Díaz, F. (1994a). Por una historia antropológica de la Antropología. In R. S. Arce (Ed.), *Antropología sin fronteras: ensayos en honor a Carmelo Lisón* (pp. 561–578). Centro de Investigaciones Sociológicas.

Del Pino Díaz, F. (1994b). Antropología e Historia. Por un diálogo interdisciplinar. *Revista de Dialectología y Tradiciones Populares, XLIX*(2), 570.

Del Pino Díaz, F. (2013). Un doble homenaje colectivo al amigo Joan Prat i Carós. *Arxiu d'Etnografia de Catalunya, 13*, 285.

Devillard, M. J. (2020). José Luis García García (1941–2020). Un antropólogo social excepcional y un humanista convencido. *Revista de Antropología Social, 29*(2), 115–123.

6 CHRONOLOGY OF A DISCIPLINE: SOCIAL AND CULTURAL... 219

Domínguez Gregorio, I. (2018). *Historia de la antropología americanista española (1892–1992)*. Universidad Complutense de Madrid.

Esteva Fabregat, C. (1969). La etnología española y sus problemas. *In Actas del I Congreso Nacional de Artes y Costumbres Populares*, 1968. (pp. 1–40) Institución Fernando el Católico.

Esteva Fabregat, C. (1984a). Antecedentes y propósito. *Ethnica, 1,* 7–11.

Esteva Fabregat, C. (1984b). Final de etapa. *Ethnica, 20,* 3–5.

Anta Félez, J. L. (2007). *Segmenta antropológica. Un debate crítico con la antropología social española*. Universidad de Granada.

Fernández Álvarez, O., & Díaz de Viana, L. (Eds.). (2020). *La discreción del antropólogo. La Antropología entre León y Tabarca: Homenaje al profesor José Luis González Arpide*. Universidad de León.

Fernández de Rota, J. A. (Ed.). (1996). *Las diferentes caras de España. Perspectivas de antropólogos extranjeros y españoles*. Universidade da Coruña.

Ferrándiz, F. J., Flores, J. A., García, M., López, J., & Pitarch, P. (Eds.). (2015). *Manuel Gutierrez Estévez. Maestro de etnógrafos (americanistas)*. Iberoamericana.

Frigolé, J. (1975). Algunas consideraciones sobre las unidades de análisis cultural. In A. Jiménez (Ed.), *Primera reunión de antropólogos españoles: actas, comunicaciones, documentación* (pp. 231–352). Universidad de Sevilla.

Frigolé, J., Narotzky, S., Contreras, J., Comes, P., & Prat, J. (1983). *Antropología, hoy. Una introducción a la antropología cultural*. Teide.

Galera Gómez, A., Puig-Samper Mulero, M. A., & Pelayo López, F. (1984). *El Darwinismo en la Sociedad Antropológica Española*. Actas II Congreso de La Sociedad Española de Historia de Las Ciencias: Jaca, 27 de Septiembre–1 de Octubre, 1982, 389–402.

Garralda Benajes, M. D. (2010). Historia de La Sociedad Española de Antropología Física. *Revista Española de Antropología Física, 31,* 67–70.

Gilmore, D. D. (1982). Anthropology of the Mediterranean Area. *Annual Review of Anthropology, 11,* 175–205.

Gómez García, P. (2000). Un siglo de cultura popular en Andalucía. *Demófilo: Revista de Cultura Tradicional, 33–34,* 11–29.

Gómez-Pellón, E. (2017). Trials, Emergence & Consolidation of Social & Cultural Anthropology in Spain. *Anthropos, 112*(1), 1–15.

González Alcantud, J. A. (2002). Fundamentos de Antropología: La antropología en sus fundamentos. *Revista de Dialectología y Tradiciones Populares, LVII*(1), 247–258.

González Echevarría, A., & Molina González, J. L. (Eds.). (2002). *Abriendo surcos en la tierra. Investigación básica y aplicada en la UAB. Homenaje a Ramón Valdés*. Universitat Autònoma de Barcelona.

González Montero de Espinosa, M. D. (1996). Orígenes de la antropología en España. *Asclepio, XLVIII*(1), 37–57.

220   M. RUBIO GÓMEZ ET AL.

Gouldner, A. W. (1973). Romanticism and Classicism: Deep Structures in Social Science. *Diogenes, 21*(82), 88–107.

Gregorio Gil, C. (2021). Formar para la práctica profesional de la antropología social, cuando el "futuro no se ve". In M. Moya & M. Rúa (Eds.), *El aprendizaje de la "práctica en la Universidad"* (pp. 159–186). Facultad de Filosofía y Letras.

Hallowell, A. I. (1974). A History of Anthropology as an Anthropological Problem. In R. Darnell (Ed.), *Readings in the History of Anthropology* (pp. 304–321). Harper & Row.

Harris, M. (1979) [1968]. *El desarrollo de la teoría antropológica: Historia de las teorías de la cultura*. Siglo XXI.

Henríquez Sánchez, M., & Clavijo Redondo, M. A. (2015). Acerca del mundo. Homenaje al profesor Fernando Estévez González. *Revista Tabona, 21*, 105–115.

Jiménez de Madariaga, C., & Checa Olmos, F. (2012). Treinta Años de Antropología En España. Memoria Desde La Gazeta. *Gazeta de Antropología, 28*(3).

Jiménez Núñez, A. (Ed.). (1975). *Primera reunión de antropólogos españoles*. Universidad de Sevilla.

Lévi Strauss, C. (1970). *Antropología estructural* (2nd ed.). Eudeba.

Lisón Tolosana, C. (1975). Panorama programático de la antropología social en España. In A. Jiménez (Ed.), *Primera reunión de antropólogos españoles: actas, comunicaciones, documentación* (pp. 149–162). Universidad de Sevilla.

Llobera, J. R. (1976). The History of Anthropology as a Problem. *Critique of Anthropology, 2*(7), 17–42.

Llobera, J. R. (1990). *La identidad de la antropología*. Anagrama.

Lowie, R. H. (1937). *History of Ethnological Theory*. Holt, Rinehart & Winston of Canada Ltd.

Mármol, C. d., Roigé, X., Bestard, J., & Contreras, J. (Eds.). (2016). *Compromisos etnográficos. Un homenaje a Joan Frigolé (Vol. 148)*. Universitat de Barcelona.

Martínez Veiga, U. (2010). *Historia de la antropología. Formaciones socioeconómicas y praxis antropológicas, teoría e ideologías*. Universidad Nacional de Educación a Distancia.

Medeiros, A. (2019). Los caminos de William Christian. *Arxiu d'Etnografia de Catalunya, 20*, 253–289.

Moreno, I. (1972). El trabajo de campo etnológico en España y el problema de elección de comunidad. *Ethnica, 3*, 165–182.

Moreno, I. (1975). La investigación antropológica en España. In A. Jiménez (Ed.), *Primera reunión de antropólogos españoles: actas, comunicaciones, documentación* (pp. 325–338). Universidad de Sevilla.

6 CHRONOLOGY OF A DISCIPLINE: SOCIAL AND CULTURAL... 221

Moreno Navarro, I. (2019). Claudio Esteva y la institucionalización de la Antropología en el Estado Español. *Arxiu d'Etnografia de Catalunya, 19*, 131–146.

Moya, M. (2021). La enseñanza de la práctica profesional en la carrera de Antropología. In M. Moya & M. Rúa (Eds.), *El aprendizaje de la "práctica en la Universidad"* (pp. 187–218). Facultad de Filosofía y Letras.

Müllauer-Seichter, M. (2016). *Claves en los inicios de la Antropología Social y Cultural Española. Temas y Autores.* Centro de Estudios Ramón Aceres: Madrid.

Narotzky, S. (2011). Las antropologías hegemónicas y las antropologías del sur: el caso de España. *Revista Andaluza de Antropología y Arqueología, 11*, 26–40.

Oliver Narbona, M. (Ed.). (1987). *Actas del IV Congreso de Antropología.* Universidad de Alicante.

Ortiz García, C. (1984). La Obra Antropológica de Don Luis de Hoyos Sainz. *Actas de las 2as Jornadas de Etnología de Castilla La Mancha,* 17–32. https://digital.csic.es/handle/10261/13161

Ortiz García, C. (1987). *Luis de Hoyos Sainz y la antropología española.* CSIC.

Ortiz García, C. (1994). Revista de Dialectología y Tradiciones Populares. In C. O. García & L. A. S. Gómez (Eds.), *Diccionario histórico de la Antropología española* (pp. 581–584). CSIC.

Ortiz García, C. (1996). Julio Caro Baroja, antropólogo e historiador social. *Revista de dialectología y tradiciones populares, 51*(1), 283–302.

Ortiz García, C. (2001). De los cráneos a las piedras: arqueología y antropolfogía en España, 1874–1977. *Complutum, 12*, 273–292.

Ortiz García, C. (2004). Antropología en España. *Anuario de Centro de Estudios Superiores de México y Centroamérica, 2003*, 13–24. https://repositorio.cesmeca.mx/handle/11595/341?show=full

Ortiz García, C., & Sánchez Gómez, L. Á. (Eds.). (1994). *Diccionario Historico de La Antropología Española.* Consejo Superior de Investigaciones Científicas.

Otero Carvajal, L. (2014). *La universdad nacionalcatólica. La reacción antimoderna.* Dykinson.

Otero Carvajal, L. (2017). *La ciencia en España, 1814–2015. Exilios, retornos, recortes.* Catarata.

Palenzuela Chamorro, P. (Ed.). (2017). *Antropología y compromiso. Homenaje al profesor Isidoro Moreno.* Universidad de Sevilla/Icaria.

Pérez Carretero, A. (2002). Anales del Museo del Pueblo Español y Anales del Museo Nacional de Antropología. Aproximación bibliométrica. *Revista de Dialectología y Tradiciones Populares, LVII*(1), 207–218.

Peristiany, J. G. (Ed.). (1965). *Honour and Shame: The Values of Mediterranean Society.* Weidenfeld and Nicolson.

Peristiany, J. G., & Pitt-Rivers, J. A. (2005) [1992]. *Honor and Grace in Anthropology.* Cambridge University Press.

Pitt-Rivers, J. (1954). *The People of the Sierra.* Weidenfeld and Nicholson.

222 M. RUBIO GÓMEZ ET AL.

Prat, J. (1983). L'antropologia cultural a Espanya. In Frigolé, J., Narotzky, S., Contreras, J., Comes, P., & Prat, J. (Eds.), *Antropolgia d'avui: Una introducció a l'antropologia cultural* (pp. 161–229). Teide.

Prat, J. (1991). Reflexiones sobre los nuevos objetos de estudio en la antropología social española. In M. Cátedra (Ed.), *Los españoles vistos por los antropólogos* (pp. 45–68). Júcar.

Prat, J. (Ed.). (1999). *Investigaciones e investigados: Literatura antropológica en España desde 1954.* Institut Tarragones d'Antropologia. Edición especial de Arxiu d'Etnografia de Catalunya.

Prat, J. (2012). A Ramón Valdés, In Memoriam. *Perifèria. Revista de Recerca i Formació En Antropologica, 16,* 1–7.

Prat, J., & Martínez, Á. (1996). *Ensayos de antropología cultural. Homenaje a Claudio Esteva-Fabregat.* Ariel.

Prat, J., Moreno, I., Martínez, U., & Contreras, J. (1992). *Antropología de los pueblos de España.* Taurus.

Pujadas, J. J. (2017). La antropología catalana y el exilio republicano español en México. *Disparidades. Revista De Antropología, 72*(2), 423–455.

Pujol i Sanmartín, J. M. (1999). Introducció a Una Història Dels Folklores. In I. Roviró & J. Monserrat (Eds.), *La Cultura* (pp. 77–106). Universitat de Barcelona.

Rivera Dorado, M. (Ed.). (1977). *Antropología de España y América.* Dosde.

Rivera Dorado, M. (Ed.). (1978). *Perspectivas de la Antropología española.* Akal.

Rodríguez Becerra, S. (2018). Mis recuerdos de Don Claudio Esteva. *Arxiu d'etnografia de Catalunya, 19,* 155–172.

Rodríguez, S., & Medina, M. D. C. (2002). La Revista Demófilo y la Antropología Cultural en Andalucía. *Revista de Dialectología y Tradiciones Populares, 57*(1), 163–194.

Roigé Ventura, X. (2019). El Etnólogo como conservador de Museo. Esteva y los Museos de Antropología. *Arxiu d'Etnografia de Catalunya, 19,* 281–290.

Romero Tejada, P. (1975). La antropología y los museos. In A. J. Núñez (Ed.), *Primera reunión de antropólogos españoles* (pp. 339–347). Universidad de Sevilla.

Sánchez Gómez, L. A. (1986). La antropología española del último tercio del siglo XIX a través de las revistas culturales de la época. *Revista de dialectología y tradiciones populares, 41,* 211–236.

Sánchez Gómez, L. Á. (1990). La Sociedad Española de Antropología, Etnografía y Prehistoria (1921–1951). *Disparidades. Revista de Antropología, 45*(1), 61–87.

Sánchez Gómez, L. Á. (1992). La antropología al servicio del Estado: El Instituto «Bernardino de Sahagún» del CSIC (1941–1970). *Disparidades. Revista De Antropología, 47*(1), 29–44.

Sánchez Molina, R. (2014). Superando el "carácter nacional": La antropología ante los retos de la globalización. *Antropología Experimental, 12,* 23–42.

Sánchez Montañés, E., & Iglesias Ponce de León, M. J. (2002). La Visión Del Otro. Breve Historia de La Revista Española de Antropología Americana. *Revista de Dialectología y Tradiciones Populares, 57*(1), 59–70.

Sánchez Gómez, L. Á. (1997). Cien años de antropologías en España y Portugal (1870–1970). Etnográfica. *Revista do Centro de Estudos de Antropologia social, 2*, 297–317.

Sánchez Gómez, L. Á. (1997). Cien años de antropologías en España y Portugal (1870–1970). *Etnográfica. Revista do Centro de Estudos de Antropologia social, 2*, 297–317.

Sanmartín Arce, R. (2002). Una historia para la creación antropológica contemporánea. La Revista de Antropología Social. *Revista de Dialectología y Tradiciones Populares, LVII*(1), 235–246.

Sanmartín Arce, R. (2020). Carmelo Lisón Tolosana. Una vocación antropológica. *Revista de. Antropología Social, 29*(2), 103–113.

Solana Ruiz, J. L. (2002). La Gazeta de Antropología: de la precariedad local al ciberespacio global. *Revista de Dialectología y Tradiciones Populares, LVII*(1), 129–138.

Soto Marata, P. (2021). Aprender colaborando. In M. Moya & M. Rúa (Eds.), *El aprendizaje de la "práctica en la Universidad"* (pp. 187–218). Facultad de Filosofía y Letras.

Stocking, G. W. (1968). *Race, Culture and Evolution: Essays in the History of Anthropology.* The University of Chicago Press.

Stocking, G. W. (2002). Delimitando la antropología: reflexiones históricas acerca de las fronteras de una disciplina sin fronteras. *Revista de Antropología Social, 11*, 11–38.

Stolcke, V. (2008). De padres, filiaciones y malas memorias. *Revista Pós Ciências Sociais, 5*(9–10), 11–62.

Tomas Cardoso, R. (2012). Notas sobre la Historia de la Antropología Física en España: Diálogos entre Antropología, Prehistoria y Arqueología en las distintas fases de formación de la Antropología Física Española. *ArqueoUCA: Revista Digital Científica Independiente de Arqueología, 2*, 125–138.

Tomé Martín, P., Valdés Gázquez, M., & Álvarez Plata, C. (Eds.). (2021). *Símbolos en la ciudad, símbolos de la ciudad. Ensayo en homenaje a María Cátedra.* Tirant Humanidades.

Úbeda, L. (2002). Historia, Antropología y Fuentes Orales. *Revista de Dialectología y Tradiciones Popu La historiografía de la antropología como historia: entre la pluralidad y ortodoxia extremas. Iztapalapalares, LVII*(1), 219–223.

Vázquez León, L. (2016). *Revista de Ciencias Sociales y Humanidades, 81*, 9–39.

Velasco Maillo, H. (1989). El umbral de lo obvio. Notas a propósito de la traducción al castellano de "The People of the Sierra". *Folk-lore andaluz, 3*, 51–58.

Velasco Maíllo, H. (2014). Las aportaciones de Julio Caro Baroja en tiempos de una antropología no institucionalizada en España. *Cuadernos de Etnología y Etnografía de Navarra, XLVI–XLVII*(89), 151–176.

Velasco Maíllo, H. (2020). Para Carmelo Lísón Tolosana. In H. Velasco (Ed.), *Maestro Lisón: conversaciones, reflexiones y ensayos como celebración en sus 90 años y más* (pp. 11–17). Fundación Lisón Donald.

Velasco Maillo, H. & Caro, C., (Eds.) (2015). *De Julian a Julio y de Julio a Julian. Correspondencia entre Julio Caro Baroja y Julian Pitt-Rivers (1949–1991).* CSIC

Velasco Maíllo, H., & Lisón, C. (1995). In memoriam: Julio Caro Baroja. *Agricultura y sociedad, 75,* 13–23.

Vicente Rabanaque, T., García Hernandorena, M. J., & Vizcaíno Estevan, A. (Eds.). (2017). *Antropología en transformación: sentidos, compromisos y utopías: Actas del XIV Congreso de Antropología.* Universitat de Valéncia.

Vila Vilar, E. (2019). Alfredo Jiménez Núñez: In Memoriam. *Minervae Baeticae. Boletín de La Real Academia Sevillana de Buenas Letras, 47,* 267–270.

CHAPTER 7

From the Regime Ethnologists to the Democratic Generation: Histories of Portuguese Anthropology

Giacomo Pozzi and Chiara Pussetti

ANTHROPOLOGIES IN PORTUGAL: POINTS OF CONTACT AND TRANSITION[1]

Ephemeral soprano voices—sampled and arranged by Philip Glass—floated in the balmy air of a late Portuguese summer in the courtyard of the Ethnographic Museum in Coimbra during the opening of the first

---

[1] This chapter is the result of a joint process of reflection between the two authors. However, sections can be divided as follows: Giacomo Pozzi—"Anthropologies in Portugal: Points of Contact and Transition"; "Building a Different Country, Imagining a Different Anthropology"; "Conclusion". Chiara Pussetti—"National Identity, Regime Ethnologists and Jorge Dias: From the End of the Nineteenth Century to the Fall of the Estado Novo"; "The Democratic Generation and Anthropologies of the Contemporary". We would also like to thank the editors of this volume, Gabriella D'Agostino and Vincenzo Matera, Miguel Vale de Almeida and João de Pina Cabral, for their precious comments. Where not otherwise stated, translations of extracts into English and Portuguese are by the authors.

G. Pozzi (✉)
Department of Humanities, IULM University, Milan, Italy
e-mail: giacomo.pozzi@iulm.it

© The Author(s), under exclusive license to Springer Nature
Switzerland AG 2023
G. D'Agostino, V. Matera (eds.), *Histories of Anthropology*,
https://doi.org/10.1007/978-3-031-21258-1_7

Congress of the European Association of Social Anthropologists (EASA), taking place between 31 August and 3 September 1990 (Eriksen, 1991, pp. 75–76). Approximately 450 anthropologists from all over Europe came together in response to the invitation launched by a small group of 19 anthropologists. They discussed Europe (the title of the congress was "Anthropology and Europe"), anthropological theory and the future of the discipline in the lecture halls of a university that was celebrating its 700th anniversary at the time. Three decades later, in a sunny July in Lisbon, the 16th EASA Congress was held: in this case, the sounds that surrounded the participants were those of computer keyboards, digital platforms and intermittent internet connections. In a Europe sadly devastated by the COVID-19 epidemic, the 30th anniversary celebration of the Association's first Congress took place entirely online. By 2020, the number of participants had grown to around 1900, but the central topic of discussion remained the same: dialogue within and beyond Europe, inspired by the motto "New anthropological horizons in and beyond Europe".

Portugal is considered a marginal country in relation to the larger European area. This is due in part to the small size of its national territory (just over 92,000 km^2, less than one-fifth of neighbouring Spain) and small population (10.28 million people). Socially, economically and politically, but also culturally, the Portuguese-speaking country belongs to Southern Europe and the even smaller circle of Mediterranean countries (Portugal, Italy, Greece and Spain, a grouping economic journalists refer to as P.I.G.S. without much irony—or at least with an irony that is largely misunderstood). As a member of P.I.G.S., the country has long been considered less than virtuous and tending to financial mismanagement. Like its Mediterranean peers, Portugal's public finances are precarious, its economic competitiveness is low, its government bond yields are minimal and its productivity is limited, all of which result in a reduced ability to repay public debt. However, in recent years—or at least until the crisis caused by the COVID-19 pandemic—the country has been able to deconstruct this image of being located at the bottom of the European ladder thanks mainly to the income generated by tourism along with a few other sectors.

C. Pussetti
University of Lisbon, Lisbon, Portugal
e-mail: chiara.pussetti@ics.ulisboa.pt

It has demonstrated—albeit admittedly in a way that has drawn some criticism—that it is possible to throw off the yoke of economic crisis and the even more violent and ferocious yoke of the "cure" imposed by Troika.[2]

There are historical causes for all of this. In general, and very briefly, the events characterising Portugal's history are inextricably linked to its particular geographical position. With its approximately 800 km of coasts facing the Atlantic Ocean, the country represents the extreme Western offshoot of the Old World. It is a strip of land with its gaze turned always towards the sea, a position that has made it a seafaring nation par excellence thanks in part to two strategic outposts in the Atlantic: the archipelagos of the Azores, Madeira and Cape Verde. Portugal represents one of the oldest political organisations in Europe and has maintained roughly the same borders since the thirteenth century. In this sense, the country has maintained an enviable and unusual stability over the centuries due to its relations with the rest of Europe. The vast Spanish territory represents a presence against which Portugal has always had to be on guard, due to the risk of absorption, and for a long time Spain acted less as a bridge and more as a wall dividing Portugal from the rest of Europe. This is part of what makes its history so unique as compared to the other European powers. This uniqueness is most evident in the role that the ocean has played in the construction of the world of Portuguese influence: rather than entertaining relations with other European nations, the country has preferred to surf the waves. This allowed it not only to build one of the greatest empires of the modern era (and the last to fall), but also to develop—in almost total isolation from the rest of Europe—its economy, politics and "culture", in relation to the ocean. The isolation resulting from its Atlantic and imperial vocation had as an extreme consequence the establishment of a fascist dictatorial regime that lasted half a century, a regime that played on the country's history of separateness to further isolate it and anchor it to political, social and economic positions that distanced it from the rest of Europe. It was not until the mid-1970s with the African wars of liberation, ensuing national independence and the fall of the centuries-old Lusophone empire that the socio-political transformations took place

---

[2] From the Russian word *тройка*, ("trio"), in the framework of European Union policy Troika represents the set of official creditors who act during negotiations with the various member countries. It consists of representatives of the European Commission, the European Central Bank and the International Monetary Fund.

leading first to the European Economic Community (EEC) and then the European Union.

It was in the country marked by all these vicissitudes, however, that European anthropology decided thirty years ago to begin to think of and construct itself as such: in a certain sense, to use a de Martinian myth, Portugal was the first place chosen to plant the *kauwa-auwa* pole (i.e. the EASA Congress) of the old world anthropologists (the Achilpas) in order to redeem the European branch of the discipline from an epistemological and geographical distress that threatened to undermine its possibilities for existence. In this sense, returning recently to the same spaces where the myth was first created has meant renewing a founding act carried out in the past, the celebration of a restless trajectory that, thanks to the pole, nevertheless manages to remain connected to the "centre".

The eccentricity and marginality of Portuguese history, including the history of the discipline, has undoubtedly played a paradigmatic role in this trajectory. As the feminist writer bell hooks repeatedly reminded us, "[M]arginality is a place of radical possibility [...]. A place capable of offering us the possibility of a radical perspective from which to look, create, imagine alternatives and new worlds" (bell hooks, 1998, p. 68). Can Portugal adequately represent this place? In a way, the nineteen founders of European anthropology believed it could.

In 1990, Portuguese anthropology was experiencing a moment of particular vitality in what are known as the "years of internationalization" (Bastos, 2014; Pina-Cabral, 1989, 1991). The generation of anthropologists trained in the first-degree courses after 25 April 1974—the year of the famous Carnation Revolution (*Revolução dos Cravos*) that brought down the pro-fascist dictatorship, one of the last great European dictatorships to persist after the Second World War—became responsible for the new anthropology courses. Many had completed their training abroad, returning to Portugal in the 1990s with a wealth of knowledge and experience acquired over the course of long periods spent in English or American departments and research centres. In an interview we conducted with him, Miguel Vale de Almeida uses the term "democratic generation" to define the anthropologists who emerged after 25 April, bringing with them baggage accumulated elsewhere. A dynamic and international panorama was created in those years, a landscape Vale de Almeida defines as "peripheral or marginal cosmopolitanism". This effervescence effectively represented the restlessness and prolificacy of European anthropology at the time: a discipline that was attempting to redefine its ethical, methodological, theoretical and epistemological premises from a post-modern perspective and in a context of increasing mobility.

Although it now operates in a different framework, this dynamism has not been lost: Portugal today represents a politically progressive vanguard in Europe and, notwithstanding its limits and issues, from the point of view of anthropology it acts as a reservoir of experimentation, exchange and contact growing out of a patchwork of "histories", traditions and schools of thought.

The "histories", traditions and schools of thought comprising Portuguese anthropology have been recounted by several authors, from different perspectives and with distinct narratives. Jorge Dias provides an initial summary of these accounts in *Bosquejo*, going back as far as the sixteenth century with its transoceanic voyages and related chronicles (Dias, 1952). Veiga de Oliveira has devoted a great deal of energy to restoring—often partially—the life of the research centres (and their researchers) created by Jorge Dias himself (Oliveira, 1968, 1984). Between the end of the 1980s and the beginning of the 1990s, João de Pina Cabral (Pina-Cabral, 1989) outlined the main stages in the history of Portuguese anthropology. Pina Cabral likewise began his account at the end of the nineteenth century, and therefore inevitably with the figure of Jorge Dias, and went on to discuss the historical, epistemological, methodological and theoretical current surfacing in the discipline until its "rebirth" at the end of the 1980s (Pina-Cabral, 1991).

If we had to identify a single person who has contributed the most to the study of the history of anthropology in Portugal, it would undoubtedly be João Leal. Investigating the period between 1870 and 1970, Leal has focused on popular culture, its impact in the construction of national identity and the social, political and cultural landscape of the periods in which the discipline took hold (Leal, 2000, 2006).

Another point of reference for our reflections here is the work of José Sobral. Sobral recently devoted an essay to the figure of Jorge Dias, significantly titled *O outro aqui tão próximo* ("The Other Here So Close"). Sobral analyses Dias's role in the history of Portuguese anthropology by linking his studies on rural communities with "construction of empire" perspectives and the research that Dias carried out among the Macondes in Mozambique, together with his wife Margot Dias, at the end of the 1950s (Sobral, 2007).

More than twenty years after his first historical overview, Pina Cabral has returned to reflect, together with Susana Matos Viegas, on anthropology's relationship during the nineteenth and twentieth centuries, with the two main poles of the broader political axis that determined the construction of the Portuguese state: the pole of the nation and that of the empire. This analysis of what the two authors have called *A encruzilhada portuguesa* ("The Portuguese Crossroads") (Viegas & Pina-Cabral, 2014, p. 316) reaches up to the present day, providing a broad overview of the consolidation of research and university teaching in anthropology. This text is part of a wider series of reflections—some offering accounts of lived experiences, others historical-analytical in character—written by thirty anthropologists who participated in 2012 in the Congress organised by Marina Pignatelli (Pignatelli, 2014) celebrating the 50th anniversary of the creation of the Centre for the Study of Cultural Anthropology (*Centro de Estudos de Antropologia Cultural* - CEAC).

In 2018, the above-mentioned José Sobral co-wrote with Cristiana Bastos a timely and effective entry for the *International Encyclopedia of Anthropology* (Bastos & Sobral, 2018) dedicated to the anthropology of Portugal. The two scholars highlight in particular how it was only after the 1974 revolution that Portuguese anthropology began to flourish and become consolidated, thanks to a renewed climate of the kind of intellectual freedom essential for the development of critical thinking.

A year later, following the interpretative line proposed by Bastos and Sobral, Paula Godinho published her own reading of the history of Portuguese anthropology between 25 April 1974 and 2018. While acknowledging the importance of the studies carried out between the end of the nineteenth and the beginning of the twentieth century and particularly those linked to the "School of Jorge Dias", Godinho focuses on the period from the late 1970s to the present, providing an exhaustive description of the work of the main Portuguese anthropologists and the cycles of expansion and contraction the discipline has undergone in recent years (Godinho, 2019).

In the following pages, these "histories"—or rather "histories of histories"—constitute points of reference leading us down a path of reflection aimed at providing the reader with an original perspective on the trajectory of a marginal and paradigmatic, eccentric and revelatory anthropology. Before proceeding with our reconstruction,[3] a note on our methods is in order: this chapter is the result of collaboration between two Italian anthropologists who, at different times and in different ways, have built their careers in dialogue with Portuguese anthropology.[4] The diversity of their personal biographies enables different views on the history of the discipline to emerge, and the following pages represent an attempt to synthesise this heterogeneity into a single account.

NATIONAL IDENTITY, REGIME ETHNOLOGISTS AND JORGE DIAS: FROM THE END OF THE NINETEENTH CENTURY TO THE FALL OF THE ESTADO NOVO

João Leal is the anthropologist who has contributed most to mapping the history of the discipline in Portugal. In his *Etnografias Portuguesas (1870–1970): Cultura Popular e Identidade Nacional* (2000), Leal outlined the history of Portuguese anthropology according to two fundamental themes: on the one hand, rural popular culture understood as the primary object of research and, on the other, the interpretation of this sphere of culture as a strategic terrain for constructing national identity and the nation as an "imagined community" (Anderson, 1991). According to Leal, the beginnings of nineteenth-century anthropology were characterised by an "ethnogenealogical" discourse on national identity that framed the nation as a community of descent in which vernacular culture, language, oral literature and popular customs complement each other to

[3] The authors presented here recognise the necessarily incomplete nature of their choices in terms of enumeration, description and analysis. As it could not be otherwise, we agree with their statement: a complete history of Portuguese anthropology would require a long list of authors and many volumes to be exhaustive. Therefore, we apologise to the colleagues omitted from this overview, as everyone is important in this discipline with its aspirations of being humane and interventionist.

[4] Giacomo Pozzi began visiting Portugal in 2010 thanks to an Erasmus grant. From that experience, he collaborated with ISCTE-IUL and the *Universidade Nova de Lisboa*. He then obtained a PhD in Urban Studies in Portugal in co-tutorship with a PhD in Cultural and Social Anthropology from the University of Milano-Bicocca. Since 2020, he has been conducting fieldwork in Cape Verde. Chiara Pussetti's link with Portugal began in the 1990s, following fieldwork among the Bijagó of Guinea Bissau. Chiara Pussetti and Lorenzo Bordonaro were among the first Italian anthropologists to start a career in Lisbon, opening a path that ended up being heavily trodden in the following years. She is currently a researcher with the *Instituto de Ciências Sociais* at *Universidade de Lisboa*.

embody an identity based on ethnogenesis and the richness of popular culture (Leal, 2000, pp. 17–18).

In another fundamental volume, *Antropologia em Portugal: Mestres, Percursos e Tradições* (2006), Leal presented four great masters of Portuguese anthropology[5]: Consiglieri Pedroso, Adolfo Coelho, Teófilo Braga and Leite de Vasconcelos. Their importance can be grasped from the historical context in which they operated, marked by the transformation—part of a wider European shift—of a vague and effervescent romantic interest in popular culture into a systematic and scientifically oriented effort to collect data.[6] These four scholars were particularly attentive to this process: Coelho, in particular, was enormously interested in fieldwork and "modern" methodologies of investigation as well as in certain emerging theories such as diffusionism, comparative mythology and evolutionism.[7]

If we were to look for a fundamental theme characterising Portuguese ethnographic production between the end of the nineteenth and beginning of the twentieth century on the basis of these four *mestres'* work, it certainly lies in the investigation of the construction of national identity and ethnogeny[8] as analysed through literature and popular mythologies. The ultimate example of this moment is the research career of José Leite de Vasconcelos, an intellectual history marked by "a back-and-forth between ethnography and archaeology" (Leal, 2006, p. 36). Through the publication of his *Etnografia Portuguesa* (Vasconcelos, 1933, 1936, 1941), the anthropologist constructed a compendium of ethnographic synthesis—based in part on a comparative perspective—of Portuguese popular culture. In this constant dialectic between past and present, the key point that emerges is the importance of popular culture understood as the "Lusitanian" foundations that accompanied the Portuguese people from prehistory to the foundation of an idea of nationhood.

---

[5] The following reflections on the book *Antropologia em Portugal: Mestres, Percursos e Tradições* are a re-elaboration of a text by Clara Saraiva published in the journal *Etnográfica* (Saraiva, 2008).

[6] Analysing, for example, Consiglieri Pedroso's compilations of folk tales and myths published in English as *Portuguese Folk Tales* (Consiglieri Pedroso, 1882).

[7] Such as Max Muller, Foustel de Coulanges, Spencer, Renan, Mommsem, Benfey, James Frazer and E.B. Tylor (Leal, 2000, pp. 31–33).

[8] This argument is confirmed in the writings of Teófilo Braga. See, for example, Braga (1867).

7 FROM THE REGIME ETHNOLOGISTS TO THE DEMOCRATIC GENERATION... 233

Amidst theoretical influences and concerns poised between defending national identity and systematically cataloguing the country's diversity and cultural richness, Portuguese anthropology reflects both anthropological traditions of the Western world of the time: the "anthropology of colonial empire-building" and the "anthropology of nation-building" (Stocking Jr, 1982). In spite of the importance of the colonial empire, the development of Portuguese anthropology was focused mainly on the question of national identity.[9] According to Leal, this orientation was determined by the weakness of Portuguese colonialism and, at the same time, the centrality of national identity issues in Portuguese intellectual life: quoting Eduardo Lourenço (2007), Leal defines this situation "as the ontological fragility of the nation". It is important to note that this interpretation is not intended to reproduce a conciliatory view of Portuguese colonialism. Portugal has often thought of itself as "the matrix of a society capable of integrating, through mestizaje, groups of different origins and for this reason of being free from racial discrimination" (Ribeiro-Corossacz, 2016, p. 137). However, this celebratory vision—culminating in Freyre's (1940) theories of lusotropicalism—has been widely critiqued by various components of civil society and the intellectual community, including Leal himself.

Despite its fragile national identity, Portugal is well known to have been a colonial empire and this fact inevitably determined the development of "its" anthropology to a large extent. After the proclamation of the Republic in 1910, a development in which several ethnographers took on politically key roles (such as Teófilo Braga, president of the Republic in 1915), the expansion of the discipline was inextricably linked to the ideology of the regime. The period of military dictatorship beginning with the 1926 military coup, also known as the Revolution of 28 May and later as the National Revolution, put an end to first Portuguese Republic by

[9] Leal analyses four fundamental stages of Portuguese anthropology between 1870 and 1970 (1870–1880; 1890–1900; 1910–1920; 1930–1970). In the first, he identifies the study of Portuguese ethnic originality; in the second, an interest in the country's internal diversity emerges (some journals, such as *Portugália* and the *Revista Lusitana*, had a national scope while others such as *A Tradição, A Ilustração Transmontana* and *Revista do Minho and Lusa* had a more local scope and regional circulation) (Leal, 2000, pp. 32–35); in the third, the republic and optimism about national destiny gave rise to nationalist ethnography with a folkloristic character; in the fourth, Jorge Dias and his team, coining the concept of "ethnography of urgency", are concerned with preserving the material and immaterial heritage of different local communities.

establishing a *Ditadura Nacional* that lasted until 1932. Both this period and the authoritarian regime established in 1933 and brought down by the Carnation Revolution of 1974, called the *Estado Novo* or Second Portuguese Republic, bore a clear colonial imprint. This colonial stamp can be seen, for example, in the public exhibitions organised to give visibility to Portuguese imperialism (Godinho, 2019, p. 6; Bastos & Sobral, 2018). During the years of *Estado Novo*, the anthropological community was essentially divided into three groups: "regime ethnologists", intellectuals who opposed the *Estado Novo* and the school of Jorge Dias.

The first grouping included ethnologists such as Vergílio Correia and others who, although not openly embracing the dictatorship, continued to practise their profession even after the *coup d'état*. It also comprised figures directly linked to the regime such as António Ferro, a great supporter of the *Estado Novo*'s cultural policy. The Salazarist euphoria of the time, conveyed by most of the regime ethnologists, celebrated rural Portugal with its rich popular culture differentiated by regional variation alongside a fierce imperialism narrating the nation as an "immense colonial empire" by virtue of the African, Asian and Eastern territories under its domination.

Most of the regime ethnologists were trained at the school of Adriano José Alves Moreira, the scholar who served as Minister of Ultramar during the period of the *Estado Novo*. This *escola* was linked to the historical institute *Escola Superior Colonial* that then became the *Instituto Superior de Ciências Sociais e Políticas* (ISCSP). Alves Moreira was director of ISCSP and shaped its curriculum by introducing the social sciences—thereby continuing the project launched by the Lisbon Geography Society—with the aim of building an institution responsible for training colonial administrators. In this case, he had clear political interests, linked to those of the dictatorship, that defined the Institute's political and ideological mission. The anthropology of the regime was not traditionally linked to the empire and little research was conducted in the countries that had been colonised. Rather, the discipline was interested in the construction of national identity on the basis of a folkloric ethnological tradition influenced by thinkers such as António Augusto da Rocha Peixoto. Archaeologist, ethnologist and naturalist, Rocha Peixoto was a leading figure in the second half of the nineteenth century. Dealing with Portuguese culture and identity, he developed a tradition of nationalist-oriented studies of how the Portuguese had represented themselves over time; later, this line of inquiry was carried forward by Jorge Dias in a way strongly influenced by German anthropology.

In these years, the intellectual vigour of the late nineteenth- and early twentieth-century ethnographers waned (Bastos & Sobral, 2018, p. 3) and ethnography placed itself at the service of the *Estado Novo*. At the same time, physical anthropology was established as a discipline in Portugal as elsewhere in Europe. Oliveira Martins, a historian and economist, was one of the first to support not only this field of study but also one of its main outcomes, the hierarchisation of "races".

Imperialist ideas influenced research in the field of physical anthropology and this was particularly so within the so-called *Escola do Porto* led by professor of medicine António Augusto Mendes Correia, coordinator of all the "anthropological missions" carried out in the colonies (Pereira, 2005). Mendes Correia founded the Portuguese Society of Anthropology and Ethnology in 1918[10] and in 1943 he published a text that became highly popular, *As Raças do Império* (Matos, 2006).[11] The book was based on a simple assumption: *mestizaje* represented a risk and "the race had to remain pure". Following this racist logic, his disciples (including Santos Júnior) used a Lombrosian approach to measure skulls[12] and presented theses on the "Negroes of the colonies".

During the *Estado Novo* years, a part of the Portuguese anthropological community adhered to the school of Jorge Dias, a figure who had played a particularly important role in the development of the discipline. Jorge Dias was born into a wealthy middle-class family in Porto. After graduating in Germanic Philology and working in Munich, he developed a passion for anthropology and went on to earn a PhD in Anthropology from the University of Munich in 1944 with a thesis entitled *Vilarinho da Furna: Um Povo Autárquico da Serra Amarela* (Sobral, 2015).

His official career as an ethnologist in Portugal began in 1947 when he was invited by Mendes Correia to direct the *Secção de Etnografia do Centro*

---

[10] The Society still exists today and publishes the journal *Trabalhos de Etnologia e Ethnologia.*

[11] Mendes Correia (from the University of Porto) and Eusébio Tamagnini (from the University of Coimbra) were part of the political elite of the time: the former became President of the Lisbon Geography Society and the Colonial School; the latter was a minister in the Salazar regime (Bastos & Sobral, 2018, pp. 4–5).

[12] Rui Pereira recounts how, in November 1945, Santos Júnior gave a speech to the settlers of Beira (Mozambique) entitled "How to study a Negro: a lesson on how to observe the descriptive characteristics of an indigenous person, identify and take the body measurements of greatest anthropological interest" (Pereira, 2005).

de Estudos de Etnologia Peninsular (CEEP), established in 1945 at the University of Porto (Oliveira, 1974, p. 12). In this period Dias formally created his school consisting of his wife, Margot Dias, as well as friends and long-time companions, Fernando Galhano and Ernesto Veiga de Oliveira, who were joined in 1959 by Benjamim Enes Pereira.

The work of Jorge Dias and his team followed the established pathways of Portuguese ethnography at the beginning of the century by focusing on three essential themes. The first concerned the rural world, investigated through a sort of "emergency" ethnography approach based on the premise that this world was at risk of disappearing from one moment to the next (Dias, 1948, 1950, 1953a). The second theme, the characterisation of Portuguese culture and ethnic psychology, was represented by three texts in particular: *Elementos fundamentais da Cultura Portuguesa* (Dias, 1953b); *Algumas considerações acerca da estrutura social do povo português* (Dias, 1955); and *Tentámen de Fixação das Grandes Áreas Culturais Portuguesas* (Dias, 1960). On the one hand, these volumes reflect the significant influence of Human Geography—represented in Portugal by Orlando Ribeiro—on the research group and, on the other, the influence of Dias's romanticism and idealism that led to framing peasants as beings of superior quality and purity and outlining representative democracy as an exemplary model of autarchic government. The third thematic area was related to the 1950s establishment of the Missions for the Study of Ethnic Minorities in Overseas Portuguese Territories (MEMEUP), a research series that marked a new interest in the anthropology of "empire-building".

Methodologically, the group favoured intensive Malinowski-style fieldwork that, in line with the functionalist perspective, was reflected in the drafting of monographs.[13] Such intensive work was also a means of highlighting the nation's cultural wealth and thus contributing to the preservation of heritage. The school's theoretical influences mirrored Dias's international academic training: the diffusionism he encountered in Germany on the one hand and the American culturalism he absorbed during a series of trips to the United States on the other.

As mentioned above, the Dias school did not coincide with what we have called "regime ethnologists". However, the link between the school's

---

[13] Such as those of Jorge Dias on two mountain communities and the phenomenon of agro-pastoral communitarianism: Vilarinho da Furna (Dias, 1948) and Rio de Onor (Dias, 1953a).

founder and the dictatorship was ambiguous and controversial (Pina-Cabral, 1991). Dias began his academic career with the support of Mendes Correia, a figure linked to the colonial and racist policies of the *Estado Novo*. Despite the pro-Nazi cast of his education, Dias never adhered to eugenic theses. At the same time, however, he did defend colonisation as a fundamental part of the Portuguese national character (Sobral, 2007) and support the lusotropicalist theses of Gilberto Freyre, the Brazilian sociologist who portrayed the Portuguese as ideal colonisers—not racists—who would use *mestizaje* to construct a harmoniously multiracial Brazil (Castelo, 1998). Dias was so inspired by this idea that he manifested an ethnocentric nationalist stance premised on the civilising superiority of Christianity and the providential mission of the Portuguese, thus fully identifying with official *Estado Novo* policy (Sobral, 2015).

The student of Dias with the most significant influence on the development of the discipline was Benjamim Enes Pereira. His career is linked to both the affirmation of anthropology in Portugal and the internal diversification of the discipline (Saraiva, 2010). As a member of the research centres founded by Dias as well as the National Museum of Ethnology (MNE), Enes Pereira was distinguished by his studies on material culture. As Leal points out, Pereira's anthropological project "anticipated to a large extent the renewed contemporary interest in material culture, or in the 'social life of things', to quote Appadurai's (1986) felicitous formulation" (Leal, 2010, p. 187).

Building a Different Country, Imagining a Different Anthropology[14]

The events of 25 April 1974 radically changed the situation of anthropology in Portugal. The Carnation Revolution[15] inaugurated a historical moment of social, political and cultural transformation and renewal. Portugal and the revolution attracted not only social scientists but also photographers and filmmakers, all looking to experience and document

---

[14] The title of this section comes from Sérgio Tréfaut's excellent documentary *Outro País* (Tréfaut, 1999) which portrays the photographers and filmmakers who documented the events of the revolution.

[15] Through which the dictatorial regime of the *Estado Novo*, in force since 1933, was deposed and a process began that would end with the establishment of a democratic regime and the establishment of a new Constitution (on 25 April 1976) marked by a strong socialist orientation

the *Revolução dos Cravos*. Some of the intellectuals, artists and art critics (such as Ernesto de Sousa), ethnomusicologists (such as Michel Giacometti) and filmmakers (such as Manoel de Oliveira and Álvaro Campos) who had produced ethnographic work "against the grain" of the *Estado Novo's* celebratory logic—and who therefore constituted one of Leal's above three groupings of anthropologists under the *Estado Novo* (in addition to the Dias school and regime ethnologists)[16]— were finally able to express themselves freely. In addition to the agrarian reform process in Alentejo, the *Plano de Trabalho e Cultura* was launched in 1975 as part of the *Serviço Cívico Estudantil*. Coordinated by Michel Giacometti, this project brought students and young university students throughout the country to ethnographic inquiry focused on collecting data about litera-ture, music, folk medicine, tools and material culture (Godinho, 2019, p. 11). These investigations left behind the nineteenth-century preoccu-pation with looking for the nation's founding identity among rural popu-lations and were instead guided by a strong focus on class struggle, characteristic of that revolutionary moment and the PREC (*Processo Revolucionário Em Curso*), the period of Portugal's transition to democ-racy. As Branco points out, "The anthropology of those years is not dedi-cated to nation-building, it does not evoke it in its essence, but rather interrogates the country with a question, sometimes contemplative, some-times non-conformist (echoing the spirit of revolution and decolonisa-tion)" (Branco, 2014, p. 376).

Expectations of a true regime reform in Portugal were fulfilled in the Marcelist period, during the *Primavera Marcelista* (Marcelista Spring)— the initial period of Marcelo Caetano's government from 1968 and 1970 characterised by a certain degree of social modernisation and political lib-eralisation. In 1972, the *Instituto Superior de Ciências do Trabalho e da Empresa* (ISCTE) was created as part of a reform of public universities supported by certain progressive sectors of the authoritarian regime. Of the many leading figures of this reform, two stand out as having played a key role in the restructuring that led to the creation of the ISCTE: Eduardo Gomes Cardoso, engineer and head of the National Institute of Industrial Research (INII); and Adérito Sedas Nunes, economist, social scientist and

---

[16] The same thing happened with the architects who, on the basis of Ribeiro's tripartite division (Ribeiro, 1963), examined popular architecture in the country from the end of the 1950s until the beginning of the 1960s (Associação de Arquitectos, 1988). The second part of *Etnografias Portuguesas* deals with this topic in a masterful way (Leal, 2000, pp. 145–223).

director of the magazine *Análise Social* and the Office of Social Research (GIS). In the 1960s, Sedas Nunes conducted a sociological study on universities in Portugal that identified their limitations as well as directions for much-needed reform with a view to making them more modern and open to society. The GIS had a considerable impact in a society where social sciences were regarded with suspicion: the history of the Institute of Social Sciences (ICS)—where Chiara Pussetti works—began with the creation of the Social Science Research Group (GIS) in 1962.

A period of expansion in research and teaching began, a time of change and hope aimed at achieving a better and more democratic future. The former colonies gained their independence in 1975. The *Instituto Superior de Ciências Sociais e Política Ultramarina* (ISCSPU)—an institution created at the beginning of the twentieth century to meet the needs of governing and administration colonial possessions, integrated post-25 April into the *Universidade Técnica de Lisboa*—went bankrupt: the professors who taught there were fired, as they were considered to be linked to the regime. The institution's mission was radically reformulated: it no longer needed anthropologically trained colonial administrators, but rather anthropologists. With the contribution of the geographer Raquel Soeiro de Brito, who trained in France with Luc de Heusch, and Augusto Mesquitela Lima[17], an anthropologist and writer from Cape Verde who in 1978 created the Department of Anthropology at the *Universidade Nova* and the Institute of African Studies, the *Universidade Técnica* took on the new name of ISCSP and managed to attract young professors trained at the former ISCSPU or abroad (such as João Leal, Rosa Perez, José Gabriel Pereira Bastos, Jorge Crespo and Yáñes Casal).

At this point, an internal, generational disciplinary war broke out. Young anthropologists and students took sides against the circle of anthropologists who, despite having collaborated with the regime, had managed to maintain their academic positions—and thus dictate lines of thought—after the fall of the dictatorship. As a result, the anthropological current linked to the regime was dismantled during the years of the revolution. In order to imagine a new course for the discipline, between 1974 and 1976 no anthropology classes were held in Portugal.

---

[17] Initially with José Carlos Gomes da Silva, a scholar who graduated in Belgium but shortly afterwards founded the Anthropology course at ISCTE and later encouraged the transfer of young teachers from FCSH to ISCTE.

240   G. POZZI AND C. PUSSETTI

João Leal was one of the main protagonists of this period. In 1979, he founded the first "post-*Estado Novo*" anthropology course in the *Universidade Nova*. The *Universidade Nova* was linked to the figure of Vitorino Magalhães Godinho, a historian and former director of the *Biblioteca Nacional*, who conceived the Department of Social Sciences. His idea was very interdisciplinary, and he founded a department that united people who distanced themselves critically from the colonial matrix of the ISCSP.

Some of the anthropologists who had begun working as professors at the *Universidade Nova*, such as Gomes da Silva, João Leal and Rosa Perez, decided to move to the ISCTE. They thus detached themselves from a certain reactionary branch of scholarship linked to the idea of studying "Ultramarine" countries that still characterised, albeit marginally, the *Universidade Nova*. Between 1982 and 1984, a strong Department of Anthropology was created at the ISCTE with a contemporary and critical character that distinguished it at the national level from the discipline's overall colonial heritage.

In a text dealing with the evolution of anthropology in Portugal since the April Revolution, Paula Godinho has suggested the half century separating us from that event should be divided into two main cycles. According to the *lisboeta* anthropologist, these cycles are defined by "waves" oscillating between phases of disciplinary expansion and contraction determined by social, political and economic fluctuations not only in the country but also in Europe and the global panorama more generally. Godinho thus identifies a first phase of openness and dynamism following the *revolução dos cravos* (1974) and Portugal's entry into the European Union (1986), a phase that lasted until approximately the beginning of the twenty-first century. A second phase, however, began with the 2008 economic recession: this represented a moment of crisis for Portuguese anthropology, the effects of which began to be severely felt between 2012 and 2013. Specifically, the funds available for teaching and research decreased drastically with dramatic consequences for students, researchers, universities and research centres, as well as for doctoral and post-doctoral fellowships. As funding for research projects declined, there were fewer and fewer opportunities to offer fellowships. An entire generation of scholars suddenly found itself unemployed, and many bright young people left the country.

Focusing on discipline's expansion and dynamism, Godinho points out that the anthropologists who began their careers in the 1980s carried forward the rural studies of Jorge Dias, reflecting Robert Redfield's theoretical influence. In general, therefore, Portuguese scholarship was characterised by an intense continuing interest in the rural world undergoing profound transformation. Examples of this approach included, for example, Brian O'Neill's study of landowners, peasants and street journalists in Trás-os-Montes, the vision of the Minho peasant world described by João Pina Cabral, and the continuation of Dias's study in the village of Rio de Onor by Pais de Brito (Godinho, 2019, pp. 12–15). Others focused instead on the theme of celebrations, taking up Benjamim Pereira's work (Pereira, 1973) on the *Ciclo dos Doze Dias* ("Cycle of Twelve Days") masks and Noémia Delgado's film illustrating them. In addition to Ernesto Veiga de Oliveira's collection of texts on cyclical festivals (Oliveira, 1984), Pierre Sanchis carried out research on pilgrimages (Sanchis, 1983) and, also in the 1980s, João Leal and Rosa Perez at the *Universidade Nova*'s Anthropology Department (FCSH) encouraged students to carry out fieldwork revisiting the *Ciclo dos Doze Dias* festivities. Finally, a group of scholars devoted their attention to studying the organisation and dissolution of family ties (due to phenomena such as emigration) and building on the work of Callier-Boisvert (1966), José Cutileiro and Caroline Bretell (1991).

The opening of the anthropology programme at FCSH was followed by the inauguration of another course at the *Instituto Superior da Ciência do Trabalho e da Empresa*. While both institutes presented an international offering with professors from abroad—some Portuguese self-exiles, others professors "from outside" (what were then significantly called "the foreigners"[18])—FCSH was shaped by the tradition of French anthropology and structuralism while the ISCTE was distinguished by Anglo-Saxon influence (Almeida, 2014; Branco, 2014; Godinho, 2019; O'Neill, 2014; Pignatelli, 2014).

In the 1980s, FCSH's programme entailed not only a four-year course of study but also an obligatory few months (or even year) of fieldwork and a written dissertation. This requirement kindled young people's interest in research at an early stage: some students, fascinated by the earlier work of the National Museum of Ethnology team, were committed to the rural studies characteristic of Portuguese anthropology while others followed

---

[18] Going "abroad" in those years meant leaving a country closed to the world by a fascist-inclined dictatorship, in addition to the many cases where people went into exile to escape persecution by the political police or to avoid going being sent to fight in the colonial war.

research paths on diverse, more topical and socially critical themes such as whaling in the Azores, a practice that was about to be banned in 1982. Many FCSH graduates were then placed as professors in the same department or in the new course created at the ISCTE.

The Democratic Generation and Anthropologies of the Contemporary

In the years that followed the regime, those anthropologists who had fled abroad were able to return and a new generation of young anthropologists established itself. Miguel Vale de Almeida (in an interview conducted on 23 November 2021) called this new wave "the democratic generation". Many of the young anthropologists who trained in these years were born before 25 April, a time when anthropology was intimately linked to its colonial vertex. Rejecting the legacy of the dictatorship, during the 1980s and the 1990s the democratic generation diversified its research foci, working with innovative approaches, methodologies, theoretical frameworks and themes. Topics included urban neighbourhoods (Graça Cordeiro), the use of psychotropic substances in raves (Luís Vasconcelos), the phenomenon of hip-hop (Teresa Fradique), elite families in Lisbon (Antónia Lima), medical anthropology (Cristiana Bastos) and gender identity (Miguel Vale de Almeida). These research paths often focused on previously less-investigated geographical settings, both inside the national territory (e.g. Cristiana Bastos and Clara Saraiva worked in the north-east of the Algarve) and the international context. In the latter case, new research areas included Morocco (Maria Cardeira da Silva), Guinea-Bissau (Clara Carvalho; Clara Saraiva), Mozambique (Rui Pereira), Brazil (Cristiana Bastos, Miguel Vale de Almeida, Susana Viegas), Angola (Nuno Porto) and Cape Verde (João Vasconcelos). It is worth noting that, in most cases, research abroad took place (and still takes place) in areas that had been part of the Portuguese empire until a few decades earlier. Scholars have chosen and continue to choose these sites because of the opportunities by a common language and, secondly, because of the ramifications of post-colonial policies and ties, thus demonstrating the deep (and sometimes unconscious) roots of colonial webs.

A fundamental arena for sharing research results, developing the discipline and building of the scientific community was represented by the anthropological journals associated with the country's various departments and research centres. *Ethnologia*, the journal of the FCSH Department of Anthropology published between 1983 and 2003, played a prominent role in these processes.[19] *Etnográfica*, published by the *Centro em Rede de Investigação em Antropologia* (CRIA), still today stands out as the main Portuguese journal of anthropology with international standing. It was first directed by João Leal (*Universidade Nova*), then Miguel Vale de Almeida (ISCTE), Manuela Ivone Cunha (*Universidade do Minho*) and now Humberto Martins (*Universidade de Trás-os-Montes*). To mark the years of internationalisation, the journal accepts publications in four languages (Portuguese, English, French and Spanish) and has become a pole of attraction for Brazilian colleagues looking to disseminate their work in Europe.[20]

The anthropological community was strengthened not only by the originality of the topics and working methods and the chance to share these through journals, but also and probably above all by the nationwide growth of anthropology degree programmes and research centres. Thanks to the contribution of lecturers recruited after 25 April as well as young doctoral students and researchers, various research institutions were founded. At the ISCTE, the *Centro de Estudos de Antropologia Social* (CEAS, 1986–2009) was created in 1986 and the *Centro de Estudos Africanos* (CEA) in 1981, later renamed *Centro de Estudos Internacionais* in 2013. At FCSH, the *Centro de Estudos de Etnologia Portuguesa* (CEEP, 1994–2007) was opened, followed shortly afterwards by the *Centro de Estudos das Migrações e Minorias Étnicas* (CEMME, 2000–2009). In Coimbra, physical and biological anthropology continued to play a leading role in the work conducted at the *Centro de Investigação em Antropologia e Saúde* (CIAS, since 1994), heir to the forensic tradition developed at that university.

---

[19] In one of its special issues (Cardeira da Silva, 1997), the periodical featured a portrait of the vitality of the department headed by Jill Dias. A specialist in ethnohistory, Dias combined deep historical knowledge with remarkable ethnographic sensitivity and, in addition to numerous publications on Africa, she also curated one of the most important exhibitions at the National Museum of Ethnology, *África and Brazil, Nas Vésperas do Mundo Moderno* (Dias, 1992).

[20] Other significant scientific journals include *Antropologia Portuguesa* by the University of Coimbra (founded in 1983); *Trabalhos de Antropologia e Etnologia*, a journal founded in 1918 and published by the *Sociedade Portuguesa de Antropologia e Etnologia* (SPAE); *Arquivos da Memória*, created by CEEPA in 1994; *Análise Social*, founded in 1963 by the Institute of Social Sciences at the University of Lisbon.

The 1997 creation of the *Fundação para a Ciência e a Tecnologia* (FCT)[21]—Portugal's national public funding agency for science, research and technology—resulted in the restructuring of research centres alongside a considerable increase in research funding. In terms of restructuring, in 2009 the CEAS joined with the CEMME and other centres to form the *Centro em Rede de Investigação em Antropologia* (CRIA) bringing together anthropologists and universities from all over the country (Trás-os-Montes, Minho, Coimbra, Lisbon and Algarve). Alongside the *Instituto de Ciências Sociais* of Lisbon University, CRIA constitutes the largest centre of anthropological research in the country.

In terms of funding, the creation of the FCT inaugurated a period of abundance in doctoral and post-doctoral fellowships. These were open to students and researchers of all nationalities, but attracted in particular candidates from Italy, France, Belgium and Germany. These were the years of internationalisation. The contribution of anthropologists trained abroad greatly enriched the Portuguese scientific community, making it one of the most lively and fertile in Europe.

A very international environment was created in this period with a strong preponderance of intellectuals belonging to what we might define as the "Lusophone axis" (using the Portuguese language as an instrument of scientific work and strengthening relations with Brazil[22] and the former Portuguese colonies in Africa) and the "Anglophone axis" (using English as a *lingua franca* for connecting Europe and the United States, creating dialogue between multiple disciplinary traditions and attracting researchers of different nationalities). Teachers, researchers and students circulated between countries and institutions, moving between different universes, feeding on multiple stimuli and expanding their research horizons. This was an effervescent environment, with "sandwich" grants (to support the movement of Brazilian students); PALOP grants (to enable students from African countries with Portuguese as their official language to study in Portugal); ERASMUS (European Region Action Scheme for the Mobility of University Students) grants; and specialist, master's, doctoral and post-doctoral grants.

---

[21] This replaced the former *Junta Nacional para a Investigação Científica* (JNICT).

[22] It was mainly after the 1990s that Portugal and Brazil developed very close relations, thanks to the research work of Portuguese anthropologists in Brazil (Cristiana Bastos, Miguel Vale de Almeida, Susana Viegas and João de Pina-Cabral, among others) and of Brazilian anthropologists in Portugal (e.g. Feldman-Branco, 2001).

7 FROM THE REGIME ETHNOLOGISTS TO THE DEMOCRATIC GENERATION... 245

Institutes, departments and research centres proved ready to welcome new researchers and projects with national or European funding. Portuguese anthropologists were particularly receptive to the foreign researchers who arrived in these years, bringing new synergies: these included, among others, Ramon Sarró, Ruy Llera Blanes, Lorenzo Bordonaro, Frédéric Vidal and Iñigo Sánchez. Unfortunately, the economic crisis of 2008 and the subsequent and inevitable fleeing of many researchers abruptly interrupted this process (Godinho, 2019).

Nevertheless, between the end of the 1990s and the first decade of the twenty-first century, the diversity of anthropological production highlights the changes that have taken place, as evidenced by Cristiana Bastos and José Sobral's detailed published in the *International Encyclopedia of Anthropology*, which we quote here in full:

> The scope of research topics and contexts expanded outside the national borders and improved in diversity and sophistication within. To outline a sample, necessarily incomplete and counting only works published until 2010, there had been research outside Portugal on Gujarat villages (Rosa Perez), Moroccan cities (Maria Cardeira da Silva), sub-Saharan African settings (Manuel Areia, A. Yanez Casal, J. Fialho Feliciano, Clara Carvalho, Manuel J. Ramos, Fernando Florêncio, Manuela Palmeirim, Amélia Frazão-Moreira, Nuno Porto, F. Ribeiro), ethnicities and kinship in China (João de Pina-Cabral, Gonçalo D. Santos), Azorean diaspora in the Americas (João Leal), Brazilian indigenous groups (Susana Matos Viegas), transnational identities and practices (Susana T. P. Bastos and José G. P. Bastos, Luís Batalha, João Vasconcelos, José Mapril, Marta Rosales), science networks (Cristiana Bastos, Nélia Dias), death rituals (Clara Saraiva), and, with a renewed approach to Portuguese issues, there were works on national identity (Luís Cunha, José Sobral, António Medeiros), borders (Fátima Amante, Paula Godinho, Humberto Martins), memory and heritage (Paula Godinho, José Sobral, Elsa Peralta), cultural policies (Vera Marques Alves), religious communities (Marina Pignatelli, Pedro Pereira, Ramon Sarró and Ruy Blanes, Clara Saraiva), labor (Paulo Granjo, Emília M. Marques), financial elites (Antonia P Lima), prisons and confinement (Susana T. P. Bastos, Manuela I. Cunha), soccer (Daniel Seabra), tourism (Paula Mota Santos, Luís Silva, Xerardo Pereiro), critical museum studies (Nuno Porto, Nélia Dias), fairy tales (Francisco Vaz da Silva), the history of anthropology (Frederico Rosa), and Portuguese anthropology (Rui Pereira, Jorge Freitas Branco, João Leal, Gonaçalo D. Santos), epistemology (Filipe Verde, Luís Quintais), environment (Ana Isabel Afonso, Jean-Yves Durand, Pedro Prista), surveillance (Susana Durão, Catarina Fróis), land reform and revolu-

tion (Margarida Fernandes, Sónia Vespeira de Almeida), fishing communities (Inês Meneses and Paulo Mendes, Francisco Oneto Nunes), spatial patterns and culture (Shawn Parkhurst), ritual and performance (Paulo Raposo), visual anthropology (Catarina Alves Costa), urbanities (Filomena Silvano, Teresa Fradique, Daniel Seabra Lopes, Paulo C. Seixas), health and illness (Cristiana Bastos, M Manuel Quintela, Elsa Lechner, Chiara Pussetti, Luís Silva Pereira), food and cuisine (Daniela Araújo, Vasco V. Teixeira, José Sobral, Nuno Domingos, Marta Rosales), ethnomusicology (Susana Sardo), and many other topics. [...] [W]hile the study of colonial issues was avoided for a long period in the new Portuguese anthropology, it would come back as a prime field, often in convergence with history, cultural, and postcolonial studies. Biological anthropology also renewed itself dramatically in the post-dictatorship decades, opening up to important research on primatology in Lisbon (Claudia de Sousa and Catarina Casanova). Yet Coimbra remains the benchmark in the teaching and research of biological anthropology and also in connection with archaeology and forensic medicine (Augusto Abade, Eugénia Cunha, Cristina Padez, among others). (Bastos & Sobral, 2018, pp. 11–12)

A new anthropological community was formed without dissolving individual specificities, creating networks, nuclei and centres that facilitated the dynamic international circulation of knowledge, practices and theoretical developments. The Portuguese model involves two parallel career paths, one based mainly on teaching and the other on research. The mission of the *Instituto de Ciências Sociais da Universidade de Lisboa*, for example, is essentially centred on research and innovation, preparing competitive research projects in international arenas, teaching at the doctoral level and coordinating post-doctoral students.

A further sign of disciplinary strengthening and institutionalisation in recent years was the 1989 founding of the Portuguese Anthropology Association (APA). The association aims to represent all the anthropologists who speak Portuguese or who work and train in Portugal. The APA counts among its members several scholars from abroad, mainly Brazil and Spain as these are the countries with which the APA has established close, collaborative relations.

The Brazilian anthropologist Carla Costa Teixeira recently wrote a very detailed history of the APA, tracing the relationship between the strengthening of the Association and the consolidation of discipline in Portugal (2021). Her exhaustive analysis maps the main stages of the establishment of the Association in an effort to understand the place held by the social sciences and anthropology in science policies in Portugal, considering the tensions that have marked the modernisation of scientific and technological knowledge production in the country since the early 1990s.

CONCLUSION

According to Pina-Cabral (1989), Portuguese anthropology is heir to circumstances that intimately tie the history of the country to that of the discipline. As we have tried to highlight in this chapter, each phase of the discipline has been accompanied by a significant historical transition. This was true of the discipline's romantic period in the nineteenth century, the work of the first ethnographers in the gestation period of the Republic, the work of Jorge Dias and his group in the 1950s and 1960s and, finally, the period at the end of the 1980s when Pina-Cabral wrotehis essay, considered the period of disciplinary development. In addition to these phases, we must certainly add the phases of disciplinary internationalisation and crisis. Pina Cabral, highlighting the ever-lively dialogue with the international currents dominating scholarship in different eras, pointed out that, in the Portuguese case, moments of vitality were always followed by "long periods of paralysis, isolation from the international dialogue and inability to produce internally innovative young scientists" (Pina-Cabral, 1989, pp. 34–35). Writing at the end of the twentieth century, with the democratic transition completed, Pina-Cabral explains that although it is no longer necessary to fight against the ideological, cultural and social isolation of the period of Salazar's dictatorship, Portugal's position remains peripheral and therefore requires a strengthening of international relations. The 1990s and beginning of the twenty-first century have witnessed the realisation of this need, with anthropology courses spread widely, research centres founded and restructured, foreign students and researchers integrated into the national system and scientific cooperation networks created at the European and world levels.

In the introduction, we asked if Portugal—in its marginality—might represent a space of synthesis and original creativity in the context of European anthropology more broadly. In the past we have tried to reconstruct here, such innovation has proven possible in some phases but not in others. We must now look to the future, a future that will be achievable if the new generations are able to project themselves into the time to come and seize the momentum of the debates, struggles and schools that have characterised the history of Portuguese anthropology. In this way, the

248   G. POZZI AND C. PUSSETTI

discipline will remain strong and lively, contributing more and more to the creation of a just, democratic and inclusive society.

REFERENCES

Almeida, M. V. (2014). Com um pé dentro e outro fora: reflexões pessoais sobre a geração dos eighties. *Etnográfica, 18*(2), 379–384.

Anderson, Benedict. (1991) [1983]. *Imagined Communities. Reflections on the Origin and Spread of Nationalism.* Verso.

Associação Dos Arquitectos Portugueses. (1988). *Arquitectura Popular em Portugal.* Associação dos Arquitectos Portugueses.

Bastos, C. (2014). A década de 1990: Os anos da internacionalização. *Etnográfica, 18*(2), 385–401.

Bastos, C., & Sobral, J. (2018). Portugal, Anthropology. In H. Callan (Ed.), *International Encyclopedia of Anthropology.* John Wiley and Sons Ltd.

bell hooks. (1998). *Elogio del margine. Razza, sesso e mercato culturale.* Feltrinelli.

Braga, T. (1867). *Antologias: Cancioneiro Popular Coimbra.* Imprensa da Universidade.

Branco, J. F. (2014). Sentidos da antropologia em Portugal na década de 1970. *Etnográfica, 18*(2), 365–378.

Bretell, C. (1991). *Homens que partem, mulheres que esperam. Consequências da emigração numa freguesia minhota.* Publicações Dom Quixote.

Callier-Boisvert, C. (1966). *Soajo: une Communauté Féminine Rurale de l'Alto Minho* (pp. 237–278). Bulletin des Etudes Portugaises.

Cardeira Da Silva, M. (Ed.). (1997). *Trabalho de Campo.* Cosmos.

Castelo, C. (1998). *O Modo Português de Estar no Mundo: O Luso-Tropicalismo e a Ideologia Colonial Portuguesa: 1933–1961.* Edições Afrontamento.

Consiglieri Pedroso, Z. (1882). *Portuguese Folk-tales.* Folklore Society.

Dias, J. (1948). *Vilarinho da Furna: Uma Aldeia Comunitária.* Imprensa Nacional Casa da Moeda.

Dias, J. (1950). Os elementos fundamentais da cultura portuguesa. *Estudos de Antropologia, I,* 1.

Dias, J. (1952). Bosquejo histórico da etnografia portuguesa. *Revista Portuguesa de Filologia, II,* 1–64.

Dias, J. (1953a). *Rio de Onor: Comunitarismo Agro-Pastoril.* Editorial Presença.

Dias, J. (1953b). Os elementos fundamentais da cultura portuguesa. *Estudos de Antropologia, I,* 135–157.

Dias, J. (1955). Algumas considerações acerca da estrutura social do povoportuguês. *Estudos de Antropologia, I,* 159–181.

Dias, J. (1960). Tentamen de fixação das grandes áreas culturais portuguesas. *Estudos de Antropologia, I,* 183–206.

Dias, J. (1992). *África e Brasil. Nas Vésperas do Mundo Moderno.* CNCDP.

7 FROM THE REGIME ETHNOLOGISTS TO THE DEMOCRATIC GENERATION... 249

Eriksen, T. H. (1991). A Community of European Social Anthropologists. *Current Anthropology, 32*(1), 75–78.

Feldman-Branco, B. (2001). Brazilians in Portugal, Portuguese in Brazil: Construction of Sameness and Difference. *Identities, 8,* 607–650.

Freyre, G. (1940). *O Mundo que o Português Criou: Aspectos das Relações Sociais e de Cultura do Brasil com Portugal e as Colónias Portuguesas.* Livros do Brasil.

Godinho, P. (2019). Antropologia Portuguesa contemporânea, casi medio siglo desde Abril. *Disparidades. Revista de Antropologia, 74*(2), 1–30.

Leal, J. (2000). *Etnografias Portuguesas (1870–1970): Cultura Popular e Identidade Nacional.* Publicações Dom Quixote.

Leal, J. (2006). *Antropologia em Portugal: Mestres, Percursos, Transições.* Livros Horizonte.

Leal, J. (2010). Os dois países de Benjamim Pereira: uma homenagem. *Etnográfica, 14*(1), 185–195.

Lourenço, E. (2007). *O Labirinto da saudade. Psicanálise Mítica do Destino Português.* Gradiva.

Matos, P. F. (2006). *As côres do império: Representações raciais no império colonial português.* Imprensa de Ciências Sociais.

O'Neill, B. J. (2014). Os anos 70 em 3D: reflexões pessoais. *Etnográfica, 18*(2), 333–340.

Oliveira, E. V. d. (1968). *Vinte Anos de Investigação Etnológica do Centro de Estudos de Etnologia Peninsular.* Instituto de Alta Cultura.

Oliveira, E. V. d. (1974). António Jorge Dias. In AA.VV., *In Memoriam António Jorge Dias, vol. I.* Lisboa: Instituto de Alta Cultura-Junta de Investigações do Ultramar.

Oliveira, E. V. d. (1984). *Festividades Cíclicas em Portugal.* Publicações Dom Quixote.

Pereira, B. E. (1973). *Máscaras Portuguesas.* Junta de Investigações do Ultramar.

Pereira, R. (2005). Raça, sangue e robustez: Os paradigmas da antropologia física colonial portuguesa. *Cadernos de Estudos Africanos, 7*(8), 209–241.

Pignatelli, M. (2014). Antropologia em Portugal nos últimos 50 anos: Introdução. *Etnográfica, 18*(2), 301–305.

Pina-Cabral, J. (1989). Breves considerações sobre o estado da antropologia em Portugal. *Antropologia Portuguesa, 7,* 29–36.

Pina-Cabral, J. (1991). A antropologia em Portugal hoje. In J. Pina-Cabral (Ed.), *Os Contextos da Antropologia* (pp. 11–41). Difel.

Ribeiro, Orlando (1963) [1945]. *Portugal, o Mediterrâneo e o Atlântico.* Sá da Costa.

Ribeiro-Corossacz, V. (2016). Una decolonizzazione mai terminata. Il modello portoghese di colonizzazione in Brasile e la costruzione dell'Altro/a africano/a nell'immaginario razzista. *Altre modernità, 16*(11), 134–147.

Sanchis, P. (1983). *Arraial: Festa de um povo.* Publicações Dom Quixote.

Saraiva, C. (2008). João Leal, Antropologia em Portugal: Mestres, Percursos, Tradições. *Etnográfica* [Online], 12(1).

Saraiva, C. (2010). Os caminhos do Benjamim. *Etnográfica, 13*(1), 161–163.

Saraiva, C., Durand, J.-Y., & Alpuim, J. (Eds.). (2014). *Caminhos e Diálogos da Antropologia Portuguesa, Homenagem a Benjamim Pereira*. Câmara Municipal de Viana do Castelo.

Sobral, J. M. (2007). O Outro aqui tão próximo: Jorge Dias e a Redescoberta de Portugal pela Antropologia Portuguesa (anos 70–80). *Revista de História das Ideias, 28*, 139–187.

Sobral, J. M. (2015). Dias, António Jorge. In *Dicionário de Historiadores Portugueses. Da Academia Real das Ciências ao Final do Estado Novo*. Link: http://dichp.bnportugal.pt/projecto.html (accessed on 17 January 2022).

Stocking Jr, G. (1982). Afterword: a view from the center. *Ethnos, 47*, 172–186.

Teixeira, C. C. (2021). Da Desconstrução da dualidade nação-império à reafirmação da antropologia em Portugal: história e desafios contemporâneos da Associação Portuguesa de Antropologia (APA). In *BEROSE International Encyclopaedia of the Histories of Anthropology*, Paris. Link: https://www.berose.fr/article2484.html (accessed on 17 January 2022).

Tréfaut, S. (1999). *Outro Pais. 70'*. Prod. SP FILMES, distribuição FAUX.

Vasconcelos, J. L. d. (1933). *Etnografia Portuguesa I*. Imprensa Nacional.

Vasconcelos, J. L. d. (1936). *Etnografia Portuguesa II*. Imprensa Nacional.

Vasconcelos, J. L. d. (1941). *Etnografia Portuguesa III*. Imprensa Nacional.

Viegas, S. M., & Pina-Cabral, J. (2014). Na encruzilhada Portuguesa: A antropologia contemporânea e a sua história. *Etnográfica, 18*(2), 311–332.

CHAPTER 8

Anthropology in Russia: From Nineteenth-Century Ethnography to the New Post-Soviet Anthropology

Pietro Scarduelli

FIRST ETHNOGRAPHICAL STUDIES IN THE NINETEENTH CENTURY

Russia has a long tradition of ethnographic studies which dates back to the nineteenth century, when travellers and explorers visited the far east of Siberia, Alaska (which was Russian territory until 1867, when it was sold to the United States for 7.2 US dollars because it was too difficult and too expensive to keep control over a territory so far away from the centre of the empire) and the north-west coast of Canada, and wrote reports on habits and customs of the native societies. The origins of Russian ethnography and American anthropology are similar: the former began in the last few decades of the nineteenth century, with the observation of the native societies incorporated in the Russian empire during its expansion to the east; in the same period, the first field research of the American anthropologists was carried out among the Indians living in the territories

P. Scarduelli (✉)
University of Piemonte Orientale, Vercelli, Italy

© The Author(s), under exclusive license to Springer Nature Switzerland AG 2023
G. D'Agostino, V. Matera (eds.), *Histories of Anthropology*, https://doi.org/10.1007/978-3-031-21258-1_8

251

conquered by the United States during the advance to the West. The Russian empire and the United States devised similar political and military plans aiming at the conquest of wide spaces envisaged as 'empty' as the native peoples were unimportant or simply a hindrance to be removed if they put up resistance. During the conquer of Siberia, the Russian army didn't meet any resistance; on the contrary, the American army fought hard against the Plain Indians; this difference marked their lot. The peoples of Siberia retained their way of life and their traditions; on the contrary, the Plain Indians were victims of a cultural ethnocide. In both cases, however, only ethnographers and anthropologists paid attention to them.

After the first settlements founded in the north-western tip of the American Continent by fur traders (which soon also became centres of colonisation and evangelisation of the natives), the Russian empire took control of Alaska in the last few years of the eighteenth century through the Russian-American Company, founded in St Petersburg in 1795 by N. P. Rezanov (as an imitation of the English East India Company) with the aim of developing trade with those far territories and exploiting their natural resources. The presence of merchants, orthodox priests, officers and civil servants furthered the arrival of travellers, explorers and scientists, who left a vast amount of ethnographic observations about Inuit, Tlingit and other ethnic groups of Alaska.

Among the many who deserve to be mentioned, the Vice Admiral Golovnin of the Russian imperial Navy stands out, who was correspondent of the Russian Academy of Sciences and carried out two journeys around the world, the former from 1807 to 1809, the latter in 1817. When he came back, he wrote a book about his journey wherein he describes his meeting with the Kodiak, a native people of the Siberian peninsula Kamchatka. More information may be found in the *History of the Russian-American Company*. The Navy lieutenant Tikhmenev was charged to write it by the Company in 1857.

The most remarkable contribution was supplied by Kirill Khlebnikov, who worked in the Russian-American Company from 1801 (a few years after its foundation) and was appointed director of the Company's office in Novji Arkangel (today Sitka), chief town of Russian Alaska; this assignment allowed him to gather a great deal of information about the history, the geography and the ethnography of the colony. His reports are regarded as the most authoritative and detailed source on Russian territories in the American Continent for the first three decades of the nineteenth century (Khliebnikov, 1836).

8 ANTHROPOLOGY IN RUSSIA: FROM NINETEENTH-CENTURY...

More information was supplied by the scientific expedition organised by Voznesenskii, who had a post in the zoological museum of the Russian Academy of Sciences; Voznesenskii sailed from Saint Petersburg on August 20, 1839, on a ship belonging to the Russian-American Company and docked at Novji Arkangel on May 1, 1840. He carried out many explorations in Russian Alaska for five years, gathering mineralogical, botanical, zoological samples and ethnographical finds, and drawing maps and sketches of species and places. He supplied scientific training to the Navy officer L.A. Zagoskin, who was charged by the Company to carry out an exploration of the inland of Alaska, which up to that time had been scarcely known; he covered thousands of miles between 1842 and 1843, also collecting information about the native peoples.

Ethnographical data were gathered not only by scientists, Company employees and Navy officers but also by orthodox priests, sent to Alaska in order to convert the natives. The most important contribution was supplied by A.V. Kamenskii, who evangelised local people in Novji Arkangel and in Canadian Manitoba, where he met the Tlingit Indians. Later he wrote a book, published in 1906: *The Indians of Alaska. Their Origin and Religion.*

The persecution of the opponents to the czarist tyranny also helped (although unintentionally) the development of Russian ethnography because many members of the intelligentsia, associated to the political groups hostile to the monarchy and sentenced to exile in the most distant lands of Siberia, devoted themselves to the observation of habits and customs of the natives. L. Y. Sternberg, opponent of the monarchy and militant of the Narodnaja Volja group (Will of the people), arrested in 1886, after serving a three-year sentence in Odessa prison, was sentenced to ten years' exile in the Sakhalin islands and sent to a far village, 80 miles from Port Aleksandrovsk, where he devoted himself to the study first of the Ainu and later of the Ghilyak, gathering worthwhile information on their language, folklore, religion and social organisation. In 1893, from the exile, he began to publish papers on a review founded a few years before, in 1889, and still existing today: *Etnograficheskoe Obozriene* (*Ethnographical Survey*). In 1917, after the Revolution, he founded with Bogoraz the first centre of ethnographical studies at the University of Saint Petersburg (Institute of the northern peoples) and carried on his research on Siberian cultures till his death in 1927, publishing many papers; his masterpiece is *Pervobytnaja religija v svete etnografii* (*Primitive Religion: An Ethnographical Perspective*), published after his death, in 1936. He may be

254 P. SCARDUELLI

deemed one of most outstanding soviet ethnographers of the first half of the twentieth century.

V. G. Bogoraz was also a revolutionary exiled in Siberia, where he devoted himself to the observation of Chukchi, analysing their language and folklore. In 1901, he took up a post at the American Museum of Natural History in New York, where, before 1889, Franz Boas (the founder of the twentieth-century American anthropology) had also worked. He returned to Russia in 1904, taught in Saint Petersburg and cooperated with Sternberg, founding the Institute of Northern Peoples together; both of them were members of the Jesup North Pacific Expedition, organised by Boas.

Another two outstanding ethnographers from the first few decades of the nineteenth century are S. M. Shirokogorov and D. A. Zolotarev. The former carried out fieldwork in Siberia along the Chinese border, among Tungus and Manchu of the Amur River and organised three expeditions in the Transbaikal region and Manchuria in 1912, 1913 and 1915–1917. He wasn't a political militant, unlike Sternberg and Bogoraz, and his works lack the Marxist theoretical outline typical of their scientific production. He left the Soviet Union and moved to China in 1922, where he carried out field research among the Yi of Yunnan. His decision to break free from his motherland is clear from his choice to publish his main works (*Social Organization of the Northern Tungus*, 1929, *Psychomental Complex of the Tungus*, 1935) in English instead of Russian.

The latter, D. A. Zolotarev, didn't work in Siberia as the majority of Russian scholars did and chose to devote himself first to the study of the Yaroslav, and later to the Sami of Carelia. He taught in Leningrad (Saint Petersburg had been renamed in honour of the father of the October Revolution), but in 1930 he left the USSR. When he came back, he was arrested and charged with neglecting the Marxist theory in his scientific production. Set free in 1933, he was arrested again two years later and sent to a concentration camp where he died.

Ethnography After the October Revolution

The two revolutions of 1917 (the first in February, the second in October) furthered the development of ethnography. After the February Revolution, a commission (as a division of the Academy of Sciences) was created for the study of the tribes living on Russian soil; its main aim was to draw an ethnic map of the country. After the October Revolution, one of the first decrees issued by the Bolshevik was the Declaration of the Rights of the Peoples of Russia, which proclaimed that all the peoples have equal rights, including the right to self-determination (even to secession) and recognised the right of national minorities to a free development.

Those who had been exiled by the czarist regime began to cooperate with the new soviet power and strengthened ties with the central political authorities which entrusted the ethnographers with the study of the so-called ethnic question and of nationalisms, which were envisaged as a threat to the internationalist ideology adopted by the new State born from the October Revolution.

In the 1920s, ethnography thrived: many research expeditions were organised, academic departments were founded, scientific reviews were published and scholars took part in international conventions. Obviously the theoretical frames used by the ethnographers were Marxism, historical materialism and the evolutionary theory of the nineteenth century, especially the theory of H. L. Morgan, whose main work (*Ancient Society*) had deeply influenced Marx and Engels. In the papers of both Sternberg (who kept up some correspondence with Morgan) and Bogoraz, the notion of 'primitive society' has the evolutionary meaning of 'ancestral'. The small societies of Siberia and northern Russia were the main object of survey and were envisaged as examples of the first stage of development of mankind. The theoretical kit also included other classic Marxist notions such as 'primitive communism', 'patriarchal society' and 'feudal society'. The study of folklore emphasised the progressive features of the native societies (in the prospect of building socialism), that is, the consciousness of being subordinate and the need to fight for emancipation. Therefore, it is not surprising that the development of soviet ethnography implied a close relationship among ethnoarchaeology, ethnohistory and field research on societies and cultures in northern Russia, Siberia and on the folklore of rural communities. This interlacement was the consequence of a theoretical frame which envisaged 'traditional', marginal societies as vestiges of the archaic stages of social development.

The most important Russian folklorist of the first half of the twentieth century is Vladimir Propp, the only one whose renown spread outside Russia, although with some delay. His masterworks are *Morphology of the Fairy Tale*, published in 1928 and *The Historical Roots of the Fairy Tales*, published in 1946. The first book, which was translated in the United States in 1958 and attained renown thanks to the paper Lévi-Strauss devoted to him in 1960, is deeply influenced by the formalist theory.

Propp commits himself to finding out the analogies among the fairy tales and brings to light their morphological structure. Propp's synchronic inquiry stimulated the interest of Lévi-Strauss, who caught the similarities with the structuralist theory. In *The Historical Roots of the Fairy Tales*, on the contrary, Propp adopted a diachronic inquiry, depicting the age and the historical-social context the fairy tales arose from. Propp's historical approach, seemingly similar to the approach previously adopted by the Grimm brothers, Max Müller, Frazer and Andrew Lang, is actually different because it is framed into the Marxist theory; Propp uses the notions of 'structure' and 'superstructure' and the evolutionary stages depicted by historical materialism.

In the first few years after the revolution, the trend that had already emerged at the beginning of the century grew stronger until there was a sharp separation between ethnography and ethnology: a very limited descriptive function was allotted to the former, while the more important task of analysing and comparing the data was entrusted to the latter. In the two-year period 1929–30, the ideological control of the academy was strengthened, and ethnology, envisaged as a discipline conflicting with Marxism, was censored and removed from the universities.

This change brought about long-term consequences: ethnography was deprived of any theoretic relevance and confined to the limited task of describing the ethnic groups. Any attempt of wide-range inferences was ruled out, and this discipline became actually very similar to *Volkskunde*; both Russian and German ethnography remained theoretically backward in comparison with American, English and French anthropology.

For decades, soviet ethnography was being allotted the task of supplying examples to support the stages of social development depicted by historical materialism: the small societies were branded as 'backward' and envisaged as relics of the past. According to this theory, ethnography developed a historiographic bias. The use of written sources was regarded as more important than empirical observation and fieldwork. However, ethnographers didn't have strong academic relationships with historical disciplines; on the contrary, more meaningful links were established with linguistics and archaeology, with the aim (biased by the ideology) of tracing the ancient history of the so-called primitive societies. The same choice of favouring the academic relationships with these disciplines was made in the same years by American anthropology. Only in the last three decades of the twentieth century, when the evolutionary paradigm became obsolete, did the relationship between soviet ethnography and archaeology lose its importance.

Elfimov (2007) pointed out that the choice of favouring the historiographic bias made soviet ethnography similar to the ethnography of Franz Boas, based on the notion of historic-cultural areas. Boas was persuaded that, when all the ethnic groups have been described, all the historic-cultural areas have been identified and the origin of every population has been traced, ethnography will have attained its aim and fulfilled its task.

The hypertrophic development of the study of ethnicity is a feature of soviet ethnography which emerged at the beginning of the 1930s and continued until the end of the Soviet Union. The priority of this kind of research was the consequence of the strengthening of the ideological grip on ethnography, which was entrusted by the political power with very specific tasks. The Soviet State (as well as the czarist empire) enclosed many ethnic and linguistic minorities within its borders, some of which being quite large (Ukrainians, Lithuanians, Latvians, Estonians, Moldavians, Georgians, Armenians, Abkhazians, Turkmenians, Tajikis, Kirghizis). Each of these ethnic and linguistic entities was fragmented in a multitude of sub-units at regional as well as local level. The soviet power was distrustful of them and feared that they could play a leading role in the awakening of nationalist, anti-soviet and secessionist movements. Nationalism was envisaged as ideologically dangerous and incompatible with the internationalist bias of Marxism; therefore, the political power regarded ethnography as a useful device for a deeper insight into a phenomenon which had to be kept under political control. Ethnographers had a higher status and academic prestige in comparison with their colleagues in western countries, where anthropology was regarded as harmless oddness.

This was the main trend of soviet ethnography; nevertheless, research into the new ritual practices that the Communist party had brought in was also carried out. After the victory in the civil war, the revolutionary power was strengthened, and Bolsheviks developed a strategy aimed at weakening the orthodox Church's influence and getting people out of the habit of attending religious services, which were regarded as a 'dark' legacy of the czarist age. Therefore, new rites of passage were organised by the State: 'red christenings', 'red marriages', 'red burials' (McDowell, 1974; Lane, 1981; Scarduelli, 2014, pp. 46–47). Their purpose was to change the perception of the social reality and to give a different meaning to the most important events of life; these events were taken out of the religious

258   P. SCARDUELLI

frame, deprived of their religious symbols and values and associated to the revolution. This plan had a twofold aim: to eradicate from the collective representations the symbolic dualism holy/secular and to weld the individual identity to the new self-image as soviet citizen, which was being created by the State's propaganda, the communist party, the Red Army and the school. The study of the new soviet ceremonies was the fourth (and less important) field of research of the soviet ethnography, the most important being ethnohistory, the study of folklore and the study of ethnicity. Research into the new rituals was carried out until the 1960s and the 1970s; some important works are *Sovremennje prazdniki i obriadi v derevne* (*Contemporary village's feast and rituals*), by L. Alekseeva published in 1968; *Obrjady vcera i segodnija* (*Rituals of yesterday and today*), written by V. I. Brudnij and published in the same year; and *Novaja zhizn. Novje prazdniki* (*New life. New feasts*), published in 1975.

The importance ethnography was vested with by the political power made it possible in the 1930s to found many academic institutions and journals. At the end of the nineteenth century, a journal had already been founded which would become the most prestigious in the field of ethnography: *Etnograficheskoe Obozrenie* (Rassegna etnografica); in 1926 its name changed to *Etnografija* and in 1931 to *Sovetskaja Etnografija*. In 1992, after the end of the USSR, the journal took back its original name. The first issue of *Sovetskaja Etnografja* in 1931 enclosed a paper by H. M. Matorin, *Sovremennji etap n zadaci etnografii* (Contemporary stage and tasks of ethnography), followed by a strongly ideologically biased paper by M. Iu. Palvedre on Finnic bourgeois ethnography and the policy of Finnish Fascism. The third paper belonged to the mainstream of the soviet ethnography (ethnic studies) and was devoted to the nationalistic bias of the Chuvashi's ethnography (an ethnic group of Turkish origin whose territory stretches along the banks of the Volga River between Nizhnij Novgorod and Kazan). The following paper, written by P. E. Bartov, was devoted to the Ifugao of Philippines, clear evidence that the study of 'exotic' cultures had not been discarded by soviet ethnography.

As time went by, the reference to the Marxist theoretical frames, so evident in the works published in the 1930s, became more and more conventional, and a trend of ethnographic pedantry and dull descriptive style grew. A good example is a paper published in *Sovetskaja Etnografija* in 1983 and devoted to the same archaic image recurring in the popular Russian embroidery.

Post-Soviet Anthropology

In 1992, after the end of the USSR, *Sovetskaja Etnografija* returned to its former name (*Etnograficheskoe Obozrenie*); however, its name was not the only change. There was a sudden, deep upheaval in ethnographic research: the working conditions in the academy, the scholars' status, the availability of research funds, the theoretical frameworks, the fields of inquiry and the training of young scholars. To understand how sudden and deep this change was, it is necessary to frame it in the wider context of the political, social and cultural changes the fall of USSR brought about (Strayer, 1998; Marples, 2004).

The disappearance of the first socialist State in the world had dramatic effects on 300 million citizens living in Russia and in the other republics of the USSR, which suddenly became independent; the change involved daily life, social practices, moral values and the image the people had of their own country. The end of the USSR was a 'catastrophic' experience not only from the point of view of material and social life but also from a cognitive point of view. This experience shared some similarities with what happened to the Aztec people when they and the *conquistadores* clashed. The sudden disappearance of the USSR brought about an earthquake in the mental landscape of Russian people, who endured the loss of the superpower status of their country, political and cultural subalternity to the United States, economic colonisation, the spread of violence and crime and the breakdown of welfare.

Obviously, the academy was also severely affected by the economic crisis of the first half of the 1990s. The universities underwent several changes from then on, the most dramatic being the cut in state funding, forcing scholars to seek private funding. The latter type of funding clearly influenced the choice of research topics. With regard to this problem, Baiburin remarks the difference between 'romantics' and 'pragmatics': the former being the scholars who didn't have any kind of funding, the latter being the scholars who tried to achieve funding by proposing research projects suitable for the market's requirements or even by carrying out research on demand. Obviously, the old scholars were more affected by the new situation because of long years spent in the soviet academy; they found it hard to adjust to the change. Furthermore, they were reluctant to accept the theoretical influence of American and English anthropology and their topics. The inevitable and necessary transformation of the Russian ethnography was therefore difficult both for objective and subjective reasons (Elfimov, 1999, 2007).

An important attempt to open the former soviet ethnography to western anthropology and to the dialogue with foreign colleagues, to acquire fresh theoretical frames, new topics and fields of research was the foundation of the *Antropologicheskii Forum* in September 2004, whose English name is *Forum for Anthropology and Culture*, an interdisciplinary, international journal including contributions within the fields of anthropology, cultural studies and cultural history. It is published by prestigious Saint Petersburg institutions—the Peter the Great Museum of Anthropology and Ethnology, the Russian Academy of Sciences and the European University of Saint Petersburg—and is supported by the European Humanities Research Centre of the Oxford University. The editorial board includes not only Russian but also American, English and French scholars; the journal also accepts contributions from foreign scholars, has an English edition published once a year which offers a choice of the most interesting Russian contributions. Furthermore, the second volume every year publishes a panel discussion on specific issues, both theoretical and methodological; for example, the ethics of field research, the future of museum ethnography, relationships among researchers and research subjects, the teaching of anthropology and Russian national identity.

The papers published by the Forum cover a wide range of issues: the typical ethnic topics of soviet ethnography but also the cultural dynamics in contemporary Russia; for instance, soviet school in the post-Stalin age, witnesses of the siege of Leningrad, prayers for rain in Central Asia, the coexistence of public and private in the economy of rural Russia, domestic strategies of the migrants (over the last twenty years a huge number of migrants have been leaving the former soviet republics bound for Moscow in search of jobs), teenagers' obsession with buying goods and the spread of drugs among young people. Contributions concerning the anthropology, the archaeology and the cultural history of geographical areas of other Continents are also published, for instance, papers on Easter Island inscriptions, Indian religious feasts and the historical memory of African Americans.

One year after the foundation of the Forum in 2005, the editorial board sent a wide range of questions to 150 scholars in many Russian universities: do foreign anthropologists quote their Russian colleagues? Do Russian anthropologists make any use of their western colleagues' works? Which theoretical frames are applied? Which are the most important fields of inquiry? The editorial board received only forty-five answers (actually not many; the vast majority of them sent from scholars of the Moscow and Saint Petersburg universities); however, these answers offer an interesting picture of the state of contemporary Russian anthropology, of the main fields of inquiry, of the training of young anthropologists and of the relationships with Anglo-American anthropology.

Some answers are detailed and exhaustive. Abashin, a member of the editorial board of the prestigious journal *Etnograficheskoe Obozrenie*, maintains that Russian ethnography is backward and slowly declining; he also asserts that outdated theories still prevail and that students receive inadequate training; there are no Russian anthropological handbooks of international standards; foreign handbooks are neither translated nor used in anthropological courses, and although many classical works have been translated (Malinowski, Kluckhohn, Evans-Pritchard, Lévy-Bruhl, Leach, Geertz, Bourdieu, Anderson), they are only studied superficially. Abashin complains about the absence of a theoretical debate, due to the lack of ideas worthy of being discussed. However, field research is still alive; he mentions the Schweitzer work (an ethnolinguistic study concerning the Russian communities settled since the seventeenth century in northeastern Siberia) and the works of Utekhin on community life (see bibliography). He and Tishkov (one of the most outstanding Russian anthropologists of the last thirty years) also point out that there is no agreement within the scientific community about what ethnography ought to be, its fields of inquiry, the problems it should focus on, the strategies that ought to be applied for the development of the discipline and the relationships with the international anthropological community (Tishkov, 1998).

Abashin strongly supports the opinion that Russian anthropologists should devote themselves to the main problems of the contemporary Russia: migrants' stream from the former soviet republics to Moscow, social inequalities, insecurity, survival strategies of the poorest people, political authoritarianism, social control, matters regarding cultural boundaries and the study of the soviet age. On the contrary most of the scholars still devote themselves to outdated issues such as ethnicity and tradition.

Relationships with the anthropological international community is a very important subject for Russian anthropologists. Many factors make these relationships difficult: the traditional distrustfulness of Russian ethnographers towards western colleagues, the fact that western anthropologists do not speak Russian and their old die-hard prejudices as regards soviet ethnography. Western scholars were persuaded that Russian ethnographers suffered a heavy political censorship, and therefore their scientific production was of no value. However, contacts between Russian and western anthropologists have increased recently; some western scholars have begun to carry out research in fields that are familiar to their Russian colleagues and to pay more attention to the works they publish (Wanner, 2011).

Ekaterina Melnikova points out that some Russian scholars are trying to enter the international market of social research and therefore to adapt their theoretic frames and their practices of inquiry to market demands. However, this attempt to conform to terminology, concepts and patterns of western anthropology clashes with the deep difference between the training of Russian anthropologists and the training of western anthropologists. The main problem underscored both by Melkinova and Abashin is the weakness of the discipline's institutional foundations; in Russian universities it is badly taught: anthropology is mainly a brand used by pro-western scholars who are in love with capitalism. Reshetov also blames the undiscriminating use of western anthropological jargon, the superficiality and the amateurism of scholars studying new issues such as conflicts and ethnopolitics.

Baiburin, editor-in-chief from 2004 to 2013 of the previously mentioned journal *Antropologicheskii Forum,* thinks, like Abashin, that Russian anthropologists' professional identity is undergoing a crisis and that there is widespread uncertainty and confusion about the current tasks of the discipline. The main subject of soviet ethnography is on the wane (Tishkov published in 2001 a book entitled *Rekviem po etnosu, Requiem for ethnos*), but the study of the contemporary world, which is one of the main topics of the anthropological research in the West, in Russia has a very slow development, partly because of the previously mentioned problems (mainly the weakness of the university teaching and of the training of the young generation of scholars), partly because this topic is monopolised by sociologists. In addition, subjects which are very important today for western anthropology, such as the new rise of nationalisms and xenophobia, in Russia are more studied by political experts than by ethnologists.

The delay in scientific updating and the poor skill in dealing with the most current topics make ethnography less and less useful both for political institutions and for private companies, which would be willing to fund research. The consequence is a widespread frustration, especially among the scholars who spent most of their academic life in the soviet age. The soviet regime was strongly interested in ethnography, and ethnographers had an important role in the carrying out of the national policy aiming to achieve a better knowledge of local ethnic groups, to strengthen the ideological control of these groups and to fight nationalisms. Today the political situation and the dominant ideology are completely different, and ethnography is no longer requested to fulfil these tasks; therefore anthropologists feel useless, even more so because they are also ousted from the new fields of research funded by the market; the private enterprises prefer to turn to sociologists and political experts.

Baiburin, like Abashin, severely criticises the way the new generations of scholars are trained. After the fall of the Soviet Union, educational standards lowered; in some universities (especially in the marginal areas and less important cities), the outdated topics of the soviet age (ethnic studies, folklore) are still taught; in other universities, most of all in the newly founded institutions and most important cities, more open to foreign influences, students are introduced to western anthropology but only receive superficial information about badly chosen and badly translated scientific literature. There is a deep disparity between centre and periphery, which concerns the availability of both information and resources. Obviously, the scholars who work in the academic institutions in Moscow and Saint Petersburg are in a better situation, while the ethnographers who work in the more remote regions endure both cultural and geographic marginalisation. Nevertheless, Baiburin maintains that even the anthropologists working in Moscow and Saint Petersburg are backward and incapable of developing a serious theoretic debate.

Russian anthropology swings between the longing for the past and attention to western anthropology; many scholars stubbornly stick to the legacy of soviet ethnography and are neither willing nor capable of self-criticism; others, on the contrary, are willing to accept the western influence but in an undiscriminating way. There is not a third option, that is, an attempt to renew the Marxist theoretical frames. A new way of applying Marxism to anthropology is hindered by the fact that during the soviet age, the use of the Marxist theory was merely conventional; ethnographers had to conform to the 'official' version of the Marxist theory established by the State's ideology. Quite paradoxically, an original use of Marxist frames in anthropological research was carried out by western anthropologists, mainly in France (Meillassoux, Godelier, Bourdieu).

264   P. SCARDUELLI

One of the most outstanding contemporary Russian anthropologists, in addition to Abashin and Baiburin, is Valerii Tishkov, who has been the director of the Institute of Ethnology and Anthropology of the Russian Academy of Sciences since 2015. Tishkov's assessment of the state of the discipline is less pessimistic in comparison with Abashin's or Baiburin's; he points out that the decline of soviet ethnography, founded on historic materialism and evolutionism hasn't led to the stagnation of research because over the last two decades a research trend with a new theoretical bias has begun to rise. This new trend focuses on the social and cultural changes which have been taking place in Russia over the last thirty years. Tishkov entrusts this new trend with a 'political' mission, the task of helping to understand the transformation process, a task that sociological and statistical research can't fulfil. Only anthropology is able to work out analytical models of the contemporary society and to interpret the behavioural patterns, the strategies of political mobilisation and legitimation of leadership (Tishkov, 2020).

Therefore, contemporary Russian anthropology also includes scholars, in addition to those who look back to soviet ethnography and those who aim to imitate western anthropology, who try to work out new theoretic perspectives and think that it is necessary to analyse Russian contemporary society discarding widespread western stereotypes such as 'the collapse of the soviet empire' and 'gulag archipelago', which originate from the ideological assumption that the Russian society is just a projection of the political regime, of its rules and values. A widespread western prejudice, shared not only by politicians and people but unfortunately also by anthropologists, asserts that the Russian society, moulded for decades by the soviet regime, is a *unicum* and that the communist ideology created a *Homo sovieticus*, radically different from western people. Tishkov underlines, on the contrary, the similarities between the private strategies of Russians and those of Western Europeans, concerning both the aspiration to comfort (or even wealth) and family dynamics, both ethnic and professional identities and psycho-deviances. It is the same argument that the English anthropologist Chris Hann supported in his work on the privatisation of the collective property, on the post-socialist economy and on the problems involved by the redistribution of the commodities that people aspire to (1993).

Both contemporary Russian society and Western European society have many inner differences, confront similar problems and have similar dynamics. An example is the social impact of the stream of migrants. Western countries must deal with a massive stream of migrants from northern Africa, whereas Russia attracts the dwellers of the former soviet republics, where, obviously, the standard of living is quite lower; Russia must cope with a migration of about four or five million young men from Azerbaijan, Armenia, Belarus, Georgia, Moldova, Ukraine and Tajikistan. These migrants are illegal and offer cheap manpower for the building industry, trade and services. Their spread to the biggest cities (Moscow and Saint Petersburg) has triggered Russian xenophobia and fostered prejudices very similar to those shared by the dwellers of western countries about north African migrants. Russians call the migrants 'chechens' or 'blacks', no matter where they come from. Europeans act in the same way when labelling people arriving from Nigeria, Eritrea or Sri Lanka as 'black'.

Tishkov has carried out an inquiry into the psychological, social and cultural problems which hinder the integration of the migrants, but he has also drawn attention to other problems regarding their displacement: people living in the former soviet republics still keep the tendency to move as freely as they did in the soviet age, also because the family bonds which go across boundaries still exist. However, the former soviet republics are now sovereign states which claim the right to control their own borders both to show off their sovereignty and to control the illegal trade of drugs and weapons. Obviously, these contrasting claims (freedom of movement and boundary control) clash. Tishkov points out that it was difficult to keep the USSR united, but it is difficult too to dismember it. The task of anthropologists, especially Russian ones, who endured the difficult transition from the USSR to contemporary Russia, is not to analyse the geopolitical implications of this change but to study the human geography, the way the cultural identities changed or remained unchanged and also the personal and social sufferings brought about by such a huge upheaval. This new task demands the critical reassessment of the old ethnic demography of the soviet age, based on the administrative classification in 'peoples', 'nations', 'ethnic groups' and the adoption of a fresh view, which allows us to understand the dynamics implied by the transformation of the collective identities, both ethnic and social; such a new view must be founded on the theoretic assumption (which the western ethnic studies acquired fifty years ago) that collective identities are not objective but self-ascribed; therefore every individual may have multiple identities and feel himself/herself, in different contexts, as a village dweller, member of a local ethnic group or of a nation.

If contemporary Russia copes with migration and problems similar to those western Europe has to face, it also deals with other ethnic problems quite different, mainly the fact that about twenty million Russians or Russian-speaking individuals live in the 'new foreign countries', that is, the republics which achieved independence after the fall of the USSR. Suddenly becoming citizens of Lithuania, Latvia, Estonia, Moldova and Kazakhstan, these Russians keep their ethnic identity, speak only Russian (many of them do not speak the official languages of the new states at all: Lithuanian, Ukrainian or Rumanian), and stay loyal to the Russian homeland, which claims the right to protect them. In addition to the problem concerning the migrants arriving in Russia from the former soviet republics, this problem is an important issue for Russian anthropologists.

Another field of inquiry that is very important for Russian anthropology is the study of material culture. The standard of living in Russia has been improving over the last twenty years; this improvement concerns food (more widespread consumption of fruit, cheese, wine, wider assortment of foods, many more restaurants, which in the soviet age were scarce) but also commodities and consumer goods: electronic devices, cell phones, TV remote controls, microwave ovens, portable computers; furthermore, Russians can now easily travel abroad, visit foreign countries and spend holidays on exotic beaches. Everyday life has completely changed: there are now new domestic devices, new interior design, luxury furniture imported from Italy and new heating systems. Profound changes have also taken place in body care, cosmetics and beauty treatments, which are now widespread. Over a period of twenty years (just one generation) hundreds of goods and commodities that were previously unknown have changed the daily lives of Russians.

One of the most important outcomes of the sudden and chaotic transition from a socialist system to the market economy at the beginning of the 1990s was the rise of a new wealthy class, with enough money (often illegally earned) to buy luxury goods and to show them off as status symbols: imported luxury cars, yachts, private aircrafts, villas in Sardinia or Monte Carlo. For the members of this new class the former soviet people's wish to have a dacha has become the aspiration to build a luxury country house with a swimming pool and private park.

As Tishkov (1999) remarks, Russian anthropologists have begun to study the transition from the soviet way of life focused on the aspiration to own commodities that are hard to come by, such as cars or refrigerators (this problem was called *defizit* in the soviet age) to a quite different way of life that is focused on the greedy consumption of imported commodities and on the aspiration to leisure and comfort. Among the studies devoted to the transformation of the behavioural patterns during the transition from the socialist society to the market economy (studies which may be labelled as the 'anthropology of everyday life') is the important book by I. Utekin, *Ocherki kommunalnogo byta* (*Studies on the Community Life*), which analyses soviet and post-soviet stereotypes, in particular the most prosaic facets of the everyday life, the semiotics of the living space, the relationships with the neighbours, the pathologies of everyday life, personal hygiene and the distribution of household tasks.

Another topic, which belongs to the field of studies labelled in the West since the 1940s as political anthropology, has been focused on by Russian anthropologists in recent years: the relationship between the State and citizenship. The anthropologists who analyse the transformation of the Russian identity after the fall of the Soviet Union have created the label 'revolution of the double refusal', which means that the overthrow of the soviet regime and the rejection of the socialist economic system are intertwined with the refusal of moral values shared by soviet citizens (however, not all Russians rejected them, and the refusal is more or less radical according to the social class and ideological bias).

The analysis of the new, post-soviet organisation of the State's power may also be included in the field of political anthropology. Russian scholars use a concept created by western political anthropology (in particular dynamic anthropology and F. Bailey) more than half a century ago, that is, the power as a 'political arena' wherein rival political subjects vie and fight for public resources. The politicians (many of whom began their career on the soviet age and still retain habits and behaviours of the former nomenklatura) have mixed old privileges (official cars, bodyguards, dachas allotted by the State) with new privileges, acquired (mainly in the 1990s, during the premiership of Yeltsin) through the plunder of the State's assets and properties. There are some similarities but mainly sharp differences between soviet politicians and the present politicians: in particular the tough selection of the nomenklatura's members worked out by the Communist Party has been replaced by a competition without rules; to win the contest it is of primary importance to achieve the support of the holders of economic power. Another difference in comparison with the soviet political system (which was based on a tough centralisation of the decision-making process) is the wide autonomy of the governors

268 P. SCARDUELLI

of the *oblasti* (regions), who through the control of the ballot can achieve strong local support.

Many Russian anthropologists tried to carry out a radical renewal of their discipline and devote themselves to the new topics (cultural change, new behavioural patterns of the Russians, migrations, Russian minorities in the former soviet republics, material culture, analysis of political power), but their attempts were seriously hindered by the lack of financial resources in the years of Eltsin's leadership, when the funding was sharply cut down and the recruitment of a new generation of researchers was undermined. The crisis of the 1990s has deeply damaged Russian anthropology, leaving an unbridgeable gap between the old scholars still sticking to old-fashioned soviet ethnography and the young inexperienced scholars. As Elfimov remarks (2007, p. 92), Russian anthropology is a tribe split into two halves which do not communicate: those who look back nostalgically on the soviet age and envisage ethnography as a calling, and the young people, who envisage the scientific research as a business, just a job. Elfimov warns that the retirement of the old generation could bring about the collapse of the discipline or its deep transformation, as it lost its institutional relationship with the State, which was so strong in the soviet age.

Anyway, in spite of the theoretical backwardness in comparison with western anthropology and the hindrances of the present situation, Russian anthropology is vital and devotes itself to a wide range of fields of research which other disciplines (sociology, political science) do not take into account. The future of Russian anthropology is yet to be written.

References

Alekseeva, J. (1968). *Sovremennje prazdniki i obrjadi v derevne* (Contemporary Feasts and Rituals). Profizdat.

Baiburin, A. (1993). *Ritual v tradizionnoi kulture* (The Ritual in the Traditional Culture). St. Petersburg.

Baiburin, A., Kelly, C., & Vakhtin, N. (Eds.). (2012). *Cultural Anthropology after the Collapse of Communism*. Routledge.

Bogoraz, V. G. (1901). The Chukchi of Northeastern Asia. *American Anthropologist, 3*(1), 28–136.

Bogoraz, V. G. (1934). *Chukchi. Sotsial'naja organizatsija (The Chukchi. Social Organization)*. Institut Naroda Severa.

Bogoraz, V. G. (1939). *Chukchi. Religija (Chukchi Religion)*. Glavsevermorput.

Brudnij, V. I. (1968). *Obrjad vciera i segodnija* (Rituals of Yesterday and Today). Moskva.

8 ANTHROPOLOGY IN RUSSIA: FROM NINETEENTH-CENTURY... 269

Dobrizhena, L. M. (1995). *Suverenitet i etnicheskoe samosoznanie, ideal, praktika* (*Sovereignty and Ethnic Consciousness, Ideal, Practice*). Institut of Ethnology and Anthropology.

Elfimov, A. (1999). The State of the Discipline in Russia: Interviews with Russian Anthropologists. *American Anthopologist, 4*, 775–785.

Elfimov, A. (2007). Russian Ethnography: Dilemmas of the Present and the Past. *Anthopological Yearbook of European Cultures, 16*, 77–100.

Hann, C. (1993). *Socialism, Ideals, Ideologies and Local Practices*. Routledge.

Kasten, E. (Ed.). (2018). *Jochelson, Bogoras and Shterberg: A Scientific Exploration of Northeastern Siberia and the Shaping of Soviet Ethnography*. Kulturstiftung Siberien.

Khazanov, A. (1996). *After the USSR: Ethnicity, Nationalism and Politics in the Commonwealth of Independent States*. University of Winsconsin Press.

Khliebnikov, K. (1836). Vzgljad na polveka moei djizni (A Look on Half Century of My Life). *Sjn otechestva, CLXXV.*

Korobkov, A. V., & Zaionchkovskaja, Z. A. (2004). The Changes in the Migration Patterns in the Post-Soviet States: The First Decade. *Communist and Post-Communist Studies, 37*, 481–508.

Koslov, V. I. (1999). *Ethnos, Nation and People*. Moscow.

Lane, C. (1981). *The Rites of Rulers: Ritual in Industrial Societies. The Soviet Case*. Cambridge University Press.

Marples, D. (2004). *The Collapse of the Soviet Union 1985–1991*. Routledge.

McDowell, J. (1974). Soviet Civil Ceremonies. *Journal for the Scientific Study of Religion, 13*(3), 265–279.

McFaul, M., & Rybov, A. (1999). *Rossiskoe obschestvo: stanovlenie demokraticheskich tsennostei? (The Russian Society: The Making of Democratic Values?)*. Carnegie Center.

Scarduelli, P. (2014). *I riti del potere*. Carocci.

Schweitze, P. (2004). *Russkie Starozhily Sibiri* (Ancient Russian Settlers in Siberia). Moskva.

Shirokogorov, S. M. (1919). *Opyt izledovanija osnov shamansta i Tungusov* (Research Experience on the Foundations of Shamanism and on Tungusov). Moskva.

Shirokogorov, S. M. (1929). *Social Organization of the Northern Tungus (Original Edition in English)*. The Commercial Press.

Shirokogorov, S. M. (1935). *Psychomental Complex of the Tungus (Original Edition in English)*. Kegan.

Slezkine, Y. (1993). Sovetskaja etnografija v nokdaune. 1928–38 (Soviet Ethnography Knocked Down. 1928–38). *Etnograficheskoe Obozrenie, 2*, 113–125.

Stecenko, S. E. (1975). Novaja zhizn. Novye prazdniki (New Life. New Feasts). *Nauka i religija, 4*, 13–19.

Sternberg, L. J. (1893). Sakhalinskie Giliak (The Giliak of the Sakhalin Island). *Etnograficheskoe Obozrenie, 2*, 1–46.

Sternberg, L. J. (1936). *Pervobytnaja religija v svete etnografii (Primitive Religion. An Ethnographic Outlook)*. Insitut narodov severa.

Strayer, R. (1998). *Why Did the Soviet Union Collapse*. Tylor & Francis.

Tishkov, V. A. (Ed.). (1997). *Migratsii i Novye Diaspory v Postsovetskikh Gosudarstvakh (Migrations and New Diasporas in Post-Soviet States)*. Institut Etnologii Antropologii Moskow.

Tishkov, V. A. (1998). The Anthropology of Russian Transformations. *Anthropological Journal of European Cultures, 8*(2), 141–170.

Tishkov, V. A. (1999). Ethnic Conflicts in the Former USSR. *Journal of Peace Research, 36*(5), 571–590.

Tishkov, V. A. (2001a). *Rekviem po etnosu (Eternal Rest for Ethnos)*. Nauka.

Tishkov, V. A. (2001b). Rossiiskaja etnologija (Russian Ethnology). *Etnograficheskoe Obozrenie, 5*, 3–23.

Tishkov, V. A. (2020). From Where Is Russian Ethnology and Where Is It Going? A Personal View in Global Prospective. *Etnograficheskoe Obozrenie, 2*, 72–137.

Tishkov, V. A., & Pivneva, E. A. (Eds.). (2018). *Istoricheskaja pamiat' i rossiiskaja identichnost (Historical Memory and Russian Identity)*. Rossiiskaja Akademija Nauk.

Tomilov, N. A. (2001). Rossiiskoe etnograficeskoe sibirevedenie 20 veka (Russian Ethnographic Studies on Siberia in the XX Century). *Etnograficheskoe Obozrenie, 3*, 92–101.

Utekin, I. (2004). *Ocherky kommunalnogo byta (Studies on Community Life)*. Odintsovskyi Gumanitarnyi Institut.

Wanner, C. (2011). An Anthropological Light: Ethnographic Studies of Russia and Ukraine in the Post-Soviet Era. *Canadian Slavonic Papers, 53*(2/4), 545–557.

CHAPTER 9

Indigenous Ethnologists, National Anthropologists, Post-colonial Intellectuals: The Trajectory of Anthropology in French-Speaking West and Equatorial Africa

Alice Bellagamba

The research and reflections underlying this chapter were developed within the framework of the Research Project of National Interest (PRIN-2017) "Genealogies of African Freedoms" (2020–2023), which the author has coordinated together with Pierluigi Valsecchi (University of Pavia), Alessandro Gusman (University of Turin) and Bruno Riccio (University of Bologna). Special thanks to Gabriella D'Agostino and Vincenzo Matera, editors of this volume, for the encouragement to consider an aspect of the history of anthropology that has proven particularly fruitful.

A. Bellagamba (✉)
University of Milano-Bicocca, Milan, Italy
e-mail: alice.bellagamba@unimib.it

© The Author(s), under exclusive license to Springer Nature Switzerland AG 2023
G. D'Agostino, V. Matera (eds.), *Histories of Anthropology*,
https://doi.org/10.1007/978-3-031-21258-1_9

271

272 A. BELLAGAMBA

In the regions of Sub-Saharan Africa conquered by France in the second half of the nineteenth century, which later became part of French West and Equatorial Africa, the development of anthropology[1] can be linked to colonial expansion. As in the British Empire, geographical knowledge was central for conquering and governing new territories but the need to identify, understand and legitimise colonial domination also drove the growth of expertise on indigenous societies, languages and cultures. For the leaders of the Third Republic (1870–1940) the creation of the first centres of metropolitan colonial erudition, such as the Musée de l'Homme (1880) or the l'École française d'Extrême Orient (1898), was meant to balance "in a civilising, if not spiritual way, a politics of imperial expansion through military conquests" (Karady, 1982, p. 23; Conklin, 1997, pp. 175–97; De L'Estoile, 2000; Wilder, 2005). The works of nineteenth-century travellers such as René Caillié (1830), who reached the city of Timbuktu in the 1820s, having studied the Arabic language and Muslim customs, provided a point of reference for the colonial officials and the missionaries sent to serve in the interior of West and Equatorial Africa by the turn of the century. Previously, these regions had been known only thanks to information gleaned from trading activities and military expeditions. With the establishment of the École coloniale in 1889 (from 1934, the École nationale de la France d'outre-mer), ethnology and indigenous languages were included among subjects taught to aspiring officials. Once in the field, one of their duties was to develop a knowledge of the "backward races" which could strengthen the understanding of human diversity as much as support the civilisation of primitive people (Mbembe, 2010, p. 166).

In addition to the contribution of Maurice Delafosse, Charles Monteil, Henri Gaden, Henri Labouret, Gilbert Viellard and Robert Delavignette,[2]

---

[1] The term "anthropology" is used differently in French than in English. By the end of the nineteenth century, "ethnology" and "ethnography" corresponded to the emerging discipline of British and American cultural and social anthropology, while "anthropology" was a generic term used to indicate the entire field of studies centred on the human sphere as much as a synonym of physical anthropology. After World War II, led by Claude Lévi-Strauss, French scholars began to speak of themselves as cultural and social anthropologists (Sibeud, 2012, pp. S83–S84).

[2] See, for example, Delafosse (1912), Monteil (1915, 1924), Gaden (1931), Labouret (1929, 1935), Viellard (1939), Delavignette (1939); more specifically on the work of Delafosse, see Amselle and Sibeud (1998) and on that of Gaden, Dilley (2014). Sibeud (2002) reconstructs the beginnings of French Africanist thought, while Coquery-Vidrovitch (2006) offers a critical assessment of developments following decolonisation, underlining how Africanists lost their central role in the French context.

appointed head of the École in 1937, and other ethnologist-officials whose work is often mentioned when discussing the beginnings of African studies in France, the "colonial library" (Mudimbe, 1988)[3] expanded thanks to the efforts of ethnographer-missionaries. This is the other great root of anthropology in French-speaking Africa (Abéga, 2006, p. 114). Both the Holy Ghost Fathers and the Missionaries of Africa[4] played a role in French colonisation, albeit their mission not always agreed with Republican ideals of civilisation. Even if it often conflicted with their religious commitment (especially in regions such as Saharan Africa and the Sahel, where evangelisation made little headway compared to Islamic proselytism), missionaries followed the rule of respecting the history, customs and habits of the peoples they worked with, attempting to spread the evangelical message through local cultures. Through the publication of the first dictionaries and the teaching of indigenous languages in the missionary schools, their contribution to linguistic standardisation was crucial. Above all, missionary ethnographic engagement triggered a process of cultural reflection and recuperation that would filter into indigenous practices and discourses, only to be "discovered anew by later anthropologists" (Cinnamon, 2006, p. 413).

When Georges Balandier met the Fang of Gabon in the late 1940s, they were involved in a process of cultural revivalism, mediated by the religious

---

[3] For Mudimbe (1988), the expression "colonial library" refers to body of texts and representations, and to the epistemology, that have "invented" the otherness and inferiority of Africa as an antithesis to Western civilisation.

[4] Founded in 1703, from 1732 the Holy Ghost Fathers (*Congregatio Sancti Spiritus sub tutela Immaculati Cordis Beatissimae Virginis Mariae*) were actively engaged in evangelising work in the Caribbean and North American French colonies and in other parts of the world with trade links to France, such as China and Siam. In 1766, the Holy See assigned them the Apostolic Prefecture of Iles Saint-Pierre et Miquelon, off the coast of Canada, followed by those of French Guiana and Saint-Louis du Sénégal. Suppressed during the French Revolution and restored under Napoleon Bonaparte, only to be immediately again suppressed, the congregation continued to operate during the 1800s, settling from the end of the century in the parts of Africa conquered by France. Holy Ghost Fathers who made important contributions to advancing African ethnology included Alexandre Leroy, with his impressive work on Bantu religions (Leroy, 1911) and numerous articles published in the journal *Anthropos*, founded in 1906 by Wilhelm Schmidt (1968–1954), a Verbite (Society of the Divine Word, SVD) missionary. The Missionaries of Africa (known as the White Fathers) are a more recent order, founded in 1868 by Cardinal Charles Martial Allemand Lavigerie, Archbishop of Algiers. Lavigerie, aware that members of the congregation were destined to live in little-known areas of Africa, made the study of local languages and cultures one of the missionaries' daily tasks. The White Fathers also published numerous articles in *Anthropos*.

274   A. BELLAGAMBA

cults, which drew on the ethnological insights of Father Henri Trilles (1912) and of the Presbyterian missionary Robert Hamill Nassau (Cinnamon, 2006, p. 414). Léon M'ba, who would go on to become the first president of the Gabonese Republic, was among the intellectuals involved in the cultural re-imagination of Fang culture and traditions. Between the two world wars, M'ba (2002) published works on Fang marriage customs and laws. His ethnological engagement, like that of many other intellectuals and politicians of his generation, stands as a reminder that it would be partial, and above all tending towards metropolitan arrogance, to overlook African contributions to the "colonial library," not just as interpreters and mediators but also as amateur researchers and authors (Labrune-Badiane & Smith, 2018, p. 29). The ethnological interest of Africans educated in colonial and missionary schools is, after all, the proper starting point for what Jean Copans (1991, p. 328) has called an "a knowledge of Africa from within," certainly subordinated to colonial scientific conventions and methodologies but nonetheless an expression of a localised patriotism that, with the fading of the empires after the Second World War, would converge in the anti-colonial struggle. François Manchuelle (1995, p. 335) traces the origins of this proto-nationalism in the early days of the colonial conquest. Taking his work as a starting point, and reviewing the available critical literature on developments in anthropology and the social sciences in the countries born out of the breakup of French West and Equatorial Africa, the following pages introduce some of the African pioneers of ethnological research. With decolonisation, history and sociology came to dominate representation of African cultures and societies. After pausing to consider the reasons that, after independence, complicated the transformation of colonial anthropology into national anthropological traditions, this overview will close with some reflections on the challenges of this new century.

Pioneers of Indigenous Ethnology: Folklore, Customs, Local History

A reconstruction of "indigenous" anthropological traditions in French West Africa could choose as its starting point the town of Saint-Louis, a historical site of French presence in this part of the continent. In the second half of the nineteenth century, France, which had previously restricted its political and commercial activity to the coast, embarked on the conquest of the inland regions. Heading up this expansion was military commander Louis Faidherbe, who in 1854 was appointed governor of the Colonie du Sénégal, in other words the settlement of Saint-Louis, and an adjacent narrow coastal strip. In the previous year of 1853, Abbot Pierre-David Boilat had published his *Esquisses senegalaises* (Boilat, 1984) which offered a detailed description of the peoples among whom he officiated, in particular the Serer and Wolof. Boilat was born of a French father and creole mother in Saint-Louis. In 1855, Frederic Carrère and Paul Holle published another ethnologically inspired work, *De la Sénégambie française* (Carrère & Holle, 1855). Holle, like Boilat, was creole. The publication added to the knowledge of Senegalese society and culture, which was expanding in the period also thanks to Faidherbe's efforts (1859, 1882, 1887). Reflecting Republican ideals, *De la Sénégambie française* fiercely criticised the feudalism of Wolof and Mauritanian society with which Saint-Louis had been in contact for centuries, evoking, as Boilat had done, a future in which Senegal would catch up with Europe socially and economically.

Fadherbe's initiatives as governor included the establishment of the École des otages (later renamed the École des fils des chefs) in order to train the offspring of indigenous rulers and aristocrats to assume positions in the colonial administration of the territories progressively included into the French sphere of influence. Yoro Dyao, the son of Fara Penda, a Wolof aristocrat allied to the French, was one of its first pupils (Boulègue, 1988, pp. 395–396). Dyao is celebrated as a pioneer by Senegalese historiographers because he provided not only one of the first French-language reconstructions of the history of the Wolof kingdoms, but also observations on the social structure, customs and habits of the Wolof, equally important from an anthropological point of view. After graduating with honours, he was appointed canton chief. His complicated relationship with the administration, which saw him repeatedly removed from office and reinstated, did not prevent him from cultivating his intellectual ambitions, starting with the publication in 1864 of an article on Wolof royalty in *Le Moniteur du Sénégal*, the colony's official journal (Dyao, 1864). Two of Dyao's notebooks were published by Gaden (1912) and the remainder by Raymond Rousseau (1930), a teacher at the Lycée of Saint-Louis to whom Gaden entrusted the task.

Dyao's work, like that of Boilat, Carrère and Holle, was inspired by a sort of emerging African patriotism, in his case focussing on the glories of the medieval Jolof Empire, which had dominated the Wolof regions of

Senegal from the thirteenth to the sixteenth century. His notebooks reflect the point of view of an aristocrat on his own society: foundation myths, social organisation, relations between the elites, slaves and endogamous professional groups, known in colonial language as "castes." Dyao criticised aristocratic vices, and while his collaborative relationship with the French was evident, he also longed for a reformed Wolof society, in which slavery would be abolished and authority exercised humanely. Other indigenous intellectuals cultivated similar historical and ethnological interests. *Chroniques du Foûta sénégalais*, published by Delafosse and Gaden (1913), was a combination of two manuscripts, the first put together by the retired interpreter Abdoulaye Kane (Abdulay Kan), former chief of the Futa Toro canton, and the second by Yahia Kane (Yahya Kan), also a canton chief. After repeated joint revisions by Gaden and Sire-Abbas-Soh, a scholar from Futa Toro, and translation and annotation by Delafosse, these materials were published with a critical introduction by the latter. Besides cooperation between indigenous figures and colonial officials on questions of common interest, the knowledge accumulated in the "colonial library" emerged also from below.

In 1916, for instance, Kane (1916) published an ethnographic article on the family genealogies of Futa Toro in the first issue of the journal of the Comité d'études historiques et scientifiques de l'A.O.F, set up in the previous year of 1915 at the behest of the governor, Marie François Joseph Clozel, with the aim of strengthening ethnological, historical and scientific studies on this part of the continent.[5] Members of the Comité included, among others, Delafosse, Gaden, Labouret, as well as Emile Durkheim, Lucien Levy-Bruhl and Georges Hardy, inspector-general of education in French West Africa. In 1913, Hardy had promoted the publication of another journal, *Bulletin de l'Enseignement de l'Afrique Occidentale Française*, with the aim of hosting many of the works published by indigenous amateur ethnologists. His innovative educational policy combined the fundamentals of French language and culture with an appreciation of local history and cultures. Indigenous teachers were

---

[5] Senegalese ethnologists and historians of note from this period include Jean-Pierre Sarr, a seminarist who gathered the first information on Serer history and customs, and Cheikh Moussa Kamara, a scholar from Futa Toro who wrote in Arabic—also a friend of Delafosse, Gaden and other French Africanists—author of *Zuhuir al-Basatin fī Ta'rikh al-Sawadin* (translated as *Florilège au jardin de l'histoire des Noirs*), consisting of over 1700 pages of genealogies, chronicles and comments written in the early 1920s (Boulègue, 1988, p. 396; Robinson, 1988, p. 100).

encouraged to conduct research into oral traditions, ethnography, folklore, arts and music both in their home places and in the areas to which they were posted. With the support of questionnaires and investigative guidelines provided by the administration, their contribution had to help explain regional particularities and cultural and linguistic differences, as much as serving as a bridge between indigenous and French culture.

Pontins is the name used for graduates of the École normale William-Ponty,[6] opened in 1903 in Saint-Louis to train an elite of African administrative auxiliaries and transferred in 1913 to the island of Gorée. Between the two world wars, many *Pontins* made a fundamental contribution to African ethnology, publishing mainly in the *Bulletin* but also in the most prestigious journals such as the *Bulletin du Comité d'Études historiques et scientifiques de l'AOF or Outre-mer* of the École Coloniale. With his 44 published contributions and five unpublished manuscripts, Mamby Sidibé, for example, ranks as one of the pioneers of Malian anthropology (Hopkins, 2013, p. 5). The son of farmers and hunters and, like many other representatives of his generation, forced to attend primary school, he finished his studies at the William-Ponty and went on to hold a variety of educational posts in French Sudan. Bobou Hama—a politician, novelist, amateur ethnologist and historian celebrated as one of the first Nigerien intellectuals (Cornevin, 1982; Laya et al., 2007)—was among his pupils at the École Primaire Supérieure de Ouagadougou. Hama's memoirs offer this portrayal of Sidibé: "he knew Africa, its folktales, its legends, its stories. The first event he explained to us was the pilgrimage to Mecca of great Emperor of Mali, Kankou Mousa, in 1325" (Hama, 1972, p. 222). Neither Sidibé nor many other *Pontins* had the benefit of formal ethnological training. They were rather self-taught social scientists with a keen awareness of methodological aspects. Critical of certain aspects of traditional society, such as slavery and war, Sidibé (1923, 1927) was familiar with the way in which the oral tradition could be manipulated. He advised learning how to converse with people discreetly, taking part in the informal discussions "through which elders contradict and correct each other"

---

[6] As a federal school, the École normale William-Ponty was attended by students from all over French West Africa. Initially it had a teacher-training function, but from the 1920s on it also prepared administrative and financial officials, as well as students from Dakar's Jules Carde School of medicine. At the time of decolonisation. The majority of political leaders in French-speaking West Africa had a William-Ponty background. Further details of the school, its educational polices, as well as the professional and political careers of its students are available in Jézéquel (2002).

(Sidibé, 1927, p. 71). Hama's other teacher at the École Primaire Supérieure de Ouagadougou was Dominque Traoré, who also favoured immersion in local customs and practices. During his studies among the Bobo-Fin of Upper Volta (now Burkina-Faso), he had no qualms about joining a local cult, taking advantage of his knowledge of similar religious practices in his home area (Labrune-Badiane & Smith, 2018, p. 275). Hama wrote of him: "he spent all his free time in Ouagadougou Zongo, the foreigners' neighbourhood. He talked with people from all ethnic groups. His investigative passion astonished us. He was also the author of a big book, *Medicine et magie en Afrique*" (Hama, 1972, p. 222; Traoré, 1965). The administration had intended for the William-Ponty pupils to act as collectors of historical and ethnological information. However, Traorè, Sidibé and other teacher-ethnologists developed an autonomous taste for research that gave a voice to an emerging intellectual and political awareness of the richness, complexity and relevance of the indigenous cultures. Putting folklore, oral traditions, uses, customs and esoteric knowledge into writing, as they were doing, was a way of recuperating and preserving for future generations a past of which they could become proud.

African and Metropolitan Researchers After the Second World War: Professional Hierarchies, Political Engagement, Scientific Innovation

From 1936, an additional contribution to the production in Africa of knowledge about Africa was made by the Institut d'Afrique Noire (later the Institut Fondamentale d'Afrique Noire), based in Dakar, then the administrative capital of French West Africa. As with the Rhodes Livingstone Institute, established by the United Kingdom in 1938 in Lusaka, the aim was to boost scientific research capable of meeting administrative demands. Whereas the British, in southern Africa, were mainly concerned with socio-economic and political changes driven by migration towards mining centres, and therefore oriented towards an applied anthropology, the French felt the need to collect, preserve and promote the records of their presence as much as indigenous traditional knowledge and objects. The Institut d'Afrique Noire was conceived of as a large database of West African cultural and natural heritage, a context for strengthening (and hierarchising) relations between metropolitan researchers and scholars operating in the colonies (Labrune-Badiane & Smith, 2018, pp. 160–161). Under its director Theodore Monod, the institute expanded its range of operations, opening regional branches in the other capitals of French West Africa. It counted on the services of William-Ponty graduate Alexandre Adandé, originally from Dahomey (Jézéquel, 2011, p. 50). Adandé directed the ethnological section and curated the institute's collections of objects, which with the independence of Senegal in 1960 would contribute to the establishment of the Musée d'Art africain de l'Institut fondamental d'Afrique noire Cheikh Anta Diop IFAN/CAD (renamed the Musée Théodore Monod d'Art africain in 2007). He published regularly and in particular on artistic questions, and took part in Radio Dakar programmes, through which the institute's researchers shared their research results with a wider audience.[7] The lack of a metropolitan qualification, however, thwarted his career within the Institute. University studies in France were in fact becoming a prerequisite for access to high-ranking administrative posts. Despite its progressive spirit, which allowed it to act as an intellectual incubator for the political debates preceding the real decolonisation process, the internal organisation of IFAN relegated the majority of African collaborators to subordinate and technical roles (Jézéquel, 2011, p. 51). They were called to act as educated informants and producers of documentation rather than of conceptual innovation. Colonial hierarchies regarded with suspicion anyone, like the Guinean Ousman Poréko Diallo, who dared travelling to France for further study without their knowledge and consent.[8] Even where circumstances opened institutional pathways to research positions, African input remained relatively untapped.

In 1944, the IFAN welcomed within its staff both Sidibé and Traorè, after a six-month training period in Dakar. Sidibé was sent to Niamey, where in the absence of a director he filled the post on an interim basis until 1948. Traoré, on the other hand, was posted to Bamako. Despite their ethnographic skills, the two struggled to obtain the same degree of scientific recognition that they had earned in their role as

---

[7] Profiles of Adandé and other William-Ponty graduates are available on the website: https://bibcolaf.hypotheses.org (last accessed: 20 February 2022).

[8] Diallo graduated from the École des Langues orientales in Paris and went on to obtain a degree in humanities. On returning to Africa in 1956, he had difficulty in obtaining a post as an IFAN assistant. After the independence of Guinea (1958), he was appointed as an assistant to the Institut National de la Recherche et de la Documentation de Guinée (INRDG) and head of the ethnology-sociology department (https://bibcolaf.hypotheses.org/notices-biographiques/ousmane-poreko-diallo-1922-1961, last accessed: 31 March 2022).

teacher-ethnologists in the interwar period. Traoré's research was received with distrust by the institute's scientific leadership, who repeatedly refused his requests for support for the publication of his extensive work in the ethno-medical field. In Sidibé's case, Monod acknowledged his abilities but considered him as a temporary second choice for the Niamey post, acceptable until a more qualified replacement arrived from Paris. Once the new director arrived, Sidibé's contribution to the institution was entirely overlooked: he returned to teaching and embarked on a career of political militancy. The knowledge that he and other *Pontins* gained of West African languages, territories and populations became crucial for mobilising the rural masses when the *Loi-cadre Defferre* (Law No. 56–619 of 23 June 1956) gave the eight colonial territories of French West Africa a governing council. Members were appointed by Territorial Assemblies elected by universal suffrage with a single electoral college (Cooper, 2014, p. 214). Politics offered tangible opportunities for career advancement that seemed far more promising than research. Set up in 1946, the Rassemblement Démocratique Africain (RDA)[9] immediately drew several *Pontins*, including Adandè, who was later involved in the foundation of the Union Progressiste Sénégalaise (UPS) and the Union Démocratique Dahoméenne (UDD). With the independence of Dahomey, he went on to occupy a number of ministerial posts in his country of origin between 1958 and 1965. Hama in turn was active in the Nigerien branch of the RDA, the Parti Progressiste Nigérien, acting as its secretary from 1956 to 1974, as well as heading the centre for the documentation of the oral traditions of Niamey.

Besides IFAN hierarchical logics, the scientific marginalisation of teacher-ethnologists and other William-Ponty graduates can also be explained by their association with a phase of French ethnology, which young IFAN researchers trained in metropolitan France, like Georges Balandier, Paul Mercier and Jacques Lombard were now contesting as unable to restore historical agency to Africa and Africans.[10]

---

[9] The Rassemblement Démocratique Africain (RDA), set up in 1946, played a crucial role in the decolonisation of French West and Equatorial Africa. It comprised a range of parties present in the various colonial territories and was dissolved in 1958 after the vote for independence. The RDA did not support secession from France, but nonetheless made anti-colonial and pan-Africanist demands.

[10] Paul Mercier, who had been a friend of Balandier since their schooldays, established the Dahomey branch of IFAN. When he was recalled to Dakar in 1951 to study urbanisation processes, Monod recruited Jacques Lombard to replace him. Lombard too devoted himself to the study of urban anthropology (Galliard, 2017, p. 10).

For Balandier, in particular, the symbolic-traditionalist approach of Griaule and scholars such as Denise Paulme (Jézéquel, 2011, p. 54), could not explain the creative interlacement between tradition and modernity, conservatism and innovation typical of 1950s and 1960s African societies. His perspective was giving voice to the demands for scientific renewal common throughout research centres and among scholars working in Africa, including African staff members, after the end of World War II (De L'Estoile, 2017, p. 909). Political engagement and scientific input mutually reinforced each other in that period. In 1947, Balandier started work at the IFAN in Dakar to later become the director of the institution's Conakry site. Here he met Madeira Keita, a technical assistant, war veteran and also a *Pontin*, who had run the institute in the absence of a metropolitan researcher. Keita became his "teacher in decolonisation," organising local meetings and introducing Balandier to a political environment where he gradually got to know "the majority of French-speaking actors of independence" (Balandier, 1977, p. 71). Keita, like other RDA militants, considered the development of an engaged knowledge capable of guiding socio-political change as a priority (Mann, 2015, p. 40). He probably accompanied Balandier to the mining centres of Siguiri, in northwest Guinea, where gold was mined using traditional methods. Balandier (1948, p. 547) admired the cosmopolitan character of the area, which in his view was a fine example of the flexibility and eclecticism of a regenerated social life outside the confines of the village, in a context dominated by market relations. As a scholar, he could grasp the emergence of a community on a non-ethnic basis, one that could inspire the efforts of Keita and other RDA members to create unity around the common cause of the party rather than ethnic and regional affinities (Mann, 2015, pp. 28–29). The exchange was mutual: just as Balandier's analysis laid down a path towards political-practical action, Keita's work provided material for his theoretical reflection. One of the few articles he wrote while at IFAN appeared in the first issue of *Etudes Guinéennes*, the journal launched by Balandier as director of the institute. Examining the question of secrecy, Keita (1947) argued that, given the speed and outreach of news diffusion in rural Africa, the value indigenous societies attached to confidentiality seemed paradoxical. When faced with a researcher, albeit indigenous, informants became reticent. What he did not mention, and what Balandier would later assess in his conceptualisation of the "colonial situation" as a totality in which colonised and colonisers participated in equal measure as historical actors (Bellagamba & Finco, 2022, pp. 36–37), was the

282   A. BELLAGAMBA

centrality of such confidentiality in the strategies of resistance (and survival) of colonised societies. Indigenous cultural institutions and practices, which the colonisers condemned from the vantage point of their supposed moral superiority, could continue a silent life behind the façade of obedient conformity with the requirements of the colonial administration (Balandier, 1955, pp. 60–61). This was the art of evasion (Bonhomme, 2017, p. 956), what Balandier termed—in relation to the legacy of slavery in the Kongo society—a "conspiracy of silence" (Bellagamba, 2020, p. 179). Neither he nor Keita seem have mastered very well the capacity to hide their engagement to political change to the colonial administration. Friendship with Keita and other RDA militants, as much as his manifest contempt for the hypocrisy of the symbolic apparatus of French domination, caused Balandier's sudden departure from Guinea. Kept under close observation, Keita was removed from public office in 1950, only to be reinstated in 1952 and transferred to Dahomey, thus ridding Guinean society of a figure that the colonial authorities considered to be a dangerous troublemaker (Mann, 2015, p. 98).

ANTHROPOLOGISTS IN INDEPENDENT NATIONS: MARGINALITY, SUBALTERNITY, DECOLONISATION

According to Paul Nchoji Nkwi (2006, p. 157), who taught social and cultural anthropology at the University of Yaounde I after obtaining his doctorate in Germany,[11] "the new nations of Africa dismissed [...] [the discipline] both as a cultivation of primitivism and as an apologetic for colonialism." National leaders and politicians looked for knowledge that could meet the needs of modernisation, and anthropology simply appeared to have little to offer in this respect. Few in numbers, African anthropologists found themselves trapped in a blind alley. The more they practised the discipline according to European and North American academic standards, the more their governments considered them useless; and the more they concentrated on objectives that made sense in terms of the ongoing processes of transformation, the more their scientific output was belittled

---

[11] With courses on the family, marriage and kinship, anthropology was one of the first disciplines taught at the Université fédérale de Yaoundé, set up on French initiative in 1962 and supported by France for a decade thereafter. The discipline took on greater importance with the reforms of the 1990s, which strengthened recruitment of students and academic staff alike (Nkwi & Sopca, 2007, p. 73 and ff.).

by their European and North American colleagues. What Paul Zeleza (2009, p. 112) has called the "golden age" of African university institutions "was characterized by the excitement of building new universities and expanding old ones, all underpinned by the triumph of African nationalism and the euphoria of independence." Sociology gained traction as a form of knowledge based on contemporary dynamics and history capable of giving back to African peoples the protagonism lost with colonisation (Atieno-Odhiambo, 2002, p. 16; Coquery-Vidrovitch, 2006, p. 110; Copans, 2010, pp. 91). In French-speaking Africa, this changeover was legitimated theoretically and conceptually by none other than Balandier (1970). Once back in Paris after his equatorial sojourn, he started to draw the outlines of an African sociology, in which the themes of dependence and emancipation with respect to recent colonial history played a central role.

Even after the achievement of independence, Paris considered interference in the internal politics of its former colonial territories to be a natural right (Schmidt, 2013, p. 166). For the new nations, relationships with the former colonial metropolis remained an open and sensitive question as the process of decolonisation generated new forms of subordination, manifested financially by the creation of two currencies, one for what had been French West Africa and another for the former equatorial colonies (Chad, the Central African Republic, Gabon and the Republic of Congo) pegged to the French franc and, from 2001 on, to the euro (Pigeaud & Sylla, 2018). Former West and equatorial colonies continued to supply essential raw materials to France, which was also their main export market, while thousands of French citizens, with state support, found work in the sub-Saharan regions, in education and in military, technical and health cooperation, not to mention private investors. In some countries, such as the Ivory Coast, France hampered the Africanisation of higher education, exercising an indirect influence over the careers of university professors and researchers, whose Marxist orientation raised suspicion of communist sympathies (Arnaud & Delaleeuwe, 2008, pp. 22–23). Continuing scientific (and educational) relations with France (Martin, 1995, p. 2; see also Olivier de Sardan, 2011; Doquet & Broqua, 2019) characterised the development of anthropology and of academic disciplines in general with African students completing their studies at French universities in order to return home to consolidate Franco-African cooperation in higher education.

With branches in various countries in French-speaking Africa, the Office de la recherche scientifique et technique outre-mer (ORSTOM),[12] established in 1953, openly acknowledged its origins in the Office de la recherche scientifique coloniale (ORSC), set up in 1943 (Coquery-Vidrovitch, 2006, pp. 118–119; Dozon, 2019, pp. 127–128). Until the 1980s at least, this was the only institution with sufficient resources to conduct serious anthropological research, as Nkwi (2006) remarks in the case of Cameroon. The ORSTOM focussed on development questions, given that cooperation on socio-economic transformation was one of the main axes of the renewed French presence in the former colonial territories (Olivier de Sardan, 2011, p. 511).

When viewed from the external perspective of Archibald Mafeje (2001, pp. 52–53), among the South African anthropologists most critical of the interconnection between anthropology and colonialism, African studies, as developed in France, give the impression of not having a colonial history from which to free themselves. From within, the situation appears more complicated. Balandier himself conducted his African research and developed his critique of colonialism while working first with the IFAN and later the Institut d'études centrafricaines (IEC) in Equatorial Africa (De L'Estoile, 2017, pp. 908–909). And, the anthropologists of the next generation, who placed Africa at the centre of their research interests, have been accused by African scholars and historians of Africa of having privileged theory over the commitment to constructing knowledge of African societies and cultures on equal terms (Gondola, 2007; Anignikin, 2014, pp. 244–245).

At the end of the 1980s, African higher education was trapped between structural reform programmes and repressive political regimes hampering freedom of expression (Zeleza, 2009, p. 112). Writing in this period of crisis, the Beninese philosopher Paulin Hountondji (1988) denounced the subaltern position of African anthropologists. Research subject matter, methodologies and interests were all other-directed by developments of the discipline in the Global North and in metropolitan France. Lack of resources for scientific research, but also the idea that African

---

[12] In 1998, the ORSTOM was converted into the Institut de recherche pour le développement (IRD), under the aegis of the French ministries dealing with research and cooperation. It was given the mandate of working in cooperation and partnership with the countries of the Global South and engaging in research in human and social, health and environmental fields. By 2018 the institute had branches in 40 countries worldwide as well as in the French overseas territories, in addition to four regional delegations in metropolitan France.

anthropologists should devote themselves to studying their own society, forced them into the role of learned informants of their western colleagues: their contribution was mainly empirical, while it was left to researchers from former colonising countries to elaborate theory. Resuming the argument developed in the 1960s and 1970s by theorists of dependence on the way in which colonisation under-developed Africa,[13] Hountondji (1988) compared the mining of knowledge with that of natural resources. What he seemed to wish for was a final separation of the development of African anthropology, and in general human and social sciences, from metropolitan epistemologies and academic knowledge-building processes. Africa should instead be taken as the starting point, with the crucial issues for African populations at the core of attention. His perspective echoed the demands for an Africanisation of knowledge that in those years animated the intellectual debates of the Council for the Development of Economic and Social Research in Africa (CODESRIA).[14] Hountondji (1997) himself contributed to this emerging field of discussion a philosophical reflection on the epistemological importance of "endogamous knowledge," in other words technical, natural and health-related knowledge and relations rooted in the historicity of the continent's cultures.

Retrospectively, his position seems symptomatic of a period when the horizons of French-speaking African intellectuals broadened towards the United States.[15] France in turn was sliding from a policy of openness aimed at the expansion of its world influence, also in cultural and scientific terms, to one refocussed on the European space and the international competition on the higher education market (Blum Le Coat, 2019, pp. 156–157). Since the beginning of this new century, the "recovery era" of African university institutions, to continue with Zeleza's periodisation (Zeleza,

---

[13] On Africa, see Amin (1972) and Rodney (1972).

[14] Founded in 1973, with its headquarters in Dakar, the CODESRIA aimed to "promote multi-disciplinary social research deriving from the experience of the continent and its inhabitants and relevant to such experience" (Olukoshi & Nymanjoh, 2006, p. 18). In addition to supporting the education of young scholars, the institution offered African researchers an important showcase for their work, which might otherwise have been condemned to submit to the scientific interests and publishing market of the Global North. Its first executive secretary was Samir Amin.

[15] For example, Mudimbe, who settled permanently in the United States in the 1980s and Achille Mbembe, who spent almost the entire next decade working in US research institutions and universities.

2009, p. 112), has relaunched the discussion on the epistemological and didactic bases for African anthropology and university education. Whether or not anthropology and the social sciences as practised in Africa can be effectively decolonised is an open question that since the 2000s has interlaced with the blossoming of post-colonial studies in France (Blanchard et al., 2005; Amselle, 2008; Mbembe, 2010; Bancel & Blanchard, 2017).

For Joseph Tonda (2012), who for many years taught sociology and anthropology at the Université Omar Bongo in Libreville (Gabon),[16] the answer is negative. Rather than shutting themselves into the ghetto of Afrocentrism, at a stage in history when scientific knowledge is practised under the banner of interconnectedness, the task for African anthropologists and intellectuals in general is rather to address, in its daily and also academic manifestations, the legacy of the unequal position of Africa with respect to the Global North and the former colonial powers. The first and most evident legacy takes the form of the social market for degrees and diplomas, where academic qualifications obtained in Africa are less valued, even in Africa, than those obtained elsewhere. Inscribed in academic environments and the social fabric, the awareness of this disparity reproduced a hierarchy between the metropole and periphery that was central to colonialism and later reproduced by French-African cooperation in the field of higher education. Tonda himself studied in France, while the first doctorate to be obtained from Omar Bongo University, by coincidence by the anthropologist Paulin Kialo (2005), was awarded in partnership with a French institution (Bonhomme, 2007, p. 111).

The second and possibly more ambiguous legacy is the politicisation of colonial ethnological and anthropological knowledge. Developed for administrative purposes, the classification of African cultures and people in terms of their specificities and differences produced a substrate of knowledge that was reborn in the African ethno-nationalisms of the end of the twentieth century, highlighting the "racial, racializing, and racist past" of anthropology (Zeleza, 2009, pp. 124–125). To explain this point, Tonda

---

[16] When it was set up in 1970, the National University of Gabon (soon renamed Omar Bongo University in honour of the president of the country) had departments of history and sociology, from which a separate department of anthropology was set up in 1997 under the directorship of a French-educated Gabonese anthropologist, Jean-Émile Mbot, and of a French oceanographer living in the country. The department organised a full programme, offering bachelor, master and doctoral degrees, quickly establishing itself as an important centre for the development of the discipline (Bonhomme, 2007, p. 2). After heading the department of sociology at Marien Ngouabi University in Brazzaville, Tonda took up his post at Omar Bongo in the early 2000s.

relies on his experience of the civil war that affected the Republic of the Congo in 1997, when the militias of President Pascal Lissouba, the "Zoulous," fought the "Cobras" of Denis Sassou Nguesso. On the barricades, Tonda met students from ethnology and anthropology courses who had taken up arms to defend themselves from the genocide threatened by their opponents: "in this situation [...] the Other was anyone belonging to the other 'camp' [...] Oddly, the 'camp' presented itself as a domain or space of 'racial' danger (in the colonial sense of race indicating ethnicity) and the people in charge of exterminating the 'races' that lived in each 'camp' were the educated ones—students whose career had been brutally interrupted by the war" (Tonda, 2012, p. 4; see also Tonda, 1998). In the violence of the conflict, the never forgotten substratum of colonial primitivist ethnology made up ground on the sociological study of cultural contamination, with a sort of "fatal regression" that revealed the political ambiguity of a human science, such as anthropology, traditionally devoted to preserving ethnic heritage and clan-based identities (Tonda, 2012, p. 5).[17]

Although denouncing the essentialist tradition that anthropology, wherever practised, inevitably tends to reproduce, Tonda has shown, through his own work, the possibility of a critical political anthropology that, starting from "the difficulties and confusions of living the everyday in African contexts," seeks to reinterpret, in a creative manner, the conceptual tool-kit of Western social sciences (Bernault & Geschiere, 2000, p. 152). Following on from Balandier (1970, p. 44), he considers society as an agglomerate moved by different temporalities, which combine and contrast in a constant dynamic of transformation. From the analysis of the ethnic dynamics that marked the equatorial conflicts of the late twentieth century (Tonda, 1998) to that of "de-parentalization" (Tonda, 2007), that is, the process of de-linking from affiliations and solidarities in favour of new urban-based social identities, Tonda places consumption at the centre of the equatorial socio-political project and proves its relevance to interrogate the limits of Western-based lifestyles and related ideologies of the self and society. To emerge from the colonial situation meant, at the time of independence, to gain access to the goods and benefits of civilisation that the colonisers had kept for themselves. Swiftly, however, the leaders of equatorial new nations movements privatised the state and its

---

[17] This essentialist drift also characterised Ivorian human and social sciences in the difficult political transition following the death of President Félix Houphouët-Boigny, who had been in power since 1963 (Arnaud & Delaleeuwe, 2008; Cutolo, 2010, p. 534 and ff.).

wealth, generating a system of subjugation as violent as, or perhaps even more violent than, the colonial system with the complacency and complicity of the former French colonial homeland. Then, from the 1990s on, a neoliberal ethos swept through countries such as the Republic of Congo and Gabon, offering the idea of free individuals who gauged themselves based on their own ability to participate in a global economy of desire (Tonda & Bernault, 2000, p. 12). The decolonisation of anthropology is for Tonda an impossible task as the figure of the white coloniser, which haunts African scholars, is only a metaphor for the market wherein they, like their colleagues of the Global North, operate thus becoming the more or less conscious agents of the expansion of a lifestyle that trades every fragment of humanity. In a way comparable to that of scholars like Michel-Rolph Trouillot (2003) and Yarimar Bonilla (2017), Tonda paves nonetheless the way to an understanding of the West whose starting point is Africa rather than the West itself.

A pristine past, before colonisation, where anthropologists could seek refuge from the internal contradictions of their own discipline, simply does not exist. Nor the solution lays in setting socio-cultural anthropology, as today taught and experienced in the Global South, apart from its developments in the Global North. Anthropologists from former colonial contexts, whether African or Caribbean, can rather help the West to unsettle its own certainties by showing that "concepts such as sovereignty, democracy, freedom, and even universalism are not neutral categories of analysis, nor simple reflections of European history [...] These are the native categories of the West as a *project*, not a place" (Bonilla, 2017, p. 334). In this respect, Tonda's analysis of contemporary equatorial dynamics of consumption does innovates, from within, the anthropological project of casting light on the processes through which certain configurations of power produce and reproduce themselves through a regime of submission actively participated by the very people they oppress and violate.

FINAL CONSIDERATIONS: CHALLENGES FOR THE NEW CENTURY

This reconstruction of developments in anthropology in French-speaking Africa cannot but end by underlining its limitations. North African countries colonised by the French and Madagascar have been left out of the discussion, as has much of the higher education and research today conducted in Senegal, the Ivory Coast, Benin and also Mali, Niger and Chad. Here, for example, the Centre de Recherches en Anthropologie et Sciences Humaines (CRASH)[18] was set up in 2005 with the aim of promoting anthropology and social research capable of contributing to national development. An appreciation of the richness and plurality of the situations through which anthropology, but also history and the human and social sciences as a whole, are practised, experienced, challenged and reformulated in the everyday life of university institutions and research centres in French-speaking African countries would be complete only by integrating with fieldwork of the desk research from which this chapter born. Some general considerations are nonetheless possible.

The first is the parallel development of the discipline in France and its former colonies, a dynamic that also occurred in the English-speaking context, considering that the first British chair in social anthropology was created at the University of Cape Town in 1921 (Kuper, 1999, p. 83). It is thus not so much a question of provincialising the history of anthropology or overturning the colonial hierarchies weighing on contemporary construction of scientific subjectivity as of emphasising, from the outset, the multi-centred patterns and multi-directional exchanges that have affected the discipline. If in the eyes of scholars such as Mafeje (2002) it is impossible to free anthropology from its racist legacy, it is also true that of the various humanistic branches of knowledge to have emerged in the industrial and imperial nineteenth century, it was anthropology that explored the possibility of being "otherly human" compared to the hegemonic models of the period. In a multi-centric approach to the developments of anthropology, coincidences can acquire a new historical meaning. *Esquisses sénégalaises* (Boilat, 1984) and *De la Sénégambie française* (Carrère & Holle, 1855) were published virtually at the same time as the pioneering work on the Iroquois by Lewis Henry Morgan (1851), seen as one of the founding fathers of North American anthropology. The work of the great ethnological officials of French-speaking Africa, including Delafosse and Gaden, grew in constant dialogue with an emerging indigenous historiography/anthropology that is today considered an important documentary source. And if the power relations and the hierarchies generated by European colonial expansion count for anything, it would be reductive to consider Dyao's contribution as a mere African reaction to the growing interest for the languages, cultures and customs of

---

[18] http://www.crash-td.net/about/1 (last accessed: 22 February 2022).

non-European populations that culminated in 1925 in the creation of the Institut d'Ethnologie in Paris (Labrune-Badiane & Smith, 2018, pp. 154–155). Lyn Schumaker (2001), by closely examining the internal work dynamics of the Rhodes-Livingstone Institute, has shown how African co-workers and the surrounding African context influenced the work of British anthropologists within the institution. The same line of reasoning is applicable to French-speaking Africa, as the brief commentary on the relationship of human and scientific exchange between Keita and Balandier is intended to show. In other words, only a cross-cutting, bottom-up perspective to the history of anthropology lets hidden intellectual interconnections and collaborations emerge out of the frustrations and humiliations generated by colonial and post-colonial situations (Tonda, 2012, p. 109).

Another aspect deserving of attention is the role played by the diaspora. "The age of crisis" of African university institutions resulted in an intellectual migration that has significantly contributed to a global reconfiguration of the profile of African studies. It is thus essential to consider whether, in dealing with the development of anthropology in sub-Saharan Africa, only scholars working in Africa should be considered or also African researchers who, from their posts in the Global North, have taken part in the overall renewal of knowledge on contemporary Africa. If their research interests remain in Africa, and if their theories take as their starting point the African terrain, this is not necessarily a negative development. In the case of French-speaking countries, for instance, the analysis should broaden to include the trajectories of scholars such as Fatoumata Ouattara (2004, 2014), who actively engaged in a discussion of their role of native anthropologists in respect with the societies they study and the French institutions within which they operate or Jean-Pierre Olivier de Sardan (2011), who has centred his intellectual endeavour in Niger. His commitment to the development of anthropological and sociological research in West Africa has resulted in the creation, together with Nigerien and Beninese colleagues, of the Laboratoire d'Etudes et de Recherche sur les Dynamiques Sociales et le Développement Local (LASDEL) with a branch in Niamey, the capital of Niger inaugurated in 2001 and another in the Northern Beninese city of Parakou in 2004. LASDEL's mission is to pursue a socio-anthropology of public interest capable of overcoming the scientifically limited horizons of development consultancy to build and share critical knowledge on contemporary African public spaces, from the question of citizenship to the daily workings of bureaucracy, health and government services. The expansion of the post-colonial debate in French-speaking contexts in this new century has encouraged an intellectual position that, in its generalising perspective, has tended to devalue the heritage of knowledge on Africa accumulated thanks to anthropology, history, sociology and other disciplines capable of delving into the analysis of concrete situations (Copans, 2019, p. 216).[19] Fierce criticism of the contemporary legacies of colonialism, including anthropology, however risks obscuring the dynamics affecting university institutions and scientific research in both metropolitan France and the former colonies, under pressure from models of neoliberal inspiration with their roots in the English-speaking North Atlantic world. In the broader framework of a global economy that is "knowledge based, innovation based" (Mbembe, 2016, p. 38), higher education is progressively denationalised through a competition for excellence that marginalises loosing institutions as second-class ones. "An entirely new era, that of global Apartheid in higher education, is unfolding" (Mbembe, 2016, p. 38; Nyamnjoh, 2019). An example of how inequality is reproduced and increased is the creation and consolidation of enormous digital databases giving instant access to scientific publications, while at the same time restricting it. Institutions are thus places in hierarchies according to their ability to pay expensive subscriptions, and individuals ranked in terms of their possibility to access the most prestigious global centres of higher education. Furthermore, whereas since the early 2000s Senegal has led the way in attempting, insofar as possible, to bring salaries of university researchers and teaching staff into line with the cost of living, in neighbouring Guinea Conakry the entire public sector is underpaid. This indirectly strengthens the world of consultancy, with its rules of scientific production that tend to privilege description over conceptualisation and critical analysis, contributing to a diminishment of the role of the scholar as a public intellectual (Olivier de Sardan, 2011; Nyamnjoh, 2019). Even where, as in the Ivory Coast, anthropology has undergone relative institutional reinforcement (with the opening of a new

---

[19] An example would be the critique by Charles Didier Gondola (2007) of how the history of Africa is practised in French-speaking as compared to North American contexts. For Gondola, who began to put forward his argument during the 1990s, French scholars dealing with colonialism cultivated a Eurocentric perspective, remaining deaf to constructive comments from both Africans and historians of the continent trained in other scholarly traditions. Mbembe (2010, p. 160), for his part, sees the lack of French interest in English-speaking post-colonial studies as the expression of an intellectual provincialism that would continue to celebrate the glories of a France with a central role in world balances of power.

292   A. BELLAGAMBA

department of sociology and anthropology at the University of Bouaké in the early 1990s, a growth in the teaching posts for anthropology and the creation of the Institut des sciences anthropologiques pour le développement [ISAD] at the University of Cocody-Abidjan) an analysis of how the discipline is locally reproduced shows a downward curve from the first to the third cycle of higher education, with very few doctoral theses produced (Gnabéli, 2011, p. 20). African sovereignty over anthropology and social and human sciences must certainly be seen as a goal for this new century, fulfilling the wishes expressed by Hountondji in the late 1980s. And it is time for Africa to become, thanks to the university institutions and research centres present on the continent, a research "object empirically, methodologically and conceptually built" within the continent (Copans, 2019, p. 218). But this re-localisation can only come about by acknowledging that African studies as a whole, including anthropology, is today "a house of many mansions, a field with diverse, complex, and fascinating disciplinary, interdisciplinary, and global dimensions. The days when one country, one centre – or one paradigm, for that matter – dominated African studies are long gone" (Zeleza, 2009, p. 133).

REFERENCES

Abéga, S. C. (2006). The Practice of Anthropology in Francophone Africa. In M. Ntarangwi, D. Mills, M. H. M. Babiker, & M. B. Ahmed (Eds.), *African Anthropologies: History, Critique and Practice* (pp. 114–136). Zed Books.

Amin, S. (1972). Underdevelopment and Dependence in Black Africa: Origins and Contemporary Forms. *The Journal of Modern African Studies*, 10(4), 503–524.

Amselle, J.-L. (2008). *L'Occident décroché. Enquête sur le postcolonialismes.* Stock.

Amselle, J. L., & Sibeud, E. (Eds.). (1998). *Maurice Delafosse, entre orientalisme et africanisme.* Larose-Maisonneuve.

Anignikin, S. C. (2014). Tendances actuelles des études africaines: l'histoire de l'Afrique entre «Africanisme» et «Afrocentrisme». In *African Dynamics in a Multipolar World: 5th European Conference on African Studies. Conference Proceedings* (pp. 234–267). Centro de Estudos Internacionais do Instituto Universitário de Lisboa.

Arnaud, K., & Delaleeuwe, N. (2008). Les «hommes de terrain»: Georges Niangoran-Bouah et le monde universitaire de l'autochtonie en Côte d'Ivoire. *Politique africaine, 4,* 18–35.

Atieno-Odhiambo, E. S. (2002). From African Historiographies to African Philosophy of History. In T. Falola & C. Jennings (Eds.), *Africanizing Knowledge* (pp. 13–64). Transaction Publishers.

9 INDIGENOUS ETHNOLOGISTS, NATIONAL ANTHROPOLOGISTS... 293

Balandier, G. (1948). L'Or de la Guinée Françaises. *Présence Africaine*, 1(4), 539–548.

Balandier, G. (1955). *Sociologie actuelle de l'Afrique noire. Dynamique des changements sociaux en Afrique centrale*. Presses Universitaires de France.

Balandier, G. (Ed.). (1970). *Sociologie de mutations*. Anthropos.

Balandier, G. (1977). *Histoire d'autres*. Stock.

Bancel, N., & Blanchard, P. (2017). Un postcolonialisme à la française? *Cités*, 4, 53–68.

Bellagamba, A. (2020). "Una cospirazione del silenzio". Georges Balandier e lo studio della schiavitù e del post-schiavitù in Africa. In V. Matera (Ed.), *Storia dell'etnografia. Autori, teorie, pratiche* (pp. 179–206). Carocci.

Bellagamba, A., & Finco, R. (2022). Introduzione: «Detesto il confinamento»: l'impegno scientifico, politico e umano di Georges Balandier. In G. Balandier (Ed.), *La situazione coloniale e altri saggi* (pp. 7–49). Meltemi.

Bernault, F., & Geschiere, P. (2000). Joseph Tonda, the social sciences and the vortex of city life in Africa. *Africa*, 92(1), 152–160.

Blanchard, P., Bancel, N., & Lemaire, S. (2005). *La fracture coloniale: La société française au prisme de l'héritage colonial*. La Découverte.

Blum Le Coat, J.-Y. (2019). Diplômés de France au Congo-Brazzaville et relations universitaires franco-congolaises (1960–2005): une étude de cas de la construction et de la rupture du lien singulier franco-africain. *Histoire de la recherche contemporaine. La revue du Comité pour l'histoire du CNRS*, 8(2), 147–159.

Boilat, D. (1984). *Esquisses senegalaises*. Karthala (ed. or. 1853).

Bonhomme, J. (2007). Anthropologue et/ou initié. L'anthropologie gabonaise à l'épreuve du Bwiti. *Journal des anthropologues*, 110–111, 1–13.

Bonhomme, J. (2017). L'art de la dérobade. Innovations rituelles et pouvoir colonial en Afrique centrale. *Cahiers d'études africaines*, 228, 951–972.

Bonilla, Y. (2017). Unsettling Sovereignty. *Cultural anthropology*, 32(3), 330–339.

Boulègue, J. (1988). A la naissance de l'histoire écrite sénégalaise: Yoro Dyao et ses modelés (Deuxième moitié du XIXème siècle, début du XXème siècle). *History in Africa*, 15, 395–405.

Caillié, R. (1830). *Journal d'un voyage à Temboctou et à Jenné dans l'Afrique Centrale, précédé des observations faites chez les Maures Braknas, les Nalous et des autres peuples, pendant les années 1824 à 1828*. Imprimerie Royale.

Carrère, F., & Holle, P. (1855). *De la Sénégambie française*. Firmin Didot Frères, Fils et Companie.

Cinnamon, J. M. (2006). Missionary Expertise, Social Science, and the Uses of Ethnographic Knowledge in Colonial Gabon. *History in Africa*, 33, 413–432.

Conklin, A. (1997). *A Mission to Civilize: Republican Ideas of Empire in France and West Africa*. Stanford University Press.

Cooper, F. (2014). *Citizenship between Empire and Nation: Remaking France and French Africa, 1945–1960*. Princeton University Press.

Copans, J. (1991). Les noms du Géer. Essai de sociologie de la connaissance du Sénégal par lui-même, 1950–1990. *Cahiers d'études africaines*, 123, 327–362.

Copans, J. (2010). *Un demi-siècle d'africanisme africain. Terrains, acteurs et enjeux des sciences sociales en Afrique indépendante*. Karthala.

Copans, J. (2019). Penser l'Afrique ou connaitre les sociétés de l'Afrique? *Cahiers d'études africaines*, 233, 215–269.

Coquery-Vidrovitch, C. (2006). French Historiography on Africa: a Historical and Personal Contextualisation. *Afrika Spectrum*, 41(1), 107–126.

Cornevin, R. (1982). Hommage à Boubou Hama. *Présence Africaine*, 123(3), 278–280.

Cutolo, A. (2010). Modernity, Autochthony and the Ivorian Nation: The End of a Century in Côte D'Ivoire. *Africa*, 80(4), 527–552.

De L'Estoile, B. (2000). Science de l'homme et «domination rationnelle»: savoir ethnologique et politique indigène en Afrique coloniale française. *Revue de synthèse*, 3–4, 291–323.

De L'Estoile, B. (2017). Enquêter en «situation coloniale». Politique de la population, gouvernementalité modernisatrice et «sociologie engagée» en Afrique équatoriale française. *Cahiers d'études africaines*, 228, 863–919.

Delafosse, M. (1912). *Haut-Sénégal-Niger: Le Pays, les Peuples, les Langues; l'Histoire; les Civilizations*. Émile Larose.

Delafosse, M., & Gaden, H. (Eds.). (1913). *Chroniques du Fouta sénégalais, traduites de deux manuscrits arabes inédits de Sire-Abbas-Soh par M. Delafosse & H. Gaden*. Leroux.

Delavignette, R. (1939). *Les vrais chefs de l'Empire*. Gallimard.

Dilley, R. (2014). *Nearly Native, Barely Civilized: Henri Gaden's Journey through Colonial French West Africa (1894-1939)*. Brill.

Doquet, A., & Broqua, C. (2019). Introduction: Formaliser la réflexion sur les relations académiques franco-africaines. *Histoire de la recherche contemporaine. La revue du Comité pour l'histoire du CNRS*, 8 (2), 122–125.

Dozon, J.-P. (2019). Entre production savante, posture critique et imperium: l'africanisme français des années 1970. *Histoire de la recherche contemporaine. La revue du Comité pour l'histoire du CNRS*, 8 (2), 126-132.

Dyao, Y. (1864). Histoire des Damels du Cayor. *Le Moniteur du Sénégal et dépendances*, 448–453.

Faidherbe, L. (1859). *Notice sur la colonie du Senegal et sur les pays qui sont en relation avec elle*. A. Bertrand.

Faidherbe, L. (1882). *Grammaire et vocabulaire de la langue peul a l'usage des voyageurs dans le Soudan*. Maisonneuve.

Faidherbe, L. (1887). *Langues senegalaises: wolof, arabe-hassaniya, soninke, serere: notions grammaticales, vocabulaires et phrases*. Leroux.

Gaden, H. (1912). *Légendes et coutumes sénégalaises. Cahiers de Yoro Dyao*. E. Leroux.

Gaden, H. (1931). *Proverbes et maximes peuls et toucouleurs: traduits, expliqués et annotés*. Institut d'ethnologie.

Galliard, G. (2017). Obituary Jacques Lombard (1926–2017): French Africanism of the Third Generation. *Modern Africa: History, Politics and Society*, 5(2), 7–26.

Gnabéli, R. Y. (2011). L'anthropologie sociale dans les universités ivoiriennes entre marginalisation et subordination. *Journal des Anthropologues*, 126–127, 17–34.

Gondola, C. D. (2007). *Africanisme: la crise d'une illusion*. L'Harmattan.

Hama, B. (together with Clair Andrée). (1972). *L'aventure d'Albarka*. Julliard.

Hopkins, N. S. (2013). Mamby Sidibé (1891–1977): Malian Anthropologist and Militant. *Mande Studies, 15*, 5–41.

Hountondji, P. (1988). Situation de l'anthropologue africain: note critique sur une forme d'extraversion scientifique. *Revue de l'Institut de Sociologie*, 3–4, 99–108.

Hountondji, P. (Ed.). (1997). *Endogenous Knowledge*. CODESRIA.

Jézéquel, J.H. (2002). Les «mangeurs» de craies. Socio-histoire d'une catégorie lettrée à l'époque coloniale. *Les diplômés de l'École Normale William Ponty (c. 1900–1960)*. Thèse de doctorat, École des Hautes Études en Sciences Sociales.

Jézéquel, J. H. (2011). Les professionnels africains de la recherche dans l'état colonial tardif: le personnel local de l'Institut Français d'Afrique Noire entre 1938 et 1960. *Revue d'Histoire des Sciences Humaines*, 1(24), 35–60.

Kane, A. (1916). Histoire et origine des familles du Fouta Toro. *Annuaire du Comite d'études historiques et scientifiques de l'A.O.F*, 1, 325–344.

Karady, V. (1982). Le problème de la légitimité dans l'organisation historique de l'ethnologie française. *Revue française de sociologie*, 23(1), 17–35.

Keita, M. (1947). Le Noir et le secret. *Etudes Guinéennes*, 1, 69–78.

Kialo, P. (2005). *Pové et forestiers face à la forêt gabonaise. Esquisse d'une anthropologie comparée de la forêt*. Thèse de doctorat en anthropologie, co-tutelle Université Omar-Bongo (Gabon) et Université Paris 5.

Kuper, A. (1999). South African Anthropology. An Inside Job. *Paideuma*, 45, 83–101.

Labouret, H. (1929). La parenté à plaisanteries en Afrique Occidentale. *Africa*, 2(3), 244–254.

Labouret, H. (1935). La sorcellerie au Soudan occidental. *Africa*, 8(4), 462–472.

Labrune-Badiane, C., & Smith, E. (2018). *Les Hussards noirs de la colonie. Instituteurs africaines et « petites patries » en AOF (1913–1960)*. Karthala.

Laya, D., Namaïwa, B., & Penel, J. D. (2007). *Boubou Hama. Un homme de culture nigérien*. L'Harmattan.

Leroy, A. (1911). *La religion des primitifs*. Beauchesne.

M'ba, L. (2002). *Écrits ethnographiques*. Editions Raponda-Walker.

Mafeje, A. (2001). *Anthropology in Post-Independence Africa: End of an Era and the Problem of Self-Redefinition*. Heinrich Böll Foundation.

Mafeje, A. (2002). *The Theory and Ethnography of African Social Formations. The Case of the Interlacustrine Kingdoms.* Codesria, Dakar.

Manchuelle, F. (1995). Assimilés ou patriotes africains ? Naissance du nationalisme en Afrique française (1853–1931). *Cahiers d'études Africaines*, 138–139, 333–368.

Mann, G. (2015). *From Empires to NGOs in the West African Sahel.* Cambridge University Press.

Martin, G. (1995). Continuity and Change in Franco-African relations. *The Journal of Modern African Studies*, 33(1), 1–20.

Mbembe, A. (2010). Faut-il provincialiser la France? *Politique Africaines*, 3(119), 159–188.

Mbembe, A. (2016). Decolonizing the University: New Directions. *Arts & Humanities in Higher Education*, 15(1), 29–45.

Monteil, C. (1915). *Les Khassonké: monographie d'une peuplade du Soudan français.* E. Leroux.

Monteil, C. (1924). *Les Bambara du Ségou et du Kaarta.* Émile Larose.

Morgan, L. H. (1851). *League of the Ho-dé-no-sau-nee, or Iroquois.* Sage & Brother, M.H. Newman & Co.

Mudimbe, V. (1988). *The Invention of Africa. Gnosis, Philosophy, and the Order of Knowledge.* Indiana University Press.

Nkwi, P. C. (2006). Anthropology in a Postcolonial Africa: The Survival Debate. In G. L. Ribeiro & A. Escobar (Eds.), *World Anthropologies, Disciplinary Transformation within Systems of Power* (pp. 157–180). Berg Publications.

Nkwi, P. C., & Sopca, A. (2007). Anthropology at the University of Yaounde I: A Historical Overview, 1962–2008. *The African Anthropologist*, 14(1–2), 65–88.

Nyamnjoh, F. (2019). Decolonizing the University in Africa. In *Oxford Research Encyclopedia of Politics*, https://doi.org/10.1093/acrefore/9780190228637.013.717

Olivier de Sardan, J.-P. (2011). Promouvoir la recherche face à la consultance. Autour de l'expérience du Lasdel (Niger-Bénin). *Cahiers d'études africaines*, 202–203, 511–528.

Olukoshi, A., & Nymanjoh, F. B. (2006). CODESRIA: 30 Years of Scholarly Publishing. *Africa Media Review*, 14(1–2), 17–26.

Ouattara, F. (2004). Une étrange familiarité. Les exigences de l'anthropologie «chez soi». *Cahiers d'études africaines*, 175, 635–657.

Ouattara, F. (2014). À l'épreuve d'une proximité. Anthropologie «chez soi» appliquée en contexte de partenariat. In L. Vidal (Ed.), *Expériences du partenariat au Sud* (pp. 183–200). Éditions de l'IRD.

Pigeaud, F., & Sylla, D. S. (2018). *L'arme invisible de la Francafrique: Une histoire du Franc CFA.* La Découverte.

Robinson, D. (1988). Un historien et anthropologue sénégalais: Shaikh Musa Kamara (A Senegalese Historian and Anthropologist: Shaikh Musa Kamara). *Cahiers d'études africaines*, 109, 89–116.

Rodney, W. (1972). *How Europe Underdeveloped Africa*. Bogle-L'Ouverture Publications.

Rousseau, R. (1930). *Le Sénégal d'autrefois. Etude sur le Oualo. Cahiers de Yoro Dyao*. Librairie Larose.

Schmidt, E. (2013). *Foreign Intervention in Africa: From the Cold War to the War on Terror*. Cambridge University Press.

Schumaker, L. (2001). *Africanizing Anthropology*. Duke University Press.

Sibeud, E. (2002). *Une science impériale pour l'Afrique? La construction des savoirs africanistes en France, 1878–1930*. Éditions de l'École des Hautes Études en Sciences Sociales.

Sibeud, E. (2012). A Useless Colonial Science? Practicing Anthropology in the French Colonial Empire, circa 1880–1960. *Current Anthropology*, 53 (Suppl_5): S83–S96.

Sidibé, M. (1923). Monographie de la subdivision de Banfora (cercle de Bobo). *Bulletin de l'Enseignement de l'Afrique Occidentale Française*, 48, oct.–dec., 52–64; 51, juil.–sept., 62–74; 52, oct.–dec., 59–69; 53, janv.–mars, 38–51; 54, avr.–juin, 40–52.

Sidibé, M. (1927). Contribution à l'étude de l'histoire des coutumes indigènes de la région de Bobo. *Bulletin de l'Enseignement de l'Afrique Occidentale Française*, 64, janv.–juin : 54–71.

Tonda, J. (1998). La guerre dans le «Camp Nord» au Congo-Brazzaville: ethnicité et ethos de la consommation/consummation. *Politique Africaine*, 72, 50–67.

Tonda, J. (2007). Entre communautarisme et individualisme: la «tuée tuée», une figure-miroir de la déparentélisation au Gabon. *Sociologie et sociétés*, 39(2), 79–99.

Tonda, J. (2012). The Impossible Decolonization of the Social Sciences in Africa. *Mouvements*, 72(4), 108–119.

Tonda, J., & Bernault, F. (2000). Introduction au thème: dynamiques de l'invisible en Afrique. *Politique Africaines*, 3(79), 5–16.

Traoré, D. (1965). *Comment le noir se soigne-t-il ? Médecine et magie africaine*. Présence africaine.

Trilles, H. (1912). *Chez les Fang: ou, Quinze années de séjour au Congo français*. Desclée, De Brouwer et Compagnie.

Trouillot, M.-R. (2003). *Global Transformations. Anthropology and the Modern World*. Palgrave MacMillan.

Viellard, G. P. (1939). *Notes sur les coutumes des Peuls au Fouta Djallon*. Larose.

Wilder, G. (2005). *The French Imperial Nation-State: Negritude and Colonial Humanism between the World Wars*. University of Chicago Press.

Zeleza, P. T. (2009). African Studies and Universities since Independence: The Challenges of Epistemic and Institutional Decolonization. *Transition*, 101, 110–135.

CHAPTER 10

A Nerve Centre of the Discipline on the Periphery of the Empire: South Africa and Anthropology in the Twentieth Century

Stefano Allovio

THE PRIMACY OF CAPE TOWN

The year 1926 was an important year for British studies on Africa: in London, thanks to funding from the Carnegie Foundation and the Rockefeller Foundation, the International African Institute was founded, and its journal *Africa* has been a point of reference for anthropology in general and African Studies in particular ever since its first publication in 1928.[1] Also in 1926, at the Azande settlements in South Sudan, Edward Evans-Pritchard began his fieldwork, which he carried out for 20 months (from 1926 to 1930) and from which he drew the invaluable data which

---

[1] In its early years, the journal *Africa* would host important programmatic contributions on the role of anthropology in Africa, including two relevant essays by Bronislaw Malinowski (1929, 1930).

S. Allovio (✉)
University of Milano Statale, Milan, Italy
e-mail: stefano.allovio@unimi.it

© The Author(s), under exclusive license to Springer Nature Switzerland AG 2023
G. D'Agostino, V. Matera (eds.), *Histories of Anthropology*,
https://doi.org/10.1007/978-3-031-21258-1_10

299

led him to publish, in 1937, one of the most important classics of anthropology: *Witchcraft, Oracles and Magic Among the Azande.*

The year 1926, although crucial, is not really the year of the "start" of British African Studies, but rather of the "restart" after the first two decades of the twentieth century in which eminent scholars from British institutions carried out ethnographic research in Africa: for instance, Edward Westermarck in Morocco and the Seligmans (Charles and Brenda) in Sudan. In fact, in 1926 there were those who, like Evans-Pritchard, arrived in Africa with enthusiasm and those who, like Radcliffe-Brown, left it somewhat disappointed.

Alfred Reginald Radcliffe-Brown was never an Africanist, yet his name is inextricably linked to the institutional development of social anthropology in Africa. Indeed, in 1920, having experienced health problems after his well-known and important ethnographic research in the Bay of Bengal, he considered it fit to go to live in Johannesburg with his brother (Gordon, 1990; Kuper, 1999). It was then that he wrote to the teacher/lecturer who had been his tutor at Cambridge, Alfred Cort Haddon, to seek advice on possible work opportunities in South Africa. Cambridge was an important training centre at the heart of the British Empire and the then Prime Minister of the South African Union, Jan Smuts, had studied at the prestigious British university as an honorary fellow of Christ's College, there meeting Professor Haddon. Haddon, who during his stay in South Africa in 1905 had already advocated establishing an institute of ethnographic studies there, informed Smuts directly of the presence in South Africa of "the most brilliant and experienced of the young students trained at the Cambridge School of Ethnology."

What Haddon's endorsement by South Africa's highest political authorities actually amounted to cannot be accurately assessed. Already at the end of the nineteenth century and throughout the first two decades of the twentieth century, there had been calls for the development of institutions for the study of the cultures and languages indigenous to southern Africa. These appeals emerged mainly from the missionary world of the time, in which there was considerable ethnographic and linguistic expertise.[2] Robert Gordon (1990, p. 17) highlights the role played by the missionary W.A. Norton, who in 1917 wrote an essay titled *The Need and Value of Academic Study of Native Philology and Ethnology*, in which he

---

[2] It is worth mentioning the work of the Swiss missionary Henri-Alexandre Junod (1863–1934) among the Tsonga (Harries, 1981; Reubi, 2004).

vehemently denounced the absurdity of ignoring, in South African academic institutions, the study of the languages and customs of the majority of the population.

Certainly Radcliffe-Brown arrived in South Africa at the right time, as did Haddon's letter which had landed on Smuts' desk: in fact, in 1920, a chair of social anthropology was established at the University of Cape Town (UTC) as the founding nucleus of the nascent *School of African Life and Languages*.[3] In this regard, in relation to the centre-periphery dynamics that have developed in the academic field of anthropology and also to the Euro-centric from which the history of British anthropology is studied, it is quite significant what an important South African anthropologist, Meyer Fortes (1956, p. 151) points out: "We can appreciate this far-sighted act [the establishment of the chair at UCT] if we remember that, until then, there was not a single full-time chair of anthropology in any British university."

Although a certain post-colonial literature has no doubts in identifying, rather too simplistically, in the Haddon–Smuts–Radcliffe-Brown nexus one of the clear proofs of the "complicity" of anthropology (of all anthropology?) in the colonial project and in the formulation of South African segregationism (Ntsebeza, 2012, cited by Arowosegbe, 2016), the situation is, to say the least, more complex. Smuts was somewhat lukewarm to the idea of funding a chair in social anthropology, preferring to promote prehistoric studies; Radcliffe-Brown himself, right from his inaugural lecture published in 1922 in *Bantu Studies*, stated, without hesitation and with little political calculation, that segregationism was not a good idea at all. On the contrary, he considered it unfeasible, since the components of South African society were strongly and irrevocably interconnected (Kuper, 1999, p. 85).

In short, Radcliffe-Brown's immediate impact on the development of South African social anthropology "appears to have been minimal, if not disastrous" (Gordon, 1990, p. 19). Within months of taking office, South African politicians and academics were disgruntled and hostile towards

---

[3] A second chair, that of Bantu Philology, was entrusted to W.A Norton. This and other historical information contained in this part of the essay is taken from the excellent essay on the beginnings of social anthropology in South Africa, written by Robert Gordon and published in *African Studies* in 1990. Among the many essays devoted to reconstructing the history of anthropology in South Africa see, for example: Pauw, 1980; Hammond-Tooke, 1997; Gordon, 1988; Gordon & Spiegel, 1993, and especially the valuable essay by Adam Kuper (1999), to which reference has often been made.

continuing to fund the "School" of Radcliffe-Brown who, in turn, complained about the socio-political context in which he found himself working. As Fredrick Barth argues, the South African experience had done nothing but reinforce the radical and anti-colonial positions of the man who was nicknamed "Anarchy Brown" (Barth et al., 2005) Perhaps he was not exactly an obscure and terrible agent in the pay of that discipline (anthropology) defined by some as the "handmaiden of colonialism" (Asad, 1973). In fact, after only five years, and having made little impact in political and academic terms, but being much appreciated as a teacher, Radcliffe-Brown decided to leave Cape Town to go to work in Sydney. In one of his last public speeches, he forcefully reaffirmed that South African nationalism had to involve both the black and white populations (Stocking, 1995, p. 327).

Many of his South African students praised his competence, methodological rigour and passion. Davidson Don Tengo Jabavu, a prominent black South African intellectual and activist, is strikingly positive in his assessment of Radcliffe-Brown as one of the best teachers (Gordon, Gordon, 1990, pp. 20–21). He, who, like his father (John Tengo Jabavu), fought for the rights of black people in a South Africa marked by inequality and discrimination, had no doubt that Radcliffe-Brown's teaching was an example to be emulated and that social anthropology was a valuable discipline to be fostered in South African universities. Jabavu himself taught courses in social anthropology at Fort Hare Native College, courses which a young Nelson Mandela attended as a student.

Even before Radcliffe-Brown left for Australia, social anthropology courses had been established in other South African universities (Johannesburg, Stellenbosch and Pretoria). At the University of Cape Town, another student of Haddon and W.H.R Rivers, Thomas Theodore Barnard, replaced him. Despite the fact that he had obtained his PhD with a thesis titled *The Regulation of Marriage in the New Hebrides*, he seems to have been much more interested in botany and horticultural systems than in social anthropology. The well-known South African anthropologist Isaac Schapera, in an interview with the Comaroffs, believes that Barnard did not have the authority to teach anthropology and relied on the notes that Schapera himself, as a student, had compiled during Radcliffe-Brown's lectures in Cape Town (Comaroff & Comaroff, 1988). Isaac Schapera took over from Barnard in 1935, and contributed to the excellence of South African anthropology: his research among the Tswana was ethnographically rigorous, and his attention to social transformations and

10 A NERVE CENTRE OF THE DISCIPLINE ON THE PERIPHERY...   303

political dynamics enabled him to make remarkable contributions to the discipline (Schapera, 1938, 1953, 1970). Schapera credits his fascination with Radcliffe-Brown's teaching skills as one of the decisive elements in his conversion to anthropology, together with the fact that from the time he was born—in a small village in the interior semi-desert region of Namaqualand where his father was a relatively unsuccessful trader—he was immersed in the Hottentot culture, in which he took a strong interest. The bond and mutual respect between Schapera and the Tswana never ceased. His books are used in courts and schools in independent Botswana and a street in the capital is named after him (La Fontaine, 2004), proving once again how simplistic is the image of a post-colonial Africa that is keeps its distance from and is suspicious of anthropology as a whole. It was precisely the children of merchants and above all of missionaries (e.g. Monica Wilson and Eileen Krige), in close contact with the indigenous peoples of South Africa, who chose anthropology and were inspired, directly or indirectly, by Radcliffe-Brown's passage through the Cape.

Working closely with the renowned British anthropologist was Agnes Winifred Hoernlé (née Tucker), considered by some to be "the mother of South African social anthropology" (Carstens, 1985; Gluckman & Schapera, 1960; Richards, 1961). After studying philosophy in Cape Town, she travelled to Europe to study anthropology and psychology at Cambridge, working with Haddon and Rivers; she later specialised in Germany and Paris with Émile Durkheim. In 1912, many years before the arrival of Radcliffe-Brown, she returned to South Africa where she carried out rigorous ethnographic research among the Nama Khoikhoi in the borderlands of Namibia (Hoernlé, 1925). Particularly attentive to the ritual and symbolic dimension of culture, she did not disdain the study of cultural change, always trying in her writings to balance the empirical-ethnographic with the theoretical.[4] From 1923 to 1938, she was *Senior Lecturer* in Social Anthropology at the University of the Witwatersrand, where her husband Alfred Hoernlé was Director of the Department of Philosophy and with whom she was heavily involved in social and population support projects. For all her importance in the development of South African social anthropology, Winifred Hoernlé did not receive the academic recognition she deserved; she certainly paid the price for being a woman in male-dominated working environments, such as academia.

---

[4] Peter Carstens, on the occasion of the centenary of Winifred Hoernlé's birth, edited a valuable collection of her essays (Hoernlé, 1985).

304 S. ALLOVIO

Peter Carstens (1985, p. 17) wisely observes that she undoubtedly deserved to replace Radcliffe-Brown as chair of social anthropology at the University of Cape Town, but was preferred to a male colleague, Barnard, with less experience and little inclination towards anthropological research. Among Winifred Hoernlé's pupils, it is worth mentioning, in addition to Max Gluckman, a group of anthropologists who distinguished themselves with their painstaking ethnographic research: Eileen Krige, who conducted fieldwork among the Lovedu, Hilda Kuper, a scholar of the Swazi kingdom, and Ellen Hellman, a pioneer of urban studies in the slums of the Johannesburg suburbs.

It should be remembered that from the 1930s onwards, Bronislaw Malinowski began to exert a strong influence on South African anthropology. The seminars he held at the London School of Economics were attended by black intellectuals (e.g. Jomo Kenyatta and Z.K. Matthews) and many English-speaking and Afrikaner South African anthropologists. Malinowski's trip to Africa in 1934 (Kuper, 1999, pp. 90–93) also strengthened this bond. After visiting his fieldwork students (Lucy Mair in Uganda and Audrey Richards in Northern Rhodesia), Malinowski went to South Africa to attend a conference on African educational systems. It was there that he met the Swazi ruler Sobhuza II, who was keen to promote, from an educational perspective, the Swazi initiation rituals and the youth groups (*emabutfo*) associated with initiation ceremonies (Kuper, 1978, pp. 104–109). It was mainly the missionaries who expressed misgivings about the ruler's proposal because they considered the values expressed by the Swazi association or regiments to be incompatible with those of the Christian faith. The English officials of the colonial administration were more favourable to Sobhuza II's proposal, but they wanted to examine its implications in depth and invited, with the sovereign's consent, Isaac Schapera and Winifred Hoernlé to look into it. In spite of their favourable report, the support of some important personalities, the formation of a new regiment, and the organisation of a nationwide *umcwasho* (rite of passage for women into adulthood) to include girls, Sobhuza II's proposal was not followed through.

This story is emblematic of the tension between processes of transformation and the valorisation of traditional practices. Malinowski spent some time at the court of the Swazi king, where Hilda Kuper, who had trained not only with Hoernlé but also with Malinowski himself, was conducting ethnographic research. Sobhuza II and Malinowski agreed on the valorisation of traditional cultures within a framework of dynamic

10 A NERVE CENTRE OF THE DISCIPLINE ON THE PERIPHERY... 305

transformation of society, which, however, should not necessarily result in a generalised Westernisation. Malinowski's rather mechanical view of cultural change, where (partly "resistant") cultures would to some extent overlap, was criticised by South African social anthropologists (especially Monica Hunter, Schapera and Meyer Fortes) who considered more appropriate Radcliffe-Brown's approach, according to which the South African context should be seen as a social arena in which individuals (and not cultures) interacted in a historically and irreversibly new situation (Kuper, 1999, pp. 92–93). As would later become clearer, the appropriateness of such an approach was, in South Africa, well-founded not only from a theoretical but also from a political point of view (in liberal terms), since segregationist practices were supported from an anthropological standpoint by Afrikaner ethnologists from the perspective of preserving cultures and fighting the Westernisation of Bantu groups. In short, British-derived social anthropology could not, in any case, have an easy time in South Africa, which was slowly constructing for itself legislation constantly and inexorably moving towards apartheid. At the time of Malinowski's trip, the Herzog government had for some years suspended funding for the research of Africanists. Until the outbreak of the Second World War, funds from the Rockefeller Foundation supported the ethnographic work of many anthropologists. Later, with the establishment of the apartheid regime, everything became incredibly complicated.

THE LABORIOUS INSTITUTIONALISATION OF THE DISCIPLINE

If Hoernlé can be considered "the mother of South African social anthropology," another woman helped to establish the discipline in the country's universities: Monica Hunter Wilson (1908–1982), born in the Eastern Cape where her father, a Scotsman from Glasgow, had moved as a missionary (Bank & Bank, 2013). Monica Hunter lived in close contact with the local people from an early age, learning the Xhosa language and showing curiosity and interest in the cultures of the region. At Cambridge, she dedicated her energies first to the study of history and then turned her attention to social anthropology. Under Hodson's guidance and with Driberg's advice, she returned to her homeland in 1931–1933 to carry out field research among the Pondas, with a view to writing her doctoral thesis. This was to form the basis of her best-known monograph, *Reaction to Conquest*, published in 1936 with a preface by the philosopher and several times South African Prime Minister, Jan Smuts.

An attentive scholar of ceremonial and ritual practices, Monica Wilson was also very interested in the processes of transformation and urbanisation of the local populations, coherently placing herself within the tradition of studies inaugurated with the teachings of Radcliffe-Brown in Cape Town; a tradition which not infrequently led her to combining research work with commitment and support for the demands of the black population of South Africa. With her husband Godfrey Wilson (also Scottish like Monica's parents) she conducted intensive fieldwork among the Nyakyusa of Tanzania from 1935 until 1938, the year before Godfrey was appointed the first director of the renowned Rhodes-Livingstone Institute in Northern Rhodesia (now Zambia).

His difficult and conflict-ridden relationships with the colonial administration and his unswerving position on the side of the African miners led Godfrey Wilson to leave the direction of the Research Institute in 1941, a few years before his tragic suicide. In 1944, Monica, alone with two children to look after, had no other solution but to return to her homeland, to the small town of Alice where her parents lived and where she managed to find a job at the University College of Fort Hare, a cherished institution that had long been dedicated to the education of black Africans and where illustrious figures who later became famous in the struggle against apartheid (e.g. Nelson Mandela, Desmond Tutu, Robert Sobukwe, Olivier Tambo) had the opportunity to study.

As mentioned earlier, social anthropology was already being taught at Fort Hare thanks to the efforts of Jabuvu and later Zachariah Keodirelang "ZK" Matthews, another prominent black activist who forged a solid partnership with Monica Wilson even when the latter left Fort Hare to take up a post as Full Professor at Rhodes University in Grahamstown in 1947 (the first woman to achieve tenure at the university).

These were certainly not easy years for a multitude of reasons. The South African Monica Wilson was establishing herself in the academic context of a country where black South Africans struggled to cling on to the right to education, let alone to teaching. As will be seen below, the community of South African anthropologists had for decades been characterised by strong internal divisions over the thorny issue of segregationism and apartheid policy. Even those who were contrary to it were accused of doing microscopic studies of individual tribal groups and of not taking sides in the name of objectivity and cultural relativism. These are, roughly speaking, the charges levelled against anthropology by the South African historian William Miller Macmillan, who accused anthropologists of being "paralysed conservatives." Nevertheless, one cannot ignore the fact that many white South Africans, whose influences could be traced back to British social anthropology, were capable of political stances in proximity to black activists. It is no coincidence that in post-apartheid South Africa, on the seafront of East London, the African National Congress government unveiled a monument with a plaque listing the hundred heroes of the Eastern Cape (Bank, 2008). Alongside legendary names such as Nelson Mandela, Steve Biko, Oliver Tambo and Govan Mbeki, it was decided to engrave also the name of Monica Hunter Wilson.

The great South African anthropologist lived with and shared the backdrop of black intellectuals' grievances and claims for redress, collaborated actively with them (especially with Matthews), explicitly valued, as did few others at the time, the crucial role of native co-workers in field research and, finally, was credited with not having abandoned South Africa in the dark decades of apartheid, as did many others. From 1952 until her retirement in 1973, Monica Wilson taught at the University of Cape Town (UCT) and went on to foster the study of social anthropology in South African universities. Her focus on the processes of detribalisation and urbanisation, that is, those very processes which demonstrated in both conceptual and practical terms the absurdity of a social project based on segregation, would remain central to her lifelong interests, together with an interest in issues related to religious systems.[5]

Indicative in this regard are her studies of Langa, a suburb of Cape Town, conducted with Archie Mafeje in the early 1960s (Wilson & Mafeje, 1963). Equally significant are the parts of her first monograph, *Reaction to Conquest* (1936), dedicated to the life of Africans on white farms and in urban settings, with a particular focus on East London, the same city where Philip and Iona Mayer (1961; Mayer & Mayer, 1962) carried out their ethnographic research, which contributed to rethinking the approach to social surveys on migration.[6]

Philip Mayer (1910–1985) was born near Berlin into a Jewish family and soon was obliged to leave Nazi Germany, taking refuge first in Switzerland and then in London, where he completed his education at

---

[5] On the occasion of her retirement, colleagues and students compiled a collection of essays in her honour whose title is significantly: *Religion and Social Change in Southern Africa* (Whisson & West, 1975).

[6] The centrality of East London in urban anthropology studies is evidenced in recent years thanks to the relevant ethnographic survey conducted by Leslie Bank (2011).

Oxford. From 1945, he and his wife Iona began working in Kenya and then, from 1949, moved to South Africa where his academic career took shape: first in Grahamstown, then at the University of the Witwatersrand and finally again in Grahamstown. In particular, the Mayers studied the processes and strategies of adaptation to the urban environment of the Xhosa. Some of them (these the Xhosa defined as *school*) chose a path of assimilation to the urban and "modern" context, others (defined by the Xhosa as *red*) showed more resistance, remaining anchored to the rural world of their origin and to traditional values (Mayer, 1961).

When a period of forceful accusations against the Mayers by liberal and Marxist intellectuals began in the 1970s, Monica Wilson's collaborator Archie Mafeje was at the forefront. In his view (Mafeje, 1971), the rigid opposition between *red* and *school* did not correspond to the reality of the situation: the two categories were porous and fluid. For Mafeje, the proposition of this dichotomy points to an idea of identity essentialism that was not only sociologically untenable, but politically "irresponsible" in the light of the segregationist proposals inherent in apartheid policy.

The institutionalisation of social anthropology in South African universities could not be separated from the progressive worsening of the socio-political situation, of which the events of the decade 1938–1948 are emblematic: an initial cut in funding, to which reference was made earlier, was followed by prohibiting social anthropologists from accessing *native reserves*, and ultimately the radicalisation of the policies of the Afrikaner nationalists in power with the institution of what would sadly go down in history as apartheid. At that point, many anthropologists decided to retire or go elsewhere: Isaac Schapera went to the London School of Economics, Hilda Kuper emigrated to the United States, a new generation of black anthropologists left the country (Absolom Vilakasi, Bernard Magubane, Archie Mafeje, Harriet Ngubane). Max Gluckman, one of South Africa's most brilliant anthropologists, was barred from entering Zulu territories after conducting important research among the Zulu people (Gluckman, 1940a, 1940b). A communist Jew, disliked by the South African political authorities for his ideas, Gluckman spent the period of the Second World War directing the Rhodes-Livingstone Institute (1941–1946), replacing Godfrey Wilson, before going on to establish a new Department of Social

Anthropology in Manchester, thus bringing the South African critique of functionalism to the heart of Britain (Kuper, 1999, p. 95).[7]

While it is true that British social anthropology was grafted onto the development of the discipline within some South African universities, it is equally true that South African anthropology went on to "fertilise" British anthropology with a disruptive force. Interestingly, Isaac Schapera, interviewed by the Comaroffs (1988, p. 557), confirmed that a sort of quartet closely linked to South Africa had been formed in Britain: Schapera, Fortes and Gluckman (South Africans) and Evans-Pritchard, an Africanist whose wife, Ioma Heaton Nicholls, was South African, being the daughter of a prominent businessman and politician who had moved to South Africa during the Anglo-Boer War.[8]

Assimilationists, Segregationists and New Developments at the End of the Twentieth Century

In the light of what has been stated thus far, it can be affirmed that Anglophone and British-inspired South African social anthropology, starting with the theories espoused by the young Radcliffe-Brown lecturing in Cape Town, has contributed to demonstrate, with more or less force and political impact depending on the case, how the process of transformation in South African society encompasses both the black and white populations. Many English-speaking South African anthropologists are progressive and "assimilationist" when it comes to the thorny issue of black-white co-existence. Emphasising the inevitability of a dynamic and hopefully inclusive society rather than individual cultures, while legitimately deserving of anthropological appreciation, is an element to be taken into account in a context such as South Africa marked by segregationist policies and by the presence of an Afrikaner nationalism closely linked to a specific ethnological school (*volkekunde*) established in some Afrikaans-speaking

---

[7] In the overall economy of this essay, it is not possible to devote as much space to the Rhodes-Livingstone Institute (RLI) as it deserves. It is sufficient to recall that the RLI, founded in 1937, was Africa's first social science research institute and that its development is probably much more connected to the South African context of radical and liberal social sciences than is acknowledged (Schumaker, 2001).

[8] Evans-Pritchard's father-in-law, George Heaton Nicholls, accompanied Lewanika, chief of the Barotse, to London to attend the coronation of Edward VII. Settling in the Natal region, George became a member of Parliament in 1920 as a Zululand member and later administrator of Natal.

universities, such as those of Stellenbosch and Pretoria. These Afrikaner ethnologists also contributed to the elaboration of apartheid policies as was denounced by many and by English-speaking South African social anthropologists themselves (Gluckman, 1975; Sharp, 1981).

As Robert Gordon (1988) points out, it is worth recalling the genealogy of Afrikaner ethnology. From the 1920s onwards, Germany was at the forefront of studies on ethnology and the languages of Africa. Connections with the Protestant missionary world and the enhancement of educational processes centred on indigenous languages characterised the approach of many German scholars. A considerable number of young South Africans whose native tongue was Afrikaans (which is a West Germanic language) went to Germany for further studies in ethnology and Bantu linguistics (among them Eiselen, van Warmelo, Engelbrecht, van Eeden, Ziervogel). It is relevant to note that this happened in the 1920s and 1930s when Germany was not only embracing the rigours of philological studies of non-European languages, but also witnessing an increasing spread of Nazi ideology which greatly influenced the young Afrikaner students. Back in South Africa, these young ethnologists adhered without hesitation to Afrikaner nationalist policies and to the revendication of the white settlers who had been defeated and impoverished by the Anglo-Boer conflict and the new order of the Union of South Africa.

Afrikaner ethnologists initially maintained cordial relations with Anglophone social anthropologists, but from the mid-1930s onwards, when the Afrikaner nationalists were firmly installed in power and segregationist policies became ever more concrete, relations became strained. The Anglophone "assimilationists" thought and practised an anthropology centred on the idea of an integrated society, particularly visible in the human events of the urbanised and de-tribalised black population; the Afrikaans-speaking "segregationists" insisted on the study of cultures and the defence of their integrity, to be guaranteed—a not insignificant detail from a political and social (!) point of view—through the creation of reserves to "protect" the identity of the Bantu groups subjected to a damaging Westernisation. It is not surprising, therefore, that some of these ethnographers played a significant role in the construction of apartheid, nor is it surprising that anthropology, conceived of as a single monolithic and culpable discipline, was viewed with great distrust by many black intellectuals and activists.

As Gordon (1988, p. 536) points out, the comparison between the two schools (Anglophone social anthropologists vs. Afrikaner ethnologists) is

10 A NERVE CENTRE OF THE DISCIPLINE ON THE PERIPHERY... 311

not only a matter of obvious social political judgement, but also a scientific and academic one: the former have produced excellent works, some of which have become classics of anthropology worldwide; they have allowed, as in few other contexts, many female anthropologists to establish themselves; and, finally, they have welcomed numerous black scholars and intellectuals into the scientific community of social anthropologists. The latter, none of this.

Academically, the most influential scholar connected with Afrikaner ethnography was Werner Max Eiselen who alternated periods of employment in universities (in Stellenbosch until 1936 and in Pretoria from 1948 to 1950) with governmental appointments aimed at drawing up guidelines for the education of black South Africans. In Stellenbosch one of his students, Pieter J. Schoeman, replaced him, while the chair of *volkekunde* at the University of Pretoria passed to Pieter J. Coertze in 1951.

A hotly debated aspect, relevant to the history of the discipline in South Africa, is the affinity between Afrikaner ethnologists and Bronislaw Malinowski, who is often quoted in their writings. This closeness is surely due to an appreciation of certain elements of Malinowski's anthropology: (1) the desire to "defend" Bantu cultures from Westernisation (even in educational programmes); (2) the appreciation of cultural diversity, that is, individual cultures conceived in holistic terms; (3) the "mechanical" vision of cultural change that would take the form of the coexistence of a traditional "culture," a Western-derived "culture" and a new urban culture. Added to this is the fact that, in a context where Afrikaner ethnologists were partly still "fighting," ideally and academically, the Anglo-Boer War (Gordon, 1990, p. 31), Malinowski was not strictly a Briton, certainly less so than Radcliffe-Brown, the theoretical reference point for South African social anthropologists.[9s] The centrality given to "cultural diversity" by Afrikaner ethnologists was a reason for affinity not only with Malinowski, but also with the American "culturalists" of the Boas school (Melville Herskovits and Ruth Benedict are frequently quoted in their works).

Having said that, one must be very careful not to proceed with erroneous arguments and easy conclusions because if it is true that American "culturalism" found admirers among Afrikaner ethnologists who were in favour of racist policies, it is also true that it was precisely the school of Boas which distinguished itself in opposing racism and discrimination

---

[9s] On the different impact of Radcliffe-Brown and Malinowski on South African politics, see also Niehaus (2017).

(King, 2019). Moreover, while it is true that some of Malinowski's theories found admirers among Afrikaner ethnologists, they themselves considered Malinowski's ethnographic method subjective, unscientific and somewhat inappropriate: "participant observation requires an intimacy of living that they found unseemly, preferring to rely on formal interviews with authority figures" (Kuper, 1999, p. 95). It is significant to note that the implosion of Afrikaner ethnology (represented by Coertze's theory of ethnos) in the 1970s was caused not only by the awareness of what was foreshadowed by apartheid, but also by the inability of ethnographers to ignore Malinowskian methodologies. In this regard, it is worth mentioning the Afrikaner ethnologist Boet Kotzé (1943–2020), one of the first who had the courage and intellectual honesty to distance himself from his masters even while studying for his doctorate and, from the early 1980s, to establish relations with English-speaking social anthropologists from Cape Town such as John Sharp, Martin West, Mugsy Spiegel (van der Waal & Sharp, 2020). Kotzé was followed by many other Afrikaner ethnologists; this fact indirectly raises doubts about dichotomous and simplified (therefore ideological) visions of reality: as in this case, thinking of a compact and granitic *volkekunde* universe opposed to an equally compact and indistinct *social anthropology* universe.

Returning to the appreciation of cultural diversity, it should be noted that it is a programmatic aspect of the discipline of anthropology, arguably the central aspect. Nevertheless, in the South Africa of segregation and apartheid regulations, cultural diversity became not only a sacrosanct object of study, but a programmatic political element endorsed by the racist state administration aided by numerous Afrikaner ethnologists. If the valorisation of cultural diversity implies, in many cases, intercultural policies focused on inclusion, equal rights and coexistence, in twentieth-century South Africa the valorisation of cultural diversity legitimised exclusions, inequalities and rules for separate coexistence. In this regard, Max Gluckman is very clear when, implicitly addressing Edmund Leach, fellow at King's College, Cambridge, and Rodney Needham at Merton College, Oxford, he writes: "It is possible in the seclusion of King's College, Cambridge (or Merton College, Oxford [...]), to lay stress primarily on persistent differences; this was not possible for 'liberal' South Africans confronted with the politics of segregation within a nation in which 'others' were regarded and treated as different and inferior" (Gluckman, 1975, p. 26, quoted in Kuper, 1999, p. 95).

In short, it is necessary to contextualise, precisely in terms of time and place, diffidence towards an anthropology strongly oriented towards the valorisation of cultural diversity. It is no coincidence that, with the collapse of the apartheid regime, the valorisation of cultural diversity seems to be gaining renewed legitimacy to the point of once again becoming—but in a different direction compared to the past—a matter of political and not just academic debate. For example, Harriet Ngubane (1929–2007), professor of Social Anthropology at the University of Cape Town and later a member of parliament for the neo-traditionalist Zulu party (Inkatha Freedom Party), strongly defended the valorisation and study of indigenous knowledge, as well as drawing attention to demands for the recognition of traditional authorities (Ngubane, 1999). Adam Kuper (1999), reflecting on the state of anthropology in a liberated late twentieth-century South Africa, notes a certain attractiveness in the discipline for many South African students. As is the case in other parts of the continent, anthropology seems to be oriented towards practical application; nevertheless, basic ethnological research also merits a revival due to the same demand coming from black students.

In late twentieth-century South Africa, anthropology had to shake off not only the anathema felt towards the study of cultural diversity, but also the accusation of being a force of conservatism. As mentioned earlier, numerous paths followed in life by English-speaking social anthropologists show that such a generalised accusation would be overly hasty. In addition, some anthropologists have actually taken the path of activism: emblematic is the tragic story of David Webster (1944–1989), a brilliant anthropologist at the University of the Witwatersrand, the son of a Copperbelt miner, who was murdered by government security forces (CCB) on 1 May 1989[10] in front of his house (James, 2009). Adam Kuper, in the final part of his 1999 essay (widely referenced in this review), as well as recalling the story of David Webster, an anthropologist engaged in activism "beyond anthropology," dedicates attention to a very fascinating figure in South African anthropology, who chooses to be an activist "through anthropology": Mamphela Ramphele (1947–).

---

[10] On the 20th anniversary of his death, a park in the city of Johannesburg was named after him. Part of the exterior wall of his house at 13 Eleanor Street, Troyeville, Johannesburg, has been decorated with a commemorative mosaic and the house has been declared a heritage site.

314   S. ALLOVIO

Before turning her attention to social anthropology, Ramphele trained as a doctor at the University of Natal where she began her anti-apartheid political activism alongside Steve Biko, a fellow fighter and her life partner for many years. In 1976, because of her anti-apartheid activities, she was first imprisoned for a few months and then confined (until 1984) in the district of Tzaneen (in present-day Limpopo) where she had the opportunity to continue her studies and the strength to implement social and health initiatives. At the end of her confinement, Ramphele moved to Cape Town where she undertook ethnographic research (from 1986 to 1988) on the desperate conditions of black workers in the dormitories of the townships of Langa, Nyanga and Guguletu with the objective of obtaining a PhD in social anthropology from the University of Cape Town (Ramphele, 1993) where she became vice-rector in 1996, the first black woman to hold this position in a South African university.

The subsequent story of her life tells of her intense political and managerial activity (top role at the World Bank, member of the boards of directors of several companies, founder of a political party), but what is of interest here is her passionate defence of anthropology and the ethnographic method. This she considers to be exhausting, especially for one like her accustomed to the world of activism, but an invaluable method that seeks to obtain a clearer understanding of the society in which one lives. Ramphele had the opportunity to interact and engage directly with the most powerful and distinguished politicians of the new South Africa (Ramphele, 1995). She had a heated discussion with Nelson Mandela, visiting him in prison just a few months before his release, about the role of indigenous authorities in the new post-apartheid order. She did not draw back from engaging in frank discussions with Thabo Mbeki, Mandela's successor as President of South Africa, seeking to convince him of the value and importance of social anthropology and ethnography in order to achieve a deeper understanding the realities of the current situation. When all is said and done, giving a methodologically rigorous account of the tragic conditions in dormitories for black workers in the urban periphery in the final years of apartheid (Ramphele, 1993), besides being very hard work (perhaps harder than activism, it would seem), is not an escape from responsibility, but a path intrinsic to academia and anthropology in order to continue to reflect on and act in the world.[11]

REFERENCES

Arowosegbe, J. (2016). African Scholars, African Studies and Knowledge Production on Africa. *Africa, 86*(2), 324–338.

Asad, T. (Ed.). (1973). *Anthropology and the Colonial Encounter*. Humanities Press.

Bank, A, & Bank, L. (2013). *Inside African Anthropology. Monica Wilson and her Interpreters*. Cambridge University Press.

Bank, A. (2008). The Life, Work and Legacy of Monica Hunter Wilson (1908–1982). *FHISER Research Series No, 9*.

Bank, L. (2011). Home Spaces, Street Styles. In *Contesting Power and Identity in a South African City*. Wits University Press.

Barth, F., Gingrich, A., Parkin, R., & Silverman, S. (2005). *One Discipline, Four Ways: British, German, French and American Anthropology*. University of Chicago Press.

Carstens, P. (1985). Agnes Winifred Hoernlé (1885–1960): The Mother of Social Anthropology in South Africa. *Anthropology Today, 1*(6), 17–18.

Comaroff, J., & Comaroff, J. (1988). On the Founding Father, Fieldwork and Functionalism: A Conversation with Isaac Schapera. *American Ethnologist, 15*(3), 554–565.

Evans-Pritchard, E. (1937). *Witchcraft, Oracles and Magic among the Azande*. Clarendon Press.

Fortes, M. (1956). Alfred Reginald Radcliffe-Brown, FBA, 1881–1955. A Memoir. *Man, 172*, 149–153.

Gluckman, M. (1940a). Analysis of a Situation in Modern Zululand. *Bantu Studies, 4*(1-30), 147–174.

Gluckman, M. (1940b). The Kingdom of the Zulu of South Africa. In M. Fortes & E. E. Evans-Pritchard (Eds.), *African Political Systems* (pp. 25–55). Oxford University Press.

Gluckman, M. (1975). Anthropology and Apartheid: The Work of South African Anthropologists. In M. Fortes & S. Patterson (Eds.), *Studies in African Social Anthropology* (pp. 21–40). Academic Press.

Gluckman, M., & Schapera, I. (1960). Dr. Winifred Hoernlé: An Appreciation. *Africa, 30*(3), 262–263.

Gordon, R. (1988). Apartheid's Anthropology: The Genealogy of Afrikaner Anthropology. *American Ethnologist, 15*(3), 535–553.

[11] He writes: "Radcliffe-Brown, Monica Wilson, the Mayers and many others have done valuable work that has left a broader and more sophisticated understanding of South African society" (Ramphele, 1995, p. 167).

316   S. ALLOVIO

Gordon, R. (1990). Early Social Anthropology in South Africa. *African Studies, 49*, 15–48.

Gordon, R., & Spiegel, A. (1993). South African Anthropology Revisited. *Annual Review of Anthropology, 22*, 83–105.

Hammond-Tooke, W. D. (1997). *Imperfect Interpreters. South Africa's Anthropologists*. Witwatersrand University Press.

Harries, P. (1981). The Anthropologist as Historian and Liberal: H.-A. Junod and the Thonga. *Journal of Southern African Studies, 88*(1), 37–50.

Hoernlé, W. (1925). The Social Organization of the Nama Hottentots of Southwest Africa. *American Anthropology, 27*(1), 1–24.

Hoernlé, W. (1985). *The Social Organisation of the Nama and Other Essays* (Centenary Volume) (P. Carstens, Ed.). Witwatersrand University Press.

James, D. (2009). David Webster: An Activist Anthropologist Twenty Years On. *Africa Studies, 68*(2), 287–295.

King, C. (2019). *Gods of the Upper Air. How a Circle of Renegade Anthropologists Reinvented Race, Sex, and Gender in the Twentieth Century*. Doubleday.

Kuper, H. (1978). *Sobhuza II. Ngwenyama and King of Swaziland*. Duckworth.

Kuper, A. (1999). South African Anthropology: An inside job. *Paideuma, 45*, 83–101.

La Fontaine, J. (2004). Isaac Schapera 19052003. *The Cambridge Journal of Anthropology, 24*(1), 59–61.

Mafeje, A. (1971). The Ideology of Tribalism. *Journal of Modern African Studies, 4*(2), 253–261.

Malinowski, B. (1929). Practical Anthropology. *Africa, II*(1), 22–38.

Malinowski, B. (1930). The Rationalization of Anthropology and Administration. *Africa, III*(4), 405–430.

Mayer, P. (1961). *Townsmen or Tribesmen: Conservatism and the Process of Urbanisation in a South African City, with Contributions by Iona Mayer*. Oxford University Press.

Mayer, P., & Mayer, I. (1962). Migrancy and the Study of Africans in Towns. *American Anthropologist, 64*(3), 576–592.

Ngubane, H. (1999). Current Politics, Development Aims, and Anthropology in Southern Africa. *Anthropological Journal on European Cultures, 8* (2) (*The Politics of Anthropology at Home II*), 129–140.

Niehaus, I. (2017). Anthropology at the Dawn of Apartheid. Radcliffe-Brown and Malinowski's South African Engagements, 1919–1934. *Focaal—Journal of Global and Historical Anthropology, 77*, 103–117.

Ntsebeza, L. (2012). African Studies at UCT: An Overview. In T. Nhlapo & H. Garuba (Eds.), *African Studies in the Postcolonial University* (pp. 1–21). University of Cape Town.

Pauw, B. A. (1980). Recent South African Anthropology. *Annual Reviews of Anthropology, 9*, 315–338.

Ramphele, M. (1993). *A Bed Called Home. Life in the Migrant Labour Hostels of Cape Town*. David Philip.

Ramphele, M. (1995). *A Life*. David Philip.

Reubi, S. (2004). Aider l'Afrique et servir la science: H. A. Junod, missionnaire et ethnographe (1863–1934). *RHN*, 197–214.

Richards, A. (1961). Agnes Winifred Hoernlé: 1885–1960: With a Portrait. *Man, 50*(1), 53.

Schumaker, L. (2001). *Africanizing Anthropology. Fieldwork, Networks, and the Making of Cultural Knowledge in Central Africa*. Duke University Press.

Schapera, I. (1938). *A Handbook of Tswana Law and Customs*. Oxford University Press.

Schapera, I. (1953). *The Tswana (Ethnographic Survey of Africa)*. International African Institute.

Schapera, I. (1970). *Tribal Innovators: Tswana Chiefs and Social Change*. Athlone.

Sharp, J. (1981). The Roots and Development of 'Volkekunde' in South Africa. *Journal of Southern Africa Studies, 8*(1), 16–36.

Stocking, G. (1995). *After Tylor. British Social Anthropology 1888–1951*. University of Wisconsin Press.

van der Waal, C. S., & Sharp, J. (2020). Boet Kotzé, a Radical and Prophetic African Anthropologist (March 4, 1943–July 8, 2020). *Anthropology Southern Africa, 43*(2), 259–265.

Whisson, M. G., & West, M. (Eds.). (1975). *Religion and Social Change in Southern Africa. Anthropological Essays in Honour of Monica Wilson*. David Philip.

Wilson, M. (1936). *Reaction to Conquest. Effects of Contact with Europeans on the Pondo of South Africa*. Oxford University Press.

Wilson, M., & Mafeje, A. (1963). *Langa: A Study of Social Groups in an African Township*. Oxford University Press.

CHAPTER 11

American Anthropology: Some Distinctive Features

Angela Biscaldi

As Alan Barnard (2000) points out, it is not always easy or possible to define precise traditions of anthropological thought along national lines, just as much of the narratives of the history of anthropology are conducted starting from the research focuses dominant at the time they were written—interests that, more or less consciously, select and underline some themes, fields, authors and, at the same time, neglect or diminish others. Even with these limitations, in this chapter I will try to outline three areas of reflection of the American anthropology that were present at its birth and which, over time, have characterised it: the accentuated empiricism, the idiographic/relativist perspective and the marked applied tendency that has accompanied it from the beginning.

The intent is to concisely explain some theoretical-methodological emergencies that today have a precise meaning for anthropologists, or constitute an essential point of reference in addressing particular research themes, as they are associated and referable to US epistemology.

A. Biscaldi (✉)
Department of Social and Political Sciences, University of Milano, Milan, Italy
e-mail: angela.biscaldi@unimi.it

© The Author(s), under exclusive license to Springer Nature Switzerland AG 2023
G. D'Agostino, V. Matera (eds.), *Histories of Anthropology*,
https://doi.org/10.1007/978-3-031-21258-1_11

319

Empiricism

It is well known that for Europeans the reflection on cultural otherness was produced, during the eighteenth and nineteenth centuries, first of all by literary imagery, the Enlightenment myth of the good savage, and then by the colonial experience—that's why at the origins of European anthropology there is an alterity experienced "at a distance" (Fabietti, 2020).

The situation in the United States, on the other hand, is very different. Not only because the country, since its birth, has been a particularly heterogeneous space where people from different continents find themselves living together, but also because these men and women have built their cultural identity by relating to the "primitives", the so-called "red Indians" who occupy the territories of the New World. The American aborigines, in fact, have played an important role in the process of building the United States of America, both in a material sense (as a presence, a physical obstacle to the occupation of new lands) and in an ideological sense. In fact, after their removal, it was necessary to legitimise, in the eyes of Europeans, the independence and existence of a new country, with a homogeneous identity. They were a problem to solve earlier, as well as an element of anthropological reflection.

We can therefore say that American civilisation elaborates a definition of itself, its own identity, in close relationship with otherness, an otherness interpreted in a complex and contradictory way, based on different moments and interests in the history of the country's constitution: the corrupt and cruel Indian, the enemy that prevents white people from expanding (Gliozzi, 1977); the Indian sinner to be redeemed (Trigger & Washburn, 1996; Abler, 1992); the irrational man in the exploitation of the land, which white people, on the other hand, are able to use better (Bergamini, 2002); or the innocent Indian, a guarantee of the positive, powerful, uncontaminated nature of the new continent (Eisen, 1977; Ronda, 2002); or even the degraded Indian to be recovered and confined in reserves (Frantz, 1999).

It is with respect to this complex and polyphonic cultural heritage (Gerbi, 2000) and within this framework that the field work of Lewis Henry Morgan (1818–1883), considered one of the fathers of American anthropology, fits in. A wealthy landowner, a lawyer, a New York state senator, defender of Indian rights in Washington in 1846, an activity whose traces remain in *The League of the Iroquois* (1851), a work that arises from the concern to demonstrate the legitimacy of Indian culture compared to the American one and the reasons why it should be considered as worthy of respect (Resek, 1960; Moses, 2009; Alliegro, 2015).

Morgan's works—*Systems of consanguinity and affinity of the human family* (1871) and *Ancient Society* (1877)—move within the evolutionary interpretative framework that was dominant in the second half of the nineteenth century.

According to the evolutionist perspective, starting from the assumption of the psychic unity of the human race, human culture is a unity that has developed progressively over time, conforming itself to all peoples essentially in the same sequence of development. Along their evolutionary path, the various peoples have moved through a sequence of fixed cultural stages, whose grades, marked by inventions and discoveries, have brought them "inexorably" from the original wildness, through the barbarian, to civilisation—represented by English society in the late nineteenth century. The cultural differences that can be observed at an empirical level are therefore attributable to the different stages reached and occupied by the various societies in their unstoppable path towards "civilisation".

In *Systems of consanguinity and affinity of the human family* (1871) the evolutionist perspective is not made explicit by the author, but acts as an implicit project to build a typology of kinship systems, on the basis of an extended and decontextualised comparison; in *Ancient Society* (1877) instead, it is explicitly used as an epistemological paradigm. This last work was particularly appreciated by Karl Marx and Friedrich Engels who recognised in it the materialistic conception of history; it was translated into many languages and is considered a fundamental text in socialist countries (thus linking the alternating fortune of Morgan's works to that of Marxism); particularly criticised, however, by those who have seen the most complete synthesis of evolutionist ideology. Nonetheless, despite being within an evolutionary perspective and with partially remote data collection, Morgan's data collection leaves the predation paradigm (disordered collection of objects and customs) and assumes an analytical planning, endowing itself with clear anthropological objectives so as to develop an adequate methodology (Alliegro, 2021).

In 1879, in the wake of Morgan's work, a research centre dedicated to the study of natives was founded, the *Bureau of American Ethnology* (Judd, 1967), directed by John Wesley Powell, a compiler of Indian languages and customs. The centre proved to be extremely prolific, with its *Annual Reports*, volumes of thousands of pages with analytical discussions of individual ethnic groups, comparative analyses and methodological reflections; moreover, in 1879 the *Anthropological Society of Washington* was founded (whose *American Anthropologist* magazine was founded ten years later, in 1889).

Those years—the second half of the nineteenth century—were important for the nascent American anthropology, marked by impressive works of ethnographic collection and description: in addition to the one already mentioned by Powell on Aboriginal myths and languages, we remember Frank Hamilton Cushing, who carried out research over almost five years, between 1879 and 1884, among the Zuni of New Mexico, studying their mythological system (Cushing, 1979; Tiberini, 1999); Alice Flecther on the initiation rites of the Pawnee Indians (1904); James Mooney on Ghost Dance, among the Sioux Indians (1896); by J. Owen Dorsey, scholar of the Siouan linguistic stock (Rigs & Dorsey, 1893).

As Enzo Vinicio Alliegro (2021) writes, well before the mainstream narrative that identifies Franz Boas and Bronislaw Malinowki as the founding fathers of the ethnographic method, the North American continent was the site of significant initiatives of great ethnographic depth: a scientific anthropological community was born, endowed with a language and with a reflexive and critical research of a specific methodology. In addition, the intense fieldwork of American anthropologists stimulated British researchers who, in 1886, under the leadership of linguist Horatio Hale, promoted an expedition for the field study of the Indians of the west coast of the Pacific. The young German Franz Boas, a physicist and geographer, participated in the study, destined to have a profound impact on the history of the new-born American anthropology, promoting a new epistemological disposition and a different ethical posture in the study of human diversity (Gruber, 1967).

Cultural Relativism

In a famous ten-page article from 1896, *The Limits of the Comparative Method in Anthropology*, Franz Boas makes the first criticism of evolutionary thought. The theoretical-methodological flaws of evolutionists are identified by the anthropologist both in the assumption of a unique factor extraneous to the functioning of the societies under consideration as an absolute criterion of interpretation (the concept of Western progress), and in the collection and use of insufficient and poorly organised data.

Boas points out that a culture is not the product of the "uniform action of uniform causes" but rather the outcome of a particular history;

11 AMERICAN ANTHROPOLOGY: SOME DISTINCTIVE FEATURES 323

apparently similar cultural phenomena, in fact, can be the product of very different historical causes. The development sequences proposed by the evolutionists remain for the author in many cases conjectures contradicted by the results of an analytical and detailed ethnographic investigation. Indeed, it is necessary to concentrate on the study of a specific cultural area and to reconstruct within it, the historical processes that have led to the formation of a cultural phenomenon and, on the outside, the processes of diffusion and exchange with neighbouring cultures or with cultures whose historical relationship can be proven. The nomothetic method of the evolutionists—a single law for all cultural phenomena—is replaced by the Boasian historical particularism, an idiographic conception, aimed at considering each culture in its specificity: the search for general laws gives way to the study of contexts and research of the different meanings attributed by communities to objects, practices, values.

At Colombia University, Boas's ideographic position faces the typological and racial tradition of the *National Museum*, of the archaeologists of the *Carnegie Institution of Washington* and of the *Peabody* of Harvard in Cambridge, the eugenics movement of Charles B. Davenport. In those years, a rift was created between the Washington-Cambridge axis on one side and Columbia University on the other, a centre from which the Boasians would soon spread to other parts of the country (Kroeber and Lowie in Berkeley, Sapir in Chicago and Yale, Hersvowitz in Evanston, Goldenweiser in New York); two real schools with different approaches that would fight over the years for research funds, the control of the AAA, the direction of the *American Anthropologist*, appointments in the nascent anthropology departments. The theoretical division (which contrasts evolutionists with historicists) also reflects different political positions on issues relevant to the time such as immigration, interventionism or isolationism during World War I, separatism or assimilationism of the Indians of America (Silverman, 1981).

The Boasian historicist paradigm, which recognises the importance of the peculiarity of cultures and therefore of their plurality, contributes to constituting the intellectual climate in which a central concept in American anthropology could be born and developed, which will fuel an important debate throughout the twentieth century cultural relativism (Biscaldi, 2009). In the preface to an edition of *Primitive Man*, Melville Herskovitz, considered the systematiser of perspective, acknowledges the merit of the master Franz Boas for having laid the foundations for the comparative study of values. He writes that the essential contribution of the book must be sought in its implicit demonstration of how, in human culture, the plurality of forms hides the unity of natural gifts, needs and aspirations common to all men, referring to cultural relativism which, arising from unity in cultural diversity, creates awareness of the attachment that all peoples have for their particular way of life. (Herskovitz in Boas, 1963). Certainly, Franz Boas's opposition to generalisations and his support for particularistic analyses of individual cultures derive from the importance that the anthropologist attributed to the ethnographic method, based on inductive reasoning and data collection (King, 2019).

The direct experience in the field—among the Inuit in 1883–1884 and then among the Indians of the north-western coast of the Pacific in 1886—directed him, in fact, towards two areas of reflection, destined to give life to two important areas of research.

The first one is the analysis of the relationship between thought, language and culture. In the *Handbook of American Indian Languages* (1911–1941), Boas argues that it is imperative to know the native language to conduct good research in the field since much information can only be obtained by listening to the conversations of the indigenous people and taking part in their daily life.

This practical necessity combined with his direct knowledge of the Eskimo language and the languages of the American Indians (in particular Bella Coola and Chinook) lead him to reflect, on a theoretical level, on the different role of language in filtering and organising, through its grammatical categories, the experience of the world of individuals: each language selects some aspects of the reality it intends to express, directing speakers towards different perceptions and evaluations of the experience. These reflections would help to strengthen the idea of the relativity of cultures and would converge in the Sapir-Whorf hypothesis, according to which the structure of the language we speak determines our vision of the world (Whorf, 1956).

For Boas, primitive peoples, despite never having systematised their thinking in a written form, possess the same mental faculties and the same ability to reason in an abstract way as civilised peoples.

The idea that culture is not so much the sum of uses and customs of a society, but rather a system of thought—concepts and groups of concepts—capable of acting as a guide for human behaviour would be the basis of ethnoscience, the study of the way in which the individual sees and categorises the natural world that would develop from the second half of the 1950s, with Floyd Lounsbury, Ward Goodenough, Harold Conklin and Charles Frake.

The second area of Boasian reflection concerns the attention to the psychological processes that operate within cultural processes, that is the attention to the way in which individuals represent themselves and react to the behavioural models proposed by their culture. This attention would lead him to reject any deterministic explanation of cultural phenomena.

For Boas, culture is not determined by geographical conditions: they can have an influence on it but in themselves, they are not creative, since the cultural manifestations of populations living in the same type of environment can show considerable differences. Culture is not determined by the economy either, as economic conditions always act on a pre-existing culture and in themselves depend on other aspects of civilisation. Equally unfounded is racial determinism, as experience has shown that members of most races placed in a given civilisation can participate in it (Boas, 1911–1941).

Culture must be understood from the inside, not from an abstract, extraneous objective point of view: Boas teaches his students that, in order to conduct valid research in other cultures, they should first develop methods that allow them to get out of the narrow limits of their ethnocentrism.

Between World Wars I and II, this teaching was at the centre of the theoretical reflection and ethnographic practice of a generation of American anthropologists who rejected the assumption of the superiority of Western culture: it became a kind of guiding light both from an epistemological and from a methodological point of view. Alfred Kroeber compares the Boasian turning point to a real Copernican revolution in anthropology, writing that the awareness of cultural diversity introduced by Boas, by distancing anthropologists from the ethnocentrism of which they were unwittingly carriers and directing them towards a relativist perspective, has revolutionised their universes of interpretation and understanding (Kroeber, 1948).

During the thirties, Boas's influence began to diversify: a line of research, which sees in its referents Alfred Kroeber and Robert Lowie, focuses its attention on the study of social processes, working to define "culture" as the object of study of anthropology, trying to give specificity to anthropological knowledge, compared to other emerging knowledge, such as sociology and psychology.

326   A. BISCALDI

Another line, the School of *Culture and Personality*, known for the figures of Margaret Mead, Ruth Benedict, Ella Deloria, Zora Deale Hurston, Abraham Kardiner and Ralph Linton, focuses on the relationship between the individual and society, on the processes of socialisation and learning, on the specific way in which cultural traits are integrated into unique models (single cultures), on the cultural determination of personalities and cultural and social roles, on the coherence of cultural models and on the possibility of the anthropologist to grasp them. Both lines of research are united by the rejection of explanations based on linear causation and generalisations on a theoretical level, an attitude that would allow the consolidation of a propensity for deconstruction and the regulatory use of concepts.

In a recent work, Charles King (2019) reconstructs the climate of the Boasian school in which a real intellectual revolution matures that question, research after research, opposing the dominant conservative vision, the concepts of race, gender, sexuality and disability, showing its character of cultural fiction, of the product of human artifice, of labels that reside in the mental frames and in the unconscious habits of a given society. King writes:

> More than anyone in his day, Boas understood that his own society's deepest prejudices were grounded not in moral arguments but rather in allegedly scientific ones. Disenfranchised African Americans were intellectually inferior because the latest research said so. Women could not hold positions of influence because their weaknesses and particular disposition were well proven. The feebleminded should be kept to themselves because the key to social betterment lay in reducing their number in the general population. Immigrants carried with them the afflictions of their benighted homelands, from disease to crime to social disorder.
>
> A science that seemed to prove that humanity had unbridgeable divisions had to be countered by a science that showed it didn't. By making Americans in particular see themselves as slightly strange—their tenacious belief in something they call race, their blindness to everyday violence, their stop-and-go attitude toward sex, their comparative backwardness on women's role in governance—Boas and their circle took a gargantuan step toward seeing the rest of the worlds as slightly more familiar...
>
> A century ago, in jungles and on ice floes, in pueblos and on suburban patios, this band of outsiders began to unearth a dizzying truth that shapes our public and private lives even today.

They discovered that manners do not in fact maketh man. It's the other way around. (King, 2019, p. 20)

Outside Columbia University and the Boasian outposts, American anthropology after the 1930s was dominated by the Washington-Cambridge axis home to physical anthropologists and the University of Chicago where, from 1931 to 1937, Radcliffe-Brown's teaching promoted the diffusion of the socio-structural approach. This perspective was destined to merge with the tradition of Chicago urban sociology and shortly thereafter, to meet Malinoswski's functionalism which was Yale from 1938 to 1942. Radcliffe-Brown and Malinowski thus introduced the British functionalist perspective into American anthropology.

In this context, the particularist position of Boas and his school seem to lose importance, since they limit the possibility of proposing general explanations of cultural phenomena, capable of identifying criteria of regularity or systematic correlations that can lead to the formulation of general laws (Harris, 1968). The idiographic approach seems to make anthropology weak knowledge, whose role appears limited to providing a detailed description of particular phenomena and the possibility of inducing an estrangement from the Western point of view.

Starting from the 1940s, under the pressure of these factors, a part of American anthropology would start to be interested in generalising nomothetic perspectives again, with theoretical emergencies such as neo-evolutionism, cultural materialism, economic substantivism and ethnoscience. But the dialogue with the relativist perspective would remain inevitable and continuous.

APPLICATIONS

Together with the ethnographic and idiographic approach, American anthropology was characterised, from its origins, by a marked applicative character, to the point that it would be possible to write a parallel history of American cultural anthropology, retracing both the political and military commitment of American anthropologists. Already in 1870, John Powell testified before the Congress of the United States of America the genocide of Native Americans caused by the westward expansion of the railway (Vincent, 1994); Powell himself would be the first director of the *Bureau of American Ethnology*, founded in 1879 to support the federal government in managing so-called Indian affairs. The expression "applied anthropology" was coined precisely in that context by James Moony in a report drawn up for the BAE in 1902 (Kedia & Willigen, 2005).

In 1907, Franz Boas, a former professor at Columbia University, was commissioned by the *Dillingham Immigration Commission* (named after its president, Republican Senator William P. Dillingham) to participate in a study on the children of European immigrants and on the impact of immigration on the American population (Boas, 1912).

The commission made up of three senators, three deputies and three "experts" chosen by President Theodore Roosevelt conducted a far-reaching three-year survey on the social effects of migration and entrusted Boas with the task of analysing changes in the physiology of immigrants. In this study, published in 1912, Boas examines the cephalic index of a sample of Jewish families from Eastern Europe and southern Italians, highlighting how the shapes of the skulls of the second generations born in the United States had slightly changed compared to those of their parents. For example, the typical "long-headed" cephalic structure of southern Italians tends over time to become "round-headed" in a land of migration. These variations are used by Boas to argue that the characteristics of immigrants, both physical and mental, are not "immutable" as the supporters of the restriction of migratory flows suggested, but instead had a strong capacity to adapt to the host society.

In a letter written to *The Nation*, "Scientists as Spies" in 1919, Boas also publicly denounces four fellow anthropologists for acting as spies in Central America during World War I, "prostituting" anthropological knowledge and seriously compromising international credibility of the discipline (Boas, 2005; Price, 2000). Boas's argument is that a social scientist who uses his research as a cover for political espionage should lose his right to be seen as such; the response of the American Anthropological Association (which at its annual meeting ten days later sanctioned Boas and invited him to resign from the national research council) inaugurates the complex debate on the political compromise of field research, on the positioning and ethics of applied anthropology (Biscaldi, 2016)

In the following years, many American anthropologists were involved in applied studies, with a strongly multidisciplinary approach, in different fields: the works in the Native American reserves, the studies on the socio-cultural basis of the industrial organisation carried out at Harvard, the studies on rural communities, sponsored by the Department of Agriculture, of the Roosevelt administration (Bennett, 1996). Various organisations were founded that employed anthropologists in different ways: the *Applied*

Anthropology Unit of Bureau of Indian Affairs (BIA), founded by John Collier, with the aim of monitoring the Indian situation after the *Indian Reorganization Act* of 1934 (van Willigen, 2002); in 1941 the *Society for Applied Anthropology*, assuming a strong professional connotation; and shortly after, the *Smithsonian Institute of Social Anthropology* under the direction of George Foster.

During World War II, about half of the American anthropologists actively engaged in various war support activities (Cooper, 1947; Price, 2000). Most worked for the *War Relocation Authority* in managing internment camps for Japanese Americans; in the *Far Eastern Civil Affairs Training School* to train the administrators who had to manage the territories conquered from the Japanese; or the *Foreign Morale Analysis Division*, which collected information on opponents on behalf of the War Department, the State and the Navy.

The use of social scientists for military purposes, destined to continue into the second half of the twentieth century, called into question not only the public credibility of the discipline in the countries concerned (Silvert, 1965), but also raised complex ethical issues (Mcfate & Laurence, 2015; Gonzàlez, 2015). Some of them are still unresolved and deal with the role of the so-called embedded anthropologists, together with the ethical-political implications of ethnographic research conducted in war scenarios (Inglese, 2016).

REFERENCES

Abler, T. S. (1992). Protestant Missionaries and the Native Culture: Parallel Careers of Asher Wrights and Silas T. Rand. *American Indian Quarterly, 1*, 25–37.

Alliegro, E. V. (2015). Lewis Henry Morgan. *Un fondatore della ricerca antropologica, Archivio di Etnografia, 8*(1), 55–100.

Alliegro, E. V. (2021). Ethnography before Ethnography: Genesis and Development of Fieldwork in North America. In V. Matera & A. Biscaldi (Eds.), *Ethnography. A Theoretical Oriented Practice* (pp. 21–49). Palgrave Macmillan.

Barnard, A. (2000). *History and Theory in Anthropology*. Cambridge University Press.

Bennett, J. W. (1996). Applied and Action Anthropology: Ideological and conceptual aspects. *Current Anthropology, 37*(1), 23–53.

Bergamini, O. (2002). *Storia degli Stati Uniti*. Laterza.

Biscaldi, A. (2009). *Relativismo culturale. In difesa di un pensiero libero*. UTET.

330 A. BISCALDI

Biscaldi, A. (Ed.). (2016). Etiche della Ricerca in Antropologia applicata. *Antropologia Pubblica, 2* (2).

Boas, F. (1911–1941). *Handbook of American Indian languages.* Smithsonian Institution.

Boas, F. (1912). *Changes in Bodily form of Descendants of Immigrants.* Columbia University Press.

Boas, F. (1963). *The Mind of Primitive Man.* The Croweller-Collier Publishing Company (First Edition Copyrighted and Published, 1911).

Boas, F. (1986). The Limitations of Comparative Method in Anthropology. *Science, 4*(103), 901–908.

Boas, F. (2005). Scientists as Spies. *Anthropology Today,* 21 (3), 27–27 (ed. or 1919).

Cooper, J. M. (1947). Anthropology in the United States during 1939–1945. *Journal de la Societé des Americanistes, 36*(1), 1–14.

Cushing, F. H. (1979). *Zuni: Selected Writings of Frank Hamilton Cushing* (H. Green, Ed.). University of Nebraska Press.

Eisen, G. (1977). Voyageurs, Black-Robes, Saints, and Indians. *Ethnohistory, 24*(3), 191–205.

Fabietti, U. (2020). *Storia dell'antropologia.* Zanichelli.

Fletcher, A. (1904). *The Hako: A Pawnee Ceremony.* Twenty-Second Annual Report of the Bureau of American Ethnology, 1900–1901.

Frantz, K. (1999). *Indian Reservation in The United States.* University of Chicago Research Papers.

Gerbi, A. (2000). *La disputa del Nuovo Mondo.* Adelphi.

Gliozzi, G. (1977). *Adamo e il nuovo mondo. La nascita dell'antropologia come ideologia coloniale: dalle genealogie bibliche alle teorie razziali (1500–1700).* La Nuova Italia.

Gonzàlez, J. R. (2015). *The Rise and Fall of the Human Terrain System,* June 25. https://www.counterpunch.org/2015/06/29/the-rise-and-fall-of-the-human-terrain-system/

Gruber, J. W. (1967). Horatio Hale and the Development of American Anthropology. *Proceedings of the American Philosophical Society, 111*(1), 5–37.

Harris, M. (1968). *The Rise of Anthropological Theory: A History of Theories of Culture.* Thomas Y. Cromwell Company.

Inglese, D. (2016). L'antropologia in Guerra. Il caso Human Terrain System. *Dialoghi mediterranei,* 18. https://www.istitutoeuroarabo.it/DM/lantropologia-in-guerra-il-caso-human-terrain-system/

Judd, N. (1967). *Bureau of American Ethnology: A Partial History.* University Oklahoma Press.

Kedia, S., & Willigen, J. (2005). *Applied Anthropology: Domains of Application.* Greenwood Publishing Group.

11 AMERICAN ANTHROPOLOGY: SOME DISTINCTIVE FEATURES 331

King, C. (2019). *Gods of the Upper Air. How a Circle of Renegade Anthropologist Reinvented Race, Sex and Gender in the Twentieth Century*. Knopf Doubleday publishing Group.

Kroeber, A. (1948). *Anthropology*. Harcourt and Brace.

Mcfate, M., & Laurence, J. H. (Eds.). (2015). *Social Sciences Goes to War. The Human Terrain System in Iraq and Afghanistan*. C. Hurst & Co.

Mooney, J. (1896). *The Gost Dance Religion and the Sioux Outbreak of 1890*. Government Printing Office.

Morgan, L. H. (1851). *League of the HO-DE'-NO-SAU-NEE, or Iroquois*. Sage & Brother.

Morgan, L. H. (1871). *Systems of Consanguinity and Affinity of the Human Family*. Smithsonian Institution Washington.

Morgan, L. H. (1877). *The Ancient Society or Research on the Line of Human Progress from Savagery, Through Barbarism to Civilization*. World Publishing.

Moses, D. N. (2009). *The Promise of Progress: The Life and Work of Lewis Henry Morgan*. University of Missouri Press.

Price, D. (2000). Anthropologists as Spies. Collaboration Occurred in the Past, and There's No Professional Bar to It Today. *The Nation*, 2 November. https://www.thenation.com/article/archive/anthropologists-spies/

Resek, C. (1960). *Lewis Henry Morgan. American Scholar*. The University of Chicago Press.

Rigs, S. R., & Dorsey, J. O. (1893). *Dakota Grammar, Texts, and Ethnography*. Contributions to North American Ethnologist, IX.

Ronda, J. P. (2002). *Lewis and Clark among the Indians*. University of Nebraska Press.

Silverman, S. (Ed.). (1981). *Totem and Teachers: Perspectives on the History of Anthropology*. Colombia University Press.

Silvert, K. H. (1965). American Academic Ethics and Social Research Abroad: The Lesson of Project Camelot. *Background, 9*(3), 215–236.

Tiberini, E. (1999). *Senza riserve. Etnologia del Nord America*. Bulzoni.

Trigger, B. G., & Washburn, B. E. (Eds.). (1996). *The Cambridge History of the Native Peoples of the Americas, Volume I: North America*. Cambridge University Press.

Van Willigen, J. (2002). *Applied Anthropology: An Introduction*. Greenwood Publishing Group.

Vincent, J. (1994). *Anthropology and Politics: Visions, Traditions, and Trends*. University of Arizona Press.

Whorf, B.L. (1956). *Language, Thought, Reality. Selected Writings of Benjamin Lee Whorf*. MIT Press; John Carroll.

CHAPTER 12

From Hegemony to Fragmentation: North American Cultural Anthropology Over the Past Fifty Years

Berardino Palumbo

But if you are concerned with tracing the movement of a discipline by packaging your experiences into emblematical units it is rather more troubling.
—Geertz *(1995, 110)*

INTRODUCTION

It is not easy, perhaps not even possible, to provide an even minimally detailed overview of developments in North American cultural anthropology over the past few decades. There are at least two reasons for such difficulty. The first is the problematic relationship between the almost hegemonic centrality this tradition of study has held in the international disciplinary arena since the mid-1980s and the fact that the author of this

B. Palumbo (✉)
University of Messina, Messina, Italy
e-mail: berardino.palumbo@unime.it

© The Author(s), under exclusive license to Springer Nature Switzerland AG 2023
G. D'Agostino, V. Matera (eds.), *Histories of Anthropology*,
https://doi.org/10.1007/978-3-031-21258-1_12

333

chapter writes from a standpoint that is "peripheral" in relation to the tradition of anthropology. The second is the observation that North American anthropology encompasses multiple theoretical positionings, research themes, and methodological choices that developed at the turn of the last two centuries, such a multiplicity that it might be more appropriate to characterize it as multiple traditions or, at any rate, multiple lines of reflection, rather than a single, compact disciplinary bloc. Mapping this complexity is central to then understanding how this tradition has related to—and sometimes clashed with—other hegemonic currents of anthropology, particularly the British and French ones.

Compounding such difficulties is the fact that, while until the very beginning of the new millennium it was perhaps still possible to trace lines of continuity and points of aggregation within the highly multi-faceted field of U.S. anthropological, since September 11, 2001, the field seems to be undergoing a process of theoretical, methodological, and thematic pulverization. On the contrary, as we shall see, the drive that now grants the field of U.S. anthropological studies its coherence is the tendency to engage with key, pressing issues of today's global landscape and adopt specific ethical-political positions. Another point to consider is that, although anthropology (or the currents of North American anthropology) has retained a hegemonic role on the discipline's global stage, there have been attempts in recent years to challenge the hegemonic line (e.g. the so-called ontological turn as manifested in Francophone and Anglophone, or at any rate European, literature) and voices (exponents of "world anthropologies") that advocate, at least on a programmatic level, for developing global and multi-centered disciplinary spaces.

Setting off from these premises, this attempt at synthesis—knowingly partial and bound to the personal positioning mentioned above—will be organized according to four chronological phases: 1973–1986 (Struggle for leadership), 1986–1990 (Transition), 1990–2001 (Hegemony), and 2001–2020 (Deflagration).[1] As suggested by my choice of terminology, this proposed chronology and phase naming are intended to evoke a Gramscian aura. In a nutshell, the first phase of U.S. anthropology involved

---

[1] In an important essay tracing the main phases and trends in U.S. anthropology, Sydel Silverman (2005, p. 346) highlights both the hegemonic status of U.S. anthropology since at least the very early 1980s and, with the new millennium, the emergence of a polycentric, international anthropological community. I would like to thank Mariella Pandolfi who suggested me the possible connection between September/11 and the process of fragmentation of the U.S. anthropological hegemony.

12 FROM HEGEMONY TO FRAGMENTATION: NORTH AMERICAN CULTURAL... 335

the emergence of multiple, often divergent, and mutually opposing, theoretical and methodological perspectives that competed to potentially determine the direction (in the Gramscian sense) of what was poised to become the globally hegemonic anthropology, seeking even to define future directions of research. The second phase, more a rather short period than a real phase, was instead a time of transition. In this period the intellectual struggles of previous decades became polarized, pitting realist positions against deconstructionist ones even as the latter were internally differentiated in terms of both the relationship between ethnography and theory and their reading of historical processes. The third phase is envisioned as the one in which the many theoretical perspectives and lines of research stabilized—albeit with certain methodological and stylistic options persisting and scholars taking on more radical political positionings—thereby enabling U.S. anthropology to play its full hegemonic role in the discipline's international arenas. Finally, in the deflagration phase, mounting political radicalism and pronounced ethical-social movement position-taking gave rise to a fragmentation of theoretical viewpoints, methodological options and, equally importantly, research foci. Indeed, research in this phase has been increasingly directly and explicitly connected to the political, economic, and cultural dynamics of a global world.

The perspective assumed by this overview and its proposed chronology are caught up with the discipline's internal debates. Anthropology probably appears to maintain a certain degree of autonomy from other disciplinary fields and from the broader intellectual, social, economic, and political context. With anthropology as with any other social science, contextualization and mutual influence between fields is quite central. The choice to reconstruct anthropological debate while abiding by its disciplinary boundaries is based on one specific consideration: as convinced as I am that keeping fields separate is an analytically arbitrary and knowledge-limiting operation, I do not believe it would be possible in this space to systematically periodize the relationships between U.S. cultural anthropology's internal trends and the larger historical-political processes shaping North American and world history and society over the past two centuries. Notwithstanding space limitations, however, the periodization of each phase can include brief contextual references borrowed from existing texts about and reflections on the social history of U.S. anthropology. I draw on the work of Thomas Patterson (2001) and his careful reading of the trajectory of U.S. anthropology from a Marxist perspective. Compared to other reviews less directly concerned with relations between academic

336   B. PALUMBO

knowledge, disciplinary field, and society (e.g. Marcus & Fisher, 1986; Geertz, 1995; Ortner, 2006), Patterson's work (2001, pp. 135–164) reframes the period between the mid-1970s and first decade of the new century examined here as an analysis of how the neoliberal era has impacted North American university institutions and social scientific knowledge.

As also argued by other scholars writing in the same period or at earlier times (e.g. Silverman, 2005, pp. 310–327; Wolf, 1972), Patterson contends that it was the 1960s political and social unrest and student protests erupting in response to the Vietnam War that fueled the profound changes sweeping over the U.S. academic system, and with it cultural anthropology, during the 1970s. More generally, he notes, that historical stage witnessed the collapse of the unwritten pact between "capital and organized labor made in the late 1940s, (under which) the capitalist class conceded some elements of a welfare system in exchange for labor peace" (ibid., p. 135). It was under this pact that U.S. anthropology had undergone its process of institutionalization and expansion. The theoretical perspectives and ethnographic research developed in the period examined here thus unfolded under macroeconomic conditions of labor market deregularization, deindustrialization, post-Fordism, and the onset of the financialization of the economy.

First Phase: Struggle for Leadership, 1973–1986

The year 1973 (and first half of that decade more generally) seems to offer a good starting point for an introduction to contemporary North American cultural anthropology. It was in 1973 that Clifford Geertz published *The Interpretation of Cultures*, a collection of his essays destined to rapidly become the founding text of the shift later known as the discipline's "interpretive turn." In those early years of 1970, the field of U.S. cultural anthropology was certainly not hegemonized by the interpretive approach; rather, it still occupied a minority, if not exactly niche, position in the disciplinary arena. The volume most directly molded by the late—1960s climate of political contestation and radicalization, Hymes, 1972 (but first published in 1969) cites Geertz and his work as an example of the analysis of a colonial situation (Hymes, 1972, p. 186) carried out with a "cultural ecology" approach (ibid., p. 271). It is likewise referenced as an incoherent attempt to construct a theory of culture based solely on relations between people in the field (ibid., pp. 373–375). Geertz had been working at Princeton's prestigious and institutional Institute for Advanced

Study since 1970, and he is certainly not numbered among the ranks of those critical voices who—as argued by the authors of the chapters in this volume—were speaking out in the late 1960s to urgently demand the disciplinary field be reconfigured to respond to the political dynamics of the time. Instead, we find Geertz along with his interpretive anthropology in a well-known essay written in 1974 by Roger M. Keesing. From his Australian standpoint well outside the tensions between political and academic fields vibrating through the positionings of his U.S. colleagues, Keesing observes the global, and especially U.S., anthropological scene in a seemingly aseptic manner. He suggests (1974, pp. 74–81) that, between the 1960s and early 1970s, U.S. anthropology was animated by "adaptive" theories of culture according to which culture and society were to be understood as systems in a dynamically adaptive relationship with the environment (take Marvin Harris' cultural materialism, for example, or the cultural ecology of Robert Carneiro, Andrew Vayda and Roy Rappaport). At the same time, there were also "ideational theories" of culture that understood "cultures" primarily as more or less autonomous systems of ideas. Keesing identifies several positions in this latter camp: those who regarded cultures as "cognitive systems" (e.g. Ward Goodenough, James Spradley or, at that time, also Stephen Tyler); those who instead conceptualized them as structural systems (and here he references Claude Lévi Strauss); and, finally, those who saw cultures as "symbolic systems" (a position represented by Geertz, but also David Schneider). Geertz occupies a specific position in this overview. In fact, the volume in which Geertz—collecting up a series of articles written in previous years—presents a systematic explanation of his explicit theory of culture and its interpretation in the opening chapter was published in 1973, that is, five years after the first edition of the volume edited by Hymes.

In 1974, it was not easy to guess which perspectives would soon become central and give rise in turn to new lines of inquiry, and which would instead end up sidelined to positions that are more marginal. And Keesing was indeed very cautious. Perhaps the extreme complexity achieved by some componential analyses, bordering on the esoteric, considered together with the fact that neuroscience and evolutionary psychology research was being rearticulated, might have suggested that the first phase of anthropological cognitivism was nearing its end. From a 1974 standpoint, however, it was more difficult to foresee the imminent waning of the cognitive force of structuralism or the fact that the dialectic between "expertise" and "execution" characterizing linguistics and social studies in that period would soon lose its significance. While Keesing maintained a neutral standpoint, Geertz on the other hand made it clear which theoretical perspectives his interpretive anthropology diverged from. The first of these was cognitive anthropology (1973, pp. 11–12), as Geertz critiqued this approach for its mentalism and belief that meaning is not public—that is, embedded in social relations—but rather private, organized according to formal patterns. The second was structuralism as developed by Levi-Strauss, in this case critiqued for its pursuit of deep structures of the human mind underlying social behavior through which to alchemically transform the romantic impulse driving ethnographic fieldwork into a utopian, formal Science of Man (ibid., pp. 358–359). Beyond this sphere of what Keesing called "ideational" theories of culture, Geertz also naturally distinguishes between his work and all forms of behaviorism, as well as—less obviously, given he also trained under Parsons—functionalist approaches. In this introductory chapter he does not, however, explicitly reference the frameworks being developed at other, prestigious U.S. universities (Columbia, the University of Michigan), namely the "adaptive theories of culture" that were contributing important ethnographic and theoretical insights as part of a realist, materialist, and scientist view of anthropological research in specifically this period between the mid- 1960s and 1970s. Even more significant is the fact that he does not mention the shift towards Marxist theoretical frameworks, by that time no longer conformist; indeed, between the 1960s and 1970s such Marxist lenses were characterizing the work of various materialist-leaning scholars (especially Eric Wolf, 1969 and Sidney Mintz, 1974). Geertz (1995, pp. 128–131) was well aware that the political and social changes taking place in the world at that time called for cognitive aptitudes and contextualization processes completely different from those adopted by the previous generation of anthropologists. Nonetheless, considering his work was strongly influenced by Max Weber, Geertz' own thinking was certainly not heading in the direction of Marx. After all, his 1970 move to the Institute of Advanced Studies at Princeton had placed Geertz in a position of visibility, and thus institutional orthodoxy, not shared by other colleagues in the discipline.

From his Marxist viewpoint, Patterson (2001, p. 138) holds that only theoretical positions influenced by Marxian materialism possessed the ability, in the early 1970s, to analytically and politically grapple with the challenges facing the social sciences following the reorganization of the U.S. labor market, educational system and society. In the same section

12 FROM HEGEMONY TO FRAGMENTATION: NORTH AMERICAN CULTURAL... 339

(ibid., pp. 138–139) he frames the emergence of "interpretive" and "symbolic" perspectives in this period as perpetuating the tendency typical of North American anthropology's idiographic tradition to separate "society" from "culture." I do not share in the radical nature of Patterson's position in the sense that I do not believe Marxist-influenced social sciences are the only ones capable of grasping the economic-political dynamics of the contemporary world. However, from the mid- 1970s to the mid- 1980s, Geertz' interpretive anthropology does seem to have represented the most institutional and ultimately conservative face of U.S. cultural anthropology's reaction to the political tensions of the previous decade. Besides the unmistakable narrative and descriptive quality of his interpretations and the strong theoretical awareness underlying them, it may have been this institutional and conservative character that helped ensure the success of Geertz's framework. And yet, even in those years such success did not go uncontested.

The main alternative to symbolic-interpretive anthropologies was a current of work that took certain materialist and ecological positions stemming from the neo-evolutionary tradition revolving around Julian Steward, some of his students (including Sidney Mintz, Eric Wolf, and Stanley Diamond) and the Universities of Michigan and New York (Columbia), and gradually transformed these positions in an explicitly Marxist direction. Alongside the spread and consolidation of a symbolic-interpretive current, therefore, there was also a developing Marxist field in U.S. cultural anthropology, the very one Patterson had advocated for in retrospect. Following the publication of a monographic issue of American Ethnologist in 1978 (AA.VV., 1978), this field has been known as Political Economy. As William Roseberry (1988) recalled a decade later in his retrospective presentation, it is closely tied to earlier Marxist anthropological approaches that flourished in Europe (the French "cerebral" Marxists including Maurice Godelier, Claude Meillassoux, and Emmanuel Terray; and British attempts to build on them in the work of Maurice Bloch) in the transition from the 1960s to the 1970s. At the same time, the anthropologists working under the umbrella of this perspective, such as Wolf, Mintz himself, Jane and Peter Schneider, and Roseberry the author of the review, but also June Nash and Eleanor Leacock, based their analyses a realist and materialist ontology and were driven by the need to understand the global scenarios contextualizing both anthropology and the various human groups it might study.

340 B. PALUMBO

Of the many ethnographies written in this theoretical framework (e.g. Mintz, 1974; Cole & Wolf, 1974; Nash, 1979), it may be interesting for our purposes here to look more closely at the monograph Jane and Peter Schneider, students of Eric Wolf, devoted to Western Sicily in 1976. *Culture and Political Economy in Western Sicily* (translated into Italian in 1993) analyzes:

> the relationship between the early colonial period (during which Sicily exported wheat and animal products) and a later neocolonial period (during which manpower is the principal energy loss). It traces the rise and development of mafia to these conditions. In addition, it analyzes cultural codes which are especially salient to contemporary social organization—codes which celebrate honor, cleverness, and friendship. We seek the origins of these codes in early adaptations of the Sicilian people to externally generated political and economic forces, and suggest that similar codes may have played similar roles in other pre-nineteenth-century colonial regions. (Schneider & Schneider, 1976, pp. ix–x)

Grounded in long-term ethnographic research in Sambuca di Sicilia, a town in the Agrigento area, the book frames the analysis of social and economic relations and the system of values observed in the local context within the broader political-economic landscape in which Sicily is and had been embedded over its long history. The Schneiders read this history through the categories of "center," "periphery," and "semi-periphery" Wallerstein (1978, 1980) had developed in that period, categories in which cultural and social factors play an important role in generating processes of increasing marginalization, with these same factors shaped by economic-political logics and national as well as global-level dynamics. This framework is the setting for a historical-anthropological analysis of how Mafia-oriented attitudes and relations developed and were perpetuated over time, understood in this case as direct consequences of Sicily's economy and society having been encapsulated in a marginal position vis-à-vis the structures of the Italian nation-state.

The Schneiders' insights and interpretations remain valid even today although, read in light of anthropology's phase of theoretical revamping in the mid-1980s, it is clear how they are anchored in the representational modes and ontological assumptions of the time. The best-known and most relevant example of this kind of sensitivity and specific theoretical

12 FROM HEGEMONY TO FRAGMENTATION: NORTH AMERICAN CULTURAL... 341

model is Eric Wolf's volume *Europe and the People without History* (1982). In this text, Wolf explicitly states his vision of the modern world:

> This book has asked what difference it would make to our understanding if we looked at the world as a whole, a totality, a system, instead of as a sum of self-contained societies and cultures; if we understood better how this totality developed over time; if we took seriously the admonition to think of human aggregates as "inextricably involved with other aggregates, near and far, in web like, netlike connections" [...]. As we unraveled the chains of causes and effects at work in the lives of particular populations, we saw them extend beyond anyone population to embrace the trajectories of others-all others. (Wolf, 1982, p. 385)

According to Wolf's vision, beginning in a certain epoch and through processes still in need of explication, the world has gradually become a unified network of relationships in which there is no point in continuing to refer to societies, cultures, or various local areas in "essentialist" terms. In the world described by Wolf, concepts such as tribe, ethnic group, and small, closed, corporate-type peasant community are no longer useful and must make way for studying the connections and flows of information and relationships in and through which different local contexts have been historically constituted. Wolf proposes ideal models meant to represent different degrees and modes of involvement as well as different form of interactions between local nodes, and proposes to investigate these nodes through micro-sociologies and micro-histories, on the one hand, and in relation to the network of the system-world on the other; indeed, his overall analysis focuses on the latter. On the economic level, he thus posits a kinship-based mode of production, tributary mode of production, and capitalist mode of production, concepts apparently derived from Marxian theory and its other anthropological reworkings. At the same time, on the sociocultural level, he identifies the types of social formation that arrange and organize labor, employing to this end, ideological forms of representation (blood, mystical and spiritual substance, class) specific to each different ideal model and representing the direct expression of the typical analytical categories of anthropological research.

The foundations underlying Wolf's approach and anthropological political economy was a "realist" epistemology, quite distinct from interpretative positions with their essentially constructionist basis. This epistemology was accompanied by a set of theoretical assumptions specific to

342   B. PALUMBO

the materialist tradition summarized by a sympathetic author a decade later as follows:

> On the level of metatheory, however, the logical reconstruction of social formations proceeds from the ontological presupposition of socially constitutive labor. In other words, for political economy, it is social labor that serves as a universal model of human action and that accounts for the self-formation of the human species in particular. [...]
>
> A Marxist political economy offers, therefore, a critical theory with universal and practical intent in linking the standard of evaluation or critique directly to a general condition of humanity, that is the ontology of labor. The universal standard by which the reciprocity of social relations can be determined is contained in the reconstruction of the meta-rules of social labor as formative and transformative, as well as in the identification of producers with their products of labor. (Ulin, 1991, pp. 74–75)

Socially determined human labor constitutes an ontological criterion on the basis of which researchers can conduct general assessments of forms of social organization and identify a foundation for forms of meta-discourse capable of representing the relationships between general and local processes. In this case as well, "realist" perspectives seemed quite distant from Geertz' interpretive anthropology. As we see in the collection of essays, published in 1999 in Italian (Geertz, 1999), this current of the discipline was not interested in constructing some systematic meta-narrative aimed at anchoring ethnographic holism to global political-economic dynamics (i.e. generalizing in cases and not through them, to echo Geertz's well-known assertion). Rather than framing the understanding of cultural texts in globally overarching structural logics, such understanding was always supposed to be embedded in kaleidoscopic processes of interpreting native interpretations of social behavior.

Supported thusly by realist epistemology, *Europe and the People without History* is both the most accomplished and the most ambitious synthesis of political economy approaches. The book shows how, from a certain point onwards, all the "other" human groups observed and investigated through the anthropological gaze took on the sociocultural configurations we associate with them through their relations/clashes with the West. In so doing, it also represents a landmark point in the development of what has been called (Dirks, 1996) the "historical turn" in U.S. anthropology. Indeed, Wolf's theoretical framework met with critique, often harsh, in the years just after it was published, critiques to be understood as part of the larger

12 FROM HEGEMONY TO FRAGMENTATION: NORTH AMERICAN CULTURAL... 343

debate on the relationships between ethnography, anthropological theory and historiographical imagination animating U.S. cultural anthropology at the time. In the second half of the 1980s, in the aftermath of this debate, what emerged was the theoretical/methodological scaffolding focused on the relationship between social practices and history that went on to characterize U.S. cultural anthropology's hegemonic phase.

SECOND PHASE: TRANSITION, 1986–1990

To understand disagreements around ways of writing an anthropological history of what Wolf ironically termed "the peoples without history" and the parallel development of a theoretical framework (multi-faceted but also organized around certain conceptual nodes) of sufficient weight to assume a hegemonic role over the course of the 1990s, we must leave the materialist field and return to the interpretive one.

In 1982, *Annual Review of Anthropology* published the lengthy essay "Ethnographies as Texts" in which George Marcus and David Cushman take stock of several emerging trends in ethnographic writing, highlighting the "genealogical" connections between these trends and previous stances as well as their possible theoretical implications for the discipline as a whole. The tone of the article would seem didactic, almost plain, were it not for the two authors' clarity in defining the epistemological, theoretical, and methodological levels involved in reflecting on forms of ethnographic representation. What stands out above all is their emphasis on the distinction between "ethnographic realism" and other forms of narrative experimentation, a distinction that went on to become canonical in North American anthropological rhetoric in the space of just a few years. Another interesting aspect of the essay is the surfacing, or we might say resurfacing, of an epistemological divide inside cultural anthropology between Enlightenment and realist-influenced ways of constructing truthfulness and forms of representation rooted in a hermeneutic, Romantic stance (Marcus & Cushman, 1982, p. 38). Not surprisingly, the essay highlights Geertz—who did indeed refer to that epistemological stance—among the authors considered to have paved the way for less traditional and more holistic forms of ethnographic representation.

After all, it was precisely Geertz's (1973, p. 19) arguments, and a seminar held in April 1984 of which a number of texts soon became classics (Clifford & Marcus, 1986; Marcus & Fisher, 1986; Clifford, 1988), that brought renewed attention to the theses presented in the 1982 essay and introduced an urgent issue in North American anthropological debate: the need to carefully analyze and radically deconstruct the rhetorical strategies through which ethnographic accounts are written. These arguments were the fruit of "experimental" work and reflections which their authors did not always take into account (such as the radically experimental work of feminist and/or black anthropologists, including Behar & Gordon, 1996; Patterson, 2001, p. 155; Pinelli, 2019, pp. 131–139), an aspect for which they came under criticism. Nonetheless, these writings gave rise to a long period of heated theoretical, methodological, and epistemological discussion marking the emergence of what later came to be called a dialogical perspective in U.S. (and international) anthropology. Grounded in an awareness of the crisis surrounding representational strategies (not only what does the ethnographer write, but also *on whose behalf* and *for whom* does he write, and how does he create and represent his "objects?" (Clifford, 1986, p. 13), the theses advocated by deconstructionist anthropology also belong to a more general postmodern cognitive inclination characterized by certain basic assumptions: first, the rejection of the idea that cultural interpretations are underpinned by "ontological" foundations and, second, the assertion that there exists no meta-theoretical and meta-discursive basis in which to anchor representations ("social facts").

These assumptions are accompanied by a rejection of the view of the knowing subject as autonomous, unified, and apodictic (Rabinow, 1986) together with the idea that social facts are not only representations and representations of representations, but also dialogically constructed in the interaction between the observer and observed. The discipline's theoretical pretensions had already been curbed and compressed into the space of ethnography in the work of Geertz; with this shift, writing ethnography was in turn reframed as the production of effective texts, that is, texts capable of reflecting on the process of co-constructing social representations. Having established that ethnographic writing could not refer to some extra-textual "reality," the task of reflecting on this writing could no longer be considered—as it had been in the realist epistemological scenario—an act performed separately from the process of representation itself. Indeed, this analysis and critical dismantling of ethnographic texts was connected to the idea that experimenting with writing and reflecting on one's own ethnographic positioning (Marcus, 1986, 1989) were key. Another aspect considered of paramount importance was the ability to convey both the "artificial," fictive nature of the institution of social objects, and—on the basis of ontological assumptions about the real

12 FROM HEGEMONY TO FRAGMENTATION: NORTH AMERICAN CULTURAL...   345

world, despite the contradiction in this move (Palumbo, 1992)—the disjointed, multi-centric and non-holistic character of contemporaneity.

This proposed dialogic and deconstructionist approach was destined to produce long-lasting effects, and it elicited bitter reactions on the part of the "realist" camp that continued throughout the decade following the publication of its founding texts.[2] To summarize a decade of theoretical and ideological disagreement, we can look at statements from exponents of each of the opposing camps. As part of a broader reflection on the notion of power, Wolf (1990, p. 587) made his epistemological beliefs explicit as follows:

> I think that it is the task of anthropology—or at least the task of some anthropologists—to attempt explanation, not merely description, descriptive integration, or interpretation. [...] Writing culture may require literary skill and genre, but a search for explanation requires more: it cannot do without naming and comparing things, without formulating concepts for naming and comparison. [...] This means that I subscribe to a basically realist position: I think that the world is real, that these realities affect what humans do and that what humans do affects the world, and that we can come to understand the whys and wherefores of this relationship. [...] But I also believe that the search for explanation in anthropology can be cumulative; that knowledge and insights gained in the past can generate new questions, and that new departures can incorporate the accomplishments of the past.

For his part, Marcus (1989, pp. 13–14) held that more recent materialist studies constituted a new form of the discipline's old realism ("new old realism"), the purpose of which was:

> to salvage some version of the holism for which traditional ethnographic accounts have strived, while turning past simplistic and hardly realizable notions of total description into a more sophisticated problematic of representation. [...] New old realism is thus the conservative end of the current trend of experimentation and critique of ethnography in that, while taking very seriously the arguments about the limits of representation and therefore of any conventional commitment to holism, it nonetheless wants to sustain

---

[2] The key texts include Keesing (1983, 1987), Schölte (1987), Moore (1987), Kapferer (1988), Tyler (1987), Wolf (1988, 1990), Roseberry (1988), Sangreen (1988), Whitten (1988), Nancel, & Pels (1989), Roth (1989), Spencer (1989), Carrithers (1990), Birth (1990), Ulin (1991), Sanjek (1991), Weiner (1992), and Friedrich (1992).

that commitment in novel ways, primarily by complexifying the definition and construction of the realities treated by ethnography. [...] The fiction of the ulterior whole [...] has moved to centre stage in the macro-micro world narrative structure of new old realism, and in so doing, has come to bear the weight of giving explanatory and moral context to ethnographic accounts.

The search for ontological and theoretical levels existing outside the inherent dialogic nature of the ethnographic relationship was viewed as an attempt to establish forms of meta-narrative and to proceed with the analysis and writing of historical processes without having first conducted a textual critique of the representations produced by anthropologists. From Marcus' point of view, proceeding in this way risked reifying reality and constructing a world the consistency of which lay in the coherence of its causal relations, a world ready to be segmented, organized, and represented as an inaccurate and historically anachronistic compact entity. Instead, anthropologists needed to utilize ethnography and experimentation precisely so as to reconfigure (in textual representation) these very forces (the forces that, according to the realist perspective, connected up different localities); in so doing, he suggested, anthropological accounts could eliminate the dichotomy micro versus macro, understood in this case as a widely used ethnographic rhetorical framework that places severe limits on the ways ethnography might be enacted and applied under the cognitive conditions of post-modernity (Marcus, 1989, p. 9). It was at the point when the exponents of these perspectives reflected on the configurations of what Ana Tsing (2000) would years later call the "global situation" that the epistemological and theoretical distance between their respective positions became evident, rendering explicit other dimensions of these contrasting approaches as well. In contrast to the realist field, the dialogical perspective no longer viewed the "global system/local realities" analytical pairing as reflecting a real dialectic between general historical processes and local realities endowed with their own strength and continuity. Viewed in this way, the pairing was transformed into a dichotomy between different forms and levels of ethnographic representation. If the goal of research was to represent the forces and processes composing the world-system in different narrative forms, and the opposition between larger system and local spaces was to be understood exclusively "as a rhetorical frame of reference," the task was no longer one of analyzing or interpreting (or perhaps explaining) the historical processes leading to the constitution of the contemporary world-system. Problems that had been theoretical, historical, scientific, political, and ethical seemed to run the risk of becoming purely questions of rhetoric.

In conclusion, it seems reasonable to argue that one of the outcomes of the debates animating contemporary U.S. anthropology's transition from a phase of internal struggle to one of external hegemony has been the extreme polarization of theoretical positions. This polarization has been accompanied by an increasingly stark separation between intellectual work—concentrated in a limited number of prestigious, mainly private, universities—and the socio-political field. Geertzian-derived interpretive anthropology had displayed a greater capacity to adapt to institutional academic settings and the elegant appearance of being above political engagement, or at any rate disinterested in providing analytically timely analyses of global and North American political-economic processes in the 1970s–1980s. Such traits continued to find expression in this transitional phase, at this point in the revisitation of issues of power and its structural dimensions as part of the textual analysis central to the new dialogical theses. Some retrospective attempts were made to provide political and personal contextualization (Clifford, 2012, p. 421). Nevertheless, in this sphere politics and economics seem to be reduced to the politics of the ethnographic text and the economics of representation. It seems that a generous segment of U.S. cultural anthropology lost the ability to have (and perhaps its interest in having) an impact on globally significant social and political processes, or simply to provide useful analyses of them—an aim that had been so evident in the early stages of the discipline (Patterson, 2001)—among the plush halls of prestigious universities (Calabretta & Palumbo, 1994).

Third Phase: Hegemony, 1990–2001

Despite the polarizations characterizing anthropology and its increasing marginalization in relation to the U.S. public arena with the consequent gradual radicalization of scholars' political positions, a new theoretical current nonetheless emerged from the debates of the 1970s and early 1980s. Regardless of internal divisions over epistemological issues, the "dialogical turn" and associated deconstructionist examination of customary ways of writing and doing ethnography ended up having a significant impact. Ethnographic writing has changed profoundly throughout the discipline since the very early 1990s, including outside the academic circles that had initially proposed the dialogical turn. This shift has not been exclusively or mainly a matter of embracing the call to deconstruct "classical" forms of representation and show their implicit authorial and power strategies; nor of reflecting on relations between research practices and the writing of ethnographic field notes (Sanjek, 1990); nor, finally, of moving towards radically experimental forms of representation—although such forms have also been deliberately asserted (e.g. Marcus, 1989, 2012; Taussig, 1993) or, more recently, even critiqued from within (Marcus, 2007, 2008). Rather, the main outcome of this "turn"—in the 1990s at least—was liberatory (Taussig, 2012, p. 515). That is, it managed to remove the patina of scientism that had coated a considerable part of anthropological literature or at any rate the most institutional parts, in and also beyond North America until at least the moment in which *The Interpretation of Cultures* was published. Of course, this did not result in the "realist" style suddenly disappearing from ethnographic and anthropological writings. For example, we still see such a style in work modeling a cognitive-evolutionist approach (Hirschfeld, 1996) or, to look to a different face of the discipline, those with a classically social anthropological slant by scholars such as Michael Herzfeld (1987, 1992, cf. Herzfeld, 2018). In the decade following the rise of reflexive positions, ethnographic texts (especially monographs, but also journal articles) become more complicated. While at this point scholars had not yet begun to reconfigure their underlying research agendas in the way that Marcus (2012) identifies as connoting North American anthropology in the first years of the 2000s, their ethnographic accounts did take on profoundly different narrative trends: hyperrealist or surrealist ones (Taussig, 1984, 1997) consciously adopting the fictions typical of literary fiction (Faubion, 1993), interested in modeling ethnographic writing on oral narrative, thereby overturning the conventional textual relationships between oral narrative and commentary (Shryoch, 1997), or pushing auto-ethnographic writing to its limits in the border zone between epistemological reflection, poetry and methodology (Behar, 1996). As also noted by Marcus and Fisher (1986, pp. 41–42), there were several specific theoretical premises underpinning this move to explore the possibility of reflecting on the construction of ethnographic accounts and shift anthropology towards cultural critique and it may be useful to consider them in greater depth.

At the end of the 1970s and beginning of the 1980s, a current of thought took root in the social sciences, including U.S. work, that eventually came to be called "French Theory" (comprising a set of authors who were quite distinct from one another but perhaps united by their common

12 FROM HEGEMONY TO FRAGMENTATION: NORTH AMERICAN CULTURAL... 349

Frenchness and the success their work enjoyed in France around the mid-1960s; they included Foucault, Derrida, Braudillard, Deleuze, and Guattari, among others: see Best & Keller, 1991; Cusset, 2008). In particular, North American anthropologists appropriated certain units of theory that had been developed in Europe. Although their adoption of these ideas was admittedly simplificatory (Creahn, 2002), it was also functional to the theoretical problems that had emerged in their own disciplinary field. Such units of theoretical thought included the Foucauldian reformulation of the notion of power with its insight that power permeates all levels of social relations and is able to shape bodies, feelings, emotions and subjectivities while also inserting itself into discursive orders,[3] Bourdieu's notion of "practice" associated with a phenomenological reading of the processes through which social actors take on tastes and styles (habitus) and their strategic capacity to move within institutionalized and competitive social spaces (fields), and, later, the Gramscian categories of "hegemony," "ideology," and "common sense".[4] More broadly, in the span of just a few years it could be said that thinkers such as Weber, Wittgenstein and Rorty, the ones appreciated by Geertz, were replaced by Foucault, Bourdieu, de Certeau or even Gramsci, authors whose work revolves around understanding power, its institutional formulations and its minute, everyday relations with human action, imagined as stratified, contextual, habitual, and predetermined but also performative and potentially innovative.

Sherry Ortner, one of Geertz' doctoral students at Chicago, was among the first to grasp these theoretical shifts in her well-known and important 1984 article "Theory in Anthropology since the Sixties." Tracking developments in anthropological theory from the 1960s to the early 1980s, Ortner (1984, pp. 158–159) chose to characterize the new phase she saw North American anthropology as poised to enter with the "key symbol"

---

[3] Foucault's work began to be translated into English with *L'Archéologie du savoir* in 1972 and continued, in addition to his works on madness, the clinic and the prison, with the three volumes of *L'Histoire de la sexualité*: vol. I 1978, vol. II 1985, and vol. III 1986.

[4] The English translation of P. Bourdieu's *Esquisse d'une Thorie de la pratique* was published in 1977 and *La Distinction* was translated in 1984, while *Le Sens Pratique* was not translated until 1990. A selection of Gramsci's *Prison Notebooks* was published in English in 1971, but it was not until 2011 that the full edition of the *Notebooks* was released. For an example of one of the earliest and most thoughtful uses of Gramsci's thought in Anglophone anthropology, see Frankenberg (1988). Regarding Gramsci and Anglophone anthropology more generally, see Frankenberg (1988) and Crehan (2002).

of the notion of "practice," although, she added, the same imminent phase could also have been denoted by the notion of "history". As revealed by this two-fold characterization and the theoretical isomorphism it indicated, the pursuit of historical processuality in the anthropological interpretations of this emerging theoretical framework was directly linked to efforts to develop new ways of reading human action.

In this context, if we examine the practice/history relationship from the perspective of social actors and their actions, cultural meanings and patterns no longer appear to be simply presupposed in individual minds (cognitivism), played out in the social arena (interactionism) or rendered textual through social action (interpretivism). Rather, they are revealed as embodied and, through processes of naturalization, woven into social actors' deepest emotional levels. At the same time, such cultural meanings and patterns can also be dis-embodied and performed in specific contexts; by virtue of being put on display, they can sometimes even be contested and transformed. In this view, practices (understood as strategic, for Bourdian-inspired scholars, or contextually performed for those building on Michel de Certeau's idea of tactics) are enacted on a much more ambiguous, fluid, and viscous motivational magma than the interactionists had been able to grasp, the structuralists had been interested in understanding, and the cognitivists had been willing to admit. The agency of subjects was no longer seen as channeled or imprisoned by the series of dichotomies that had distinguished and blocked previous theoretical frameworks: norm versus action, meaning versus function, competence versus execution, conscious versus unconscious, objectivism versus subjectivity, and group versus individual. Unconscious, habitual, embedded levels of action were revealed to coexist with conscious, rational, strategic levels as part of an emotional, social, political, and historical dialectic that anthropology could no longer afford to observe solely from a distance. Social poetics—the expressive face of a practice, the ways and social styles through which it is enacted (Herzfeld, 1985)—help to define fundamental dimensions (emotional, social, political) of subjects themselves and their being in the world; at the same time, such poetics underscore the limits of subjects' universes of meaning and scopes of action, sometimes reconfirming their breadth and at other times enlarging them, depending on the specific context and power relations at play. Or, as Ortner herself later noted (2005, p. 59) in a paper that revisits some of Geertz's theses in an effort to take stock of two decades of social research, individual agency:

12 FROM HEGEMONY TO FRAGMENTATION: NORTH AMERICAN CULTURAL... 351

But the idea of agency itself presupposes a complex subjectivity behind it, in which a subject partially internalizes and partially reflects upon—and finally in this case reacts against—a set of circumstances in which she finds herself.

Viewing the practice/history relationship from the perspective of power reveals how this relationship actually unfolds, the different forms it takes in different contexts, and how it operates as part of specific technologies of control and mechanisms for disciplining bodies and genders, behavioral patterns, sensations and emotions (e.g. Comaroff, 1985; Ong, 1987). By permeating the gears of social life, driving and constituting them, power gives rise to productive effects, structuring the fields that determine habitus and people's predispositions to act. It generates forms of hegemony and defines common sense. People react to the everyday operation of power in various ways, accommodating or even resisting it more or less consciously and in more or less embodied ways, reactions that in turn serve to modify practices and their meanings.[5] On the other hand, anthropologists "face power" (Wolf, 1990, 1999, 2001) by also analyzing its manifestations in state and structural settings through innovative theoretical frameworks incorporating an historical lens (Herzfeld, 1987, 1992; Handler, 1988; Kertzer, 1988; Rabinow, 1989; Gupta, 1995).

Once the notions of agency (action, practice), gender,[6] subject/individual/self/person/body[7] and power had been reformulated between the mid-1970s and early 1980s, history—or, more precisely, reflections on anthropological ways of interpreting, representing, and imagining history (what Comaroff and Comaroff call "the historical imagination" [1992])—came to play an important role in shaping the theoretical landscape of North American anthropology in the developmental phase I have defined as hegemonic. After all, the processes of historicizing anthropology (Ohnuki-Tierney, 1990) and politicizing culture (Wright, 1998) characterize in some ways this hegemonic landscape. In the second half of the 1980s, at least two significant debates involving leading figures in U.S. anthropology erupted around this very question of history. The first

---

[5] For a presentation of developments in the Anglophone arena of political anthropology between 1970 and the first decade of the new century that is both useful and dense, see Gledhill (2009).

[6] See Ortner & Whitehead (1981); Rosaldo (1984, pp. 147–157); Strathern (1988); Lutz & Abu-Lughod (1990); Cohen (1994); Battaglia (1995).

[7] For an introduction to this node of work, key sources include Lock (1993); Scheper-Hughes (1994); Pizza (1998); Csordas (1999).

revolved around the strictly culturalist (and partly structuralist) theses outlined by Sahlins in his *Islands of History* (1985) to which Appadurai (1986) and Friedman (1988, with Sahlins' response published the same year: Sahlins 1988) responded from more or less critical positions. The second, triggered specifically by Wolf's, 1982 book, involved publications by Talal Asad (1987) and then Michael Taussig (1989), with Taussig writing to express misgivings about the kind of historical anthropology Wolf was proposing and Wolf himself (together with Sidney Mintz [1989]) then publishing a response to the arguments posed by his critics.

Differences of theoretical positioning notwithstanding, in general the key issue for these various critics was that these works of anthropological political economy as summed up by Wolf's volume ended up viewing human action as structurally and systematically determined (Taussig, 1989, pp. 141–144). Both Ortner in 1984 and Taussig a few years later went on to posit a definite link between the mechanicity of historical contexts and processes as reconstructed by political economy scholars and their outdated or careless treatment—or even outright neglect—of human agency. Addressing this point in more depth, Michael Taussig (1987b, pp. 111–112) called on anthropologists to move beyond political economy scholars' representations of capitalism imagined as reproducing itself continuously, mechanically and positivistically in the scene-world. He suggested they instead employ other concepts and lines of interpretation developed as part of the Marxian tradition, proposing concepts such as "commodity fetishism" and others inspired by Walter Benjamin's theses on history. Such concepts, he argued, had the potential to generate interpretations attentive to the phantasmal dimensions of the historical dialectic and interested in its grasping the "non-rational," occult, repressed and mimetic levels, the ones deriving from gaps and exchanges of power among various historical actors. It was also Taussig (ibid., p. 112) who had mounted significant opposition to the "realist" perspective and its attendant risk of framing cultural, symbolic, and imaginary dimensions of history as mere forms of ideological concealment or mystification of the relations of production. His monographs *The Devil and Commodity Fetishism* (Taussig, 1980) and *Shamanism, Colonialism, and the Wild Man* (1987) came to represent turning points in the development of a current of historical anthropology capable of subverting political economy research's linear—and, according to Taussig, *mechanical*—type of narrative. At the same time, his work also enriched the anthropological understanding of the historical dialectic by introducing a recognition of the

12 FROM HEGEMONY TO FRAGMENTATION: NORTH AMERICAN CULTURAL... 353

complexity, including symbolic-cultural complexity, of the forces and powers involved in this dialectic, thereby transcending the textual self-referentiality of contemporary deconstructionist literature in the discipline.

In the same period, critiques of realist readings of the relations between global history and local histories, between economic-material structures and cultural dynamics, were also being advanced by scholars representing more classical faces of the discipline. In the preceding decades, Marshall Sahlins had been engaging with neo-evolutionary perspectives while he then came to terms in some ways with the various currents of Marxist anthropology in an important volume (Sahlins, 1976). Influenced by the work of Lévi-Strauss, as early as 1981 (*Historical Metaphors and Mythical Realities:* Sahlins 1981) and even more emphatically with *Islands of History* (1985) Sahlins went on to propose innovative readings of the historical dialectic and relations between the West and other worlds. Although he acknowledged the almost monumental value of Wolf's book, based on his own fieldwork in Polynesia Sahlins considered it of central importance to understand the cultural patterns ("structure") through which different groups had participated in historical processes during the encounters/clashes with Europeans phase, thus helping to define the scope, meanings, and effects of these interactions. Only by carefully analyzing these cultural structures and historical contingencies, he argued, could anthropologists define an event and its effects in non-Eurocentric terms, thus recognizing the various social actors' capacity to act, often in mutually contradictory and conflicting terms, that had seemingly been denied them by materialist readings of the historical dialectic.

As we shall see, in the late 1990s Sahlins went on to revisit these critiques (in two essays: Sahlins 1999a, 1999b), but this time no longer addressed to realist and materialist interpretations of history; in this later case, his target was instead the postmodern and deconstructionist stances prevailing in U.S. anthropology. The issues he identified included the politicization and consequent annihilation of the notions of culture and tradition, the abandonment of the concept of structure, and researchers' loss of interest in cultural diversity. One of his critiques, moreover, was against the trend of mechanically and/or moralistically subsuming various "others" in conceptualizing the history of Western political-economic expansion and associated tendency to instrumentalize others, thereby analytically denying them the capacity to act in their own right and to develop their own spaces and ways of adjusting. Meanwhile, Sahlins' theses gave rise to a proliferation of ethnographic work during the late 1980s and

1990s investigating other people's histories, the cultural forms through which these histories are culturally modulated (Lambek, 1998, 2002) and the poetics through which they are enacted (Herzfeld, 1991). There were also numerous publications devoted to analyzing conceptions and poetics of time (Ohnuki-Tierney, 1990; Trautmann, 1992; Munn, 1992; Boyarin, 1994; Owen Hughes & Trautmann, 1995).

The work of Jean and John Comaroff proved particularly theoretically important in this phase. South African-born and British-trained (London School of Economics and Manchester) scholars, the Comaroffs had relocated to the U.S. where they taught for more than 30 years (1979–2012) at the University of Chicago before moving to Harvard. The two anthropologists displayed a thorough awareness of the problems and theoretical debates of those years revolving around the relationships between ethnography, history, and power. This sensitivity is clear in Jean Comaroff's (1985) ethnographic monograph devoted to analyzing how the members of a South African group, and especially the women, shaped their relationships with the colonial and postcolonial world by reconfiguring their perceptions of themselves/themselves and their bodies; it is also evident in their two jointly written volumes (1991; 1997) providing historical-anthropological reconstructions of the political and cultural relations between blacks and whites in South Africa's colonial period. In the introductory chapter of the first of these two volumes using a historical-anthropological approach to trace the ways Twana groups (1991) have adapted to the colonial system and the introduction to a collection of essays also published in 1992 as part of a series the Comaroffs edited together with Pierre Bourdieu and Maurice Bloch, the two scholars make their proposed theoretical framework explicit. The discipline's renewed anthropological and ethnographic attention to historicity not only requires careful reflection on the complexity of how the cultural and structural (economic-political) dimensions of the historical dialectic relate, they suggest; it is also essential that anthropologists be able to grasp the articulation of human agency and its embodied stratification and to investigate the spaces of freedom and/or constraining forces enabling or limiting expressions of agency. Viewed in this way, history/historicity can be seen as not (only) an external process that has imposed itself on the lives of "others", thereby shaping them, and neither as the outcome of the dialectical confrontation between the cultural structures that organize the meaning of events and processes. Rather, it can be recognized as the result of intimate dynamics, embodied in and enacted through individual and

12 FROM HEGEMONY TO FRAGMENTATION: NORTH AMERICAN CULTURAL... 355

collective action within the space allowed by specific political-economic constraints and unfolding on the basis of mutable and moldable cultural patterns. It is not surprising, therefore, that to meet this interpretive challenge the Comaroffs sought to enlarge their store of analytical instruments. In addition to Marxian concepts, Sahlins' theses, and deconstructionist inclinations, they also enriched their theoretical armory with notions such as those of habitus, formulated by Bourdieu, and hegemony/ideology, drawn (indirectly) from Antonio Gramsci. What these concepts share is an underlying scaffolding stemming from a felt need to consider the relationship between constraint (habitual, hegemonic, and embodied) and freedom (experienced, ideological and performed). From the Comaroffs' theoretical perspective, the relationships between action, contexts and power relations are inevitably filtered through subjects, understood as socially constructed bodies deconstructed through processes of meaning-incorporation. Practice, they showed, can no longer be read as exclusively conscious (rational, strategic, and manipulative) or unconscious (structural, mechanical, and normative). Rather, it must be seen as enacted along a continuum spanning conscious, objectified, ideological and instrumental dimensions of human action and unconscious, naturalized, hegemonic and habitual ones. These insights clearly comprised a profoundly different theoretical arena than the 1970s and early 1980s framework. This new arena determined the contours of a significant segment of U.S. anthropological research during the following decade. As Jane Comaroff and her husband John clearly argued (1991, p. 29):

> Much more plausible is the notion that social knowledge and experience situate themselves along a chain of consciousness once again a continuum whose two extremes are the unseen and the seen, the submerged and the apprehended, the unrecognized and the cognized. It hardly needs pointing out that the one extreme corresponds to the hegemonic pole of culture, the other to the ideological. And just as hegemonies and ideologies shift over time and space, so the contents of consciousness are not fixed. On the one hand, the submerged, the unseen, the unrecognized may under certain conditions be called to awareness on the other, things once perceived and explicitly marked may slip below the level of discourse into the unremarked recesses of the collective unconscious.

The analytical space delineated by the intersecting of theories of praxis, conceptualizations of power, cultural constructions of the self, gender, and subjectivity, and the historiographical and ethnographic imagination (with ethnography understood as practice and a critical awareness of forms of representation) was central to a great deal of anthropological research in the 1990s and beginning of the following century. It would be impossible to trace the multiple lines of inquiry growing out from this conceptual space with even moderate accuracy, especially considering they developed along the threads of the different specializations (e.g. medical, political, economic, and feminist anthropology and the anthropology of gender) into which the disciplinary field has branched over time. Here I will try to outline a few of them that, while not addressing the full scope of the theoretical space outlined above, are useful for articulating and shedding light on some of its nodes.

One concept that U.S. anthropologists engaged widely in the transition from the 1980s to the 1990s is that of resistance.[8] Foucault (1976, pp. 125–127) had theorized the structural nexus between power and resistance ("l'autre term, dans les relations de pouvoir": ibid., p. 127) in the mid-'70s while, even earlier, Marxist historiography had investigated the implicit, every day, minute and unconscious ways that peasant and proletarian revolts oppose power (Hobsbawm, 1965; Thompson, 1963; Wolf, 1969). In line with this latter work and situating himself between anthropology, political studies, and the then-emerging field of cultural studies, James Scott (1985, 1990) made the concept of resistance the lynchpin of some of his now-classic publications. Scott framed forms of resistance as "hidden transcripts" unfolding in the "infrapolitical" dimension and, therefore, implicitly opposed to official political registers and regimes. His theses apparently posed several problems, the first of which was defining what constitutes "resistance." The answer provided by Scott (1986, p. 22) focused on the objectives of subaltern actors' actions, leaving somewhat unresolved the problem of determining how conscious and deliberate an individual or collective action had to be in order to be defined as "resistance". That is, the issue lay in determining whether or not intimately hidden, incoherent acts detached from any conscious or organized will to bring about change—such as those of subaltern classes—can be considered as having explicitly political significance (Scott, 1990, ch. 4). Configured differently and posed as part of other theoretical paradigms,

---

[8] See Urla and Helepololei (2014) for a reading of the rise and fall of the concept of resistance in U.S. anthropology between 1980 and the 2000s. For a careful introduction to this aspect in work in Italian, see Saitta (2015).

12 FROM HEGEMONY TO FRAGMENTATION: NORTH AMERICAN CULTURAL... 357

these same problems had been central to political anthropology in previous decades beyond the United States as well.[9] They had been a key focus of the Manchester school (Max Gluckman, in primis), for instance, and so it is no coincidence that Jean and John Comaroff's theoretical reflection and historical-ethnographic research would engage with them and form cognitive perspectives different that Scott's. They sought to investigate the dialectic between "hegemony" and "ideology" (between habitus and creative performance, acceptance and contestation, revelation, and revolution) through thick ethnography and a historical-anthropological investigation taking into account the reformulation of certain basic notions of twentieth-century social theory (body, self, individual, group, ethnicity, and identity). As such, their work essentially constituted an anthropological response to the same problems being posed by both Scott and the set of critical perspectives that were coming together in that period under the label of cultural studies.

The debate around resistance/power relations was particularly charged in early 1990s U.S. anthropology. In 1990, Lila Abu-Lughod—author of an earlier, notable monograph on Bedouin women's social poetics and forms of resistance (Abu-Lughod 1986)—published a remarkable essay critiquing studies on resistance that begin by inverting their own guiding questions. Instead of romantically pitting instances of resistance against a generic form of power and asking whether and how they might become "real" forms of political action, she suggests, why not investigate what places and spaces of resistance (along with anthropological studies of them) can tell us about power itself (Abu-Lughod, 1990, p. 41)? Abu-Lughod uses the practices of resistance enacted by Bedouin women, both nomadic ones and those sedentarized in Egyptian settings, as a "diagnostic of power" (Ibid., p. 42). In so doing, she manages to pose some remarkably keen theoretical questions, each of which calls into question prior theoretical frameworks: how to prevent Bedouin women's creative and minute practices of resistance from being attributed consciously political meanings (that they do not have) or, in the opposite direction, from being regarded as pre-political and archaic (here, Abu-Lughod challenges an ideological feminist lens)? How to avoid analytical representations that depict these women as trapped in forms of "false consciousness", given that their actions actually unfold in the grey area between implicit

---

[9] For Italy, for example, similar issues churned in Lombardi Satriani's (1966) Gramscian-oriented rereading of folklore as a culture of implicit contestation.

contestation and explicit support of the forms of (male) power under which they are subjugated (challenging Scott and certain Marxist positions)? How to prevent women's spaces of implicit contestation from being attributed merely ritual value as an outlet for their frustration (challenging functionalist stances)? And finally, in the final section of the essay Abu-Lughod shows how this proposed approach can be used to articulate the power/resistance dialectic diachronically as well; resulting analyses could thus map the workings of power (in its institutional, habitual, and ideological manifestations) in cultural, dynamic, creative terms rather than merely deterministic ones.

The questions posed by Abu-Lughod paved the way for innovative lines of thought and inquiry. A few years later, Sherry Ortner (1995, p. 174) reiterated the centrality of ethnography for understanding the dynamics surrounding forms of resistance and the tendency, evident in polity and cultural studies approaches, to produce "thin" ethnographies, lacking in fine-grained depth and substance and thus unable to ensure even minimal degrees of holistic contextualization. Ortner's position was shared by other contemporary anthropologists (Kaplan & Kelly, 1994) and she herself revisited the same arguments the following year in an essay analyzing the relationship between cultural constructions of agency and spaces of resistance. Her stated purpose in this piece was to reassert the key importance of interpretive and Geertzian-derived holism when carrying out any anthropological interpretation of relations among power, subjectivity (Ortner, 2005) and human praxis. At the same time, many North American anthropologists of the time stressed the central role of what might be defined as cultural mediation in relationships among forms of power, practices, and constructions of subjectivity (a stance that granted prominence to Gramsci's thought from the mid-1980s onward) so as to distance themselves from reductionist readings of historical processuality. In so doing, this literature sought to create a kind of *cordon sanitaire* against the increasingly invasive spread of cultural (and subaltern) studies.

Not long after, Herzfeld (2005) similarly staked out a divergent position, in this case distinct from Scott's theses proposed in a 1998 volume analyzing the organizational, classificatory, and "governmental" abilities of the state, in a special forum in *American Anthropologist*. It is useful to outline these positions in order to map the standpoint taken by a significant segment of U.S. anthropology on the theoretical issues highlighted just above. At the same time, this discussion serves to introduce one of the domains around which U.S. anthropologists generated key insights in the field's hegemonic phase, namely the state. In Scott's view (1998, pp. 4–5), the state is an entity that presents itself as an expression of rational, universalist knowledge, part of a modernist ideology that controls and organizes nature and society through its technical mechanisms. It can take on more or less authoritarian forms, and states leaning towards authoritarianism seek to shape civil society in such a way that it will be amenable to the workings of the state and incapable of mounting forms of resistance. Scott then posits another, opposite face to the state's technical-administrative function: *metis*, the array of practical skills and forms of individual ingenuity that have the potential to generate forms of resistance while also giving rise to local knowledge and spaces of action (ibid., pp. 316–317). From Herzfeld's perspective, however, this view of the state appears too rigid. On a general level, Scott acknowledges that "formal schemes" of state order are related to the aspects "of practical knowledge that the former tend to reject" (1998, p. 7). Herzfeld (2005) nonetheless raises several objections to this view, critiquing its quasi-oppositional polarization between state and localness and between governmental technologies and practical ingenuity, and the fact that it has trouble identifying spaces of mutual, performative compromise between the two poles, thereby resulting in a tendency to grant the idea of resistance a central analytical position while largely overlooking social actors' intentionality. Moreover, Herzfeld specifically (ibid., pp. 370–371) shows that, in contemporary settings, local spaces (with their forms of *metis* and practices, granted an implicit oppositional role and/or status as alternative to constrictive state action in Scott's lens) are often the product of heritage-valorization policies enacted by state agencies themselves. He likewise stresses (ibid., pp. 372–373) that the apparatuses of the state and its concrete representatives sometimes provide social actors (civil society, local contexts) with spaces of and tools for manipulating and interacting with the state, spaces and tools the state itself must have in order to operate.

Herzfeld's objections to Scott's framework mirror other reactions to certain social theories that had proposed rigid, mechanical, and unidirectional readings of the relations between power, practices, culture, and subjectivity. Most importantly, however, Herzfeld implicitly references various strands of research developed during the 1990s and the years immediately following. In two different theoretical volumes (1992; 1997), for example, Herzfeld himself reflected on how bureaucracy and the performative sharing of symbols, stereotypes and emotions between social actors and state structures often plays a decisive role in nation-state operation. It is only when a set of people share none of those common symbolic roots that enable mutual, reciprocal, and operational compromise between bureaucrats and citizens, Herzfeld (1992) argues, that a state's ideological aspirations to bring reality in line with its technical-administrative classifications have the potential to produce dramatic effects. On the other hand, the spaces of "cultural intimacy" built by localities to signal boundaries and define spaces of action are "disemic" and, in reality, the supposedly rigid opposition characterizing them—as reiterated by the state versus local area relationship—is actually continually reproduced by the performative manipulation of the same stereotypes that underpin it (Herzfeld, 1997). Like Scott, Herzfeld also recognizes states as organizing, classifying, administering, enforcing and/or claiming to enforce a pure, modern rationality even while simultaneously producing spaces of cultural sharing by employing and transforming symbols derived from elemental domains (family, kinship, and blood). In this way, the state ensure that its symbols can be interpreted in multiple directions, ambiguously offering opportunities for the manipulation of these symbols that allow citizens and local places to construct levels of social autonomy and forms of accommodation leading to co-participation. Whether adopting a Weberian framework like the one Herzfeld ultimately employs or embracing a Marxian and Gramscian perspective, many ethnographies produced in that period precisely investigated these issues. That is, they explored the spaces of cultural signification through which the relationships between power structures (the state, of course, but also gendered structures and, more and more often, those of transnational agencies), processes of subjectivity embodiment and construction (Ortner, 2005), and individual and collective agency are made fluid and manipulatable or instead reinforced to such an extent as to trigger dramatic points of rupture.

Imagining a hypothetical continuum, we might identify one pole as holding ethnographies such as Herzfeld's on Greece (1985; 1991) that present such relationships as being embedded in a dialectic that allows room for maneuvering, accommodation, and mutual—sometimes covert—recognition between the parties involved. Other examples that come to mind are Akhil Gupta's (1995; 2005) work on the Indian state and the ways it produces "meaningful representations and practices" that enable citizens, even marginal ones living in rural India, to ascribe cultural meaning and enjoy spaces for action (Gupta, 2005, p. 188). Such representations include corruption and related narratives that "help shape people's expectations of what states can and will do, and how bureaucrats will respond to the needs of citizens" (ibid., p. 190).

12 FROM HEGEMONY TO FRAGMENTATION: NORTH AMERICAN CULTURAL... 361

Another is Shryoch's (1997) aforementioned ethnography analyzing the relationship between Bedouins' genealogical and oral history and the imagination (official and written) of the Jordanian nation. This analysis demonstrates the profound structural distance between the oral history of Bedouin groups and the local social/political structure generated by their narrating this history, on one hand, and the official historiographical imagination of the Kingdom of Jordan, on the other. At the same time, Shryock also highlights the dense interweaving these two historiographies, one oral and intimate and the other written and official, constructed through the efforts of intellectuals/politicians capable of moving and mediating between the two.

Abu-Lughod's ethnographic and reflexive trajectory could be placed at a somewhat intermediate point on the continuum. In *Veiled Sentiments*, her 1986 monograph that swiftly became a classic, the Palestinian/American scholar (one of the "halfies" who helped enrich U.S. anthropology in that generation) presents a rather traditional account of the social and political structure of the Bedouin group she studied (typically patrilineal and ideologically male-centered) juxtaposed in an almost oppositional way to a careful, participatory analysis of the ways women in this group made use of certain spaces, modes and social poetics (oral poetry, veiling). In 1993—after the article critiquing the notion of resistance and an essay raising questions about the concept of culture itself, which I will address shortly—she published a second monograph, a collection of the stories of some women and men in this same Bedouin group. For theoretical reasons that Abu-Lughod explicates in a dense introduction (1993, pp. 1–35), this work is intentionally fragmentary compared to the 1986 monograph. The reasons for this choice lie at the intersection of multiple impulses and issues: the need to develop innovative forms of ethnographic representation capable of accounting for the power differentials involved in the observer/observed relationship; a critique of certain implicit assumptions in feminist analyses and the tendency of this literature to fail to recognize how figures of the "self" (e.g. Western, male) and the "other" (female, predominantly non-Western) are defined by specific power relations; and the resultant critique of the tendency to "generalize" and to construct categories that create sharp distinctions (between observer and observed, between self and other) and end up taking fluid processes and scenarios and rendered them homogeneous, internally consistent and timeless. In line with her 1991 essay, one of the concepts Abu-Lughod challenges is the very notion of "culture," and this book's fragmentary and fluid storytelling style is thus a way of writing "against culture."

362   B. PALUMBO

Another example of research that could be situated at this midpoint of the continuum is the work of Veena Das (another "halfy"). In a 1995 monograph, Das focuses on a number of events that each represents a critical juncture for cultural and social politics in contemporary India. The critical social situations she addresses (including women who were kidnapped but chose to remain with their abductors, or Sikh militants and the construction of their subjectivity) highlight internal contradictions in relations among the state, the community, and individuals, thus offering scholars the chance to recount such contradictions. If the act of kidnapping women, the violence they endured, and the memory of such incidents become matters of national and ideological interest, how can we grasp the feelings and accounts of the victims whose choice to remain living with their captors places them outside of official discursive orders (Das, 1995, p. 9)? How can we capture the mechanisms and emotions of the people living in communities whose very existence is based on embracing collective violence and the accumulated memory of such violence (ibid., pp. 13–14)?

Neither of the ethnographic endeavors in these monographs set out to uncover the complicit interweaving of (state) power and spaces of everyday life. They do not question the reciprocal ways state actors and marginal groups and individuals—or those simply subjected to state power—produce phantasmatic images of each other, as described in Taussig's (1987a, Taussig, 1997) accounts. As we are about to see, they also do not set up communities or individuals with their "cultural intimacy" or local *metis*, in opposition to (state, patriarchal) power. Rather, they seek to identify fractures, critical points and forms of friction (Tsing, 2004) that might shed light on the complexity and interstices of those relations and the ways in which they challenge the categorical claims of structured powers (ethnographic authorship included) with their essentialist lack of flexibility.

If studies privileging the dialectical dimension of relations between power and subjects comprise one pole, on the opposite end we can instead find research that, often conducted in contexts of intensely rigid power differentials and marked violence, instead highlights the confrontational and conflicting aspects of relations among power, social groups, subaltern or marginal groups, and individuals. An exemplar of such positioning is Nancy 1993 monograph dedicated to what she calls the "routinization of human suffering" (ibid., p. 16) in a poor community in Northeastern Brazil, where the author outlines her theoretical stance on this intersection

12 FROM HEGEMONY TO FRAGMENTATION: NORTH AMERICAN CULTURAL... 363

with awareness and transparency. The U.S. scholar focuses in particular on the structural violence associated with conditions of economic poverty and political marginality that causes poor mothers to become numb and emotionally resigned to losing their children. The research begins as a social work and international cooperation project (Scheper-Hughes first engages with the community that later becomes her research participants when working in this area as a social worker trying to improve mothers' living conditions). It then gradually takes on the form of an ethnography as she broadens her theoretical focus to also consider the structural relationships between central powers, violence, poverty, and hunger, on one hand, and cultural constructions of illness, emotions, and practices among women living in these marginalized conditions, on the other:

> But more positively, as my *companheiras* and *companheiros* of the Alto pulled me toward the "public" world of Born Jesus, into the marketplace, to the *prefeitura*, to the ecclesiastical base community and rural syndicate meetings, the more my understandings of the community were enriched, and my theoretical horizons and political orientations expanded. The everyday violence of shantytown life, and the madness of hunger, in particular, became the focus of my study, of which the specific case of mother love and child death was one instance. (Scheper-Hughes, 1993, p. 18)

In the face of the hunger, misery, and structural violence that constitute the local manifestations of the state, it is impossible for the researcher to cling to neutrality, be it political, theoretical, or even methodological. The anthropologist might initially imagine she will be able to maintain a separation between her position as a scholar and the activist one she held as a social worker, but in reality, the local community demands direct and explicit engagement. The women and men of the *favela* call on Scheper-Hughes to share in their struggles and the tactics of resistance they deploy against the institutional violence and structural abandonment of the more or less democratic state and federal government. Scheper-Hughes shifts her positioning, adjusting her conceptual apparatuses to the demands made of her. The resulting analyses thus unfold within this political framework and corresponding theoretical choices. An illustrative example is her reading of the complex ethnomedical constellation *nervos*. Scheper-Hughes reconstructs the symbolic and semantic linkages of this category, showing its history in the area under investigation and its close connection with endemic hunger, also examining local cultural representations of hunger and comparing them with medico-nutritionist analyses (1993, ch. 3). This work is distinct from a symbolic-interpretive interpretation designed to map the forms of coherence or ambiguity in a symbolic/ritual system; it likewise diverges from reductionist analyses that tend to view *nervos* and its various manifestations as indicating a pathological condition that masking and concealing the problem of hunger with its evident physical, physiological, and psychological repercussions. Scheper-Hughes instead proposes a reading that is both phenomenological and political: phenomenological in that it shows how the bodies and minds of women and men in this community inhabit everyday, deep-rooted conditions of suffering, precarity, and hunger to themselves become "battlefields" (ibid., p. 187) in which external forces come face to face with the (symbolic and cultural) ways individual subjects live and experience them. Political in that *nervos* is an idiom through which the poor residents of northeast Brazil are able to express their anger in acceptable ways (Scheper-Hughes, 1993, p. 195). Scheper-Hughes also treats the political field surrounding this folk medical category as a dynamic, historically variable space in which the state, along with the concrete mechanisms through which medical science operates in the context of the *favela*, is able to medicalize the category of *nervos*. This process acts as a gateway through which local powers are able to effectively take this embodiment of suffering, anger, and hunger and deprive it of its inherently critical, contestatory, and subversive qualities, translating manifestations of discomfort that are simultaneously bodily, emotional, and psychological into the terms of mental illness (ibid., p. 211).

Building on Gramsci, Foucault and Basaglia, Scheper-Hughes' monograph calls for the democratization of medicine; only a biased reading of her arguments would suggest she seeks to eliminate or deny biomedicine. As such, it stands as mentioned above on the more ideological-political pole of the continuum of conceptualizations of the dialectic between powers, subjectivity, agency, historiographical imagination and reflections on ethnography that distinguished North American anthropological research in the phase I have called "hegemonic." However, as with other studies cited here, some features come to light that, embraced or criticized, went on to become central in the next phase, U.S. anthropology's "explosion." Ethical and political engagement is a trait the author consciously asserts here as constitutive of ethnographic fieldwork positioning and the kind of interpretation anthropologists ought to provide. The anthropologist-activist comes to understand by participating and involving herself in the struggles of the people with whom she lives.

12 FROM HEGEMONY TO FRAGMENTATION: NORTH AMERICAN CULTURAL... 365

Another theoretical feature can also be found in Abu-Lughod's monograph that went on to fuel debates at the onset of the new century: the critique of the concept of culture so key to the development of twentieth-century anthropology. As in an earlier essay, in her efforts to write "against culture" (Abu-Lughod, 1991) she actually returns to a line of thought whose roots can be traced back to at least the work of Edmund Leach and Fredrik Barth with their tendency to reflect critically on the constructed character of the relationship between (a) culture and (a) society and the essentializing inclinations of cultural holism. Like Wolf in his 1982 volume, Abu-Lughod holds that "culture" (or even "society") is a concept that takes complex historical processes and subjective dynamics and frames them as rigid. Moreover, since the 1970s, "culture" understood in the anthropological sense had come to be commonly used term in the international political lexicon, serving to indicate, assert and often construct social and identity aggregations cast in essentialist terms. Numerous examples of anthropological research have reflected on this process, including Herzfeld's work (1982, 1987) on European and Greek intellectuals, social scientists, and politicians' construction of "contemporary" Greek culture, Richard Handler's (1988) research on the relationships among nationalism, cultural politics, and cultural objectification in Quebec and, more radically, the critique of differentialist culturalism posed by Verena Stolcke (1995) and Douglas Holmes' (2000) analysis of essentialisms and identity fundamentalisms among Europe's new neo-fascist right-wingers. This issue (the essentialization of culture and how it is used in more or less discriminatory, differentialist, and identity-based ways) is also one of the themes that ended up being addressed in the discipline's next phase. Scholars went on to engage it in different ways, from the anthropology of heritage-making processes (Collins, 2008, 2015) to the anthropology of the state and nationalisms (Herzfeld, 1987; Foster, 1991; Carrier, 1995; Gupta & Ferguson, 1997).

Before moving on to an inevitably brief presentation of the final phase, however, there is one last issue of note that became central in the 1990s and, albeit under different names and within different conceptual frameworks, during the first decade of the new century as well: globalization. Anthropologists arrived at this issue from a variety of trajectories: first through the mediation of more broadly oriented work (Harvey, 1989; Giddens, 1990; Sassen, 1991), then through a gradual transformation of existing theoretical frameworks such as the ones proposed by Wallerstein and Wolf, the latter in more complex and specifically anthropological terms. Michael Kerney (1995) taking stock of studies on globalization and transnationalism, identified several lines of research: urban anthropology and new migrations, forms of de-territorialization, the implosion of the world's earlier political configurations, media and spatio-temporal compression, tourism, the cultural dynamics of globalization, and the production of diasporic communities. A few years later, Jonathan Xavier Inda and Renato Rosaldo (2001) were already able to offer a thoughtful overview of the fruit of a season of ethnographic work. According to the two editors of a volume presenting the research carried out over the last decade, anthropologists' main contribution to the study of globalization lay in addressing the cultural dimensions of these ongoing processes (Xavier Inda & Rosaldo, 2001, p. 5). Echoing other theoretical work cited above (Giddens, Harvey), they argued that globalization entails the compression and radical reconfiguration of space-time relationships (ibid., pp. 6–8). This reconfiguration has accelerated economic, human, and cultural flows, produced constraints that interconnect and transcend previous political-institutional boundaries, extended social, economic, and political practices across those same boundaries, and intensified processes of interconnection between the global sphere and local contexts (ibid., p. 9). Since cultural flows cut across local spaces, there is no longer that close connection between (a) culture and (a) place that had been central to the twentieth-century anthropological imaginary (Xavier Inda & Rosaldo, 2001, pp. 10–12). Ethnographic research has thus focused on processes of cultural de-territorialization and, at the same time, complementary processes of re-territorialization. Local spaces are not absorbed and annihilated by the expansion of Western-centered globalization, researchers find; rather, they are reshaped and reorganized into new social and cultural forms. Anthropological studies, according to Xavier Inda and Rosaldo, have revealed a more complex and dynamic world than scholars from other disciplines hypothesized: globalization has neither homogenized nor Westernized the world. It has instead reconfigured and re-centered relations between the West and "other" worlds. Local places and those very forms of knowledge cast as peripheral by other interpretive schemes have proven capable of producing sentiments of belonging and reshaping economic, social, media and hence cultural flows. These latter, for their part, no longer follow the directions and trajectories rigidly predetermined by previous theories charting the global expansion of the Euro-Atlantic economic system.

12 FROM HEGEMONY TO FRAGMENTATION: NORTH AMERICAN CULTURAL... 367

Without delving into the arguments of individual ethnographic studies, we can identify two fixed points in the field of anthropological studies of globalization: one theoretical and the other methodological. On the theoretical level, the most prominent contribution remains the insights Arjun Appadurai presented in 1996 with *Modernity at Large*. In this volume, Appadurai (1996, p. 33) precisely pinpoints the frames (technoscape, financescape, mediascape, and ideoscape) organizing the global flows that traverse and reconfigure relations between local areas, describing the specific characteristics and functioning of each frame. He also reflects (ibid., pp. 188–198) on certain social and cultural disjointures produced by the circulation of these flows, including the breakdown of the bond between nation-states, localities and neighborhoods that plays a decisive role in determining the living conditions of large masses of people in late modernity.

The other lynchpin of anthropological explorations of globalization, the level of methodology, is represented by Marcus' work. In a number of essays published between 1989 and 1997 and later collected along with other articles in a 1998 volume, Marcus (1998) proposes a series of methodological innovations and experimental tactics for situating ethnographic research in the global contexts of post-modernity, beginning from the critical, dialogical stance that had been taking root in North American anthropology since *Writing Culture*. Faced with the challenge of imagining the global ecumene in ethnographic terms (*The Whole*: 1989), Marcus (1995) proposed the innovative strategy of multi-sited ethnography, a method that spread so widely in following years as to become all but standard. While in a 1997 (Marcus, 1997) paper he emphasized the importance of complicity in co-constructing ethnographic representations, in later work co-written with Holmes (2005; 2006) Marcus proposed the idea of refunctioning ethnography altogether via dialogue with para-ethnography, that is, the self-descriptions produced for technical reasons by various institutional actors.

At the end of the 1990s and beginning of the 2000s, one of the outcomes of anthropological reflections and ethnographic research on globalization conducted within this theoretical and methodological space was to render the "global situation" a shared frame—if not exactly a new master narrative, then at least a background setting within which to situate more or less experimental ethnographies. Indeed, Tsing (2000, p. 328) writing at the beginning of the new millennium provided the following definition of the "global situation," thereby foreshadowing the shift from globalization studies to neoliberalism studies that U.S. anthropology was poised to make shortly thereafter:

> Market enthusiasms have replaced communism; national governments prostrate themselves before international finance; social movements market "culture" on a global scale. How should social scientists analyze these changes? This question is muddied by the fact that social science changes too. "Global" practices challenge social scientists to internationalize their venues, as North American and European scholars are brought into discussion with scholars from the South. Social science theories no longer take Western genealogies for granted but, rather, require fluency with a wider range of perspectives, from Latin American dependency theories to South Asian subaltern studies. The excitement of this internationalization of scholarship encourages many of us to throw ourselves into endorsements of globalization as a multilayered evolution, drawing us into the future. Sometimes our critical distance seems less useful than our participation. And yet, can we understand either our own involvement or the changing world without our critical skills? This chapter argues that we cannot.

FOURTH PHASE: DEFLAGRATION, 2001–2020

Drawing distinct lines between the different phases is obviously an arbitrary operation. After all, the only way of identifying them as phases is by considering them in retrospect and from afar. Viewed from a present-day perspective, North American anthropology seems to have undergone a process of theoretical, methodological, and thematic fragmentation. From a standpoint further back in time, however, we can discern not only points of innovation and fractures but also important lines of continuity. As we have seen, the cornerstones around which scholars developed their theoretical approaches in the final two decades of the last century included theories of practice, a focus on agency in relationship to power, and the mechanisms through which subjectivity is constructed. Interest in these issues certainly did not wane with the turn of the century but it did become more finely honed, with analyses delving more deeply into various aspects. A particularly interesting example of this development is Saba Mahmood's, 2005 monograph on women in the Egyptian piety movement, part of a more general Islamic revival involving the Muslim world since the 1970s.[10]

---

[10] Thank you to Barbara Pinelli for having brought to my attention the theoretical relevance of Mahmood's work.

This dense ethnography is fueled by a dual critique targeting both a number of feminist theories and the notion of agency itself. The case of women choosing to subject themselves to Islamic rules of public and private behavior poses political problems for feminist theories and, at the same time, theoretical problems for anthropological approaches to agency and resistance (Mahmood, 2005, pp. 5–10). Mahmood (2005, pp. 14–15) argues that the element underlying these (apparent) contradictions in both cases is the uncritical acceptance of cultural assumptions bound up with the Western tradition's conceptualization of subjectivity, freedom and constraint. Indeed, both feminist and anthropological theories assume that what constitutes agency is either a gradual act of asserting the self or a form of resistance to constrictive mechanisms. The way anthropological and feminist theory understand agency is thus based on a political, teleological, and liberatory conception of the self. Such a conception is not remotely a given, however; it represents the construct of a specific moral economy which was in turn produced over the course of a particular cultural history. To anthropologically understand Egyptian Muslim women's desire to subject themselves to norms, we must thus question the different ways in which individual human actions inhabit norms (ibid., pp. 14–15):

> if the ability to effect change in the world and in oneself is historically and culturally specific (both in terms of what constitutes 'change' and the means by which it is effected), then the meaning and sense of agency cannot be fixed in advance, but must emerge through an analysis of the particular concepts that enable specific modes of being, responsibility, and effectivity. Viewed in this way, what may appear to be a case of deplorable passivity and docility from a progressivist point of view, may actually be a form of agency— but one that can be understood only from within the discourses and structures of subordination that create the conditions of its enactment. In this sense, agentival capacity is entailed not only in those acts that resist norms but also in the multiple ways in which one *inhabits* norms.

Mahmood's ethnography seeks to understand the actions and emotions of Egyptian women who, driven by an avowed sense of devotional piety, actively adhere to a revival of the Islamic faith. Where theories of agency and resistance see forms of subjugation, she instead chooses to investigate culturally determined forms of subjectification (differing from the ones presupposed by Western theories of agency) and other historical constructions of subjectivity. In taking this path she was guided by the theoretical suggestions Talal Asad (1993, 2003) offers as part of his genealogical reading of the cultural-historical processes involved in constructing categories such as "secularization," "secularism," "violence," and "public space," the ways subjectification effects are produced, and the more general "moral economies" they give rise to.

Looking for an element of novelty in this phase of U.S. anthropology, we find it precisely in this more radical focus on critically deconstructing the discipline's analytical categories and reconstructing the genealogies behind these categories, prior to or as part of conducting ethnographic research. In fact, this phase seems to involve a more pronounced politicization of anthropologists' gaze on the world in general and the worlds in which they work while at the same time their analytical frameworks are likewise more deeply politicized. At first glance, this tendency might appear to be a consequence of the fact that U.S. anthropologists have been more systematically and mechanically employing the above-mentioned theoretical bloc developed by European thinkers outside of the discipline, comprising so-called French Theory (but also Italian thinkers), by applying categories developed by Foucault, Gramsci and, more recently, Agamben. Indeed, this is the thesis Marshall Sahlins argued with keen foresight in two 1999 essays published later collected in a 2002 volume (Sahlins, 2002). With an eye on the past and concern for the future of the discipline, in these articles Sahlins fiercely critiques the trends he saw emerging at the time, labeled with obvious disdain as "afterologies". He sees these stances as generating a number of misguided interpretative tendencies: abandoning the notion of culture and consequently losing interest in cultural diversity—imagined, like the notion of tradition itself, as only ever a figment of the researcher's invention—at the very moment when social actors in other worlds, worlds which are by no means disappearing, are asserting precisely this notion; the disappearance of the concept of structure, resulting in the prevalence of moralistic and/or political readings of cultural and social facts (Sahlins calls this "redemptive cultural critique"—1999b, p. V); the move to adopt an abstract, pervasive and corrosive idea of cultural complexity, mediated by uses of the Foucauldian notion of discourse in place of the old anthropological idea of culture ("So nowadays all culture is power"—ibid., p. VI); and the tendency to view other individuals and cultures as having lost the capacity to act when they intersected the history of Western political-economic expansion and associated tendency to instrumentalize others, objectifying them as mere players in our Western games, processes and destinies.

12 FROM HEGEMONY TO FRAGMENTATION: NORTH AMERICAN CULTURAL... 371

Sahlins' provocatory analysis identified aspects and trends that, as we have seen, were indeed taking place in North American anthropology, and were expressed even more radically in later years. For example, the shift from the narrative meta-context represented by the concepts of globalization and late liberalism, central to the 1990s, to accounts framed by the notion of neoliberalism does seem to have involved a politicization and ideologization of scholars' positionings, both theoretical and methodological. In a thoughtful overview of the anthropological studies carried out under the label of neoliberalism, Tejaswini Ganti (2014, p. 94) notes how it this framework had gained ground since 2005:

> Anthropological engagements with the topic of neoliberalism begin in earnest in a post-9/11 world where the impact of various market-oriented economic reforms, policy prescriptions, financial crises, and the global War on Terror became more palpable in anthropologists' field sites.

The many ethnographic studies conducted with the neoliberal arena as their main rhetorical and organizational meta-context have pursued different directions. One was a more "materialist" direction linked to the political economy perspectives of the 1980s or at any rate interested in economic and political dimensions, such as those presented in the volume *Millennium Capitalism* edited by John and Jean Comaroff in 2001 as well as Herzfeld's (2009) ethnography on the effects of gentrification in a neighborhood in the city of Rome. A second was the direction more directly influenced by Foucauldian theses on governmental mechanisms and processes of subjectification. An illustrative example of this is Aihwa Ong's (2003) work on the governmental effects of U.S. welfare on the bodies and self-perceptions of Cambodian immigrant women; Ong (2006, p. 12) also exemplifies this approach in not necessarily considering the spread of neoliberal ideologies, policies and techniques as a homogeneous process with predefined and constricting results, directed by the West toward other worlds. On a different level, this second thread can also be seen in Jean and John Comaroff's (2009) reflections on the commodification and patrimonialization of culture, ethnicity, and other forms of collective identity construction.[11]

---

[11] In addition to Ganti (2014), discussions of the different versions of the neoliberalism/anthropology relationship can be found in Lomnitz (2008), Hirsch (2010), Hilgers (2012), Wacquant (2012), and Carrier (2016).

This move to embed ethnographic research and anthropological interpretation in the various scenarios of neoliberalism, as well as tendency for scholars choosing this narrative horizon to formulate positions Sahlins called "afterological," has triggered debates and reactions, oftentimes critical. In the first part of a realist—if not quite materialist—oriented volume analyzing the relationship between neoliberalism, anthropological theory and its (supposed) crisis, for instance, James Carrier, systematically reflects on anthropology in the neoliberal context and relations between anthropological research and neoliberalism, concluding by accusing a significant segment of North American research of being an intimately neoliberal anthropology (2016, pp. 39–61). Unquestionably, both Sahlins' early, biting critiques and Carrier's more nuanced and inevitably more up-to-date reflections capture some critical aspects of recent anthropological research (especially in the U.S.).Some ethnographic research is not particularly dense, and it is often organized around projects and on the basis of methodological choices preemptively conceived as experimental; it is often guided by deconstructionist-leaning theoretical apparatuses and, framed in a historical, institutional and economic-political scenario presented as neoliberal, such research can indeed give the impression of being pre-packaged cognitive bundles set up to be displayed, or sold, in an elite academic marketplace that is itself driven by neoliberal logics.[12] Having acknowledged that tendency and taken into account the unavoidably varying density of different ethnographic endeavors, however, if nothing else an overview of the research carried out in this phase reveals the vitality of North American anthropological research.

In an essay intended to re-present and update the arguments of her 1984 article, Ortner (2016) addresses specifically the conceptual and narrative space generated by relations between (U.S.) anthropological research and neoliberalism in an effort to map its contours. In her view (2016: 48), research carried out between 1984 and the first decade of the 2000s can be divided into "dark anthropologies," "anthropologies of the 'good'" and work involving the "re-emergence of the study of resistance." Considering the labels she uses and reading the essay as a whole, Ortner's classification—while effective—appears to be based more on capturing studies' political, ethical and emotional content and tones than on tracing

---

[12] For a critical presentation of some such research, limited to the Italian context, see Palumbo (2018, pp. 189–206).

their theoretical and methodological differences as she had done in her 1984 essay.

These "dark anthropologies," according to Ortner (2016, pp. 51–58) reflect cases in which neoliberal logics have been imposed on the (often colonial) worlds studied by anthropologists and the ethnographies must thus analyze these logics' processes, mechanisms and governmental effects, charting repercussions on local subjects that are primarily constrictive but sometimes also creative. The research focus of "dark anthropologies" thus revolves around power in its economic, cultural, and ideological dimensions, with anthropologists revealing its inequality-producing applications and sometimes repressive capacity to exert control.

"Anthropologies of the good" look instead at the "ethical choices and moral dilemmas" that individual social actors face when maneuvering in the same political-economic arenas that constitute the settings of "dark" research (ibid., p. 60). Moreover, while "dark" studies tend to focus on suffering subjects brought face to face with the workings of coercive powers (the state, transnational agencies, the patriarchy), "anthropologies of the good" (predominantly British rather than North American in origin) instead revolve around the idea of "effervescent" (Robbins, 2015: 219) subjects capable of taking action and choosing "a life truly worth living" (Throop, 2015, p. 46).

The third emerging stance Ortner identifies is one that innovatively revisits the discipline's interest in various forms of resistance. This renewed anthropological interest tends to privilege collective and political forms of resistance rather than building on the threads of thought highlighted above to conduct an in-depth theoretical investigation of the relationships between power, subjectivity, agency, and historical dialectics. Apart from research that carries forward the critical anthropologies of previous decades, this new work on "resistance" focuses on collective subjects or the individuals acting within collective entities, organized into movements with explicit political and ethical goals. The ethnographers carrying out these new analyses of resistance almost never position themselves outside of the movements under investigation; rather, they take sides, become involved, and stake out positions based on ethical and political commitments they share with the movement participants themselves.

Ortner's three-part classification captures some trends that became established in the next few years. Indeed, the anthropology of social and political movements in which it was considered important for the researchers to be directly involved was one of the themes most widely addressed in the first decade of the 2000s (Hale, 2006; Casas-Cortés et al., 2008, 2013; Collins, 2012). Equally central was work distanced itself from anthropologies of power and constraint to instead investigates subjects' openness to the future and capacity to look ahead (Appadurai, 2013) along with the emergence of an anthropology of ethics and morality (Faubion, 2011; Mattingly & Throop, 2018). These are not the only issues to have attracted the attention of North American anthropologists over the past few decades, however. Other foci have appeared one after another or, more often, overlapping in the same period almost as if to suggest a stormy sea traversed by different and successive waves of interest. We can get an idea of this by browsing the presentations of current trends provided in a specific section of American Anthropologist that surveys both theoretical and public, applied work published each year in major U.S. journals. In 2008, foci included neoliberalism investigated in terms of its political-economic and epistemological-intellectual aspects (Richland, 2009) and, on a more public level, war, climate change, environmental disasters, human rights, disparities in the health care system, and racial inequalities in the U.S. (Checker, 2009). In 2009 research again addressed the financial crisis, civil rights and race relations in the U.S., climate change, cultural heritage, and political engagement (Brondo, 2010). In 2010, scholars showed theoretical interest in indigenism, multispecies ethnography, the nature-culture relationship, security and a focus on the thought of Deleuze and Guattari (Hamilton & Placas, 2011); on the public level, they investigated collaboration, engagement, political activism and advocacy (Mullins, 2011). For the following year, Dole (2012) identifies the relationship between secularism and liberalism, the politics of affect and care, and the politics of space and time as central themes; Baer (2012) instead finds industrial globalization, power differentials in the global world, climate change and disasters, the emergence of indigenism, and the need to reflect on the relationship between public and engaged anthropology as central to public anthropology studies. In 2012, Muehlebach (2013) finds that the central theme of U.S. anthropological research has been precarity, as part of a more general interest in ethics. In the area of public engagement (Gomberg-Muñoz, 2013), anthropologists addressed reactions to the Occupy movement, relations between local communities and migrants, migration policies and migrants' rights.

We could continue the list to cover more recent years as well, including, for example, the ecological-political issues captured by the notion of anthropocene (Mathews, 2020), energy resources and surrounding politics (Boyer, 2019), or Elizabeth Povinelli's (2016) radical, innovative perspective on "geontopower" and the end of late liberalism. Besides certain nascent spaces of reflection (with Povinelli's seemingly among the most innovative), however, extending the list would not make recent work appear any more coherent or unified in terms of theoretical frameworks, themes, and objects of research. It is, however, characterized by underlying trends such as researchers' political and ethical engagement with social actors, their involvement with existential and social conditions, and their consequent focus on pressing, publicly gripping issues.

Where, then, might we find coherence and commonality in an anthropology that has been described (Jobson, 2019) as "burning"? Perhaps it is to be found in the arguments John Comaroff deployed in 2010 to counter the idea that anthropology was entering a crisis or even coming to an end. In response to objections raised about anthropological research, Comaroff reiterated the constitutive features of the discipline:

> While we ground our work in its various epistemic operations, there is every reason to believe that we shall not kill ourselves off by trivialization, irrelevance, or indistinction, which is more or less assured by a retreat into neo-empiricism, cryptoculturalism, or brute localism. Or by repudiating ethnography altogether, which has manifested itself in a few powerful places of late. For me, there is no such thing as a postethnographic anthropology just as there is no such thing as a posttheoretical one. (John Comaroff, 2010, p. 533)

> All of them evince a capacity to estrange, to ground their theory in an ethnographic optic at once wide angled and close up, to demystify received orthodoxies. By these means does our own verb-to-be become a proper noun. By these means does the critical practice of ethnography become Anthropology, upper case. So (...) anthropology, into which I was initiated on that grim day in South Wales in 1971, is not about to die. Nor is it "in suspension." It is very much alive, producing new kinds of knowledge, new theorywork, new empirical horizons, new arguments. The future of the discipline, in short, lies, as it always will, in its indiscipline. (ibid., p. 534)

References

AA.VV. (1978). Political Economy. *American Ethnologist, 5*(3).
Abu Lughod, L. (1993). *Writing Women's Worlds: Bedouin Stories.* University of California Press.

376 B. PALUMBO

Abu-Lughod, L. (1986). *Veiled Sentiments. Honor and Poetry in a Bedouin Society.* University of California Press.

Abu-Lughod, L. (1990). The Romance of Resistance: Tracing Transformations of Power through Bedouin Women. *American Ethnologist, 17*(1), 41–55.

Abu-Lughod, L. (1991). Writing Against Culture. In R. G. Fox (Ed.), *Recapturing Anthropology. Working in the Present* (pp. 137–162). School of American Research Press.

Appadurai, A. (1986). Theory in Anthropology. Center and Periphery. *Comparative Study in Society and History, 28*(2), 356–361.

Appadurai, A. (1996). *Modernity at Large. Cultural Dimensions of Globalization.* University of Minnesota Press.

Appadurai, A. (2013). *The Future as Cultural Fact. Essays in the Global Condition.* Verso Books.

Asad, T. (1987). Are There Histories of Peoples Without Europe? *Comparative Study in Society and History, 29*(3), 594–607.

Asad, T. (1993). *Genealogies of Religion. Discipline and Reasons of Power in Christianity and Islam.* The Johns Hopkins University Press.

Asad, T. (2003). *Formations of the Secular: Christianity, Islam, Modernity.* Stanford University Press.

Baer, H. (2012). Engaged Anthropology in 2011: "A View from the Antipodes in a Turbulent Era". *American Anthropologist, 114*(2), 217–226.

Battaglia, D. (1995). Problematizing the Self: A Thematic Introduction. In D. Battaglia (Ed.), *Rhetorics of Self-Making* (pp. 1–15). University of California Press.

Behar, R. (1996). *The Vulnerable Observer. Anthropology That Breaks Your Heart.* Beacon Press.

Behar, R., & Gordon, D. (1996). *Women Writing Culture.* University of California Press.

Best, S., & Keller, D. (1991). *Postmodern Theory. Critical Interrogations.* Red Globe Press.

Birth, K. (1990). Reading and the Righting of Writing Ethnographies. *American Ethnologist, 17*(3), 549–557.

Boyarin, J. (Ed.). (1994). *Remapping Memory: The Politics of Timespace.* University of Minnesota Press.

Boyer, D. (2019). *Energopolitics: Wind and Power in the Anthropocene.* Duke University Press.

Brondo, K. V. (2010). Practicing Anthropology in a Time of Crisis: 2009 Year in Review. *American Anthropologist, 112*(2), 208–218.

Calabretta, V., & Palumbo, B. (1994). Antropologia, storia e politica. Intervista a George Marcus. *Ossimori, 4,* 131–136.

Carrier, J. (1995). Introduction. In J. G. Carrier (Ed.), *Occidentalism: Images of the West* (pp. 1–32). Clarendon Press.

12 FROM HEGEMONY TO FRAGMENTATION: NORTH AMERICAN CULTURAL... 377

Carrier, J. (Ed.). (2016). *After the Crisis: Anthropological Thought, Neoliberalism and the Aftermath*. Routledge.

Carrithers, M. (1990). Is Anthropology Art or Science? *Current Anthropology, 31*(3), 263–282.

Casas-Cortés, M., Osterweil, M., & Powell, D. (2008). Blurring Boundaries: Recognizing Knowledge-Practices in the Study of Social Movements. *Anthropological Quarterly, 81*(1), 17–58.

Casas-Cortés, M., Osterweil, M., & Powell, D. (2013). Transformations in Engaged Ethnography. Knowledge, Networks, and Social Movements. In J. Juris & A. Khasnabish (Eds.), *Insurgent Encounters. Transnational Activism, Ethnography, and the Political* (pp. 199–227). Duke University Press.

Checker, M. (2009). Anthropology in the Public Sphere, 2008: Emerging Trends and Significant Impacts. *American Anthropologist, 111*(2), 162–170.

Clifford, J. (1986). Introduction: Partial Truths. In J. Clifford & J., Marcus, G. (Eds.), *Writing Culture. The Poetics and Politics of Ethnography* (pp. 1–26). University of California Press.

Clifford, J. (1988). *The Predicament of Culture*. Harvard University Press.

Clifford, J. (2012). Feeling Historical. *Cultural Anthropology, 27*(3), 417–426.

Clifford, J., & Marcus, G. (1986). *Writing Culture. The Poetics and Politics of Ethnography*. University of California Press.

Cohen, A. P. (1994). *Self-Consciousness. An Alternative Anthropology of Identity*. Routledge.

Cole, J., & Wolf, E. (1974). *The Hidden Frontier: Ecology and Ethnicity in an Alpine Valley*. Academic Press.

Collins, J. (2008). But What if I Should Need to Defecate in Your Neighborhood, Madame? *Cultural Anthropology, 23*(2), 279–328.

Collins, J. (2015). *Revolt of the Saints. Memory and Redemption in the Twilight of Brazilian Racial Democracy*. Duke University Press.

Collins, J. (2012). Theorizing Wisconsin's 2011 Protests: Community-based Unionism Confronts Accumulation by Dispossession. *American Ethnologist, 39*(1), 6–20.

Comaroff, J. (1985). *Body of Power, Spirit of Resistance. The Culture and History of a South African People*. University of Chicago Press.

Comaroff, J., & Comaroff, J. (1992). *Ethnography and the Historical Imagination*. Westview Press.

Comaroff, J., & Comaroff, J. (1997). *Of Revelation and Revolution. The Dialectics of Modernity on a South African Frontier, Vol. 2*. University of Chicago Press.

Comaroff, J., & Comaroff, J. (Eds.). (2001). *Millennial Capitalism and the Culture of Neoliberalism*. Duke University Press.

Comaroff, J., & Comaroff, J. (2009). *Ethnicity, INC*. University of Chicago Press.

Comaroff, J., & Comaroff, J. (1991). *Of Revelation and Revolution. Christianity, Colonialism and Consciousness in South Africa, Vol. 1*. University of Chicago Press.

378   B. PALUMBO

Comaroff, J. (2010). The End of Anthropology, Again: On the Future of an In/Discipline. *American Anthropologist, 112*(4), 524–538.

Creahn, K. (2002). *Gramsci, Culture and Anthropology*. University of California Press.

Csordas, T. (1999). Embodiment and Cultural Phenomenology. In G. Weiss & H. F. Haber (Eds.), *Perspectives on Embodiment: The Intersections of Nature and Culture* (pp. 143–162). Routledge.

Cusset, F. (2008). *French Theory. How Foucault, Derrida, Deleuze, & Co. Transformed the Intellectual Life of the United States*. Minnesota University Press.

Das, V. (1995). *Critical Events. An Anthropological Perspective on Contemporary India*. Oxford University Press.

Dirks, N. (1996). Is Vice Versa? Historical Anthropologies and Anthropological Histories. In T. McDonald (Ed.), *The Historical Turn in the Human Sciences* (pp. 17–51). University of Michigan Press.

Dole, C. (2012). Revolution, Occupation, and Love: The 2011 Year in Cultural Anthropology. *American Anthropologist, 114*(2), 227–239.

Faubion, J. (1993). *Modern Greek Lessons. A Primer in Historical Constructivism*. Princeton University Press.

Faubion, J. (2011). *An Anthropology of Ethics*. Cambridge University Press.

Foster, R. (1991). Making National Cultures in the Global Ecumene. *Annual Review of Anthropology, 20*, 235–260.

Foucault, M. (1976). *Histoire de la sexualité 1. La volonté de savoir*. Gallimard.

Frankenberg, R. (1988). Gramsci, Culture, and Medical Anthropology: Kundry and Parsifal? Or Rat's Tail to Sea Serpent. *Medical Anthropology Quarterly n.s., 2*(4), 324–337.

Friedman, J. (1988). No History is an Island. *Critique of Anthropology, VIII*(3), 7–39.

Friedrich, P. (1992). Interpretation and Vision: A Critique of Cryptopositivism. *Cultural Anthropology, 7*(2), 211–231.

Ganti, T. (2014). Neoliberalism. *Annual Review of Anthropology, 43*, 89–104.

Geertz, C. (1973). *The Interpretations of Cultures*. Basic Books.

Geertz, C. (1995). *After the Fact: Two Countries, Four Decades, One Anthropologist*. Harvard University Press.

Geertz, C. (1999). *Mondo globale, mondi locali. Cultura e politica alla fine del ventesimo secolo*. Il Mulino.

Giddens, A. (1990). *The Consequences of Modernity*. Stanford University Press.

Gledhill, J. (2009). Power in Political Anthropology. *The Journal of Power, 2*(1), 9–33.

Gomberg-Muñoz, R. (2013). 2012 Public Anthropology Year in Review: Actually, Rick, Florida Could Use a Few More Anthropologists. *American Anthropologist, 115*(2), 286–296.

Gupta, A. (1995). Blurred Boundaries: The Discourse of Corruption, the Culture of Politics, and the Imagined State. *American Ethnologist, 22*(2), 375–402.

12 FROM HEGEMONY TO FRAGMENTATION: NORTH AMERICAN CULTURAL... 379

Gupta, A. (2005). Narrating the State of Corruption. In D. Shore & C. Haller (Eds.), *Corruption. Anthropological Perspectives* (pp. 211–242). Pluto Press.

Gupta, A., & Ferguson, J. (Eds.). (1997). *Culture, Power, Place: Explorations in Critical Anthropology.* Duke University Press.

Hale, C. (2006). Activist Research v. Cultural Critique: Indigenous Land Rights and the Contradictions of Politically Engaged Anthropology. *Cultural Anthropology, 21*(1), 96–120.

Hamilton, J., & Placas, A. (2011). Anthropology Becoming ...? The 2010 Sociocultural Anthropology Year in Review. *American Anthropologist, 113*(2), 246–261.

Handler, R. (1988). *Nationalism and the Politics of Culture in Quebec.* University of Wisconsin Press.

Harvey, D. (1989). *The Condition of Postmodernity. An Enquiry into the Origins of Cultural Change.* Sage.

Herzfeld, M. (1982). *Ours Once More: Folklore, Ideology and the Making of Modern Greece.* University of Texas Press.

Herzfeld, M. (1985). *The Poetics of Manhood: Contest and Identity in a Cretan Mountain Village.* Princeton University Press.

Herzfeld, M. (1987). *Anthropology Through the Looking Glass: Critical Ethnography in the Margins of Europe.* Cambridge University Press.

Herzfeld, M. (1991). *A Place in History: Social and Monumental Time in a Cretan Town.* Princeton University Press.

Herzfeld, M. (1992). *The Social Production of Indifference. Exploring the Symbolic Roots of Western Bureaucracy.* Chicago University Press.

Herzfeld, M. (1997). *Cultural Intimacy. Social Poetics in the Nation-State.* Routledge.

Herzfeld, M. (2005). Political Optics and the Occlusion of Intimate Knowledge. *American Anthropologist, 107*(3), 369–376.

Herzfeld, M. (2009). *Evicted from Eternity. The Restructuring of Modern Rome.* The University of Chicago Press.

Herzfeld, M. (2018). Anthropological Realism in a Scientistic Age. *Anthropological Theory, 18*(1), 129–150.

Hilgers, M. (2012). The Historicity of the Neoliberal State. *Social Anthropology, 20*(1), 80–94.

Hirsch, E. (2010). Property and Persons: New Forms and Contests in the Era of Neoliberalism. *Annual Review of Anthropology, 39*, 347–360.

Hirschfeld, L. (1996). *Race in the Making. Cognition, Culture, and the Child's Construction of Humankinds.* MIT Press.

Hobsbawm, E. (1965). *Primitive Rebels: Studies in Archaic Forms of Social Movement in the 19th Century.* Norton Library.

Holmes, D. (2000). *Integral Europe. Fast Capitalism, Multiculturalism, Neofascism.* Princeton University Press.

Holmes, D. R., & Marcus, G. E. (2005). Cultures of Expertise and the Management of Globalisation: Towards a Re-functioning of Ethnography. In A. Ong & S. Collier (Eds.), *Global Assemblages: Technology, Politics and Ethics as Anthropological Problems* (pp. 235–252). Blackwell.

Holmes, D. R., & Marcus, G. E. (2006). Fast-capitalism: Para-ethnography and the Rise of the Symbolic Analyst. In M. Fisher & G. Downey (Eds.), *Frontiers of Capital: Ethnographic Perspectives on the New Economy* (pp. 34–57). Duke University Press.

Hymes, D. (Ed.). (1972). *Reinventing Anthropology.* Pantheon Books. (First ed. 1969).

Jobson, R. (2019). The Case for Letting Anthropology Burn: Sociocultural Anthropology in 2019. *American Anthropologist, 122*(1), 1–13.

Kapferer, B. (1988). The Anthropologist as Hero. Three Exponents of Post-Modern Anthropology. *Critique of Anthropology, VIII*(2), 77–104.

Kaplan, M., & Kelly, J. (1994). Retinking Resistance. Dialogics of 'Disaffection' in Colonial Fiji. *American Ethnologist, 21*(1), 123–135.

Keesing, R. (1974). Theories of Culture. *Annual Review of Anthropology, 3,* 73–97.

Keesing, R. (1983). Exotic Readings of Cultural Texts. *Current Anthropology, 30*(4), 459–479.

Keesing, R. (1987). Anthropology as Interpretative Quest. *Current Anthropology, 28*(2), 161–176.

Kerney, M. (1995). The Local and the Global: The Anthropology of Globalization and Transnationalism. *Annual Review of Anthropology, 24,* 547–565.

Kertzer, D. (1988). *Ritual, Politics, and Power.* Yale University Press.

Lambek, M. (1998). The Sakalava Poiesis of History: Realizing the Past Through Spirit Possession in Madagascar. *American Ethnologist, 25*(2), 106–127.

Lambek, M. (2002). *The Weight of the Past: Living with History in Mahajanga, Madagascar.* Palgrave.

Lock, M. (1993). Cultivating the Body: Anthropologies and Epistemologies of Bodily Practice and Knowledge. *Annual Review of Anthropology, 22,* 133–155.

Lombardi Satriani, L. (1966). *Il folklore come cultura di contestazione.* Peloritana edizioni.

Lomnitz, C. (2008). Narrating the Neoliberal Moment: History, Journalism, Historicity. *Public Culture, 20*(1), 39–56.

Lutz, C., & Abu Lughod, L. (Eds.). (1990). *Language and the Politics of Emotions.* Cambridge University Press.

Mahmood, S. (2005). *Politics of Piety: The Islamic Revival and the Feminist Subject.* Princeton University Press.

Marcus, G. (1986). Contemporary Problems of Ethnography in The Modern World System. In J. Clifford & G. Marcus (Eds.), *Writing Culture. The Poetics and Politics of Ethnography* (pp. 165–193). University of California Press.

Marcus, G. (1989). Imagining the Whole. *Critique of Anthropology, IX*(3), 7–30.

12 FROM HEGEMONY TO FRAGMENTATION: NORTH AMERICAN CULTURAL... 381

Marcus, G. (1995). Ethnography in/of the World System: The Emergence of Multi-Sited Ethnography. *Annual Review of Anthropology, 24*, 95–117.

Marcus, G. (1997). The Uses of Complicity in the Changing Mise-en-Scène of Anthropological Fieldwork. *Representations, 59*, 85–108.

Marcus, G. (1998). *Ethnography Through Thick and Thin*. Princeton.

Marcus, G. (2007). Ethnography Two Decades after Writing Culture: From the Experimental to the Baroque. *Anthropological Quarterly, 80*(5), 1127–1145.

Marcus, G. (2008). The End(s) of Ethnography: Social/Cultural Anthropology's Signature Form of Producing Knowledge in Transition. *Cultural Anthropology, 23*(1), 1–14.

Marcus, G. (2012). The Legacies of Writing Culture and the Near Future of the Ethnographic Form: A Sketch. *Cultural Anthropology, 27*(3), 427–445.

Marcus, G., & Cushman, D. (1982). Ethnographies as Texts. *Annual Review of Anthropology, 11*, 25–70.

Marcus, G., & Fisher, M. (1986). *Anthropology as Cultural Critique: An Experimental Moment in the Human Sciences*. University of Chicago Press.

Mathews, A. (2020). Anthropology and the Anthropocene: Criticisms, Experiments, and Collaborations. *Annual Review of Anthropology, 49*, 67–82.

Mattingly, C., & Throop, J. (2018). The Anthropology of Ethics and Morality. *Annual Review of Anthropology, 47*, 475–492.

Mintz, S. (1974). *Caribbean Transformations*. Aldine Press.

Mintz, S., & Wolf, E. (1989). Replay to Michael Taussig. *Critique of Anthropology, IX*(1), 25–31.

Moore, F. (1987). Explaining the Present: Theoretical Dilemmas in Processual Ethnography. *American Ethnologist, 14*(4), 727–736.

Muehlebach, A. (2013). On Precariousness and the Ethical Imagination: The Year 2012 in Sociocultural Anthropology. *American Anthropologist, 115*(2), 297–311.

Mullins, P. (2011). Practicing Anthropology and the Politics of Engagement: 2010 Year in Review. *American Anthropologist, 113*(2), 235–245.

Munn, N. (1992). The Cultural Anthropology of Time: A Critical Essay. *Annual Review of Anthropology, 21*, 93–123.

Nancel, L., & Pels, P. (1989). Critique Reflexivity in Anthropology. A Report on the Bob Sholte. Memorial Conference, Held in Amsterdam December 1988. *Critique of Anthropology, 9*(3), 81–85.

Nash, J. (1979). *We Eat the Mines and the Mines Eat Us: Dependency and Exploitation in Bolivian Tin Mines*. Columbia University Press.

Ohnuki-Tierney, E. (Ed.). (1990). *Culture Through Time. Anthropological Approaches*. Stanford University Press.

Ong, A. (1987). *Spirits of Resistance and Capitalist Discipline: Factory Women in Malaysia*. State University of New York Press.

Ong, A. (2003). *Budda Is Hiding: Refugees, Citizenship, the New America*. University of California Press.

382   B. PALUMBO

Ong, A. (2006). *Neoliberalism as Exception: Mutations in Citizenship and Sovereignty*. Duke University Press.

Ortner, S. (1984). Theory in Anthropology Since the Sixties. *Comparative Studies in Society and History, 26*(1), 126–166.

Ortner, S. (1995). Resistance and the Problem of Ethnographic Refusal. *Comparative Studies in Society and History, 37*(1), 173–193.

Ortner, S. (2005). Subjectivity and Cultural Critique. *Anthropological Theory, 5*(1), 31–52.

Ortner, S. (2006). *Anthropology and Social Theory: Culture, Power, and the Acting Subject*. Duke University Press.

Ortner, S. (2016). Dark Anthropology and Its Others: Theory Since the Eighties. *Hau: Journal of Ethnographic Theory, 6*(1), 47–63.

Ortner, S., & Whitehead, H. (Eds.). (1981). *Sexual Meanings. The Cultural Construction of Gender and Sexuality*. Cambridge University Press.

Owen Hughes, T., & Trautmann, T. (Eds.). (1995). *Time. Histories and Ethnologies*. University of Michigan Press.

Palumbo, B. (1992). Immagini del mondo. Etnografia, storia e potere nell'antropologia statunitense contemporanea. *Meridian, 15*, 109–140.

Palumbo, B. (2018). *Lo strabismo della DEA. Antropologia, accademia e società in Italia*. Ed. Museo Pasqualino.

Patterson, T. (2001). *A Social History of Anthropology in the United States*. Berg.

Pinelli, B. (2019). *Migranti e rifugiate. Antropologia, genere e politica*. Raffaello Cortina.

Pizza, G. (1998). Introduzione. In Pizza, G. (ed.), Figure della corporeità in Europa. *Etnosistemi, V*(5), 2–8.

Povinelli, E. (2016). *Geontologies. A Requiem to Late Liberalism*. Duke University Press.

Rabinow, P. (1986). Representations Are Social Facts: Modernity and Post-Modernity. In J. Clifford & G. Marcus (Eds.), *Writing Culture* (pp. 234–262). University of California Press.

Rabinow, P. (1989). *French Modern. Norms and Forms of the Social Environment*. MIT Press.

Richland, J. (2009). On Neoliberalism and Other Social Diseases: The 2008 Sociocultural Anthropology Year in Review. *American Anthropologist, 111*(2), 170–176.

Robbins, J. (2015). On Happiness, Values, and Time. The Long and the Short of It. *Hau: Journal of Ethnographic Theory, 5*(3), 215–233.

Rosaldo, M. (1984). Toward an Anthropology of Self and Feeling. In R. A. Shweder & R. A. La Vine (Eds.), *Culture Theory. Essays on Mind, Self, and Emotion* (pp. 147–157). Cambridge University Press.

Roseberry, W. (1988). Political Economy. *Annual Review of Anthropology, 17*, 161–185.

Roth, P. A. (1989). Ethnography Without Tears. *Current Anthropology*, 30(5), 555–569.

Sahlins, M. (1976). *Culture and Practical Reasons.* The University of Chicago Press.

Sahlins, M. (1981). *Historical Metaphors and Mythical Realities: Structure in the Early History of the Sandwick Islands Kingdom.* The University of Michigan Press.

Sahlins, M. (1985). *Islands of History.* The University of Chicago Press.

Sahlins, M. (1988). No History is an Island. *Critique of Anthropology*, VIII(3), 41–51.

Sahlins, M. (1999a). Two or Three Things that I Know About Culture. *Journal of the Royal Anthropological Institute*, 5(3), 399–421.

Sahlins, M. (1999b). What is Anthropological Enlightenment? Some Lessons of the Twentieth Century. *Annual Review of Anthropology*, 28, I–XXIII.

Sahlins, M. (2002). *Waiting for Foucault, Still.* Prickly Paradigm Press.

Saitta, P. (2015). *Resistenze. Pratiche e margini del conflitto quotidiano.* Ombrecorte.

Sangreen, S. (1988). Rhetoric and the Authority of Ethnography. *Current Anthropology*, 3(29), 405–436.

Sanjek, R. (1990). *Fieldnotes. The Making of Anthropology.* Cornell University Press.

Sanjek, R. (1991). The Ethnographic Present. *Man n.s.*, 26(4), 609–628.

Sassen, S. (1991). *The Global City: New York, London, Tokio.* Princeton University Press.

Scheper-Hughes, N. (1993). *Death Without Weeping. The Violence of Everyday Life in Brazil.* University of California Press.

Scheper-Hughes, N. (1994). Embodied Knowledge: Thinking with the Body in Critical Medical Anthropology. In R. Borofsky (Ed.), *Assessing Cultural Anthropology* (pp. 229–242). McGraw-Hill.

Schneider, J., & Schneider, P. (1976). *Culture and Political Economy in Western Sicily.* Academic Press.

Scott, J. (1985). *Weapons of the Weak: Everyday Forms of Resistance.* Yale University Press.

Scott, J. (1986). Everyday Forms of Peasant Resistance. *The Journal of Peasant Studies*, 13(2), 5–35.

Scott, J. (1990). *Domination and the Arts of Resistance: Hidden Transcripts.* Yale University Press.

Scott, J. (1998). *Seeing Like a State: How Certain Schemes to Improve the Human Condition Have Failed.* Yale University Press.

Sholte, B. (1987). The Literary Turn in Contemporary Anthropology. *Critique of Anthropology*, VII(1), 33–47.

Shryoch, A. (1997). *Nationalism and the Genealogical Imagination. Oral History and Textual Authority in Tribal Jordan.* University of California Press.

Silverman, S. (2005). The United States. In F. Barth et al. (Eds.), *One Discipline, Four Ways: British, German, French, and American Anthropology* (pp. 255–347). University of Chicago Press.

384   B. PALUMBO

Spencer, J. (1989). Anthropology as a Kind of Writing. *Man n.s., 24*(1), 145–164.

Stolcke, V. (1995). Talking Culture, New Rhetorics of Exclusion in Europe. *Current Anthropology, 36*(1), 1–24.

Strathern, M. (1988). *The Gender of the Gift: Problems with Women and Problems with Society in Melanesia.* University of California Press.

Taussig, M. (1980). *The Devil and Commodity Fetishism in South America.* University of North Carolina Press.

Taussig, M. (1984). History as Sorcery. *Representations, 7,* 87–109.

Taussig, M. (1987a). *Shamanism, Colonialism, and the Wild Man: A Study in Terror and Healing.* The University of Chicago Press.

Taussig, M. (1987b). The Rise and Fall of Marxist Anthropology. *Social Analysis: The International Journal of Social and Cultural Practice, 21,* 101–113.

Taussig, M. (1989). History as Commodity in Some Recent American (Anthropological) Literature. *Critique of Anthropology, IX*(1), 7–23.

Taussig, M. (1993). *Mimesis and Alterity. A Particular History of the Senses.* Routledge.

Taussig, M. (1997). *The Magic of the State.* Routledge.

Taussig, M. (2012). Excelente Zona Social. *Cultural Anthropology, 27*(3), 498–517.

Thompson, E. P. (1963). *The Making of the English Working Class.* Victor Gollancz.

Throop, J. (2015). Ambivalent Happiness and Virtuous Suffering. *Hau: Journal of Ethnographic Theory, 5*(3), 45–68.

Trautmann, T. (1992). The Revolution in Ethnological Time. *Man n.s., 27*(2), 379–397.

Tsing, A. (2000). The Global Situation. *Cultural Anthropology, 15*(3), 327–360.

Tsing, A. (2004). *Friction: An Ethnography of Global Connection.* Princeton University Press.

Tyler, S. (1987). Still Rayting. Response to Sholte. *Critique of Anthropology, VII*(1), 49–51.

Ulin, R. (1991). Critical Anthropology Twenty Years Later: Modernism and Postmodernism in Anthropology. *Critique of Anthropology, 11*(1), 63–89.

Urla, J., & Helepololei, J. (2014). The Ethnography of Resistance Then and Now: On Thickness and Activist Engagement in the Twenty-First Century. *History and Anthropology, 25*(4), 431–451.

Wacquant, L. (2012). Three Steps to a Historical Anthropology of Actually Existing Neoliberalism. *Social Anthropology, 20*(1), 66–79.

Wallerstein, I. (1978). *The Modern World-System, Vol. I: Capitalist Agriculture and the Origins of the European World-Economy in the Sixteenth Century.* Academic Press.

Wallerstein, I. (1980). *The Modern World-System, Vol. II: Mercantilism and the Consolidation of the European World-Economy, 1600–1750.* Academic Press.

Weiner, F. J. (1992). Anthropology contra Heidegger. Part 1: Anthropology's Nihilism. *Critique of Anthropology, 12*(1), 75–90.

12 FROM HEGEMONY TO FRAGMENTATION: NORTH AMERICAN CULTURAL... 385

Whitten, N. E. (1988). Toward a Critical Anthropology. *American Ethnologist, 15*(4), 732–742.

Wolf, E. (1969). *Peasant Wars of the Twentieth Century*. Harper and Row.

Wolf, E. (1972). American Anthropologists and American Society. In D. Hymes (Ed.), *Reinventing Anthropology* (pp. 99–115). Pantheon Books.

Wolf, E. (1982). *Europe and the People Without History*. University of California Press.

Wolf, E. (1988). Inventing Society. *American Ethnologist, 15*(4), 725–761.

Wolf, E. (1990). Distinguished Lecture: Facing Power—Old Insights, New Questions. *American Anthropologist, 92*(3), 586–596.

Wolf, E. (1999). *Envisioning Power Ideologies of Dominance and Crisis*. University of California Press.

Wolf, E. (2001). *Pathways of Power: Building an Anthropology of the Modern World*. University of California Press.

Wright, S. (1998). The Politicization of 'Culture'. *Anthropology Today, 14*(1), 7–15.

Xavier Inda, J., & Rosaldo, R. (2001). Introduction: A World in Motion. In J. Xavier Inda & R. Rosaldo (Eds.), *The Anthropology of Globalization: A Reader* (pp. 1–34). Blackwell.

CHAPTER 13

Trajectories and Subjects of Brazilian Anthropology

Valeria Ribeiro Corossacz

The Past up in Smoke

On 2 September 2018, a fire destroyed Rio de Janeiro's Museu Nacional, a natural history, ethnology and anthropology museum associated with the Universidade Federal do Rio de Janeiro (UFRJ). Founded in 1818 and considered the oldest scientific institution in the country, the Museu hosted the first hub of development for anthropological studies in Brazil. It is also the seat of a prestigious programme founded in 1968 and funded in part by the Ford Foundation, the Programa de Pós Graduação em Ciências Sociais (PPGAS) at UFRJ. During the years of military dictatorship (1964–1985), this programme generated research foci in indigenist, rural and urban anthropology central to the discipline. The Museu was located inside the Palácio de São Cristóvão, the former residence of the

---

I would like to thank Patricia Pinho for her invaluable comments on an early draft of this chapter.

V. R. Corossacz (✉)
University Roma Tre, Rome, Italy
e-mail: valeria.ribeirocorossacz@uniroma3.it

© The Author(s), under exclusive license to Springer Nature Switzerland AG 2023
G. D'Agostino, V. Matera (eds.), *Histories of Anthropology*,
https://doi.org/10.1007/978-3-031-21258-1_13

387

Portuguese royal family and later the Brazilian imperial family, and showcased the intertwining of anthropology and European colonial history as well as the colonisation of lands, communities and ecosystems in this region of Abya Yala.

The destruction of the Museu Nacional is a sad yet significant starting point for examining the history of the discipline and, at the same time, grasping some of the elements that mark its more recent developments. Indeed, the fire and consequent loss of ethnological collections whose value to humanity cannot be measured, along with the volumes, letters and archives of the Francisca Keller Library of Cultural Anthropology, reflect the recent climate of institutional neglect in Brazil. A state of neglect so marked at times that it would seem to express outright hostility towards knowledge, particularly anthropology (Cabral de Oliveira & Marini, 2020) because of the discipline's commitment to studying and defending Brazil's most historically oppressed populations. Like a cloud of ominous omens, the fire foreshadowed the effects that Jair Bolsonaro's election as President of the Republic a few months later ended up having on both the worlds studied by anthropology and the academic life of the discipline.

The work carried out at PPGAS at UFRJ has encompassed the main research foci and themes of Brazilian anthropology based on field research covering the country's vast territory. This research has investigated exploitative relations in rural areas, *quilombos* (communities of escaped slaves and their descendants), transformations among indigenous peoples, their languages and ontologies, the role of racism in forming the nation, the whitening policies aimed at purging the country of black people, and Afro-Brazilian culture, to name but a few areas. These research activities documented the various forms of oppression and resistance enacted during the dictatorship period and forged a disciplinary commitment to social engagement and militancy that went on to characterise Brazilian anthropology even after the transition to democracy. Finally, Marshall Sahlins' gesture of bequeathing his books to the Museu after his death in 2021 so as to rebuild the library lost in the fire testifies to the close links between Brazilian anthropology and various scientific communities in other countries and simultaneously speaks to hopes for reconstruction and the vitality of the anthropological community as it engages directly with the nation's transformations.

DELVING INTO THE ORIGINS OF ANTHROPOLOGY

A number of *museus nacionais* sprang up in Brazil's main cities (Rio de Janeiro, São Paulo, Salvador da Bahia and Recife) at the end of the nineteenth century. Founded even before the country's universities, these institutions had the mission of fostering the production of knowledge considered scientific around issues at once biological and ethnographic. The theoretical approach of most of the research carried out in these institutions was strongly influenced by the current of social Darwinism developed in Europe and the deterministic tendency to posit biology as the cause of social, cultural and economic conditions, especially in the field of racial studies (Schwartz, 1993). Indeed, the paradigm of biological determinism provided a framework that, using language perceived as scientific, could be used to legitimise the hierarchical structure of Brazilian society despite its differences from European society. The initial development of the field we now call cultural anthropology was linked to these institutions and, in particular, the work of racially classifying the different communities residing in Brazil. Researchers considered their research to be a scientific contribution to the effort of forging a nation perceived at the time as ailing and often racially degenerate, that is, not sufficiently white. A second stage in the growth of anthropological studies took place in the country's Faculties of Medicine in the first decades of the twentieth century. Edgar Roquette-Pinto, Arthur Ramos, Thales de Azevedo and René Ribeiro—well-known figures in Brazilian anthropology—were educated in these departments (Laraia, 2014). Given this disciplinary genealogy, Corrêa has argued that the first Brazilian anthropologist was the forensic coroner Raymundo Nina Rodrigues (1862–1906) whose work provided a hub for the formation of the "Nina Rodrigues school," bringing together illustrious anthropologists specialised in the study of Afro-Brazilian cultures and religions (Corrêa, 1998). Nina Rodrigues investigated the origins of the slaves brought from Africa to Bahia, the Afro-Brazilian cultures found in the country's north-east and the physical characteristics of criminals and Afro-descendant Brazilians. He claimed that only legal experts had the competency and standing "to evaluate in each individual the consequences of racial crossbreeding" (Corrêa, 1998, p. 175), that is, the consequences of subverting social categorisations. As this statement clearly illustrates, biological determinism was the paradigm of reference in these first studies on topics considered to be anthropological. It is worth noting, in fact, that research on *negros* (the direct descendants of enslaved Africans) and Afro-Brazilian cultures—both considered to be a "problem" for the country—represents one of the legendary and foundational branches of the discipline (Corrêa, 2013). The proximity between medicine and anthropology (seen in the *continuum* between physical and cultural anthropology) stems precisely from the interest that physicians from that period had in the habits of everyday life. As Corrêa notes: "It is no coincidence that case studies, genealogical research and the comparative method were common procedures in the scientific work of physicians before becoming a methodology used by the social sciences" (1998, p. 93). The approach we now call "ethnographic," based on the direct observation of shared, recurring acts, collective memories and ritual practices, thus represents a sort of original trunk from which anthropology went on to branch out, gradually abandoning explanations based on biological nature as a causal factor to instead explain the world through the prism of culture.

ANTHROPOLOGY IN AND OF BRAZIL[1]

It was not until the 1920s and '30s that real anthropological knowledge began to take shape, not yet completely distinct from sociology and clearly influenced by the ideas being formulated in Europe and the United States. The commonly used term at the time was instead ethnology, as the first tradition of studies to develop was indigenist ethnology followed by what Cardoso de Oliveira termed the anthropology of national society (1986). The field of anthropological studies was not yet institutionalised in this phase, although several anthropologists were already engaging in field research. These two faces of the discipline were led by two "mythical" figures: Curt Nimuendajú (1883–1945) and Gilberto Freyre (1900–1987). The first, who had come to Brazil from Germany, focused his studies on the native populations and especially the Guaraní. He lived with them for extended periods of time, taking an approach that might today be defined as advocacy and an effort to protect their rights (Corrêa, 2013).[2] The second, trained in the Boas school, studied the colonial and slave-owning structures of Brazilian society, valorising its African and indigenous-origin populations in a narrative aimed at normalising the subordinate position of the country's natives and descendants of African slaves by asserting the

[1] This expression is borrowed from Peirano, 2000.
[2] The Nimuendajú Curt archives were destroyed in the 2018 fire.

positive value of *mestiçagem*.[3] As Corrêa argues, "the anthropological tradition in Brazil was born out of this intersection between natives who were interested in studying 'foreigners' (the 'Negro settlers', as they were called by the physician Nina Rodrigues), and foreigners who were interested in natives" (1988, p. 80). This was a dynamic time marked by the intense interweaving of links with foreign countries in which France was progressively replaced by the United States.[4]

A famous photo from 1939, taken in the Jardim da Princesa of the Museu Nacional in Rio and featuring Claude Lévi-Strauss, Ruth Landes, Charles Wagley, Heloísa Alberto Torres, Luís Castro Faria, Raimundo Lopes and Edson Carneiro, testifies to the vibrancy of Brazilian anthropological studies. Torres was the director of the Museu Nacional from 1938 to 1955, the first woman to teach anthropology at this institution and a member of the group that founded the Associação Brasileira de Antropologia (ABA) in 1955. She conducted fieldwork among indigenous people, the most notable being carried out in 1930 on the island of Marajó (Pará) at a time when anthropology was such an exclusively male universe that Cardoso de Oliveira, referring specifically to her fieldwork, recalls how highly unexpected it was at the time to encounter a woman anthropologist (1986, p. 231). It was thanks to Torres' work of encouraging visiting researcher exchanges that the photo includes Landes and Wagley. Recommended to her by Boas, these scholars went on to become central figures in the history of Brazilian anthropology.[5] Together with Lévi-Strauss, who at the time was coming to the end of his stay in Brazil and preparing to move to the United States, these foreigners illustrate the importance of international ties in defining the national character of the

[3] For a more detailed discussion of Freyre, please refer to Pallares-Burke, 2005, and Ribeiro Corossacz, 2005.

[4] The United States also went on to become a reference point for much research on racism—see Oracy Nogueira's famous essay *Preconceito racial de marca e preconceito racial de origem* (1954), thus becoming "our privileged, almost *civilizing* Other" (Peirano, 2000, p. 227).

[5] Unlike Wagley, Landes had a very rocky academic trajectory. Fiercely attacked by Ramos and Herskovits to discredit her scientifically ("Their calumnies were symbolic rape on me," in Corrêa, 1995), she remained outside the university for quite some time (Cole, 1995). Landes was anomalous as a field anthropologist in Brazil in that period in that she worked "alone," that is, without having ventured into the field as the "wife of" someone (Corrêa, 2000). Her nationality and whiteness were resignified by her gender and independence.

discipline.[6] Finally, Carneiro's presence in the photo points to an absence, namely the lack of Afro-Brazilians; having represented a privileged research object during the development of the discipline, for a long time Afro-Brazilian scholars were not recognised as legitimate producers of anthropological knowledge.[7] As Corrêa notes, Carneiro never held a university position despite his seminal anthropological work precisely because of "his political battle for the rights of blacks and African-descended religious associations in Salvador" (2013, p. 6). Torres and Carneiro are exceptions that offer us a window into a discipline, composed of white men, that was progressively gaining ground. This homogenous racial makeup reflected the larger structure of Brazilian society and was long considered insignificant for understanding the social conditions behind the discipline's production of scientific knowledge.[8] The first university professorships in social and cultural anthropology were established in this phase and it was already clear that field activity was central to distinguishing Brazilian anthropology from other social sciences, with empirical research representing the basis for the discipline's theoretical analysis. The 1939 photo should not lead us to think that Rio de Janeiro was the sole centre of development for the discipline, however. On the contrary, anthropological knowledge in those years was developing in other regions as well, sometimes around museum institutions or particularly active figures or movements such as the movement for the defence of folklore launched in the city of Natal by Câmara Cascudo. The Afro-Brasileiros Congresses, held in Recife and Salvador between 1934 and 1937, are another example of this activity. Organised by Freyre and Carneiro, respectively, they brought together researchers from different disciplines and scholars interested in the cultural and religious expressions of the black population. The conferences were also attended by exponents of Afro-Brazilian religious communities that were suffering persecution on the part of state authorities.

[6] In addition to Lévi-Strauss, other foreign anthropologists also taught in Brazil in the 1930s and 1940s. They included the less-well-known Dina Dreyfus (Lévi-Strauss' wife), who also conducted fieldwork, and Radcliffe-Brown (Cardoso de Oliveira, 1986). Roger Bastide taught at the University of São Paulo from 1938 to 1955.

[7] Carneiro was an indispensable companion in Landes' research in Salvador, as she explained (1970).

[8] Torres' unusual institutional trajectory is partly related to the fact that she was the daughter of a very important scholar of the time, Alberto Torres, and was viewed as a kind of mother figure by the young researchers of the Museu (Corrêa, 1995).

The period between the 1950s and '70s is remembered as a time of disciplinary consolidation and institutionalisation. Anthropology gained institutional ground in the late '60s with the establishment of postgraduate study programmes that provided professional, systematic training for entire generations of anthropologists. According to Peirano, at this stage anthropology considered itself a "genuine social science" (2000). Several authors have noted that public funding, as well as grants from foreign foundations—primarily based in the United States—have contributed substantially to growing Brazilian anthropology since the 1930s, allowing young anthropologists to access grants to carry out their studies and field investigations and to consolidate research lines and foci (Laraia, 2014; Corrêa, 2013). A noteworthy example is the UNESCO project (1951–1952) engaging foreign and Brazilian scholars in collaborative work: it was created with the aim of studying Brazil, a country envisioned at the time as free of racism and thus a helpful case to understand in order to build a new West based on "harmony between races."[9] Several important volumes were published in the 1950s regarding what was defined at the time as "racial prejudice": *Brancos e Negros em São Paulo* (1955) by Bastide and Fernandes, *O Negro no Rio de Janeiro* (1953) by Costa Pinto, and *As Elites de Cor, um estudo de ascenção social* (1955) by Thales de Azevedo. At this point we can perceive a specific feature of Brazilian anthropology, namely the fact that it established itself as a community of scholars conducting field research in their own country, "among us" (Cardoso de Oliveira, 1986, p. 236; Peirano 2000), as part of a renewed drive to analyse and understand the nation. Another element that stemmed in part from this internal focus was the production of essays written in Portuguese that engaged with the writings of foreign authors. On one hand, this tendency led to forced "internal interlocution" (Peirano, 2000); on the other hand, however, it made it possible for Brazilian scholars to dialogue with other Portuguese-speaking communities. Indeed, this intra-lusophone dialogue was later sought out and valorised in the 2000s as part of a new epistemological endeavour to cultivate south-south scientific relations.

---

[9] In reality, an awareness of the existence of racism in Brazil was circulating among Brazilian researchers, as attested to by the results of many UNESCO studies (see Maio, 1999).

OLD AND NEW LINES OF RESEARCH

As noted above, indigenous studies was one of the first research areas to be established and has remained central to the discipline over time. The study of indigenous communities was obliged to grapple with a rather intrusive state institutional apparatus: in 1910, the state had set up the Serviço de Proteção aos Índios (SPI)[10] in which the positivist military played a central role and whose policies were characterised by a guardianship regime (Pacheco de Oliveira, 1988). The SPI was later joined by the Conselho Nacional de Proteção ao Índio (1939) and then definitively replaced by the Fundação Nacional do Índio. Anthropologists working in this context were well aware of the importance of staking out a clear position, including by taking part in the SPI, in support of indigenous people and their struggles to defend their rights in the face of continuous land invasions, murders and forms of violence at times perpetuated in the name of "pacification, [and] civilization."[11] Darcy Ribeiro (1922–1997) was a key figure in such work, not only for his engagement in defending indigenous lands but also because he organised specialisation courses in indigenist ethnology, including a programme at the Museu do Índio in 1953. Laraia highlights the paradoxical fact that this period of disciplinary consolidation took place specifically in the 1970s, under the regime of the military dictatorship. Even as violence, torture and persecution intensified following the approval of Decree AI-5,[12] the 1968 Sucupira reform allowed universities to launch numerous post-graduate programmes. Thanks to this institutional consolidation, anthropologists were able to carve out valuable spaces for defending the communities they studied. On multiple occasions the ABA brandished its particular expertise to speak out in opposition to shameful governmental choices, including by taking a clear stand against the *Emancipação das Comunidades Indígenas* project (1978) that the state sought to use to avoid taking responsibility for protecting indigenous peoples (Laraia, 2014) and helping to scuttle it. At the same time, ABA also demanded that anthropologists be granted access to the indigenous lands from which state authorities had barred them. In this

---

[10] The SPI was closed in 1967 following major corruption scandals and human rights violations.

[11] The 1964 coup put an end to institutional collaboration.

[12] Enacted in 1968, this decree—considered the harshest law passed by the military regime—also resulted in the forced retirement of professors, such as anthropologist Florestan Fernandes, classified as militant activists.

period, burgeoning investigation into the rural world and political struggles of farmers (see the work of Moacir Palmeira and Lygia Sigaud, to name just two) was joined by other new lines of research and teaching; one such line was urban anthropology with its array of insights, including reflections on ethnography. Based on his ethnography of the lower-middle-class Copacabana apartment building where he lived, Velho considered the implications of studying a familiar sphere and noting that being familiar with something does not automatically entail knowing it (Velho, 1978). The topics he addressed in this area make for an extremely rich field: old age/youth, housing and forms of residence, family transformations, forms of deviance from the social norm, middle-class lifestyles, urban violence and drug trafficking. Also worth mentioning is the powerful influence of Roberto DaMatta's work: DaMatta forged new spaces and crossed borders (Velho 2011), particularly through his work on the national ethos, rituals and national myths.

Another field of studies also emerged during the years of the dictatorship: the "anthropology of women," later extended into "anthropology of gender," took shape in this period thanks to stimuli generated by the discipline's encounter with feminism (Heilborn, 1992; Corrêa, 2001). This field, extremely heterogeneous in terms of approaches and topics and animated in particular by women anthropologists, was distinguished from previous investigations into women's roles by the impact of and exchanges with feminist practice and theories as well as its dialogue with the homosexual movement.[13] Corrêa notes that several anthropological studies from as early as the 1970s deconstructed the polarised vision of male and female and denaturalised perceived differences between them. Many studies by female anthropologists were conducted in interdisciplinary research groups, a common feature of gender and feminist studies. Also during the 1970s, Brazilian anthropology not only continued to welcome a considerable number of foreign professors and researchers but also made its appearance on the international scene (Corrêa, 2013).

With the end of the dictatorship and process of democratic transition, the Assembléia Nacional Constituinte (1987–1988) was established involving all the country's social movements and indigenous communities as well as ABA. Through this involvement, the association has managed to maintain a continuous dialogue with social movements, contributing to

---

[13] The continuous availability of tailored funding has contributed to the development of this area of anthropological studies.

396   V. R. COROSSACZ

defending the interests of indigenous communities (Pacheco, 2006) and carrying forward the anthropological community's involvement in building a new vision of society and nation. This involvement has continued up to the present, for instance, with ABA's participation in the 2021 campaign against the *marco temporal* (Milestone Thesis[14]). On this occasion as well, Brazilian anthropologists supported indigenous peoples' claims that the right to land is a right to life (significantly, the encampment organised before the Supreme Court in August 2021 was named "Struggle for Life"). Anthropologists have always played a crucial role in the process of demarcating indigenous lands (and *quilombolas*; see Hoffman French, 2003), not only in the sense of implementing administrative procedures, but also and especially in the sense of using their disciplinary perspective, based on ethnographic methodology, to argue that the criterion to follow when recognising these peoples' right to land, and therefore to demarcation, is their specific forms of social reproduction and organisation[15].

FROM OBJECTS TO SUBJECTS OF ACADEMIC ANTHROPOLOGICAL THEORY

At the 2000 ABA meeting, only 15 out of 1500 attendees were black, a proportion that matched the national average of black faculty (1%) in Brazilian universities that year (Carvalho, 2005). Carvalho fittingly characterises Brazilian universities, and anthropology itself, as racially segregated and further notes that the topic of "race relations" has historically been dealt with by white anthropologists who did not consider their whiteness to be a relevant factor in formulating theories about racism or Brazilian society in general: these were seen as *simply* "anthropological discussions." The anthropologist also observes that no one engaged in theorising or ethnographic production since the 1950s had managed to enact a minimum of reflexivity or self-analysis regarding their own whiteness. Thanks to the introduction of quotas in public universities for public school students, and for students in this population defining themselves as

---

[14] This measure was designed to invalidate the land claims of indigenous groups who were not physically occupying their lands on the day the new constitution was signed in 1988. The measure has been defended by representatives of agrobusiness and large estate owners and supported by the Bolsonaro government. As of the end of 2021, the Supreme Court (Supremo Tribunal Federal) had still not ruled on this measure.

[15] See the ABA document at the following link: http://www.aba.abant.org.br/files/20201203_5fc963f23a347.pdf

black and indigenous,[16] the racial composition of the academic community is changing: in 2018, 51.2% of graduates were black (ABA, 2021). Furthermore, new universities were set up under the Partido dos Trabalhadores governments (2003–2016) in more peripheral parts of the country, which also fostered the study of anthropology. The inclusion of lower class, black and indigenous students gave rise to discussions about how to transform the production of anthropological knowledge, taking into account the way racism and coloniality, in intersection with other forms of oppression, structure academic spaces, teaching practices and curricula. However, the number of black professors remains limited (23.6% of the total faculty in 2019) and there is still a tendency to exclude or "overlook" the work of black researchers in bibliographical references, a form of isolation often resulting from these scholars' anti-racist political engagement and critique of white studies on racism (Figueiredo & Grosfoguel, 2007; see also Ratts, 2006).

These considerations help explain the long academic marginality of scholars such as Lélia Gonzalez (1935–1994), a feminist anthropologist and activist in the Movimento Negro Unificado whose work was not considered properly anthropological precisely because it broke with the discipline's traditional canons, first and foremost by virtue of her racial and gender positioning. Gonzalez was one of the first to address the imbrication of the social relations of gender and race in Brazilian culture and society (1983), prefiguring the approach that later became internationally known as "intersectionality" through the dissemination of African American feminist publications (see Lasa Forum, 2019). Her career offers a window into the processes through which non-white anthropologists, especially women, have been rendered invisible and/or marginalised, pointing to the urgent need to consider what kinds of scholars are legitimated to formulate anthropological theory (and which theories are granted value) in the academy and for what population of learners. This context of transformation in both the country's social structure and university student bodies is also the setting for Pacheco de Oliveira's insights into the consequences of Brazilian anthropology's having developed as a "peripheral" national tradition stemming from the importation of Eurocentric anthropological models treated as if they were universal, particularly regarding indigenous visibility and the need to decolonise

---

[16]The first laws were enacted at the individual state level in 2002, leading to the approval of the federal law no. 12.711 in 2012.

knowledge ethnographically, theoretically and epistemologically (2018). On one hand, therefore, the challenge is to recognise the implications of the fact that Brazilian anthropology has long studied an "other" who, unlike in European contexts, has been defined as an "internal other"; on the other hand, the task is to acknowledge the repercussions of a radical social change process in which the objects have become the subjects of anthropological knowledge production inside universities and thus unveiled the internal coloniality of Brazilian society and academia[17]. It is no longer a matter of studying "cultural differences," but rather of investigating the historical and social relations and epistemologies that have produced these "differences." Researchers studying indigenous communities have taken up this challenge by consulting community leaders on what fieldwork will involve and how the collected data will be used, a process in which researchers are pushed to consider the needs of these communities and thus abandon a position of "neutrality" (Pacheco de Oliveira, 2018). The same issues also concern Brazil's *quilombolas* populations and the way anthropological studies of them are used (Cavignac, 2020)[18].

Despite enormous difficulties due to federal funding cuts, attacks and persecution,[19] anthropologists in recent years have continued to produce research in new ways that take into account new links between those conducting the research and the communities and practices under investigation, deconstructing and overcoming this dualism. The ABA has continued to take a stand against forms of structural oppression such as racism through its document calling for the need to maintain and reinforce legally mandated quotas for black, indigenous and public school students. This text expresses support for a law defined as a "device for social inclusion"

---

[17] Indeed, there have always been black researchers and intellectuals both male and female, but they have faced resistance from hegemonic sectors of the Brazilian academy unwilling to recognise "the black subject—woman or man—as a producer of thought" (Ratts, 2006, p. 31).

[18] Beatriz Nascimento (1942–1995), a black professor, researcher, and activist, studied the concept of *quilombo* from a historic and anthropological perspective. Her work provides both an example of "forgetfulness," that is, the tendency for white academics to overlook research carried out by black women, and a goldmine for current investigations into *quilombos* (in English, see the special issue of the journal *Antipode*, 2021).

[19] Debora Diniz, a professor of Anthropology at the University of Brasilia, left Brazil in 2018 following death threats trigged by her research on reproductive rights and abortion rights in particular. See Ribeiro Corossacz and Lenzi Grillini, 2021, for a wider discussion of the socio-political context that led to Bolsonaro's election and its effects on research and academia.

and considered necessary for democratising academic institutions by recognising other forms of knowledge and implementing new kinds of teaching (ABA, 2021). Given the spread of Covid-19 in an already severely impoverished country and institutional management designed not to protect the country's population, especially its most vulnerable members, it is more important than ever to develop an anthropology embedded within networks of theoretical, affective and political relationships.[20] Such an approach to producing anthropological knowledge is not dissociated from the feelings and material conditions of the bodies producing it; rather, it is fed by a growing awareness of the dramatic effects of ultraliberal capitalism, especially on the lives of non-white, poor and non-straight people and, through climate and environmental changes, on the ecosystems and people of this land called Brazil.

REFERENCES

ABA. (2021). *Nota Técnica da Associação Brasileira de Antropologia sobre as ações afirmativas consignadas na Lei 12.711 de agosto de 2012*, http://www.portal.abant.org.br/2021/12/10/nota-tecnica-da-associacao-brasileira-de-antropologia-sobre-as-acoes-afirmativas-consignadas-na-lei-12-711-de-agosto-de-2012-e-atualizada-pela-lei-13-409-de-dezembro-de-2016/

Antipode. (2021). *"In Front of the World"*: *Translating Beatriz Nascimento*, 53, 1, https://antipodeonline.org/2021/01/21/translating-beatriz-nascimento/

Cabral de Oliveira, J., & Marini, M. (2020). Why Is the Bolsonaro Government Afraid of Anthropology? *Hot Spots Cultural Anthropology, Bolsonaro and the Unmaking of Brazil*, https://culanth.org/fieldsights/why-is-the-bolsonaro-government-afraid-of-anthropology

Cardoso de Oliveira, R. (1986). O que é isso que chamamos de Antropologia Brasileira? *Anuário Antropológico, 10*(1), 227–246.

Carvalho, J., J., de (2005–6). O confinamento racial no mundo acadêmico brasileiro. *Revista Usp, 68*, 88–103.

Cavignac, J. (2020). Threatened Rights and Resistance: For a Politically Engaged Anthropology. *Hot Spots Cultural Anthropology, Bolsonaro and the Unmaking of Brazil*, https://culanth.org/fieldsights/threatened-rights-and-resistance-for-a-politically-engaged-anthropology

Cole, S. (1995). Ruth Landes and the early ethnography of race and gender. In R. Behar & D. Gordon (Eds.), *Women Writing Culture* (pp. 166–185). University California Press.

---

[20] See, for example, the online LGBTI+ seminar *Desafios e cidadania em tempos de pandemia* organised by the ABA Gender and Sexuality Committee, held 30 June 2021.

400 V. R. COROSSACZ

Corrêa, M. (1988). Traficantes do exêntrico: os antropólogos no Brasil dos anos 30 aos anos 60. *RBCS, 3*, 79–98.

Corrêa, M. (1995). A natureza imaginária do gênero na história da antropologia. *cadernos pagu, 5*, 109–130.

Corrêa, M. (1998). *As Ilusões da Liberdade. A Escola de Nina Rodrigues e a Antropologia no Brasil.* Bragança Paulista: Instituto Franciscano de Antropologia, Universidade de São Francisco.

Corrêa, M. (2000). O mistério dos orixás e das bonecas: raça e gênero na antropologia brasileira. *Etnográfica, IV, 2*, 233–265.

Corrêa, M. (2001). Do feminismo aos estudos de gênero no Brasil: um exemplo pessoal. *cadernos pagu, 16*, 13–30.

Figueiredo, Â., & Grosfoguel, R. (2007). Por que não Guerreiro Ramos? Novos desafios a serem enfrentados pelas universidades públicas brasileiras. *Ciência e Cultura, 59*(2), 36–41.

Gonzalez, L. (1983). Racismo e sexismo na cultura brasileira. *Ciências Sociais Hoje, Anpocs, 2*, 223–244.

Heilborn, M. L. (1992). Fazendo gênero? A antropologia da mulher no Brasil. In A. C. de Oliveira & C. Bruschini (Eds.), *Uma questão de gênero* (pp. 93–126). Rosa dos Tempos/Fundação Carlos Chagas.

Hoffman French, J. (2003). Os quilombos e seus direitos hoje: entre a construção das identidades e a história. *Revista de História, 149*(2), 45–68.

Landes, R. (1986). A Woman Anthropologist in Brazil. In P. Golde (Ed.), *Women in the Field: Anthropological Experiences* (pp. 119–142). University California Press.

Laraia, R., de Barros. (2014). Os Primórdios da Antropologia Brasileira (1900-1979). *ACENO, 1*(1), 10–22.

Lasa Forum. (2019). *Dossier: El pensamiento de Lélia Gonzalez, un legado y un horizonte*, 50, 3, https://forum.lasaweb.org/past-issues/vol50-issue3.php

Maio, M. Chor. (1999). O projeto UNESCO e a agenda das ciências sociais no Brasil dos ano 40 e 50. *Revista Brasileira de Ciências Sociais, 14*(41), 142–157.

Pacheco de Oliveira, J. (1988). *O nosso governo: Os ticuna e o regime tutelar.* Editora Marco Zero.

Pacheco de Oliveira, J. (2006). Uma ABA indigenista? Notas para uma experiência singular do fazer antropológico. In C. Eckert & E. Pietrafesa de Godoi (Eds.), *Homenagens: Associação brasileira de antropologia: 50 anos* (pp. 71–78). ABA, Nova Letra.

Pacheco de Oliveira, J. (2018). Desafios contemporâneos para a antropologia no Brasil. Sinais de uma nova tradição etnográfica e de uma relação distinta com os seus "outros". *Revista Mundaú, 4*, 140–159.

Pallares-Burke, M. L. (2005). *Gilberto Freyre: um vitoriano dos trópicos.* Editora Unesp.

Peirano, M. (2000). A Antropologia como Ciência Social no Brasil. *Etnográfica, IV, 2,* 219–232.

Ratts, A. (2006). *Eu sou atlântica. Sobre a trajetória de vida de Beatriz Nascimento.* ImprensaOfical, Instituto Kuanza.

Ribeiro Corossacz, V. (2005). *Razzismo, meticciato, democrazia razziale. Le politiche della razza in Brasile.* Rubbettino.

Ribeiro Corossacz, V., & Lenzi Grillini, F. (2021). Conflitos e resistências no Brasil nos tempos do bolsonarismo. *Confluenze. Rivista di Studi Iberoamericani, 13*(1), 1–31.

Schwarcz Moritz, L. (1993). *O Espetáculo das Raças. Cientistas, instituições e questão racial no Brasil, 1870–1930.* Companhia das Letras.

Velho, G. (1978). Observando o familiar. In E. de Oliveira Nunes (Ed.), *A aventura sociológica* (pp. 1–13). Zahar.

Velho, G. (2011). Antropologia urbana: interdisciplinaridade e fronteiras do conhecimento. *Mana, 17*(1), 161–185.

CHAPTER 14

From the Study of Indigenous Cultures to the Critics of Modernity: On Anthropology *made in* Colombia

Alessandro Mancuso

INTRODUCTION

Not only is Colombia varied in terms of both its geography and population; it is also marked out by great conflicts and inequalities resulting from its colonial and post-colonial history.

Anthropological studies have closely intertwined with this complex history characterized by continuous tensions between the main projects and discourses on the construction of national identity, on the one hand, and, on the other, the structuration of social hierarchies based on the interplay between people's "race", ethnicity, gender and class (Arocha & de Friedemann, 1986; Correa, 2006; de Friedemann, 1987; Jimeno, 2005, 2007; Pérez, 2017). Especially in the key moments of the national development of the disciplinary field, Colombian anthropologists have

A. Mancuso (✉)
University of Palermo, Palermo, Italy
e-mail: alessandro.mancuso@unipa.it

© The Author(s), under exclusive license to Springer Nature
Switzerland AG 2023
G. D'Agostino, V. Matera (eds.), *Histories of Anthropology*,
https://doi.org/10.1007/978-3-031-21258-1_14

403

repeatedly brought to the fore the situation of violence, conflict and injustice in which they carried out their research and work.

In recent years, the historiography of Colombian anthropology (Restrepo et al., 2017; Rojas & Jaramillo, 2020; Tocancipá-Falla, 2016a) has firmly insisted on a distinction between anthropology *about* Colombia and anthropology *made in* Colombia. The latter can be defined as that "produced in the country, which constitutes an empirical, methodological, or conceptual contribution for new anthropological works or debates in Colombia. Forms of relationality (in methodological terms), production and appropriation are all essential facets of this definition" (Restrepo et al., 2017, p. 12).

Talking about anthropology "made in" Colombia therefore means underlining the importance of sharing the concern for the historical and current limits of full access to citizenship rights with the socio-politically oppressed subjects *with whom* the research is carried out without this involving the closing in a "nation-centric" perspective (Caviedes, 2007; Rojas & Jaramillo, 2020). If anything, through the reworking of distinctions between "empire-building" anthropologies and "national", "metropolitan" and "peripheral" anthropologies, including those belonging to the "northern" or, instead, to the "southern" globalised world system (Hannerz, 2011; Krotz, 1997; Ribeiro, 2014; Stocking, 2001; Uribe, 2005), in the light of an overall consideration of "world Anthropologies" (Restrepo, 2017), anthropology "*made in* Colombia" is to be seen as a special "node" within the global articulation of academic and non-academic networks in various "places" around the world (Restrepo et al., 2017). Nowadays, such an articulation can be noticed in the increasing relations with other national traditions from Latin American anthropology, in terms of research interests, debates, as well as collaborations and publications (i.e. Mejias, 2017).

The present study is based on the recognition of and considerations on the history of anthropology *made in* Colombia as suggested by Colombian scholars. Of course, these considerations have been filtered by a personal point of view as an "external" (even European) observer, not to mention all the limits and advantages of such a distance. However, my fieldwork and life experience in Colombia, although limited over time, has been crucial for my reading of this history. As I am writing a chapter especially intended for non-Colombians, I feel it is necessary to provide the reader with some basic information about the history of Colombia and put it first, before moving on to the history of anthropology made in Colombia.

HISTORICAL BACKGROUND

Colombia has a surface area of over a million square kilometres and a population of nearly fifty million people. According to the 2018 census, nearly two million declared themselves to be indigenous, while nearly three million claimed to be Afro-Colombian.

Colombia hosts a large variety of ecosystems which makes it the country with the second-highest biodiversity rate in the world (over 50,000 animal and plant species) in relation to its surface. Generally, the country is divided into six "macro-regions": Amazonía, Orinoquía, Andina, Pacífica, Caribe and the Insular region. These regions can only be partly identified on the basis of their "natural" features, especially resulting from historic events which eventually moulded their specific socioeconomic, ethnical and cultural features. If anything, it is necessary to point out, against any prospect of environmental determinism, how historical processes—especially those related to the construction of national identity—have played a crucial role in the shaping of the territory and its regionalisation (Arias, 2017; Serje, 2016; Silva, 1994).

In Colombia and all over America, the European conquest had a devastating impact on the lives of indigenous people from its very beginning (Arocha & de Friedemann, 1986).

When it comes to territory exploitation and the consolidation of political control over the populations, colonisation is to be considered as a centuries-long process that did not take place until the twentieth century in certain areas, such as the majority of the Amazon region and the Guajira peninsula.

The early consolidation of the Spanish domination in the first half of the sixteenth century was marked by the foundation of the urban centers of Santa Marta (1525), Cartagena de Indias (1533) and Santa Fé de Bogotá (1538), along with the implementation of a *Real Audiencia* in the latter city. Colombia was home to a multitude of distinct indigenous groups with different cultures, languages and social organisations, although many of them were connected to each other by trade linkages. Furthermore, these populations lacked political integration. However, some of them, like the Tairona from the Caribbean region, and especially the Muisca who inhabited the Andean Altiplano, were organised in loose confederations housing around 600,000 people (see Langebaek, 2019). By virtue of soil fertility and their agricultural methods, both the Muisca and the Tairona could benefit from remarkable food production and were also well known for their goldsmith's craft.

Other additional ethnonyms are also mentioned by fifteenth- and sixteenth-century historians, and some of them are associated to indigenous peoples (e.g. Guajiros/Wayuu, Katío/Emberá, Kuna/Tule, Chimila/Ette Eneka, Guahibo/Sikuani. Motilones/Barí and Yukpa; Tunebo/U'wa) currently living in Colombia.

Even after the early stages of the *Conquista*, the actual imposition of Spanish colonial rule mainly involved the Andean region and a large part of the Caribbean area. Colonisers believed that these regions could be easily occupied to exploit their agro-pastoral potential and move on to hunt for gold deposits and other precious metals. The indigenous peoples living in these areas were often dispossessed of their lands or forced to pay taxes through the *encomienda* system, as well as provide workforce for the non-indigenous landowners' *haciendas* or in mines during prearranged periods of the year (*mita* system) (Safford & Palacios, 2001). Additional means to keep control over the populations included their concentration (*reducción*) in nucleated settlements (*pueblos*, including *pueblos de indios*, where Spaniards would not officially be lodged with the exception of missionaries) or in reserves known as *resguardos*, where the indigenous communities often managed to keep their own autonomy (Herrera, 2002).

A significant reduction in the indigenous population size during the first century following the coming of the Conquistadores and a ban on indigenous slavery (which was often overturned) were the main factors that led to a flow of slaves from Africa in order to meet the need for necessary workforce to run colonial economy properly (McFarlane, 1993). Cartagena de Indias, on the Caribbean coast, became the main entrance port for slaves in Nueva Grenada (present-day Colombia) starting from the seventeenth century. As far as socio-political justification is concerned, the colonial elites put the accent on the "racial" purity of their European ancestry ("pure" Spanish descendants were named *criollos*) which co-existed with the development of reproductive unions between European, African and indigenous populations. This resulted in a difficult classification of "mixed-races" only partially associated with an invariable social hierarchy, except for the highest levels (such as officials of the Spanish empire, representatives of the catholic Church and *criollos*) and the lowest positions (slaves and "pure" indigenous) (Jaramillo Uribe, 1968).

Following the declaration of Independence from Spain (1819), Nueva Grenada changed its name to the Republic of Gran Colombia. In terms of national unity, divisions, hierarchies and regional conflicts, ethnic components and different social groups, the new state inherited the current situation towards the end of the colonial period (Helg, 2005). Rivalries among the colonial elite factions appeared with the secession of Venezuela and Ecuador (1830), later followed by Panama (1903), and there was a constant tension between the forces promoting the reinforcement of the Andean region as the major axis of the country's political and economic development, and those claiming a federalist model instead, as it was more responsive to the peculiarities of each region (Bushnell, 1993).

Before the promulgation of the 1991 Constitution, the Colombian ruling classes had held their official belief that building a nation and a sense of common belonging involved going through a biological and cultural blending of the three original components—European, indigenous, and African—of the new state. Actually, the elite policy was pushing towards a process of *blanqueamiento* of the whole population to meet the criteria of a European urban "civilization". At the same time, the elite looked to preserve the colonial hierarchies along with the privileged status of European bloodlines, thus discriminating the indigenous and African-descent populations, including the *mestizas*, especially when they resisted assimilation and refused subordination (Múnera, 2005). To this day, according to official statistics, Colombia has the most unequal distribution of household income and properties in the world.

Social inequality and political rivalries between "liberals" and "conservatives" as well as the persistent refusal of national elites to acknowledge dignity and legitimacy to any political agenda that could affect their privileged position have all led to recurrent violent clashes over the last two centuries (Bushnell, 1993; Safford & Palacios, 2001). Among these, the *Guerra de los Mil Días* (1899–1902), those following the massacre of striking banana workers from the United Fruit Company carried out by the army (1928–1930), and those from *La Violencia* period (1948–1957) which reportedly caused 175,000 deaths and approximately two million internally displaced people (nearly one-fifth of Colombian population at that time) were the longest and most widely spread conflicts until the mid-twentieth century. This undeclared civil war caused mass killings of civilians, numerous targeted murders of political leaders, trade unionists and students, atrocious tortures and body mutilations, as well as proximity between the army and paramilitary units. These incidents also occurred in the most violent phase of what became known as "the internal armed conflict" (between 1990 and 2010), and will be discussed later.

In 1958, the two main parties (liberal and conservative), whose supporters clashed with each other during the civil wars from Independence onwards, negotiated an agreement to take turns to exercise power. The agreement was effective until 1974, but it was not a solution to the weak social bases of the Colombian political system (Palacios, 1995). Generally, 1964, the year in which two Marxist-inspired guerrilla groups, FARC (Fuerzas Armadas Revolucionarias de Colombia) and ELN (Ejercito de Liberación nacional) were born (followed by liberal democratic M-19, Movimiento 19 de Abril in the 1970s, which would lay down its weapons in 1990), is reported to be the beginning of the "internal armed conflict", whose ceasefire was secured with the 2016 peace agreement between the government and FARC.

After their inception during 1970s, in the following decade drug production and trafficking grew so exponentially that they wielded enormous influence on the entire Colombian economy, society and politics. Between the mid-1980s and the following ten years, drug cartels responded to the State's enforcement action (as urged on by the USA) by causing an indiscriminate outburst of violence. They murdered some prominent public figures and carried out several car bomb attacks among civilians. In spite of the fact that some leaders were arrested or killed (e.g. Pablo Escobar, in 1993), drug trafficking continued to flourish in the following decades until it became one of the major triggers for a new and deep resurgence of the internal armed conflict (Piccoli, 2005).

The persistence of the latter considerably halted or distorted the political implementation process of those innovative principles (referenced below) that were established with the Political Constitution adopted in 1991. From the mid-1980s to 2010, the flare-up of the internal armed conflict happened concurrently with the rise and development of paramilitary units that fought against the leftist guerrillas even in the matter of drug trafficking control and profits. In the earliest phase of this period, following several failed attempts of negotiating peace with the government, the guerrillas' sphere of influence increased as well as their military power, since they could finance their activities through kidnappings, extortions, as well as their involvement in drug trafficking.

By means of a new scorched-earth policy (often covertly or overtly supported by the army and the economic/political elites) against the guerrillas and their support bases, the paramilitary units began to dispute territorial control of many areas with them. The paramilitaries, with the tacit consent and complicity of a large part of the local elites, achieved these results by spreading terror among a sizeable portion of the urban and rural population. From 1990 to 2010 targeted murders of peasant leaders, indigenous and union representatives grew significantly in number along with massacres of civilians, often combined with tortures, rapes, mutilations and concealment of dead bodies. Suspicions about connections with guerrillas were often used as an excuse to persuade residents to leave and/or give away their lands, which were to be acquired by paramilitaries, or (as further discussed later) vacated in order to facilitate the implementation of major projects of economic development.

During President Uribe's eight years in office (2002–2010), the government—with military support from the USA—was able to severely weaken the guerrillas and, at the same time, negotiate an agreement with paramilitaries about their demobilisation. This was followed by the beginning (even if surrounded by ambiguity and uncertainty) of peace negotiations, investigation processes and judgement of responsibilities of all the crimes committed by the armed groups, including reparation programmes for the victims (Ley de Justicia y Paz, 2005; Ley de Victimas, 2011). The most significant fact marking a change of direction towards a "post-conflict" scenario for Colombia was the peace deal with FARC in 2016, followed by the demobilisation of their military apparatus.

The huge number of victims of the "internal armed conflict", almost all civilians (nearly 300,000 deaths, 164,000 *desaparecidos*, 7 million internally displaced people between 1964 and 2016), is only one of its complicated consequences at the present time (Vargas, 2019). Colombia is still affected by substantial inequalities and contrasts. A great number of former paramilitaries have set up organised criminal groups with mafia-like control over the territory in several areas infiltrating the very heart of "legal" economy on the side. Social movements demanding more justice and respect of constitutional rights are still subject to violent repression through targeted murders of indigenous, Afro-Colombian and environmentalist leaders, including a recent indiscriminate use of special riot control measures.

Finally, it is important to mention two crucial elements which have contributed to the development of the current scenario since 1990: "neo-extractivism" and government policies aimed to facilitate access to international markets and the entry of major foreign corporations into the country. The increased extraction of precious metals and hydrocarbons, and the implementation of extensive plantations of African oil palm and biofuels, along with ambitious dam and hydropower development plans,

410 A. MANCUSO

have all affected the areas that were historically occupied by indigenous, Afro-Colombian and peasant (*campesinas*) populations. This inevitably interfered with the recognition of their territorial rights and disrupted their livelihoods. Moreover, the local populations did not receive any kind of benefits from the implementation of these megaprojects either in terms of job opportunities or in terms of royalty payments by the companies. Any legal restrictions to the implementation of economic development megaprojects included in the 1991 Constitution about the indigenous and Afro-descendant peoples under a regime of *resguardos*, along with the provision stating that the implementation is subject to prior, free and informed consultation (FPIC) with the populations, have often been bypassed. This happened by means of approval of other laws, general corruption at the highest echelons of politics, public administration, and even acts of violence and terror carried out by paramilitaries in order to force residents to leave their lands (Houghton, 2008; Rodríguez-Garavito & Orduz, 2012).

An Attempt at Periodisation

Any periodisation of a disciplinary tradition appears as a simplification of both its continuities and discontinuities, not to mention the combination of distinctive theoretical and research directions that go beyond the periodization itself, which is indeed not immune to those "presentist" partialities that often come along with all retrospective reflections: the same goes for Colombia (Correa, 2006; Tocancipá-Falla, 2016b). Almost all recent reflections and evaluations on anthropology *made in* Colombia, as mentioned at the beginning of the present chapter, lead to identify three main periods in the history of Colombia on the basis of the crucial moments of its academic and public institutionalisation, including research areas, theoretical frameworks and the main scholarly methods used in each of these periods. Such reinterpretations of historiography point out that this periodisation goes with different phases in the relations between the creation of a disciplinary field and the projects for the construction of the State and national society, situated in turn within the processes of structuring a world system order of political, economic, social and cultural relations, characterised by the asymmetry between "centers" and "peripheries".

The rise and early development of the discipline is generally associated with the birth of the Instituto Etnológico Nacional (IEN), in 1941. Until about the mid-sixties, research interests seemed to be primarily (though

14 FROM THE STUDY OF INDIGENOUS CULTURES TO THE CRITICS... 411

not exclusively) focused on indigenous populations. A lot of researchers became involved in government indigenist policies fostering integration into the national society in compliance with modernisation and economic development models. This period ended approximately between 1968 and 1971 when, as a consequence to wider socio-political processes, the long-established comparison between "basic" and "applied" research ultimately drew criticism and reached a crisis point.

In the second period which went from these years to those following the promulgation of the 1991 Constitution, the number of anthropologists with academic training increased considerably. At the same time, a new orientation embedded in a Marxist-influenced theoretical framework (and, especially, by dependency theories) began to spread out and was often put into practice: one of the main tasks for anthropologists included being involved in "social and political engagement" supporting collective subjects. These latter were in fact the indigenous groups, as well as Afro-descendants, peasants and urban working classes, who were striving to change their subaltern condition through rights and social justice movements. Starting from about 1980, this new way of understanding and performing anthropological work would reach a crisis point for several reasons which will be discussed later, although its enduring contributions to the recognition of new citizenship rights to indigenous minority and Afro-descendants must not be underestimated.

The most recent period, from 1991 until the present day, began with the emergence of a new theoretical and research perspective, namely *Antropología en la Modernidad*, which would gain academic hegemony over the following decades. This perspective is identified with the reception of some relevant debates in contemporary social and cultural theory; not only did it focus on the connections among culture, discourse, power and subjectivity, but it also promoted the opening of new fields of research which marked a definitive rejection of the idea of Colombian anthropologists having to deal mainly with "indigenous cultures". From an academic point of view, this was the moment when the discipline grew rather significantly as well as the number of those who earned a degree in anthropology. However, this also caused the downgrading of undergraduate degrees in terms of the level of knowledge and skills achieved as well as employment opportunities in a range of professional areas. Other than that, there have been significant changes in the relations between academic roles and how the acquired "knowledge" can be applied within a professional setting. This has also led to a change in the anthropologists' political roles.

412   A. MANCUSO

The following sections provide further descriptions of the core features of each period.

INSTITUTIONALISATION AND CONSOLIDATION

Ethnographic and linguistic evidence about indigenous populations in Colombia date back to the colonial period, and it can be traced back to the work of chroniclers, missionaries, explorers or travellers who sometimes provide useful information (beyond prejudice) to reconstruct their history as well as the changes these populations went through in the centuries following the arrival of Europeans. From this point of view, the Chorographic Commission's work (1850–1859) led by Agustín Codazzi as well as the study on *Tribus indígenas del Magdalena* (1884) carried out by famous writer Jorge Isaacs rank among the most outstanding achievements in the nineteenth century. In the early decades of the twentieth century, several foreign ethnologists (especially German, such as Koch-Grünberg and Preuss) led ethnographic and archaeological expeditions which produced some important documentation, without however building lasting relationships with Colombian institutions.

Through their descriptions and analyses of the country's different environments and populations, the works of some prominent intellectuals, scholars and men of science from the eighteenth and nineteenth centuries (i.e. Humboldt, Mutis, Sandoval and Caldas) had a deep impact on the concepts of otherness, savage, civilisation, race, environment, miscegenation, centre/periphery, territory, frontier and nation which have shaped the dominant biopolitical order in Colombia during most of the twentieth century (Castro-Gómez, 2005; Cunin, 2003; Múnera, 2005; Serje, 2011; Wade, 1997a, 1997b, 2011).

The Instituto Etnológico Nacional (IEN) was founded in 1941, during the years of the *República Liberal* (1930–1946), so called after the liberals kept their grip on power during all the period, pushing through several reforms of many administrative institutions. In addition to that, in this period there was a modernisation of the higher education system, which had been previously grounded on traditional "liberal arts" and under strong clerical influence.

In 1937, the Escuela Normal Superior was established and it became the first institution in higher education to award diplomas in ethnology. In 1938, Gregorio Hernández de Alba—who had taken part in an ethnographic and archaeological investigation campaign with other US researchers in the Caribbean region in 1935 (Hernández de Alba, 1936)—founded the Servicio Arqueológico Nacional and the Museo Arqueológico Nacional. Three years later, he was also responsible for the creation of the IEN, together with Paul Rivet, formerly founder and director of the Musée de l'Homme in Paris. Rivet held in fact the position of director of the IEN until 1943, when he moved to Mexico where he had been nominated cultural advisor for De Gaulle's government in exile (Lauriére, 2008).

Hernández de Alba had met Rivet in 1939, when the latter was visiting Colombia. He spent a study period at the Museé de l'Homme at the invitation of Rivet himself. After the German occupation in France, the French scholar, who was also an active member of the Socialist Party, had to leave the country to find refuge and hospitality in Colombia, where, in collaboration with Hernández de Alba, he established the IEN. Later, other young European expat scholars such as Gerardo Reichel-Dolmatoff, Juan Friede and Ernest Guhl joined the IEN as members.

From its very early years, the IEN encouraged research and teaching activities in compliance with a model promoting a connection between different branches of the "science of humankind": ethnology, archaeology, linguistics and pre-history. The integration among these disciplines was supposed to help the development of a general anthropology that could also deal with Rivet's primary interest, namely the largely unknown origins of American settlement and the cultural developments that had taken place there prior to the European conquest. Between 1942 and 1943 thirteen anthropologists (including six women) graduated from the IEN: Luis Duque Gómez, Alicia Dussan, Virginia Gutiérrez, Roberto Pineda Giraldo, Milciades Chávez, Graciliano Arcila and Blanca Ochoa; they were all bound to play prominent roles in the academic and institutional consolidation of the discipline.

According to Rivet, a general ethnographic and archaeological research programme on indigenous cultures and societies in Colombia had to be based on the combination of diffusionist and functionalist positions, along with those of the French sociological school and the US "culturology", this latter being especially useful for the purposes of the studies on "acculturation" that had followed on from the arrival of Europeans in the Americas.

In 1943 Hernández spent a study period in the United States, where he met Julian Steward. This earned him a participation in the writing of some entries in the *Handbook of South American Indians* led by Steward himself. More importantly, it catalysed the introduction of neo-evolutionist

414   A. MANCUSO

and cultural ecology approaches in Colombian anthropology and archaeology.

In 1943, Hernández and Antonio García also founded the National Indigenist Institute (INI) affiliated with the Inter-American Indian Institute (III), to work on "applied anthropology" on behalf of the State, in order to elaborate assimilation policies of Colombian indigenous populations, as well as to reduce their economic and social gap with the dominant society. A great number of IEN members also carried some research on behalf of this new institution; in the following twenty years the National Indigenist Institute edited and financed the publication of over twenty works on the social condition of indigenous communities, before that indigenist politics in Latin America went under radical criticism towards the end of the 1960s (Giraudo, 2009).

The careers of the married couple Pineda Giraldo and Gutiérrez de Pineda simplify in different ways the frequency of passages between "pure" research and "applied" research. In 1947, the two anthropologists took part in the research expedition in the Guajira peninsula among the *guajiros/wayuu*, and published two monographs which remained the main ethnographic source of information about this indigenous people for several decades (Gutiérrez de Pineda, 1950; Pineda Giraldo, 1950). Later, Pineda Giraldo and Gutiérrez de Pineda, together with Hernández de Alba, contributed to the studies carried out by a team of US researchers in the Cauca Department with the aim of comparing the class structure in Popayán (the capital city of the Department) with that in the Mexican city of Querétaro (Whiteford, 1963); the work is considered as the first experiment of urban anthropology in Colombia (Blanco, 2016). After they had been forced to abandon the region due to a deteriorating political situation, the couple spent some time in the United States, where they met Kroeber, Lowie and Foster.

Pineda Giraldo later worked at the Instituto de Seguridad Campesina, the Instituto de Crédito Territorial and in the Centro Interamericano de Vivienda, and conducted research on social relations in tobacco plantations in the Santander region as well as on the housing projects for internal migrants in the urban areas; he then collaborated with the Organization of American States (OAS) and was the director of the Instituto Colombiano de Antropología (ICAN) between 1982 and 1986 (Echeverri, 2008; Pineda Camacho, 2008).

Virginia Gutiérrez de Pineda became Professor of Medical Anthropology at the Universidad Nacional in Bogotá where she taught for thirty years.

Even if she published some works on "popular medicine" in Colombia she is most known for her studies on the Colombian family and its forms, of which she suggested a classification in a number of types. Gutiérrez de Pineda argued that each of these family types was associated with a specific region and/or ethnic group and differentiated from the others according to the historic mechanism of its formation, organisation and the roles of women (i.e. Gutiérrez de Pineda, 1994, 1999). These works gave her great public notoriety to such an extent that an image of the anthropologist's close-up can be found on the ten thousand-pesos banknotes that began circulating in 2016.

Retrospectively, it can be said that a division of labour was retained and sometimes resulted in a contrast between the IEN studies producing urgent ethnographic knowledge on the basis of the predicted disappearance of the "traditional cultures" of the indigenous groups (Dussán de Reichel, 2017 / 1965) and the INI "applied" researches. The latter could be placed within a project of "organic indigenism" in which researchers had to provide their contribution to the design and execution of programmes to improve living and health conditions as well as access to land of the indigenous communities (not uniquely, as shown) in order to encourage the development of "modern" forms of socio-political organisation (Restrepo et al., 2017, pp. 23–24).

These two ways of conceiving the relationship between anthropological research and indigenous populations caused disagreement between Hernández de Alba (who believed priority had to be given to "applied" research) and Rivet (who conversely advocated the prominence of "pure" research). The quarrels persuaded Rivet—prior to his departure for Mexico—to choose Luis Duque over Hernández as a director of the IEN. Duque carried out significant research on pre-Columbian archaeology mainly in the famous area of San Agustín, declared a UNESCO World Cultural Heritage Site in 1995 on his impulse.

Between the 1960s and 1980s he held the position of director of the Gold Museum (containing some of the most remarkable pre-Columbian gold artefacts which survived both the Conquistadores destruction and the tomb raiders' illegal trafficking) and of the new Fundación de Investigaciones Arqueológicas Nacionales; he was also dean of the Universidad Nacional and president of the Colombian Academy of History.[1] His career proves how he and the other IEN members intended

---

[1] See Duque Gómez (2005 [1955]), and the bibliography of his works therein.

416   A. MANCUSO

to let the history, the past—and, to a lesser extent, the present—of indigenous populations seep into the historiographic conscience of Colombians as a key element for the building of their national identity. From this standpoint, Duque favoured investigation on the pre-Columbian past and advocated its integration within Colombia's art history and cultural heritage, in a suitable perspective for the elite ideology and that could be easily translated into greater appreciation of such a past in the official cultural policies.

Among the pioneers of Colombian anthropology, Juan Friede, who provided some key analyses and documents about colonial history (Friede, 1947, 1953, 1963, 1974), conversely highlighted how the colonial relationships influenced the persistent "indigenous question" in Colombia as it stands.

After founding the Instituto Etnológico del Cauca in 1946, Hernández de Alba himself steered the activities promoted by the new organisation towards "organic indigenism" and came to involve a Guambian native Francisco Tumiña. In 1950, Hernández was forced to leave office and abandon the region, after a bomb was detonated in front of his home as an act of retaliation for exposing the murder of a group of Paeces people from the Tierradentro *resguardo*. In 1960, following the end of *La Violencia*, during which the elites had shown their hostility towards any kind of anthropological research resulting from applicative or theoretical interests, Hernández de Alba promoted the creation of División de Asuntos Indígenas and later became its director. The governmental institution took on a prominent role in directing the indigenist policy primarily towards "social integration" and then "development" goals. Hernández's actions within this organisation came under a barrage of criticism: at the beginning he took advantage of the scenario following the Agrarian Reform Act (1961) and supported the protection of existing *Resguardos* as well as the implementation of new areas under this regime; however, in the second half of the decade he adopted a favourable attitude towards their gradual dissolution, maybe because he was pressured by the landowners' lobby. In addition to this, Hernández gave the green light to the entry of the Summer Institute of Linguistics in 1962 and the US protestant missions into many indigenous territories out of the urge to conduct research on lesser-known endangered indigenous languages and balance the influence of catholic missions (Correa & Acero, 2013; Perry, 2006; Troyan, 2007).

Reichel-Dolmatoff's Controversial Legacy

Among the generation who pioneered anthropology in Colombia, the most prominent scholar at an international level, and still the most controversial—especially in Colombia—is Reichel-Dolmatoff, whose works wove together archaeology, historiographic investigation, ethnography and theoretical consideration.

Between 1946 and 1950, six regional branches of the IEN were established in several administrative departments: Antioquia, Atlantico, Boyacá, Cauca and Magdalena. Austria-born Reichel relocated to Colombia before the beginning of World War II and became the director of the Magdalena branch from its foundation. Over the following twenty years, he carried out archaeological, ethnographic and ethnohistorical research in the Caribbean region which sometimes involved the participation of his wife, Alicia Dussán. His self-financed work on the Kogi people from Sierra Nevada in Santa Marta, first published between 1950 and 1951 (Reichel-Dolmatoff, 1985), is the most relevant result of his ethnographic research in the 1945–1960 period. Other than providing extensive ethnographic records, Reichel carried out a comprehensive analysis of the relations between the cosmology of this people and its ecological implications. His interpretation of these relations, which later resulted in research (i.e. Reichel-Dolmatoff, 1978), strongly influenced the construction of the Kogi public image as the embodiment of the "ecological native", whose political uses have been recently discussed from several points of view (Colajanni, 2008; Ulloa, 2004; Uribe, 2006). Furthermore, his thesis on a strong continuity between contemporary indigenous cultures of Sierra Nevada and the pre-Columbian Tairona culture—supported by archaeological and historiographic studies (Reichel-Dolmatoff, 1951, 1953)—was equally influential. In the early 1960s, starting from his findings in some archaeological areas of Northern Colombia, Reichel was one of the scholars who led the debate on more complex hypotheses on the sequences of cultural development between the central American, Andean and Amazon areas (Langebaek, 2005).

In 1952, the IEN changed its name to ICAN (Instituto Colombiano de Antropología). In 1963, both the first undergraduate program and Department in Anthropology were opened at Universidad de Los Andes, the most important private university in the country. Reichel was appointed director of both. During the same years, a specialisation in Anthropology was established within the degree course in Sociology at the Universidad

Nacional, Colombia's most prominent public university. There, in 1966, the programme at the Department of Anthropology started to be successful, so it was duplicated in 1967 at the Universidad de Antioquia (Medellín) and in 1970, at the Universidad del Cauca (Popayán). Until 1990, these eight or ten-semester-structured programmes, including a compulsory period to be devoted to carry out fieldwork with the purpose of writing a final monograph, would remain the only existing ones in Colombia, as well as the main wellspring for the "intermediate" generation of anthropologists working in the following decades. Each of these departments promoted the edition of one or more specialist journals (currently publishing issues), to be added to the *Revista Colombiana de Antropología*, published by the ICAN.

After becoming director of the Department of Anthropology at the Universidad de Los Andes, Reichel established its educational and research goals, with "basic" research taking priority over "applied" research, "primitive" cultures acting as the main study field of the discipline and a special focus on indigenous cultures (here "primitive" was to be intended as premodern or of "peoples without writing"). Reichel received criticism from the students who urged anthropology and its practice both to show interest in the various segments of Colombian society, including peasants and the working class in a subaltern condition, and to offer tangible support to transform such a condition. As a response, he hit back by defending his positions on "basic research" into indigenous populations, arguing that this could actually help to understand and value forms of cultural diversity that need to be urgently documented. In fact, if, on the one hand, these forms were disappearing, on the other hand, their study was not only of academic interest, as they provided useful instruments to understand some major issues, such as the relationship with the environment that the whole of humanity is actually facing today.

Apparently, the students thought this view about the knowledge of "other cultural worlds" preceding and "illuminating", if not guiding, political action was intellectualistic, not overly persuasive, elite-oriented, and not actually paying attention to the need for the emancipation of subaltern social subjects. The criticism urged them to seek students' participation in tailoring the academic curriculum, which eventually caused Reichel to resign as a director in 1968 (Pérez, 2017).

In the same year he published *Desana*, an account of the cosmology of this indigenous group from Colombian Amazonia that was not based on "fieldwork", but on data from interviews with Desana native Antonio

Guzmán, which took place in Reichel's office at the Universidad de Los Andes, integrated by the scholar's interpretative commentaries (English translation: Reichel-Dolmatoff, 1974). *Desana* was greeted enthusiastically as very innovative by the majority of experts in Amerindian ethnology, such as Lévi-Strauss, and it paved the way for a long season of "field" research among the indigenous groups of Colombian Amazonia, to which both Reichel (i.e. Reichel-Dolmatoff, 1996a, 1996b, 1997) and other Colombian anthropologists (i.e. Cabrera et al., 1999; Cayón, 2013; Correa, 1996; Londoño, 2004; Van der Hammen, 1992) as well European and US ones (Colajanni, 2014) have provided further important contributions. Even today, *Desana* remains a reference work in the ethnology of Indigenous North Western Amazon (see Descola, 2013).

Some of Reichel's (who joined the University of California after leaving the Universidad de Los Andes despite keeping Colombia as his home and work base) hypotheses on Amazonian indigenous cultures resulting from the combination of his Amazonian as well as Kogi ethnography and his reinterpretation of Colombia's pre-Columbian past, all sparked off an intense debate (i.e. Correa, 1993; Descola, 2013; Langebaek, 2005). These hypotheses include the "ecological" orientation of several Colombian indigenous cosmologies (Reichel-Dolmatoff, 2017) and especially the consideration of the shaman as a regulator of the reciprocal relationships with the environment, who could already be found in pre-colonial indigenous cultures of Colombia, as evidenced by iconographic sources (Reichel-Dolmatoff, 1988).

As previously mentioned, Reichel-Dolmatoff raised a storm of controversy among Colombian anthropologists which is still stirring debate today. His concept of anthropology has come under vigorous attack for scientific and political reasons: the privilege of an idea of indigenous cultures completely abstracted from everything that, throughout history and especially today, has transformed them following their subaltern integration into a dominant society of colonial origins; the consequent equation between cultural difference and indigenous cultures verging on an essentialist understanding of cultural values; a concept of ethnographic practice and writing which overall emphasises the anthropologist's role as the ultimate source of research authority and its results (and yet, looking retrospectively at his research with the Kogi, he wrote: "the Kogi introduced me to a new view of what I thought ethnology was. They did not expect me to ask the tricky or banal questions of the ethnologist, but instead took the initiative and questioned me, questioning my ability to answer them, testing my ability to understand their way of thinking" (Reichel-Dolmatoff, 1991, p. 83).[2]

All these elements together have been more or less rightfully considered to be part and parcel of the colonial heritage of the discipline over the last decades, and they are even thought to have undermined Reichel-Dolmatoff's interpretations on the "ecological" implications of indigenous cosmologies. Even when, in *The People of Aritama* which he co-wrote with his wife Alicia (Reichel-Dolmatoff & Reichel-Dolmatoff, 1961), he looked into contexts where interethnic, status relations and hierarchies were strongly intertwined and had connections with the negotiation on the identity of people's indigenous origins, his verdict about the indigenous Kankuamo from the Sierra Nevada actually being on the verge of extinction due to high levels of "acculturation" was considered to be part of the neo-colonial inclination to single out as "indigenous" only those groups exhibiting distinctive traits of "traditional culture". In addition to this, his conclusion was proven wrong by the Kankuamo themselves, who went into action and successfully earned legal recognition as "indigenous people" (Gros, 2000; Morales, 2000).

His connections with the Nazi SS in his early youth did not emerge until ten years after his death, occurred in 1994 (Colajanni, 2014), and were exposed as the primal and permanent mark—though not blatantly visible—of his theoretical work (Uribe, 2017b). This argument has been firmly rejected by other eminent social scientists in Colombia, who denied the fact that his remote past might have added any significant elements to the comprehension and evaluation of his theoretical and ethnographic legacy (Langebaek, 2017).

From "engaged" Anthropology to the 1991 Constitution

Despite being structured around a fourfold scheme of education in general anthropology following the US model, the Anthropology degree programmes that appeared between 1960 and 1970 had a number of different curricula. Unlike that of Los Andes, the programme at the Universidad

---

[2] In the same work, he describes his own ethnology as one that "began to take indigenous thinkers seriously, starting from the recognition that there were such thinkers, that there were intellectuals in the jungle or philosophers in the mountains" (Reichel-Dolmatoff, 1991, p. 24).

Nacional, for instance, was designed to enable its graduates to "take care" of the country's "social issues" from an anthropological point of view (Pineda Camacho, 2008). Its implementation originating from the Sociology curriculum is relevant, especially when considering that the latter was established by Father Camilo Torres (who later became a member of the ELN and was killed in a battle) and Orlando Fals Borda. With his influential research on the *Violencia* period in Colombia, seen as a "social process" (Fals Borda, 1962–1964), Fals Borda would become known in the following decades for giving shape to the theoretical-political and methodological concept of Participatory Action-Research, applied through his work with peasant movements and organisations, and for experiments of sociological and historiographical writing (e.g. Fals Borda, 1979–1986; cf. Rappaport, 2015); in 2008, prior to his death, he received the prestigious Malinowski Award from the Society of Applied Anthropology in the United States (which had repeatedly refused to give him an entry visa for USA for years) (Fals Borda, 2008).

Fals Borda's perspective was part of a large-scale transformation trend regarding the sense of anthropological knowledge and practice, and especially the epistemological, ethical and political values of the relationships between researchers and the people among whom they carry out research.

This is the idea behind the first meeting of the "Barbados group" and his final Declaration (1971). On that occasion, not only were the work of religious missions among the indigenous groups equated with an ethnocide (Bonfil-Batalla et al., 1971), but the "assimilationist" structure of indigenous policies was also criticised, as well as the use of research methods disconnected from any actual analyses of or intervention in the domination these groups had been facing.

Similarly, the foundation (1971) of the Consejo Indígena del Cauca (CRIC) and the introduction of its seven-point programme to demand indigenous people's rights in Colombia had an impact as well. The points demanded: broadening and enforcing of the *resguardos'* regime, that is of the lands collectively owned by the indigenous communities, as well as of the self-government institutions based on colonial *cabildo*; abolition of the requirement to perform unpaid labour (*terraje*) in the landowners' estates; protection and recovery of indigenous history, language and custom; formation of indigenous teachers and development (established by Decree 1142 of 1978, which marked the end of the Church control over indigenous education) of "ethnoeducation" (Gros, 1991).

422 A. MANCUSO

During the 1970s, the majority of the anthropologists of this "intermediate-generation" joined Marxism as a theoretical and practical perspective to change society and dominance-based relationships: "the concepts of exploitation, domination, subordination and oppression replaced those of acculturation, deculturation, cultural depersonalisation and the [consequent] reduction of indigenous peoples as mere cultures" (Correa, 2006, p. 34, cf. Uribe 2017a).

Likewise, the dissemination of Liberation Theology, of Paulo Freire's "pedagogy of the oppressed", as well as of debates around the strategies aiming to achieve social transformation and the defeat of the capitalist and neo-imperialist orders—including the role of guerrilla, trade unionism, left-hand parties and social movements—led to put "science neutrality", "technocratism" and applied anthropology all in question. On the other hand, the idea that anthropological research, and especially fieldwork, had to give priority to active collaboration with social movements gained a foothold. This collaboration, especially with the indigenous movements, was intended to provide knowledge and useful instruments to put forward their demands and organisations, develop their historical consciousness and identity along with their whole social struggles (de Friedemann, 1987). Going beyond the option between speaking *of* and *on behalf* of indigenous groups, this perspective had as a result a lot of experiences in collaborative research and fieldwork, some of which have had enduring influence (i.e. Findji, 2019 [1992]; Vasco Uribe, 2002; Dagua et al., 1998)[3]. This influence can also be detected in the conspicuous prominence that the recognition of indigenous rights achieved in Colombia with the new 1991 Constitution. In addition to that, both this work and Fals Borda's remain without a doubt a source of reference, even as the objects of critical re-examination, for later experiences of collaborative research with direct or indirect political goals (i.e. Archila et al., 2015; Escobar, 2010; Rappaport, 2005).

Caviedes (2002, 2007, cf. Londoño, 2013) reconstructed this way of doing anthropology through a series of detailed interviews with a vast number of participants (anthropologists and indigenous leaders) in this season. He carried out his research in the south-western region of the country, home to some indigenous peoples, such as the Paeces and the Guambianos, with a stronger and ancient tradition of political

---

[3] See also Vasco Uribe's website, www.luiguiva.net, and Jaramillo, and Rojas (2019, pp. 799–953).

14 FROM THE STUDY OF INDIGENOUS CULTURES TO THE CRITICS...   423

mobilisation. Caviedes proposed to call this way of doing anthropology "apocryphal" anthropology, since much of this work manifested more through frequent unsigned articles published in the magazines and bulletins of indigenous, political and union organisations, rather than academic publications, as well as in audiovisual practices (e.g. talking maps, available aids for indigenous teachers), rather than written practices. At the same time, Caviedes showed the debates and disputes which took place among the indigenous organisations (especially between the CRIC, in certain moments of its history, and the AISO, Autoridades Indígenas de Suroccidente), among the researchers, but also between the former and the latter in relation to defining a political agenda. The main points of discussion included: integration of indigenous struggles and their objectives within those of trade unions and non-indigenous movements versus definition of their autonomy and irreducibility to class struggle—and how to understand the researchers' roles in supporting the movements. Caviedes also suggests a distinction between "collaborators" who were in line with the first option, and "supportive" researchers, generally closer to the second option.

In the late 1970s, a combination of circumstances took anthropologists back to social movement activities with a partial return to "academic" commitment or work in public institutions. With the National Security Statute (1978), social movements and their supporters ended up being subjected to firm state repression, since they were basically matched to subversive armed groups. As a reaction to this policy, the guerrillas, along with a large number of leftist political and union forces all opted for a Lenin-type "avant-garde" strategy to carry on social struggles, where key decisions were made by top leaders. Guerrillas, in particular, reignited military conflicts to fight back against the State institutions and ruling classes. In such conditions, many social movement supporters were forced to choose between upholding legality (and running the risk of being persecuted or arrested) or embracing illegality. Furthermore, in 1980, some indigenous organisations that would soon (1982) give life to ONIC (National Indigenous Organization of Colombia) made a public declaration against the presence of external activists within the communities they represented. Lastly, the coming of drug trafficking and paramilitaries definitely made "field-work" impossible especially in rural areas for the years to come.

Several Colombian anthropologists lived out these events through what Nina de Friedemann (1987) called an experience of "*conmoción*", namely shock and disorientation as well as disillusion with the perspectives of political changes that had animated the previous decade. Such collective discomfort emerged and sparked off heated debates on the occasion of the first Congress of Anthropology in Colombia in 1978[4]. Nevertheless, new theoretical reflections surfaced in this period. A reconsideration of the indigenous peoples' conditions and their new organising process fuelled an argument, aware of its potential political consequences about the use of concepts like "ethnic minorities", "super-ethnicity", "nations", in which the relational nature of ethnic identity construction and a complex articulation of its reproduction and integration within a capitalistic economy as well as the national state were highlighted (Correa, 2006). The *Encrucijadas de la Colombia Amerindia* collective volume (Correa, 1992, cf. de Friedemann & Arocha, 1985), published shortly after the new 1991 Constitution, expresses the new approaches under several aspects.

In spite of the fact that, in the 1980s, state policies and the ICAN overall promoted archaeological research, in 1975 new "stations" for ethnographical research were opened in those areas of the country that had remained peripheral even to sociocultural anthropology research, namely Amazonia and Orinoquia. In 1988, the Centro Colombiano de Estudios de Lenguas Aborígenes (Ccela) was founded at the Los Andes University and it was meant to make up for the limited number of researches on indigenous languages carried out by academic institutions (Landaburu, 2005). In 1978, the first urban anthropology course was implemented at the Universidad Nacional; in the following decades this research field would achieve significant growth mainly due to studies that might provide instruments for urban planning and the design of internal migrants' integration policies in rural areas on behalf of public bodies (Blanco, 2016).

Eventually, starting from 1980, Nina de Friedemann (e.g. de Friedemann, 1984) prompted a research campaign on Colombian populations of African descent and pointed out how they were almost completely "invisible" within anthropological, sociological and historical studies on Colombia, despite making up a significant portion (also demographically) of the national population. In the following years, Jaime Arocha and de Friedemann herself (who prematurely died in 1998) published a series of monographs as a result of in-depth field research on particular "Afrodescendant" populations, such as those from San Basilio de Palenque and

---

[4] To this day seventeen national congresses of anthropology have been held in Colombia. The last one took place in Cali in 2019.

the Pacific region. In their works, particular emphasis was placed on elements of cultural continuity with some African populations (called "huellas de africanía" by the two researchers) (i.e. Arocha, 1999; Arocha & de Friedemann, 1986; de Friedemann & Patiño, 1983).

Between Criticism of Modernity, Post-structuralism and Alignment with Neoliberal Hegemony

For several reasons (as previously discussed), the new 1991 Constitution, resulting from the efforts of a Constituent Assembly inclusive of some political actors that had been previously excluded from political life, was both an end point and a horizon to open new spaces for reinforcement of democracy in Colombia. I have already hinted at the wide recognition of rights for indigenous peoples and Afro-descendant communities, which happened when the principle of assimilation was finally turned down in favour of cultural pluralism as a bedrock of the nation; the reinforcement of a regime of territorial protection;[5] "affirmative action" measures in favour of ethnic minorities; the obligation of a free, prior and informed consultation of indigenous and Afro-descendant groups before economic development projects were carried out in their territories and any policy involving them was taken.

I have also pointed out how the period following the Constitution was marked by intense, violent conflicts and incidents to such an extent that numerous features of the programme to strengthen Colombia's fragile democracy were nullified or distorted. The development of an economic model, as well as a neoliberal governance with its complementary

---

[5] Today, on paper, 25% of Colombia's surface area is made up of *resguardos*, and with Law 70 of 1993, the possibility of collective land ownership was extended to Afro-descendant communities, starting from those settled in the Pacific region. This legal recognition doesn't tally with actual indigenous and Afro-descendant sovereignty in these territories for reasons that cannot be explained in detail here. These include the fact that the State owns the subsoil and its resources, the lack of administrative autonomy as well as the intrusion of illegal armed groups and organised crime associated with drug trafficking as well as the presence of military bases owned by the Colombian army.

426 A. MANCUSO

expressions such as neo-extractivism and "state multiculturalism",[6] ambiguously intersected the "internal armed conflict" along with the role that the Colombian state, the political elites and the paramilitaries took on in the conflict with the apparent aim of removing any obstacle to the imposition of such a model.

Colombian anthropology had to face this scenario from several points of view. As for theoretical framework and research fields, the rise and consolidation of a new perspective called "anthropology of modernity" intentionally marked a discontinuity in relation to the past. This new perspective was initially put forward by some anthropologists like Maria Victoria Uribe, Mauricio Pardo and Eduardo Restrepo, who occupied pre-eminent positions within the ICAN at that time. In 1997, this institution started to be controlled by the newly born Ministerio de Cultura, and in 1999, following the merging with the Instituto de Cultura Hispánica, it was renamed ICANH (Instituto Colombiano de Antropología e Historia) and divided into four sections: Social Anthropology, Archaeology, History and Heritage (Rojas & Jaramillo, 2020).

In the prefaces to some collective works of a new editorial collection published by ICANH and purposely called "Anthropology of modernity", the editors presented a sort of manifesto of the new perspective. The old Colombian anthropology was criticised for preserving an obsolete concept of culture as its main theoretical framework. Such a concept had essentialised sociocultural and ethnic identities and alterities without further critical scrutiny. Not only did this tendency reportedly appear in the equation between anthropological studies and "indiology", but it was also visible in research projects on other social subjects (especially Afro-descendants) based on the "culturalist" and "orientalist" models that had been used in

---

[6] In Colombia, and generally in Latin America as a whole, anthropologists (e.g. Bocarejo, 2011; Chaves, 2011) use the expression "state multiculturalism" to highlight the fact that the State one-sidedly defines—assuming that there is always a close correspondence between "ethnicity" and the "integrity" of a "traditional culture"—the criteria to recognise special territorial, linguistic and cultural rights to indigenous and Afro-descendant groups, whose existence must be "certified" by the State itself. Other than leaving the non-indigenous domination process and its influence on the indigenous and Afro-descendant "cultures" in the background, as a consequence of "state multiculturalism", the retention of "cultural diversity" is opposed to any change and adjustment to dominant sociocultural, economic, political forms. Similarly, the broad mass of small peasants is excluded from recognition of special rights and protections.

researches on indigenous groups (Restrepo et al., 2017; Restrepo & Uribe, 2000; Uribe & Restrepo, 1997).

Implicitly, the "Anthropology of modernity" deliberately took its distance from the orthodox Marxist vision of connections between domination, cultural processes and social subjectivities. References to post-structural perspectives and especially Foucault, cultural studies (i.e. Aparicio, 2011; Rojas, 2011), subaltern studies, as well as the theory of intimate links between modernity and "coloniality" (i.e. Mignolo & Escobar, 2010), are thought to be strategic in order to critically analyse the articulation between class, ethnic and gender subjectivities, and draw attention to both discourse, knowledge/power devices of colonial/modern origin at the heart of this articulation, as well as "dislocation" and resistance strategies used to react to them.

The consequences of adopting such an approach can be listed as follows: a huge expansion of the subjects and fields of research as the new forms of eco-governmentality (i.e. Escobar, 1999, 2010; Ulloa, 2004); experiences and multifarious dynamics of violence, armed conflict, memory and oblivion in Colombia (and elsewhere) and the creation of "victim", "witness", "reparation" categories (i.e. Castillejo, 2016; Jaramillo, 2014; Jimeno et al., 2012; Restrepo, Rojas, and Saade, vol. II, pp. 397–537); the deconstruction of development discourses and practices combined with the analysis of emerging potential "alternatives to modernity" (i.e. Escobar, 1998, 2014); the connections between gender, body, ethnicity and violence (see Vigoya, 2017).

As discussed earlier, the critical analyses of the concepts of culture, identity and tradition espoused by post-1991 "multicultural" policies put into effect by the State and their connection with new forms of neoliberal governmentality are an additional significant topic to consider theoretically and critically from the standpoint of the "anthropology of modernity" new paradigm. The Foucauldian "genealogical" approaches have fostered the intersection between anthropology and history in the analysis of the above-mentioned topics, resulting in a critical reconsideration of the role of archaeological research, its interpretive frameworks (i.e. Langebaek & Gnecco, 2005; Gnecco, 2016) and the current patrimonialisation policies (Chaves et al., 2014).

Some previously investigated research fields have been scrutinised in light of new theoretical perspectives. These are urban anthropology, medical anthropology, social movements (i.e. Archila & Pardo, 2001; Oslender, 2008) and the indigenous and "Afro-descendant" people's cultural life

428 A. MANCUSO

and social conditions (i.e. Chaves & Del Cairo, 2012; Restrepo, 2016b; Rojas, 2011; Ulloa, 2010), with a special attention to previously neglected aspects for the latter, such as ethnic identification processes, the relationships with the State, leadership and new forms of organisation and political representation, racism and discrimination, and urban scenarios.

A glance at congress meetings and articles published in numerous academic journals over the past ten years (e.g. "Revista Colombiana de Antropología", "Antípoda", "Maguaré", "Boletín de Antropología") has put a spotlight on the fact that all these research problems and their resulting theoretical issues must be situated in the continental dimension of Latin America. Such a tendency reflects a rising awareness of history and the current situation which, beyond all national peculiarities, puts Latin American anthropologies together, even when it comes to re-balancing the relationships between what have become known as Central or "north-Atlantic" anthropologies and "peripheral" or "Southern" anthropologies.

Anthropology has significantly gained relevance as an academic discipline in Colombia since 1997. Not only have the bachelor's programmes increased in number from four to twelve (six in public universities and six in private universities), four MA programmes and three doctoral degree programmes have also been launched. The creation of post-graduate programmes has opened up the opportunity to obtain a second-cycle degree or a PhD in Anthropology without having to pursue one's studies abroad as was common in the past, or enrol in a post-graduate programme based on other social sciences. The number of anthropology graduates in Colombia rocketed from 240 in 1979 to over 1000 by the end of the following decade, and reached 4928 in 2015; yet another 535 with a MA or post-graduate qualification must be added.

A considerable number of the new academic programmes in anthropology no longer revolves around the traditional articulation between socio-cultural anthropology, archaeology, linguistic anthropology, biological anthropology in compliance with the U.S. model, as there is now an inclination to privilege the first field and "contemporary anthropologies" (Tocancipá-Falla, 2016b). As identified by Restrepo (2016a), after the development of MA and doctoral programmes there has been both a decrease ("minimalization": ibid, p. 74) in the standards required for first-degree students to achieve the qualification, and a sharp decline in the importance of fieldwork as a final achievement and assessment of graduate competencies. The implication behind this is that in order to complete their theoretical and methodological training and experience field research, students are supposed to continue their graduate and doctoral studies. Moreover, considering that the majority of new *pregrado* programmes has been launched by private universities whose admission fees are prohibitively expensive to most Colombians, the effect has been a new "elitization" of anthropologists (ibid, p. 76).

The increased number of career opportunities for anthropologists, including both academic and especially non-academic positions in public or private sectors, cannot hide the fact that those vacancies are unable to absorb a large number of graduates, not to mention that they mainly refer to precarious work with fixed-term employment contracts that are strictly regulated by employers.

Leaving academic positions aside, qualified anthropologists are often hired by public institutions, private companies and NGOs to fill various positions: consultancy on and expertise in free, prior and informed consultation (FPIC) processes, in sociocultural studies, in designing and developing cultural heritage policies, in urban design and territorial organisation; mediation between major corporations and local populations in "corporate social responsibility programmes"; archaeological prospections in areas destined to large development and infrastructure projects; assistance for internally displaced people (*desplazados*) from the "internal armed conflict", and in the "reparation" processes for the victims of and the "communities" affected by the armed conflict; "cultural management"; marketing and consumer research.

The vocabulary used clearly shows the significant transformations behind this transition of the role of anthropologists from active political, social engagement and activism in social, political, trade union and "civil society" movements to occupations such as "advisors", "experts", "managers", "mediators" and "service providers". Paradoxically, only those with open-ended, stable academic jobs are given the opportunity to remain more faithful to the very first model of "professional role". Even in this case, however, the severe limitations caused by the increase of fixed-term contracts, as well as the need to comply with "quality", "productivity", "accreditation" formats imposed by a management and neoliberal model of knowledge and higher education must also be taken into consideration, over and above the significant research funding cuts, whose distribution and expense are subject to requirements established by state bureaucratic apparatus (Pérez, 2017).

430 A. MANCUSO

Eduardo Restrepo, one of the leading figures behind the significant "turn" resulting from the programme of "anthropology of modernity", passed judgement on the current situation (ostensibly not limited to Colombia). Although he acknowledges that this "turn" should be welcomed for having refreshed theoretical debate and led anthropologists to explore new fields of research, so de-provincialising anthropology in Colombia, Restrepo notes that the proposal of "*theorising* politics" and "*politicising* theory" did not actually result either in an empowerment of cultural critique or in an increased influence of the anthropologists on the course of the recent socio-political processes that have taken place in Colombia as well as on the country's public opinion. Instead, the real people's struggles with which anthropologists usually identified with, have been inevitably pushed away (Restrepo, 2016a, p. 71). Pessimistically, he concludes that "generally, anthropology in Colombia has evolved into a flexible discipline, bowing to both governmentality and market logics" (ibid, p. 82).

Looking towards the future, Andrea Pérez states that albeit in a country full of conflicts and inequalities, "disagreements" have arisen within the Colombian anthropology at different times (often related to difficult and unpredictable life choices for the people that had expressed it) over the preservation of the status quo, as well as the hegemonic influence of North-Atlantic anthropologies. With regard to the unprecedented power of current neoliberal capitalism in transforming social and political relationships as well as producing an introjection of its own logics (especially among anthropologists and subaltern subjects) and also pointing out that "technocracy [...] has become the main penchant of today's anthropological practice" (*ibid*, p. 116), Pérez is nonetheless aware of the fact that there is widespread dissatisfaction among a considerable amount of students, researchers and teachers. Pérez goes on to ask: "Could it be that these [voices] are a plea to stop to think about this dead-end competition that pits people against each other? Should we maybe pay more attention to dissident voices that may turn out to be a fertile ground in order to deal with this crossroads of the new apolitical, individualist, technocratic anthropology, as happened in the past?" (ibid, p. 119).

REFERENCES

Aparicio, M. (2011). Sobre deseos, intervenciones y trayectorias: la antropología y los estudios culturales en Colombia. *Tabula Rasa, 15*, 13–31.

14 FROM THE STUDY OF INDIGENOUS CULTURES TO THE CRITICS... 431

Archila, M., & Pardo, M. (2001). *Movimientos sociales, estado y democracia en Colombia*. CES-UN.

Archila, M., et al. (2015). *Hasta cuando soñemos. Extractivismo e interculturalidad en el Sur de la Guajira*. CINEP.

Arias, J. (2017). La regionalización de la diferencia. In E. Restrepo, A. Rojas, & M. Saade (Eds.), *Antropología hecha en Colombia. Vol. II* (pp. 13–47). UniCauca.

Arocha, J. (1999). *Los ombligados de Ananse. Hilos ancestrales y modernos en el Pacífico colombiano*: UN.

Arocha, J., & de Friedemann, N. (1986). *De sol a sol. Génesis, transformación y presencia de los negros en Colombia*. Planeta.

Blanco, D. (2016). Seis décadas de investigación antropológica urbana en Colombia. In J. Tocancipá-Falla (Ed.), *Antropologías en Colombia: Tendencias y debates* (pp. 269–331). UniCauca.

Bocarejo, D. (2011). Dos paradojas del multiculturalismo colombiano: la espacialización de la diferencia indígena y su aislamiento político. *Revista Colombiana de Antropología, 47*, 97–121.

Bonfil-Batalla, G., et al. (1971). Por la liberación del indígena (Declaración de Barbados). *Problemas del desarrollo, 2*(8), 169–174.

Bushnell, D. (1993). *The Making of Modern Colombia: A Nation in Spite of Itself*. University of California Press.

Cabrera, G., Franky, C., & Mahecha, D. (1999). *Los Nukak, nómadas de la Amazonía colombiana:* Ediciones Universidad Nacional

Castillejo, A. (2016). Guerra, cotidianidad y los órdenes globales: notas antropológicas para una relectura de la violencia en Colombia. In J. Tocancipá-Falla (Ed.), *Antropologías en Colombia: Tendencias y debates* (pp. 125–165). Ed. UniCauca.

Castro-Gómez, S. (2005). *La hybris del punto zero: ciencia, raza e ilustración en la Nueva Granada. (1750-1816)*. Ed. Pontificia Universidad Javeriana.

Caviedes, M. (2002). Solidarios frente a Colaboradores: Transformaciones de la antropología en el Cauca en las décadas de 1970 y 1980. *Revista Colombiana de Antropología, 38*, 237–260.

Caviedes, M. (2007). Antropología apócrifa y movimiento indígena. Algunas dudas sobre el "sabor" propio de la antropología hecha en Colombia. *Revista Colombiana de Antropología, 43*, 33–59.

Cayón, L. (2013). *Pienso, luego creo: la teoría Makuna del mundo*. ICANH.

Chaves, M. (Ed.). (2011). *La multiculturalidad estatalizada: Indígenas, afrodescendientes y configuraciones de estado*. ICANH.

Chaves, M., & Del Cairo, C. (Eds.). (2012). *Perspectivas antropológica sobre la Amazonía contemporanea*. ICANH-Ed. Universidad Javeriana.

Chaves, M., Montenegro, M., & Zambrano, M. (Eds.). (2014). *El valor del patrimonio. Mercado, políticas culturales y agenciamentos sociales*. ICANH.

432   A. MANCUSO

Colajanni, A. (2008). Il pensiero locale sullo sviluppo. Riflessioni sul cambiamento socio-economico pianificato in due società indigene (Kogi e Aruaco) della Sierra Nevada de Santa Marta (Colombia). In A. Colajanni & A. Mancuso (Eds.), *Un futuro incerto. Processi di sviluppo e popoli indigeni in America Latina* (pp. 143–202). CISU.

Colajanni, A. (2014). Un pensatore indigeno dell'Amazzonia e un antropologo a colloquio nella grande città delle Ande. In G. Reichel-Dolmatoff (Ed.), *Il cosmo amazzonico* (pp. 339–364). Adelphi.

Correa, F. (Ed.). (1992). *Encrucijadas de la Colombia amerindia.* Colcultura.

Correa, F. (Ed.). (1993). *La selva humanizada. Ecología alternativa en el trópico húmedo colombiano.* CEREC.

Correa, F. (1996). *Por el camino de la anaconda remedio.* UN-Colciencias.

Correa, F. (2006). Interpretaciones Antropológicas sobre lo "Indígena" en Colombia. *Universidad Humanística, 62,* 15–41.

Correa, F., & Acero, S. (2013). Proyecciones del Instituto Indigenista de Colombia en la División de Asuntos Indígenas. *Baukara, 3,* 83–98.

Cunin, E. (2003). *Identidades a flor de piel. Lo "Negro" entre apariencias y pertenencias: categorías raciales y mestizaje en Cartagena.* IFEA-ICANH-Uniandes-Observatorio del Caribe.

Dagua, A., Aranda, M., & Vasco, L. (1998). *Guambianos: hijos del arcoiris y del agua.* CEREC.

Descola, P. (2013). *Beyond nature and culture.* University of Chicago Press.

Duque Gómez, L. (2005) [1955]. *Colombia: Monumentos históricos y arqueológicos.* Academia Colombiana de Historia.

Dussán de Reichel, A. (2017) [1965]. "Problemas y necesidades de la investigación etnológica en Colombia", In E. Restrepo, A. Rojas, M. Saade (Eds.), *Antropología hecha en Colombia. Vol. I.* (pp. 285–315). Ed. Unicauca.

Echeverri, L. (2008). Homenaje a Roberto Pineda Giraldo. *Nómadas, 29,* 202–205.

Escobar, A. (1998). *La invención del Tercer Mundo: construcción y deconstrucción del desarrollo.* Norma.

Escobar, A. (1999). *El final del salvaje. Naturaleza, cultura y política en la antropología contemporanea.* CEREC-ICAN.

Escobar, A. (2010). *Territorios de diferencia. Lugar, movimientos, vida, redes.* UniCauca.

Escobar, A. (2014). *Sentir-pensar con la tierra. Nuevas lecturas sobre el desarrollo.* Unaula.

Fals Borda, O. (1962-1964). *La Violencia en Colombia. Estudio de un proceso social.* Tercer mundo.

Fals Borda, O. (1979-1986). *Historia doble de la Costa. Voll. I-IV.* Carlos Valencia.

Fals Borda, O. (2008). The Application of the Social Sciences. Contemporary Issues to Work on Participatory Action Research. *Human Organization, 67*(4), 360–362.

14 FROM THE STUDY OF INDIGENOUS CULTURES TO THE CRITICS... 433

Findji, M. T. (2019 [1982]). "Movimiento indígena y "recuperación" de la historia". In E. Jaramillo, A. Rojas (Eds.), *Pensar el Suroccidente. Antropología hecha en Colombia. Vol. III* (pp. 391–408). UniCauca.

Friede, J. (1947). *El Indio en lucha por la tierra. Historia de los resguardos del macizo central colombiano.* Instituto indigenista de Colombia.

Friede, J. (1953). *Los Andakí, 1538-1947. Historia de la aculturación de una tribu selvática.* Fondo de Cultura Económica.

Friede, J. (1963). *Los Quimbayas bajo la dominación española.* Banco de la República.

Friede, J. (1974). *Los Chibchas bajo la dominación española.* Banco de la República.

de Friedemann, N. (1984). Estudios de negros en la antropología colombiana: presencia e invisibilidad. In N. de Friedemann & J. Arocha (Eds.), *Un siglo de investigación social en Colombia* (pp. 507–572). Etno.

de Friedemann, N. (1987). Antropología en Colombia: después de la conmoción. *Revista de Antropología, 3*(2), 142–164.

de Friedemann, N., & Patiño, C. (1983). *Lengua y sociedad en el palenque de San Basilio.* Instituto Caro y Cuervo.

de Friedemann, N., & Arocha, J. (Eds.). (1985). *Herederos del jaguar y de la anaconda.* Carlos Valencia.

Giraudo, L. (2009). *La questione indigena in America Latina.* Carocci.

Gnecco, C. (2016). La arqueología en Colombia en el nuevo milenio. In J. Tocancipá-Falla (Ed.), *Antropologías en Colombia: Tendencias y debates* (pp. 63–84). UniCauca.

Gros, C. (1991). *Colombia indígena.* CEREC.

Gros, C. (2000). *Políticas de la etnicidad.* ICANH-CES.

Gutiérrez de Pineda, V. (1950). Organización social en la Guajira. *Revista del Instituto Etnológico Nacional, 3*(2), 1–255.

Gutiérrez de Pineda, V. (1994) [1968]. *Familia y Cultura en Colombia.* Universidad de Antioquia.

Gutiérrez de Pineda, V. (1999) [1975]. *Estructura, función y cambio de la familia en Colombia.* Universidad de Antioquia.

Hannerz, U. (2011). *Anthropology's World.* Pluto Press.

Helg, A. (2005). *Liberty and Equality in Caribbean Colombia 1770-1835.* University of North Carolina Press.

Hernández de Alba, G. (1936). *Etnología guajira.* Imprenta nacional.

Herrera, M. (2002). *Ordenar para controlar. Ordenamiento espacial y control políticoenlasLlanurasdelCaribeyenlosAndesCentralesNeogranadinos.* UniAndes.

Houghton, J. (Ed.). (2008). *La tierra contra la muerte: conflictos territoriales de los pueblos indígenas en Colombia.* CECOIN-OIA.

Jaramillo, E., & Rojas, A. (Eds.). (2019). *Pensar el Suroccidente. Antropología hecha en Colombia. Vol III.* UniCauca.

434 A. MANCUSO

Jaramillo Uribe, J. (1968). *Ensayos sobre historia social colombiana*. Ed. Universidad Nacional.

Jaramillo, P. (2014). *Etnicidad y victimización. Genealogías de la violencia y la indigenidad en el norte de Colombia*. UniAndes.

Jimeno, M. (2005). La vocación crítica de la antropología en Latinoamérica. *Antípoda, 1*, 44–65.

Jimeno, M. (2007). Naciocentrismo: tensiones y configuración de estilos en la antropología sociocultural colombiana. *Revista Colombiana de Antropología, 43*, 9–32.

Jimeno, M., Murillo, S., & Mártinez, M. (2012). *Etnografías contemporáneas. Trabajo de campo*. CES-UN.

Krotz, E. (1997). Anthropologies of the South. Their rise, their silencing, their characteristics. *Critique of Anthropology, 13*(3), 237–251.

Landaburu, J. (2005). Las lenguas indígenas de Colombia: presentación y estado del arte. *Amerindia, 29-30*, 3–22.

Langebaek, C. (2005). De los Alpes a las selvas y montañas de Colombia: el legado de Gerardo Reichel-Dolmatoff. *Antípoda, 1*, 139–171.

Langebaek, C. (2017). Gerardo Reichel, a la luz de su obra. *Invención del indigenismo y ecologismo en Colombia. Antípoda, 27*, 17–34.

Langebaek, C. (2019). *Los muiscas. La historia milenaria de un pueblo chibcha*. Editorial Debate.

Langebaek, C., & Gnecco, C. (2005). *Contra la tiranía tipológica en arqueología: Una visión desde Suramérica*. UniAndes.

Lauriére, C. (2008). Paul Rivet: hombre político y fundador del Museo del Hombre. *Revista Colombiana de Antropología, 44*(2), 481–507.

Londoño, C. (2004). *Muinane: un proyecto moral a perpetuidad*. UniAntioquia.

Londoño, W. (2013). Tres momentos de la escritura antropológica en Colombia. *Antípoda, 16*, 281–311.

McFarlane, A. (1993). *Colombia Before Independence*. Cambridge University Press.

Mejias, A. (Ed.). (2017). *Antropologías del sur: cinco miradas*. BDLA.

Mignolo, W., & Escobar, A. (Eds.). (2010). *Globalization and the Decolonial Option*. Routledge.

Morales, P. (2000). El Corpus Christi en Atánquez. Identidades diversas en un contexto de reetnización. *Revista Colombiana de Antropología, 36*, 20–49.

Múnera, A. (2005). *El fracaso de la nación. Región, clase y raza en el Caribe colombiano*. Planeta.

Oslender, U. (2008). *Comunidades negras y espacio en el Pacífico colombiano. Hacia un giro geográfico en el estudio de los movimientos sociales*. Ed. Universidad Nacional.

Piccoli, G. (2005). *Colombia, il paese dell'eccesso*. Feltrinelli.

Pérez, A. (2017) [2010]. "Antropologías periféricas: una mirada a la construcción de la antropología en Colombia" In E. Restrepo, A. Rojas, M. Saade (Eds.), *Antropología hecha en Colombia. Vol. I.* (pp. 89–122). UniCauca.

14 FROM THE STUDY OF INDIGENOUS CULTURES TO THE CRITICS... 435

Perry, J. (2006). *Caminos de la antropología en Colombia: Gregorio Hernández de Alba.* Uniandes.

Pineda Camacho, R. (2008). Los campos de investigación de la Antropología en Colombia (1941-2008). *Jangwa Pana, 6*(7), 6–19.

Pineda Giraldo, R. (1950). Aspectos de la magía en la Guajira. *Revista del Instituto Etnológico Nacional, 3*(1), 1–164.

Rappaport, J. (2005). *Intercultural Utopias: Public Intellectuals, Cultural Experimentation, and Ethnic Pluralism in Colombia.* Duke University Press.

Rappaport, J. (2015). Introducción a la edición especial de Tabula Rasa: Orlando Fals Borda e la Historia doble de la Costa. *Tabula Rasa, 23,* 11–21.

Reichel-Dolmatoff, G. (1951). *Datos histórico-culturales sobre las tribus de la antigua Gobernación de Santa Marta.* Banco de la República.

Reichel-Dolmatoff, G. (1953). Contactos y cambios culturales en la Sierra Nevada de Santa Marta. *Revista Colombiana de Antropología, 1,* 15–122.

Reichel-Dolmatoff, G. (1974) [1968]. *Amazonian Cosmos: The Sexual and Religious Symbolism of the Tukano Indians.* Chicago University Press.

Reichel-Dolmatoff, G. (1978). The Loom of Life: A Kogi Principle of Integration. *Journal of Latin American Lore, 4*(1), 5–27.

Reichel-Dolmatoff, G. (1985) [1950]. *Los Kogi-Una tribu de la Sierra Nevada de Santa Marta. Two volumes.* Procultura.

Reichel-Dolmatoff, G. (1988). *Orfebreria y chamanismo. Un estudio iconografico del Museo del Oro.* Villegas editores.

Reichel-Dolmatoff, G. (1991). *Indios de Colombia: Momentos vividos. Mundos concebidos.* Villegas Editores.

Reichel-Dolmatoff, G. (1996a). *The Forest Within. The World-view of the Tukano Amazonian Indians.* Themis.

Reichel-Dolmatoff, G. (1996b). *Rainforest Shamans. Essays on the Tukano Indians of the Northwest Amazon.* Themis.

Reichel-Dolmatoff, G. (1997). *Yurupari. Studies of an Amazonian Foundation Myth.* Harvard University Press.

Reichel-Dolmatoff, G. (2017) [1976]. "Cosmología como análisis ecológico: una perspectiva desde la selva pluvial". In E. Restrepo, A. Rojas, M. Saade (Eds.), *Antropología hecha en Colombia. Vol. I.* (pp. 125–142). UniCauca.

Reichel-Dolmatoff, G., & Reichel-Dolmatoff, A. (1961). *The People of Aritama. The Cultural Personality of a Colombian Mestizo Village.* Routledge & Kegan.

Restrepo, E. (2016a). La antropología en Colombia en el nuevo milenio. In J. Tocancipá-Falla (Ed.), *Antropologías en Colombia: Tendencias y debates* (pp. 63–84). UniCauca.

Restrepo, E. (2016b). "Estudios afrocolombianos" en la antropología: tres décadas después. In J. Tocancipá-Falla (Ed.), *Antropologías en Colombia: Tendencias y debates* (pp. 167–217). UniCauca.

436 A. MANCUSO

Restrepo, E. (2017). Antropologías del mundo: perspectiva analítica y política. In A. Mejias (Ed.), *Antropologías del sur: cinco miradas* (pp. 99–126). Mérida.

Restrepo, E., Rojas, A., & Saade, M. (Eds.). (2017). *Antropología hecha en Colombia. Voll. I e II.* UniCauca.

Restrepo, E., & Uribe, M. T. (2000). Introducción. In E. Restrepo & M. T. Uribe (Eds.), *Antropologías transéuntes* (pp. 9–22). ICANH.

Ribeiro, G. L. (2014). World Anthropologies: Anthropological Cosmopolitanism and Cosmopolitics. *Annual Review of Anthropology, 43,* 483–498.

Rodríguez-Garavito, C., & Orduz, N. (2012). *Adiós río. La disputa por la tierra, el agua y los derechos indígenas en torno la represa de Urrá.* Dejusticia.

Rojas, A. (2011). Antropología y estudios culturales en Colombia. *Tabula rasa, 15,* 69–93.

Rojas A., & Jaramillo, E. (2020). Trayectorias, tensiones y propuestas de la Antropología hecha en Colombia. *Gazeta de Antropología, 36* (2), artículo 7.

Safford, F., & Palacios, M. (2001). *Colombia: Fragmented land, Divided Society.* Oxford University Press.

Serje, M. (2011). *El revés de la nación. Territorios salvajes, fronteras y tierras de nadie.* UniAndes.

Serje, M. (2016). Márgenes y periferias en el pensamiento antropológico colombiano (siglo XIX). In J. Tocancipá-Falla (Ed.), *Antropologías en Colombia: Tendencias y debates* (pp. 99–112). UniCauca.

Silva, R. (Ed.). (1994). *Territorios, regiones, sociedades.* UniValle-CEREC.

Stocking, G. W. (2001). *Delimiting Anthropology.* University of Wisconsin Press.

Tocancipá-Falla, J. (Ed.). (2016a). *Antropologías en Colombia: Tendencias y debates.* UniCauca.

Tocancipá-Falla, J. (2016b). Introducción: antropologías en Colombia. Retrospectiva y prospectiva. In J. Tocancipá-Falla (Ed.), *Antropologías en Colombia: Tendencias y debates* (pp. 17–60). Popayán: UniCauca.

Troyan, B. (2007). Gregorio Hernández de Alba (1904-1973): The Legitimization of Indigenous Ethnic Politics in Colombia. *European Review of Latin American and Caribbean Studies, 82,* 89–106.

Ulloa, A. (2004). *La construcción del nativo ecológico: complejidades, paradojas y dilemas de la relación entre movimientos indígenas y el ambientalismo en Colombia.* ICANH-Colciencias.

Ulloa, A. (2010). Reconfiguraciones conceptuales, políticas y territoriales en las demandas de autonomía de los pueblos indígenas en Colombia. *Tabula Rasa, 13,* 73–92.

Uribe, C. A. (2017a) [1980]. "La antropología en Colombia". In E. Restrepo, A. Rojas, M. Saade (Eds.), *Antropología hecha en Colombia. Vol. I* (pp. 43–66). UniCauca

Uribe, C. A. (2005). Mimesis y paideia antropológica en Colombia. *Antípoda, 1,* 67–78.

14 FROM THE STUDY OF INDIGENOUS CULTURES TO THE CRITICS... **437**

Uribe, C. A. (2006). «Y me citarán por muchos años más». El modelo interpretativo de Gerardo Reichel-Dolmatoff y la Sierra Nevada de Santa Marta. In A. Abello (Ed.), *El Caribe en la nación colombiana* (pp. 277–289). Bogotá: Museo Nacional y Observatorio del Caribe Colombiano.

Uribe, C. A. (2017b). De Gran Jaguar a Padre Simbólico: la biografía "oficial" de Gerardo Reichel-Dolmatoff. *Antípoda, 27*, 35–60.

Uribe, M. T., & Restrepo, E. (Eds.). (1997). *Antropología en la Modernidad*. ICAN.

Van der Hammen, C. (1992). *El manejo del mundo: naturaleza y sociedad entre los Yukuna de la Amazonía colombiana*. Tropenbos.

Vargas, A. (2019). *Colombia: antropologia di una guerra interminabile*. Rosenberg & Sellier.

Vasco Uribe, L. (2002). *Entre selva y páramo: viviendo y pensando la lucha india*. ICANH.

Vigoya, M. (2017). La antropología colombiana, el género y el feminismo. *Maguaré, 31*(2), 19–60.

Wade, P. (1997a). *Race and Ethnicity in Latin America*. Pluto Press.

Wade, P. (1997b). *Gente negra. Nación mestiza. Dinámica de las identidades raciales en Colombia*. UniAntioquia, ICANH, Siglo del Hombre, Uniandes.

Wade, P. (2011). Multiculturalismo y racismo. *Revista Colombiana de Antropología, 47*(2), 15–35.

Whiteford, A. (1963). *Popayán y Querétaro: comparación de sus clases sociales*. Universidad Nacional.

CHAPTER 15

History of Anthropology in Mexico: From Nation Building to the Recognition of Diversity

Rodrigo Llanes Salazar

In memoriam
—Luis Vázquez León *(1951–2021)*

INTRODUCTION: MEXICAN ANTHROPOLOGY AS A TRADITION?

Studies on Mexican social anthropology usually agree that it has its own profile that distinguishes it from other anthropologies in the world. Unlike European and North American anthropologies, it has focused on the study of the "otros internos" (the other from within), mainly indigenous peoples and peasants. Emerging from the Mexican Revolution of 1910,

---

R. L. Salazar (✉)
National Autonomous University of Mexico, Yucatan, Mexico

© The Author(s), under exclusive license to Springer Nature Switzerland AG 2023
G. D'Agostino, V. Matera (eds.), *Histories of Anthropology*,
https://doi.org/10.1007/978-3-031-21258-1_15

439

440   R. L. SALAZAR

it has been closely associated with the Mexican nation state and has been what George Stocking Jr. (1982) called "anthropologies of nation-building"; as a consequence of its relationship with the Mexican state, it has had an applied tradition, of solving the "great national problems"; and has contributed with original theories and ideas on indigenous politics and on Mesoamerica.[1] Due to these characteristics, José Lameiras, in an influential essay on the subject, wrote that "Mexican anthropology has had, during its historical process of formation, characteristics that, with respect to other disciplines of the social sciences developed in the country, allow us to confer on it the character of nationality and justify for it, at an early age, the title of Mexicanity" (Lameiras, 1979, p. 109).

To a large extent, this tradition, or national character, of anthropology in Mexico developed from the Revolution of 1910 came to a symbolic end in 1968, when the Mexican state repressed the student movement that demanded a series of political and civil rights. In recent works, this period has been characterized in different ways. For example, for Claudio Lomnitz (2014), anthropology was the "queen" of the social sciences in Mexico, due to the influence it had in the discussion and attention to public problems, particularly the so-called indigenous problem, but also in areas such as agrarian politics and education; Néstor García Canclini (2019) refers to this stage as the formation of the post-revolutionary nation in which anthropology sought to integrate indigenous peoples.

For his part, Federico Besserer (2019) characterizes this stage as an "international" one—due to the foundation of the *Escuela Internacional de Arqueología y Etnologías Americanas* (International School of American Archeology and Ethnologies) and the relationship between Manuel Gamio and Franz Boas—although he agrees that the anthropology of this period was marked by a sense of "Mexicanity". From the perspective of anthropology as a profession, Luis Reygadas (2019) defines this period as that of the "professionalization of anthropology in Mexico City", the country's capital.

Thus, it was in this period of nation building that the *Escuela Internacional de Arqueología y Etnologías Americanas* (1910), the *Dirección de Antropología* (Division of Anthropology) (1917), *el Departamento de Asuntos Indígenas* (Department of Indigenous Affairs)

---

[1] These ideas have been developed in the studies of Villoro (1979), Comas (1976), Lameiras (1979) and Beals (1993). Critical reviews of these ideas can be found in Medina (2004), Krotz (2006) and Vázquez León (2014a).

(1936), *el Instituto Nacional de Antropología e Historia* (National Institute of Anthropology and History, INAH) (1939), *la Escuela Nacional de Antropología e Historia* (National School of Anthropology and History) (1942), *el Instituto Nacional Indigenista* (National Indigenist Institute) (1948) and the current headquarters of the *Museo Nacional de Antropología* (National Museum of Anthropology) (1964) were established. In this period, paradigmatic works of Mexican anthropology were published, such as *Forjando patria* (Forging a Nation) (1916) and *La población del Valle de Teotihuacán* (The Population of the Valley of Teotihuacán) (1922) by Manuel Gamio; *Formas de gobierno indígena* (Indigenous Forms of Government) (1953), *El proceso de aculturación* (The Acculturation Process) (1957) and *Regiones de refugio* (Regions of Refugee) (1967) by Gonzalo Aguirre Beltrán, which contributed to the theory and practice of indigenism, ideas that were "exported" to other Latin American countries.

However, since the 1960s, this tradition of Mexican anthropology—a nationalist anthropology linked to the State dedicated to solving the indigenous problem—was severely questioned on various fronts. A new generation of anthropologists argued that anthropology was at the service of power, questioned the heavy institutional burden that limited anthropological research to indigenous issues and Mesoamerican heritage and declared themselves supporters of the decolonization movements of the time (see Warman, 2002). This critical rupture had important consequences in the theoretical and thematic diversification of Mexican anthropology, since the Marxist and ethnicist trends gained strength, as well as the studies on peasants, workers and popular sectors. Several studies agree that this "political rupture", as Carlos García Mora and Andrés Medina (1983) called it, represented the beginning of a new stage in Mexican anthropology. For García Canclini (2019), at this stage, under the influence of Marxism, anthropology studied peasants to contribute to their emancipation, a process by which the indigenous people, as rural workers, would be merged with the migrants, urban poor and university students. Besserer (2019) has characterized this stage as "multinational", in which theoretical frameworks and researchers trained in other parts of the world were incorporated and joined their demands with the indigenous demands of the country. The arrival of researchers exiled by the dictatorships in South America also contributed to the theoretical discussions in Mexico at this time.

This period, which has been characterized as that of a "critical" or "committed" anthropology, had among its main features the questioning of the indigenist theory and politics of the previous stage, although it did not renounce indigenism, but rather sought to transform it. Thus, new indigenist proposals emerged, such as "participatory indigenism". In addition, original theoretical proposals also emerged, such as Ángel Palerm's (1980) work on multilinear evolution and the articulation of peasant and capitalist modes of production, and Guillermo Bonfil's theory of cultural control, which supported one of the most important anthropological works of the time, *México profundo: una civilización negada* (1987). But, in addition to the theoretical and thematic consequences, the political breakdown of 1968 also had consequences for the professional practice of Mexican anthropology. On the one hand, as Reygadas (2019) observes, the fact that in 1968 for the first time an anthropologist graduated outside Mexico City, characterizes this stage (1968–1987) as that of the "expansion of the training of anthropologists in Veracruz, Yucatán, Michoacán, Puebla and the State of Mexico" (Reygadas, 2019, p. 44).

On the other hand, the political breakdown also represented a rupture in the anthropological community. According to Luis Vázquez León (2014b), this moment meant a split between, on one side, an ethnological tradition, linked to the governmental sphere (mainly embodied by INAH), and which has been organized in the *Sociedad Mexicana de Antropología* (Mexican Anthropology Association) and, on the other side, a sociocultural tradition, sheltered in academic institutions, whose main professional association is the *Colegio de Etnólogos y Antropólogos Sociales* (Ethnologists and Social Anthropologists Association, CEAS). As Luis Vázquez León (2002), Juan Luis Sariego (2007), Esteban Krotz and Luis Reygadas (2020) observed that in the 1970s a process of "academization" of anthropology began in Mexico, that is, the number of anthropology study programmes and research centres in the country increased quantitatively, and, above all, academic anthropology gained greater visibility.

Several studies have associated the establishment of the neoliberal model in Mexico since 1982 with a new stage in the country's anthropology profession. Besserer (2019) characterizes this period as "transnational", marked by the end of nationalism and by the emergence of research topics—such as migration—that shorten the radical distance between the "anthropological Self" and the "ethnographic Other". According to Besserer, in this stage, the demography and structure of the discipline, the way in which anthropology knows the reality it studies as well as the way in which reality is conceived or conceptualized have changed. Undoubtedly, as Angela Giglia, Carlos Garma and Ana Paula de

Teresa (2007) observe, this stage is characterized by greater theoretical and thematic diversity that can't be grouped into one or two paradigms as in previous periods. It was in this period that, as Aguirre Beltrán (1990) pointed out, the indigenous paradigm "collapsed". In 2003, INI became the *Comisión Nacional para el Desarrollo de los Pueblos Indígenas* (National Commission for the Development of Indigenous Peoples, CDI), an organization in tune with the multicultural ideology of this period. In 2018, the CDI was transformed into the *Instituto Nacional de los Pueblos Indígenas* (National Institute of Indigenous Peoples).

Regarding the professional field, Reygadas (2019, p. 40) states that the period from 1988 to 2007 is "a stage marked by the intensification of globalization and by the massification of the training of anthropologists", a trend that continues from 2008 until today and that the author calls "growth, diversification and precariousness of the anthropological profession" (Reygadas, 2019, p. 55). For Vázquez León (2002), at this stage, academic anthropology continues to be hegemonic; however, another type of anthropology began to become visible, which he called "post-academic", which is practiced from the private sphere, such as consulting services. Furthermore, as Reygadas' periodization proposal indicates, in the last four decades of the professional practice of anthropology, there is an increase in the study programmes and anthropologists with professional degrees. Additionally, the precariousness of the working conditions has worsened in the discipline.

Thus, currently, in Mexico there are 25 undergraduate, 19 masters and 9 doctoral programmes in anthropology, and it is estimated that there are more than 7000 anthropologists. "The vast majority—says Reygadas (2019, p. 11)—are young people who graduated in the present millennium." However, they face unstable jobs and a general lack of social security. More than half (53.8%) of the anthropologists lack a permanent position and 63% do not have any benefits (Reygadas, 2019). Thus, there is "a strong imbalance of the different sectors of professional anthropologists in terms of visibility, representation and defense of labor interests" (Krotz & Reygadas, 2020, p. 409). Likewise, as Krotz observes, the quantitative growth of academic anthropology does not go hand to hand with a greater public presence of anthropology. On the contrary, according to Lomnitz (2014), since the 1980s, the prestige of social anthropology in Mexico has gradually fallen. Anthropology went from being the "queen" of social sciences in the country to "Cinderella". Lomnitz (2014) suggests that even in public debates on topics considered "classics" of

444 R. L. SALAZAR

anthropology, such as culture, anthropology has been conspicuous by its absence in recent years.

If we take into consideration Carmen Bueno's (2011, p. 398) assessment that Mexico "no longer prioritizes national identity and/or the criticism of the status quo, but rather focuses on its positioning in a world disrupted by global networks of trade and governed by a neoliberal State", it is worth asking, what are the results of the tradition of Mexican anthropology today? In what follows, I will address how anthropology has contributed to the nation building in México and how, based on this political project, it has adapted and transformed theoretical ideas generated in the North, particularly in the United States. To do this, I will elaborate on ideas developed by some of the most notable Mexican anthropologists: Manuel Gamio, Gonzalo Aguirre Beltrán and Guillermo Bonfil. Finally, I will explore the legacy of this tradition in the current context of violence in Mexico.

NATION BUILDING

The Mexican Revolution was a heterogeneous armed movement against the dictatorship of Porfirio Díaz (who ruled the country uninterruptedly between 1884 and 1911) that involved two antagonistic groups: middle classes who demanded greater democracy (such as the no re-election of the president) as well as rural sectors demanding the distribution of land. One of its main legacies was the Constitution of 1917, which recognized the nation as the owner of the land and subsoil (Article 27), the maximum working day of eight hours, the legalization of unions and the right to strike (Article 123) and public education (Article 3), among others (Garciadiego & Kuntz Ficker, 2010). After the armed conflict, the post-revolutionary governments needed, in addition to building a new State, to formulate the foundations of the Mexican nation.

Of course, nation building was not an exclusive project of anthropology, but included several other notable individuals and institutions: the *Secretaría de Educación Pública* (Ministry of Public Education), especially under the direction of José Vasconcelos, who sought to build a national identity, a new healthy, moral and productive man, and to spread the national language; the philosophy of Samuel Ramos, who analysed the components of the Mexican national identity; the literature and muralism of Diego Rivera, José Clemente Orozco and David Alfaro Siqueiros, who portrayed the history of Mexico and the country's popular struggles; and the music of Carlos Chávez and Agustín Lara.

According to several works on the history of Mexican social anthropology, one of the distinctive features of this discipline is the contribution to the nation-building project. Manuel Gamio (1883–1960), considered to be the first professional Mexican anthropologist, entitled one of his most influential works *Forjando patria. Pro-nacionalismo* (Forging a Nation: Pro-Nationalism). The first works on the history of Mexican anthropology, written by Juan Comas and Gonzalo Aguirre Beltrán, positioned Gamio as the founding father of what Aguirre called "Mexican school of anthropology". Gamio headed the Anthropology Department of the Ministry of Agriculture and Development (created in 1917)[2] and published two crucial works for the early development of Mexican anthropology, the previously mentioned *Forjando patria* and the extensive study *La población del valle de Teotihuacán*.

However, this early historical view of the origin of Mexican anthropology obscures important aspects of the development of the discipline. In her study *Entre el campo y el gabinete. Nacionales y extranjeros en la profesionalización de la antropología mexicana (1877–1920)* (Between the Field and the Cabinet. Nationals and Foreigners in the Professionalization of Mexican Anthropology [1877–1920]), Mechthild Rutsch (2007) challenges the idea that Mexican anthropology is the child of the Mexican Revolution and claims that "the not very controversial myth of the original foundation of Mexican anthropology by Manuel Gamio is, in fact, the result of an ideological position shared by the majority of our current scientific community" (Rutsch, 2007, p. 22). Following this idea, it is worth noting that both Juan Comas and Gonzalo Aguirre Beltrán were collaborators of Gamio and shared to a large extent his vision of anthropology. In her study, Rutsch locates the origins of Mexican anthropology to the reorganization of the National Museum in 1877 (the Museum was founded in 1825). A scientific community was formed within this institution. It was mainly composed at first by *criollo* men, doctors and natural scientists, followed by lawyers and engineers, who carried out ethnographic, archaeological, historical, physical and linguistic research, as well as teaching.

Rutsch also highlights the role of researchers such as Nicolás León and Andrés Molina Enríquez, both eclipsed by the figure of Gamio. It was

---

[2] Krotz (2010) views the creation of this Anthropology Department as the starting point of Mexican anthropology.

446   R. L. SALAZAR

León who taught the first ethnology lecture at the National Museum in 1906. He also conducted field research with the Popoloccas of Puebla and Oaxaca (Rutsch, 2007, p. 108). In 1907, Molina Enríquez replaced León. Before Gamio, Molina had a "political and revolutionary vision of Mexican ethnology" (Rutsch, 2007, p. 148) and believed that ethnology was "the science of governing" (Rutsch, 2007, p. 262). As Luis Vázquez León (2002) observed, Molina Enríquez began a tradition of critical anthropology in Mexico, according to which the discipline should remedy the "great national problems". Precisely, one of Molina's most influential works was entitled *Los grandes problemas nacionales* (*The Great National Problems*) (1909). He was also a pioneer in dealing with the issue of the "territorial rights of indigenous tribes" based on property relations. However, Vázquez León (2014a, p. 123) wrote, "[I]t has become common that Andrés Molina Enríquez does not appear among the illustrious figures of Mexican anthropology, an exclusion caused by the indigenist historiography of Juan Comas with his well-intentioned anti-racial spirit".

Although the beginnings of Mexican anthropology with Molina Enríquez and Gamio clearly had a nationalist objective—to attend to "national problems" and to "forge a nation"—the "national" character of anthropology in Mexico was also forged from the relationship with foreigners. The *historia patria* (national history) cultivated in the National Museum, and in the archaeological and ethnological research on heritage and indigenous peoples, largely responded to the looting of archaeological pieces (Rutsch, 2007). The German anthropologist Eduard Seler was hired at the National Museum to classify and catalogue the museum's objects. Molina Enríquez took up the influential work of Lewis Henry Morgan, but also criticized unilinear evolutionism, identifying diverse paths in the evolution of peoples. Likewise, it was Franz Boas—considered the founding father of anthropology in the United States—who had the idea and initiative to create the International School of American Archaeology and Ethnology in Mexico, founded in 1910.

Thus, we can see how some researchers at the National Museum took up anthropological and sociological theories from the North and reformulated them according to national ideological purposes and goals. The case of Molina Enríquez is illustrative. Molina drew on the social Darwinism that enjoyed certain popularity at the time, but unlike the hegemonic interpretations, he did not consider the white or European "race" as the most "suitable" to lead the new revolutionary national project. For Molina, the descendants of the Spanish in Mexico focused their interests abroad, while the indigenous populations turned their interests to their own local communities. It was the mestizo group that was the most "suitable" to carry out the new nation-building project. Thus, he reformulated social Darwinism based on an ideology considered by some as "mestizophilia" (Basave, 2011; Vázquez León, 2002).

Regardless of whether he is considered the founding father of Mexican anthropology or not, we can find elements in Gamio's life and work that give Mexican anthropology its hallmark (Krotz, 2010, p. 6). Born in Mexico City, Gamio spent time on a rubber plantation in Santo Domingo, Veracruz, near the Gulf of Mexico. In this farm, Gamio lived an experience that awakened his anthropological vocation, perhaps analogous to the one Boas experienced among the Inuit. As the historian Ángeles González Gamio relates:

> [H]e is fascinated with this other Mexico he is discovering [… and] once he realizes how useless it is to try to make the farm produce, he gets to know the people who live in the area, learns their language: Nahuatl and begins to be deeply concerned about the problems they suffer; there he awakens that vocation that drives him throughout his life to undertake a sometimes quixotic struggle to improve the lives of indigenous groups. (González Gamio, 1987, p. 21)

Gamio himself acknowledged that "I became interested in the indigenous population when I lived for about three years on my family's ranch, called 'Santo Domingo'" (in González Gamio, 1987, p. 21). From this experience he wrote the short story "José Antonio" (1906), as well as texts that would become part of *Forjando Patria*, such as "Redemption of the indigenous class". In these pages he argues that the Indians have "intellectual aptitudes comparable to those of any race" (1960, p. 21), but that they are shy, lack energy and aspirations and always live in fear that the "people of reason", white men, will scorn them. For Gamio, the Indians will not "awaken spontaneously", but "it will be necessary that friendly hearts work for your redemption" (1960, p. 21). From these moments it is clear that indigenism will not be a policy formulated by the Indians to solve their problems, but by the non-Indians, the "friendly hearts", who will redeem the Indian.

After his experience at the Santo Domingo farm, Gamio joined the National Museum, where he had Nicolás León as a teacher, with whom he felt "a special attachment" (González Gamio, 1987, p. 25). In 1908 he

448   R. L. SALAZAR

carried out archaeological work in Chalchihuites, Zacatecas, and in 1909 he went to New York to study at Columbia University under the direction of Franz Boas. In 1917, when he was in charge of the Department of Anthropology, he began the Teotihuacán project, work for which he received his PhD from Columbia in 1922. Under the supervision of Eduard Seler, he carried out the "first stratigraphic exploration of Mexico" (De la Peña, 1996, p. 47).

The case of Gamio is illustrative in understanding how hegemonic anthropologies are received and assimilated in local contexts. Gamio did not faithfully reproduce the ideas of his professor Boas. For Guillermo de la Peña (1996), the Mexican anthropologist was an "intellectual intermediary" between American and Mexican anthropologies. Intellectual intermediaries are those individuals who make "intelligible and acceptable to an intellectual community the scientific ideas and research methods of a foreign intellectual community. This is not a mere work of translation, but an innovative practice; in turn, innovation is not simply imitative of what is foreign: it achieves a new synthesis" (De la Peña, 1996, p. 44). In this regard, Gamio took up Boas' stratigraphic method to establish cultural sequences in the Teotihuacán Valley and also adopted the thesis of independence among culture, race and language. Like Boas, Gamio questioned some of the racist ideas of his time. In *Forjando Patria*, he quotes Boas' *The Mind of Primitive Man* and states that "there is no pretended innate inferiority" of the Indians of the country, but that their problems of backwardness are due to "causes of education and environment" (Gamio, 1960, p. 23). Therefore, what must be done to solve the problems of the Indians is "to provide them with the education and the environment inherent to the culture they are trying to spread" (1960, p. 24). However, the nation-building project and the liberal ideology of progress led Gamio to adapt Boas' culturalist approaches. For example, he did not fully accept the doctrine of North American cultural relativism, because, like Molina Enríquez, he believed that there was a superior cultural form, the mestizo population, the only one capable of forging the Mexican homeland. As De la Peña (1996, pp. 61–62) wrote:

> The nation, [Gamio] argued, is a superior type of spiritual unity that must be built through the application of scientific laws. To achieve that unity, development should not be imposed on the different cultural areas that make up the nation; on the contrary, each of them must follow its own rhythm. Thus the discipline of anthropology, with the help of other sciences,

would be a crucial instrument in the nation-building process. However, the last goal was the "incorporation" of indigenous cultures into modernity.

Thus, as Cynthia Hewitt observed, Gamio made a "liberal reinterpretation of ethnographic particularism" (1988, p. 27). Hewitt agrees with Comas, Aguirre Beltrán and other historians of Mexican anthropology that with Gamio's work "the modern practice of anthropology in Mexico started" (1988, p. 27).

The role of the modern mestizo nation-building project in the readaptation of anthropological ideas produced in the North can also be seen in the work of Gonzalo Aguirre Beltrán (1908–1996), one of the most influential theorists of Mexican indigenism. Physician by training, he met Gamio when he took up a position as a biologist in the Demographic Department of the Ministry of the Interior in 1942. Two years later, he studied anthropology at Northwestern University under the tutelage of Melville Herskovits and Irving Hallowell. According to Aguirre (1994, p. 11), these anthropologists "leave a deep impression on my mind, precisely because of my proclivity for acculturative studies". Due to his intellectual capacities, Herskovits recommended that he dedicate himself to academia, but Aguirre preferred politics. In his own words: "When I returned from Northwestern after studying with Herskovits, I had two paths to follow: to dedicate myself to university teaching and research in search of an academic position, or dedicate myself to public administration, that is, to politics, to participate in the destiny of the people and to transform it. … I chose the last alternative" (Aguirre Beltrán, 1990, p. 11).

Aguirre's work must be understood in the context of Mexico's "modernization" process. In the framework of the so-called glorious thirties (1940–1970), the country experienced what has been known as the "Mexican miracle". During those decades there was an important population growth (from 26 million Mexicans in 1950 to 49 million in 1970), as well as the growth of industry, the modernization of agricultural activities and the construction of large hydraulic and electrification works. All this happened under the leadership of a strongly centralized State (in the federal and executive governments), which, through a corporate and clientelist structure, controlled the business, labour and peasant sectors (Loaeza, 2010). As Luis Aboites and Engracia Loyo (2010) note, one of the consequences of the Revolution was the entry of the masses into the political life of the country through the formation of agrarian committees and leagues, unions, political parties, chambers, unions and federations.

450   R. L. SALAZAR

Thus, in this period, several sectors of the Mexican population experienced a process of upward mobility that had not been previously seen in the country.

Thus, upon his return to Mexico, Aguirre served as head of the Demographic Department of the Ministry of the Interior—a position previously held by Gamio—and, thanks to a recommendation letter from Herskovits, he was appointed head of the Department of Indigenous Affairs (DAI), an institution created in 1936 by Mexican President Lázaro Cárdenas, and one of the preceding institutions of the National Indigenist Institute. During Cárdenas' presidency, one of the most important events for indigenism in Latin America was held, the First Inter-American Indigenist Congress in Pátzcuaro, Michoacán, in April 1940. According to Aguirre, this event established "the norms of the integrative indigenist policy, in the background of the philosophy that, based on cultural relativism, seeks the integral development of ethnic groups" (Aguirre Beltrán, 1994, p. 12).

In 1946, the DAI (its personnel and functions) was transferred to the Ministry of Public Education. It was under these conditions that Aguirre received Indigenous Affairs. In this institution he invited the anthropologists Julio de la Fuente, Carlos Basauri and Calixta Guiteras, as well as the pedagogue Vicente Casarrubias and the agronomist Cesáreo García Villareal to work with him. From this institution, they conducted research in different indigenous regions to provide technical and economic training to indigenous communities. In 1948 the National Indigenous Institute (INI) was created. Its first director was Alfonso Caso, who invited Aguirre to join the Institute. From this organization, Aguirre put into practice his ideas on the acculturation process and the integration of indigenous communities into the Mexican nation. In 1951 he founded the first *Centro Coordinador Indigenista* (Indigenous Coordinating Center, CCI) in San Cristóbal de las Casas. The CCIs were "government organizations created by presidential decree, which had under their charge the implementation of an integral type of action in the intercultural refugee regions" (Aguirre Beltrán, 1976, p. 27). This definition requires several clarifications.

The first is that, as Aguirre stated in one of his first major works, *Formas de gobierno indígena*, "Mexico is a country that struggles to reach the degree of homogeneity that will allow it to lay the solid foundations of a nationality" (Aguirre Beltrán, 1991, p. 15). But three obstacles stood in the way of the formation of the Mexican nation: the hostile geography, the ethnic-linguistic diversity and the accentuated feeling of ethnocentrism of the indigenous communities, whose sense of belonging were reserved to the community and did not extend beyond these boundaries to the nation. "Reality shows—wrote Aguirre (1991, p. 15)—with clear evidence that the Indians are not Mexican citizens, because they do not feel like Mexicans or enjoy the forms of the national culture. According to an accurate and incisive expression, they are foreigners in their own country." Both Aguirre and his collaborator Julio de la Fuente, two of the main theorists of indigenism, agreed that the ethnocentrism of the indigenous communities was a problem for the construction of the Mexican nation. And, as for Molina Enríquez and Gamio, the mestizo population was "the only sector of the population around which Mexican nationality could really be created" (1991, p. 17).

In his early works, as in *Formas de gobierno indígena*, Aguirre argued that knowledge of these forms of government was crucial to "find the appropriate formula so that the psychological adjustment that the indigenous will have to carry out in order to integrate into the forms of national culture takes place without serious frustrations or deep emotional conflicts" (1991, p. 19). Although, as we will see later, Aguirre took up Herskovits' concept of acculturation, in 1932 Richard Thurnwald had already observed the socio-psychological dimension of acculturation: that any acceptance of a new cultural element implies a change in the attitudes, social behaviour or even in the institutions of the receiving people. "This process of adaptation to new conditions of life is what we call acculturation" (Thurnwald, 1932, p. 557).

It is in this context that we can understand that, for Aguirre, indigenism was "a policy not formulated by the Indians for the solution of their problems, but that of the non-Indians with respect to the heterogeneous ethnic groups that receive the general distinction of Indians" (Aguirre Beltrán, 1992, pp. 24–25). In a similar way to Molina Enríquez and Gamio, Aguirre thought that the indigenous could not carry out an indigenist policy because "the scope of their world was reduced to a parochial, homogeneous and preclassist community, where the Indian had a very vague sense and notion of nationality" (Aguirre Beltrán, 1992, p. 25).

Aguirre stated on several occasions that his approach was "integrative and acculturative" (1994, p. 16). He took up the concept of "acculturation" from Herskovits, who, in an influential article with Robert Redfield and Ralph Linton, wrote: "Acculturation comprehends those phenomena which result when groups of individuals having different cultures come into continuous first-hand contact, with subsequent changes in the

452   R. L. SALAZAR

original cultural patterns of either or both groups" (Redfield et al., 1936, p. 149). What is noteworthy is that he interprets the concept of acculturation within the framework of what he called the "Mexican school" of anthropology. In this regard, in his book *El proceso de aculturación*, he wrote:

> The general development of anthropological theory and the application of its postulates in Mexico, in favor of the social changes produced by the Revolution, have created an ideological content, a system of norms and a wealth of experiences that are giving the Mexican school its distinctive profile and have allowed the implementation of an induced cultural change. (Aguirre Beltrán, 1992a, p. 44)

Although Aguirre finds "the cultural approach to the acculturation process" useful (1992a, p. 47), he questions "its ostensible tendency to consider culture as a super-organic entity [in reference to the famous approach of Alfred Kroeber, R.Ll.], independent of society and of the individuals who create and carry it" (1992a, p. 47). Therefore, he also considers the "social" and "integral" dimension, and approaches the concept of acculturation "according to the integral criterion that the Mexican school maintains emphatically, and that summarizes the apparent duality that exists between culture and society, between cultural exchange and social interaction, between levels of acculturation and levels of association or integration" (1992a, p. 50).

In this sense, the post-revolutionary nationalist ideology, which gave rise to the "Mexican school of anthropology", as well as the influence of the works of Donald Brand, Robert West and Daryl Forde, led Aguirre to adapt the concept of acculturation in a regional social framework. For Aguirre, the object of research and action of indigenism should not be the community, but the region, particularly what he called, taking up Frank Lorimer, the "region of refuge". These are intercultural regions in which "the structure inherited from the Colony and the archaic culture of the pre-industrial content, have found shelter against the onslaught of modern civilization" (Aguirre Beltrán, 1991a, p. 31). These colonial relations of domination are marked by racial segregation, political control, economic dependence, unequal treatment, social distance and evangelical action in favour of the non-indigenous population and to the detriment of indigenous communities. In other words, the social, educational, agrarian and health policies of the Mexican Revolution have not yet arrived in the

15 HISTORY OF ANTHROPOLOGY IN MEXICO: FROM NATION BUILDING... 453

refugee regions. Why was it so important to integrate the indigenous people into the nation? For Aguirre (1991a, p. 52):

> [A]t the level of the nation, there are no serious obstacles that prevent the member of an ethnic minority from integrating into the majority, as long as it was his wish; but, at the regional or local level, the domination mechanisms deny equality, interfere with mobility, seek the isolation of the group and maintain the status quo of the colonial situation by preserving, within the class society, totally anachronistic caste relations.

As we will see later, from the decade of the 1960s, a new generation of anthropologists denounced the indigenism of integration as a form of ethnocide, that is, the destruction of indigenous cultures. However, for Aguirre (1994, p. 22), "integration does not intend to destroy Indian ways of life and culture; on the contrary, it seeks the preservation of the vernacular language and the reconstruction of ethnic territoriality, that is, of land and language, the instruments of cultural continuity and of modernization and economic development as an adventure in the hands of ethnic peoples".

CRITICAL RUPTURE AND THE CONSTRUCTION OF A PLURICULTURAL NATION

In the 1960s, a new generation of social scientists severely questioned the dominant anthropology and indigenism of the time. In 1962, the young anthropologist Guillermo Bonfil Batalla formulated a critique of applied anthropology in Mexico, which he described as "conservative"; in 1963, the sociologist Pablo González Casanova published the article *Sociedad plural, colonialismo interno y desarrollo* ("Plural Society, Internal Colonialism and Development"), in which he analysed the relationship between indigenous communities and "national" society as a form of colonialism, and, in 1965, his influential book *La democracia en México* (Democracy in Mexico) was published, in which he argued that the country's political system does not meet the characteristics to be considered democratic (see González Casanova, 1965); in 1966, the anthropologist Rodolfo Stavenhagen published *Siete tesis falsas sobre América Latina* ("Seven Erroneous Theses About Latin America"), in which he questioned the hegemonic social theories on the region's development (see Stavenhagen, 1967). Probably the text that ultimately had the greatest impact on anthropology was the collective work entitled *De eso que llaman*

454   R. L. SALAZAR

antropología mexicana, published in 1970.[3] This new generation of social scientists was located in a context in which various social movements in Mexico—that of the railroad workers, doctors and nurses, the peasants and, above all, students—questioned the lack of civil and political liberties in the country. They were also influenced by the Cuban Revolution (1959) and the Marxist, anti-imperialist and anti-colonial currents developed in several parts of the world.

De eso que llaman antropología mexicana includes five texts written by young anthropologists: Arturo Warman, Guillermo Bonfil, Margarita Nolasco, Mercedes Olivera and Enrique Valencia, all of them trained at the National School of Anthropology and History. In these texts we find strong questioning of the anthropology practiced by Gamio, Aguirre Beltrán and Julio de la Fuente, among other anthropologists from the first half of the twentieth century. For Warman, the "Mexican anthropological tradition" contributed "effectively" to the disintegration of indigenous groups (Warman, 2002, p. 10) and Gamio, far from representing a revolutionary break with the dictatorship of Porfirio Díaz, embodied the continuity of the previous regime. According to Warman: "Gamio synthesized in his proposal all the currents of Porfirian indigenism: the racist, the culturalist, the educational and the economic [...] he proposed that the Indian should cease to be an Indian. To achieve this expensive ideal, the author designed what seemed to be an original and novel path: that of integration" (2002, p. 21). One of Warman's main criticisms of Gamio is that, from him, "anthropology voluntarily chained itself to the service of power, laying the foundations for the marriage to become a concubinage. And today we are paying for it" (2002, p. 22). In tune with González Casanova's and Stavenhagen's approaches on internal colonialism, Warman argued:

> Anthropology in Mexico has always been linked to expansionist processes of groups attached to Western culture. First it served the imperial metropolis and then the national sectors launched into internal colonialism and connected with international powers. Although it has always been justified in the supposed defense of the colonized, Mexican anthropology has always served the colonizer. (2002, p. 28)

---

[3] For Aguirre Beltrán (1990), the rupture was initiated by González Casanova with *La democracia en México*, where he proposes the concept of "internal colonialism".

15 HISTORY OF ANTHROPOLOGY IN MEXICO: FROM NATION BUILDING... 455

Probably the most influential essay included in *De eso que llaman antropología mexicana* is Bonfil's, *Del indigenismo de la revolución a la antropología crítica* ("From Revolution's Indigenism to Critical Anthropology"). Bonfil incorporates the work of social scientists from the "Third World" (Fanon, Memmi, Kenyatta) and critical currents from First World countries. He argues that "contemporary Mexican indigenism must recognize the 1910 revolution as its starting point" (Bonfil Batalla, 2002, p. 34) and that the most notable Mexican indigenists, from Gamio to Aguirre Beltrán, were formed in that process. And he challenges: "[T]he ideal of redemption of the Indian, translates, as in Gamio, into the denial of the Indian. The goal of indigenism, brutally said, is to achieve the disappearance of the Indian" (2002, p. 36).

From Bonfil's essay we find one of the early reformulations of the Mexican national project as a pluricultural nation. Although Bonfil adopted some Marxist ideas, he distanced himself from the approaches that supported revolution led by the proletarian or peasant class and, instead, he argued that an alternative project of nation could be built on the basis of indigenous cultures. In his words, "indigenous cultures have alternatives outside this system [Western and capitalist], because they do not base their legitimacy in terms of national culture but in their own and different past and in a history of exploitation as indigenous peoples; and it is precisely having been exploited as indigenous peoples that has allowed the survival of their own different culture" (2002, p. 43). Thus, in tune with some of the anti-colonial movements of the time, Bonfil claimed for indigenous peoples the right that was "historically established, to decide for themselves their own destiny" (2002, p. 46). As a result, Bonfil reached an "*inevitable*" conclusion: the perspective of a pluricultural state for Mexico" (2002, p. 47). But, in order to build "a plural state", a necessary condition is "the liberation of minority ethnic groups from the system of asymmetrical relations to which they are and have been subjected by the dominant society" (2002, p. 48). Throughout his career, Bonfil worked to understand the survival of the indigenous peoples' own culture, the possibilities of their self-determination and the construction of an alternative to the current system. A paragraph from his 1970 essay accurately illustrates his position:

> By exposing the irrationality of many current structures, by demonstrating that others are not necessary but rather mere contingency—and they are, on the other hand, irrational—by exhibiting their gratuitous and erratic

456 R. L. SALAZAR

character, critique is excercised, but utopia is also founded. It is the inevitable counterpart of criticism, constructive action, and gestation of models that eliminate at the root the deficiencies of the present whose causes and dynamics have been perceived. Utopia is the organization of anti-values where the current evaluative framework has demonstrated its historical ineffectiveness; it is the imagination of new and better ways of doing things, of doing life. In the forging of utopias, ethnology has much to contribute because its field encompasses the multiplicity of human experience, because it registers the alternatives that man has lived, because it demonstrates the viability of as many projects as societies with a distinctive culture have existed. There is much to learn from the Indians, from the "primitives" all over the world. (Bonfil Batalla, 2002, p. 52)

Later in his career, Bonfil drew on the anthropological approaches of Georges Balandier, as well as those from anti-colonial theorists and Latin American social scientists, and formulated the "theory of cultural control" to understand the cultural processes that take place when dominant and subaltern groups interact. One of the objectives of this theory was to establish a new cultural policy that would allow subaltern and popular groups to strengthen their "own culture". What was important for Bonfil was not only the cultural elements produced by the groups, but, above all, their collective decision-making capacity. Thus, the "cultura propia" encompasses both of the groups that make their own decisions on cultural elements that they produce ("autonomous culture"), and of the groups that make decisions about foreign cultural elements ("appropriate culture") (Bonfil Batalla, 1991). Likewise, the theory of cultural control was the basis of Bonfil's most important book, which would become one of the most influential in Mexican anthropology in the last three and a half decades: *México profundo. Una civilización negada* (1987). This work was written in a period of a serious economic crisis that the country suffered in 1982, in a context of poverty, inequality and "aggression against nature", from which neoliberal policies began to be implemented—mainly the privatization of state companies, as well as public services and natural resources. It is in this circumstance that Bonfil proposed to build a new alternative project of nationhood for Mexico.

In *México profundo*, Bonfil criticizes the "Imaginary Mexico", a project that the dominant elites have copied from models of other countries (Spain, France, United States) and, in contrast, vindicates the "Deep Mexico", in which a "cultural matrix" of Mesoamerican origin remains

15 HISTORY OF ANTHROPOLOGY IN MEXICO: FROM NATION BUILDING... 457

with a series of knowledge, techniques, forms of social organization and use of natural resources, and which is manifested not only in the indigenous communities but also in the popular and subaltern sectors of the cities. It is from this Mesoamerican cultural matrix that Bonfil proposed a "national project organized on the basis of cultural pluralism", in which "pluralism is not understood as an obstacle to overcome, but as the very content of the project, which legitimizes it and makes it viable", a "pluricultural nation" (Bonfil Batalla, 2005, p. 232). In this project, Bonfil does not attempt "to globally deny the West or pretend to isolate ourselves from its presence" (2005, p. 235), but rather "we must learn to see the West from Mexico instead of continuing to see Mexico from the West" (2005, p. 235).

Bonfil's ideas in *México profundo* are currently present in Mexican social anthropology, although its institutional, professional and practical conditions have been remarkably transformed in the last five decades. As I have already noted, critical anthropology coincided with a rupture in the national anthropological community, especially between governmental and academic anthropology. Despite the severe criticisms that Bonfil and Warman made of the governmental anthropology represented by Gamio, Caso and Aguirre Beltrán, Bonfil and Warman held important governmental positions.[4] Both were key figures in the modification of Article 4 of the Constitution in 1992 which, in tune with the demands of indigenous organizations and movements and international law on the rights of indigenous peoples, recognized that "the Mexican nation has a pluricultural composition originally supported by its indigenous peoples".

However, it should be noted that the recognition of the pluricultural composition of the Mexican nation occurred within the framework of what Charles R. Hale (2002) called "neoliberal multiculturalism"; that is, at the same time that the State legalizes certain indigenous claims—such as the recognition of cultural difference or indigenous language—it excludes others that may threaten the reproduction of capital—such as

---

[4] Bonfil was director of the National Institute of Anthropology and History (1972–1976), of the CIS-INAH (INAH Higher Research Center) (1976–1980), founder and director of the National Museum of Popular Cultures (1981–1985) and was head of the SEP's Department of Popular Cultures. Warman was director of the National Indigenous Institute (1988–1992), head of the Agrarian Attorney's Office (1992–1994), Secretary of Agriculture, Livestock and Rural Development (in 1994) and Secretary of Agrarian Reform (1994–1995 and 1995–1996). According to Luis Vázquez (2014a), Warman represents the "brilliant twilight of government anthropology".

collective rights to lands and territories. Thus, the reform of Article 4 of the Constitution coincided with the modification of Article 27, which opened the possibility of privatizing and commercializing ejido lands. The Mexican State has also issued mining and energy bills that have intensified the development of extractive megaprojects in indigenous regions. By 2017, there were 24,709 mining concessions covering an area of 20.79 million hectares in Mexican territory (Fundar, 2018). According to various studies, the main socio-environmental conflicts in Mexico are caused by mining projects (Cisneros & Espinosa, 2016; Castellanos, 2018; Centro Mexicano de Derecho Ambiental, 2018).

On the other hand, as I pointed out in the introduction to this chapter, the critical anthropology proposed by Bonfil not only meant a break with the dominant anthropology and indigenism, but also coincided with an expansion of anthropological teaching and research institutions in Mexico, as well as with a split in the national anthropological community. With the institutional expansion of anthropology and the questioning of the indigenist paradigm, a theoretical and thematic diversification also took place in Mexican anthropology (Medina, 2004, p. 231; Portal Ariosa & Ramírez Sánchez, 2010, p. 270), two of the most notable being Marxism and Ethnicism (see Hewitt de Alcántara, 1988). Eventually, it would be the ethnicist approach, defended by Bonfil, that would be the most influential in Mexican anthropology at the end of the twentieth century and the beginning of the twenty-first century, as well as in policies towards the indigenous communities.

The anthropology practiced in universities and research institutions has gone through what Vázquez León (2002) and Juan Luis Sariego (2007) called a process of "academization", in which the academic field has become the most valued and prestigious. This process has deepened since the 1980s, when science and technology evaluation policies gained greater strength, as well as the neoliberal university model, with the prioritization of quantitative accountability criteria (see Merry, 2011; Krotz, 2014; Díaz Crovetto & Oehmichen-Bazán, 2020). However, the academic expansion of Mexican anthropology has not been able to provide a job and positions for the growing number of anthropologists trained in Mexico in the last four decades. Regarding the problem of labour precariousness of anthropologists outside the academy, in 2014 the round table "The situation of the professional practice of anthropology in the face of labor flexibilization" was organized as part of the III Mexican Conference of Social Anthropology and Ethnology. From this event, the group *Antropólogos por un mercado laboral y digno* ("Anthropologists for a decent labour market") was founded. It is mainly composed of young anthropologists with a Marxist influence. This group has joined forces with other initiatives that have explored and studied the conditions of anthropologists working outside the academy. One of the initiatives was the "Survey on the professional practice and working conditions of anthropologists in Mexico" in 2016. The group has also called for professional anthropologists to use the Ethnologists and Social Anthropologists Association as a tool to improve the working conditions of the profession (see Legarreta Haynes, 2016). Likewise, based on these experiences, from the academy, Krotz and Reygadas (2020) have called for the "de-academization" of anthropology. Their proposal "is not about opposing segments of the anthropological community, but to make it stronger through a visibility strategy, including the interests of the majority of the graduates in our professional organizations and diversification of the professional practice of anthropology" (Krotz & Reygadas, 2020, pp. 414–415). The dignity of professional practice and the de-academization of anthropology are still pending tasks and constitute one of the main challenges of the discipline today.

The Legacy of a Tradition?

Current Mexican social anthropology, practiced by more than 7000 anthropologists, can hardly be reduced to a single epistemological, theoretical or political approach. In Mexican academia, topics as diverse as interspecies ethnographies, film audiences, (neo)extractivism and the exploration of outer space are currently being addressed. However, as some scholars of Mexican anthropology have observed, the discipline is currently engaged in "a substantial effort to transcend the nationalist matrix in which it is formed" (Medina, 2004, p. 232), or, as María Ana Portal and Xóchitl Ramírez have written (2010, p. 277), "there is a movement that went beyond the interest in 'making a nation'—that is, a nationalist anthropology anchored in the country—to what we could think of as an anthropology of 'being in the world' based on networks, cultural interconnections and multiplicity of analytical views". If the nation-building project has been abandoned, what is left of the "Mexican school of anthropology" or the "Mexican anthropological tradition"?

Returning to Bonfil's ideas, it is now a matter of building a pluricultural nation. Indigenous peoples continue to be one of the main actors in this project, although in recent years, Afro-Mexican populations and migrant groups have also gained visibility. Likewise, for the new generations of anthropologists, the building of a pluricultural nation no longer depends mainly on government action, but through collaborative work with civil society organizations and social movements. Gamio's idea that there should be "friendly hearts" that redeem the indigenous and Aguirre Beltrán's that the solution of indigenous problems should be formulated by non-indigenous people have been left behind. Since the uprising of the *Ejército Zapatista de Liberación Nacional* (Zapatista Army of National Liberation) in 1994, and epistemological, theoretical and methodological proposals emerged such as the decolonial turn and collaborative research, which are currently present in Mexican anthropology today, indigenous people and other subjects of study must be the protagonists in the solution of their problems. Although anthropologists from the North continue to be cited, these studies are increasingly influenced by epistemological and theoretical proposals from the global South, such as the work of Boaventura de Sousa Santos (2009) on epistemologies of the South, ecology of knowledge and the emancipatory use of law, as well as the programme of modernity-coloniality and the decolonial turn (Escobar, 2003).

An important difference with previous periods is that the project of building a pluricultural nation is taking place in a context of profound violence and inequalities in Mexico.[5] Since the war that the Mexican State declared against organized crime in 2006, more than 350,000 people have been murdered in the country and more than 72,000 have disappeared (Pardo Veiras & Arredondo, 2021). Specifically, events such as the massacre of 72 Central American migrants in San Fernando, Tamaulipas, in 2010; the judicial executions of 22 young civilians in Tlatlaya, Estado de Mexico, and the forced disappearance of 43 rural students from Ayotzinapa, Guerrero, in 2014; as well as the thousands of femicides committed in the country have shocked various sectors of the population, including the anthropological one. In this setting, there has been an increase in research on the phenomena of violence and security in the country, but also epistemological, theoretical and methodological reflections on the practice of anthropology in violent contexts.[6] For example, the Colectivo Tardes Etnográficas has

---

[5] According to Gerardo Esquivel (2015), the fortune of the 16 richest Mexicans in the country is equivalent to the accumulated income of 20 million inhabitants of Mexico.

[6] See, for example, issue 91 of *Nueva Antropología* journal, about public security and privatization of security and issues 58, 62 and 63 of *Alteridades* journal about violence and (in) security.

developed the "Security Protocol for anthropologists in the field", in which they propose to carry out ethnographic work in a network to reduce risks (see Del Río Vithe et al., 2020). Research on violence and human rights violations has also privileged testimony as a source of information and a way of producing anthropological knowledge, as well as proposals for action such as anthropological expertise and the *Amicus Curiae*.[7]

In this context, we can find in the last two decades some innovative epistemological, theoretical and methodological proposals committed to the construction of a pluricultural nation. One of them is "communality", as it has been formulated by the Mixe indigenous anthropologist Floriberto Díaz. According to Díaz, "communality" is a livelihood practiced by Mesoamerican communities. It refers to the collectivist nature of indigenous life in Oaxaca and to an underlying energy, to spiritual existence and to the "immanence of the community" (Díaz, 2007, p. 39); "expresses universal principles and truths regarding indigenous society [characterized by notions of] the communal, the collective, complementarity and integrality" (Díaz, 2007, p. 40); its defining elements are the Earth as mother and as territory, consensus in assembly (against the principles of market competition), free service as an exercise of authority, collective work as an act of recreation, and rites and ceremonies (Díaz, 2007, p. 59); likewise, communality is marked in an important way by orality, which implies social relations and direct communication (Díaz, 2007, p. 216).[8] Interestingly, Díaz points out that he is not the creator of the notion of communality; its original authors are the indigenous communities. In this sense, according to Leif Korsbaek (2009), it represents a "new paradigm" in Mexican anthropology, while with communality "indigenous people have the possibility of producing the knowledge that was previously the privilege of anthropology and put it to the use of their own project formulated by the indigenous people themselves, and not as before by non-indigenous people who occasionally had a strongly anti-indigenous mentality" (Korsbaek, 2009, p. 120).

---

[7] See issues 57 and 62 of the journal *Desacatos*, dedicated to "Dilemmas of Cultural Expertise" and "Uses and Destinations of Testimony in Latin America", respectively.

[8] For Juan José Rendón Monzón (2003), another defender of communality, this has as fundamental elements the communal territory, communal work, communal political power and communal festival. In both Díaz's and Rendón's formulations we can appreciate, as Korsbaek (2009: 118) has done, the prominence of material elements (territory, work and political power) and the marginalization of other elements that are more important for anthropologists, such as language and worldview.

In addition to the emergence of indigenous anthropologies and the proposal of communality, a trend that has gained strength in contemporary Mexican social anthropology is "co-labor" research. This type of research is heir to different proposals developed in Latin America, such as participatory action research (Fals Borda, 2007), critical pedagogy and popular and liberating education (Freire, 1970), the Modernity/Coloniality research programme (see Escobar, 2003), the epistemology of the South of the Portuguese sociologist Boaventura de Sousa Santos (2009) as well as the collaborative research proposals of Charles R. Hale (2006). Co-labour research, as defended by Xóchitl Leyva and Shannon Speed (2008), implies collaboration with those traditionally called "study subjects" throughout the research process, from the definition of the project objectives to the production of the results and their uses.

Illustrative examples of collaborative research and indigenous anthropologies in Mexico can be found in the three-volume collegiate work, *Prácticas otras de conocimiento(s). Entre crisis, entre guerras*, coordinated by Xóchitl Leyva Solano (2015). The books bring together research with organized indigenous women, peasant teachers, young urban indigenous artists, community communicators and indigenous academics who question the knowledge practices of the neoliberal academic system. From the *"other practices of knowledge"* elaborated by these subjects, the three volumes are intended to challenge the modern regime of knowledge/power. Particularly the initiatives of co-theorization with indigenous researchers stand out, as well as the recognition of indigenous epistemologies and ontologies for "the defense of the pluriverse" (Leyva Solano, 2015, p. 63).

Collaboration with indigenous communities, organizations and movements for the construction of a pluricultural nation has taken various theoretical, methodological and political forms in contemporary Mexico. One of them is "militant" anthropology, as proposed by Orlando Aragón Andrade (2019). This type of anthropology starts "from the collaboration with a determined public and the intervention of critical legal knowledge in their struggle", and has "at its core the enterprise of thinking in order to act or intervene and thus try to respond to the challenges and problems that [the indigenous community of] Cherán faced" (2019, p. 30). Militant anthropology has been particularly visible in the political and legal advocacy to defend indigenous people's rights. Likewise, Laura Valladares (2021) has proposed the existence of a "community anthropology", in which it is the indigenous communities and organizations themselves that invite anthropologists to carry out research on a certain problem in a horizontal and collaborative relationship.

Finally, we can highlight the greater visibility that feminist anthropologists have gained in Mexico. In this regard, Marisa Ruiz Trejo (2022) identifies two trends in the new generations of feminist anthropologists, including several indigenous, Afro-Mexican, lesbian, non-binary and *muxhes*[9] anthropologists: epistemologies and movements for the defence of life and the earth, and transfeminist thought. These trends coincide in the analysis and complaints of violence against women and in the emphasis on the relationship between the body and the territory (see Leyva Solano, 2019). In many of these works, the influence of the work of Donna Haraway (2016) can be appreciated: her critiques of the Anthropocene and Capitalocene, as well as her proposals for an ethic of care and generating "oddkin" or odd kin with other beings that inhabit the Earth. But also, as in the cases of communality and co-labour research, the conceptualizations of indigenous women's movements are taken up again, such as the concept of "terricidio" (terracide), which refers to the processes of dispossession and destruction of the Earth by capitalist, colonialist and patriarchal practices.

The Mexican anthropological tradition has been characterized by its contributions to the nation-building project, first a mestizo nation, which sought to integrate the heterogeneous indigenous population into the national society, and later a pluricultural nation, in which research has sought the recognition of cultural diversity in a context of inequality and violence. From these political projects, theoretical contributions generated in the North have been reinterpreted and, in some cases, Mexican anthropologists have formulated original theoretical proposals. Currently, Mexican social anthropology is no longer exclusively a governmental anthropology. Its most visible and prestigious field is practiced within academia. However, outside academia, working conditions are often precarious, a setting in which proposals have been made to dignify the professional practice of anthropology in Mexico. A critical review of the legacy of Mexican social anthropology reminds us that it is not possible to have an absolutely plural society if relations of inequality and exploitation persist. This is valid not only regarding the fields studied by anthropology but also within the discipline itself.

---

[9] As Elvis Guerra explains: "Muxhe is a gender identity that has to do with people who are born biologically male and eventually adopt another gender different from the one they were born" (Cultural Survival, 2019).

References

Aboites, L., & Loyo, E. (2010). La construcción del nuevo estado, 1920–1945. In *Nueva historia general de México* (pp. 357–386). El Colegio de México.

Aguirre Beltrán, G. (1976). Estructura y funciones de los Centros Coordinadores. In G. Aguirre Beltrán, A. Villa Rojas, & A. Romano Delgado (coords.), *El indigenismo en acción* (pp. 27–40). Secretaría de Educación Pública/Instituto Nacional Indigenista.

Aguirre Beltrán, G. (1990). Derrumbe de paradigmas. *México Indígena, 9*, 5–16.

Aguirre Beltrán, G. (1991). *Obra antropológica IV. Formas de gobierno indígena.* Universidad Veracruzana/Instituto Nacional Indigenista/Gobierno del Estado de Veracruz/Fondo de Cultura Económica.

Aguirre Beltrán, G. (1991a). *Obra antropológica IX. Regiones de refugio. El desarrollo de la comunidad y el proceso dominical en Mestizoamérica.* Universidad Veracruzana/Instituto Nacional Indigenista/Gobierno del Estado de Veracruz/Fondo de Cultura Económica.

Aguirre Beltrán, G. (1992). Un postulado de política indigenista. In *Obra antropológica XI. Obra polémica* (pp. 21–28). Universidad Veracruzana/Instituto Nacional Indigenista/Gobierno del Estado de Veracruz/Fondo de Cultura Económica.

Aguirre Beltrán, G. (1992a). *Obra antropológica VI. El proceso de aculturación y el cambio socio-cultural en México.* Universidad Veracruzana/Instituto Nacional Indigenista/Gobierno del Estado de Veracruz/Fondo de Cultura Económica.

Aguirre Beltrán, G. (1994). *El pensar y el quehacer antropológico en México.* Benemérita Universidad Autónoma de Puebla.

Aragón Andrade, O. (2019). *El derecho en insurrección. Hacia una antropología jurídica militante, desde la experiencia de Cherán, México.* Universidad Nacional Autónoma de México.

Basave, A. (2011). *México mestizo: análisis del nacionalismo mexicano en torno a la mestizofilia.* Fondo de Cultura Económica.

Beals, R. (1993). La antropología en el México contemporáneo. In *Dos lecturas de la antropología mexicana* (pp. 5–29). Universidad de Guadalajara.

Besserer, F. (2019). Prólogo. Repensando la antropología y la mexicanidad en el siglo XXI. In M. A. Portal (Ed.), *Repensar la antropología mexicana del siglo XXI: viejos problemas, nuevos desafíos* (pp. 19–24). Universidad Autónoma Metropolitana.

Bonfil Batalla, G. (1991). Lo propio y lo ajeno: una aproximación al problema del control cultural. In *Pensar nuestra cultura* (pp. 58–67). Alianza.

Bonfil Batalla, G. (2002). Del indigenismo de la revolución a la antropología crítica. In A. Warman et al. (Eds.), *De eso que llaman antropología mexicana* (pp. 33–54). Comité de Publicaciones de los alumnos de la Escuela Nacional de Antropología e Historia.

15 HISTORY OF ANTHROPOLOGY IN MEXICO: FROM NATION BUILDING... 465

Bonfil Batalla, G. (2005). *México profundo: una civilización negada*. Debolsillo. (English version: Bonfil Batalla, G. (1996). *México Profundo: Reclaiming A Civilization*. University of Texas Press).

Bueno, C. (2011). *La antropología en México: veinte años después. Inventario Antropológico. Anuario de la Antropología Mexicana, 9*, 397–414.

Castellanos, L. (2018). Los planes del gobierno de AMLO podrían enfrentar cientos de conflictos territoriales. *The New York Times en español* (on line), November 29. Retrieved November 29, 2018, from https://www.nytimes.com/es/2018/11/29/amlo-conflictos-ambientales/

Centro Mexicano de Derecho Ambiental. (2018). *Informe anual sobre la situación de personas defensoras de los derechos humanos ambientales en México, 2017.* Centro Mexicano de Derecho Ambiental.

Cisneros, I., & Espinosa, E. (2016). Megaproyectos. Van 80 agresiones a pueblos indígenas. *El Universal* (on line), November 5. Retrieved November 5, 2016, from http://www.eluniversal.com.mx/articulo/periodismo-deinvestigacion/2016/11/5/megaproyectos-van-80-agresiones-pueblos-indigenas

Comas, J. (1976). *La antropología social aplicada en México. Trayectoria y antología*. Instituto Indigenista Interamericano, Serie Antropología Social, 16.

Cultural Survival. (2019). Ser Muxhe en Juchitán, México. *Cultural Survival Quarterly Magazine*, December. Retrieved June 16, 2022, from https://www.culturalsurvival.org/es/publications/cultural-survival-quarterly/ser-muxhe-en-juchitan-mexico

De la Peña, G. (1996). Nacionales y extranjeros en la historia de la antropología mexicana. In M. Rutsch (comp.), *La historia de la antropología en México. Fuentes y transmisión* (pp. 41–81). Universidad Iberoamericana/Plaza y Valdés/Instituto Nacional Indigenista.

de Sousa Santos, B. (2009). *Una epistemología del sur: la reinvención del conocimiento y la emancipación social.* Consejo Latinoamericano de Ciencias Sociales/Siglo XXI.

Del Río Vithe, M., Morales, M. C., & Monreal Quistián, O. (2020). *Protocolo de seguridad para antropólogas y antropólogos en campo.* Colectivo Tardes Etnográficas/Universidad Autónoma Metropolitana-Itzapalapa. https://www.academia.edu/47772617/Protocolo_de_Seguridad_para_Antropologas_y_Antropologos_en_Campo_Colectivo_Tardes_Etnograficas

Díaz Crovetto, G., & Oehmichen-Bazán, C. (2020). Las antropologías latinoamericanas ante el giro a la derecha: primeras aproximaciones. *Plural. Antropologías desde América Latina y el Caribe, 3*(6), 15–32.

Díaz, F. (2007). *Escrito: comunalidad, energía viva del pensamiento mixe. Ayuujktsënää yën -ayuujkwënmää ny-ayuujk mëk äjtën* (S. Robles, & R. Cardoso, comps.). Universidad Nacional Autónoma de México.

466 R. L. SALAZAR

Escobar, A. (2003). "Mundos y conocimientos de otro modo". El programa de investigación de modernidad/colonialidad latinoamericano. *Tabula Rasa, 1*, 51–86.

Esquivel, G. (2015). *Desigualdad extrema en México. Concentración del poder económico y político.* Oxfam México/Iguales.

Fals Borda, O. (2007). La investigación-acción en convergencias disciplinarias. *LASA Forum 2007, 38*(4), 17–22.

Freire, P. (1970). *Pedagogía del oprimido.* Siglo XXI.

Fundar. (2018). *Las actividades extractivas en México: minería e hidrocarburos hacia el fin del sexenio. Anuario 2017.* Fundar.

Gamio, M. (1960). *Forjando patria. Pro-nacionalismo.* Porrúa.

García Canclini, N. (2019). Prólogo. In M. A. Portal (Ed.), *Repensar la antropología mexicana del siglo XXI: viejos problemas, nuevos desafíos* (pp. 11–18). Universidad Autónoma Metropolitana.

García Mora, C., & Medina, A. (Eds.). (1983). *La quiebra política de la antropología social en México.* Universidad Nacional Autónoma de México.

Garciadiego, J., & Kuntz Ficker, S. (2010). La Revolución mexicana. In *Nueva historia general de México* (pp. 537–594). El Colegio de México.

Giglia, A., Garma, C., & de Teresa, A. P. (comps.). (2007) *¿Adónde va la antropología?* Universidad Autónoma Metropolitana-Iztapalapa.

González Casanova, P. (1965). Internal Colonialism and National Development. *Studies in Comparative International Development, 1*, 27–37.

González Gamio, A. (1987). *Manuel Gamio. Una lucha sin final.* Universidad Nacional Autónoma de México.

Hale, C. R. (2002). Does Multiculturalism Menace? Governance, Cultural Rights and the Politics of Identity in Guatemala. *Journal of Latin American Studies, 34*(3), 485–524.

Hale, C. R. (2006). Activist Research v. Cultural Critique: Indigenous Land Rights and the Contradictions of Political Engaged Anthropology. *Cultural Anthropology, 21*(1), 96–120.

Haraway, D. (2016). *Staying with the Trouble: Making Kin in the Chthulucene.* Duke University Press.

Hewitt de Alcántara, C. (1988). *Imágenes del campo. La interpretación antropológica del México rural.* El Colegio de México.

Korsbaek, L. (2009). El comunalismo: cambio de paradigma en la antropología mexicana a raíz de la globalización. *Argumentos, 22*(59), 101–123.

Krotz, E. (2006). Mexican Anthropology's Ongoing Search for Identity. In G. L. Ribeiro & A. Escobar (Eds.), *World Anthropologies. Disciplinary Transformations Within Systems of Power* (pp. 87–109). Berg.

Krotz, E. (2010). Evolution of the Anthropologies of the South: Contributions of Three Mexican Anthropologists in the Latter Half of the Twentieth Century. In R. Darnell & F. Gleach (Eds.), *Histories of Anthropology Annual Volume 6* (pp. 1–17). Lincoln.

15 HISTORY OF ANTHROPOLOGY IN MEXICO: FROM NATION BUILDING... 467

Krotz, E. (2014). Las ciencias sociales frente al 'Triángulo de las Bermudas'. Una hipótesis sobre las transformaciones de la investigación científica y la educación superior en México. *Revista de El Colegio de San Luis, 1*(1), 18–46.

Krotz, E., & Reygadas, L. (2020). ¿Hacia la desacademización de la antropología mexicana? Una idea para la discusión gremial y para el VI Congreso Mexicano de Antropología Social y Etnología. *Plural. Antropologías desde América Latina y el Caribe, 3*(6), 409–419.

Lameiras, J. (1979). La antropología en México. Panorama de su desarrollo en lo que va del siglo. In V. Autores (Ed.), *Ciencias sociales en México: desarrollo y perspectiva* (pp. 107–180). México.

Legarreta Haynes, P. (2016). Medio siglo después de la crítica: disputas política y el papel de la antropología mexicana en la división del trabajo social. *EntreDiversidades* (Special issue), 15–54.

Leyva Solano, X. (Ed.). (2015). *Prácticas otras de conocimiento(s). Entre crisis, entre guerras.* Cooperativa Editorial Retos/Programa de Democracia y Transformación Global/Grupo Internacional de Trabajo sobre Asuntos Indígenas/Talleres Paradigmas Emancipatorios-Galfisa/Proyecto Alice/Taller Editorial La Casa del Mago.

Leyva Solano, X. (2019). "Poner el cuerpo" para des(colonizar)patriarcalizar nuestro conocimiento, la acadmiea, nuestra vida. In X. Leyva & R. Icaza (coords.), *En tiempos de muerte: cuerpos, rebeldías y resistencias* (pp. 339–363). Cooperativa Editorial Retos/Consejo Latinoamericano de Ciencias Sociales/International Institute of Social Studies/Erasmus University Rotterdam.

Leyva Solano, X., & Speed, S. (2008). Hacia la investigación descolonizada: nuestra experiencia de co-labor. In X. Leyva, A. Burguete & S. Speed (coords.), *Gobernar (en) la diversidad: experiencias indígenas desde América Latina. Hacia la investigación de co-labor* (pp. 65–107). Facultad Latinoamericana de Ciencias Sociales/Centro de Investigaciones y Estudios Superiores en Antropología Social.

Loaeza, S. (2010). Modernización autoritaria a la sombra de la superpotencia, 1944–1968. In *Nueva historia general de México* (pp. 387–411). El Colegio de México.

Lomnitz, C. (2014). La etnografía y el futuro de la antropología en México. *Nexos,* November 14. Retrieved November 15, 2014, from https://www.nexos.com.mx/?p=23263

Medina, A. (2004). Veinte años de Antropología Mexicana. La configuración de una Antropología del sur. *Mexican Studies/Estudios Mexicanos, 20*(2), 231–274.

Merry, S. E. (2011). Measuring the World. Indicators, Human Rights, and Global Governance. *Current Anthropology, 52*(S3), S83–S95.

Palerm, A. (1980). *Antropología y marxismo.* Nueva Imagen.

Pardo Veiras, J. L., & Arredondo, I. (2021). Una guerra inventada y 350,000 muertos en México. *The Washington Post,* June 14. Retrieved June 16, 2021, from https://www.washingtonpost.com/es/post-opinion/2021/06/14/mexico-guerra-narcotrafico-calderon-homicidios-desaparecidos/

Portal Ariosa, M. A., & Ramírez Sánchez, P. X. (2010). *Alteridad e identidad. Un recorrido por la historia de la antropología en México*. Universidad Autónoma Metropolitana/Juan Pablos.

Redfield, R., Linton, R., & Herskovits, M. (1936). Memorandum for the Study of Acculturation. *American Anthropologist, 38*(1), 149–152.

Rendón Monzón, J. J. (2003). *La comunalidad. Modo de vida en los pueblos indios*. Consejo Nacional para la Cultura y las Artes.

Reygadas, L. (2019). *Antropólog@s del milenio. Desigualdad, precarización y heterogeneidad en las condiciones laborales de la antropología en México*. Universidad Autónoma Metropolitana/Instituto Nacional de Antropología e Historia/Centro de Investigaciones y Estudios Superiores en Antropología Social/Universidad Iberoamericana/Colegio de Etnólogos y Antropólogos Sociales/Red Mexicana de Instituciones de Formación de Antropólogos.

Ruiz Trejo, M. G. (2022). Etnografías feministas en México: críticas de las nuevas generaciones de antropólogas. *Alteridades, 32*(63), 81–94.

Rutsch, M. (2007). *Entre el campo y el gabinete. Nacionales y extranjeros en la profesionalización de la antropología mexicana (1877–1920)*. Instituto Nacional de Antropología e Historia/Universidad Nacional Autónoma de México.

Sariego, J. L. (2007). La academización de la antropología en México. In A. Giglia, C. Garma, & A. P. de Teresa (Eds.), *¿Adónde va la antropología?* (pp. 111–127). Universidad Autónoma Metropolitana-Iztapalapa.

Stavenhagen, R. (1967). *Seven erroneous theses about Latin America*. New England Free Press.

Stocking, G., Jr. (1982). Afterword: A View from the Center. *Ethnos, 47*(1–2), 172–186.

Thurnwald, R. (1932). The Psychology of Acculturation. *American Anthropologist, 34*(4), 557–569.

Valladares, L. (2021). La antropología comunitaria. Una nueva relación de investigación en y con los pueblos indígenas. *Alteridades, 31*(62), 13–24.

Vázquez León, L. (2002). *Quo vadis anthropologia socialis?* In G. de la Peña & L. Vázquez León (Eds.), *La antropología sociocultural en el México del milenio: búsquedas, encuentros y transiciones* (pp. 51–104). México.

Vázquez León, L. (2014a). *Historia de la etnología. La antropología sociocultural mexicana*. Primer Círculo.

Vázquez León, L. (2014b). Ciento cuatro años de antropología mexicana. *Revista Antropologías del Sur, 1*, 119–131.

Villoro, L. (1979). *Los grandes momentos del indigenismo en México*. Centro de Investigaciones Superiores del Instituto Nacional de Antropología e Historia.

Warman, A. (2002). Todos santos y todos difuntos. Crítica histórica de la antropología mexicana. In A. Warman et al. (Eds.), *De eso que llaman antropología mexicana* (pp. 5–31). Comité de Publicaciones de los alumnos de la Escuela Nacional de Antropología e Historia.

CHAPTER 16

Social Anthropology in India: Studying the Self in the Other

Sara Roncaglia

The attainment of this position has been a slow growth, obstructed
[accompanied] *at every point by established errors.*
—Linton *(1936, p. 320)*

Anthropology became established in India during the British colonisation. Subsequently, in the early years of the twentieth century, it was given official recognition in major universities throughout the country with courses on social anthropology and sociology, which led to a progressive

---

S. Roncaglia (✉)
University of Milano, Milan, Italy

© The Author(s), under exclusive license to Springer Nature
Switzerland AG 2023
G. D'Agostino, V. Matera (eds.), *Histories of Anthropology*,
https://doi.org/10.1007/978-3-031-21258-1_16

469

470 S. RONCAGLIA

professionalisation of the discipline.[1] Our aim here is to understand the process of transposing a "Western science" into an Indian context, with its attending political, ethical and cognitive consequences (Uberoi et al., 2007, p. 10). This chapter is, therefore, meant less as an exhaustive account of all the major figures who have shaped the history of anthropology in India, than as an analysis "focusing on the intersection of knowledge, institutions and practices in a specific geographical locale" (Uberoi et al., 2007, p. 8). We will be considering both the Indian protagonists who played a pivotal role in the discipline and the salient debates that shaped its development. While the link between colonialism and anthropology in India is unquestionable, an attempt is made here to bring out, within a chronological framework and in a multifaceted perspective, the disciplinary positioning of different scholars: their relations to the subjects studied and the roles they played in the epistemological transformations before and after independence. One such transformation has to do with the blurred disciplinary distinction between social anthropology and Indian sociology, whose boundaries seem to coincide if read within a Western context. As Andre Béteille has pointed out, however:

> [...] what anthropology is to an American will be sociology to an Indian, and what sociology is to an American will be anthropology to an Indian. The distinction will work only so long as all societies, Western and non-Western, are studied only by Western scholars. It becomes meaningless when scholars from all over the world begin to study their own as well as other societies. (Béteille, 1974, p. 11)

Such a hazy disciplinary distinction also occurs in another momentous area of inquiry about anthropology in India, namely the study of Indian society itself, with a view to exploring its multiple social and cultural layers, its religious and linguistic pluralities, as well as the political, economic and

---

[1] In the 1950s, Dhirendra Nath Majumdar identified three main periods in the history of anthropology in India: formulationary (1774–1911), constructive (1912–1937) and critical (1938–) (Majumdar, 1950). In the early 1970s, Surajiit Sinha distinguished between the British colonial period (1774–1919), the pre-Independence period (1920–1949) and the post-Independence period (1950–) (Sinha, 1971). In the late 1970s, Lalita Prasad Vidyarthi identified the formative period (1774–1919), the constructive period (1920–1949) and the analytical period (1950–) (Vidyarthi, 1978). In the same years, Ramkrishna Mukherjee pointed out some reference groups of the discipline as the pioneers (1920–1940), the modernisers (1950), the insiders (1960), and the pace-makers and non-conformists (1970) (Mukherjee, 1979).

16 SOCIAL ANTHROPOLOGY IN INDIA: STUDYING THE SELF IN THE OTHER   471

educational changes encapsulated in the familiar "unity in diversity" catch-phrase. For Indian anthropological knowledge did take shape within the birth of an independent nation-state, in the progressive building of inclusive epistemologies of self-study. Mysore Narasimhachar Srinivas characterised this direction as a study of the "self-in-the-Other":

> When an Indian anthropologist is studying a different caste or other group in India, he is studying someone who is both the Other and also someone with whom he shares a few cultural forms, beliefs, and values. That is, he is studying a self-in-the-Other and not a total Other, for both are members of the same civilisation, which is extraordinarily complex, layered, and filled with conflicting tendencies. I consider the study of one's own society not only feasible but essential, for it is best that a culture is studied by both outsiders and insiders. Alone, neither is complete. [...] [*In research*] the clash of multiple subjectivities would, to my mind, be better than a single subjectivity, whether that of the insider or outsider. (Srinivas, 1997, pp. 22–23, *the italics are mine*)

As highlighted more recently by Gopala Sarana and Dharni P. Sinha, Srinivas' sensitivity successfully anticipated some of the most current issues on the reflexive value of national anthropology:

> One of our greatest drawbacks is the lack of other-culture studies by Indian anthropologists. [...] However, what has until now been our weakness will prove to be a source of strength in the very near future. We do not think there is any other country in the world where anthropological self-study has been conducted by native-born anthropologists for almost seven decades. Before long, anthropologists of all countries, particularly the developing countries, will have to start studying their own culture. We cannot anticipate the kinds of problems these native anthropologists will face. This new aspect of anthropology in almost every country will encounter growing pains. The only exception then will be anthropology in India, which has long passed that stage. (Sarana & Sinha, 1976, p. 217)

THE ANTHROPOLOGY OF COLONIAL ADMINISTRATION

Anthropology in India developed alongside colonisation and the implementation of ten-year censuses, conducted from the second half of the nineteenth century with the dual purpose of enhancing scientific knowledge of the country and reinforcing British rule. This task was entrusted to the Imperial Civil Service, whose members were officials in the service of the British Crown who performed administrative, military and educational duties. The growing need to gather information about the social, religious and economic life of India's diverse population served as a stimulus for promoting anthropological research, interpreted within the framework of "a firm commitment to positivism, to methods of empirical observation, and verification" (Dhanagare, 1993, p. 35).

Among the leading anthropologists in British India was Herbert Risley (1851–1911), a civil servant for 39 years. In 1885 he was commissioned to carry out an ethnographic survey of the vast province of Bengal, which then included what is now West and East Bengal (Bangladesh), Bihar, Jharkhand and parts of Orissa (Odisha), covering a population of nearly 70 million people. Risley availed himself of about 190 assistants, mostly Indian, who were given specific memo directives on the subjects to be explored: physical features, caste affiliation, religion, people occupation, as well as local customs and traditions. It all resulted in the 1891 publication of the volumes *The Tribes and Castes of Bengal: Anthropometric data* and *The Tribes and Castes of Bengal: Ethnographic glossary* (Risley, 1891a, 1891b). In the preface to this work Risley explained that he had endeavoured to apply the methods of research enshrined in modern European anthropological science to Indian ethnography. He also accompanied the text with an introduction, an alphabetically ordered ethnographic glossary describing individual tribes and castes, and a detailed index (Risley, 1891a, 1891b; Fuller, 2017).

A substantial part of data collection consisted in anthropometric analysis of the various local populations, that is, the measurement of body features, especially those related to nose shapes, on which the so-called nasal index calculation was based. Analysis outcomes led Risley to postulate a racial origin of caste, founded on an alleged correlation between somatic features and social status. Also, such correlation appeared to be arranged hierarchically, in the distinction between a "higher" order, represented by the light-skinned Arya, and a "lower" order, represented by the dark-skinned Dravida (Fuller, 2017; Bayly, 1997).

William Crooke (1848–1923) and Denzil Ibbetson (1847–1908), and also ICS officials in the late Victorian period, were of different views. Ibbetson oversaw the 1881 census as superintendent for the Punjab, in which capacity he issued the ethnographic survey entitled *Report of the Census of the Panjab 1881*, on Punjabi castes and tribes classified mainly on the basis of occupation (Ibbetson, 1883). In 1893 Crooke, who edited the commemorative edition of Risley's *The People of India*, was commissioned to carry out an ethnographic survey in north-western provinces and Oudh (from 1902 the united provinces of Agra and Oudh, currently Uttar Pradesh and Uttarakhand), with a population of 47 million. He too relied on many Indian assistants, including the scholar Ram Gharib Chaube (1850–1914). Although Crooke was also an advocate of anthropometry, in his *Tribes and Castes of the North Western Provinces* (Crooke, 1896), he noted that the nasal index applied to the populations under study showed negligible differences. He accordingly concluded that the caste system should be taken mainly as a by-product of an evolution in the division of labour (Fuller, 2017).

Alongside colonial governmental anthropology, a few non-governmental institutions contributed to the development of the discipline by promoting ad hoc research projects and a dissemination of their results. Prominent among these were the Asiatic Society of Bengal and the Anthropological Society of Bombay. Although not all sources agree on the role that the Asiatic Society of Bengal played as an anthropological institution in India, it is clear that it vigorously promoted the study of civil and natural history, antiquities, arts, sciences and literature of Asia. Founded in 1784 by William Jones (1746–1794), who was a judge in Calcutta and an orientalist, the Asiatic Society was the vehicle for cultural relations aimed at promoting the knowledge of Sanskrit and of the many aspects of Indian culture. From 1832 onwards, the main organ for disseminating such knowledge was the *Journal of the Asiatic Society of Bengal*, whose aim was "to give publicity to such oriental matters as the antiquarian, the linguist, the traveller and the naturalist may glean, in the ample field open to their industry in this part of the world, i.e. Asia" (Chaudhuri, 1956, p. viii; Kejariwal, 1988).

The Anthropological Society of Bombay was founded in 1886 by a group of European, mostly British, scholars, who were later joined by a fair number of Indian scholars, including Jivanji Jamshedji Modi (1854–1933). The association had "the purpose of promoting the prosecution of anthropological research in India, by investigating and recording facts relating to the physical, intellectual and moral development of man, and more especially of the various races inhabiting the Indian Empire" (Shah, 2014, p. 355). This was done via the publication of the *Journal of the Anthropological Society of Bombay* (issued regularly until 1936 and then sporadically until 1973) and the establishment of a library and museum.

A key vector for the diffusion of anthropological knowledge was in fact the institution of museums, which for historian Tapati Guha-Thakurta exemplified "the idea of the imperial archive" (Thakurta, 2004, p. 45), that is, colonial constructs aimed at collecting in one place the natural and cultural heritage of India with the main purpose of educating the "natives". To this end, in this initial phase, museums were primarily devoted to the display of archaeological finds documenting the ancient history of India, to the exploration of the pantheon of the main deities that animate its religious history, as well as to the cataloguing of animal and vegetable samples that characterise its natural history. It should be pointed out that this process was not merely heterodirected or passively endured, because Indian personnel made significant contributions to it. Important instances of this archival-popularising effort were also the museum founded in 1814 in Calcutta by the Asiatic Society of Bengal, with the primary goal of collecting "all articles that may tend to illustrate Oriental manners and history or to elucidate the peculiarities of art and nature in the East" (Basa, 2016, p. 467). Later, there also came the Madras Museum, founded in 1851, which featured a small ethnographic section, as well as the Victoria and Albert Museum in Bombay, established in 1857 (since 1975 Bhau Daji Lad Museum).

India's Pioneers

Many prominent figures in this early pioneering phase of anthropological research in India lacked specific training but came from other fields of study or other professional experiences. They included Ananthakrishna Iyer, Rai Bahadur Sarat Chandra Roy and Bhimrao Ramji Ambedkar.

The vital role of Iyer (1861–1937) in the emerging Indian anthropology was epitomised by the term "Ananthropology", coined by Srinivas (Ram, 2007, p. 64). Having graduated from Christian College in Madras in 1883, Iyer became a science teacher at Victoria College in Palghat, Kerala. In 1902, Dewan's secretary, aka Prime Minister of Cochin, Achuta Menon, asked Iyer to conduct an ethnographic survey of Cochin State as part of the 1901 colonial state census operation. As was customary, Iyer was to collect data according to a set of predefined categories, originally drafted by Risley. In applying these rules, Iyer adapted their format, based on his first-hand prior knowledge of the region. He simplified the layout of questions, focusing on a few specific themes: the origin and tradition of the caste or tribe, habitation, marriage rituals, cycle of life, hereditary system, magic, witchcraft and diet (Ram, 2007).

16 SOCIAL ANTHROPOLOGY IN INDIA: STUDYING THE SELF IN THE OTHER   475

While he fell short of contesting the concept of race, he did omit anthropometric surveys from his research. Also, dissatisfied with data obtained via questionnaires, he personally travelled to villages to meet and interview inhabitants directly. Thanks to his knowledge of local languages, he was able to collect an extensive amount of highly detailed data. The results of his early research were published by the Ernakulam government press between 1904 and 1906 in the form of monographs about individual castes and tribes and were later collected in the volumes *Cochin Tribes* and *Castes* published between 1908 and 1912 (Ram, 2007).

After studying the Syrian Christian communities of Malabar, Cochin and Travancore, in 1924 Iyer resumed ethnographic research in the principality of Mysore and completed it in 1936 with the publication of a four-volume work, *The Mysore Tribes and Castes*. From the 1920s, he became a professor of anthropology, history and culture of ancient India at the University of Calcutta, a role he carried out with great dedication. As he himself wrote in the preface to *The Mysore Tribes and Castes*, he established the main lines of anthropological study in India for a whole new generation of scholars.

While not an anthropologist by profession, Roy (1871–1942), who John H. Hutton (Mills, 1942) dubbed as the "Father of Indian ethnology", inscribed his life and his work around political and academic turning points which were crucial to the discipline. His pivotal figure embodies the contradictory status of scholars during the colonial period: researchers, tireless promoters of the study of anthropology and defenders of the rights of tribal peoples. After graduating from Calcutta University with a law degree, in 1898 he left for Ranchi, Bengal, where he taught English at the Gossner Evangelical Lutheran Missionary School. He spent a good part of his life there, becoming a lawyer and official interpreter in government disputes and thus gaining a thorough knowledge of the traditions and customs of the Chota Nagpur people in Bengal.

In 1912, he published his first monograph entitled *The Mundas and Their Country*, which delved into the history and origin of the Munda because, as he wrote, their conspicuous historical and cultural heritage remained largely unknown:

In India, we have vast fields for historical research as yet lying unexplored or but partially explored. The early history of the so called Kolarian Aborigines of India is one of those obscure tracts that have hardly yet been rescued from the darkness of oblivion. [...] And yet these are peoples whose remote ancestors were once masters of Indian soil,—whose doings and sufferings, whose joys and sorrows, once made up the history of the Indian Peninsula. The historian of India generally dismisses from consideration these and other aboriginal tribes as 'an unclaimed ignoble horde' who occupy the background of Indian History as the jungle once covered the land to prepare the soil for better forms of life. (Roy, 1912, pp. 1–2)

According to Roy, the interweaving of history, ethnography and geography was crucial for reconstructing the cultural forms of the Munda, given the close historical continuity between population, climate and territory. After the arrival of the Arya around the sixth century BCE, the Kolarian tribes, of Dravidian origin and to which the Munda belonged, migrated to settle in the more remote areas of present-day Jharkhand, where, in a context of geographical isolation, they developed social and cultural institutions of their own. Contact with the Hindu Raja, the Mughal state, and British colonial forces gradually destroyed their ancient political system, at least until the early twentieth century, when the Bengal government finally adopted land tenure laws that took into account the traditional patrilineal *khuntkatti* land system. Such laws, however, sparked a fierce conflict between Munda farmers and Hindu landowners.

In the wake of his very successful first publication, Roy subsequently obtained a grant presented by the Government of Bihar on the initiative of its governor, Edward Gait, to conduct research on the Oraons of Chota Nagpur, a population on which he would later write two monographs: *The Oraons of Chota Nagpur*, published in 1915, and *Oraon Religion and Customs*, which appeared in 1928. The former addressed their historical origin and cultural organisation, while the latter their magical-religious setup. His second monograph records a clear epistemological shift in the practice of participant observation, which began to include excerpts from interviews, personal observations, as well as the transcription of legends and songs (Dasgupta, 2007).

In the 1930s, as a member of the Bihar and Orissa Legislative Council, Roy proposed that the Aborigines of Chota Nagpur should not be excluded from Indian nation-building but should instead be treated as a minority with special rights. As such, they needed both protection against usury and adequate legislation for preserving their land rights. Roy also advocated greater inclusion of Aborigines in legislative processes and parliamentary democracy, since he held that tribal life did not take place in a *vacuum* but was rather an integral part of a larger social system. He also wrote several articles to refute the notion that these peoples were primitive, and even changed his terminology: he no longer defined them as *tribe*, but as *Aborigines*, founders of the villages of Chota Nagpur and holders of ancestral rights over their lands (Paidipaty, 2010; Roy, 1946).

The final phase of his scientific production saw the emergence of a more definite syncretic tension between the ideas of the ancient Indian philosophers and the anthropological concepts of Western derivation. In the 1938 article *An Indian Outlook on Anthropology* published in the journal *Man in India*, which he himself had founded in 1921, Roy thought that the essence of Indian thought lay in a reflexive process of "sympathetic immersion" with other cultures and that this attitude could be profitably associated with ethnography, making it an indispensable tool for Indian nation building (Guha, 2018). In a national framework aimed at self-determination, anthropology could support unity in diversity, highlighting the ties that existed between all the people who inhabited the subcontinent.

> Thus, the objective methods of investigation of cultural data have to be helped out, not only by historical imagination and a background of historical and geographical facts, but also by a subjective process of self-forgetting absorption or meditation (*dhyana*) and *intuition* born of sympathetic immersion in, and self-identification with, the society under investigation. The spread of this attitude by means of anthropological study can surely be a factor helping forward the large *unity-in-diversity through sympathy* that seems to an Indian mind to be the inner meaning of the process of human evolution, and the hope of a world perplexed by a multitude of new and violent contacts, notably between Eastern and Western civilizations. [...] The anthropological attitude while duly appreciating and fostering the varied self-expression of the Universal Spirit in different communities and countries, and not by any means seeking to mould them all in one universal racial or cultural pattern, is expected to help forward a synthesis of the past and the present, the old and the new, the East and the West. (Roy, 1938, p. 150)

Although not traditionally counted among India's leading anthropologists, Ambedkar (1891–1956), leader of the *Dalit* and father of the Indian Constitution, gave a significant contribution to the establishment of the discipline. Despite his financial difficulties, he managed to study at Columbia University in New York, where in 1916 he wrote *Castes in India: Their Mechanism, Genesis and Development*. The paper addressed the origin and functioning of the caste system in India as a complement to the anthropology seminar given by Alexander Goldenweizer. By critically appropriating the issues put forth by Franz Boas, Ambedkar rejected the notion of a supposed fixity of racial identities and hierarchies, and stigmatised the practice of untouchability as a cultural, rather than a racial, question. As seen above, the racial explanation of caste in India and Europe in the early twentieth century was widely accepted and endorsed by scholars such as Risley and Weber.

For Ambedkar, instead, the people of the subcontinent were characterised by such an ethnic mix that any alleged "racial differences" were irrelevant. Despite the intrinsic diversity of the Indian population, there was still, in his opinion, a common cultural identity signalled by the ubiquity of caste, an institution that must be understood as a crucial factor in relations of production. By rejecting the very concept of race, Ambedkar concurrently repudiated the notion that ascribed social divisions to alleged biological grounds. He explained, in fact, that in ancient India, some social groups had turned into closed endogamous groups, the castes, mainly in order to secure privileges accrued via class division. On account of their dominant position, the Brahmanas were probably the first, and were later emulated by the other classes (Cháirez-Garza, 2018). As he himself wrote:

> Endogamy or the closed-door system, was a fashion in the Hindu society, and as it had originated from the Brahmin caste it was whole-heartedly imitated by all the non-Brahmin subdivisions or classes, who in their turn, became endogamous castes It is 'the infection of imitation' that caught all these sub-divisions on their onward march of differentiation and hasturned them into castes. The propensity to imitate is a deep-seated one in the human mind and need not be deemed an inadequate explanation for the formation of the various castes in India. (Ambedkar, 1916, p. 18)

This explanation, arguably the result of a bracketing of Ambedkar's personal experience of marginalisation with reflections drawn from his socio-economic studies, epitomised the evolution of a theory capable of connecting class oppression to the yokes of caste and race. It is a tension that can also be found in more recent debates of socio-anthropological discourse in India.

Professionalisation

Between 1910 and 1950, Indian anthropology set out on a path of gradual professionalisation, thanks to the institutionalisation of the discipline in the country's major universities. In 1919, an anthropology programme was activated within the sociology department at the University of Bombay. Under the guidance of Patrick Geddes (1854–1932), biologist and urban planner, the programme included courses in human geography and urban planning. In this early phase of the history of academic anthropology, the influence of Cambridge University and of scholars such as John Hutton and William Rivers was particularly far-reaching (Sinha, 1991). A member of the Civil Service from 1908 to 1938, Commissioner for the Indian Census of 1931, Hutton (1885–1968) was Professor of Social Anthropology at Cambridge University from 1938 to 1950. Rivers (1864–1922), professor of Psychology, acquired a solid reputation in the field of Indian anthropology following the 1906 publication of the monograph entitled *The Todas* (Rivers, 1906). At the end of 1901, he spent five months among the Toda, a herding population inhabiting southwest India in the Nilgiri Hills who based their livelihood on buffalo, an animal held sacred. It was Rivers himself who encouraged Roy to pursue his monograph-style studies on the populations of Bihar. It was also under Rivers' supervision that Kshitish Prasad Chattopadhyay (1897–1963) and Govind Sadashiv Ghurye (1893–1983) were awarded their PhDs from Cambridge in 1923.

After Geddes's retirement, Ghurye became the director of the Sociology Department of the University of Bombay, which had set up a School of Research in Economics and Sociology in order to examine social changes brought about by rising industrialisation and urbanisation. Born into a Saraswat Brahman family, Ghurye pursued a model of sociology somewhat influenced by his previous training in the study of Sanskrit as well as by his research on diffusionism at Cambridge. A revised version of his doctoral thesis *Ethnic Theory on Caste* was issued in 1932 under the title *Caste and Race in India*.

Through a systematic analysis of classical texts, ethnographic accounts and evolutionist theories, Ghurye provided a historical survey of the caste system, starting from ancient history up to modernity. For Ghurye, caste was the outcome of the unbroken contact between different races/ethnic groups which, via a process of assimilation and conflict, gave shape to a dynamic and constantly evolving system. There remained, however, a few

480 S. RONCAGLIA

ideal typical features which enabled its reproduction within a fixed canon, traceable to the four *varna, Brahmana, Kshatriya, Vaishya* and *Shudra*. Caste was thus configured as a self-contained institution, based on birth within a specific caste and on a complex internal division ordered into mutually exclusive segments, or *jati*. The system was based on hierarchy: it entailed restrictions in the sphere of social interactions rooted in the distinction between pure and impure (with special regard to food sharing) but also invested in the entire sphere of rights and duties. Also, since caste was hereditary and assigned at birth, caste inevitably restricted occupational choice. Finally, caste entailed stringent restrictions on marriage (Ghurye, 1932).

Ghurye was partially opposed to the correlation between caste and race promoted by Risley, because he held that the anthropometric data collected were limited to northern India, where the Arya invasion had produced relative homogeneity, mainly due to a stricter application of endogamy. Adopting a diffusionist perspective, Ghurye claimed that the caste system had spread across India through a historical process of acculturation, which could not possibly be traced to differences in somatic features of the kind invoked by an alleged "racial character" of caste membership. Its apparent "fixity" was ultimately an arbitrary construct, the product of a British process of objectification of racial differences brought about by census (Upadhya, 2007; Cohn, 1990).

In 1921, the Department of Anthropology was established at the University of Calcutta, joined in 1926 by Biraja Sankar Guha (1894–1961). Guha obtained his doctorate from Harvard and was the first Indian director of the Anthropological Survey of India from 1945 to 1954. Dhirendra Nath Majumdar (1903–1960) and Nirmal Kumar Bose (1901–1972) were trained in anthropology in Calcutta, while in the same years the city of Lucknow became a nerve centre for the study of social sciences under the leadership of Radhakamal Mukherjee (1889–1968). The teaching staff of the same university were joined in 1922 by Dhurjati Prasad Mukerji (1894–1961) and in 1928 by Majumdar. The latter eventually became the head of the anthropology department (Vidyarthi, 1978).

A versatile scholar keen to explore different fields of anthropological knowledge, Majumdar pursued his Cambridge PhD with a study on the Ho tribe in Chota Nagpur, where he came into contact with Roy. Two of his publications powerfully convey the versatility of his interests: *Race Elements in Bengal* and *Social Contours of an Industrial City* (Majumdar, 1960a, 1960b). The first was in the wake of Risley's work on physical anthropology, which Majumdar studied in depth at Cambridge with Geoffrey Morant and Reginald Ruggles Gates, carrying out extensive anthropometric and serological surveys among the tribes and castes of Bengal to analyse their social stratification. The second volume lies more firmly within the field of social anthropology and traces the emergence of Kanpur as an industrial city, addressing the various historical phases that marked its development. Through an extensive, questionnaire-based data collection, Majumdar investigated living conditions in the factories, the socio-cultural heritage of workers and the effects of industrialisation on female fertility.

Mukerji, instead, was one of the pioneers of sociology in India: he contributed to the development of economic anthropology, social ecology and working-class studies in Indian academia. He approached sociology as a social philosopher, adopting Marxism as an analytical method for interpreting the history of the subcontinent. His effort to dialectically combine Indian tradition with modernity led him to delve historically into India's cultural and social change. In 1947, in the wake of independence and the Partition, he re-issued *Modern Indian Culture: A Sociological Study* (previously published in 1942), with a view to understanding the reasons for division, communitarianism and violence (Madan & Sarana, 1962).

According to Triloki Nath Madan, a former student of Mukerji's and later an eminent sociologist, Mukerji believed that there had been a complex historical process of mutual adaptation, culminating in the coexistence of Hindus, Buddhists and Muslims. This process had been profoundly altered by British rule, which upset the foundations of India's social economy with radical reforms in agriculture, trade and education. Contrary to the Marxist view, which posited British colonisation as the alleged engine of India modernisation, Mukerji held that Indian history should be "made" by Indians themselves, striving to actively understand the changes that opened up areas of contiguity between tradition and change. Tradition in this sense was understood not merely as an orientation towards the past, but also as a sensitivity to the specific shifts taking place within Indian society. It was thus a living tradition, able to evolve over time and to establish a bridge between past and present. Mukerji believed that each culture had its own peculiar mechanism of change. And in the Indian tradition this was based on three unique generative principles: *shruti* (the Vedic tradition based on listening), *smriti* (the post-Vedic tradition based on memorisation) and *anubhava* (the tradition based on the realisation of the individual). The latter, belonging to sphere of personal experience, was in

482   S. RONCAGLIA

his view the most revolutionary principle, because it flowed from the individual into collective experience, where it gave impetus to major transformations. Mukerji's sociological speculation led him to question the uncritical adoption of Western models of development and to consider the modernisation of Indian society as a historical process capable of expanding the self-awareness of its citizens. In his view, supine emulation of the West would instead seriously undermine the ability of the Indian people to choose the nation's future (Madan, 2007). In *On Indian History: A Study in Method*, he wrote:

> Our sole interest is to write and to act Indian History. Action means making; it has a starting point—this specificity called India; or if that be too vague, this specificity of the contact between India and England or the West. Making involves changing, which in turn requires (a) a scientific study of the tendencies which make up this specificity, and (b) a deep understanding of the Crisis [...]. In all these matters, the Marxian method [...] is likely to be more useful than other methods. (Mukerji, 1945, p. 46)

In the late 1930s, the University of Pune opened a Department of Sociology and Anthropology, later headed by Irawati Karve (1905–1970). A student of Ghurye and a PhD student at the Kaiser Wilhelm Institute of Anthropology at the University of Berlin, she was the first female Indian anthropologist in an almost exclusively male world. Indologist, philosopher and a scholar of *Mahabharata*, and *Ramayana,* she was influenced by the cultural and social context of Maharashtra and of the University of Bombay, and by the colonial ethnological tradition of anthropometry applied to the subdivision of castes and tribes. Her entire career was animated by a marked propensity towards fieldwork. Some of the themes that would accompany her throughout her scientific career were highlighted in her 1953 book *Kinship Organisation in India*: namely the relevance of physical anthropology, of the study of kinship and of the oral tradition. As she wrote in the first chapter:

> I moved from region to region taking measurements, blood samples and collecting information about kinship practices and terminology. The contacts were established through friends, students and Government officials. [...] so I travelled from place to place never knowing where my next step was to be nor where my next meal was to come from [...] Rest pauses between work, meal times, travel in buses full of people and in third class railway compartments filled with men and women gave me the opportuni-

ties I sought for collecting kinship material. A small begining would suffice to set the ball rolling and each would come out with his or her stories. I had naturally to tell also all about myself, my husband and children and the parents-in-law and the others would tell about their kin. At such times it was not always possible or advisable to take notes. Kinship terms and situations involving personal narratives or family usages, scraps of song and proverbs were, however, taken down. (Karve, 1953, pp. 18–19)

Although Karve did not like to be defined as "a feminist anthropologist" (Sundar, 2007, p. 398), in the 1990s Patricia Uberoi highlighted her pioneering role in promoting the feminist perspective on the Indian family and in pointing the way for gender studies to new generations:

[...] A pioneer of an indigenous 'feminist' perspective on the Indian family. Her central contrast of north and south Indian kinship revolved around difference in marital arrangements as seen from the viewpoint of women: marriage with kin versus marriage with strangers; marriage close by versus marriage at a distance [...] Similarly, she evaluated modern changes in family life—for instance the modification of Dravidian marriage practices in the direction of the northern model—from the viewpoint of their possible effects on women's life. (Uberoi, 1993, p. 40)

Towards Independence

A major part of administration-based colonial anthropology revolved around tribal pacification strategies and border management. As they endeavoured to delineate the social framework of tribal populations, British officials developed a vocabulary in which terms such as tribe and caste were not interchangeable but labelled distinct social categories. These positions were supported by theories such as the one put forth by Lieutenant John Briggs. In the course of several conferences held in 1852 at the Asiatic Society, he argued that the so-called Indian tribes constituted a single race, that is, that of the original inhabitants of the subcontinent. Their social system differed from the caste system in various aspects of cultural life, such as the greater freedom accorded to women, fewer dietary restrictions, the diversity of religious and funeral rites, as well as the use of writing (Briggs, 1852). The tribes were therefore portrayed as the subcontinent's primitive, indigenous communities, forced to migrate to more inaccessible areas to escape relentless encroachment upon their lands. The term *tribe*, in line with that of *race*, thus took on a meaning of immanence, of aboriginality.

Some colonial administrators such as William George Archer (1907–1979) and John H. Hutton believed that such tribes, precisely because they were "primitive", were incapable of coping with the complexities of modernity, that is, of a social system based on contracts, electoral systems and courts. Laws such as the Scheduled Districts Act of 1874 were therefore enacted to prevent extinction and protect "tribal areas". As a result, large swathes of Indian territory were placed under the special tutelage of British officials, tasked with administering justice, borders and internal disputes. Beginning in 1920, a front against British tribal policy began to develop within the Indian anti-colonial movement. The main accusation that its proponents levelled at the British administration was that of segregating the tribes culturally and politically, in order to distance them from growing Indian nationalism (Guha, 1998). Scholars such as Bose, Chattopadhyay, Majumdar and Ghurye therefore saw the tribal question as a quintessentially political issue, closely tied to aspirations towards national self-government. Accordingly, they promoted a development of Indian anthropology envisioned in the model of a nationwide science, meant to promote the progressive building of an independent State.

Controversy between Verrier Elwin (1902–1964) and Ghurye erupted within such a transitional context. Having arrived in India as a missionary, Elwin joined the Christa Seva Sangh of Pune, a spiritual movement of Christian renewal very close to Gandhian positions. Later, however, he abandoned the cassock to devote himself to ethnography, conducting research on the Baiga, Muna and Agaria of Madhya Pradesh, and devoting the rest of his life to defending their rights. In 1939, Elwin published the ethnographic monograph *The Baiga* (Elwin, 1939) and in 1941, the pamphlet *Loss of Nerve* (Elwin, 1941), in which he argued the need to apply government measures for safeguarding tribal populations against the exploitative schemes of modern civilisation. Based on his 20 years of fieldwork among tribal communities, during which he witnessed the gradual deterioration of their traditional way of life caused by unrelenting outside interference, Elwin proposed the creation of national parks dedicated to their preservation. Indian independence leaders, however, dismissed these parks as "anthropological zoos", set up for the sole use and consumption of anthropologists.

In 1943, Ghurye attacked Elwin's positions in an essay entitled *The Aboriginal-So Called-and their Future* (reissued after Independence under the title *The Scheduled Tribes*) (Ghurye, 1959). He argued that the isolation of the tribal people was mainly due to ghettoisation policies upheld by the colonial administration. Primitive societies seemed anachronistic: out of touch with the country's idea of modernisation. Hence the need to reintegrate them into the Indian social body. In order to refute the very notion of primitive/tribe applied to the most isolated communities, a thorough, critical overhaul of the terms used until then was deemed necessary. Ghurye thus parsed the ample body of colonial administrative writings and concluded that there lay a fundamental misunderstanding under the distinction between caste and tribe. The alleged originality of the tribes was historically inaccurate, since from a racial and cultural point of view these people appeared similar to the rest of the Indian people. The very definition of *tribal* or *aboriginal* set up an artificial separation, quite out of line with the historically recorded ability of Hindu society to integrate the different fringes of its population. Ultimately, according to Ghurye, there existed a line of continuity between caste and tribe. While the social backwardness of the latter was an undeniable fact, its cause was to be found in their forced isolation, which had prevented access to education and modernity. In view of this, Ghurye called for a policy of integration and accommodation of cultural minorities under the aegis of a single Indian nation (Singh, 1996; Sinha, 2005a, 2005b; Guha, 1996a, 1996b).

This academic and political-administrative debate occurred during the terminal phase of British colonial rule and paved the way to a renewed thrust in the field of Indian anthropology. Cultural diversity was now framed within the unitary framework of the state, which needed a new historical, cultural and social reconstruction under the banner of syncretism. Ghurye' own epistemological legacy lies within this paradigm, further developed and expanded by some of his students, such as Srinivas and Akshay Ramanlal Desai (1915–1994).

THE VILLAGE AND THE NATION

The Independence of 1947 saw a substantial rise in the popularity of sociology and social anthropology, which were seen as effective tools to meet the growing demand for information on the diverse socio-economic conditions of the new state. The creation of the National Planning Commission, the ten-year population census, the development of demographic and anthropological-social institutions such as the Central Social Welfare Board, the Office of the Commissioner for Scheduled Castes and Tribes, the Tribes Research Institute, the Indian Council of Science Research, the Anthropological Survey of India, the social promotion drive of the Ford Foundation in India and the introduction in each state of the Community Development Program, all required new skills as well as an ever-increasing commitment from social science scholars (Vidyarthi, 1978). As Nirmal Kumar Bose wrote in 1972 in *Anthropology and Some Indian Problems*:

> An anthropologist does not merely play the part of an observer in a game of chess. He has a greater and a deeper commitment, namely, that in India he has to draw a lesson from what he observes, so that he can utilise his knowledge in the attainment of the equalitarian ideal which our nation has set before itself as its goal. If he accepts this ideal then, with his superior analytical apparatus, and the use of comparisons and sympathetic thinking, he can suggest many modifications in the ways in which the government or leaders of society are trying to bring about justice where injustice prevails today. And this is where applied anthropology has a significant role to play and a heavy responsibility to bear. (Bose, 1972, pp. 5–6)

As research facilities proliferated, there also occurred a momentous shift in the theoretical blueprint of Indian social anthropology. Most notably in the 1950s and 1960s, research on villages was placed at the centre of anthropological, sociological, economic and political reflection. In the national discourse, villages marked a point of interesection in the thought of three eminent figures. For his part, Mahatma Gandhi repeatedly described the village as the quintessential repository of the values of Indian civilisation, a foundational social unit whose solidity was an indispensable precondition for self-government and autonomy. Unlike Ghandi, Jawaharlal Nehru stigmatised the village as the very emblem of backwardness; while for Ambedkar, the village was above all the symbolic site of caste oppression on the part of the *Dalit* (Chatterjee, 1995; Jodhka, 2002).

From a geopolitical point of view, the village figured prominently in the ideological debate that emerged from the political settlement at the end of World War II; a time characterised by the Cold War and the start of decolonisation. After the 1955 Bandung conference, the political agenda of so-called Third World countries was marked by development plans for rural society, which seemed helpless in the face of challenges posed by massive population and by an agricultural sector beset by low productivity.

16 SOCIAL ANTHROPOLOGY IN INDIA: STUDYING THE SELF IN THE OTHER

As a consequence, to ensure progressive modernisation, the new states were forced to gain a firmer grasp of their social structures. The impetus to agricultural production provided by the so-called green revolution gave rise to multidisciplinary research focused on peasants and the effects of progress.

From an anthropological point of view, research on villages marked a new phase in the history of social sciences in India, which finally distanced themselves from a long-held association with the study of "primitive tribes". Against the notion of "primitive tribes" as compact and relatively homogeneous communities, research on villages now enabled the social sciences to zero in on their social fabric, with a special focus on caste. For the structure of the caste system could not be circumscribed within the territorial boundaries of a single village. The study of castes was instead bound to extend from a given village to a selected group of villages, then to a specific region and would eventually yield a broad overview of the whole nation.

Malinowskian field research was consolidated and relied on field *view*, that is, a scientific method able to describe and interpret the village as a microcosm, reflecting the essentially plural character of India (Jodhka, 1998). At the same time a new generation of scholars, actively involved in nation-building on the principle of India's structural unity, also emerged. The theoretical underpinnings of this paradigmatic change were manifold, starting with the influence of the work of Robert Redfield, who in the 1930s had published *Tepoztlán, in Mexican Village*, then *Little Community*, in 1955, and *Peasant Society and Culture*, in 1956. William Henricks Wiser's monograph *The Hindu Jajmani System* of (1936) had a major impact on the analysis of inter- and intra-caste relations in rural contexts. Analysing the system of professional obligations called *jajmani*, Wiser applied the conceptual notion of reciprocity to the interdependence between different groups, subsuming the reading of caste relations under the banner of an equitable exchange of mutual services (Wiser, 1936). In the wake of these studies, three books were published in 1955: *Village India: Studies in the Little Community*, edited by McKim Marriott under the direct supervision of Redfield; *India's Villages*, edited by Srinivas and finally *Indian Village*, by S.C. Dube.

Shyama Charan Dube (1922–1996) embodied this crucial epistemological shift in Indian anthropology on account of the many roles, at times contradictory, that he took on in the course of his career: scholar and administrator; a witness to the shift in studies from tribal to village studies, with the attending nationalist tensions in the social sciences; a moderniser and a critic of development; and a writer in English and Hindi (Dube, 1960; Dube, 1996). Raised in Chhattisgarh, he studied at the University of Nagpur, earning his doctorate in anthropology in the 1940s with a thesis on the Kamar tribe, a population of the Chhattisgarh state that was originally made up of hunter-gatherers and would later consist predominantly of farmers. After teaching at the University of Lucknow, in the 1950s, he took up service at the University of Osmania in Hyderabad where he studied in the village of Shamirpet, in the Telangana region. The year-long project involved a team of scholars from various disciplines, including agricultural, educational, veterinary, medical and sociocultural sciences (Dube, 2007).

On the basis of a preliminary census, Dube's anthropological investigations focused on the study of a sample of more than 100 families of different caste, religion, education and income level; on the collection of 11 biographies; and on multiple episodes and accounts of community life (which included data on diets, agricultural techniques and animal care). The aim of this survey was to describe the social, economic, ritual and family structures of villages. The project resulted in the publication, in 1955, of *Indian Village*, a volume in which Dube combined an extensive account of the rural community with a functional analysis of its historical transformations. The book resonated powerfully with Anglo-Saxon scholars such as Morris Opler and Edmund Leach, who hailed it the emblem of a new young and independent India, which aimed at building change through the cooperation of social scientists engaged in multidisciplinary and organic projects around national development. Opler himself invited Dube to collaborate on the Cornell India Project, a project that focused on social change in the villages of northern India. In 1954–1955, together with a large number of Indian scholars, including his wife, the anthropologist Leela Dube analysed the village of Rajput, with a population of just over 5000 people, and the village of Tyagi, with about 750 inhabitants. 1958 saw the publication of *India's Changing Villages: Human Factors in Community Development*, in which the cultural dynamics of villages were bracketed with the ongoing efforts to build the Indian nation by developing rural communities. The monograph became one of the pillars of administrative programmes in emerging nations, as it brought back into focus the actions and the themes of modernisation (Dube, 2007).

Another scholar who gained prominence in the field of village studies was Mysore Narasimhachar Srinivas (1916–1999), although his

16 SOCIAL ANTHROPOLOGY IN INDIA: STUDYING THE SELF IN THE OTHER   489

contribution to the anthropological debate went far beyond this field. After graduating in sociology from Bombay with Ghurye, he went on to study at Oxford, working with Alfred Reginald Radcliffe-Brown and Edward Evan Evans-Pritchard. This period had a strong impact on his view of anthropology, on the central role he gave to participatory observation and on the issues he considered worth pursuing. At Oxford, on the initiative of Evans-Pritchard, he undertook the ethnographic study of the village of Rampura, in the state of Karnataka, near the city of Mysore, where he himself had been born into a family of Tamil-speaking Brahmans. He spent 11 months there in 1948, returning repeatedly for short periods between 1948 and 1964 (Srinivas, 1997). The publication of *The Remembered Village* came many years later, in 1976, combining structural analysis of the village with his own personal memories. Srinivas retrospectively interpreted the choice to study Rampura as the desire to approach a context that he knew only in part: even though his family did own rice fields close the village, as a city-dweller he felt removed from it all. Moreover, that village was small in size and had a complex caste stratification.

After an introduction to the place and his main interlocutors/informants, Srinivas described the cyclical pattern of agricultural practices, such as sowing, use of water and relations to animals, as well as the structure of social relations, divided into various family and caste relationships. By bringing out the complex interdependencies at work within a small settlement, he highlighted both the strictly hierarchical codification of the caste system and its controlled fluidity. Caste was not described as a fixed structure, but as a dynamic set of resources based on daily interactions and rituals, which were deployed in various ways and to different ends. Here Srinivas relied on the notion of *Sanskritisation*, which had become a major theoretical touchstone for Indian anthropology after its initial definition in the mid-1950s. The term indicated the emulation of upper caste ritual practices on the part of lower castes seeking upward mobility.

> When an individual jati (a local endogamous unit of the caste system), or a section of a local jati, captured political power or became wealthy, over a period of time he or the group emulated the customs, ritual, and lifestyle of a higher caste. Eventually a myth, or purana, came into existence claiming noble origins for the caste and changing the caste's name by adding a suffix characteristic of one or another twice-born varna [a hierarchical division of

490   S. RONCAGLIA

Vedic society into four orders: Brahmin (priests), Kshatriya (wariors), Vaishya (traders), and Shudra (menials)]. This is the classic form of Sanskritisation. Sanskritisation occurred right from the earliest times in Indian history [...]. (Srinivas, 1997, p. 16)

The Remembered Village represented from the start a crucial point of reference for the Indian social sciences, due to the relevance it granted to the application of structural-functionalist theories, to the practice of participatory observation and to the tension towards salvage ethnography. The book was also found to feature some degree of reflexivity, expressed in Srinivas' explicit mention of his own position as a Brahmin within the community and the effects this had on his research. By presenting both himself and the reactions of his interlocutors in his own field reports, Srinivas introduced a subjective character to his writing, which occasionally gives rise to a sort of self-criticism.

I realize only too clearly that mine was a high caste view of village society' (Srinivas, 1976, p. 219). Though I knew several Muslims and Harijans well, I did not know these two sections of village society as intimately as I wanted to. I would have obtained a new angle on the village if I had spent more time in their areas. [...] I must also list other failures. (Srinivas, 1976, p. 56)

In 1966 he published *Social Change in Modern India*, in which he juxtaposed the phenomenon of sanskritisation to the issue of social mobility and its implications. Among them was Westernisation, a legacy of the changes introduced during British colonisation and perpetuated in independent India. This multidimensional concept implied, especially for the high castes, the adoption of Western lifestyles following an increase in schooling, secularisation and urbanisation (Srinivas, 1966):

Westernisation is a multifaceted concept, and different groups might choose a facet congenial to it. In the context of modem India, mobility involves not only Sanskritisation but also Westernisation. In several parts of the country, the higher castes took the lead in Westernizing their life-style, and while the higher castes were Westernizing, the so-called lower ones were Sanskritizing. This should not be interpreted to mean that the upper castes were throwing out their traditional culture or that the lower were not Westernizing. Both were occurring in each category, but since Western education had spread more widely among the upper castes and more of them were in white-collar jobs, Westernisation was more conspicuous among them. (Srinivas, 1997, p. 17)

Srinivas combined his commitment to theoretical speculation with that of teaching, first at the University of Baroda and then at the University of Delhi. In his lectures, as he championed the ethnographic method, he also voiced a certain reluctance to bend the social sciences to utilitarian ends. With these assumptions, he shaped the next generation of Indian social scholars, including B.S. Baviskar (1930–2013), Arvind M. Shah (1931–2020) and Béteille (1934).

The Anthropological Frontier

The years in which research on villages started to gain ground also saw a steady growth in the well-established line of ethnographic studies on tribal people. This aimed to combine academic speculation with the nation's achievements in modernisation. In this context, the border area designated as the North East Frontier Agency (now Arunachal Pradesh)—a key buffer zone between British territories in India and the British area of influence in Tibet during colonial times—attained unprecedented relevance. Beginning in the 1950s, this area acted as the backdrop to sensitive negotiations over the definition of the Sino-Indian border: it was reorganised by Prime Minister Nehru, who instituted the North East Frontier Area or NEFA, under the administrative supervision of the Assam Governor and with the assistance of Verrier Elwin, by virtue of his official role as Adviser of Tribal Affairs (Guha, 1998, 2007). It was in fact the Scottish anthropologist, by then a naturalised Indian, who outlined the anthropological and political framework which was to underpin the establishment of NEFA. In the 1957 volume *A Philosophy for NEFA*, Elwin resumed his debate with Ghurye and defended his previous proposals, such as banning evangelisation and trade in that area to preserve tribal cultures. He added, however, that such isolation would only be temporary and that it would soon be advisable to lay out a path to assist tribal integration in the Indian nation.

Elwin explained this course correction in explicit terms:

We are agreed that the people of NEFA cannot be left in their agelong isolation. We are equally agreed that we can leave no political vacuum along the frontier; that we must bring to an end the destructive practices of inter-tribal war and head-hunting and the morally repugnant practices of slavery, kidnapping of children, cruel methods of sacrificing animals and opium-addiction, none of which are fundamental to tribal culture. We wish to see

492   S. RONCAGLIA

that the people are well-fed, that they are healthy and enjoy a longer span of life, that they have better houses, a higher yield for their labour in the fields, improved techniques for their home industries. We would like them to be able to move freely about their own hills and have easy access to the greater India of which at present they know little [...] Above all, we hope to see as the result of our efforts a spirit of love and loyalty for India, without a trace of suspicion that Government has come into tribal areas to colonise or exploit. (Elwin, 1959, p. 53)

This position, shared by Nehru, was part of a broader attempt to address the growing conflicts along the border: the insurrectionary movement among the Naga tribes and the karst tensions with China, aggravated in 1959 by the Dalai Lama's flight to India. At the same time, this orientation marked a new testing ground for tribal integration policies, aimed at promoting the right to growth in harmony with "one's own genius" (Nehru, 1959, p. iii) within a controlled development setting. The slow exposure to modernity was thus to be mediated by a sizable army of field officers tied to the establishment of the Indian Frontier Administrative Services. These officers were appointed directly by Elwin and were expected to live with the tribal peoples as much as possible, sharing their lifestyles, customs and even material deprivations. A prerequisite for performing their duties was participation in a two-week training and teaching course which covered subjects such as social anthropology, tribal policy and social psychology. The course was meant to enhance cultural sensitivity, which would expand both the officers' knowledge of the area and their appreciation of local customs, dances, architecture and songs. Anthropology featured in this context as a "philanthropology": a science for the benefit of human beings, aimed at fostering good relations between the central state and its periphery by mediating possible disputes or insurrections (Elwin, 1959).

In 1962, NEFA's political project suffered a major setback as the Chinese army simultaneously attacked two sensitive points along the Sino-Indian border. It happened in response to New Delhi's so-called India *forward policy*, itself a reaction to the Chinese construction of a military road inside the disputed territory of Aksai Chin. Chinese troops gained ground in both Ladakh and Arunachal Pradesh. Woefully unprepared to fight in impassable mountainous areas with inadequate gear, Indian troops were forced to retreat first inland and then to flee Shilong, NEFA's capital. In November of the same year, despite the Indian army's substantial losses, the Chinese government itself declared a ceasefire, restoring the original control area along the border. The Chinese had in fact achieved their political aim: to persuade the Indian government of China's unwillingness to grant unilateral border changes (Elleman, 2001). In the wake of this conflict, harsh criticism was levelled in the political debate of the time against the idealistic NEFA vision promoted by Elwin and Nehru. They were held responsible for the fragility of the frontier, which had been made vulnerable to external attacks by the failed development of transport and communication infrastructures, as well as by a scanty deployment of forces capable of safeguarding the nation (Guha, 2007). The Chinese attack thus marked a split in the promotion policy of tribal autonomy in the Northeast, ending Elwin's experimental project along with his vision of anthropology as a tool for governance.

This was the context of anthropologist Bose's lecture on the resident populations of Assam, Manipur, Nagaland, NEFA and Tripura held at the University of Calcutta in 1966, when he opposed the project of cultural preservation and political separation devised by Elwin, because he felt it was based on a static notion of culture (Bose, 1967a, b). On the basis of experience gained over long years of research under Roy's leadership in Chota Nagpur, Bose argued that tribal culture had never stood still, but was rather continually subject to historical change. This position had been previously outlined in *Structure of Hindu Society*, which first appeared in Bengali and was later republished in English. There, Bose illustrated the historical process of tribal assimilation into the caste system, the so-called Hindu method of tribal absorption. Caste was thus for Bose a stabilising force, which had structured India's history through a dynamic process of incorporation of minorities. The caste structure, a sophisticated expression of the division of labour between mutually dependent groups, thus endowed all social bodies with economic security, within uncompetitive relations of cooperation (Bose, 1949, 1969).

As a professor of anthropology in Calcutta, director of the Anthropological Survey of India from 1959 to 1964, activist of the Gandhian movement, politician and editor of the journal *Man in India*, Bose was also sensitive to the instances of injustice to which tribal peoples were subjected (Bose, 2007). These must be addressed, however, within the broader framework of a national collective action, which should also include the hardships of other oppressed categories such as the *Dalit*, other minorities and the working class. Bose believed that the tribal question must be reformulated within the democratic framework, by steering the country's development along the primary assertion of civil rights enshrined in the Constitution. Ghurye himself had dismantled the semantic distinction between caste and tribe, thus laying the foundations for post-independence tribal policies which entailed guaranteeed political representation quotas for Scheduled Tribes. Accordingly, equal economic opportunities and cultural diversity could form the basis of a new national paradigm for anthropological research (Bose, 1967a, 1967b). In the stance taken by Bose one senses the Gandhian inspiration, which saw in science, and thus also in anthropological science, a vehicle for emancipation. But one cannot help to register, in Bose, also a certain underestimation of the unequal power relations, coercions and tensions that beset Indian society in those years. For these marked the crucible which was to forge the countercultural social movements of the seventies, as well as the breeding ground for the development of a "bottom-up" historiography in the 1980s. On the political level, these tensions resulted in the uprisings of groups inspired by Maoist doctrine, such as the Naxalites (named after the village of Naxalbari, near Siliguri, in northern Bengal), who from 1967 onwards raged in Bengal, Andhra Pradesh, Orissa and Bihar and signalled a new phase in the struggle of oppressed communities.

INTERPRETATIONS OF INDIANITY

By the 1950s and 1960s, research on the village had become the theoretical field of reference for clearing the tangles left by the anthropological legacy of the nineteenth century. The drive to promote the establishment of a strong national identity had elected it as the privileged field for projecting narratives which took the village as the epitome of Indian civilisation: a setting in which one could grasp its alleged, essential features, such as social harmony, primitive democracy and egalitarianism. In the same years, however, this approach began to come under fire, for instance in the criticism voiced by Louis Dumont (1911–1998) and David Pocock. In a paper entitled *Village Studies*, published in 1957 in *Contributions to Indian Sociology*, Dumont and Pocock contested the heuristic value of the village as a basic unit for understanding Indian society. They also questioned the applicability of the concept of "community" to rural reality, given the deep and pervasive effect of caste divisions (Dumont & Pocock, 1957).

The English publication of Dumont's *Homo Hierarchicus* in the 1970s marked the apex and the inexorable theoretical decline of village studies, since Dumont's influential research unequivocally identified hierarchy as the main structuring principle of Indian society (Fuller & Spencer, 1990). Caste was thus much more than a special form of social structure: it was rather a state of mind, which profoundly shaped the cultural spheres of values and of ideas. Drawing inspiration from Émile Durkheim and Claude Lévi-Strauss, Dumont conceived these spheres as foundational categories of thought which, once codified into relational practices, became an integral part of cognitive systems. His theory, based on the exegesis of Vedic texts that ordained the fourfold social model of *varna* according to the oppositional dialectic of pure/impure, made it possible to analyse ethnographic data on marriage, commensality and power as manifestations of an ideological structure marked less by inequality than by hierarchy (Dumont, 1966; Berger, 2012).

Homo Hierarchicus catalysed further development in social anthropology and sociology studies in India, sparking an imposing debate which reached far and wide. In 1957, Dumont and Pocock founded *Contributions to Indian Sociology*. The journal, which from 1967 would be edited by Madan (1933–), gave ample coverage of the ongoing transformations in the Indian social sciences. In the article *For a Sociology of India*, published in 1957, Dumont claimed that the sociology of India resulted from a convergence between sociology and indology, and that the latter pointed unmistakably to caste as a core structural unit in the institutions of Indian society. The latter was thus based on the complex hierarchical ranking of a vast range of social conditions encoded between an upper and a lower limit (Dumont, 1967). *For a Sociology of India* was to become a permanent feature of the journal, opening up an arena in which Indian and international anthropologists and sociologists could discuss methodological, theoretical and critical issues around the discipline (Jain, 1985).

One of the most debated issues was an exhortation to indigenise the social sciences, freeing them from the influx of Western hegemony. In the new independent state, decolonisation and the strengthening of institutions relied not solely on industrialisation and the development of an autonomous national economy, but also on a general overhaul of the social sciences, with an eye on theories better aligned to national, independent and sovereign aspirations. Thus, an umbrella term like *indigenisation* came to accommodate multiple voices: scholars who would not subscribe to a united theoretical or epistemological manifesto nevertheless shared a common aspiration to build an independent scientific tradition, decolonised from the exoticising and essentialising gaze of the West. This project advocated the testing of autonomous thought patterns, via indigenous languages and new practices rooted in local resources (Atal, 1981; Alatas, 2006). Indian anthropologists were by then well aware of how the themes on which their discipline was based, such as caste, social stratification, kinship, religious rites, folklore, tribe and village were the outcome of an *entanglement* with the Orientalist project (Patel, 2002).

In this regard, already in the fifties, Bose, in the article *Current Research Projects in Indian Anthropology*, wrote:

> There does not seem to be any problem which Indian anthropologists have made peculiarly their own. Anthropologists in our country have, on the whole, followed the tracks beaten by anthropologists in the more powerful countries of the West. What they do, we generally try to repeat on the Indian soil. (Bose, 1952, p. 133)

The search for an indigenous anthropology proved more problematic than expected, however, because Indianness was not an ontological entity, but rather an ongoing process. How to give voice to Indian specificity in relation to the common history with the West? How could anthropology, daughter of the colonial project, be the interpreter of this specificity? Although the language of the indigenous social sciences strove to free itself from Western universalism, it nevertheless ended up bringing epistemological research back within the fold of the colonial nation-state. The problematisation of Indianity triggered further sets of questions: namely what its constituent elements were and how Indianity could be translated into a unitary project, given that the heterogeneity of Indian social life— which had always been juxtaposed to the monolithic vision of colonialism—now appeared like an impediment (Sinha, 2005a, 2005b).

To understand the complexity and contradiction of this process, Sujata Patel proposed the discursive term/concept of *colonial modernity*, or the way in which "colonialism constituted ideas, ideologies and knowledge systems of the 'natives' to refract and make invisible the 'modern' contours of everyday experience of the people who were colonised" (Patel, 2021, p. 10). As the sociologist pointed out, the project of indigenous anthropology paradoxically reproduced the language of colonialism, making the episteme of colonial modernity an inseparable part of doing anthropology and sociology in India. In the 1980s, the term "indigenisation" finally fell into disuse, but survived as an emblem of the ideological opposition to Eurocentrism and of the drive to give historical articulation

16 SOCIAL ANTHROPOLOGY IN INDIA: STUDYING THE SELF IN THE OTHER

to one's ties with the West. Along this line, the revisitation of the interweave between anthropology, colonialism and nationalism also formed the backdrop to the studies on subordination and feminism in India which characterised the last quarter of the twentieth century.

FEMINISM AND GENDER

The period from the late 1970s to the early 1990s marked a critical juncture for the redefinition of the social sciences in India. Embracing the innovative demands coming from society, they were forced to come to terms with new methodological and theoretical challenges. The growth of social movements raised fundamental questions about the nature of the state and society, while positive discrimination policies enabled a new generation of students from disadvantaged groups to access higher education. Their presence in academic institutions, coupled with the impact on these institutions of women movements, tribal and *Dalit* communities formulated a new language of rights, whereby Indian anthropology began to address issues of discrimination, exclusion and subordination within the various spheres of the nation's communal life.

The 1974 report *Towards Equality*, submitted to the Indian Government by the Committee on the Status of Women in India (CWSI), made people realise the entrenched marginalisation of women in the sectors of health, employment and political participation. Following its publication, research projects and study programs on women's condition were promoted across universities, upon explicit request of the Indian Council of Social Science Research (ICSSR). The SNDT Women's University of Bombay was among the first institutions to implement these guidelines. In 1974, they established one of the first research centres entirely dedicated to these issues (Desai & Patel, 1989). In 1981, the Indian Association of Women's Studies (IAWS) was born: a platform open to female scholars, academics and activists for implementing, sharing and disseminating research and publications. Subsequently, at the turn of the 1980s, independent research centres such as the Institute of Social Studies Trust and the Center for Women's Development Studies (CWDS) were founded in Delhi, to promote "bottom-up" research aimed at supporting the welfare of vulnerable communities from a gender perspective. The shared orientation of these scientific projects was towards developing a multidisciplinary knowledge system capable of understanding, explaining and historically theorising the experiences of women in different places throughout the world. A complementarity was thus established between research, teaching and political action, since research findings were placed within the framework of social activism.

Women studies first and gender studies at a later stage introduced a critical revision of conventional readings of caste, the family and the religious structure of Indian society. Debates about the unequal distribution of power and knowledge, as well as methodological questions about the importance of subjectivity in field research expanded the boundaries of social anthropology and sociology, paving the way to an international exchange between scholars and activists from different post-colonial contexts, particularly from the global South. The formulation of a debate on gender and the questioning of the roles ascribed to it in society have gradually untethered Indian social sciences from the burden of insularity, tied to the colonial legacy, and from the need to outline the "uniqueness" of Indian social and cultural structures (Patel, 2016).

By using the concepts of gender and patriarchy as lenses for shedding light on the dominant trends of Indian society, women studies have brought back to centre stage the debate on the influence of colonialism on nationalism and on the political formation of independent India. That, in turn, has led to a reassessment of the dialectic between modernity and tradition. As it introduced new forms of inequality between the various groups and between genders, the colonial State legitimised its power structure and its attending hierarchies via narratives inscribed in the rhetoric of "tradition". This rhetoric also favoured the modernisation of the legislative apparatus and would later become the preserve of India's nationalist elite and of their ideological armoury. In fact, post-independence policies paradoxically reinstated the instruments of coercion against minorities and women, thereby justifying institutional and family asymmetries and inequalities (Agarwal, 1988). Kumkum Sangari (1951) and Sudesh Vaid (1940–2001) have spoken clearly on the matter:

> Both tradition and modernity have been, in India, carriers of patriarchal ideologies. [...] Both tradition and modernity are eminently colonial constructs. [...] We think it's time to dismantle this opposition altogether [...] Change has continued to occur [...] we need to see how woman and womanhood are inserted into and affected by social change, and how change is made to appear as continuity. That is the ideologies of women as carriers of tradition often disguise, mitigate, compensate, contest actual changes taking

16 SOCIAL ANTHROPOLOGY IN INDIA: STUDYING THE SELF IN THE OTHER   499

place. Womanhood is often part of an asserted or desired, not an actual cultural continuity. (Sangari & Vaid, 1989, p. 17)

Leela Dube (1923–2012), after Karve, and along with scholars such as Neera Desai (1925–2009) and Vina Mazumdar (1927–2013), played a crucial role in the formulation of gender anthropology in India. They helped outline an emerging field of study concomitant with women's social movements. A student at Nagpur University, in the 1940s Dube studied Gond women in the southern part of Chhattisgarh. From 1957 to 1975 she became a lecturer in anthropology at Sagar University, and in 1974 she played a crucial role in the writing of the report *Towards Equality*. From 1976 to 1993, she was chairperson of the Commission on Women of the International Union of Anthropological and Ethnological Sciences, bringing gender studies to the centre of the academic scene in India (Patel, 2012).

In the wake of the public debates of feminist movements on Personal Laws, the Uniform Civil Code, dowry and domestic violence, Dube, or Leeladee, as she was affectionately called, meticulously studied the complex interrelation between gender and kinship from an explicitly feminist perspective, highlighting the impact of patriarchal culture on the role of women and on Indian society. In *The Construction of Gender: Hindu Girls in Patrilineal India*, Dube pinpointed some of the key issues on which her anthropological reflections hinged:

The process of growing up female in the patrilineal, patrivirilocal milieu of Indian society has received inadequate attention from social scientists. The many subtleties and complexities of the process have been missed out. What does it mean to be a girl? At what age does a girl become conscious of the constraints under which she will have to live, of the differential value accorded to male and female children, and of the justifications behind it? When and how does she learn the content of roles appropriate to her? What are the mechanisms through which women acquire the cultural ideas and values that shape their images of themselves, and inform the visions they have of the future? How do they acquire sensitivity towards the contradictions in values and norms presented to them and towards the limits with in which they have to function, necessitating the adoption of particular strategies? In other words, how are women produced as gendered subject? (Dube, 1988, p. 11)

Dube acknowledged that her scientific interests were shaped by her family background and that her positioning as a researcher could not be divorced from that of a woman raised in a Brahmin family in Maharashtra. This marked tendency towards self-reflexivity may well figure among the contributions of 1970s feminism. Via the well-known slogan "the personal is political", the feminist perspective acknowledged autobiography as a practical way of grasping the dynamics of society (Dube, 2000). The collection of essays *Anthropological Explorations in Gender: Intersecting Fields* encompasses her decades-long intellectual path. In it, she uses the prism of gender as a reading key to explore various forms of female subordination (Dube, 2001). Drawing on a wide plurality of sources, ranging from ethnographic to biographical, from folklore to religion, this volume examined issues pertaining to the construction of gender in the Hindu context; the diversity of parental structures in India and Southeast Asia; the female role in the reproduction of caste structure; and the complex rituals and languages that from early childhood shape public and personal expectations around the female gender (Dube et al., 1986).

Subalternity and Historiography

At the turn of the seventies and eighties, the group of scholars headed by historian Ranajit Guha (1923), around the journal *Subaltern Studies* and the Centre for Studies in Social Sciences in Calcutta, embarked on a critical rethinking of the official historiography of the Indian subcontinent. Through an analysis of peasant insurrections in the eighteenth and nineteenth centuries, Guha exposed the Eurocentric nature of historical accounts, first the preserve of British colonisers and later also of nationalist elites. Along with scholars such as Shahid Amin (1936), Partha Chatterjee (1947), Dipesh Chakrabarty (1948), Bernard Cohn (1928–2003), David Hardiman (1947), Gyanendra Pandey (1949), Edward Said (1935–2003) and Gayatri Spivak (1942), he highlighted the (often-implicit) strategies of representation of subalterns and the failure to recognise their role in the formation of the independent nation (Ludden, 2002).

As recounted in the 1982 Preface of *Subaltern Studies I. Writings on South Asian History and Society*, the term "subaltern" came from the work of the Italian Marxist philosopher and politician Antonio Gramsci. In the translation given by the *Concise Oxford Dictionary* its meaning was that "of inferior rank" (Guha, 1982, p. vii). Only a limited selection of Gramsci's writings was available in English at the time, since a full

16 SOCIAL ANTHROPOLOGY IN INDIA: STUDYING THE SELF IN THE OTHER 501

translation of his work was only made available in later years. In Gramsci, subalternity underpinned the formulation of a revolutionary political project. In the reading of Indian scholars, the term was used instead to set up a historical research programme based on the analysis of groups which by class, caste, age or gender were subordinate to British hegemony or to local powers which had joined the colonisers. The view promoted by Guha and the Subaltern Studies collective placed the dichotomy between dominant and dominated subjects at the very core of historical research. The former were both "foreigners" (officials, industrialists, merchants, missionaries) and "indigenous" (bureaucrats, representatives of the mercantile and industrial bourgeoisie, landed feudal lords). The latter, defined by subtraction, were "the demographic difference between the total Indian population and all those whom we have describe as 'elite'" (Guha, 1982, p. 8).

Reworked and adapted to the Indian context, subalternity was thus injected into the historical reconstruction of independence, which relied on two different interpretations of events: either as a reaction to British imperialism or as a result of initiative from a restricted group of leaders: Gandhi, Nehru and Jinna, who had led the revolt. Guha pointed out that both interpretations shared a common bias whereby "the making of the Indian nation and the development of the consciousness—nationalism—which informed this process were exclusively or predominantely elite achievements" (Guha, 1982, p. 1). What was omitted was the constitutive role of the mass of Indian subalterns, consisting of the peasantry and the urban proletariat, who implemented forms and modes of resistance and insurrection distinct from those of the Indian bourgeoisie. In fact, according to Guha, mobilisation of the lower classes had been achieved either horizontally, after the coventional model of kinship and territoriality, or along associative forms related to class, which depended on the degree of proximity between the people involved (Guha, 1982).

Within this shortcoming, or failure, of Indian historiography, the Subaltern Studies collective inscribed its own task, namely, to "rewrite the history of colonial India from the distinct and separate point of view of the masses, using unconventional or neglected sources in popular memory, oral discourse, previously unexamined colonial administrative documents" (Guha & Spivak, 1988, p. vi). Popular autonomy must be recognised within the framework of its cultural, religious and political references. In the 1983 essay *The Prose of Counter-Insurgency*, Guha highlighted the discursive strategies of peasant insurrections, thereby providing a between-the-lines reading of colonial historiography. He used techniques drawn from the semiotics and structural linguistics of Roland Barthes, Émile Benveniste and Roman Jacobson, to distinguish three discursive genres, called primary, secondary and tertiary, arranged chronologically but in an order that differed from historical sources. The three genres were characterised less by complementarity than by the fact that they relied on the same assumptions: namely the identification of an exogenous cause for explaining peasant rebellions (Guha, 1983).

The first included texts describing events as they first occurred. For example, the letters British officials wrote about the rebellions they could witness first-hand or that took place in their close vicinity. These showed strong identification between writers and the colonial regime, whose direct intervention for defensive purposes was invariably called for. The second, which included texts written years after the events, did not aim to quash the rebellions but to trace their possible causes. For all its self-proclaimed impartiality, historical reconstruction systematically left out the voice of insurgents, who were featured in colonial narratives as awkward figures the administration must deal with in order to preserve its rule. Finally, the third genre included texts around the historiography of independence. Although it sided with the insurgents, this type of discourse also failed to grasp their voice in full, due to the Marxist and secularist ideology it embraced. The rebels' awareness of the past was replaced by the historians' awareness of the present (Guha & Spivak, 1988, p. 77), a glaring failure, painfully obvious for instance in their inability to understand the role of religion in uprisings, generally dismissed as "fanaticism" (Guha & Spivak, 1988, p. 78).

Awareness of the constant omission, avoidance, and mystification of the subalterns' voice triggered a debate on the possibility of reconstructing them as historical subjects. Criticism against Guha's contrapuntal (Said, 1994, pp. 66–67) and circumstantial method of reading archival sources hinged on the fact that his reading made it impossible for the voice of subalterns to break through, since the imperial narrative self lay unequivocally at the very heart of the records collected in colonial archives. Gayatri Chakravorty Spivak qualified Guha's failure as an (im)possible reformulation of subalternity (Spivak, 1988). An Indian philosopher and literary critic, Spivak earned a degree in English Literature in Calcutta, then went on to study in the United States, where, after her PhD, she taught at Columbia University in New York. International fame came thanks to the translation of Jacques Derrida's work, *De la Grammatologie*, published in English in 1976.

In the 1988 essay *Can The Subaltern Speak?*, subsequently reissued and expanded in the wake of the wide debate it generated, Spivak found in the figure of the subaltern native woman the absolute impossibility of speaking or being listened to. Her foreclosure is the precipitate of an insuperable historiographical absence and aphony. Spivak historically reconstructed this invisibility within the power relations dictated by the international division of labour, which since the very onset of imperialism and colonialism have made women the subject of exploitation par excellence. Each attempt to give the subaltern native woman a voice turned out to be an instance of exploitation, because in any effort at relaying it either by "speaking for", *vertreten*, or by "representing", *darstellen*, there always lies an absence, that of the acting subject at the instant of its own representation.

To flesh out her argument, Spivak deconstructed the British introduction of the 1829 law on the abolition of widows' sacrifice on their husband's funeral pyre, a ritual called *sati*. Contrary to the common perception of the issue in terms of a predictable narrative of "white men save brown-skinned women from brown-skinned men", this move marked a crucial identity shift in the British presence in India: from a mercantile and commercial entity to an imperial and administrative power. The redefinition of legality in this specific area shifted the frontier of colonial intervention from the public to the private sphere. By espousing the cause of women's protection, colonial imperialism mystified its own role, identifying it with the civilising mission inscribed in patriarchy. To exemplify this process, Spivak described the figure of the young activist Bhuvaneswari Bhaduri. In 1926, at the age of about 17, she was found hanged in her father's apartment in Calcutta. She was menstruating at the time of death, a sign that the decision to commit suicide was not caused by an illicit pregnancy. An initial reconstruction of events attributed the cause of death to a sort of melancholy, due to the fact that it was impossible for her to become a wife. After about ten years, however, thanks to a letter Bhuvaneswari herself had sent to her sister, the reason for her act came to light. A member of an Indian independence group, she had decided to take her own life after failing to assassinate a politician. Spivak read her suicide as:

> an unemphatic, ad hoc, subaltern rewriting of the social text of *sati*-suicide as much as the hegemonic account of the blazing, fighting, familial Durga.

504   S. RONCAGLIA

> The emergent dissenting possibilities of that hegemonic account of the fighting mother are well documented and popularly well remembered through the discourse of the male leaders and participants in the independence movement. The subaltern as female cannot be heard or read. (Spivak, 1988, p. 308)

Bhuvaneswari's gesture, the quintessential token of self-erasure, led Spivak to assert that "the subaltern cannot speak. There is no virtue in global laundry lists with 'woman' as a pious item. Representation has not withered away. The female intellectual as intellectual has a circumscribed task which she must not disown with a flourish" (Spivak, 1988, p. 308).

Intellectuals in the collective also posed a challenge to more recent historiography, because "Indian history continues into the present" (Guha & Spivak, 1988, p. viii). While it reached its intellectual maturity after independence, this generation of female and male scholars is thoroughly aware of the hold that economic and intellectual imperialism maintains, under ever new guises, over the countries that were colonised by the West. Among the outcomes of this epistemic shift, for instance, are Indian nativist policies which since the 1960s used the "India to Indians" slogan to propagate identity politics tied to an exasperated model of Hindu nationalism. And this became the leading ideological strategy for policies based on *hindutva*. Such policies explicitly target "those who recognize India as a sacred homeland", thereby excluding Muslims and Christians from the Indian (Hindu) social body. In 1992, however, the destruction of the Ayodhya mosque, built on the remains of a Hindu temple, and the political success of Hindu fundamentalism led some scholars to start reconsidering, in historical terms, the violence that had been unleashed and the gradual deterioration of relations between Hindus and Muslims. At that time, Sumit Sarkar (1939) levelled serious criticism at the Subaltern Studies collective: he distanced himself from them and exposed their epistemological failure (Sarkar, 1997).

Since the 1990s, the collective has gathered new impetus in facing postcolonial issues. Within the group, the ascendancy of British and Continental Marxism has gradually given way to the influence of American poststructuralism. Via the contribution of intellectuals from the so-called Indian diaspora, most notably the philosopher and theoretical critic Homi K. Bhabha (1949), exponents of this current of anthropological studies have outlined both the historical processes that moulded the distinctive features of contemporaneity—following the demise of a colonialist mindset—and the subsequent restoration of a sense of subjective identity to colonised peoples. Their voices recounted experiences of transnationalism, decentralisation, dislocation and fragmentation typical of diaspora cultures. In these hybrid spaces, novel questions have arisen, which have called for theories that are able to rephrase dominant paradigms, to voice an underlying tension towards the exploration of syncretism, of chaos and of the cultural disorientation of contemporaneity. In a 2012 essay devoted to the history of the collective, Partha Chatterjee initiated a reflection over the legacy of Subaltern Studies. While the project was in fact able to reinterpret and renew itself over time, Chatterjee proposed that it should be abandoned, for "Subaltern Studies was a product of its time; another time calls for other projects" (Chatterjee, 2012, p. 49).

INFINITE STIGMA

At the beginning of the 2000s, also in the wake of a broader rethink on the history of *Dalits* in India (Rawat, 2006), a far-reaching scholarly debate sparked off among activists, politicians and scholars, following the insertion of the caste discrimination issue in the agenda of the Third United Nations World Conference Against Racism—World Conference Against Racism, Racial Discrimination, Xenophobia and Related Tolerance (WCAR), in Durban, South Africa from 31 August to 7 September 2001. The move was promoted by the National Campaign on Dalit Human Rights (NCDHR)—a coalition of activists and academics for the rights of *Dalits*—by the Indian Institute of Dalit Studies and by several NGOs supported by sections of the Indian public opinion. According to the various NGOs, the prerogative to appeal to the United Nations, and in particular to the United Nations Committee on the Elimination of Racial Discrimination (CERD), was endorsed by the Indian government's ratification of the International Convention on the Elimination of All Forms of Racial Discrimination (ICERD)—1965 (Thorat, and Umakant, 2004).

The "caste is race plus" statement paved the way to a renewed understanding of difference, focused on the universal occurrence of discrimination dynamics rather than on a philology of social hierarchy based on religion. To this end, a reformulation of the concepts of caste and race has been put forth, with the aim to eschew analytical categories on caste proposed by postcolonial research and Subaltern studies. For, even though they were strongly critical of the entire historical-cultural dynamics of imperialism, research orientations of the latter kind turned out to be somewaht entrenched in the body of disciplines that fixed key reference categories for Orientalist discourse. Such studies ultimately failed to transcend the boundaries of a stringent critique against colonialism (Natrajan & Greenough, 2009, 34–38). Drawing on this background experience of historical caste discrimination and on its complex ideological burden, caste and race theory proponents have tried to emancipate debate from the narrow religious framework within which caste discrimination had been traced. Their aim was to turn it into a platform for a political and cultural activism capable of transcending the Indian scenario. The debate zeroed in on two fundamental questions: Is caste race? Can we possibly compare caste discrimination to racial discrimination?

In the world of social activism, Ambrose Pinto (1951–2018), director of the Indian Social Institute in New Delhi argued that the *Dalits*, Ambedkarians and many academics in India have never equated the concepts of caste and race in strict semantic terms. Rather, in their endeavour they have highlighted the issue of descent-based or occupation-based discrimination. Ambedkar himself clearly refuted the caste-race correlation. And Pinto himself added his own reflection on the issue in the 2001 article *Caste is a Variety of Race*, which aimed to disentangle the idea of race from a merely biological model:

> Whether it is caste or race, the status is entirely ascribed, the status one obtains at birth. Segregation exists in both the systems. [...]In both caste and race those in the lowest rung are not only discriminated against but cursed to do menial jobs. Endogamy is another feature of both. Marriages are rare and few both among different racial and caste groups. Both are stratifications, a hierarchical ordering of social categories, supported by social institutions. Inequality is intergenerationally transmitted in caste and race. Prejudice and discrimination are both a part of race and caste. And what is worse is that such prejudice and discrimination are not merely personal but institutional, a part of the structure and processes of whole society [...] How do those who oppose the linkage of caste with race explain this? Though skin colour or physical differences may not all the time play a significant part in distinguishing caste as in race, social descent and occupation does. Apartheid exists in both. (Pinto, 2001)

A wide range of positions emerged in the political and especially in the academic world, in a pressing debate between scholars who opposed the idea of caste discrimination as a form of racial discrimination and, implicitly, the idea of caste as a form of race. Among them was Dipankar Gupta

(1949), an anthropologist and sociologist at Jawaharlal Nehru University, New Delhi. In his article *Race and Caste: Divergent Logics of Mobilisation*, first published in 2000 and later reissued with revisions and expansions under the title *Caste, Race, Politics*, Gupta argued that "caste should not be seen as another variant of race" and that consequently "casteism is not racism under a different name" (Gupta, 2000, 2001). Having long been exposed to an obsessive use of the race concept during British colonialism, anthropologists and sociologists have long held that the "caste-race" thesis was unfounded. According to Gupta, reiterated support for this correlation in recent years has two main causes: the persistent influence over time of an arbitrary reading of the Vedic texts by early Western Orientalists, and the presence of similarities between the forms of segregation adopted against African Americans in the United States and South African apartheid on the one hand and the treatment of so-called untouchables in India on the other.

After dismantling the phenotypic and genetic underpinnings of the caste-race correlation, Gupta pointed out the different social structures generated by the two classifications. Race used the colour continuum as a hierarchical device: as a gradient that raises light-skinned people to the top and relegates those with dark complexions to the bottom. Caste-based stratification, however, is not *readable* on the basis of mere skin colour and gives rise to identity processes quite distinct from those of racial identity. This system has produced a society characterised by multiple hierarchies, where competition between castes is structural.

Ultimately, Gupta addresses the political aspect of the equation between caste and race. Instrumental use of this comparison has made the category of caste immutable. On the other hand, from a historical and economic point of view, we have witnessed crucial changes in recent years, which have brought about a shift in caste relations resulting in a system of dynamic alliances. As the logic of race was applied to caste, caste identities de facto became a reservoir of votes for political use. So much so that politicians turned out to be less interested in eliminating caste identities than in turning them into a pattern of proportionate representation for acquiring power and services. A caste policy was thus configured, of which the Mandal Commission is a striking example. Established in the 1980s during the Morarji Desai government to devise measures for improving the conditions of socially backward groups, it was named after the politician Bindeshwari Prasad Mandal. Directions given in the final report of the Mandal Commission listed quotas that the State should reserve in the civil service for Other Backward Classes (OBCs), on the basis of caste identity, tied to those already laid out in the Constitution for Scheduled Castes and Scheduled Tribes.

After the Durban conference, several meetings, debates and studies continued and expanded the ongoing discussion over the concepts of caste and race. The impact of the UN World Conference Against Racism turned out to be more enduring than expected, because it sparked an exchange between scholars and activists, who identified common causes in an international struggle against discrimination. Their reflections converged into a collective volume tellingly entitled *Against Stigma. Studies in Caste, Race and Justice since Durban*. The book records a wide range of attempts to articulate new theorisations of caste and race via a critical approach which collates the plight of communities segregated and oppressed on account of such stigmas. That made it possible to unpack the social processes generated by these stigmatisations in an intersectional perspective on the themes of identity, gender, power, citizenship, human rights, policies and economic changes (Natrajan & Greenough, 2009).

As Balmurli Natrajan and Paul Greenough explain at length in their introduction, through this lens scholars have addressed caste in at least three relatively new perspectives: the first within the language of social construction; the second within the framework of comparative analysis, which takes into account other features of social differentiation such as gender, class, and ethnicity; the third as *critical caste theory*, following the example of *critical race theory*, that is, a theoretical approach that brings together the studies of intellectuals and academics on the systemic and legal presuppositions of discrimination and the proposals of activists aimed at expanding the conditions for the application of universal human rights. Critical caste theory has exposed the ubiquitous application of caste in India: a system which encompasses even common forms of abuse and violence. By doing so, it has demonstrated that while the ideological constraints of caste have loosened, caste as a systemic principle of social inequality based on exclusion and discrimination endures.

The Durban conference also had political momentum in India, so much so that on 27 December 2006, India's then Prime Minister Manmohan Singh openly stated for the first time that the *Dalit* had been subjected to a unique form of discrimination in Indian society akin to a form of legal apartheid. Durban also produced unforeseen outcomes, for instance in the 2014 public gathering for the 85th anniversary of Martin Luther King's birth in Washington, D.C., which called for an end to the oppression and

16 SOCIAL ANTHROPOLOGY IN INDIA: STUDYING THE SELF IN THE OTHER 509

enslavement of *Dalits* in India. Through this public action, representatives of families who descended from African slaves expressed their political closeness to the *Dalits*. They also recalled the sermon given at Ebenezer Baptist Church on 4 July 1965, in which Dr. King, reflecting on his trip to India, pointed out the similarities between African Americans and *Dalits*, and concluded: "Yes, I am an Untouchable, and every Negro in the United States of America is an Untouchable".

INTERDISCIPLINARY FIELDS

A provisional conclusion to this brief historical survey of social anthropology in India must necessarily touch upon its inevitable shortcomings, theoretical developments still *in the making* that may possibly offer insights into the current state of this itinerant knowledge. Among the various fields of study now emerging, albeit still within the same wide range of studies of the anthropology of South Asia surveyed here, is interdisciplinary research on the contemporary identities of the *Adivasi* ("Aborigines"). The very designation of "Aborigines", in itself contentious, is ideologically amphibious in nature, because it references both the British Raj and the policies of the post-colonial state, as enshrined in the 1950 Constitution. It is used alongside those of "tribes" and "indigenous peoples"—which are now given a global connotation, although they are originally colonial terms—or those of *Vanvasi* and *Janjati*, which according to Uday Chandra are Indian neologism coined by Hindu right-wing parties and the post-colonial state, respectively (Chandra, 2015, p. 122).

The study of *Adivasi*, as a subject of anthropological analysis in an interdisciplinary direction, envisages three possible future perspectives. Firstly, it enables us to rethink ethnographic research conducted in the past, re-reading the categories used by pre-colonial, colonial and post-colonial historiography. Secondly, it serves as a prism for repositioning the view of the *Adivasis* role both in the recent literature of subaltern studies—where they are described as the most authentic anti-colonialists opposed to the Raj and the nationalist bourgeoisie—and in the culturally essentialist literature used in modern India politics to reify specific social groups. Thirdly and finally, the study of the *Adivasi* provides a critical analysis on the identity affirmation of global indigenism. This phenomenon does overcome class solidarity by crossing national borders. However, as it paves the way to a shared struggle for social, economic, environmental transformations, necessary for the planet's future, it also incautiously evokes colonial stereotypes about tribal primitivism (Chandra, 2015).

Arjun Appadurai (1949), one of the leading contemporary anthropologists, has taught us that we need to think of imagination as a collective practice, capable of playing a key role in the production of locality (Appadurai, 1996). In this perspective, "the local [... *is*] always a sustained work in process, an emergent that required not only the resources of habit, custom, and history, but also the work of the imagination" (Appadurai, 2013, p. 287, *italics mine*). Transcending the limits of the nation state, imagination binds culturally and spatially disparate elements, pulverising modernity. To imagine reality is to continually create and recreate it, shaping an interdisciplinary field of study that is forever unfinished, an "epistemology of perpetual unpacking" which has no centre, no core and no origin. This theory ultimately marks a radical departure from the emphasis on culture as a logic of reproduction, understanding it rather as a space of creative and communicative flows in the making, alive and multiform in their complex interactions. More recently, as he studies ethnographically the everyday life of slum dwellers in Mumbai, a (de)cosmopolitan city and his hometown, Appadurai ties this protean thrust of the imagination to its political equivalent: hope, that is the ability to envisage and develop active aspirations. It is a significant theoretical shift, which makes it possible to shape an anthropological approach to the future.

The account given so far falls within this groove, one step away from the unknown.

REFERENCES

Agarwal, B. (1988). *Structures of Patriarchy: State, Community and Household in Modernising Asia*. Sage.

Alatas, S. F. (2006). The Autonomous, the Universal and the Future of Sociology. *Current Sociology, 54*(7), 7–23.

Ambedkar, B. R. (1916). Castes in India: Their Mechanism, Genesis and Development. In V. Moon (Ed.), *Dr. Babasaheb Ambedkar: Writings and Speeches, 1979–2006* (Vol. 1). Education Department, Government of Maharashtra.

Appadurai, A. (1996). *Modernity at Large: Cultural Dimensions of Globalisation*. University of Minnesota Press.

16 SOCIAL ANTHROPOLOGY IN INDIA: STUDYING THE SELF IN THE OTHER 511

Appadurai, A. (2013). *The Future as Cultural Fact: Essays on the Global Condition*. Verso.

Atal, Y. (1981). The Call for Indigenisation. *International Social Science Journal, 33*(1), 189–197.

Basa, K. K. (2016). Anthropology and Museums in India. In G. Robbins Schug & S. R. Walimbe (Eds.), *A Companion to South Asia in the Past* (pp. 465–481). Wiley Blackwell.

Bayly, S. (1997). Caste and 'Race' in the Colonial Ethnography of India. In P. Robb (Ed.), *The Concept of Race in South Asia* (pp. 165–218). Oxford University Press.

Berger, P. (2012). Theory and Ethnography in the Modern Anthropology of India. *Hau: Journal of Ethnographic Theory, 2*, 325–357.

Béteille, A. (1974). *Six Essays in Comparative Sociology*. Oxford University Press.

Bose, N. K. (1975 [1949]). *The Structure of Hindu Society*. Orient Longman.

Bose, N. K. (1952). Current Research Projects in Indian Anthropology. *Man in India, 3*, 121–133.

Bose, N. K. (1967a). *Culture and Society in India*. Asia Publishing House.

Bose, N. K. (1967b). National Seminar On Hill People. *Man in India, 47*(1), 1–7.

Bose, N. K. (1969). The Tribal Situation. *Man in India, 49*(3), 217–223.

Bose, N. K. (1972). *Anthropology and Some Indian Problems*. Institute of Social Research And Applied Anthropology.

Bose, P. (2007). The Anthropologist as 'Scientist'? Nirmal Kumar Bose. In P. Uberoi, N. Sundar, & S. Deshpande (Eds.), *Anthropology in the East: Founders of Indian Sociology and Anthropology* (pp. 290–329). Permanent Black.

Briggs, J. (1852). Two Lectures on the Aboriginal Races of India as Distinguished from the Sanskritic or Hindu Race. *Journal of the Asiatic Society of Great Britain and Ireland, 13*, 275–309.

Cháirez-Garza, J. F. (2018). B.R. Ambedkar, Franz Boas and the Rejection of Racial Theories of Untouchability. *South Asia: Journal of South Asian Studies, 41*(2), 1–16.

Chandra, U. (2015). Towards Adivasi Studies: New Perspectives on 'Tribal' Margins of Modern India. *Studies in History, 31*(1), 122–127.

Chatterjee, P. (1995). *The Nation and Its Fragments: Colonial and Postcolonial Histories*. Oxford University Press.

Chatterjee, P. (2012). After Subaltern Studies. *Economic & Political Weekly, 1*(35), 44–49.

Chaudhuri, S. (Ed.). (1956). *Index to the Publications of the Asiatic Society, 1788–1953*. Asiatic Society.

Cohn, B. S. (1990). *An Anthropologist Among the Historians*. Oxford University Press.

Crooke, W. (1896). *The Tribes and Castes of the North-Western Provinces and Oudh, 4 Vols*. Government Printing.

512   S. RONCAGLIA

Dasgupta, S. (2007). Recasting the Oraons and the 'Tribe': Sarat Chandra Roy's Anthropology. In P. Uberoi, N. Sundar, & S. Deshpande (Eds.), *Anthropology in the East: Founders of Indian Sociology and Anthropology* (pp. 132–171). Ranikhet.

Desai, N., & Patel, V. (1989). *Critical Review of Researches Women's Studies.* Research Centre For Women's Studies.

Dhanagare, D. N. (1993). *Themes and Perspectives in Indian Sociology.* Rawat Publication.

Dube, L. (1988). On the Construction of Gender: Hindu Girls in Patrilineal India. *Economic & Political Weekly, 23*(18), 11–19.

Dube, L. (2000). Doing Kinship and Gender: An Autobiographical Account. *Economic & Political Weekly, 35*(46), 4037–4047.

Dube, L. (2001). *Anthropological Explorations in Gender: Intersecting Fields.* Sage.

Dube, L., Leacock, E., & Ardener, S. (1986). *Visibility and Power: Essays on Women in Society and Development.* Oxford University Press.

Dube, S. (2007). Ties that Bind: Tribe, Village, Nation, and S.C Dube. In P. Uberoi, N. Sundar, & S. Deshpande (Eds.), *Anthropology in the East: Founders of Indian Sociology and Anthropology* (pp. 444–495). Permanent Black.

Dube, S. C. (1960). *Manav Aur Sanskriti.* Rajkamal.

Dube, S. C. (1996). *Samay Aur Sanskriti.* Vani.

Dumont, L. (1957). For a Sociology of India. *Contributions to Indian Sociology, 1*(1), 8–22.

Dumont, L. (1980 [1966]). *Homo Hierarchicus: Le système des castes et ses implications.* Gallimard.

Dumont, L., & Pocock, D. F. (1957). Village Studies. *Contributions to Indian Sociology, 1*, 23–41.

Elleman, B. A. (2001). *Modern Chinese Warfare, 1795–1989.* Routledge.

Elwin, V. (1939). *The Baiga.* John Murray.

Elwin, V. (1941). *Loss of Nerve: A Comparative Study of the Contact of People in the Aboriginal Areas of Bastar and The Central Provinces of India.* Wagle Press.

Elwin, V. (1959). *A Philosophy for Nefa.* Sachin Roy.

Fuller, C. J. (2017). Ethnographic Inquiry in Colonial India: Herbert Risley, William Crooke, and the Study of Tribes and Castes. *Journal of the Royal Anthropological Institute, 23*(3), 603–621.

Fuller, C. J., & Spencer, J. (1990). South Asian Anthropology in the 1980s. *South Asia Research, 10*(2), 85–103.

Ghurye, G. S. (1932). *Caste and Race in India.* Kegan Paul & Co.

Ghurye, G. S. (1959). *The Scheduled Tribes.* Popular Prakashan.

Guha, A. (2018). *In Search of Nationalist Trends in Indian Anthropology: Opening a New Discourse.* Institute of Development Studies Kolkata.

Guha, R. (1982). Preface. In R. Guha (Ed.), *Subaltern Studies I. Writings on South Asian History and Society* (pp. Vii–Viii). Oxford University Press.

Guha, R. (1983). The Prose of Counter-Insurgency. In R. Guha (Ed.), *Subaltern Studies II* (pp. 1–42). Oxford University Press.

Guha, R. (1996a). Savaging the Civilised: Verrier Elwin and the Tribal Question in Late Colonial India. *Economic & Political Weekly, 31*, 2375–2389.

Guha, R. (1996b). *Savaging the Civilised: Verrier Elwin, his Tribes and India.* Oxford University Press.

Guha, R. (2007). *India After Gandhi: The History of the World's Largest Democracy.* Macmillan.

Guha, R., & Spivak, G. C. (Eds.). (1988). *Selected Subaltern Studies.* Oxford University Press.

Guha, S. (1998). Lower Strata, Older Races, and Aboriginal Peoples: Racial Anthropology and Mythical History Past and Present. *The Journal of Asian Studies, 57*(2), 423–441.

Guha-Thakurta, T. (2004). *Monuments, Objects, Histories: Institutions of Art in Colonial and Post-Colonial India.* Permanent Black.

Gupta, D. (2000). Race and Caste: Divergent Logics of Mobilisation. In D. Gupta (Ed.), *Interrogating Caste: Understanding Hierarchy and Difference in Indian Society* (pp. 86–115). Penguin.

Gupta, D. (2001). Caste, Race, Politics. *Seminar, 508.* https://www.india-seminar.com/2001/508/508%20dipankar%20gupta.htm#top

Ibbetson, D. C. J. (1883). *Report of the Census of the Panjab 1881.* Central Gaol Press.

Jain, R. K. (1985). *Social Anthropology of India: Theory And Method.* Indian Council of Social Science Research Survey of Research in Sociology and Social Anthropology. Satvahan.

Jodhka, S. S. (1998). From 'Book View' to 'Field View': Social Anthropological Constructions of the Indian Village. *Oxford Development Studies, 26*(3), 311–321.

Jodhka, S. S. (2002). Nation and Village: Images of Rural India in Gandhi, Nehru and Ambedkar. *Economic & Political Weekly, 37*(32), 3343–3353.

Karve, I. (1953). *Kinship Organisation in India.* Deccan College.

Kejariwal, O. P. (1988). *The Asiatic Society of Bengal and the Discovery of India's Past.* Oxford University Press.

Linton, R. (1936). Error in Anthropology. In J. Jastrow (Ed.), *The Story of Human Error* (pp. 292–321). Appleton-Century.

Ludden, D. (Ed.). (2002). *Reading Subaltern Studies. Critical History, Contested Meaning and Globalisation of South Asia.* Anthem South Asian Studies.

Madan, T. N. (2007). *Search for Synthesis. The Sociology of D.P. Mukerji.* In P. Uberoi, N. Sundar, & S. Deshpande (Eds.), *Anthropology in the East: Founders of Indian Sociology and Anthropology* (pp. 256–289). Permanent Black.

Madan, T. N., & Sarana, G. (Eds.). (1962). *Indian Anthropology. Essays in Memory of D. N. Majumdar.* Asia Publishing House.

514 S. RONCAGLIA

Majumdar, D. N. (1950). Anthropology Under Glass. *The Journal of Anthropological Society of Bombay, 14*, 120.

Majumdar, D. N. (1960a). *Social Contours of an Industrial City: Social Survey of Kanpur 1954–56*. Asia Publishing House.

Majumdar, D. N. (1960b). *Race Elements in Bengal: A Quantitative Study*. Asia Publishing House.

Mills, J. P. (Ed.). (1942). *Essays in Anthropology: Presented to Rai Bahadur Saral Chandra Roy*. Lucknow.

Mukerji, D. P. (1945). *On Indian History: A Study in Method*. Hind Kitabs.

Mukherjee, R. (1979). *The Sociology of Indian Sociology*. Allied Publishers.

Natrajan, B., & Greenough, P. (Eds.). (2009). *Against Stigma: Studies in Caste Race and Justice Since Durban*. Orient Blackswan.

Nehru, J. (1959). *Foreword to the Second Edition*. In V. Elwin (Ed.), *A Philosophy for NEFA*. Sachin Roy.

Paidipaty, L. P. (2010). Tribal Nation: Politics and the Making of Anthropology in India, 1874–1967. Columbia University UMI Dissertation Publishing.

Patel, S. (2002). The Profession and its Association: Five Decades of the Indian Sociological Society. *International Sociology, 17*(2), 262–284.

Patel, S. (2016). Feminist Challenges to Sociology in India: An Essay in Disciplinary History. *Contributions to Indian Sociology, 50*(3), 320–342.

Patel, S. (2021). Nationalist Ideas and the Colonial Episteme: The Antinomies Structuring Sociological Traditions of India. *The Journal of Historical Sociology*.

Patel, V. (2012). Prof. Leela Dube (1923–2012): Gendering Anthropology. *Social Change, 42*, 443–445.

Pinto, A. (2001). Caste is a Variety of Race. *The Hindu*, 27 March.

Ram, K. (2007). Anthropology as 'Ananthropology'. L.K. Ananthakrishna Iyer (1861–1937), Colonial Anthropology, and the 'Native Anthropologist' as Pioneered. In P. Uberoi, N. Sundar, & S. Deshpande (Eds.), *Anthropology in the East: Founders of Indian Sociology and Anthropology* (pp. 64–105). Permanent Black.

Rawat, R. S. (2006). The Problem. *Seminar, 558*. http://Www.Indiaseminar.com/2006/558/558%20the%20problem.Htm

Risley, H. H. (1891a). *The Tribes and Castes of Bengal: Anthropometric Data, 2 Vol*. Bengal Secretariat Press.

Risley, H. H. (1891b). *The Tribes and Castes of Bengal: Ethnographic Glossary, 2 Vol*. Bengal Secretariat Press.

Rivers, W. H. R. (1906). *The Todas*. Macmillan.

Roy, S. C. (1912). *The Mundas and their Country*. Kunialine.

Roy, S. C. (1938). An Indian Outlook on Anthropology. *Man in India, 38*(172), 146–150.

Roy, S. C. (1946). The Aborigines of Chota Nagpur: Their Proper Status in the Reformed Constitution of India. *Man in India, 26*, 120–136.

16 SOCIAL ANTHROPOLOGY IN INDIA: STUDYING THE SELF IN THE OTHER 515

Said, E. (1994). *Culture and Imperialism*. Vintage.

Sangari, K., & Vaid, S. (1989). Recasting Women: An Introduction. In K. Sangari & S. Vaid (Eds.), *Recasting Women: Essays in Colonial History* (pp. 1–26). Kali for Women.

Sarana, G., & Sinha, D. P. (1976). Status of Social-Cultural Anthropology in India. *Annual Review of Anthropology, 5*, 209–225.

Sarkar, S. (1997). The Decline of the Subaltern in Subaltern Studies. In S. Sarkar (Ed.), *Writing Social History* (pp. 82–108). Oxford University Press.

Shah, A. M. (2014). Anthropology in Bombay, 1886–1936. *Sociological Bulletin, 63*(3), 355–367.

Singh, K. S. (1996). G. S. Ghurye, Verrier Elwin and Indian Tribes. In A. R. Momin (Ed.), *The Legacy of G. S. Ghurye: A Centennial Festschrift* (pp. 39–45). Popular Prakashan.

Sinha, A. C. (1991). Indian Social Anthropology & its Cambridge Connections. *The Eastern Anthropologist, 44*(4), 345–354.

Sinha, A. C. (2005a). Colonial Anthropology Vs Indological Sociology: Elwin and Ghurye on Tribal Policy in India. In B. Subba & S. Som (Eds.), *Between Ethnography and Fiction: Verrier Elwin and the Tribal Question in India* (pp. 71–85). Orient Longman.

Sinha, S. (1971). Is there an Indian Tradition in Social/Cultural Anthropology: Retrospect and Prospects. *Journal of Indian Anthropological Society, 6*, 1–14.

Sinha, V. (2005b). 'Indigenizing' Anthropology in India: Problematics of Negotiating an Identity. In J. Van Bremen, E. Ben-Ari, & S. F. Alatas (Eds.), *Asian Anthropology* (pp. 139–161). Routledge.

Spivak, G. C. (1988). Can The Subaltern Speak? In C. Nelson & L. Grossberg (Eds.), *Marxism and the Interpretation of Culture* (pp. 271–313). Macmillan.

Srinivas, M. N. (1966). *Social Change in Modern India*. University of California Press: Berkeley-Los Angeles.

Srinivas, M. N. (1976). *The Remembered Village*. Oxford University Press.

Srinivas, M. N. (1997). Practicing Social Anthropology in India. *Annual Review of Anthropology, 26*, 1–24.

Sundar, N. (2007). In the Cause of Anthropology. The Life and Work of Irawati Karve. In P. Uberoi, N. Sundar, & S. Deshpande (Eds.), *Anthropology in the East: Founders of Indian Sociology and Anthropology* (pp. 360–416). Permanent Black.

Uberoi, P. (1993). Introduction. In P. Uberoi (Ed.), *Family, Kinship and Marriage in India* (pp. 1–44). Oxford University Press.

Uberoi, P., Deshpande, S., & Sundar, N. (2007). Introduction: The Professionalisation of Indian Anthropology and Sociology: People, Places, and Institutions. In P. Uberoi, N. Sundar, & S. Deshpande (Eds.), *Anthropology in the East: Founders of Indian Sociology and Anthropology* (pp. 1–63). Permanent Black.

Umakant, T. S. (Ed.). (2004). *Caste, Race, And Discrimination: Discourses In International Context*. Rawat Publications.

Upadhya, C. (2007). The Idea of Indian Society: G. S. Ghurye and the Making of Indian Sociology. In P. Uberoi, N. Sundar, & S. Deshpande (Eds.), *Anthropology in the East: Founders of Indian Sociology and Anthropology*, (pp. 195–255). Permanent Black.

Vidyarthi, L. P. (1978). *The Rise of Anthropology in India, 2 Vol.* Concept.

Wiser, W. H. (1936). *The Hindu Jajmani System*. Lucknow Pub. House.

CHAPTER 17

The Diverse Accounts of Anthropology in Viet Nam

Elena Bougleux

HISTORICAL AND METHODOLOGICAL PREMISE

Historical literature on anthropology's status as a discipline in Viet Nam presents a tangle of narratives and reconstructions, to some extent independent from each other and barely integrated. This reflects the country's complex history and the decisive role of the various international agents who, since the mid-nineteenth century, have contributed to its institutional and academic layout. It may be broadly accurate to claim that in the history of their national anthropologies, the anthropologies of the "elsewhere", former colonial contexts invariably bear traces of the influence exerted by the anthropological tradition of colonising countries. Yet, it is also true that for Viet Nam these influences are as deep as they are discordant: they rely on clashing political views, often driven by the explicit aim to cancel previous legacies and "replace" one tradition with another. Since such intervention is both culturally and institutionally impossible, it has given rise to a variegated scenario that is both theoretically fragmented

E. Bougleux (✉)
University of Bergamo, Bergamo, Italy
e-mail: elena.bougleux@unibg.it

© The Author(s), under exclusive license to Springer Nature Switzerland AG 2023
G. D'Agostino, V. Matera (eds.), *Histories of Anthropology*,
https://doi.org/10.1007/978-3-031-21258-1_17

517

and exceptionally diverse. As a consequence, this chapter does not outline a single or coherent history of the discipline and its schools, nor does it seek to highlight discontinuities of thought or method, which are at times more signalled or rehashed than actually implemented. Rather, I set out to render the fragmentary quality of anthropology's onset in Viet Nam by using heterogeneous sources, and in the awareness that no set of sources can ever be thorough.

Mere chronology could arguably provide some objective kind of continuity. In fact, each narrative tracing the history of the discipline actually turns out to uphold its own distinctive chronological phases and different key junctures, depending on whether the reconstruction of events is given in French area studies, Vietnamese and Asian studies or English-speaking area studies. Periodisation itself or the identification of turning points ultimately reflects the diverse political or cultural sensibilities of those involved in historical reconstruction. This chapter addresses these three levels of information simultaneously and with equal focus, by interleaving narratives in a logical-chronological order that does not paper over inevitable shifts in point of view. Francophone literature of the first half of the twentieth century is in fact clearly colonial, aimed as it is to documentation and promotion in a self-congratulatory key: it is indeed a *mise en valeur* of the archaeological, linguistic and mythical heritage of the Vietnamese area within the wider context of the Protectorate of Indochina (1862–1945).[1] A close link with French ethnology was established at the time, and subsequently consolidated in a solid relationship with the Musée de l'Homme, which opened its headquarters in Hanoi in 1927 and with the École française d'Extrême-Orient (EFEO), whose scientific status steadily increased and also involved Vietnamese scientific personnel since 1939, in the last years of activity.

At the end of the Second World War, under the leadership of Ho Chi Minh, Viet Nam repudiated the 1883 colonial treaties which had established the French Protectorate in Indochina. There ensued a ten-year war against France, aimed at putting an end to the colonial era. Cultural institutions at the time went through a distinct yet discontinuous phase of

---

[1] Having gained control of Cochinchina in 1867, in 1872 the French initiated military campaigns towards the rest of the country. In 1883 France concluded the Tonkin campaign, with the treaty of Hué, which required the Vietnamese court to set up protectorates over Annam and Tonkin (Protectorat d'Annam and Protectorat du Tonkin). The Franco-Chinese war (1884–1885) ensued, and the victory the French marked at the beginning of a period of extensive rule over Vietnam.

transition, so much so that some scholars speak of an "abandonment" of the EFEO on the part of France (Dang Nguyen Anh, 2019).

The Indochina War (1945–1954) ended with formal independence from France,[2] and a partition of the country into two opposing national entities: Northern Viet Nam and its capital Hanoi, its main cultural centre, under the political and cultural clout of the Soviet Union; and Southern Viet Nam, effectively controlled by the United States, which replaced France and settled in Saigon. The two decades following the partition of the country (1955–1975) marked a split within both scientific and educational institutions. Ethnology and anthropology, along with other social sciences, were most affected by the differing political climate of the Democratic Republic in the North and the Vietnamese State in the South. These disciplines took on the role of intellectual and cultural driving forces in the progressive radicalisation of their respective positions. These two decades witnessed a veritable relocation of cultural and museum institutions, a widespread renaming and redefining of scientific agendas and objectives, directed at maximising differences in socio-political outlook (Dang Nguyen Anh, 2019; Davis, 2017).

As is known, political opposition between the two Viet Nam states quickly escalated into full-scale military conflict. Hence nearly twenty years of war involved the whole region (Cambodia, Laos) and ended in 1975 with the defeat of the United States and the reunification of the Viet Nam.[3] Permanence of a unified country within a progressively weakened Soviet orbit lasted only until 1986, the year in which the Sixth Congress of the Vietnamese Communist Party inaugurated Doi Moi (Đổi mới,

---

[2] The Geneva Conference of 1954 put an end to the Indochina War and marked the demise of the French Protectorate. Four independent nations were established: Cambodia, Laos, Viet Nam of the North and Viet Nam of the South, separated by a formal boundary along the seventeenth parallel. The partition imposed on Viet Nam was *de facto* endorsed for opposing reasons by all the political actors involved in the Conference: the United States, China, the Soviet Union and France itself. The partition marked the onset of a phase of internal migration and anticipated intense emigration of Vietnamese people from both halves of the country. The Vietnamese general elections planned in the Geneva treaties for 1956, and meant to end the temporary partition set up by the Conference, never took place. On the contrary, from 1959 the Ho Chi Minh government in the North began to officially support Viet Minh guerrillas in the South.

[3] In the texts of many American authors, the Viet Nam War is called the Second Indochina War, whereas history texts of the Democratic Republic of Vietnam do not refer to the country's partition but rather mention the "occupation of southern regions by American military forces".

Renovation), a phase of economic liberalisation and social reforms that took shape in the 1990s and that led the country to the institutional and cultural configuration it retains to this day. It should be noted that the rapid series of political changes following the reunification in 1975 left recursively planned overhauls of culture and institutions largely unfinished. That undoubtedly accounts for the inconsistent quality of historical reconstructions. Because of all this, most recent trends in Vietnamese anthropology derive from an internal framework that may be defined as multilocal: multiple and polyphonic. At the same time, engagement with global studies since the 1990s inevitably introduced novel features, namely postcolonial criticism—which served at once to denounce French colonialism and the strong influence and actual presence of the Soviet Union—and a critique of ethnicity, an identitarian and foundational feature within the historically multi-ethnic context of Viet Nam.

I would underline that, attuned as it is to the global anthropological debate, the (re)-definition of contemporary anthropology in Viet Nam also allows unexpected methodological continuities to emerge between the different historical phases briefly outlined above: for instance, the repeated reliance on ethnographic museums as crucial tools for a collective (re)-working of national identity. A dense schedule of temporary exhibitions and installations of ethnographic museums that are either permanent or at least designed to be permanent characterises the history of Viet Nam in the twentieth century. Their underlying thrust is to objectify representation and boost self-recognition via recurrent exhibitions set up by heterogeneous groups of social and political actors. It is not uncommon to witness periodic relocations of objects and collections, separated and then reassembled so as to build an ever-changing narrative (Nguyen Van Hui, 2019).

Before Anthropology

Nguyễn Phuong Ngoc, director of the Institute for Asian Studies (IrASIA) at the University of Aix-Marseille, has devoted much research (Nguyễn Phuong Ngoc 2006, 2012, 2017) to chart the progressive voicing of anthropologists in Viet Nam. She has woven together the history of the country with the history of the discipline and defined current Vietnamese anthropology as "the dynamic result of a tension between opposing actors and visions" (Nguyễn Phuong Ngoc, 2017, p. 200). That is complicated by the fact that Vietnam is a multi-ethnic assemblage, bracketing the region of Tonkin in the north, under the obvious sway of China with Thai minorities; the central Annam region, populated mainly by mountain ethnic groups—the *montagnards* of colonial French literature; and Cochinchina in the south, which counts a sizable Khmer population.

Nguyễn Phuong Ngoc's reconstruction identifies a generic period "before anthropology" which recalls the time preceding French entrenchment in the administrative mesh of the country. Before anthropology, the relationship with Europe was established on the initiative of Napoleon III who invaded Cochinchina (1857–1958) for reasons largely dictated by the need to consolidate French industrialisation and to open new markets, even though initial steps of the Cochinchina campaign were ostensibly taken to protect communities of Catholic missionaries in southern Vietnam as early as the seventeenth century. As a matter of fact, we owe early transcriptions of Vietnamese from Chinese spelling (*Nam âm*, 南音, "*Southern sound*") into the Latin script (*chữ Quốc ngữ*, "*script of the national language*") to the work of Portuguese Catholic missionaries from the first half of the seventeenth century. Formalisation of the *chữ Quốc ngữ* followed the publication of the Dictionarium *Annamiticum Lusitanum et Latinum* in 1651, a trilingual dictionary aimed at translating the Catholic liturgy into Vietnamese for use by missionaries (Gaudio, 2019). *Quốc ngữ* was not instantly adopted as the main alphabet. Rather, it was used along the Chinese script and remained largely limited to the religious sphere until French administrators *de facto* enforced it.

According to Nguyễn Phuong Ngoc, starting with 1867 we may speak of a *first stage* in the history of Vietnamese anthropology: "research" on Viet Nam of this period was closely tied to the needs of conquest first and later to the establishment and consolidation of colonial administration. Most demographic data published at this stage was the result of research by French army personnel, administrators and missionaries, but also of some Vietnamese writers from a cultured and doubly educated elite well-versed in both Mandarin and Latin. These contributed to enrich the initial treasure trove of field knowledge assembled in works of lexicography, popular literature, history and geography. Contributions written in Latinised Vietnamese proved essential for strengthening control over the colony (Nguyễn Phuong Ngoc, 2012; Nguyen Van Chinh, 2019). We find references, occasionally quite censorious, to the works of Pétrus Trương Vĩnh Ký and Paulus Huỳnh Tịnh Của, who worked on standardising and simplifying Latin characters for writing Vietnamese. In their role as language officers for the Protectorate, they gave a substantial

522   E. BOUGLEUX

contribution to the success of the *Quốc ngữ* (simplified into *quoc ngu*), as an alphabet for drafting administrative documents in the colony for use by local staff.

Interestingly, even though French administration in Indochina also extended to the areas of present-day Cambodia and Laos, transcription of Cambodian and Laotian into Latin characters was never carried out, or rather never took roots, either on a social or on an institutional level. This may be due to the fact that, in addition to the contribution of Vietnamese linguists, Vietnamese transcription was endorsed by the last ruling Nguyen dynasty (阮, Nguyễn) in Hanoi, whose attitude was largely at variance with that of cultured Khmer aristocracy. The latter opposed the introduction of French or any form of Latinisation, and even promoted enhanced adoption of the Khmer alphabet, which in the very final decades of the nineteenth century was "purged" of Thai influences and embraced the spelling and lexical forms it retains today (Sasagawa, 2015; Harris, 2008).

An important institutional step in this phase was the founding of the *Société d'Études Indochinoises* in 1883 in Saigon. The Society involved both French and Indochinese personnel: for seventy years, until its final closure in 1953, it issued the *Bulletin de la Société des études indochinoises*. Despite chronic underfunding, the *Société d'Études Indochinoises* did open the very first core of a Vietnamese archaeological and ethnographic museum on the premises of its own headquarters in Saigon in 1888, following the collection of Khmer and Cham archaeological pieces obtained through a donation from the Governor General of Annam.

BETWEEN COLONIALISM AND ARCHAEOLOGY (1898–1929)

In the years between 1898 and 1901, a leading cultural institution was established in Saigon: for a long time and with lasting ascendancy, it shaped modes of knowledge and the structuring of knowledge sets for colonial France and for the many ethnic groups of Indochina. The École Française d'Extrême-Orient (EFEO) was born as a joint initiative between the eastern branch of the *Académie des inscriptions et belle-lettres* based in Paris and the government of French Indochina. It was pursued by Paul Doumer, *gouverneur général* of the colony since 1897, who entrusted its management to Luis Finot, former director of the Archaeological Mission in Indochina, which eventually converged into the new École. Colonial management in Indochina at the time was neither consistent nor unwavering, also due to political instability in France after 1870, which led to frequent changes in the top management of various colonial administration bodies (Cooper, 2005). Nonetheless, EFEO's mission was meant primarily to foster unification on a cultural level.[4] While the colonial state was never to achieve the desired consistency or even a single identity tied to an imagined "Indochinese empire", and official political discourse would merely record "relative uniformity" among the various ethnic and cultural entities that made up the region (Cooper, 2001, 2005), the EFEO cultural project was clearly intended to enhance Indochinese heritage as a whole, in its archaeological, linguistic, artistic and later also ethnic senses (Sarraut, 1929). In this first phase, ethnological research was actually carried out "on tiptoes": scholars were warned not to delve into political issues and to devote instead to the themes of "historical and philological beauty". They were to restrain investigation about the social field, avoiding issues that might damage the interests of the French authority (LeFailler, 2000, pp. 6–7).

Already in 1902, the EFEO headquarters were moved to Hanoi, to ensure proximity to the most promising archaeological area of Tonkin, and to China. In that phase, Saigon represented "modernity", endowed with immaterial culture and social themes rather than with classical finds. EFEO studies focussed instead on the two monuments-symbols and vestiges of great civilisations, Angkor (Cambodia) and Champa (along Vietnam's coast), both taken as testimonies of ancient and complex systems of language and politics. From the first decade of the twentieth century, the wealth of ancient civilisations spawned ambitious projects around what was essentially an assimilationist colonial policy: the peoples of Indochina—a concept bracketing the descendants of ancient civilisations—could be civilised; they were encouraged to abandon native customs and adopt French ways and institutions to become French (Betts, 1961).

---

[4] Most sources attest that the extent of administrative and fiscal control over the five regional units of French Indochina continued to change and featured quite different profiles even after Paul Doumer set up authorised agencies in all five areas of the protectorate. Cochinchina was administered directly by France, while the four protectorates were to a certain extent ruled by their respective monarchs: in Annam and Tonkin the Vietnamese emperor had to accept French civilian personnel into his central and regional government, which effectively created a parallel administration; the monarchies of Cambodia and Laos remained in power symbolically with very limited roles, while officials occupied the highest posts and reported to the French *Résident supérieur* (Devillers, 1952; Lam, 2000; Cooper, 2001).

Yet, in the following decade administered by Albert Sarraut, governor general from 1911 to 1913 and again from 1917 to 1919, a different EEFO policy prevailed, whereby "the French on the one hand, and Cambodians, Laotians and Vietnamese on the other, should work together without sacrificing their cultural identities for mutually beneficial growth", in order to allow "the natives to preserve the 'valid' features of their local culture and to ensure [at the same time] social cohesion and political stability" (Kratoska, 1999, p. 273; Del Testa, 2002, p. 185).

Enhancement was the keyword of these years, as methodical collections and census campaigns were launched not only for works of art but also for everyday tools, objects of worship and clothes. Sarraut introduced the principle that "each race should evolve within its own traditions and should therefore be governed differently" (Sarraut, 1923, p. 94). That meant spreading the notion of "civilisation growth" associated with a "rational, scientific and progressive colonial development program", in which the state played a key organisational role (Conklin, 1997, p. 43). The civilising mission that France undertook thus extended well beyond Indochina to include the neighbouring civilisations of Asia: a wider regional scope which was reflected in the frequent and ever-increasing installation of new museums.

But while EFEO maintained a political and cultural mission defined from above in erudite terms, the staff carrying out much of the "field" work during this new phase (1910–1929) may be defined as amateurish (Nguyn Phuong Ngoc, 2017). For these were *correspondents* appointed by EFEO among those holding various roles: explorers, military officers, colonial administrators and missionaries, each with local jobs and specific interests (Clementin-Ojha, 2000), and their interests would obviously be mirrored in the type of finds and the news that went with them. Some *correspondents* did achieve fame for the accuracy of their collections and for the extensive information they assembled. Their works are cited to this day: Leopold Cadière, a missionary in the province of Hué and central Annam, introduced a *de facto* ethnographic method for learning the local language, culture and religion, by experiencing village life over a long time (Cadière, 1958). In 1913 he founded the *Association des Amis du Vieux Hue*, and his work converged into his *Anthropologie populaire annamite*, published by the *Bulletin de EFEO* in 1915 (BEFEO 15/1, pp. 1–103). His methodology foreshadows later developments in Western anthropology, whereby researchers live with the people they study (Kleinen, 1996). Another example of an effective *correspondent* is Auguste

Bonifacy, a military officer in Indochina, credited as one of the first to carry out ethnographic work in Tonkin. His textbook *Ethnography of Indochina* was also used in the first ethnology and geography courses at the University of Indochina in Hanoi, which in fact turned out to be a purely symbolic and short-lived institution (Bonifacy, 1919; Trinh Van Thao, 1995; Hoàng Lương, 2007). Subsequently, a whole generation of intellectuals from the so-called Franco-native school began to issue early studies on Vietnamese society. These appeared mainly in the journals *Đông Dương tạp chí* (1913–1919) and *Nam Phong* (1917–1934), compiled by brilliant groups of assistants who had a good command of Vietnamese, Chinese and French.

In 1929 in Saigon the *Société des études indochinoises* inaugurated the Musée Blanchard de la Brosse.[5] That was a highly coveted milestone after a long series of unfinished projects and forced removals. The Musée Blanchard inherited the collection of the first 1888 core exhibit of the *Société*, and remained the only ethnographic museum in Saigon until 1956 (Pairaudeau et al., 1998), when it was renamed National Museum of Viet Nam (*Viện bảo tàng Quốc gia Việt Nam*), under the management of the South Vietnamese Ministry of Education.

The Blanchard Museum of Saigon, curated by Luis Malleret, future director of EFEO, was eminently archaeological. There is no doubt that ethnologists who studied Indochina also contributed to the museum's installation and realisation. It is however at the time that divergent narratives began to emerge about what art is, what civilisation is, what are the objects that represent both and how these ought to be displayed (Dias, 2014). The debate mirrored in a colonial setting what was actually happening in Paris, where Paul Rivet had taken over the direction of the Trocadéro Ethnological Museum (1925) after very uncertain times for those collections. Rivet was convinced of the cultural continuity between material objects, linguistics and archaeology as integrated manifestations of human activity (De L'Estoile, 2010), and it was along these lines that he set out to open the Musée de l'Homme in the new headquarters in

---

[5] From the name of the official who authorised its establishment, Governor General of Cochinchina from 1926 to 1929, Paul-Marie Blanchard de la Brosse signed the decree for the opening of the Musée de Saigon; later Musée Blanchard de la Brosse; from 1953 to 1975 National Museum of Vietnam; finally, after the unification, Vietnam History Museum in Ho Chi Minh City, under the direction of the Vietnam History Museum in Hanoi.

Paris, and to inaugurate the brand new Musée de l'Homme in Hanoi (Pinna, 2017).

Consolidation of the EFEO (1929–1945)

A third period in the history of anthropology in Viet Nam may be dated from 1929, when a memo was signed to allow admission of Vietnamese personnel with assistant roles to the EFEO. It was a formal act which finally acknowledged "a relatively autonomous role for the anthropology of Vietnam" (Nguyen Phan Ngoc, 2017, p. 202). A salient feature was the informal network of relations that tied French administrators to Vietnamese staff at this stage, for that led to the broader development of "grey" anthropological literature, scattered across a plethora of non-scientific journals, archives and libraries. Several cultural journals were issued in Vietnamese, such as *Đông Thanh* (1932–1934) and *Tri Tan*, edited by Nguyễn Văn Tố, e *Thanh Nghị* (1941–1945). In the same years the French *East* (1939) and *Indochine* (1940–1945) were also published, and finally the *Bulletin de la Société d'Enseignement Mutuel du Tonkin* (1920–1938), issued in both languages and also edited by Nguyễn Văn Tố. Each of these journals partakes of an ongoing debate between authors and is rooted in a notion of coordinated investigations on Indochina to be conducted without a set agenda. Even daily newspapers such as *Echo Annamite* and *Avenir du Tonkin* devoted space to descriptions and reflections of an ethnological nature; on *Annam Nouveau* Nguyễn Văn Vĩnh issued a series of influential articles on Annamite customs, institutions and names (February–September 1931), which would be quoted extensively by Pierre Gourou in *Les paysans du delta Tonkinois: étude de géographie humaine* (1936). Many of the publications were the result of joint work between Indochinese and French scholars; among them Nguyễn Văn Tố, Nguyễn Văn Khoan, Nguyễn Thiệu Lâu and Trần Văn Giáp, who were also associate members of the EFEO. And having obtained his doctorate from the Institute of Ethnology in Paris, Nguyễn Văn Huyên became the first non-European full member of EFEO. Together with Paul Levy, Nguyễn Văn Huyên founded the *Institut Indochinois pour l'Étude de l'Homme* (1938–1945), where Vietnamese and French scholars cooperated as equals, unlike EFEO, where salary gaps continued (Lévy, 1939; Clementin-Ojha, 2000).

The relationship between Pierre Gourou and Võ Nguyên Giáp[6] is well known, and convergent opinions were expressed on the issue of method (Đào Duy Anh, 1938, 1989; Thrin Van Thao, 1997) which must become more scientific and exact while also ensuring a broader and deeper critical understanding (Trần Văn Giáp, 1936).

The subject of that literature was relatively new, since its main interest shifted from grand civilisations to minority ethnic groups, mainly located in the mountainous Annam region. These were obviously not the first research projects carried out on the "peoples who inhabited the highlands" (see for instance *Proverbes et Chansons Populaires* by Nguyễn Văn Ngọc, 1928). It was however at that time that such ethnic groups were finally elected as topics of interest and research by the EFEO. Collection of systematic data on the cultures and languages of highlanders was once again started in conjunction with plans for a new museum, this time overtly ethnographic in character, which was meant to have a markedly comparative and demonstrative quality attesting the equal "value of all races" (Rivet, 1933).[7] In fact, the official French term in colonial discourse on Indochina whereby all minor ethnic groups were identified as *montagnards*, a single, non-distinctive label considered only slightly less derogatory than *mọi*, used by most (Viet or Kinh, Khmer and Cham) to mark those who were "savage" or "different". In actual fact, refinement of French ethnological analysis served to entrench the pre-existing division between "evolved" coastal ethnic groups and "less developed" mountain ethnic groups. And the resulting split that would later lead to yet another instance of objectification: a rigid subdivision of minority ethnic groups, via a classification which was clearly designed for social control (Salemink, 2003) and failed to render the fluid, largely undifferentiated clustering of minority ethnic groups (Trocki, 1999). Increased anthropological interest for minority ethnic groups led to the paradoxical outcome of considering them as units at risk, threatened by a hypothetical "modernisation" brought about by the Vietnamese of the coast and of the cities. For the

---

[6] In 1954, Võ Nguyên Giáp became known beyond the anthropological sphere as General Giáp in the Battle of Điện Biên Phủ, which put an end to the Indochina War.

[7] It should be noted that EFEO embraced this new course of scientific research in an exceptionally contentious political climate around French colonial management. In Paris, disputes emerged on the opening of the Colonial Exhibition of 1931. Many Vietnamese were arrested, most of whom were students attending a meeting with Nguyen Van Tao, a newly formed Central Committee member of the Indochinese Communist Party (Lebovics, 1992, p. 98).

latter were by now Frenchised, and thus potentially dangerous as holders of cultural features that were no longer ethnic and no longer "pure" (Pels & Salemink, 1999; Salemink, 2003). That is the climate in which Paul Rivet's mission in Indochina took place, whose purpose was to select and train ethnologically competent *correspondents* (Rivet, 1936). They were expected to be specifically proficient in using the *Instructions sommaires pour les collecteurs d'objets ethnographiques,* designed in Paris by the Trocadéro Museum for the data collection of the Dakar-Djibouti Mission (1931–1933). They must also be ready to implement a method for effective cataloguing: two copies for each object, numbered identification plates, standard in size and even in colour (Dias, 2014, p. 197). As a result, ethnology grew clearly at variance with archaeology, because along with different objects (and subjects) of analysis, now the two disciplines also embraced different methods. Collaboration between EFEO and the Paris Institute of Ethnology in 1933 produced a new *Notes pour les collecteurs de l'enquête ethnographique,* which differed from the previous *Instructions sommaires* because, for each card of each object, it encouraged researchers to include information on the urgency of "ethnographic salvage" and the risk factor for ethnic groups threatened with extinction by contact with "foreigners" (Dias, 2014, p. 196; De L'Estoile, 2012).

The *Musée de l'Homme* of Hanoi opened in 1938. It was coordinated by George Coedès, but only as part of the wider *Musée Maurice Long,* a much wealthier commercial and industrial museum with plenty of installation spaces, as noted by some not without a hint of sarcasm (Dias, 2014).

The 1930s did witness enhanced production and greater professionalisation in the field of scientific colonialism, largely due to increased EFEO funding. That led first to an expansion of staff, and then to a rise in professional opportunities for ethnologists, archaeologists and historians from all over the world, which ultimately resulted in an ever-wider pool of qualified scholars. One should not forget, however, the key role still granted to museum institutions, of an ethnological, historical or institutionally celebratory type. And these competed over collections by moving, reorganising and reinterpreting the same objects over and over again (Hobbs, 1952; Sherman, 2004). In the meantime, inauguration of EFEO Ethnology Division in 1937 served to promote new research by Vietnamese anthropologists, who were increasingly focused on the study of themselves: a move found in similar colonial contexts and a harbinger of cultural independence. Accurate reports were accordingly issued on Vietnamese society and its manifold expressions: *Précis of Vietnamese*

Civilization (Đào Duy Anh, 1938), *Annamite Civilisation* (Nguyễn Văn Huyên, 1944) and *Vietnamese Society* (Lương Đức Thiệp, 1944). The scholars themselves and their work methods also became the subject of analysis (Trần Văn Giáp, 1940–1941; Ngô Tất Tố, 1941).

Nguyễn Phuong Ngoc rightly observes that the notion of Viet Nam appeared earlier in ethnographies than in real life: there was no country called "Vietnam" until 1945 (there only existed its parts separately administered within a protectorate); yet field study had already "created" Vietnam in the scientific literature (Nguyễn Phuong Ngoc, 2012, pp. 215–216).

In 1932 the First Congress of Prehistory of the East was held in Hanoi,[8] which anticipated the First International Congress of Anthropological and Ethnological Sciences in London, in 1934 (Clementin-Ojha, 2000). On these two occasions, scholars of Indochina had the chance to compare their work and its political and social value at an international scale. But in that context, the event was rather meant to pave the way to the spreading and the rooting of Communist thought. That was to be achieved via a rhetoric of equality and common destiny among peoples (ethnic groups) that characterised the national agenda of countries within the Soviet orbit, among which Vietnam would be placed after independence.

Institutions at the Time of Transition (1945–1954)

Following the end of the Second World War, the clash between French administrators and Vietnamese resistance, built around the growing Viet Minh movement, turned into a full-scale war of independence. Many of the French EFEO scholars still present on the ground sympathised with the Vietnamese resistance: Paul Levy, who was to be the last EFEO director; Georges Condominas, author of the classic *Nous avons mangé la forêt de la Pierre-Génie Gôo* (Condominas, 1954); Marcel Ner, correspondent in 1937, 1940, 1943 (see Embree, 1948). Despite their support, field research became progressively arduous and rare. In August 1945, in a solemn ceremony, President Ho Chi Minh appointed Nguyen van Nguyen as director of the new Vietnamese Institute of Oriental Studies in Hanoi, an institute which in fact overlapped with the EFEO. It was a purely

---

[8] https://www.jstor.org/stable/pdf/42927609.pdf, Communication from THE FAR-EASTERN PREHISTORY ASSOCIATION In *Asian Perspectives*, Vol. 1, No. 1–2, 1957, pp. 6–11.

530   E. BOUGLEUX

formal appointment, because the EFEO continued to be overseen by French personnel in a parallel stance of mutual non-acknowledgement which lasted until 1957, a good three years after independence (Clémentin-Ojha & Manguin, 2001, p. 217; LeFailler, 2000, p. 37).

The movement for Vietnam independence from France, which sparked the Indochina War, went through many alternating and complex phases which climaxed in the partition between the Democratic Republic of Vietnam in the north and the Republic of Vietnam in the south, sanctioned by the Geneva conference in 1954.[9] The institutional setup of the two separate and politically opposed countries started to differ and departed quite significantly in the decades following independence. The same happened to official narratives of the time meant to chart their respective academic and scientific histories, which were often steered by ideological concerns. In both cases, we are dealing with informationally dense narratives that are now hard to pin down to a single line of development. That is especially true for the fields of the social sciences and anthropology, the very ground on which clashing political views of the self and the world inside the two states were built and ingrained. It is only via a geopolitical localisation of sources, along with a chronological approach, that this tangled double narrative may to some extent be unravelled.[10]

The history of the social sciences in current Vietnam has inherited both narratives. Yet, greatest continuity may unquestionably be found by starting from the cultural institutions of the Democratic Republic (DRV), which in turn are to be approached with caution and with a critical eye on

---

[9]Among the key events contributing to the end of the Indochina War was the defeat of France by the Viet Minh led by General Võ Nguyên Giáp in the Battle of Dien Bien Phu. Võ Nguyên Giáp had been a student at the French university of Indochina in the 1930s, and he must have known Phan Bội Châu (see note 22).

[10]A wide and discontinuous range of sources, often at odds with each other, have gone into the writing of this section: rare articles on Viet Nam issued in the leading Soviet ethnographic journal (called *Sovyetskaya Etnografia* between 1931 and 1991, the years I focus on) available in translation only with regard to some years; Soviet studies journals (*Soviet Anthropology and Archaeology*, renamed *Anthropology and Archaeology of Eurasia* in 1992); the institutional websites of the Vietnam Academy of Sciences and the National University of Vietnam in Hanoi and Ho Chi Minh (in Vietnamese and English) and related historical archives only for sections available in electronic format (some of which I have translated); records of a historical-ethnographic nature, de-classified in 2005, and for use by the American Defense Department during the Vietnam War (1968–1975, or the Second Indochina War, according to the most frequent wording in the American literature).

the different foundational events pertaining to the Academy of Sciences and the National University. The former, *Vietnam Academy of Social Sciences* (VASS), was set up in 1953 and developed in close interdependence with the political framework. It was in fact a watchdog and an executive body established by decree by the Vietnamese Workers' Party.[11] Its mission was *"contributing to fostering Marxist-Leninist ideology and the Party revolution line; Enhancing the Vietnamese people's spirit of patriotism and proletarian internationalism; Criticizing wrong, reactionary ideologies and viewpoints".*[12]

During the years of the Vietnam War (1955–1975) the scientific mission of the *Vietnam Academy of Social Sciences* was even more explicitly rephrased as "research on topics that serve the political tasks of the Party and the State".[13] And starting from 1967, again by decree of the Workers' Party, VASS itself was renamed *Vietnam Social Sciences Committee*, which was a full-fledged political committee. The Institute of Ethnology was founded only in 1968 within the newly renamed *Vietnam Social Sciences Committee*, formerly VASS, and its political role is obvious. The story of the founding of the National University of Vietnam (VNU) differs. Decreed in 1945, therefore before the Indochina War and the partition of the country, the VNU was initially to inherit the French educational institutions present at the time in both Hanoi and Saigon. After the partition, however, Hanoi became the only officially designated VNU. Within the university, anthropology neither had nor acquired autonomous status. No training courses in anthropology were offered until the early 2000s and for the final three decades of the twentieth century the discipline was only marginally practiced as a specialisation of history, and within the areas of linguistics and geography (Nguyen Van Chinh, 2019, pp. 94–95).

---

[11] In 1976 the Workers' Party (*Đảng công nhân Việt Nam*) merged with the National Liberation Front, and with the People's Revolutionary Party of Vietnam (South, *Đảng Nhân dân Cách mạng Việt Nam*, established in 1962 in support of the Viet Minh) and joined the Communist Party of Vietnam (*Đảng Cộng sản Việt Nam*).

[12] Institutional website in English of the *Vietnam Academy of Social Sciences*. Last accessed 04/2022. http://en.vass.gov.vn/noidung/gioithieu/pages/lich-su-phat-trien. aspx?ItemID=3.

[13] Ibid., http://en.vass.gov.vn/noidung/gioithieu/cocautochuc/Pages/thong-tin-don-vi.aspx?ItemID=103&PostID=66.

532   E. BOUGLEUX

As for the Republic of South Vietnam, at the end of the Indochina War French colonial institutions were handed over to "Diem's puppet regime"[14] of Cochinchina, in 1946, and subsequently to the government of the United States (1955–1960) (Mac-Duong, 1977, p. 83). Mac-Duong devoted a detailed article to the fate of anthropological institutes in Saigon during the decades of the country's partition (*Principal Stages in the Development of Ethnographic Knowledge in Vietnam*, published in 1970 on *Sovietskaya Etnografia*, and then in 1977 in an English translation on *Soviet Archaeology and Anthropology*).

An archaeology institute was founded in Saigon in 1958, in which ethnography, very much like sociology, was relegated to the status of a "division" with the evident aim of favouring studies on the ancient world. It was only between 1960 and 1961 that direction of the institute was taken over by ethnographer Chan van-Thuan. In 1960, a geography department was opened at the University of Hue, and the Society for the Study of Asian Cultures was founded with American support in Saigon. At this apparently thriving juncture, most Vietnamese-language journals were shut down: the only one to be published continuously was the *Bulletin d'études de L'Indochine*, in French and under the supervision of French scholars. A new *Center for the Study of Vietnam*, opened at the American Embassy, dealt mainly with translating social science texts by American classics into Vietnamese, to be later adopted for teaching anthropology at the University of South Vietnam: "The historians and ethnographers functioning legally in South Vietnam obsequiously speak against the teachings of Marxism-Leninism. Durkheim, Freud, and others are authorities in the eyes of these scholars". Lévi-Strauss was also labelled as "anti-Marxist and anti-historicist" (Mac-Duong, 1977, pp. 83–84).

According to Mac-Duong, the ethnographic division of the Saigon Institute of Archaeology was mainly concerned with studies on religion, Buddhism and its role in the contemporary life of the Vietnamese, with much attention paid to the "activities of magicians and astrologers and seers" (*ibidem*). It also addressed Christianity "whose import was exaggerated, together with the role of European Catholic missionaries who had

[14] Ngô Đình Diệm was the self-appointed president of the Republic of South Vietnam from 1955 to 1963. A former official of the French administration, in 1954 he opposed the Geneva conference's decision to launch a referendum aimed at the reunification of the country. With the support of a Catholic minority, Diệm established a pro-US government in southern Vietnam, supported especially by the million Catholics who had left the Democratic Republic of Vietnam after the establishment of the Communist government in Ho Chi Minh.

allegedly helped shape the conscience of the Vietnamese people". With the end of Diệm's regime, research in the Ethnography division shifted towards "an exaltation of Confucianism, described as the greatest virtue of the peoples of Asia and compared to a form of *traditional humanism*, deeply imprinted in Vietnamese and Chinese psychology" (*ibidem*). The purpose of this scientific project, which placed religions at the very core of research, was to cast rural populations as perfectly aligned to traditional village life, in a "petty bourgeois and reactionary" view of society (Mac-Duong, 1977, p. 85) which yielded no progress (Trinh Van Thao, 1990). The study of urbanised ethnic groups and the plains was, on the contrary, left to foreign anthropologists: British, American and Australian. Mac-Duong noted as much as an overt accusation when, together with DRV anthropologists of the Soviet school, he claimed that "the construction of a socialist country calls for an ethnography of all rural nations and agricultural populations; the study of ethnographers must focus on the material dimensions of culture, on the creation of a toolset based on an interdisciplinary approach that also embraces geography and sociology" (*ibidem*, pp. 85–86).

This is the very quality ethnographic research took on at the time in the Democratic Republic of Vietnam, where it was seen as natural that anthropology should lose its academic role and be approached instead as a social and practical activity "oriented to the progress of culture and economy".

PARTITION OF THE COUNTRY (1955–1975)[15]

Beyond the official narrative and institutional chronology, North Vietnam was clearly affected by its proximity to the Communist bloc, especially to the Soviet Union, which provided teachers, textbooks and higher education all across the academic world (Nguyen Van Chinh, 2019, p. 89). Vietnamese students were offered the chance to complete their studies in the USSR; leading anthropologists of the Moscow Academy such as M.V. Kriukov and S.A. Arutiunov engaged in repeated ethnographic missions (Arutiunov, 1959; Kriukov, 1976; Dragazde, 1978) and took on teaching roles in the DRV (Nguyen Van Chinh, 2019, p. 90). Literature on the rise of ethnology as a discipline in postcolonial Vietnam seems to

---

[15] This period covers the years of the Vietnam War, which is referred to as the Second Indochina War in American literature, and as *War of Resistance Against America* in history texts of the DRV.

suggest that Russian influence was the decisive and distinctive feature in North Vietnam research institutes at the time (Nguyễn Phuong Ngoc, 2012). No consensus however exists on the academic impact of that account. For example, Van Chinh notes that despite the significant influence of foreign (French and Soviet) schools, "[T]he first chair of the University of Hanoi's history department Trần Văn Giàu recalled that upon obtaining his position as chair, he wished to develop a branch of ethnology and archaeology in the Department of History. Actually, he was unable to recruit staff with adequate knowledge of these disciplines"[16] (Nguyen Van Chinh, 2019, p. 87). What was often pointed out was the brevity of nearly all Soviet ethnographic missions in Vietnam "which in any case does not affect their accuracy" (Dragazde, 1978, p. 68). There were about thirty-five theses by Vietnamese students who completed their studies in the USSR; most of them were carried out without returning to do fieldwork in Vietnam. Some of these scholars—Phan Hữu Dật, Đặng Nghiêm Vạn and Bế Viết Đẳng—will become professors and leading anthropologists in the DRV (Nguyen Van Chinh, 2019, p. 89).[17]

Quite different and certainly more effectively practical was the role Soviet anthropology played in orienting research at the Institute of Ethnology and its attendant economic policies on the basis of ethnic criteria. During the War of Resistance Against America,[18] the Institute of Anthropology carried out research on ethnicities of Vietnam under the title "Basic Research About Ethnicities and Ethnic Cultures". Ethnicity-specific features were identified in language, cultural character and self-awareness (*human self-consciousness*) (Arutiunov & Cheboksarov, 1972). Research was conducted on the field, "moving between many provinces, meeting ethnic groups of the country with a view to exploring and investigating".[19] A first-hand account in this sense came from A. Mukhlinov, who embarked on the second ethnographic mission inside the DRV in 1962 to complete the writing of *The Peoples of Vietnam (Narody*

---

[16] The Department of History was inaugurated at the National University of Hanoi in 1956 and remained the leading Humanities department until reunification.

[17] The author dwells rather critically on the academic training provided to students in the Soviet orbit during their three-year stay in the USSR: the first year was devoted to learning Russian, the second to the principles of Marxism-Leninism, and only the third engaged the study of the discipline itself (Nguyen Van Chinh, 2019, p. 91).

[18] In the institutional narrative, the Vietnam War (*War of Resistance Against America*) is said to take place from 1955 to 1975.

[19] https://vass.gov.vn/Pages/Index.aspx Last accessed 04/2022.

V'etnama) (Mukhlinov, 1977), part of his extensive work on *Peoples of Southeast Asia (Narodi Yugo-Vostok-noi Azii)* published later (Mukhlinov, 1983). The purpose of the expedition was to gather information on "minority nationalities" of the highlands. The style of the article is rhetorical and inflated, and ethnographic data only occasionally come to the surface amid undiluted praise for the successes of socialism. The actual object of study is the revolutionary movement of ethnic minorities: their role in the War of Resistance[20] and their contribution to the revolutionary process. Ethnic specificity is however treated with due consideration and focus: different cooperative methods are listed to reflect different ethnicities, languages or the existence of scripts, in accordance with their respective Thai, Khmer or Austronesian origins (Mukhlinov in *Sovietskaia Ethnography,* 1964, pp. 51–52). Mission ethnographers published their results in the journal *The Nation (Dân Tộc)* edited by the Central Committee for National Minority Affairs. Rather nonchalantly, Mukhlinov described a project to relocate nearly 1 million inhabitants of the Red River Delta to the mountain regions, planned between 1960 and 1965. The plan was allegedly justified for one by the overcrowding of the Delta region and for another by the need to "harmonise ethnic groups of the highlands, familiarising them with the Viet ethnic group" (Mukhlinov, 1964, p. 53). This familiarisation zone was named *Việt Bắc Autonomous District* and was but one of the areas of social experimentation implemented in the DRV (Mukhlinov, 1965).

In 1968 the Institute of Anthropology started issuing the journal *Vietnamese Studies,* in English and French (Michaud et al., 2002, 312), followed by *A Brief Introduction About Ethnic Groups of Tày, Nùng, Thái in Vietnam* (1968), *Dao ethnic minority in Vietnam* (1971), *Ethnic Groups in South Asian Linguistic in Northwest Vietnam* (1972) and *Problems of Identifying Component of Ethnic Minorities in Vietnam* (1975). The ostensible goal of these works was still "facilitating understanding and support between ethnic groups, thus contributing to the implementation of the ethnic policy of Party and State". Such endeavours were to converge in the publication of the *Table of Vietnam's Component of Nationalities,* which included fifty-four ethnic groups, of which fifty-three were confirmed by the Institute of Anthropology. Despite its controversial motives, the

---

[20] The denomination of Indochina War of 1945–1954 was adopted throughout the DRV.

success of ethnolinguistic mapping is widely recognised and debated to this day.[21]

Even in the planning and management of ethnographic museums we come across a "vital assistance and support to the efforts of ethnologists engaged in *Museum Studies*" by Soviet colleagues (Nguyễn, 2002, p. 89). The same author cites especially "Phạm Mai Hùng, a former director of the Museum of the Vietnamese Revolution, recalling the Soviet museologist, Professor Vampilov, who came to Hanoi in 1957 to provide assistance in the creation of the museum" (Nguyễn, 2002, pp. 89–90). The role of ethnographic museums thus re-emerged in the literature as an exhibit space, but also as the space for the construction and assertion of identity. Within the Soviet sphere of influence, the Democratic Republic of Vietnam fostered a staunch nationalist spirit and an evolutionist view of the concept of nation whereby different ethnic groups, regardless of their historical background, concur to the "liberation of the people and to self-determination" (Mukhlinov, 1964, p. 59). All was underpinned by a rhetoric of affirmed equality between social strata, not invariably matched by reality, as reported extensively in the Selected Papers by Russian Scholars in Vietnam (Russian Academy of Sciences, 2014). On the contrary, South Vietnam, initially ruled by France and later by the United States at war with the DRV, experienced colonial and then substantially neo-colonial occupation, which contributed to sharpen social and ethnic conflict.[22] To chart a sense of nationhood in South Vietnam from this fragmented picture is a much more complex matter.

---

[21] What needs to be looked into is the possible reason for the importance attributed to ethnolinguistic mapping of the mountain areas of Tonkin, that is the North of Vietnam. Squeezed between the expansions of the Chinese empire from the North and Thai incursions from the West, this mountain region featured a heterogeneous ethnic makeup, layered over time on account of the flights or migrations to the highlands by successive waves of populations who had different languages, ethnicities, and histories. Trade between these groups over such rough terrain was difficult or non-existent, and both in colonial and in Soviet times, the kingdoms and empires of the plains found it hard to oversee or tax the whole region. Missions to impose control via mapping were attempted repeatedly throughout the twentieth century. A rich selection of ethnolinguistic maps documenting all this may be found in Michaud et al., 2002.

[22] Military aid that played a decisive anti-colonial role came from the Khmer and Laotians, while the territory of the South was ravaged by both regular guerrillas, the Viet Minh of North Vietnam and irregular bands. Each militia had its own dominant ethnic group, in a context of increasing fragmentation of social as well as the political conflict.

Dân Tộc: The Nation

According to B.C. Davis, the introduction of the term *dân tộc* was debated in Indochina as early as the 1940s, even though the concept of nation remained remarkably and understandably absent from the political and anthropological lexicon of colonial Vietnam (Davis, 2017). The very concept of nation was dubious for a context which had historically inherited the notions of society (社會, transliterated into Romanised Vietnamese *xã hội*), sovereignty (主權, transliterated as *chủ quyền*) and politics (政治, transliterated as *chính trị*) from a celestial, millennial and multi-ethnic empire. Phan Châu Trinh and Phan Bội Châu, two intellectuals and philosophers who were near contemporaries,[23] argued over the meaning of *dân tộc* for the Vietnamese context starting from very different positions (Davis, 2017, 256): Phan Châu Trinh, who had a solid European training in philosophy, saw possible parallels between Rousseau and Herder, Confucius and Mencius. He trusted in the autonomous development of a sense of nation by the Vietnamese people, once freed from the colonial yoke. Phan Bội Châu, of Confucian training, rejected instead any philosophical mediation between East and West, and deemed it impossible to assert a single and plural concept of nation starting from individualities and subjects (Davis, 2017, 256–58). Be it as it may, the concept of *dân tộc* remained unsuccessful, at least until Hoàng Xuân Hãn, a linguist and student of Husserl, introduced the two concepts (and new terms) *ethnos* and *nation* in the *Vocabulaire scientifique* he edited (1942), with explicit reference to *Volk* (民族, nation, in the sense of people) (Nguyễn Phuong Ngoc, 2012, p. 40; Davis, 2017, p. 254).

In the Democratic Republic of Vietnam, the concept of nation/ethnicity/state was politically crucial. It was seen through a Marxist-Leninist lens and expressed via a Stalinist lexicon and vocabulary. The subsidiary link between the nation issue and Marxism was reasserted by distinguishing two different models of nationhood: a bourgeois nation, the spawn of capitalism bound to disappear from history (Xã Tội Tư Sản); and the Soviet nation, which could also accommodate many nations within itself, in the sense of *Dân Tộc*. According to Truong Chin, an intellectual and a

---

[23] Phan Bội Châu (1867–1940), patriot and nationalist, turned to Japan for anti-French support; Phan Châu Trinh (1872–1926), nationalist and revolutionary, anti-monarchist and anti-militarist, opposed the Japanese intervention in Vietnam.

538   E. BOUGLEUX

leading figure in the Vietnamese Communist Party,[24] Vietnam was a country of many nations, some of which also preserved (could preserve) fair organisational autonomy from the Communist system, as for instance in the areas of the Northwest, of predominantly Thai ethnicity (Mukhlinov, 1964, p. 57; Nguyễn Phuong Ngoc, 2012, p. 45). The *Table of Vietnam's Component of Nationalities* (completed in 1979, as seen above) changed the official names of ethnic groups in favour of denominations chosen by the group themselves, against derogatory, cumulative or pseudo-geographical terms used in colonial times (Davis, 2017, p. 261): "Mèo" was changed to "Hmong" or "Hơ Mông", based on how different groups of Hmong speakers call themselves; "Man", the term for "savage", was no longer attributed to speakers of the Mien language, who became Dao, also pronounced "Yao" (Khong Dien, 2002).

Different and less anthropologically intricate circumstances surround the strategy of *nation-building* promoted in South Vietnam, where ethnographic discourse and related terms were carefully eschewed and replaced by a theoretical focus on archaeology, not without a (mocking) reference to the Ancient Common Tradition bundling mountain ethnic groups together as "derived from the same egg". What was being sought was a discourse of national unity that was both anti-colonial and anti-Communist. Enlightening to this end was the publication of *Phong- Tục Tập- Quán Đồng Bào Thượng* ("Habits and Customs of Our Upland Cousins"), edited by the *President's Office for Upland Societies* of Saigon in 1959 (cited in Davis, 2017, pp. 259–260). In any case, the shared objective of the two nationhood projects in the North and in the South was inclusion of mountain ethnic groups (*"uplanders"*, *"montagnards"*) into the modern narrative, understood along the ideological perspective of the metropolitan areas of Hanoi and Saigon.

UNIFICATION (1975–1986)

In a period characterised by successful national unification but riddled with economic gloom, the Hanoi Institute of Ethnology witnessed an expansion of scientific activity, and the systematic inclusion of research

---

[24] First secretary of the PCV, author in 1953–1956 of a major agrarian reform designed for the benefit of rural ethnic groups, with a view to overhauling the still feudal setup of the land. The reform was in fact disastrous and caused hunger and famine. It was one of the publicly acknowledged failures of PCV policies.

areas only partially addressed until 1975.[25] On the one hand, research on ethnic groups and ethnic cultures of the mountains and plateaus continued. Protracted missions were conducted and led to the publication of predominantly descriptive work: *Historical and Social Material of Thai Minority* (1977); *Contributing to the Capability of Studying and Identifying Ethnicities in Vietnam* (1980); *Overview of Ede and Mnong Ethnic Minorities in Dák Lák* (1982); and *Cultural Life of Ha Nhi, Lo Lo Minorities* (1985). On the other hand, in cooperation with external researchers, the Anthropology Institute concluded the publication of the two volumes which featured all fifty-three recognised ethnic minorities in Vietnam, laid out into two sections on *Ethnic Minorities in Vietnam— North Areas* (1978) and *Ethnic Minorities in Vietnam—South Areas* (1984). The first "encyclopaedia" on ethnic Vietnam was thus successfully completed.

The Institute also opened a new section on "Economic and Social Research for the Development of the Country"; it took an increasingly active part in national economic development programmes and secured its role as the scientific-political wing of the *Vietnam Academy of Social Science*. Official narratives mention "exceptional scientific results" achieved in this direction, duly presented in two reports of an applied nature: "Construction of Scientific Arguments for the Completion of Policies Towards Ethnic Minorities and Economic and Social Development in Mountain Areas" (KX.04.11) and "Nuances of Local Cultures and Ethnic Groups in the Country's Development Strategy" (KX.06.05).[26] In particular, the second report heralded a crucial change in the policies of Vietnamese *nation-building*, introducing the notion of "blending" the Vietnamese national character with ethnic features. The trend has become progressively more significant in recent years, with the development of

---

[25] According to the official historical page of the VASS, http://en.vass.gov.vn/noidung/gioithieu/pages/lich-su-phat-trien.aspx?ItemID=3. (Last accessed 04/2022).

[26] Cited documents are available in the archive of the Institute of Anthropology and may be consulted on the website upon request. Consultation was made possible via digital translations. Even though we are dealing with a rough translation, it is reasonably certain that relations were of technique-based rather than ethnographic, provided ethnography is understood as resulting from an immersive or prolonged presence in the field. Descriptions dwell on work tools used in the fields, on the surge in agricultural productivity thanks to the introduction of machinery and on the increased quantity of rice available to each family. Interactions with rural populations are undocumented, and no quantitative distinctions emerge, either of thought or of beliefs. Distinctions and classification operate on a purely linguistic basis (Last accessed 04/2022).

environmental protection and tourism policies, "assigned" to the ethnic component of the population.

It should be underlined that not all of Hanoi's anthropology revolves around the life of the Institute: Truong Huyen Chi, former academic at VNU in Hanoi, carefully charted the biography of Nguyen Tu Chi, a non-aligned, non-academic and marginal anthropologist, and thus helped restore an important part of the history of Vietnamese anthropology in the 1970s and 1980s (Truong Huyen Chi, 2014). Nguyen Tu Chi studied anthropology in Hanoi at what was then the French school at the end of the 1950s: his early years led him to teach in French Guinea, in Conakry, where he came into contact with the literature of classic structuralist anthropology: Frazer, Levi Strauss, Mauss. On his return to Vietnam the political climate drastically changed, and his biographical story grew more entangled: he fell out of favour with party politics and was charged with having "a bourgeois approach to the study of society" (Truong Huyen Chi, 2014, pp. 94–95), which forever banned him from academia. Nonetheless, his self-arranged and self-financed ethnographic research among the Hmong did not stop. Assistance to students in their theses and publications actually intensified, and his *bohemian* lifestyle in the cafes of Hanoi made him a very popular public figure. His slovenly appearance and flaunted informality became the distinctive features of an anti-Soviet and anti-institutional way of practicing ethnology and ethnography, "in a modern overlap between *preterrain*, ethnographic opportunities and ethnographic tradition" (Truong Huyen Chi, 2014, p. 15; Pels & Salemink, 1999).

Doi Moi, the Renovation (1986–1997)

In 1986, the VI Congress of the Vietnamese Communist Party (PCV) marked the end of the controlled economy regime and inaugurated the period of *Đổi mới* (*Doi Moi*, Renovation): a momentous series of both political and economic reforms aimed at introducing the free market. In Vietnamese society, such reforms signalled at once the end of the Soviet era and the rise of China's economic sway. The Doi Moi entailed an acceleration of social change and profound transformation in the country; among its outcomes there was the normalisation of relations with the United States in 1995. In September 1995 the University of Social Sciences and Humanities was founded in Hanoi as a separate section of the Vietnam National University, which remains to this day the primary and most prestigious training and research centre in the country. In the same year the *Vietnam National University* was opened in Ho Chi Minh City.

During the Doi Moi, the Social Sciences as a whole sought emancipation from political discourse. Academic anthropology, in particular, pursued emancipation from History. The need to reflect on one's contemporary society rather than on a purely ethnic classification is now clashing with a decade-long distrust towards Western anthropological literature, which provides only "bourgeois models" for this type of scientific practice. According to Nguyen Van Chin, it is necessary to overcome an ideology-driven view of anthropology and of social science readings: a certainly arduous task. He identifies four types of hurdles in the current debate which hinder development in the discipline (Nguyen Van Chinh, 2019, pp. 96–97): the failure to distinguish between ethnology and anthropology; the belief that there is a perfect overlap between ethnology and anthropology; the view that Vietnam need not develop anthropology because ethnology already effectively covers it.

The Vietnam Ethnological Museum (VME) was founded around the same time. Starting with 1997, it was directed by Nguyen Van Huyên, a leading figure in anthropology already mentioned elsewhere in this chapter, as a member of the EFEO involved in Indochina's ethnographic museum project. The VME was created expressly to overcome the notion of museum of traditional arts intended as exhibit of exotic items, and instead promote museums as places where the testimonies of daily material culture may be preserved, "with large open spaces accommodating reconstructed models of traditional homes" (Nguyen Van Huy, 2019, p. 222). The Museum management undertook the difficult task of setting up an exhibition on the life of the Vietnamese in the course economically controlled decades, prior to Doi Moi: a very recent past. The chance to display daily life, with its adversities, its shortages and the need for change, represents a political but also a cultural challenge. In the words of director Nguyen Van Huyên, "this may well serve to shift the attention of the middle class and the urbanised population from ethnic minority groups to the social life of current Vietnamese, effectively marking a transition between ethnology and anthropology" (Van Huy, 2019, p. 229).

Following long and tortuous negotiations with the Institute of Anthropology, with the Museum of the History of the Vietnamese Revolution and with the PCV, the exhibition "*Life in Hanoi in the State Subsidy Period, 1975–1986*" was finally inaugurated in 2006. Beyond the documentary value and the success of the exhibition itself, Nguyen Van Huy's account of it remains highly informative, because it records a thorny relationship with the Institute of Anthropology, an official body still very much controlled by the PCV unlike the new museum. What emerges is that the Institute of Anthropology actually expelled non-aligned members, leaving them free to pursue the VME, still seen as an unscientific and non-academic endeavour. What also comes to the surface is subordination to the Museum of the History of the Vietnamese Revolution, which became a partner of VME for installation of the exhibit, with a clearly political and controlling role (Van Huy, 2019, p. 230).

The exhibition displays realia and everyday objects from that historical period, which also make up the raw material of the collections in the Museum of the Revolution:[27] selections made for the VME exhibition favour technology items, of Soviet industrial manufacture, emblems of a (swiftly fading) modernity, to be shown as belonging to history, via a process of ethnicisation or perhaps tribalisation of decades passed under Soviet influence. To be sure, the exhibition narrative addresses the material dimension of life in the decade of controlled economy, with nearly obsessive emphasis on food shortages, food queues and ration cards needed to obtain any, even staple, goods. Yet, no reference is made to ideology, to the control of opinions, to restrictions of freedoms or to censorship. It should be noted that one of the prevailing concerns reported by exhibition curators lay in presenting the history of the controlled economy decade without pre-packaged opinions: visitors were to be given the chance to position themselves more or less freely in terms of content analysis. However, to think that objects are neutral and attest to the neutrality of curators is a weak and untenable proposition. One cannot possibly claim neutrality in the presentation of such controversial content, although the debate reported by Van Huy would seem to witness a truly open, controversial and culturally momentous process.[28]

---

[27] Interestingly, the Vietnamese Revolution History Museum was to be absorbed by the National History Museum in 2011.

[28] In any case, it is unrealistic to imagine Vietnam as uniformly represented by any of its museums, not even with regard to museums that are meant as unmediated expressions of the socialist period. The meaning that the term *socialist* has taken on in Vietnam must be understood "situationally", as placed within a context and at a particular juncture that intersects an anti-colonial and anti-French thrust later rephrased as anti-American.

Debate on the socialist past in Vietnam, or rather on the failed experiment of socialist society that lasted only three decades (1954–1986), seems ultimately much more nuanced and far reaching inside a museum than in the static pages of a history book. Objects on display are selected together with citizens. Each window or caption is the result of a negotiation. And the power of public negotiation remains strong because it is also exerted in the act of not stopping to look or read. This experience of collective representation has made it possible to develop only a small part of that nostalgia for the Socialist Past: *Ostalgie*, a well-known *leitmotiv* in the history and memory of unified Germany against the decades of the German Democratic Republic.

On the other hand, even the convoluted history of the Musée de l'Homme in Paris—founded in the same period and by the same scholars who set up ethnographic museums in Indochina—with its partial confluence into the new, controversial Musée du Quai Branly in 2006, testifies to the difficulty of unequivocally managing the relation between history, identity and self-representation.

THE CURRENT PICTURE

Along its unique and specific paths, anthropological reflection undoubtedly reaches deep into the contemporary debate around Vietnamese culture. In 1998, the Council on Folk Art of Hanoi published a volume which suggested that the multiple ethnic groups within the nation should be assigned the role "of protecting and promoting cultural heritage, and the wealth of their own and other minority ethnic groups in the mountainous regions of Vietnam" (Dang Nguyen Anh, 2019, 283). A few years later, in 2005, the Ministry of Culture and the Committee for Strengthening Cultural Exchanges in Mountain and Ethnic Minority Areas described tourism development at once as a risk and an economic opportunity for local populations (Dang Nguyen Anh, 2019). Even from an institutional point of view we are witnessing a remarkable growth of anthropological studies: in 2004 the University of Social Sciences and Humanities in Hanoi celebrated the opening of a new Museum of Anthropology; since 2005 anthropology studies may be undertaken in *bachelor*'s degree programmes, *master's degree* courses or a PhD. In 2010 the Department of Anthropology was established at the University of Social Sciences and Humanities. In 2012 the same University set up the Centre for Vietnamese Language and Culture and the Research Centre on Gender, Population, Environment and Social Issues. In 2021, an independent University of Social Sciences was inaugurated in Ho Chi Minh City, offering a Master's degree in Ethnology and Anthropology and a PhD programme in Ethnology.

REFERENCES

Arutiunov, S. A. (1959). Poezda vo V'etnam (Trip to Vietnam). *Sovietskaya Etnografia, 3.*

Arutiunov, S. A., & Cheboksarov, N. N. (1972). *Peredacha informatsii как mekhanizm sushchestvovaniia emosotsial'nykh i biologicheskikh grupp chelovechestva* [*Transfer of information as a mechanism for the existence of emo social and biological human groups*]. Nauka.

544   E. BOUGLEUX

Betts, R. F. (1961). *Assimilation and Association in French Colonial Theory, 1890–1914.* Columbia University Press.

Bonifacy, A. (1919). *Gouvernement General de l'Indochine, and Enseignement Superieur d'Indochine. Cours D'ethnographie Indochinoise.* Imprimerie d'Extrême-Orient.

Cadière, L. (1958). *Croyances et Pratiques Religieuses des Vietnamiens [Beliefs and Religious Practices of the Vietnamese]* (Vol. 1). Publications De L'École Française D'extrême-Orient, Nouvelle d'Extrême-Orient.

Clementin-Ojha, C. (2000). *Les ethnologies de l'école francaise d'extrême-orient.* Comptes rendus de l'Academie des Inscriptions et Belles-Lettres IV, pp. 1507–1513.

Clémentin-Ojha, C., & Manguin, P.-Y. (2001). *Un siècle pour l'Asie. L'École Française d'Extrême Orient.* Les Éditions du Pacifique.

Condominas, G. (1954). *Nous avons mangé la forêt de la Pierre-Génie Gôo.* Mercure de France.

Conklin, A. (1997). *A Mission to Civilize. The Republican Idea of Empire in France and West Africa, 1895–1930.* Stanford University Press.

Cooper, N. (2001). *France in Indochina: Colonial Encounters Oxford-New.* Berg.

Cooper, N. (2005). Disturbing the Colonial Order: Dystopia and Disillusionment in Indochina. In K. Robson & J. Yee (Eds.), *France and «Indochina»: Cultural Representations* (pp. 79–94). Lexington.

Dang Nguyen Anh. (2019). Assessing Doi Moi (Renovation) Anthropology in Vietnam. In E. C. Thompson & V. Sinha (Eds.), *Southeast Asian Anthropologies. National Traditions and Transnational Practices* (pp. 276–291). National University of Singapore Press.

ĐÀO Duy Anh. (1938). *Việt Nam văn hóa sử cương [Histoire culturelle du Vietnam].* Quan Hải tùng thư.

ĐÀO Duy Anh. (1989). *Nhớ nghĩ chiều hôm [Souvenirs et réflexions au crépuscule. Mémoires].* Ed. Tre.

Davis, B. C. (2017). Between Ethnos and Nation: Genealogies of Dân Tộc in Vietnamese Contexts. In R. Darnell & F. W. Gleach (Eds.), *Historicizing Theories, Identities, and Nations. Histories of Anthropology Annual* (Vol. 11). University of Nebraska Press.

De L'Estoile, B. (2010). *Les goût des Autres. De l'Exposition coloniale aux Arts Premiers.* Flammarion.

De L'Estoile, B. (2012). Internationalization and «Scientific Nationalism»: The International Institute of African Languages and Cultures Between the Wars. In H. Tilley & R. J. Gordon (Eds.), *Ordering Africa. Anthropology, European Imperialism and the Politics of Knowledge* (pp. 95–116). Manchester University Press.

Del Testa, D. W. (2002). Workers, Culture, and the Railroads in French Colonial Indochina, 1905–1936. *French Colonial History, 2,* 181–198.

Devillers, P. (1952). *Histoire du Viêt-Nam de 1940 à 1952.* Seuil.

17 THE DIVERSE ACCOUNTS OF ANTHROPOLOGY IN VIET NAM   545

Dias, N. (2014). Rivet's Mission in Colonial Indochina (1931–1932) or the Failure to Create an Ethnographic Museum. *History and Anthropology, 25*(2), 189–207.

Dragazde, T. (1978). Anthropological fieldwork in the USSR 61–70. *Journal of the Anthropological Society of Oxford, 9*(1), 61–70.

Embree, J. F. (1948). Anthropology During the War: X. Anthropology in Indochina Since 1940. *American Anthropologist, 50, 4,* 714–716.

Gaudio, A. (2019). A Translation of the Linguae Annamiticae seu Tunchinensis brevis declaratio: The First Grammar of Quốc Ngữ. *Journal of Vietnamese Studies, 14*(3), 79–114.

Harris, I. (2008). *Cambodian Buddhism: History and Practice.* University of Hawaii Press.

Hoàng Lương (Ed.). (2007). *Đề Án Đào Tạo Thạc Sĩ, Tiến Sĩ Ngành Nhân Học— Xã Hội Đạt Trình Độ Quốc Tế.* Hà Nội.

Hobbs, C. (1952). *An Account of an Acquisition Trip in the Countries of Southeast Asia.* Cornell University, Southeast Asia Program.

Khong Dien. (2002). *Population and Ethnodemography in Vietnam.* Silkworm.

Kleinen, J. (1996). Ethnographic Praxis and the Colonial State in Vietnam [*Thuc Tien Dan Toc Hoc Duoi Che Do Thouc Dia O Viet Nam*]. In P. Le Failler & J. M. Mancini (Eds.), *Viet Nam: Sources Et Approaches* (pp. 15–48). Publications de l'Université de Provence.

Kratoska, P. (1999). Nationalism and Modernist Reform. In I. N. Tarling (Ed.), *The Cambridge History of Southeast Asia* (pp. 245–320). Cambridge University Press.

Kriukov, M. V. (1976). *Evoliutsiia etnicheskogo samosoznaniia i problema etnogeneza, «Rasy i národy», 6,* 42–63.

Lam, T. B. (2000). *Colonialism Experienced: Vietnamese Writings on Colonialism, 1900–1931.* University of Michigan Press.

Lebovics, H. (1992). *True France. The Wars over Cultural Identity 1900–1945.* Cornell University Press.

LeFailler, P. (2000). *L'école Française d'Extrême-Orient à Hanoi, 1900–2000: Regards Croisés Sur Un Siècle De Recherches / Viện Viễn Đông Bác Cổ Pháp Tại Việt Nam, 1900–2000: Nhìn Lại Một Thế Kỷ Nghiên Cứu Khoa Học.* Nhà xuất bản Văn hóa thong tin.

Lévy, P. (1939). Préhistoire et Ethnologie en Indochine. *Cahiers de l'École Française d'Extrême-Orient, 18,* 47–52.

Lương Đức Thiệp. (1944). *Xã hội Việt Nam.* Liên-hiệp.

Mac-Duong. (1977). The Principal Stages of the Development of Ethnographic Knowledge in Vietnam. *Soviet Anthropology and Archeology, 15*(4), 74–89. (or. ed. *Soviet Ethnography, 2,* 1970, pp. 91–99).

Michaud, J., et al. (2002). Mapping Ethnic Diversity in Northern Vietnam. *GeoJournal, 57,* 305–323.

546   E. BOUGLEUX

Mukhlinov, A. I. (1964). A Trip to Democratic Republic of Vietnam in 1962. *Soviet Anthropology and Archeology, 3*(2), 51–60.

Mukhlinov, A. I. (1965). Material on the Ethnography of the Highland Peoples in Nghe An Province (Democratic Republic of Vietnam). *Sovietskaya Etnografia, 5*, 45–56.

Mukhlinov, A. I. (1977). *Proiskhozhdeniye iranniye etapy etnicheskoy istoriyi vietnamskogo naroda* [*The Origin and Early Stages of the Ethnic History of the Vietnamese People*]. Nauka.

Mukhlinov, A. I. (1983). Avstroaziatskie narody V'etnama. Etnicheskaya obshchnost' Khamu [Austro-Asiatic ethnic groups of Vietnam, Ethnic community Khamu]. In *Malye narody Indokitaja* [*Small ethnic groups of Indo-China*] (pp. 123–136). Nauka Publishing House.

Ngô Tất Tố. (1941). *Lều chõng*. Mai Linh.

Nguyễn Hương Thị Thu. (2002). *Redefining the Museum in Modern Vietnam: A Case Study of the Vietnam Museum of Ethnology*. Columbia University Press.

Nguyễn Phuong Ngoc. (2012). *À l'origine de l'anthropologie au Viet-Nam: Recherche sur les auteurs de la première moitié du XXe siècle*. Aix-en-Provence Presse Universitaire de Provence.

Nguyễn Phuong Ngoc. (2017). Adopting Western Methods to Understand One's Own Culture: Social and Cultural Studies by Vietnamese Scholars of the French Colonial Era. In R. Darnell & F. W. Gleach (Eds.), *Historicizing Theories, Identities, and Nations. Histories of Anthropology Annual* (Vol. 11, pp. 199–218). University of Nebraska Press.

Nguyễn Phuong Ngoc. (1928). Tục-ngữ phong-dao (Dictons et chansons populaires), 2 volumes, 360 p. + 274 p., Hanoi.

Nguyen Van Chinh. (2019). Vietnamese Anthropology at the Crossroads of Change. In E. C. Thompson & V. Sinha Vineeta (Eds.), *Southeast Asian Anthropologies. National Traditions and Transnational Practices* (pp. 83–107). National University of Singapore Press.

Nguyen Van Huy. (2017). *Life in Hanoi in the State Subsidy Period: Questions Raised in Social Criticism and Social Reminiscences*. In R. Darnell & F. W. Gleach (Eds.), Historicizing Theories, Identities, and Nations. Histories of Anthropology Annual (Vol. 11, pp. 219–251). University of Nebraska Press.

Nguyễn Văn Huyên. (1944). *La civilisation annamite*. Direction de l'Instruction publique de l'Indochine.

Pairaudeau, N., et al. (Eds.). (1998). *Saïgon 1698–1998 Kiến Trúc/Architectures Quy Hoạch/Urbanisme*. Nhà Xuất Bản Thành Phố Hồ Chí Minh.

Pels P., & Salemink O. (1999). Introduction: Locating the Colonial Subject of Anthropology. In *Colonial Subjects: Essays on the Practical History of Anthropology* (pp. 1–52). The University of Michigan Press.

Pinna, G. (2017). Musée de L'Homme, un dramma in tre atti. *Museologia Scientifica, 11*, 125–137.

17 THE DIVERSE ACCOUNTS OF ANTHROPOLOGY IN VIET NAM   547

Rivet, P. (1933). Les Océaniens. *Bulletin de l'École française d'Extrême-Orient*, *33*, 492–496.

Rivet, P. (1936). Ce qu'est l'ethnologie. In L. Febvre & A. de Monzie (Eds.), *L'Encyclopédie française* (Vol. 7). Comité de l'Encyclopédie française, Librairie Larousse.

Russian Academy of Sciences. (2014). *Russian Scholars on Vietnam*. Selected Papers, Forum Publishing House, Moscow.

Salemink, O. (2003). *The Ethnography of Vietnam's Central Highlanders: A Historical Contextualization 1850–1990*. University of Hawaii Press.

Sarraut, A. (1923). *La mise en valeur des colonies françaises*. Payot et Cie.

Sarraut, A. (1929). Préface. In G. Maspéro (Ed.), *Un Empire colonial français. Indochine* (pp. XI–XXII). Les Éditions G. Van Oest.

Sasagawa, H. (2015). The Establishment of the National Language in Twentieth-Century Cambodia: Debates on Orthography and Coinage. *Southeast Asian Studies*, *4*(1).

Sherman, D. J. (2004). «Peoples Ethnographic»: Objects, Museums, and the Colonial Inheritance of French Ethnology. *French Historical Studies*, *27*(3), 669–703.

Trần Văn Giáp. (1936). Cổ tích của người Việt Nam ở Huế: Chua Thien Mụ [Contes de fées vietnamiens à Hue: Chua Thien Mu]. BSEM, January–June, pp. 97–109.

Trần Văn Giáp. (1940–1941). *Lược khảo về khoa cử Việt Nam từ khởi thủy đến khóa Mậu Ngọ (1918)*. Bulletin de la Association pour la Formation Intellectuelle et Morale des Annamites, pp. 41–92.

Trinh Van Thao. (1990). *Vietnam du confucianisme au communisme*. Harmattan.

Trinh Van Thao. (1995). *L'école française en Indochine*. Éd Karthala.

Trinh Van Thao. (1997). Hoàng Xuân Hãn: Essai d'un itinéraire intellectuel. *Approche Asie*, *15*, 105–111.

Trocki, C. A. (1999). Political Structures in the Nineteenth and Early Twentieth Centuries. In N. Tarling (Ed.), *The Cambridge History of Southeast Asia* (pp. 75–126). Cambridge University Press.

Truong Huyen Chi. (2014). The Margin Contextualized: Nguyễn Từ Chi (1925–1995) and an Alternative Ethnography in the Socialist Vietnam. *Moussons*, Les "passeurs", 44.

CHAPTER 18

Australian Anthropology in Its Colonial Context

Dario Di Rosa

THE COLONIAL BACKGROUND

The Australian continent and the island of New Guinea played a major role in the development of the discipline of anthropology and ethnographic practice well before their professionalization.[1] It was after the British Crown had a solid footing on the coastal areas of Australia that the

---

A previous Italian version of this chapter was co-authored with Franca Tamisari in a volume in press. I acknowledge this initial collaboration with Franca, whose expertise on Australian Aboriginal ethnography has informed some of the views I express here. I am solely responsible for any shortcomings.

[1] When the term 'New Guinea' is used in this essay without any further qualifier, I refer to the territories of the contemporary nation-state of Papua New Guinea and the Indonesian province of West Papua. Given the complex history of colonial domination of New Guinea, in this chapter I use the historically appropriate names when referring to the various colonial territories.

D. Di Rosa (✉)
The University of South Pacific, Suva, Fiji
e-mail: dario.dirosa@usp.ac.fj

© The Author(s), under exclusive license to Springer Nature Switzerland AG 2023
G. D'Agostino, V. Matera (eds.), *Histories of Anthropology*,
https://doi.org/10.1007/978-3-031-21258-1_18

549

exploration of the interior of the continent began, producing a wealth of ethnographic material through the encounter with Aboriginal communities. In 1788, the British Crown established a penal colony in what is now New South Wales and from here the British influence on the continent slowly but steadily expanded along the coastlines. Only after a solid footing on the coastal areas had been established, and the continent had officially been claimed as a British colony in 1827, did a systematic exploration of the continent's interior begin. Highly influential works emerged during this period, for example Fison and Howitt's (1880) study of kinship systems—inspired by Morgan's (1871) work in North America—and Spencer and Gillen's (1899) monograph on Aboriginal societies in Central Australia, which provided much ethnographic material for Durkheim's (1912) influential study on totemism. These examples show two instances of the characteristic give and take relationship between the theoretical advancement of the discipline and this region of the world. At the turn of the nineteenth and twentieth centuries, British academic anthropology saw a progressive shift from the so-called armchair anthropology to the first-hand collection of ethnographic 'data'. Symbolic of this shift is the 1898 *Cambridge Anthropological Expedition* to the Torres Strait (between Australia and New Guinea), an expedition that saw the participation of leading scholars such as Haddon, Rivers and Seligman, whose results were published in six volumes (*Reports of the Cambridge Expedition*: 1901–1908). It was during this expedition that Rivers (1910) elaborated the 'genealogical method', which is still a cornerstone of the collection in the field of kinship terminology. Nearly a decade later in the Solomon Islands, Rivers and Hocart conducted their fieldwork on matrilineal kinship which was pioneering for their relatively long stay (six months) and its multi-situated nature that allowed the two ethnographers to grasp the importance of inter-pelagic relations among different social groups (see Hviding & Berg, 2014). These few examples demonstrate that the South Western Pacific region had a key place in the development of ethnographic practice well before its canonization by Malinowski (1922).

It was from this British imperial milieu that Australian anthropology emerged, thanks to the role played by Hubert Murray, the Lieutenant-Governor of the Territory of Papua from 1908 to 1940. He promoted a policy for administering the 'natives', which, albeit paternalistic, aimed at enabling the coexistence of the colonisers and the colonised, whilst protecting and maintaining the cultural differences that were deemed acceptable to the sensibility and the political goals of the colonisers. While this policy was in line with the changing international perception of colonial practices, provoked by a marked liberal turn at the end of the nineteenth century (Stoler & Cooper, 1997, pp. 29–33), the specific historical experience of Australian colonialism had an undeniable weight. After much pressure from its Australian colonies, especially Queensland, the British Crown declared the south-eastern portion of New Guinea a British Protectorate in 1884. In 1901, the British colonies on the Australian continent federated into the Commonwealth of Australia, becoming the Crown's dominion, and in 1906 the administration of the south-eastern portion of New Guinea officially passed from British to Australian hands, becoming the Territory of Papua. Looking back at its recent colonial past stained in blood, among the emerging Australian middle class formed the opinion that the Territory of Papua should not become the same kind of frontier that for decades constituted the setting for violent clashes between Aborigines and colonisers (see Di Rosa, 2017). The nineteenth century image of the "doomed race" that characterised discourses on Australian Aborigines slightly morphed into a similar discourse at the turn of the century, tainted by psychological tones, attributing the causes of the depopulation in Melanesia to a loss of a will to live due to the rapid cultural change colonialism entailed for the local population (Rivers, 1922). If the demise of the Aboriginal population in Australia, though lamentable, meant *de facto* an easier access to land where colonists could settle, the depopulation of the south Pacific meant a serious threat to the labour supply in habitats that the science of the time deemed dangerous for the health of "whites" (Anderson, 2006). These were some of the moral and practical preoccupations the Lieutenant-Governor Murray had in mind when promoting his 'native policies', hence he turned to the young discipline of anthropology to address them.

Murray deemed it his administration's duty to find meaningful substitutes to those local cultural complexes and practices considered unacceptable under colonial rule, which nonetheless provided meaning to the lives of the colonised; first and foremost, any kind of homicide linked to important social functions like ceremonies or sorcery accusations were substituted with alternative practices which were acceptable to the colonisers (Chinnery, 1919). Although Murray believed in the usefulness of anthropology as a scientific tool for the colonial administration, his relations with young ethnographers conducting fieldwork in the Territory were less than idyllic. Malinowski's notorious diary registers a marked shift in his perception of the Lieutenant-Governor during the time between his first

552   D. DI ROSA

fieldwork at Mailu and his subsequent one in the Trobriand Islands (Malinowski, 1989, pp. 74–75; pp. 109–110). Reo Fortune also had frictions with Murray when the anthropologist refused to provide information about his informants' sorcery practices which were the subject of his research at Dobu (Gray, 1999). Sorcery, in fact, was one of those "traditional" practices the colonial administration outlawed for its dangerous anti-social effects. The administration of justice in relation to local customs became the battleground for a lively debate between the anthropologist Pitt-Rivers and Murray on the pages of the journal *Man* (Pitt-Rivers, 1929, 1930; Murray, 1930, 1931). There is little doubt that Murray saw in the discipline of anthropology a *practical* instrument and had little patience for theoretical discussions; this was especially true for positions of British Functionalism championed by Malinowski, which, on theoretical grounds, deemed any intervention on local social institutions as doomed to fail and actually harmful to the social mechanisms keeping a society together. It comes as no surprise that Murray lobbied for a position of Government Anthropologist as part of the administrative apparatus: someone with his feet on the ground rather than in the corridors of academic institutions.

The imperial milieu as well as family ties connected Murray to British academia.[2] Prominent figures of the early generation of ethnographers, such as Haddon and Marrett, supported Murray's project to establish the position of Government Anthropologist and suggested potential candidates for such a position to him. It was only in 1921 that, after some hesitation, F. E. Williams was appointed Government Anthropologist, a position he would keep until his death in combat in 1943. From his enviable position, Williams produced a wealth of detailed monographs published by the *Oxford University Press*, often prefaced by scholars of the calibre of Haddon, Marrett, and Seligman. Moreover, Williams could criticise the evermore-influential functionalist paradigm from his direct experience of the impact of colonialism and socio-cultural change on local societies (Williams, 1976). Despite the fact that Murray found in Williams a strong ally for his view of anthropology as a practical tool of colonial administration, evidence shows that the Lieutenant-Governor was seldom open to the practical suggestions of his Government Anthropologist when it came to increasing the colony's expenditure on "native affairs" (Griffith, 1977). Murray was also instrumental in lobbying the Australian

---

[2] Murray's brother, Gilbert, was Professor of Greek at Oxford University.

Government to create a position of Government Anthropologist for the Mandate Territory of New Guinea: the north-eastern part previously under German rule and entrusted to Australia by the League of Nations at the end of World War I. In 1924, this position was assigned to one of the most qualified candidates for the position in the Territory of Papua, Chinnery, who, besides conducting his own research and attending to his duties of part of the administration, acted as the gatekeeper for researchers such as Mead, Bateson, and Fortune himself.

Murray's search for scientific legitimation of his style of colonial administration led to the creation in 1926 of the first Chair of Anthropology at the University of Sydney, held by A.R. Radcliffe-Brown, R. Firth (1931–1932) and A.P. Elkin (1932–1956). The newly funded department was explicitly established in order 'to provide a training in anthropology for cadets of the administration Territory of New Guinea, and to give other special intensive courses for the benefit of senior officers of the Mandated Territory, Papua and other administrations' (Firth, 1932, p. 2). The courses offered insisted on social structures, considered of primary practical value for the colonial administration, as stressed by Firth (1932, p. 7):

> As an ideal, one might look forward to an anthropological compendium listing every tribe or group of tribes of the Territory, and the principles of their cultural system, into which a harassed official might delve as a guide to his elucidation of cases of land tenure, return of presents and custody of children in divorce, and the like.

The training of the colonial personnel was the main source of income for the Department and thus crucial to its viability, but, thanks to funding from the Rockfeller Foundation, much research was conducted among Aboriginal communities in Australia of less practical orientation. The outcomes of such research found a publication venue in the Department's journal, *Oceania*.[3]

At this historical conjuncture, Australian anthropology was caught in a paradox. On one hand, the anthropology department at the University of Sydney was created with the clear goal to provide "technical" training to the colonial administration's personnel in the two Australian territories of

---

[3] It is instructive to look at the impressive list of anthropological publications in just over a decade of the Department's life listed in Elkin, 1943.

554   D. DI ROSA

New Guinea. On the other hand, the research interests of two of the Department's directors—Radcliffe-Brown and Elkin—were clearly oriented towards Aboriginal ethnography. As Peterson (1990) has astutely noted, it is in this period that a division of ethnographic labour in Australian academic anthropology began to gain its contour, progressively marginalising studies on Australian Aboriginal communities. A declining evolutionist paradigm, which saw in the Australian Aborigine the quintessential "primitive" and as such a precious source for the study of mankind's remote past, was still clutching onto this ethnographic area (Cowlishaw, 1987).[4] Meanwhile the territories of New Guinea and Papua were a laboratory for the functionalist paradigm, better suited for the purpose of administering colonies through "indirect rule" (Foks, 2018).

The bifurcation of Australian anthropology into Aboriginalist and Melanesianist ethnography was definitively marked by the outbreak of World War II in the Pacific theatre. When Japanese forces bombarded Pearl Harbour, the east-Asian country used its colonies in Micronesia as military bases and invaded the northernmost part of eastern New Guinea. Australia whose troops were engaged in other war theatres of the global conflict responded by regrouping in the Territory of Papua, which passed under military administration and repelled the enemy after a long military campaign that gathered the two territories under a single administration for the first time (Toyoda & Nelson, 2006). In this period, the role of social scientists was limited (Gray, 1994), but what is relevant is that a new generation of anthropologists was recruited by the military administration, thus bypassing the "anthropological monopoly" of the University of Sydney. In 1946, the Australian National University (hereinafter ANU) was founded in the national capital, Canberra, and the Research School of Pacific Studies (hereinafter RSPaS) was created (Firth, 1996), clearly marking the Government's priorities in terms of security.

The post-war years coincided with the "opening" of the Highlands of Australian New Guinea, an area that was barely reached by the colonial administration when the war broke out. With the return of the civil administration in the colony, the process of geographical exploration, contact and pacification of the groups of the island's interior could commence again. Melanesia, already a locale imbued with exoticism in Western imagination, promised a "virgin" field for a generation of anthropologists who

---

[4] On the links between ethnographic areas and theoretical agendas see Appadurai, 1988a, 1988b; Fardon, 1990.

could study societies that were barely influenced by the usual colonial agents.[5] As M. Strathern (1990) has convincingly argued, the relevance of the ethnographies of Papua New Guinea Highlands' societies resided in the empirical challenge it provided to the dominant paradigm of the descent groups elaborated by Africanist anthropologists (Fortes & Evans-Pritchard, 1940; see Barnes, 1962; Wagner, 1974), and provided anthropological theory with new models of political leadership such as the "big men" (A. Strathern, 1971). Yet, as Knauft (1990, 1993) points out, the overwhelming attention paid to the Highlands region of Papua New Guinea led to a disinterest in many coastal areas, which had experienced almost a century of colonial contact. This caused not only a mischaracterisation of the region, as the Highlands came to constitute an ideal-typical yardstick, but also the neglect of important socio-cultural phenomena like the local adoption of Christian practices and beliefs (Barker, 1990, 1992; Douglas, 2001a, 2001b).

The ANU, through the institution in 1961 of the New Guinea Research Unit (hereinafter NGRU) in Port Moresby, played a key role in facilitating research in the Australian colony of Papua and New Guinea at the wake of its independence which was achieved in 1975.[6] The long list of NGRU publications gives a snapshot of the variety of practical research conducted during this period. Amongst them we find two important monographs penned by M. Strathern, one of the most influential contemporary anthropologists and whose work has in part shaped the so-called ontological turn. These ethnographies, one about formal and informal village courts and the other on the experience of Hageners' urban migration to Port Moresby (respectively 1972; 1975), have a very different tone from her more famous and influential *The Gender of the Gift* (M. Strathern, 1988). This is another instance of the give and take relation of this ethnographic area and academic infrastructure with the wider theoretical advancement of the discipline globally.

The anti-communist hysteria of the Cold War also shaped the post-war era of Australian anthropology. In 1951, the Menzies Government called for a referendum to outlaw the Australian Communist Party and, more broadly, give power to the Federal Government to deal with communist affiliations. Although the referendum did not pass, there were other ways

---

[5] A valuable retrospective on this period can be found in Hays, 1992.

[6] With independence, the NGRU became, after a few changes of name, Papua New Guinea's National Research Institute (see May, 2013).

in which the Government applied limitations to scholars with overt or suspected connections with or sympathies for communist parties. Worsley, following Gluckman's suggestion to head to the ANU for his doctorate, was denied an entry permit to New Guinea, where he was meant to conduct fieldwork, on the ground of MI5 (the British secret service) reports of his activities in Africa (Worsley, 2008, pp. 79–83; Gray, 2015). Worsley eventually completed his doctorate at the ANU, shifting his field site to the Gulf of Carpentaria and working on the Aboriginal kinship system, while much of the preliminary research he did for his fieldwork in Melanesia flowed into his seminal work on the so-called cargo cults (Worsley, 1957). Worsley's decision to make his case public made the Australian Government and ANU authorities more cautious in their handling of scholars suspected of communist sympathies (Gray, 2020). Gluckman was also denied entry to the Territory of Papua and New Guinea, even if only for a brief period of time. A.L. Epstein and his wife T. Scarlett also faced some difficulties conducting research in New Guinea. A.L. Epstein was part of the "Manchester School", and he came to the attention of the MI5 for his work with trade unionists in Northern Rhodesia (today Zambia) while conducting his pioneering urban ethnography. Scarlet was also suspected of communist sympathies from her early life in Vienna. Eventually the Epsteins obtained permission to work in New Guinea on the condition that they would not engage in active propaganda in the colony (Gray, 2020, p. 67), and held a position at the ANU from 1958 to 1972, when they moved back to Great Britain. It is worth pausing this historical account to take note of how the Aboriginalist/Melanesianist divide played out in the Government's perception of a threat from Indigenous people within the Australian colonial borders: 'Anthropologists planning to work in PNG [Papua New Guinea] were subject to vetting by ASIO [Australian Security Intelligence Organisation], but this was relaxed for Australian field sites' (Gray, 2020, p. 61). The case of Worsley is particularly instructive in this respect: denied access to New Guinea, he instead conducted research with Australian Aboriginal communities. Yet, the trajectory of Frederick Rose's anthropological career complicates such a simple dichotomy. English-born, Rose moved to Australia in 1937 where he first worked as a chemist and then for the Bureau of Meteorology. He conducted his fieldwork with Australian Aborigines alongside his job. Rose joined the Australian Communist Party in 1942 and left Australia in 1956 to join his wife in the German Democratic Republic, where he took a post in the anthropology department at Humboldt University, after appearing twice before a royal commission on suspicion of being a Soviet spy (Monteath & Munt, 2015). Yet, Rose's academic trajectory out of Australia seems to be less tied to the potentially subversive influence on Aborigines than to his activities as a Commonwealth citizen.

If the Red Scare meant policing of the "internal" affairs through close scrutiny of scholars working in Australia and its colonies, at the international level, the political turmoil in nearby Indonesia was no less of a preoccupation. In 1949, after four years of military and diplomatic struggles, Holland recognised Indonesia as an independent nation state. Despite this recognition, the western half of New Guinea (today West Papua) remained a matter of bitter contestation between the former colonial power and the now independent Indonesia for two decades. In 1965, an attempted coup led by the PKI (Communist Party of Indonesia) threatened the long presidency of Sukarno. The Major General Suharto crushed the PKI through a violent anti-communist purge which passed to history as the Indonesian mass killings of 1965–1966. Suharto capitalised on this course of events and eventually took Sukarno's place in 1967. It was under Suharto's regime that, in 1969, West Papua became part of Indonesia as the province of Iran Jaya after a vote on the Act of Free Choice and the passing of United Nations Resolution 2504 (XXIV). The referendum was highly contentious and the Free Papua Movement has engaged in pro-independence confrontations with the Indonesian state ever since.[7] The combination of violent decolonisation, the threat of communist infiltration, and the instability in West New Guinea, which shares only an imaginary border with the soon to become independent Papua New Guinea, gave impetus to the addition of an Indonesianist specialisation to Australian anthropology (Robinson, 2009).

AFTER DECOLONISATION

With the expansion of the tertiary education sector in the 1960s and 1970s, anthropology programmes in Australia boomed and spread across the country. Following the genealogies and trajectories of each Department goes beyond the scope of this chapter. In what follows, I sketch some of the major trends in Australian anthropology, with no pretence of being exhaustive. In the Pacific region, the official end of colonial control over territories did not mean a complete break of ties between newly

---

[7] An agile and informed overview can be found in Pouwer, 1999.

independent states and former colonial powers. Australia is no exception. Not only did it maintain close relations with Papua New Guinea, but it also extended its influence to other neighbouring Melanesian countries.

In the years when the process of decolonisation was on its way in Australia's overseas territories, a surge of Aboriginal activism swept the country. After much campaigning, Australian Aborigines, no longer "ward of the state" could vote for the Federal Government for the first time in 1963. In 1966, a group of Gurindji stockmen, led by their elders, walked off the Wave Hill station in the Northern Territory to claim their own land and to end the racially sanctioned overexploitation of their labour. The Gurindji Strike lasted until the recognition from the newly elected Labour government of their land rights in 1973 (Ward, 2016). This episode, along with other equally powerful actions such as the setting up of the "Tent Embassy" in front of the Parliament House in Canberra to highlight how Aboriginal people felt strangers in their own country, were important catalysts for the passing of the *Aboriginal Land Rights Act* of 1976 (limited, though, to the Northern Territory). Considering these long-brewing social, economic, and political issues, it is striking how Aboriginalist ethnography in those years still largely focused on "classic" themes and "traditional" communities.[8] As Cowlishaw (2017, p. 325 original italics) aptly notes, 'The social lives of *changed* Aboriginal people [...] has never evoked the intellectual excitement of what was once known as primitivity and now as radical alterity'. Indeed, 'The foundational role of Aborigines in Australia's rural prosperity is rarely acknowledged, and pastoral workers held little interest for the disciplinary elite' (Cowlishaw, 2017, p. 335).[9] An important exception to the "classicism" of the time is Berndt's (2004) study of how people of Elcho Island tried to direct and negotiate change induced by colonial forces, especially Christianity (more recent examples of works bringing in the colonial framework of interlocutors' lives are Beckett, 1990; Rose, 1991). Stanner's collection of essays (1979) is an apt example of how the ambiguity of much mainstream Australian Aboriginalist anthropology, caught between the denunciation

[8] It is important to signal the existence of a north/south regional variety within Aboriginalist ethnography; as Cowlishaw and Gibson (2012, p. 4) aptly noted, 'Work among Aboriginal people in the south of the continent [...] has always attended to the disruptions and changes to what anthropologists had mostly represented as a coherent, unified entity called Aboriginal culture'.

[9] A common feature to Australian Aboriginalist and Melanesianist ethnography is the relative absence of class analysis.

of Aborigines' present conditions and a nostalgic idea of a "pure" Aboriginal culture that, once degraded, led to the present state of affairs. As Cowlishaw (2017, p. 330) aptly puts it, for many anthropologists 'From noble savages they [Aborigines] were rapidly transforming into the pathetic poor'. It was the work of historians such as Rowley (1970, 1971a, 1971b) and Reynolds (1981, 1999) to break "the great Australian silence" (Stanner, 1969), disquieting a placid public consciousness and embittering its conservative component, thus leading to the historiographical debate known as the "history wars" (Macintyre & Clark, 2003; see Cowlishaw, 2018). In 1982, a group of Meriem people (Torres Strait) lodged a land claim with High Court of Australia and the sentence passed overturned the legal fiction of the *terra nullius* leading to the Native Title Act of 1993. The passing of this Act meant a renewed scope for "classicist" Aboriginalist ethnography as anthropologists became expert witnesses and consultants for many land right claims. Issues of "authenticity" emerged, splitting the Australian anthropological community, such as the "Hindmarsh Island Bridge affair" (Weiner, 1995, 1997; Brunton, 1996; Tonkinson, 1997). Similar issues of the legal definition of landownership rights emerged also in Papua New Guinea bringing to the fore the issue of the "entification" (Ernst, 1999) of more fluid processes of the formation of social groups through the legal category of *Incorporated Land Group* (Weiner, 2013).

If Aboriginalist ethnography confronted issues of Indigenous sovereignty, in Papua New Guinea, where extractive capitalism is a major source of the State's revenues, conflicts between communities, corporations, and the State provided reasons to look for anthropological expertise.[10] Possibly the most striking episode was the civil war sparked by the harsh State repression of local protests against the Panguna mine, which led to difficult peace negotiations with the separatist movement in the Bougainville Province. Canberra-based scholars followed the development of the events as they were unfolding, from 1988 to 1998, and their rippling effects into the very recent present (Filer, 1990; Regan, 1998; Denoon, 2000). The significance of the conflict sparked by the Panguna mine, though, goes beyond the region; as Cochrane (2017) shows, this episode re-oriented Rio Tinto's policies towards local communities in its other operations.

---

[10] It is worth noting that this is one of the few themes where the two geographical areas of expertise received sustained comparison (Rumsey & Weiner, 2001a, 2001b; Weiner & Glaskin, 2007).

560   D. DI ROSA

The presence of numerous mining activities in Papua New Guinea, paired with its characterisation as the *locus classicus* of anthropology, has led many anthropologists outside Australia to conduct their research on issues connected to resource extraction (Kirsch, 2006, 2014; Golub, 2014; Jacka, 2015). The geographical centrality of this area of the world for the anthropology of mining is best signalled by the fact that two Australian authors penned a landmark article on the *Annual Review of Anthropology* (Ballard & Glenn, 2003).

Australian academia has offered a crucial, though unsung, contribution to the no man's land that is historical anthropology. The ANU was the epicentre of this process after World War II, with the appointment of Davidson to the first chair of Pacific History in 1950. This historiography, in the programmatic statement of its founder (Davidson, 1955), marked a shift from the metropolitan focus of British Imperial History to the islands themselves (hence the name "island-oriented history"), looking in particular at the interactions between Islanders and Europeans; 'Our preponderant concern', writes Davidson (1966, p. 13), 'has been [...] with the study of multi-cultural situations' which forced the practitioners of this historiography 'to use new forms of evidence, to involve himself in other men's ways, and to avoid interpreting men's actions in terms of patterns of his own culture' (ibid., p. 10). For Pacific historians, first-hand knowledge of the islands was highly desirable and even essential for those who incorporated oral narratives in their histories; one of the most sophisticated monographs that thread the fine line between oral history and ethnographic fieldwork is *Not the Way It Really Was* (Neumann, 1992). Since the late 1970s and 1980s, a group of historians at La Trobe University which Geertz (1990) dubbed "the Melbourne Group", played a significant role in the process of rapprochement between history and anthropology (Cohn, 1981).[11] The practice of "ethnographic history" (Isaac, 1980), akin to the Geertzian "thick description" (Geertz, 1973), contributed to the development of reading colonial texts against the grain in order to recover traces of local agency or what Douglas (2009) has called "Indigenous countersigns". For anthropologists of the Pacific, though, the name Dening is the most famous. Dening's work on cross-cultural encounters that the Marquesas Islands (Dening, 1980) mustered—the

---

[11] Leading figures of the "Melbourne Group" were Inga Clenninden, Greg Dening, Rhys Isaac, and Donna Merwick.

clear differences between the two kinds of symbolic anthropology not-withstanding—a long-lasting intellectual exchange with Sahlins, who in the same decade published his influential *Historical Metaphors and Mythical Realities* and *Islands of History* (Sahlins, 1981, 1985).

From the mutual influence of these two centres of historical research on the past of Pacific societies, a generation of historians has contributed to a grounded critique of the discipline arguing for a radical historicization of anthropological analysis (Thomas, 1996). Attending to the colonial formation of exchange practices deemed "traditional" by some anthropologists, Thomas (1991) has significantly contributed to the field of economic anthropology and the de-exoticisation of the region (see Carrier, 1992, 1995). From the same academic milieu emerged pioneering debates over the "invention of tradition" and its ideological function in the post- and neo-colonial present (Keesing & Tonkinson, 1982; Keesing, 1989; Jolly, 1992). As already mentioned above, the removal from the picture of what Balandier called "the colonial situation" (1951) made the local adoption of Christianity a blind spot for many anthropologists (Barker, 1990, 1992). As Douglas (Douglas, 2001a, 2001b) has argued, for many Melanesians, Christianity was indeed a "local" religion, and the few ethnographic works on Christian practices focused on spectacular rituals of possession more congenial to the ethnographic imagination than more mundane practices resulting from close to a century of interactions with missionaries. Interestingly, such critique prefigures some of the shortcomings of the recent sub-discipline of the "Anthropology of Christianity" championed by Robbins (2004) with his ethnography of Urapmin's conversion to Pentecostal Christianity in Papua New Guinea without the direct mediation of missionaries. The Urapmin's relatively recent colonial encroachment since the 1950s, most importantly the pacification of the area and the consequent disintegration of the ritual complex tying the Min living in this area of Papua New Guinea, the absence of a direct missionary presence, and the charismatic variety of Christianity Urapmin people converted to are all elements of that "gothic theatre" (Douglas, 2001b) that made Christianity a viable topic of ethnographic inquiry. The stress on conversion as a moment of radical rupture from the past, which Robbins (2007) vigorously and skilfully wields to challenge anthropology's "continuity thinking", is also the product of a particular historical conjuncture; the same emphasis is not to be found in other communities where Christianity has long since been adopted and internalised in more mundane ways. Perhaps the insistence on "rupture" is one of the reasons why the other ethnographic region examined in this chapter has not entered the canon of the Anthropology of Christianity despite its ethnographic documentation among Australian Aborigines (Swain & Rose, 1988; see Schwartz & Dussart, 2010).

In lieu of a Conclusion

The case of Australian anthropology provides an apt testing ground for the relationship between the discipline and colonialism (including its new forms), and the knowledge/power nexus more generally. While the discipline's colonial past is now something widely acknowledged (Leclerc, 1972; Asad, 1973; Anthropological Forum, 1977) a historical investigation of the *nature* of such a relationship complicates the image of simple subservience. Colonial practical preoccupations mobilised funds to create institutions and Government positions in search of practical applications for anthropological knowledge, which seldom came to any substantial practical effect, as the case of Williams' experience as Government Anthropologist attests. The mutual legitimation between functionalism and colonial "indirect rule" hardly translated into complicity on the ground, as Fortune's case makes clear. Moreover, paying attention to the post-War years, rather than taking a broad temporal leap from pre-World War II to the present as much critique of the discipline does, enables a better appreciation of the continuities and discontinuities engendered by changed historical circumstances. The search for the exotic, which has characterised the research choices of anthropologists working with Australian Aborigines and in Melanesia, is another important node to grapple with when dealing with anthropology's search for legitimation. This calls into question the continuing centrality of the concept of "culture" as an explanatory tool (Cowlishaw, 2018, pp. 44–46) at the expense of in-depth historical and social analysis. One of the key lessons to be drawn from the Australian case is that it is the State (imperial, colonial, or however we want to label our current political forms) that enabled the space in which anthropological knowledge could be created, whether through universities and research institutes, or consultancy jobs which are particularly attractive to fund-starved universities. It therefore becomes imperative for the discipline to bring to the fore the politico-economic conditions of its own past and present existence.

REFERENCES

Anderson, W. (2006). *The Cultivation of Whiteness: Science, Health, and Racial Destiny in Australia.* Duke University Press.

Anthropological Forum. (1977). Anthropological Research in British Colonies: Some Personal Accounts (Special Issue). *Anthropological Forum, 4*(2).

Appadurai, A. (1988a). Introduction: Place and Voice in Anthropological Theory. *Cultural Anthropology, 3*(1), 16–20.

Appadurai, A. (1988b). Putting Hierarchy in Its Place. *Cultural Anthropology, 3*(1), 36–49.

Asad, T. (Ed.). (1973). *Anthropology & the Colonial Encounter.* Humanity Books.

Balandier, G. (1951). La situation coloniale: Approche théorique. *Cahiers Internationaux de Sociologie, 11*, 44–79.

Ballard, C., & Glenn, B. (2003). Resource Wars: The Anthropology of Mining. *Annual Review of Anthropology, 32*, 287–313.

Barker, J. (Ed.). (1990). *Christianity in Oceania: Ethnographic Perspectives.* University Press of America.

Barker, J. (1992). Christianity in Western Melanesian Ethnography. In J. C. Carried (Ed.), *History and Tradition in Melanesian Anthropology* (pp. 144–173). University of California Press.

Barnes, J. A. (1962). African Models in the New Guinea Highlands. *Man, 62*, 5–9.

Beckett, J. (1990). *Torres Strait Islanders: Custom and Colonialism.* Cambridge University Press.

Berndt, R. M. (2004). *An Adjustment Movement in Arnhem Land: Northern Territory of Australia.* University of Sydney.

Brunton, R. (1996). The Hindmarsh Island Bridge: And the Credibility of Australian Anthropology. *Anthropology Today, 12*(4), 2–7.

Cambridge Anthropological Expedition to Torres Straits. (1898). *Reports of the Cambridge Anthropological Expedition to Torres Straits: 1901–1935.* Cambridge University Press.

Carrier, J. C. (1995). Maussian Occidentalism: Gift and Commodity Systems. In J. C. Carried (Ed.), *Occidentalism: Images of the West: Images of the West* (pp. 85–108). Clarendon Press.

Carrier, J. G. (Ed.). (1992). *History and Tradition in Melanesian Anthropology.* University of California Press.

Chinnery, E. W. P. (1919). The Application of Anthropological Methods to Tribal Development in New Guinea. *The Journal of the Royal Anthropological Institute of Great Britain and Ireland, 49*, 36–41.

Cochrane, G. (2017). *Anthropology in the Mining Industry: Community Relations after Bougainville's Civil War.* Palgrave Macmillan.

Cohn, B. S. (1981). Toward a Rapprochement. *The Journal of Interdisciplinary History, 12*(2), 227–252.

564 D. DI ROSA

Cowlishaw, G. (1987). Colour, Culture and the Aboriginalists. *Man*, *22*(2), 221–237.

Cowlishaw, G. (2017). Tunnel Vision: Part One—Resisting Post-colonialism in Australian Anthropology. *The Australian Journal of Anthropology*, *28*(3), 324–341.

Cowlishaw, G. (2018). Tunnel Vision: Part Two—Explaining Australian Anthropology's Conservatism. *The Australian Journal of Anthropology*, *29*(1), 35–52.

Cowlishaw, G., & Gibson, L. (2012). Introduction: Locating an Australia-Wide Anthropology. *Oceania, 82*(1), 4–14.

Davidson, J. W. (1955). *The Study of Pacific History: An Inaugural Lecture Delivered at Canberra on 25 November 1954*. Australian National University.

Davidson, J. W. (1966). Problems of Pacific History. *The Journal of Pacific History, 1*, 5–21.

Dening, G. (1980). *Islands and Beaches: Discourse on a Silent Land: Marquesas, 1774–1880*. Melbourne University Press.

Denoon, D. (2000). *Getting Under the Skin: The Bougainville Copper Agreement and the Creation of the Panguna Mine*. Melbourne University Press.

Di Rosa, D. (2017). A Lesson in Violence: The Moral Dimensions of Two Punitive Expeditions in the Gulf of Papua, 1901 and 1904. *Journal of Colonialism and Colonial History, 18*(1).

Douglas, B. (2001a). Encounters with the Enemy? Academic Readings of Missionary Narratives on Melanesians. *Comparative Studies in Society and History, 43*(1), 37–64.

Douglas, B. (2001b). From Invisible Christians to Gothic Theatre: The Romance of the Millennial in Melanesian Anthropology. *Current Anthropology, 42*(5), 615–650.

Douglas, B. (2009). In the Event: Indigenous Countersigns and the Ethnohistory of Voyaging. In M. Jolly, S. Tcherkézoff, & D. Tryon (Eds.), *Oceanic Encounters: Exchange, Desire, Violence* (pp. 175–198). ANU E Press.

Durkheim, E. (1912). *Les Formes élémentaires de la vie religieuse: le système totémique en Australie*. Presses Universitaires de France.

Elkin, A. P. (1943). Anthropology and the Peoples of the South-West Pacific: The Past. *Present and Future. Oceania, 14*(1), 1–19.

Ernst, T. M. (1999). Land, Stories and Resources: Discourse and Entification in Onabasulu Modernity. *American Anthropologist, 101*(1), 88–97.

Fardon, R. (Ed.). (1990). *Localizing Strategies: Regional Traditions of Ethnographic Writing*. Scottish Academic Press.

Filer, C. (1990). The Bougainville Rebellion, The Mining Industry and The Process of Social Disintegration in Papua New Guinea. *Canberra Anthropology, 13*(1), 1–39.

Firth, R. (1932). Anthropology in Australia 1926–32—And After. *Oceania, 3*(1), 1–12.

Firth, R. (1996). The Founding of the Research School of Pacific Studies. *The Journal of Pacific History, 31*(1), 3–7.

Fison, L., & Howitt, A. W. (1880). *Kamilaroi and Kurnai: Group Marriage Customs and Relationship, and Marriage by Elopement Drawn Chiefly from the Usage of the Australian Aborigines; Also, The Kurnai Tribe, Their Customs in Peace and War.* George Robertson.

Foks, F. (2018). Branislaw Malinowski, "Indirect Rule," and the Colonial Politics of Functionalist Anthropology, c. 1925–1940. *Comparative Studies in Society and History, 60*(1), 35–57.

Fortes, M., & Evans-Pritchard, E. E. (Eds.). (1940). *African Political Systems.* Oxford University Press.

Geertz, C. (1973). *The Interpretation of Cultures: Selected Essays.* Basic Books.

Geertz, C. (1990). History and Anthropology. *New Literary History, 21*(2), 321–335.

Golub, A. (2014). *Leviathans at the Gold Mine: Creating Indigenous and Corporate Actors in Papua New Guinea.* Duke University Press.

Gray, G. (1994). "I Was Not Consulted": A. P. Elkin, Papua New Guinea and the Politics of Anthropology, 1942–1950. *Australian Journal of Politics & History, 40*(2), 195–213.

Gray, G. (1999). "Being Honest to My Science": Reo Fortune and J.H.P. Murray, 1927–30. *The Australian Journal of Anthropology, 10*(1), 56–76.

Gray, G. (2015). "A Great Deal of Mischief Can Be Done": Peter Worsley, the Australian National University, the Cold War and Academic Freedom, 1952–1954. *Journal of the Royal Australian Historical Society, 101*(1), 25–44.

Gray, G. (2020). "In My File, I Am Two Different People": Max Gluckman and A.L. Epstein, the Australian National University, and Australian Security Intelligence Organisation, 1958–60. *Cold War History, 20*(1), 59–76.

Griffith, D. (1977). *The Career of F.E. Williams, Government Anthropologist of Papua, 1922–1943.* Australian National University.

Hays, T. E. (Ed.). (1992). *Ethnographic Presents: Pioneering Anthropologists in the Papua New Guinea Highlands.* University of California Press.

Hviding, E., & Berg, C. (Eds.). (2014). *The Ethnographic Experiment: A.M. Hocart and W.H.R. Rivers in Island Melanesia, 1908.* Berghahn Books.

Isaac, R. (1980). Ethnographic Method in History: An Action Approach. *Historical Methods: A Journal of Quantitative and Interdisciplinary History, 13*(1), 43–61.

Jacka, J. K. (2015). *Alchemy in the Rain Forest: Politics, Ecology, and Resilience in a New Guinea Mining Area.* Duke University Press.

Jolly, M. (1992). Specters of Inauthenticity. *The Contemporary Pacific, 4*(1), 49–72.

Keesing, R. M. (1989). Creating the Past: Custom and Identity in the Contemporary Pacific. *The Contemporary Pacific, 1*(1/2), 19–42.

566   D. DI ROSA

Keesing, R. M., & Tonkinson R. (Eds.). (1982). Reinventing Traditional Culture: The Politics of Kastom in Island Melanesia. *Man, 13*(4). (Special Issue).

Kirsch, S. (2006). *Reverse Anthropology: Indigenous Analysis of Social and Environmental Relations in New Guinea.* Stanford University Press.

Kirsch, S. (2014). *Mining Capitalism: The Relationship between Corporations and Their Critics.* University of California Press.

Knauft, B. M. (1990). Melanesian Warfare: A Theoretical History. *Oceania, 60*(4), 250–311.

Knauft, B. M. (1993). *South Coast New Guinea Cultures: History, Comparison, Dialectic.* Cambridge University Press.

Leclerc, G. (1972). *Anthropologie et colonialisme: Essai sur l'histoire de l'africanisme.* Fayard.

Macintyre, S., & Clark, A. (2003). *The History Wars.* Melbourne University Press.

Malinowski, B. (1922). *Argonauts of the Western Pacific: An Account of Native Enterprise and Adventure in the Archipelagoes of Melanesian New Guinea.* Routledge & Kegan Paul.

Malinowski, B. (1989). *A Diary in the Strict Sense of the Term* (New ed.). Stanford University Press.

May, R. J. (2013). From the New Guinea Research Unit to the National Research Institute. In L. Crowl, M. Tuinekore Crocombe, & R. Dixon (Eds.), *Ron Crocombe: E Toa! Pacific Writings to Celebrate His Life and Work* (pp. 303–311). USP Press.

Monteath, P., & Munt, V. (2015). *Red Professor: The Cold War Life of Fred Rose.* Wakefield Press.

Morgan, L. H. (1871). *Systems of Consanguinity and Affinity of the Human Family.* Smithsonian Institution.

Murray, J. H. P. (1930). Papuan Criminals and British Justice. *Man, 30*, 132–132.

Murray, J. H. P. (1931). Justice and Custom in Papua. *Man, 31*, 117–118.

Neumann, K. (1992). *Not the Way It Really Was: Constructing the Tolai Past.* University of Hawaii Press.

Peterson, N. (1990). "Studying Man and Man's Nature": The History of the Institutionalisation of Aboriginal Anthropology. *Australian Aboriginal Studies, 2*, 3–19.

Pitt-Rivers, G. (1929). Papuan Criminals and British Justice. *Man, 29*, 21–22.

Pitt-Rivers, G. (1930). Papuan Criminals and British Justice. *Man, 30*, 211–212.

Pouwer, J. (1999). The Colonisation, Decolonisation and Recolonisation of West New Guinea. *The Journal of Pacific History, 34*(2), 157–179.

Regan, A. J. (1998). Causes and Course of the Bougainville Conflict. *The Journal of Pacific History, 33*(3), 269–285.

Reynolds, H. (1981). *The Other Side of the Frontier: An Interpretation of the Aboriginal Response to the Invasion and Settlement of Australia.* James Cook University.

Reynolds, H. (1999). *Why Weren't We Told?: A Personal Search for the Truth about Our History.* Viking.

Rivers, W. H. R. (1910). The Genealogical Method of Anthropological Inquiry. *The Sociological Review, 3*(1), 1–12.

Rivers, W. H. R. (Ed.). (1922). *Essays on the Depopulation of Melanesia.* Cambridge University Press.

Robbins, J. (2004). *Becoming Sinners: Christianity and Moral Torment in a Papua New Guinea Society.* University of California Press.

Robbins, J. (2007). Continuity Thinking and the Problem of Christian Culture: Belief, Time, and the Anthropology of Christianity. *Current Anthropology, 48*(1), 5–38.

Robinson, K. (2009). Anthropology of Indonesia in Australia: The Politics of Knowledge. *RIMA: Review of Indonesian and Malaysian Affairs, 43*(1), 7–33.

Rose, D. B. (1991). *Hidden Histories: Black Stories from Victoria River Downs, Humbert River and Wave Hill Stations.* Aboriginal Studies Press.

Rowley, C. D. (1970). *The Destruction of Aboriginal Society.* Australian National University Press.

Rowley, C. D. (1971a). *Outcasts in White Australia.* Australian National University Press.

Rowley, C. D. (1971b). *The Remote Aborigines.* Australian National University Press.

Rumsey, A., & Weiner, J. F. (2001a). *Mining and Indigenous Lifeworlds in Australia and Papua New Guinea.* Crawford House Publishing.

Rumsey, A., & Weiner, J. F. (2001b). *Emplaced Myth: Space, Narrative, and Knowledge in Aboriginal Australia and Papua New Guinea.* University of Hawaii Press.

Sahlins, M. (1981). *Historical Metaphors and Mythical Realities: Structure in the Early History of the Sandwich Islands Kingdom.* University of Michigan Press.

Sahlins, M. (1985). *Islands of History.* University of Chicago Press.

Schwartz, C., & Dussart, F. (Eds.). (2010). Christianity in Aboriginal Australia Revised (Special Issue). *The Australian Journal of Anthropology, 21*(1).

Spencer, B., & Gillen, F. J. (1899). *The Native Tribes of Central Australia.* Macmillan.

Stanner, W. E. H. (1969). *The 1968 Boyer Lectures: After the Dreaming.* Australian Broadcasting Corporation.

Stanner, W. E. H. (1979). *White Man Got No Dreaming: Essays, 1938–1973.* Australia National University Press.

Stoler, A. L., & Cooper, F. (1997). Between Metropole and Colony: Rethinking a Research Agenda. In F. Cooper & A. L. Stoler (Eds.), *Tensions of Empire: Colonial Cultures in a Bourgeois World* (pp. 1–56). University of California Press.

Strathern, A. (1971). *The Rope of Moka: Big-Men and Ceremonial Exchange in Mount Hagen New Guinea.* Cambridge University Press.

Strathern, M. (1972). *Official and Unofficial Courts: Legal Assumptions and Expectations in a Highlands Community*. New Guinea Research Unit, Australian National University.

Strathern, M. (1975). *No Money on Our Skins: Hagen Migrants in Port Moresby*. New Guinea Research Unit, Australian National University.

Strathern, M. (1988). *The Gender of the Gift: Problems with Women and Problems with Society in Melanesia*. University of California Press.

Strathern, M. (1990). Negative Strategies in Melanesia. In R. Fardon (Ed.), *Localizing Strategies: Regional Traditions of Ethnographic Writing* (pp. 204–216). Scottish Academic Press.

Swain, T., & Rose, D. B. (Eds.). (1988). *Aboriginal Australians and Christian Missions: Ethnographic and Historical Studies*. Australian Association for the Study of Religions.

Thomas, N. (1991). *Entangled Objects: Exchange, Material Culture, and Colonialism in the Pacific*. Harvard University Press.

Thomas, N. (1996). *Out of Time: History and Evolution in Anthropological Discourse* (2nd ed.). University of Michigan.

Tonkinson, R. (1997). Anthropology and Aboriginal Tradition: The Hindmarsh Island Bridge Affair and the Politics of Interpretation. *Oceania, 68*(1), 1–26.

Toyoda, Y., & Nelson, H. (Eds.). (2006). *The Pacific War in Papua New Guinea: Memories and Realities*. Rikkyo University Centre for Asian Area Studies.

Wagner, R. (1974). Are There Social Groups in the New Guinea Highlands? In M. J. Leaf (Ed.), *Frontiers of Anthropology: An Introduction to Anthropological Thinking* (pp. 95–122). Van Nostrand.

Ward, C. (2016). *A Handful of Sand: The Gurindji Struggle, After the Walk-Off.* Monash University Publishing.

Weiner, J. F. (1995). Anthropologists, Historians and the Secret of Social Knowledge. *Anthropology Today, 11*(5), 3–7.

Weiner, J. F. (1997). "Bad Aboriginal" Anthropology: A Reply to Ron Brunton. *Anthropology Today, 13*(4), 5–8.

Weiner, J. F. (2013). The Incorporated What Group: Ethnographic, Economic and Ideological Perspectives on Customary Land Ownership in Contemporary Papua New Guinea. *Anthropological Forum, 23*(1), 94–106.

Weiner, J. F., & Glaskin, K. (Eds.). (2007). *Customary Land Tenure and Registration in Australia and Papua New Guinea: Anthropological Perspectives*. ANU E Press.

Williams, F. E. (1976). Creed of a Government Anthropologist. In E. Schwimmer (Ed.), *The Vailala Madness and Other Essays* (pp. 396–418). University of Queensland Press.

Worsley, P. (1957). *The Trumpet Shall Sound: A Study of 'Cargo' Cults in Melanesia*. MacGibbon & Kee.

Worsley, P. (2008). *An Academic Skating on Thin Ice*. Berghahn Books.

CHAPTER 19

Five Paths for a History of the Pacific Islands

Adriano Favole

Considering the anthropology[1] *of* and *in* Pacific Islands, pluralising *stories* rather than reconstructing a canonical history, involves a significant expansion of the visual spectrum. Due to its brevity, this chapter cannot claim to thoroughly trace institutional paths, intellectual biographies, theoretical debates, thematic fields, clashes and encounters between different disciplinary visions that have spanned more than a century of Oceanian anthropology. I will therefore attempt to summarise the fertility of an approach which, by distancing itself from a teleological and unitary vision of the anthropology *of* and *in* Pacific Islands, restores some aspects of complexity that can be put into perspective with the other areas, regions and countries

---

Reference is made in this chapter to Pacific Islands societies. Specific attention is devoted to Australia in the contribution by Dario Di Rosa (in this volume).

[1] Unless otherwise specified, I shall use the term "anthropology" with reference to cultural or social anthropology (or ethnology in French-speaking contexts).

A. Favole (✉)
University of Torino, Turin, Italy
e-mail: adriano.favole@unito.it

© The Author(s), under exclusive license to Springer Nature   569
Switzerland AG 2023
G. D'Agostino, V. Matera (eds.), *Histories of Anthropology*,
https://doi.org/10.1007/978-3-031-21258-1_19

570   A. FAVOLE

analysed in this volume, into five *paths*. Paraphrasing one of the most famous expressions of Epeli Hau'ofa, an anthropologist of Tongan origin whom we will have the opportunity to meet several times in these pages, we could say that we find ourselves faced with a "sea of [anthropological] islands" (1993), intertwined and connected by synchronic transversal networks and deep chronological relationships. I invite the reader to cross this rich sea, full of currents, starting from a short bibliography,[2] summarised in its essential features, which is intended merely as a starting point for further and deeper investigation.

Path One: The Origins

The first humans to set foot on the islands of remote Oceania spoke Austronesian languages and made pottery known as "Lapita" (Sand & Bedford, 2010). Their ancestors had left Southeast Asia, particularly Taiwan, around 5000 years ago. They took artefacts, food plants and animals with them on their long voyages of exploration, along with knowledge and imagery about the environment, human beings and their relationships (Borgnino, 2020). If we intend to read the history of anthropology in the plural form, we cannot avoid noting that, since the arrival of people, there have been "anthropologies" at work in the South Pacific (i.e. conceptions and representations of mankind in his relations with the environment). These native anthropologies, stratified in the languages that were gradually formed and in the history of encounters and clashes, creatively transformed by each generation and, at the end of the day, by each human life, can also be found today in the gestures, rituals and lifestyle of the *Pacific Islanders*. After all, it is precisely this ancestral imprint, embedded in everyday experience, that anthropologists (academically speaking) from Oceania claim as a specific quality of their perspective,[3] as opposed to that of their colleagues from elsewhere (Hau'ofa, 1975). As we shall see, the debate and conflict between *outsiders and insiders* is one of the characteristic traits of contemporary Pacific Islands anthropology (and not limited exclusively to the Pacific, of course). No society is devoid of anthropological thought (Remotti, 1997), although, of course, it is good to distinguish between the human representations found in every society

---

[2] I would like to thank Alexander Mawyer of the University of Hawaii at Manoa for his valuable bibliographic suggestions.
[3] See *Path four*.

and anthropology understood as specialised knowledge that has been developing in Western academies since the end of the nineteenth century. Anthropology should not, however, be considered as a separate "sector", as, since its inception it has been part of a circular relationship with native epistemologies, creating streams of knowledge that come and go between the two poles of academia and local societies, creating what we could call a "circular economy of knowledge". Terms like *kustom* (*coutume* in French-speaking areas), "tribe", "gift" and "tabu"—to mention just a few examples—have long travelled between academies and local society.

If we look at representations of South Pacific societies by European authors from the second half of the eighteenth century onwards, and for much of the century that followed, we encounter a complex variety of sources and texts. They express the views of Westerners, but are influenced from the outset by the types of tangible and intangible exchange taking place in the field. Cultures and objects, as Nicholas Thomas writes, are always *entangled* (1991). *Stories* of the Pacific, such as the monumental trilogy by geographer Oskar H. K. Spate (1979, 1983, 1988), were *written* mostly from the point of view of Europeans, yet even in this case it is necessary to avoid a purely passive vision of the natives who, at every meeting, chose which elements of their society to give away, to talk about and to reveal, even in situations characterised by the technological and military pre-eminence of "whites". There is also a wide range of "native" sources that describe the great colonial "encounter": from memory and spoken traditions, songs and plastic/artistic expressions—such as carvings on bamboo in New Caledonia (Colombo Dougoud, 2013)—through to the first notebooks and books written by Pacific Islanders.

The European and scriptural perspective on the anthropology of the Insular Pacific is therefore inevitably incomplete, despite having had and continuing to have a profound influence at local level, on movements to revitalise indigenous knowledge and traditions that have taken place throughout the Pacific since the 1970s, for example (Aria, 2007). The first European sources were reports by explorers and travellers, traders, colonial administrators and especially those referred to in Pacific literature as *beachcombers*. These were Europeans like William Mariner in Tonga (1827), Thomas Williams and James Calvert in Fiji (1858), who arrived in the Pacific for the most diverse reasons (for trade, as mutineers, because they were attracted by the legend of the South Sea Paradise) and settled there, becoming so intimate with the local societies that they became "almost" natives (or so the legend surrounding them says). Similar figures

572   A. FAVOLE

can be found on many islands and some of them (mostly men) have left written accounts. The literature and missionary archives (the London Missionary Society and the Société de Marie being the two main examples) are sources that are far too well-known and extensive to go into here. We need only mention the first attempt at a systematic *survey* of Melanesian societies by the Anglican missionary Robert Henry Codrington (1891). Even in the mid-twentieth century, the most distinguished French scholar of French-speaking Oceania (New Caledonia/Kanaky in particular) was considered to be the ethnologist-missionary Maurice Leenhardt (1937, 1947). In this quick and partial overview of sources, we must remember the literary production encouraged by the ambivalent legend of the South Seas (the paradise of beaches and *vahiné*, the inferno of the cannibals), which attracted figures such as Herman Melville, Robert Louis Stevenson, Jack London, Paul Gaugin and Victor Segalen. In the same way that we must remember the circulation of objects, human beings and knowledge promoted by the great metropolitan, European, American and Australian museums (as well as those in France, Germany, Switzerland and Italy), which see the South Pacific as an ideal place to collect primitive and exotic "treasures".

Path Two: Professional Anthropology and National Traditions

At the turn of the nineteenth century, the first generation of professional anthropologists, or those who had trained with the aim focusing on indigenous societies, entered the Pacific scene. From this point of view, two institutions were ahead of their time, revealing a first surprise in these *stories* of Pacific anthropology: the Polynesian Society was founded in Auckland in 1892, while the Bishop Museum was established in Honolulu in 1889 at the behest of the royal family, at a time when the Kingdom of Hawaii was still recognised internationally before its American annexation.[4] From the earliest beginnings, we find an anthropology *in* Oceania which precedes the development of an anthropology *of* the Pacific by the colonising countries, at least with regard to institutions and research centres. Although, in the early days, they united a diverse group of enthusiasts of Pacific antiquities and traditions, who were also looked to for the purpose of providing younger generations of natives with an education related

[4] The Société des Etudes Océaniennes was founded in Tahiti in 1917.

to their own cultures, these two institutions would soon attract professional scholars and act as a driving force for the development of anthropology in Oceania. *The Journal of Polynesian Society*, which is still active today, began publication in 1892; as we shall see, the Bishop Museum was the most important funder of ethnographic research and publisher of monographs (in the famous Bulletin series) between the 1920s and the end of the 1930s.

The professionalisation of anthropology in Europe was accompanied by the birth and development of national traditions of varying importance in world research. Even today, those who work in Oceania find it surprising how difficult it is for English-speaking traditions to interact with French-speaking ones, not to mention the fact that the works of Japanese, Italian or Spanish authors are almost completely unknown in the dominant English-speaking anthropology, and that the "French-speaking" islands are little known (James Clifford's work on Leenhardt and New Caledonia, 1982, is the exception that confirms the rule). The pioneering expedition to the Torres Strait organised by Cambridge University in 1898 is one of the most famous events in the history of anthropology (not only of the Pacific), both in terms of the methods used, the knowledge produced and the names of some of the participants who were to become the masters of the first generations of British oceanists: Alfred Cort Haddon, Charles Gabriel Seligman and, above all, William H. R. Rivers (see his work dated 1914). If we add the name of John Layard, who worked in Vanuatu (1942), we have an overview of the emerging British anthropology of Pacific Islands.

The period between the wars saw the consolidation or creation of institutions that played an important role in encouraging and supporting ethnographic research in the Pacific. As mentioned above, starting from the 1920s, the Bishop Museum of Honolulu encouraged a wide range of expeditions and research on the various islands and archipelagos, with the aim of mapping the societies and cultures of the Pacific, with the publication of ethnographic monographs (the first issue of the Bulletin was published in 1922) covering the Marquesas, Samoa, Niue, Fiji, Australia, Society, Cook, Tuamotu, Wallis, Futuna and Tokelau. As written by the director of the Museum, Sir Peter Buck—an important figure in the history of the Pacific, whom we will meet again in a moment—in 1945 "the field survey on Polynesia has been practically completed" (cit. in Howard, 1983, p. 77). Anthropology *made in USA*—Hawaii was an incorporated territory of the United States at the time—like that which took shape in

New Zealand, with their emphasis on material culture, history and the relationship between culture and psychology, is significantly different from the approach of the British, dominated by the functionalist theory of Bronislaw Malinowski, founder of the *new* field research in the Trobriands, and Alfred Reginald Radcliffe-Brown. It was the latter who founded the Department of Anthropology in Sydney in 1926, which promoted research mainly in Australia, New Guinea and Melanesia. The first issue of *Oceania*, still one of the most prestigious journals in the area, was published in 1930. The first Ethnology researcher in New Zealand (Otago University) took up his post in 1919. His name was Henry Skinner, and he was a pupil of Haddon and Rivers.

While the United States, the United Kingdom, New Zealand and Australia lead the research, we must remember the less extensive tradition of French Oceanian studies, linked particularly to the four old colonies: New Caledonia, Wallis and Futuna, French Polynesia and the New Hebrides, the latter an unheard of joint Franco-British dominion until 1970. There is no shortage of German-speaking scholars, in the wake of a colonial project that fizzled out after World War I; they were very interested in material culture and fond of diffusionist perspectives, who entrusted many of their contributions to the journal *Anthropos*. If the first professional Italian anthropologists working in Oceania from the 1960s onwards were Remo Guidieri (Solomon, academically based in France), Giancarlo Scoditti (Trobriand) and Valerio Valeri (Hawaii), we should not forget the pioneering figure of Lamberto Loria, recently re-evaluated by Sandra Puccini (2005) and Fabiana Dimpflmeier (Puccini & Dimpflmeier, 2018), but whose importance is not yet recognised sufficiently at international level.

It is worth bearing in mind that, at least until the late 1950s, when people speak of national and professional anthropologies in Oceania, they are referring to a small number of scholars, only a very tiny number of whom were women. As documented in an interesting essay by Howard (1983)—which I have drawn on for much of the information contained in this paragraph—it was not until the early 1960s, particularly in the USA, that there was a *real surge* of interest in the South Pacific. Between 1962 and 1982, seventy PhD theses relating to research in Oceania (including Australia and New Guinea) were discussed in the English-speaking world, fifty-seven of them in American universities (Harvard, Chicago and Oregon being the main ones): the remaining thirteen were distributed among Australia (seven theses, Sydney), New Zealand (two, Auckland), the United Kingdom (three, one at the London School of Economics and two at Oxford) and Canada (one thesis at McGill University) (Howard, 1983). So even at the height of its popularity, Pacific European anthropology was a minority current: in this context, together with his teacher Malinowski, whom he succeeded at the London School of Economics, the best-known and most committed scholar to the institutional development of the discipline in the Pacific (both between the wars and after World War II), was Raymond Firth, a New Zealander of *Pākehā* origin. His monographs on the Tikopia (Solomon), the most famous of which is *We, the Tikopia* (1936), are still some of the most influential works on Pacific Islands anthropology. The first Oceanian to obtain a PhD in Social Anthropology, Fijian Rusiate Nayacakalou, was a student of Firth and worked in the Radcliffe-Brown Department in Sydney until his premature death at the age of 45 in 1972.

The anthropological *boom* of the 1960s is mainly linked to the substantial funds that were allocated by the US administration and military government in Micronesia with the aim of gaining a better understanding of local societies, acculturation processes and the possible spread of Marxist or otherwise critical perspectives on colonial powers (Douglas Oliver and Georges Murdock were essentially the coordinators). Until the early 1980s, as Howard again notes, anthropology mostly turned its gaze to the relationship of populations with island environments; to social structure (the study of cognate forms of kinship took on particular area-level importance); to the evolution of leadership and political systems; and, to a lesser extent, to social change and acculturation processes (Howard & Borofsky, 1989). The explosion of the so-called cargo cults at the end of World War II, with their (often implicit) anti-colonial slant, fuelled a vast literature, only partly critical of European imperialist processes: it is no coincidence that the author of the most famous and incisive work on the subject, Peter Worsley (1957), was denied research permits in Papua New Guinea by the Australian government.

If the panorama of Oceanian anthropology between the 1960s and the 1980s is therefore dominated by the United States, by New Zealand institutions increasingly oriented towards the Māori world, by Australian institutions that look towards the Indigenous Australians and Natives of the Torres Strait and Papua New Guinea for strategic reasons, and by British institutions, there is no lack of "incursions" by authors from other countries, such as Jean Guiart, who monopolised French anthropological interest for a long time. An important role in the development of linguistic and

576 A. FAVOLE

then anthropological research was later played in France by the founding, in 1976, of the Laboratoire Langue et Civilisation à Tradition Orale (LACITO of the Centre national de la recherche scientifique (CNRS) in Paris) and the work of Office de la recherche scientifique et technique outre-mer (ORSTOM) (now Institut de recherche pour le développement (IRD), an institute straddling research and applied sciences for cooperation). A handful of authors of Swedish, Danish, Canadian, Dutch and, as mentioned above, Italian origin were able to exert a certain amount of international influence. However, leaving the stories of these figures and the academic traditions from which they came behind, I would now like to devote some thought to an institution founded in the 1960s which is in many ways paradigmatic of the fate of anthropology in the South Seas: the University of South Pacific (USP) in Suva, Fiji.

Path Three: The USP in Fiji, Sociology or Anthropology?

I will now move from broad, indeed very broad perspectives such as those discussed in the first two paths, to some more specific reflections. Kim Andreas Kessler's recent archival and ethnographic research (2021) on the trajectories of cultural anthropology at the University of South Pacific (USP) is very interesting in terms of tracing and interweaving *stories* of the discipline in the South Seas. The USP was founded in 1968, following exploratory reports on the potential for a university to serve a number of newly independent island countries, and the granting of land by the New Zealand Air Force at Laucala Bay, Suva (Fiji). This is an institution funded by the governments of the Cook Islands, Fiji, Kiribati, Marshall, Nauru, Niue, Samoa, Solomon Islands, Tokelau, Tonga, Tuvalu and Vanuatu. The main objective of this English-speaking university was to provide the young generations of newly independent countries with a set of knowledge and skills that would enable them to become agents of a rapid modernisation of their islands of origin. Due to its international character, the USP was and is a microcosm of the Pacific, a place for meeting and rebuilding a *Pacific way* broken by colonial borders, a hotbed of future political and cultural leaders.

As of the preliminary reports, English, Linguistics (the Pacific and, particularly, Melanesia is an area with a very high density of indigenous languages), Economics, Mathematics, Physics, Chemistry and Biology emerged as the pillars of the University's curriculum. The humanities and social disciplines were entrusted to the School of Social and Economic Development. It was within this School or Department that anthropology was placed in a decidedly ambivalent position, literally between being and not being. The three-year degrees offered by the School were, from the outset, Geography, History and Sociology, joined by three interdisciplinary degree courses, that is, South Pacific Studies, Development Administration and Rural Development (ibid., p. 39). The reports preceding the founding of the university do not contain any explicit passages on the reasons why the degree in Sociology was preferred to that in Anthropology, a discipline that was therefore, in many ways, forged in the South Pacific. Why this decision? Kessler suggests three reasons: firstly, anthropology appeared in that context as a rather "outdated" discipline, linked to the pioneering names of Malinowski, Mead and Firth (who actually played an important role in training future USP lecturers), to "traditional" approaches to research, which seemed ill-suited to an institution set up to "modernise" the islands (despite the fact that the native elites of Fiji and other countries were developing the ideology of the *Pacific Way* at the time, which found much nourishment in studies on traditional societies). A second reason was the colonial echo of the term "anthropology". Two of Kessler's informants, former lecturers at USP, emphasise this theme. John Harré, an anthropologist and one of the first lecturers at the academy, stresses:

> The decision to use the term 'sociology' was significantly related to the idea that 'anthropology' could be conceived as a colonial concept ... We [the founding staff] made the assumption that the word 'anthropology' may have a negative connotation for our students at a time when the ten countries we served were in the process of emerging from colonial status and had in the past been subject to anthropological research by expatraite scholars (ibid., 37).

The idea that "anthropology" resonated as a colonial term is also supported by Michael Howard (an author we have already met in the previous pages, 1983), who argues his thesis with reference to a counter example. The University of Papua New Guinea, founded in 1965, was also established with the aim of modernisation, yet a degree in anthropology was created, as it was considered suitable for training the future managers of a country still de facto under Australian control. At the USP, on the other hand, the product of a consortium of independent countries, there was no place for anthropology—at least as a term. I will come back to this point shortly, but not before indicating the third reason why the name "anthropology" was dropped: the idea that it is an impractical and very abstract discipline, and therefore not suitable for an audience of native students called upon to play a leading political and cultural role in the modernisation process (an idea, as we will see later, also contested today by some native authors).

We might note, however, that the fate of anthropology at the USP was not to be completely marginalised or excluded: it was rather an *ante litteram* application of the label of "politically incorrect" to the word "anthropology". It should be noted that of the 17 sociology teachers who taught at the USP between 1969 and 1981, 8 had trained as cultural (or social) anthropologists. In 1982, the School was directed by one of the best-known names in Pacific anthropology, Grant McCall; moreover, the Chair of Social Anthropology was created as early as 1974, with the faculty being enriched with the name of Oceania's most famous native anthropologist, Epeli Hau'ofa, in 1983. *Stories* of anthropology in the Pacific reveal a second surprise here: in investigating the fate of the discipline in the Pacific, we need to distinguish a *nominal* approach (the use of the term "anthropology", accompanied or otherwise by the adjectives *cultural* or *social*) from an approach that I will call "substantive" for the sake of convenience. Even though they were studying for a degree in Sociology, Pacific students explored themes, methodologies and disciplinary genealogies that had a lot to do with anthropology, at least more with anthropology than with sociology as this discipline developed in the West. Something similar can be said about a line of studies that USP was instrumental in developing, *Pacific Studies*, of which Ron Crocombe was a first-class teacher for 20 years.

Ron Crocombe was a very important figure in the panorama of "Pacific" academic knowledge. Born in New Zealand in 1929, after working as a New Zealand government official in the Cook Islands, he came relatively late to university education, obtaining a doctorate in History in 1961 from the Australian National University (ANU) in Sydney. After teaching in Papua New Guinea from 1962 to 1969, he joined the USP in the year of its foundation and taught *Pacific Studies* there for 20 years. A staunch supporter of "native" scholars, extremely wary of anthropologists and non-Pacific academics in general, Crocombe was instrumental in the creation of two important institutions linked to USP: the South Pacific Creative Arts Society (SPCAS) and the Institute of Pacific Studies (IPS).

The first institution (SPCAS), founded in Suva in 1972, played a very important role in fostering the emergence of Oceania's first generation of writers. Authors such as the Samoan Albert Wendt (and his pupil Vilsoni Hereniko), Tongan poet and academic Konai Helu Thaman, Fijian critic and essayist Subramani and Epeli Hau'ofa himself can be listed among the best-known names. SPCAS edited the magazine *Mana. A South Pacific Journal of Language and Literature*. As well as providing an important impetus for the development of post-colonial Pacific Islands literature (Keown, 2007), SPCAS allows us to highlight a third surprise in reconstructing the *stories* of anthropology in the Pacific. Many indigenous anthropologists (undoubtedly including Wendt, Hereniko and Hau'ofa) would choose *fiction* (novellas, poems, novels and theatre) as their format for anthropological dissemination. For these authors, it is non-fiction, with its "cold", abstract and detached language, with its theories far removed from the experience of the natives, that conveys the colonial legacy of anthropological studies. The decolonisation of knowledge in the Pacific passed through this literary turning point, well exemplified by a text like Hau'ofa's *Tales of Tikongs* (1983). This same author wrote in an article in 1975: "Essentially, what Pacific peoples expect of us is to be more of the novelist and the social historian and less of the scientist who speaks in jargon" (p. 284).

Crocombe's other "creature", the Institute of Pacific Studies (1976), took an alternative route, encouraging thousands of Pacific authors to write "their own" story and anthropology in non-fiction language. I still remember being astonished when I received a copy of a book that had just come out: *Futuna. Mo ona puleaga sau*, literally "Futuna. Our two kingdoms" (Huffer & Leleivai, 2001), published by the IPS in Fiji. On the cover and inside, in good resolution, were the photographs that I had taken in the field in 1996 and 1997, sending them all to my friends and collaborators. The book, edited by Elise Huffer (who was teaching *Pacific Studies* at the USP at the time) and Petelo Lelivai, one of my references in Futuna and a member of the Service des Affaires Culturelles de Futuna, contained 12 short chapters written by 12 Futunians on topics such as the origin of royalty on the island, religion, politics, Futunian housing, rituals and aspects of daily life on the island. It had the look and feel of an "old" ethnographic monograph. The Preface states: "The ISP, whose main role is to encourage oceanic peoples to express themselves about their society,

580   A. FAVOLE

launched this project in 1998 (...) A first phase of the project was animated by Professor Ron Crocombe" (p. 5). Over 2000 Pacific Islanders authors have written for the publications of the ISP, one of the most prolific institutions in encouraging native scientific production. While the SPCAS has promoted indigenous narrative writing, the ISP has moved into the area of scientific writing more in line with the standards of Western social sciences, while trying to counterbalance the pre-eminence of external academics by using almost exclusively authors from the islands. Crocombe has been accused of a "paternalistic" attitude, of a reifying view of Pacific cultures and of encouraging a dichotomous "us"/"others" opposition. Indeed, as we shall see in the next paragraph, it is not so simple and straightforward to define the profile of Pacific indigenous anthropologists.

PATH FOUR: NATIVE ANTHROPOLOGISTS

Clearly, anthropology in its academic form is a knowledge and a way of looking at things that, as one would say in the Polynesian language of Futuna, is *mei tai*, from "overseas", originating in those European and Western countries such as the United Kingdom, France and the United States that were the protagonists of the colonisation of the Pacific. If it is true, as we have noted from the outset, that each society processes representations of the human, meaning indigenous "anthropologies" or "epistemologies", the question of the adoption or rejection of the academic discipline of anthropology by native authors deserves a paragraph of its own. In many colonised countries, it was during fight for independence or in the early stages of post-colonialism that native intellectuals and politicians expressed positions of aversion towards researchers and disciplines of foreign origin or, by contrast, set up instruments (training schools, universities and research centres) to incorporate and "indigenise" anthropological knowledge (as is the case in many Latin American states). The histories of Pacific Islands anthropology present us with a new surprise, at least if we look at a country like New Zealand, where pioneering figures of Pacific-born anthropological scholars (though not academics in the strict sense of the word) were already prominent at the beginning of the twentieth century, in the aftermath of the first dissemination of professional anthropology in Oceania. It should be noted at this point that this is not a condition that can be generalised to the whole of the Pacific Islands and that the trajectories of indigenous anthropology vary in time and space.

19 FIVE PATHS FOR A HISTORY OF THE PACIFIC ISLANDS   581

Neither you nor I had any special training in ethnology in our university days; yet we both have a field experience that few, in any, ethnologists have been favoured with … Neither the ethnologists of the old school like Peehi [Eldson Best] nor the younger generation like Skinner could tackle the things that you or I know to be of importance. (Sorrenson, 1982, p. 7)

So wrote Peter Buck to his lifetime friend Apirana Ngata, in a letter dated 10 January 1932. In an article entitled "Polynesian Corpuscles and Pacific Anthropology: The Home-made Anthropology of Sir Apirana Ngata and Sir Peter Buck" (from which the previous quote is taken and which inspires the first part of this paragraph), Maurice P. K. Sorrenson analyses the formation, the political and cultural role and the friendship between the two Māori scholars, highlighting "the belief of Ngata and Buck that their Māori ancestry and upbringing gave them a unique advantage over *Pākehā* in understanding Māori culture" (ibid., p. 7).

Peter Buck was born in 1887. Also known by his Māori name, Te Rangi Hiroa, he was the son of an Anglo-Irish immigrant, William Henry, and a Māori woman, Ngarongo-ki-tua, who belonged to the *iwi* Ngāti Mutunga. His biological mother was Rina, a relative of Ngarongo-ki-tua who consented to a surrogate pregnancy to make up for Ngarongo-ki-tua's presumed infertility and died shortly after giving birth. Apirana Ngata, born in 1874, was also of Māori descent, belonging to the *iwi* Ngāti Porou. His father was a traditional Māori leader, an expert in oral literature, and his mother was of Scottish descent on her father's side. Buck and Ngata met at the famous Te Aute (Hawke's Bay) college, where an entire generation of future Māori leaders was educated. Ngata went on to study at Canterbury University, majoring in political science; Buck became a doctor at Otago Medical School. Both were among the top students of their generation, and after some professional experience, both became members of parliament (Ngata in 1905 and Buck in 1909). The political arena brought them into contact with that first generation of *Pākehā* anthropologists who settled in New Zealand (Percy Smith and Elsdon Best among others), with whom they shared a strong passion for oral traditions and Māori material heritage. In 1909, Ngata was one of the promoters of a Manifesto for the Young Māori Party, which stressed the need to defend the Māori language, poetry, traditions, arts and crafts, and to promote anthropological and ethnological research (Ngata, 1909). Both enthusiastically participated in the recruitment of natives for the Pacific Battalion which served in Europe and the Middle East during World War I (Buck was decorated for heroism at Gallipoli).

The period between the wars witnessed a rise in the careers of the two Māori men. Ngata was a Member of Parliament for 38 years and became Minister for Native Affairs in 1928. His career was marked by strong defence of Māori rights and values, even though his land reform proposal inspired by indigenous conceptions of land (Ngata, 1931) was rejected, challenged and suspected of alleged parental favouritism. Buck soon left politics, however. A meeting in Melbourne with the then Director of the Bishop Museum of Hawaii, Herbert Gregory, earned him an invitation to join the Museum's staff in 1927. He became its Director in 1935, taking on one of the most important roles in guiding ethnographic research on Oceania (see above). The biographies of these two figures feature numerous other interesting traits that we cannot analyse here. Instead, I would like to focus on their relationship with the anthropological schools of the time.

Buck and Ngata were anything but scholars confined to their native island. Ngata's political activity and Buck's role as a professional anthropologist at the Bishop Museum took them on frequent trips throughout the Pacific and to the US, and to attend international conferences where they met many contemporary exponents of anthropology. In 1933, for example, Buck was Visiting Professor at Yale and met Franz Boas, who was 75 years old at the time. As Sorrenson (1982) points out, the two scholars had been inspired by the first generation of Pacific anthropologists in their approach to diffusionist issues and material culture. They turned their attention towards an in-depth study of the origins and trajectories of the Polynesian peoples and towards attentive research into the tangible and intangible heritage of Māori cultures. While they remained personally sceptical of the emerging Malinowskian functionalist school, they played an active and driving role in fostering and supporting the careers of two key figures in Pacific anthropology, Felix Keesing (whom Ngata sent to study in Hawaii with a grant from the Ethnological Board and who became the first holder of an anthropology professorship there) and Raymond Firth (for whom Buck tried in vain to create a professorship in New Zealand after his doctorate at London School of Economics (LSE) with Malinowski). In their correspondence, Ngata and Buck are not without their doubts regarding the approaches of these and other *Pākehā* anthropologists, and their difficulties in understanding native "psychology", being without Māori "blood" (as Buck wrote to Ngata, ibid., p. 17), and yet they did not deny their support for the consolidation of a Pacific anthropology, imagining a coexistence of *outsiders* and *insiders*. What is most striking about the approach of these two authors and public figures is their ability to intercept the theoretical and methodological transformations of early twentieth-century anthropology, creatively readapting it to the need to promote the Māori component of an almost independent multicultural state such as New Zealand/Aotearoa.

The attentive approach to psychology and to the "personality" of Boas and his school, for example (Sorrenson, 1982), is explored in its ability to promote Māori "psychology". Ngata reacted very negatively to the statements of Best who, in the wake of Lévy-Bruhl's theory of mentality (1922), considered the Māoris incapable of abstract thought. On the other hand, he was favourably impressed by the work of Paul Radin (1927) on the "philosophical" capacities of primitives. The creative action of the two Māori anthropologists, however, took place primarily in the areas of acculturation and applied anthropology. Both Ngata and Buck campaigned for the anthropological training of New Zealand's leaders. In 1931 Firth, who was a researcher in Sydney at the time, suggested to Ngata that a Department of Anthropology be set up to train officials committed to *Native Affaires*, a project which collapsed due to lack of funds. The applied anthropology used by Ngata in his political action, and which Buck theorised in the sense of valuing native knowledge, is a far cry from the anti-colonial attitudes and hostility to the presence of Western researchers that were to be found in native anthropologists of the 1960s and 1970s. Ngata and Buck were intellectuals and politicians within and "organic" to a multicultural state in which the Māoris were a minority and conceived their role as champions and defenders of the indigenous imprint on the country, definitely not as the theorists of a Māori "ethnic" state.

However, the promising beginnings of native anthropology did not meet with much response elsewhere in the Pacific Islands (except, and only partially, in Papua New Guinea). In 1975, Epeli Hau'ofa, who would later become the best-known South Pacific native anthropologist and writer, published a damning indictment of academic anthropology, of which he felt he was fully a part (so much so that he used "we" anthropologists alongside "we, natives"). Hau'ofa, born in 1939, was the son of a couple of Tongan missionaries who moved to Papua New Guinea. As he points out in the article cited above (1975), he was the second indigenous scholar to obtain a Doctorate in Anthropology (from the ANU) and to work as a professional anthropologist (first at the University of Papua New

584   A. FAVOLE

Guinea and then at the USP in Fiji), after Rusiate Nayacakalou, whom we have already mentioned. In his article, Hau'ofa reflects on his dual and problematic status as a native *and* an anthropologist, starting with the many adverse reactions to anthropology and anthropologists that he gathered among Oceanians. "Anthropologists don't really understand us"; "they don't present a complete picture of us"; "they don't know how we *feel*" (1975, p. 283—my addition of italics). The inability to capture the native emotional dimension is one of the accusations picked up and adopted by Hau'ofa, but it is by no means the only one. In their work, Western anthropologists have used titles deemed offensive (Malinowski's *The Sexual Life of Savage* is an example), arguments that reproduce colonial stereotypes, such as those of an evolutionary "racial" nature that Marshall Sahlins used to contrast the Melanesian *big man* with the Polynesian "chief".

After decades of anthropological field research in Melanesia we have come up only with picture of people who fight, compete, trade, pay brideprices, engage in rituals, invent cargo cults, copulate and sorceries each other. There is hardly anything in our literature to indicate whether those people have any such sentiments as love, kindness, consideration, altruism, and so on. We cannot tell from our ethnographic writing whether they have a sense of humour (1975, p. 286).

The cumbersome presence of generations of anthropologists "from outside" the Pacific is identified as the primary cause of the native "disillusionment" with the discipline, which, even in a new-born university like that of Papua New Guinea, was received with great enthusiasm in the 1960s, so much so that the introductory course in Social Anthropology was the most popular! Hau'ofa condemns the absence of important themes, the partiality of the representations, the often abstruse and incomprehensible non-fiction language, the paternalistic tendency to use native "informants" instead of striving to train future colleagues from the islands. The situation is such, he writes, that some countries are denying research permits to anthropologists who lose "the sense of immediacy of the lived in reality" and are unable to grasp "the deep appreciation of the nuances of their own language" (ibid., p. 288). How to break out of this impasse?

Hau'ofa anticipates some later trajectories of anthropology in Oceania when he observes that "Pacific people expect of us to be more of the novelist and the social historian and less of the scientist who speaks in jargon" (p. 284). As we have already noted, many indigenous scholars approaching anthropology will tend to embrace the research and communication style of *Cultural studies* or, as we have already seen, become writers, playwrights, poets, transitioning from the language of non-fiction to that of *fiction*, the novel and the novella. The Tongan scholar does not express an anti-anthropological position, nor does he dismiss anthropology as the servant of colonialism, but proposes a model of shared, participatory, circular anthropology, between *outsiders* and *insiders*. According to Hau'ofa, the training and recruitment of a new generation of native anthropologists would allow the development of collaborative research, in which the "field" of external anthropologists would be complemented by the internal linguistic and cultural knowledge of Pacific natives. "To humanise our study of the conditions of Man in the Pacific": the final sentence of the article summarises an approach that favours a humanistic definition of anthropology—a knowledge which, as seen by the natives, should be rightfully placed among the *humanities* rather than in the *social sciences*—and which, as we shall see in the last part of this chapter, problematises and relativises the cornerstone of the anthropological method, namely *fieldwork*.

PATH FIVE (BY WAY OF CONCLUSION): "GOING INTO" OR "STAYING ON" THE FIELD?

Reflecting on the *stories* of anthropology in the plural form also has the effect of "exploding" the category of the Pacific Islands, along with that of native anthropologists. Seen up close, the stories of the South Pacific islands show quite different trajectories, which help explain the different reception of the discipline of anthropology. Oceania, which in pre-colonial history had no towns and cities, is now a highly urbanised *Blue Continent*,[5] but there are many rural areas that present peculiar dynamics and remarkable specificities compared to urban environments. In Oceania, we find islands inhabited almost exclusively by native populations (such as Wallis and Futuna, where I have worked, and where the Polynesian component exceeds 95%); multi-ethnic islands, where the native population is a minority (Hawaii, New Caledonia and Fiji to name but a few); large independent states inhabited predominantly by native and rural populations (Solomon Islands, Papua New Guinea and Vanuatu); overseas countries or territories still linked to a European *metropole* (such as French Polynesia, a

[5] The expression "Blue Continent" is spreading at regional level and is used to indicate the Pacific Islands area (Borgnino & Giordana, 2020).

country which is, in turn, extremely differentiated internally). Writing the stories of anthropology in Oceania therefore means addressing the different outcomes of colonialism and post-colonialism, globalisation processes and diasporas, tourism and "autarkic" and "radical" choices (in the sense of favouring a presence in the places of origin) of some islands and groups.

Similarly, "native anthropologist" is a label often claimed by authors who define themselves as such, but it should not be essentialised. Oceania's (few) native anthropologists have indeed expressed and continue to express different sensitivities and theoretical and methodological stances. To give just one example: we have seen how, with the birth of the University of South Pacific, the political leaders of the new Pacific states and the local intellectual elites had created training courses based on an "applied" vision of academic disciplines, oriented towards the "development" of their respective countries, which had recently become independent. Anthropology has often been accused by native scholars of using an overly specialised, formal and self-referential language, concerned with theory rather than with capturing the moods, emotions, feelings and desires of the Pacific peoples (in some ways this is Hau'ofa's position, as outlined above). Yet, among native scholars, 'Okustino Māhina has advocated a somewhat opposing view (1999). The Tongan scholar, a qualified philosopher, sociologist and anthropologist, is critical of those who argue that the education of Pacific students should be based on "usefulness" and the application of the knowledge and skills they have acquired. According to Māhina, it is the study of philosophy, the theoretical exploration of Western social sciences and humanities and the connection between these and indigenous epistemologies that should shape the curricula of Pacific universities. And it is to this idea that an interesting Tongan institution, the Atenisi Institute, is dedicated. Beginning with its name ("Atenisi" is the Tongan version of "Athens"), it evokes the importance of classical studies, the possibility of reciprocal cross-fertilisation between Western philosophical and humanistic thought and Polynesian thought and rhetorical skills. The Atenisi Institute was founded in the 1970s by Futa Helu, a Tongan of aristocratic origin who had studied philosophy in Sydney with the empiricist John Anderson, and is still an active institution in the Kingdom of Tonga.

What conclusions can be drawn from the encounter between anthropology and the islands of Oceania, and what future scenarios can we imagine? This is the question that fuels an interesting contribution written at the beginning of the millennium by Geoffrey M. White, an American anthropologist specialising in the Solomon Islands who was working in Hawaii at the time, and native Hawaiian anthropologist (Kānaka 'ōiwi), Ty Kāwika Tengan (2001). The starting point is once again the observation of the absence or scarce presence of native anthropologists, albeit in the knowledge that other fields of research, such as *Cultural Studies* and *Native Studies*, have embraced themes and perspectives that we would not hesitate to define as "anthropological" elsewhere. Where does this native "resistance" to anthropology, or at least to the word "anthropology", come from? The two authors of the essay reprise some of the criticisms now customary to the discipline or at least to its beginnings: the portrayal of the Pacific as a set of "isolated" islands or socio-political "laboratories" ideal as places of study, essentialism, an overly "traditional" vision, incapable of looking at the phenomena of innovation and creativity. These criticisms are only partly founded: if we look at the extensive debate on the "inventions of tradition" that has opened up in the Pacific since the 1980s (Bellagamba & Paini, 1999), the positions are sometimes reversed. Anthropologists like Roger Keesing, who emphasised the "political strategies" of renewed discourses on *kustom*, and numerous Western researchers who emphasised the "invention" of tradition, or at least its presentation in increasingly new forms, were countered by many native scholars who emphasised the "authenticity" (and ultimately persistence) of cultural traditions in the Pacific.

It is true that *Cultural Studies* and *Native Studies* are perspectives that are inclined to embrace the transformations of Pacific societies, with their focus on media, writers, art and film production, and phenomena of "hybridisation" or cultural syncretism. White and Tengan however argue that these are studies that are more widely received in urban and highly schooled contexts. And of course, as many European anthropologists have argued, these are approaches that are disinclined to develop lengthy and in-depth field investigations.

And herein lies the last of the surprises in our quick glance at the stories of anthropology in the Pacific. One of the targets of recent native criticism of the discipline is precisely *fieldwork*, or at least the opposition it evokes between *outsiders* and *insiders*; it is precisely the idea that looking "from afar" is virtuous; it is precisely the idea of "going to" and "returning from" the field that is the problem.

Anthropology's valorisation of outsiderness as a strategy for culture learning, seen as a core value from inside the discipline, is often seen by others as evidence of separation and detachment, of separate values and

588   A. FAVOLE

interests. Given the palpable legacy of power differentials between natives and non-natives in a region with a long and present colonial history, it should not be surprising that "separate" is often read as divergent and conflicting (White & Tengan, 2001, pp. 395–396).

To assume that the ethnographic perspective is virtuous precisely because it is external, to defend the Malinowskian revolution that places participatory observation practised by *outsiders* at the heart of the method, is both politically and methodologically critical. Many native scholars point out that *fieldwork* as a research method assumes that, unlike the anthropologist, native communities are "stationary" and immersed in their atavistic cultures or at least in their island contexts. According to the traditional, Malinowskian idea of *fieldwork*, only the *outsider* has the capacity to understand "others" by detaching himself from his own culture or at least by bringing out the points of friction, as if colonial-era exchanges and movements had not existed; ancient and modern diasporas; as if Oceania were not inhabited by what James Clifford (2001) has called "indigenous cosmopolitans", Oceanians who systematically break down boundaries and cultural differences.

Is it possible to deny that a native of a certain society and culture can become an anthropologist of it? Can it be denied, all the more so, for societies that, precisely because they have been colonised, have found themselves living *between* several worlds and several languages, that have assimilated religions, lifestyles, foreign political ideologies, and that have also had bodily experience of the pluralism of cultural worlds? Is an indigenous anthropology politically engaged in a perpetual work of decolonisation of knowledge not virtuous? On the other hand, is it possible to deny that those who are "outside" a society can practice field research? Wouldn't denying this be a bit like claiming forms of native sovereigntism? The Native Hawaiian anthropology analysed by White and Tengan opposes not only the paternalistic attitude that relegates natives to the role of "informants" or "collaborators" of the anthropologist, but also the popular idea that there can be a virtuous marriage between the external "theory-giving" anthropologist and the internal ethnographer who provides in-depth linguistic and cultural knowledge of their society. To ward off the risk of academia becoming "the last plantation" (ibid., 398), White and Tengan propose looking at anthropology and its methods as a moving landscape, plastic and malleable in its reception in new contexts. As shown by Hau'ofa's career, it is possible to move between a canonical transcultural ethnography, literary fiction and cultural criticism. "The difficulty – and perhaps opportunity – is that none of these terms is fixed: not *fieldwork*, not *anthropology*, not *indigenous culture*, and not *cultural studies*" (ibid., p. 404). A good proposal for the future would seem to be that of placing anthropologists of external origin who are willing to "take root", capable of practicing forms of the field that are marked by "staying" or at least by "returning" rather than "entering" and permanently "leaving" the field, side by side with native anthropologists trained in the academies, brought up in multicultural environments, who have experienced first-hand the confrontation and conflict between different cultural horizons. Twenty years after White and Tengan's essay, in areas such as Hawaii, French Polynesia and Aotearoa/New Zealand, these collaborations, which are still quite rare, seem to be bearing fruit.

Anthropology of European origin *in* Pacific Islands has been the subject of love, friction and bitter opposition. It is not only an academic discipline with its own methods and topics, but a field of conflict or at least an arena of confrontation between different ideas of culture, civilisation, colonialism and decolonisation. It is anything but a fixed configuration. Anthropology in Oceania takes the form of non-fiction and *fiction*; of "observation from a distance" and from within; it has been *salvaged anthropology* (as in the projects promoted by the Bishop Museum) or the study of the creative transformations of island societies; it favours the perspective of those in diaspora or, on the contrary, of those who have decided to live on the islands from which they originate. In short, it is a travelling anthropology with unpredictable outcomes, just like the destinies of the Pacific island wayfinders who wandered the Pacific some thousands of years ago in search of new places to live and new forms of human beings.

REFERENCES

Aria, M. (2007). *Cercando nel vuoto*. Pacini.

Bellagamba, A., & Paini, A. (Eds.). (1999). *Costruire il passato. Il dibattito sulle tradizioni in Africa e Oceania*. Paravia/Scriptorium.

Borgnino, E. (2020). Transported landscapes. In A. Favole (Ed.), *L'Europa d'Oltremare* (pp. 43–58). Milano.

Borgnino, E., & Giordana, L. (2020). Oceania. Il Blue Continent. In A. Favole (Ed.), *L'Europa d'Oltremare* (pp. 149–165). Cortina.

Clifford, J. (1982). *Person and myth: Maurice Leenhardt in the Melanesian World*. University of California Press.

590   A. FAVOLE

Clifford, J. (2001). Indigenous articulations. *The Contemporary Pacific, 13*(2), 468–490.

Codrington, R. H. (1891). *The Melanesians: Studies in their anthropology and folklore*. Clarendon Press.

Colombo Dougoud, R. (2013). Les bambous gravés, objets ambassadeurs de la culture kanak. *Journal de la Société des Océanistes, 136–137*, 119–132.

Firth, R. (1936). *We, the Tikopia*. Allen & Unwin.

Hau'ofa, E. (1975). Anthropology and Pacific Islanders. *Oceania, 45*(4), 283–289.

Hau'ofa, E. (1983). *Tales of Tikongs*. University of Hawaii Press.

Hau'ofa, E. (1993). Our sea of islands. *Contemporary Pacific, 6*(1), 148–161.

Howard, A., & Borofsky, R. (1989). *Developments in Polynesian ethnology*. University of Hawaii Press.

Howard, M. C. (1983). A preliminary survey of anthropology and sociology in the South Pacific. *Journal of Pacific Studies, 9*(1), 70–132.

Huffer, E., & Leleivai, P. (Eds.). (2001). *Futuna. Mo ona puleaga Sau*. Institute of Pacific Studies.

Keown, M. (2007). *Pacific islands writing*. Oxford University Press.

Kessler, K. A. (2021). Anthropology at the University of the South Pacific: From past Dynamics to Present Perceptions. *The Australian Journal of Anthropology, 32*, 33–53.

Layard, J. W. (1942). *Stone men of Malekula*. Chatt & Windus.

Leenhardt, M. (1937). *Gens de la grande terre*. Gallimard.

Leenhardt, M. (1947). *Do kamo. La personne et le mythe dans le monde mélanésien*. Gallimard.

Lévy-Bruhl, L. (1922). *La mentalité primitive*. PUF.

Māhina, O. (1999). Theory and practice in anthropology: Pacific anthropology and Pacific Islanders. *Social Analysis: The International Journal of Social and Cultural Practice, 43*(2), 41–69.

Mariner, W. (1827). *An account of the natives of the Tonga Islands, in the Pacific Ocean*. Hurst, Chance.

Ngata, A. (1909). Draft statement of the aims and objectives of the Young Maori Party. *Maori purposes fund boards papers*. Alexander Turnbull Library.

Ngata, A. (1928). Anthropology and the government of native races in the Pacific. *The Australasian Journal of Psychology and Philosophy, VI*(1), 1–14.

Ngata, A. (1931). Land Development Report. *Appendices to the Journal of the House of Representatives* G-10.

Puccini, S. (2005). *L'itala gente dalle molte vite*. Meltemi.

Puccini, S., & Dimpflmeier, F. (2018). *Nelle mille patrie insulari. Etnografia di Lamberto Loria nella Nuova Guinea britannica*. CISU.

Radin, P. (1927). *Primitive man as a philosopher*. Appleton.

Remotti, F. (Ed.). (1997). *Le antropologie degli altri*. Scriptorium Paravia.

19 FIVE PATHS FOR A HISTORY OF THE PACIFIC ISLANDS   591

Rivers, W. H. R. (1914). *The history of Melanesian society.* Cambridge University Press.

Sand, C., & Bedford, S. (Eds.). (2010). *Lapita. Ancêtres océaniens.* Somogy-Musée du Quai Branly.

Sorrenson, M. P. K. (1982). Polynesian corpuscles and Pacific anthropology: The home-made anthropology of Sir Apirana Ngata and Sir Peter Buck. *The Journal of the Polynesian Society, 91*(1), 7–27.

Spate, O. (1979). *The Spanish Lake.* University of Minnesota.

Spate, O. (1983). *Monopolists and freebooters.* Pergamon Book.

Spate, O. (1988). *Paradise found and lost.* Pergamon Book.

Thomas, N. (1991). *Entangled objects: Exchange, material culture, and colonialism in the Pacific.* Harvard University Press.

White, G. M., & Tengan, T. K. (2001). Disappearing worlds: Anthropology and cultural studies in Hawai'i and the Pacific. *The Contemporary Pacific, 13*(2), 381–416.

Williams, T., & Calvert, J. (1858). *Fiji and the Fijians.* Heylin.

Worsley, P. (1957). *The trumpet shall sound.* MacGibbon & Kee.

CHAPTER 20

Chinese Perspectives on Anthropology and Ethnology

Roberto Malighetti

As early as 1939 Bronislaw Malinowski made a very positive judgment on Chinese anthropology and ethnology. In the preface of the book *Peasant Life in China: A Field Study of Country Life in the Yangtze Valley* (1939) by Fei Xiaotong, his PhD student at the London School of Economics, he identified the relevance and originality of Chinese anthropology. Malinowski mentioned a meeting with Wu Wenzao, a founding father of the discipline, and argued that "independently and spontaneously" there had been organized in China "an attack on the real problems of culture change and applied anthropology, an attack which embodies all my dreams and desiderata" (Malinowski, 1939, p. XXII). The preface presented Fei's monograph, stemming from the PhD thesis under Malinowski's supervision, as a functionalist analysis of Chinese rural society, defined as "a landmark in the development of anthropological fieldwork and theory", and appreciated for his ability to broaden the disciplinary boundaries

---

R. Malighetti (✉)
Department of Human Sciences, University of Milano-Bicocca, Milan, Italy
e-mail: roberto.malighetti@unimib.it

© The Author(s), under exclusive license to Springer Nature Switzerland AG 2023
G. D'Agostino, V. Matera (eds.), *Histories of Anthropology*,
https://doi.org/10.1007/978-3-031-21258-1_20

593

to the study of complex societies "outward from savagery to civilization" (Malinowski, 1939, p. XXII).

This consideration was rescued from oblivion by Maurice Freedman more than 23 years later, on October 30, 1962, in the Third Malinowski Memorial Lecture at the London School of Economics, under the chairmanship of Raymond Firth. Freedman quoted the views of the Polish master, reasserting the importance of the visit of Wu Wenzao and of Fei Xiaotong's book and foresaw the coming of "a Chinese phase in social anthropology" (Freedman, 1963).

Both views were elaborated in a very complex historical context, determined by major historical events. Malinowski's statements were made between the fall of the Manchu Qing imperial dynasty (1644–1912), the Republic of China (1912–1949), the conflict against the Japanese invasion (1937–1945) and the Civil War (1927–1949). Freedman's opinion on Chinese social anthropology was pronounced after the end of the Second World War (1945) and the foundation of the People's Republic of China (1949). In particular, they were made ten years after the reform of higher education of 1952, which abolished anthropology (人类学 ren lei xue lit. "study of man") as a "bourgeois pseudoscience" along with other social sciences such as sociology, political, legal and religious sciences. Moreover, Freedman's judgment came just after the 1957 "campaign against the right-wing elements" and "bourgeois scholars", which affected major anthropologists (Yang Shengmin, 2017). Anthropology was integrated into the discipline of ethnology (民族学 minzu xue), conceived as the study of minzu (民族), a composite and polysemic notion that can be alternatively and inaccurately translated with the terms "nation" and "nationality", "ethnicity" and "ethnic group", "clan" and "minority".

As a matter of fact, Freedman's predictions did not refer much to the researches produced by the generation mentioned by Malinowski. Freedman's statement mainly focused on the Anglo-Saxon anthropology of China, produced by authors like W. H. Newell from Oxford, G. W. Skinner from Cornell and M. H. Fried from Columbia and Isabel Crook. These scholars primarily worked on the oriental part of the country where the American and British influences were strong. They concentrated on Taiwan and on Hong Kong islands, seen as surrogates of China and laboratories for the anthropological study of its society and culture. [1] Using the model of the modern European nation-states, founded on a cultural, ethnic, linguistic, and economic homogeneity, they produced an abstract image of a culturally uniform China. They did not take into proper consideration the internal differences in mainland China as well as the significant works about minorities produced by the Chinese tradition.

THE SINICIZATION OF ANTHROPOLOGY AND ETHNOLOGY

The formation of a scientific school is the complex outcome of the mixture and confusion of a multiplicity of theoretical, cultural, economic, political and ideological factors. This view overcomes the essentializing oppositions between internal and external influences, thought in terms of authenticity, purity and well-defined borders. As it has been acknowledged by several Chinese scholars (Wang Mingming, 2008; Xu Xinjian, Wang Mingming, and Zhou Daming, 2008), the theoretical approaches, like any other form of tradition, are to be understood as hybrid results of the merging of different elements, as articulations, inexorably local, of transglobal, transversal and transdisciplinary discourses. From this horizon, Chinese anthropology can be seen as the outcome of constant re-elaborations of original perspectives based on a complicated dialogue, creative and critical, with the anthropologies, in turn themselves "confused", coming chiefly from Japan, Europe, the United States and the Soviet Union.

Chinese anthropology and ethnology interacted, throughout their history, with the major paradigmatic changes that marked the evolution of the discipline. The European impact, anticipated by the pioneering works of Marcel Granet (1884–1940), was at first conjugated with the influences of Japanese authors. The term "ethnology" arrived in China in 1895 with the translation of Thomas H. Huxley's book *Evolution and Ethics*. In 1902 an account by an historian, Wang Shunan, on the origins of European

---

[1] The development of anthropology in Taiwan followed the colonial history: the Dutch and the Japanese influences were replaced by the British. The major contemporary institutions such as the National Taiwan University and the Taiwan Tsinghua University, were created in the Fifties. Significantly, in Hong Kong, the British, at first, did not establish any department of anthropology in the University they created in 1911. The institutional history of the discipline in Hong Kong started in the Eighties, as a result of the intellectual exchange between the department of anthropology of Sun Yat-sen University (Guangzhou, China) and the Chinese University of Hong Kong (Hu Hongbao, Wang Jianmin, and Zhang Haiyang, 2006).

ethnic groups was published in Zhongwei (Ningxia), as well as the translation of a work by the Japanese scholar Ariga Nagao, based on the analysis of the evolutionary theories contained in Lewis Morgan's *Ancient Society* and in Herbert Spencer's *Principles of Sociology* (Ariga, 1882). The following year different important works were printed: the first book on anthropology, by the German scholar Michael Haberland (1898), translated by Lin Shu and Wei Yi; the text *Chinese Ethnography* (Liu Shipei, 1903); Lin Kaiqing's translation of the book *Ethnography*, written by the Japanese anthropologist and ethnologist Ryuzo Torii. In 1910, the volumes of the Soviet researcher Alexaner Pozdneev on his research (1892–1893) in Mongolia (Pozdneev, 1896–1898) and the text by N. N. Krotkov on the Xibo people of the Jilin province (Krotkov, 1912) were translated. The first Chinese scholar who originally used the word "anthropology" was Sun Xuewu, in an article dealing with the state of the art of European and American anthropology, published in 1916 by the journal of the Chinese Academy of Sciences (Sun Xuewu, 1916). In 1918 Chen Yinghuang's text entitled *Anthropology* was released (Chen Yinghuang, 1918) and, in 1921, Guo Yaogen's study on the evolution of man was printed (Guo Yaogen, 1921). Emile Durkheim's *Les Règles de la méthode sociologique* and Edward Alexander Westermark's *The History of Human Marriage*, were printed, in 1925, in the Chinese language (Song Shuhua, 2004; Hu Hongbao, Wang Jianmin, and Zhang Haiyang, 2006; Liu Mingxin, 2014).

In China, as in many other parts of the globe, anthropology and ethnology consolidated around the nation-building project. The events that marked the transition from the end of the Qing dynasty (1912) to the People's Republic of China (1949), made it strategically necessary to expand the knowledge of the ethnic groups that populated the borders of the country (Ma Changshou, 1947). From the very beginning, the two main schools of this period, the School of the South and the School of the North, did not limit themselves to the reproduction of the positions of the foreign masters. Through a creative dialogue with different traditions of thought, they started developing a specific and heterogeneous style for Chinese anthropology.

During the Republican period, the discipline was initially promoted by the *Academia Sinica*, a government institution created in 1928 by the regime and, in particular, by the work of the founder of Chinese ethnologist, Cai Yuanpei (1868–1940). Cai combined his academic role with his positions as Minister of Education of the provisional nationalist government (1912) and as Dean of Peking University (1917–1922). His work is based on a solid education completed in Europe, at the University of Leipzig (1906–1909), where he graduated in philosophy and anthropology and deepened in the course of the repeated visits to Germany and France studying, principally, the diffusionist theories (1911–1915). As Minister of Education he promoted the consolidation of the universities of the Republic of China and encouraged the development of the so-called new sciences in which he included anthropology and ethnology, appreciated for their contributions to the needs of the nationalist project. In an article he wrote in 1926, Cai Yuanpei defined the meaning of the term "ethnology" (minzu xue 民族 学) in a way that identified the discipline with the study of the country's ethnic minorities. In 1934 he established and directed an anthropology department inside the *Academia Sinica* together with his students and colleagues who shared strong links with the Western social sciences: Fu Sinian (1896–1950), the first director of the Institute of History and Philology of the *Accademia Sinica*, PhD in experimental psychology at the University College London (1920–1923); Li Ji (1896–1979), PhD from Harvard University in 1923, the first director of the Archeology Department of the *Academia Sinica* and the First Professor of Anthropology at the Human Sciences Department of Nankai University and then at Tsinghua University; Ling Chunsheng (1902–1981), PhD from University of Paris in 1926 and then founding director of the Department of Ethnology at the Academia Sinica Institute of Taiwan (Song Shuhua, 2004; Hu Hongbao, Wang Jianmin, and Zhang Haiyang, 2006; Liu Mingxin, 2014).

The *Academia Sinica* encouraged the ethnological studies of the interactions and mutual influences among groups. Its members examined migrations, forms of transmission and cultural fusions in order to demonstrate the unitary character of the Chinese community in geographical, cultural, and historical terms, traced back to the first imperial Qin dynasty (221–206 BC), from which they derived the same name "China". As a government office, the *Academia Sinica* supported the projects of the Chinese Nationalist Party (*Guomindang*). The researches were strongly influenced by the nationalist opposition to the idea of plurality and focused on the national integration along with the origins of what they called the "Chinese race". The School of the South supported the obscure nationalism of Chiang Kai-shek, founded on the principle of the descent of all the Chinese people from a common ancestor and on the consideration of the ethnic minorities as lineages of the Han (Gu Jiegang, 1937).

Historians contrast the perspectives of the School of the *Academia Sinica* with the works of the so-called School of the North, located in Peking at Yanjing University. Being a private academy, created in 1919 by the joint efforts of the North American and British missionary societies, it had no ties with the nationalist government. As a matter of fact, it opposed the nationalist ideology and its interpretation by the *Academia Sinica*. As different authors maintain (Yang Qingmei, 2017; Wang Mingming, 2018), although the war against the Japanese invasion (1937–1945) brought the members of Yanjing University and of the *Academia Sinica* in close contact, both hidden in the mountain regions of the Southwest, the dialogues between them did not succeed in producing a shared vision (He Guoqiang, and Tang Kaixun, 2005). Indeed, the civil war led the two schools to take sides on the rival and conflicting political positions: Fei Xiaotong, for example, was forced to take refuge in the US embassy to escape the republican repression; many members of the *Academia Sinica*, after the Liberation, fled to Taiwan.

Yanjing anthropologists interpreted the theories of British and American authors with whom they studied. The founder and director of the School, Wu Wenzao (1901–1985) obtained his PhD at Columbia University in 1928, under the supervision of Franz Boas, after having graduated from Tsinghua University (Beijing) in 1923. Wu was the promoter of an intense activity of academic internationalization. On the one hand he encouraged the international mobility of students, facilitating their relationships with the most influential anthropologists of the time. He supported the doctoral education of his students: Fei Xiatong at the LSE (PhD 1938) with Malinowski; Lin Yaohua (1910–2000) at Harvard (PhD 1940) under the direction of Raymond Firth who introduced the publication of his thesis in English (Lin Yaohua, 1948); Li Anzhai (1900–1985) in the United States: first at Berkeley University, where he worked with Alfred Kroeber and Robert Lowie and then at Yale University where, under the supervision of Edward Sapir, he earned his PhD in 1947.

The School of the North, from the very beginning, combined the functionalist perspectives with the historical ones in an approach subsequently defined by the Chinese scholars as "historical functionalism" (Qiao Jian, 2008). Its members developed an original model to consider the national question, opposing both the Chinese nationalist policies as well as the European theories founded on the homogeneous coincidence between the Nation and the State. Wu Wenzao thought the reality of China using the principle of the "political oneness of plural nations" (Wu Wenzao,

1942; Wang Mingming, 2012). Overcoming the perspectives that contributed to his own education, Wu Wenzao conceived China as an example of a state composed of a variety of nations. Already in his first article entitled *Nation and State*, published on the *Chinese Overseas Chinese Student Union Journal*, in 1926, when he was a student at Columbia University, Wu foreshadowed the concept of a multinational or multiethnic state (Wang Mingming, 2014; Malighetti, and Wang Mingming, 2014).

Wu's ideas were later taken up and elaborated by Fei Xiaotong, certainly the leading figure of Chinese anthropology. Inspired by the master's theories, Fei critically discussed the European idea of a nation-state and proposed a "multiethnic" concept, understood as a "pluralistic and unified configuration" or as a "pattern of diversity within unity" (Fei Xiaotong, 1988a, 1988b). This paradigm, widely used by Fei in the 1950s, as he himself wrote in his memoirs (Fei Xiaotong, 1997), emphasizes the idea of mixture and fusion. The theory applies to the concept of nation as well as to minorities, similarly thought without using essentialist principles such as territorial or linguistic and cultural authenticity and purity (Fei Xiatong, 1989). In the studies of what he called the Tibet-Yi corridor, Fei refused to consider as isolated units those passages that start in the north, on the border between Gansu, Qinghai and Sichuan, and end in southeastern Tibet and in north-western Yunnan. Instead, he thought of these areas as places of ancient and intense contacts between cultures, populated by ethnic groups and nationalities closely interrelated by history and constantly interpenetrating each other (Fei Xiaotong, 1989; Wang Mingming, 2014; Ma Guoqing, 2020a).

Under the direction of these leaders, The School of the North elaborated pioneer perspectives, different from the Eurocentric approaches which, in the same period, were engaged in comprehending their objects of analysis inside closed and well-defined units and in the global imposition of their model of the nation. The northern scholars laid the foundation of the following Chinese theoretical elaborations on the nation-state and, to a certain extent, they anticipated the recent deconstructions of the concepts of culture, identity, community, and ethnicity, produced by theories based on complexity (Hannerz, 1992) and on hybridizations (Canclini, 1990).

The Ethnic Identification Programme

Chinese anthropology and ethnology, from the very beginning, developed specific features that persisted over time. The combination of ethnographic, historical and applied researches was initially used to serve the needs of the nation-building process which, after the failure of the Nationalistic Government and the end of the civil war, was successfully carried out by the People's Republic of China. To this end, a fundamental role was played by the realization of the "Ethnic Identification Project", one of the major anthropological enterprises ever realized, aiming at recognizing and mapping the Chinese ethnic minorities. It was coordinated and implemented, between 1953 and 1979, by the state power, which promoted and supported the applied ideal of anthropology and ethnology. The programme was based at the Central Institute or College for Nationalities/the Central University for Nationalities (later renamed Minzu University of China) established by the government, in 1952, to host the headquarters of the project. This institution absorbed the main researchers after the reform of higher education which integrated anthropology inside the discipline of ethnology. A leading role was played by Wu Wenzao and Fei Xiaotong, assisted by scholars like Pan Guangdan and Wu Zelin, from the Anthropology Department of Tsinghua University, and Yang Chengzhi from Sun Yat-sen University (Yang Shengmin, 2017). Under their guidance, the researchers were included in other government initiatives aimed at the understanding of Chinese ethnic groups and at the construction of national unity: the "Research Project for the Histories of Ethnic Minorities" and the publications dedicated to ethnic issues, namely, the volumes of the "Translation Series of Ethnic Issues" and "The Collected Papers on China's Ethnic Issues".

Initially, the project adopted a Soviet model, in opposition to the European and North American "old bourgeois ethnology", considered unable to produce real empirical scientific researches and accused of idealism, collusion with colonialism and racism. Under the Soviet influence, ethnology was classified as part of history and integrated into the departments of history. From Marxist-Leninist and Stalinist perspectives, Chinese scholars used the principles of historical and dialectical materialism to elaborate their articulations between ethnographic and historical researches and to address the activities of ethnic identification as well as the socialist construction of the country (Fei Xiatong and Lin Yaohua, 1956). Many scholars studied in the USSR and many Soviet professors went to China.

Among these, one of the most important is Sergei M. Shirokogoroff (1887–1939), who taught the basics of Soviet ethnology to the post-revolutionary generation of Chinese students (Shirokogoroff, 1924; Yu Bromley, 1974; Gu Dingguo, 2000). The Maoist interpretation of Soviet historical teleology and the conjugation of Morgan's conception of social evolution with that of Engels were adopted to elaborate a "proletarian ethnology", based on class analysis. In this period, which lasted until 1958, when the relations between the PRC and the USSR were interrupted, Chinese anthropologists concentrated on perspectives that primarily came from the socialist world, including East Germany, Bulgaria, Czechoslovakia, Romania as well as North Korea and Vietnam.

The Ethnic Identification Programme began by recognizing groups through their ethnonyms. that is, by means of self-definitions of social actors. At the outset, it worked on more than 400 ethnonyms, classified on the basis of the categories already used in the definitions of Soviet ethnic minorities, that is to say, according to the so-called four commons, as they had been defined by Joseph Stalin: common language, common territory, common mode of production, common psychological conformation (later defined by the term "culture"). The research led to the different quantifications and definitions of the ethnic groups that, in addition to the Han, make up the PRC: 38 in 1953 (6.06%—35,320,360 people—total population 582,603,417); 53 in 1964 (5.78%—39,883,909 people—total population 694,581,759); 55 in 1965 and 1979 in 1982 (6.67%—67,233,254 people—total population 1,008,175,288). Peoples who did not fit into the categories of the project were considered sub-ethnicities of the Han majority or reunited with other minorities (National Bureau of Statistics of PRC, 2013; Wang Linzhu, 2015).

Due to the deterioration of political relations between the PRC and the USSR after 1958, Soviet anthropology lost its centrality, blamed of being a "bourgeoise revisionist ethnology disguised under the red coat" and a traitor of Marxism (Shi Jin, 1964). Soviet ethnology was united with the "old Chinese Ethnology" and with "Western Ethnology" and defined as "reactionary" and "bourgeoise". These positions marked a substantial closure of Chinese ethno-anthropological studies in themselves and their replacement with "ethnic studies", based on the analysis of the "class struggle" and on the Maoist interpretation of Marxism.

Fei Xiatong's intellectual career reflects the crucial moments that signed Chinese history. Over the course of time, Fei articulated various theoretical positions. At first he conjugated Malinowski's ethnography with

Radcliffe-Brown's structuralism-functionalism and with Robert Park's human ecology. At the beginning of the 1950s, as vice president of the Central University for Nationalities (1951) he adopted a Marxist-Leninist paradigm and worked, along with Li Yaohua, at the Ethnic Identification Project. After the campaign against the right-wing elements (1957), Fei lost his importance, accused of "reactionary functionalism", and of being a "lackey of imperialism" and "a traitor of the peasant class" (Yang Shengmin, 2017). His influence regained strength at the end of the cultural revolution (1966–1976), which created heavy hindrances to the ethno-anthropological research. Fei's work became hegemonic in the academies and inside the government and turned him into the most important and well-known Chinese anthropologist worldwide. In the aftermath of the opening policies launched by Deng Xiaoping (1904–1997) in 1978, he critically rethought the work of ethnic identification and took a certain distance from the Stalinist criteria for defining nationalities and from historical materialism. The articulation of his thought continued throughout the 1980s until his death and included the study of Max Weber and Richard Tawney (Wang Mingming, 2014).

Reforms and Reopenings

With the end of the Cultural Revolution (1966–1976) and the beginning of the so-called period of "reform and opening", anthropology and ethnology were rehabilitated together with the dialogue with the traditions that accompanied the birth and development of Chinese social sciences. From that moment, universities, associations and research centres began an intense organizational and propulsive phase.

Sun Yat-sen University (Guangzhou) was the first to reopen the anthropology department in 1981, under the direction of Liang Zhaotao (1916–1987). Three years later it organized the "International Symposium on Anthropology and on the 60th Anniversary of Sun Yat-sen University" entitled "the Characteristics of Southern Chinese culture" (Ji Wen, 1985). In 1981 The Chinese Anthropological Society was founded in Xiamen University (Fujian) where it organized "The First National Academic Symposium of Anthropology". The following year the University opened a master's degree in anthropology and, in 1984, a new department of anthropology (Wang Shuling, 1993). In 1987, Yunnan University created an anthropological programme in the History Department. At the end of 1989 the "First International Symposium on Urban Anthropology" was held in Beijing, promoting the spread of this specialization and the relations with scholars from different parts of the world (Zhang Shuyun, 1990).

In the Nineties, Chinese anthropology further expanded, both in terms of national and international presence. In June 1992, the China Union of Anthropological and Ethnological Sciences (CUAES) was established and the following year it joined the International Union of Anthropological and Ethnological Sciences (IUAES). Always in 1992, Peking University created the Center for Anthropology and Folklore and in 1995 hosted the "First Advanced Seminar on Chinese Social & Cultural Anthropology", which became an annual meeting for international discussion, organized with the joint support of the Chinese Ministry of Education, the Ford and the Wenner-Gren Foundations (Zhou Xing, 1995).

New departments were established in many universities in subsequent years. Leading national social science research institutions, including the Chinese Academy of Social Sciences (CASS), organized several anthropology programmes. In 1995, the Institute of Ethnology of the Yunnan Academy of Social Sciences established the Film Center of Visual Anthropology and, in 1999, organized several advanced courses in visual anthropology, attended by international students and professors. In 1996 the Chinese Society of Literary Anthropology was founded (Yang Shengmin, 2017).

During this period, the problem of the specificity of Chinese anthropology gained greater prominence, prompted by debates that centred around what was called the "localization" or "sinization" of Chinese anthropology. In September 1999, an "International Symposium on the Localization of Anthropology" was held at the Institute of Ethnology and Anthropology of Guangxi University for Nationalities. The seminar was attended by numerous international scholars from the United States, Great Britain, France, and Japan (Gao Chong, Zou, Qiong, and Yang Shengmin, 2017). The following year Fei Xiaotong (2000, 2004), put forward the idea of using what he called "cultural self-awareness" as a tool to understand Chinese anthropology and its participation in international debate.

At the beginning of the twenty-first century, Chinese anthropology continued to increase its activities and contributions. In 2001 it was recognized by the Ministry of Education as a "national key subject" (Zhang Jijiao and Wu Yue, 2021, p. 7). Several universities established anthropology institutes and programmes, such as the Institute of Anthropology at Renmin University of China (2003) or the Nanjing University Institute of Social and Cultural Anthropology (2005). Other universities developed specializations, like the Historical Anthropology Research Center in Sun Yat-sen University (2001) or the Health and Human Development Center (2002) and the Tourism Anthropology Research Center (2004) in Xiamen University (Zhang Jijiao and Wu Yue 2021, p. 8).

The participation of Chinese ethnology and anthropology in the international debate took place in the context of events of global importance. In July 2000, the China Urban Anthropology Association (CUAA) hosted in Beijing the Inter-Congress of the International Union of Anthropology and Ethnology (IUAE) entitled "Urban Ethnic Culture: Preservation and Interaction". In December of the same year, the "International Conference on Sustainable Urban Development in the 21st Century and Commemoration of the Centenary of Chinese Anthropology" was held at the University of Sun Yat-sen: besides the subject of urban development the conference discussed the characteristics of Chinese anthropology (Mei Fangquan, 2002). In 2007, a Chinese delegation participated in the 106th annual meeting of the American Anthropological Association: on that occasion the two associations decided to organize a "Chinese-American Anthropology and Ethnology Advanced Forum" to be held in China in 2009 (Yang Shengmin, 2017). The internationalization of Chinese anthropology and ethnology was ratified by hosting, in July 2009, the sixteenth world congress of the International Union of Anthropological and Ethnological Sciences (IUAES) in the campuses of Yunnan University and Yunnan Minzu University (Kunming, Yunnan). About 5000 scholars and students from over 100 countries gathered in the campuses of Yunnan University and Yunnan Minzu University (Kunming, Yunnan) and took part in the congress entitled "Humanity, Development, Cultural Diversity" (Yang Shengmin, 2017).

In August 2010, the China Union of Anthropological and Ethnological Sciences (CUAES) organized "The First Joint Meeting of Heads of Chinese Anthropology and Ethnology" at Sun Yat-sen University. The conference discussed the directions of Chinese anthropological and ethnological researches (Huang Jin and Liu Chuming, 2010). In October of the same year "The First Asian Anthropology and Ethnology Forum" promoted dialogue among scholars from different Asian countries. In 2013, "The Comprehensive Survey of Economic and Social Development in China's Ethnic Minority Areas at the beginning of the 21st Century" was realized by the Institute of Ethnology and Anthropology of the Chinese Academy of Social Sciences.

20 CHINESE PERSPECTIVES ON ANTHROPOLOGY AND ETHNOLOGY 605

Since then, the international meetings organized by Chinese ethno-anthropological institutions followed one another in a consistent way. They contributed to the definition of China's position in the dialogue with the international scientific community. The protagonists of these processes exercised their critical approach towards the main trends of thought produced by contemporary anthropology.

ANTHROPOLOGIES FROM CHINA: BEYOND GLOBALIZATION AND LOCALIZATION

Anthropology originated in Europe in the nineteenth century with the expansion of European economic and political interests. It established itself as the specific perspective of modernity, the tradition that defined its scientific apparatus in univocal and all-encompassing ways. The new form of rationality focused on the understanding of what is not modern, subtracting itself from analysis, just as the eye cannot see itself. It interpreted a division of labour between anthropology and sociology that followed the motto "sociology studies the West, anthropology all the rest". The evolutionist school forged an object connoted as "primitive" and analysed with an allochronic approach, cancelling the spatial and cultural differences inside a time scale (Fabian, 1983). Subsequently, the functionalist perspective reduced its objects into discrete and homogeneous unis, represented in monographic forms. It conceived cultures and societies as homeostatic systems made of interrelated elements, according to modalities consistent with the pragmatism of the colonial administrations, based on the policies of *indirect rule* and on the co-optation of indigenous leaderships (Malighetti, 2021a).

When, after the Second World War, the centre of the world moved from Europe to the United States, the general headquarters of knowledge also migrated there. Profound political, economic and socio-cultural changes substantially modified the discipline. Processes such as decolonization, the nationalisms of the new independent states, the Cold War had a strong impact on anthropology, opening new spaces and new research strategies (Malighetti, 2018). The anthropology of the last part of the last century does not define its objects of study *via negativa*, using oppositions (complex-simple, rational-irrational, scientific-magical, etc.) and does not limit the discipline to the investigation of "premodern" societies. Rather, it transformed modernity into an object of science, analysing its form of rationality and its technology as well as the strategies of concealment of its inevitable culturality (Feyerabend, 1975; Dumont, 1983; Ardener, 1985; Manganaro, 1990). Anthropology took the form of a transversal point of view that crosses all cultures and societies, including those that shaped scientific thought. The North-American anthropological analysis of complex societies opened spaces for studying the complexity of every society and culture (Malighetti, 2021b).

Today the centres of the world are growing and multiplying, overcoming colonial dichotomies. In this context, the anthropological traditions once ignored or considered "marginal" are acquiring increasing authority and centrality. Contemporary anthropology mixes and merges complicated conceptual reference structures produced by authors coming from different parts of the world: assemblages (Rosaldo, 1989), hybrid paradigms (Canclini, 1990), complexity (Hannerz, 1992), multiple modernities (Comaroff, and Comaroff, 1993), *scapes* (Appadurai, 1996), articulations (Clifford, 1997), and connections (Amselle, 2001). Scholars investigate the historical, the economical, the political and the linguistic spaces of exchanges in which the cultures define and form themselves. They deconstruct the connections and disconnections of the constitutive elements of identitarian policies, ethnic affiliations and nation-building processes.

This perspective prompts a serious revaluation of the pioneering theoretical elaborations of Chinese anthropologists of the past as well as of the findings of the present researches (Malighetti, 2014). The rapid development processes that characterize contemporary Chinese history are posing new challenges and new opportunities for anthropology (Liu Xin, 2004; Zhou Daming, 2012; Ping Song, 2017; Ji Zhe and Liang Yongjia, 2018; Ma Guoqing, 2020b). Chinese researchers are ethnographic witnesses of global dynamics from the standpoint of an emerging global and globalizing power with a long history of mergers and fusions and with an increasingly political, economic and cultural significance (He Ming, 2016; Pan Tianshu, 2019). They can study how China articulates tradition and modernity in original terms, as well as how it combines its modernity with other traditions (Malighetti and Wang Mingming, 2014; Malighetti and Yang Shengmin, 2017). Elaborating the conceptual tools offered by the founding fathers, the recent works study the intercultural interactions, the exchanges and the mergers that have always characterized every culture and society since the first humans ventured out of Africa 60,000 years ago. The ethnographies of the intercultural relations in the corridors and in the areas of intersections are providing insights in the cross-cultural influences and determinations. They overcame the idea of "isolated units" and they show how the mountains, the steppes, the coastal plains and the islands have been crossed by trade routes where different cultural processes overlap and mingle (Li Xingxing, 2008; Wang Mingming, 2008; Ding Hong, 2014; Wang Yanzhong, 2014).

The experiences of the past supply the potential for new proposals and synthesis. They allow to read the complex contemporary world from the point of view of its intricate flows, connections, mixtures and traffics. The positions that began to develop in the Thirties offer specific skills to investigate the processes of globalization as a phenomenon that made human history. Various points of view contradict the attempts to assert a pacified ideology of globalization as something inevitable and already accomplished, which resolves conflicts and contradictions. They oppose the mechanical substitutions of the traditional with the modern and subtract the global from an abstract universality and a single logic of homologation. Rather the ethnographies present the complexity of the micro-processes of everyday life, emancipated from a single logic of homogeneity. They place the global inside its real articulations, necessarily local and particular. They explore how the globalizing ideas and action are appropriated and re-inserted into local practices, scattering modernity in its different forms and manifestations, constantly proliferating. They elaborate the idea of negotiating realities produced by the co-belonging of modernity and tradition, the global and the local.

Combining historical research with fieldwork (Ding Hong and Min Junqing, 2012; Wang Chao, 2013; Wang Mingming, 2014), many works reinterpret concepts such as "society", "culture", "nation" in a complex way. The contemporary debates on the culturally composite reality of the Chinese Nation start from the works of Wu Wenzao and Fei Xiaotong and are influenced by some epochal events like the collapse of the USSR and of Yugoslavia in the early Nineties, as well as the terrorism that hit China. A growing number of authors are defining China in plural terms and try to comprehend the important differences that permeate its society. They see China as a complex mixture of cultures and civilizations and investigate the relations between centre and periphery as well as between the nation and ethnic minorities. They propose models that think of the nation from a complex perspective beyond multicultural or pluralistic models (Yang Shengmin, 2003a; Ma Rong, 2004; Xie Lizhong, 2014; Ma Rong, 2017; Ma Guoqing, 2017; Aga Zoushi, 2018).

From this standpoint Chinese anthropology thinks societies as arenas in which different worldviews, interests and powers connect, oppose and collude. It interprets the centrifugal and centripetal forces that characterize the contemporary world and analyses its problems: the transnational flows of cultures, people, capital and goods as well as the spread of the new media (Zhou Yongming, 2005; Zhang Shichao, 2018; Chen Xiangjun, 2018; Gong Shiyao and Chen Gang, 2019); the new consumption models (Pun Ngai, 2003; Li Zhang, 2004a; Ren Hai, 2013); the impact of tourism (Zhang Chaozhi, Zhou Xiaofeng, and Song Xiaowei, 2018; Wang Xiongzhi and Chaozhi Zhang, 2020; Zhang Chaozhi and Zhu Minmin, 2020). Relevant contributions come from the study of environmental issues (Li Yiyuan, 2003; Yang Shengmin, 2003b; Chen Xiangjun, 2017); from the researches on development, inside China (Zhu Xing, 2004; Zhu Tan, 2010; Wang Yangzhong, 2014), or outside, mainly in Africa (He Wenping, 2010; Ye Jingzhong, 2011; Zhao Yongjun, 2013; Zhao Suisheng, 2014; Niu Zhongguang, 2016; Zhao Chunming, Ma Long, and Xiong Zhenqin, 2021); from the exploration of Chinese investments abroad and the commercialization of artefacts, as well as of the spread of the so-called traditional Chinese medicine (Li Anshan, 2011; Lai Lili, 2016) or of religious practices (Ji Zhe, 2016; Jiang Ting and Zhang Chaozhi, 2019; Yu Dan Smyer, 2020).

Interesting researches have been focused on internal migrations, a field of study that refers to over 150 million of so-called *floating people*. They examine individuals and groups who have left the residence where they are officially registered by the government, especially in the countryside, to migrate into the city in search of job opportunities. Contemporary scholars go beyond the analysis produced in the Nineties about the internal migrations towards the coastal cities and the simplistic dichotomies between city and countryside. They investigate the confusions of boundaries between rural and urban environments, the changes in village communities, as well as the mixing of agricultural, industrial and post-industrial scenarios that characterize the extended urban regions (Liu Xin, 2000; Yan Hairong, 2003, 2004; Gao Yongjiu, 2004; Lai Lili, 2004; Li Zhang, 2004b; Zhou Daming, 2005). Different researches investigate the urbanization processes as well as the urbanized minorities. They analyse the new urban spaces as places of transnational connections, as well as the spatialization of the socio-economic differences. They consider the growing polarization between rich and poor and the dynamics between inclusion and exclusion, discrimination and marginalization, the new forms of urban poverty (Liu Xin, 2002; Xiang Biao, 2002; Zheng Tiantian, 2004; Zhu, Xing, 2004; Pan Tianshu, 2005).

Chinese anthropology has recently fostered ethnographic studies outside China (Liu Xin, 2010). Encouraged by the Belt and Road Initiative the ethnographers have shown growing interest in combining studies on cross-border communities and on Chinese immigrants abroad (Ding Hong, Li Rudong, and Hao Shiyuan, 2015). In April 2014, the Chinese journal "World Ethno-National Studies" created a column for "overseas ethnography" (Shi Lin, 2021). At the same time, the Committee for Cultural Research Abroad of the Chinese Union of Anthropological and Ethnological Sciences was established, and a "Seminar on cultural exchanges and research abroad" was organized (Yang Shengmin, 2017).

The perspectives of Chinese anthropology and ethnology are slowly but progressively attracting the interest of scholars who study the complexity of the contemporary world and the dynamics that go through it. The increasing authoritative presence of Chinese anthropologists and ethnologists contributes to enlarge significantly the scientific horizons and to overcome ethnocentric and autoreferential hegemonies. The greater attention that the international scientific community is gradually dedicating to Chinese scholars, albeit still not with the intensity they deserve, is not only fulfilling Malinowski's and, to a different extent, Freedman's early predictions. It can also help in bringing the dialogue and cooperation between scientists against the dangerous divisions that are threatening the world.

REFERENCES

Aga Zhousi. (2018). The "Minzu" Conjecture. Anthropological Study of Ethnicity in post-Mao China. *Cargo, Revue Internationale de Anthropologie Culturelle & Sociale (The New Chinese Anthropology)*, 8, 83–108.

Amselle, J. L. (2001). *Branchements. Anthropologie de l'universalité des cultures.* Flammarion.

Appadurai, A. (1996). *Modernity at large: cultural dimensions of globalization.* University of Minnesota Press.

Ardener, E. (1985). Social anthropology and the decline of modernism in Reason and Morality. In J. Overing (Ed.), *Reason and Morality* (pp. 44–70). Tavistock.

Ariga, N. (1882). *Shakaigaku (Sociologia)*. Asahi Shimbun.

Cai Yuanpei. (1926). "说民族学" *Shuo Min ZuXue*一般*Yi Ban*, 478–634 (Talking About Ethnology. In *An Anthology of Cai Yuanpei* (Cai Yuanpei). Taibei: Wenxing Bookstore 41–43.

610   R. MALIGHETTI

Canclini, G. N. (1990). *Culturas Hibridas: Estrategias para Entrar y salir de la Modernidad*. Banco de la Republica.

Chen Xiangjun. (2018). 影视人类学 (Anthropology of media: film and television) «应用人类学», 科学出版社, 213-227.

Chen Xiangjun. (2017). «阿尔泰山游牧者:生态环境与本土知识» (Nomads in Altai Mountains: Ecological Environment and Local Knowledge). 北京: 社科文献出版社.

Chen Yinghuang. (1918). 人类学 (Anthropology), 商务印书馆.

Clifford, J. (1997). *Routes*. Harvard University Press.

Comaroff, J., & Comaroff, J. (1993). *Modernity and its Malcontents, Ritual and Power in post-Colonial Africa*. University of Chicago Press.

Ding Hong. (2005). A Comparative Study in the Cultures of Dungan and the Hui people. *Asian Ethnicity, 6*(2), 135–140.

Ding Hong. (2014). La localizzazione dell'Islam. Una prospettiva antropologica. In R. Malighetti (Ed.), *Antropologie dalla Cina* (pp. 103–127). Seid Editore.

Ding Hong, & Min Junqing. (2012). 伊斯兰教与中国穆斯林社会现代化进程 (The Modernization of Islam and China's Muslim Society). 北京》中央民族大学出版社.

Ding Hong, Li Rudong, Hao Shiyuan. (2015). 国家社科基 大项 目"少数民族海外华人研究"开 实录 (An Introduction to the National Social Science Foundation's Major Project "Study on Ethnic Minority Overseas Chinese). 广西民族大学学报(哲学社会科学版), 6, 47–58.

Dumont, L. (1983). *Essais sur l'individualisme: Une Perspective anthropologique sur l'idéologie moderne*. Seuil.

Fabian, J. (1983). *Time and the Other, How Anthropology Makes its Object*. Columbia University Press.

Fei Xiaotong. (1939). *Peasant Life in China: A Field Study of Country Life in the Yangtze Valley*. Routledge & Kegan Paul.

Fei Xiaotong. (1981). *Towards a People's Anthropology*. New World Press.

Fei Xiaotong. (1989). *Zhonghua Minzu Duoyuan Yiti (The Plurality and Organic Unity of the Zhongghua Minzu)*. Zhonggua Renmin Xueyuan Chubanshe.

Fei Xiaotong. (1988a). Plurality and Unity in the Configuration of the Chinese People. *The Tanner Lectures on Human Values*. Hong Kong: The University of Hong Kong.

Fei Xiaotong. (1988b). The Formation and Development of the Chinese Nation with Multi-ethnic groups. *International Journal of Anthropology and Ethnology, 2017, 1*(1), 1–31.

Fei Xiaotong. (1997). A Brief Introduction of My Experience and Thinking on Ethnic Studies. *Journal of Beijing University, 2*, 5.

Fei Xiaotong. (2000). New challenges facing Chinese anthropology in the 21st century. *Journal of Guangxi University for Nationalities: Philosophy and Social Sciences, 5*, 1–37.

20 CHINESE PERSPECTIVES ON ANTHROPOLOGY AND ETHNOLOGY   **611**

Fei Xiaotong. (2004). 论人类学与文化自觉 (On Anthropology and Cultural Consciousness). 北京: 华夏 出版社.

Fei Xiaotong. (2017). The Formation and Development of the Chinese Nation with Multi-ethnic Groups. *International Journal of Anthropology and Ethnology, 1*(1), 1–31.

Fei Xiaotong, & Lin Yaohua. (1956). *A Few Tasks in Ethnography Posed by Current Ethnic Work. People's Daily. Collected Papers on China Ethnic Studies*, 6.

Feyerabend, P. (1975). *Against Method*. New Left Books.

Freedman, M. (1963). A Chinese phase in social anthropology. *The British Journal of Sociology, 14*(1), 1–19.

Gao Chong, & Zou Qiong. (1999). 从本土走向全球的中国人类学 (Chinese Anthropology from Native to Global). 广西民族大学学报.

Gong Shiyao, & Chen Gang. (2019). 他山之石或可攻玉. 当影视人类学遇见新媒体 (Visual anthropology and new media) 广西民族研.

Gu Dingguo. (2000). *Unofficial History of Chinese Anthropology*. Social Sciences.

Gu Jiegang (1937). The Solidarity of the Chinese Nation. *Shen Daily*, 7-11.

Guo Yaogen (1921). 人类进化之研究 (The Study of Human Evolution), 商务印书馆.

Haberland, M. (1898). *Volkerkunde*, («民种学». 北京: 京师大学堂官书局,1903)

Hannerz, U. (1992). *Cultural Complexity*. Columbia University Press.

He Ming. (2016). 全球化及其人类学论题 (Globalization and its anthropological issues), 思想战线.

He Guoqiang, & Tang Kaixun. (2005). 析中国民族学北派和南派的学术倾向.以吴文藻、杨成志为例 (On the Academic Tendency of the Northern and Southern Chinese Ethnology. Taking Wu Wenzao and Yang Chengzhi as Examples). 思想战线, 5, 132–140.

He Wenping. (2010). China's aid to Africa: Development feature, functions and challenges. *West Asian and Africa, 7*(1), 12–19.

Hu Hongbao. (2006). 中国人类学史 (*History of Chinese Anthropology*). Beijing.

Huang Jin, & Liu Chuming. (2010). 届中国人类学民族学学科 责人联席会综 (A Review of the First Joint Meeting of Heads of Chinese Anthropology and Ethnology in China). 广西民 族大学学报(哲学社会科学版).

Huxley, T. H. (1894). *Evolution and Ethics*. Macmillan & Co..

Ji Wen. (1985). "中山大学人类学学术会纪略" (History of the Anthropology Symposium of Sun Yat-sen University). *民族研究. Ethno-national Studies, 3*, 3–64.

Ji Zhe (2016). *Temporalité religieuse et temporalité moderne. Une sociologie du bouddhisme Chan contemporain.* .

Ji Zhe, & Liang Yongjia. (2018). Introduction. Toward a New Chinese Anthropology. *Cargo, Revue Internationale de Anthropologie Culturelle & Sociale (The New Chinese Anthropology), 8*, 7–16.

Jiang Ting, & Zhang Chaozhi. (2019). "世俗与神圣的交集: 禅修旅游体验的核" ("The intersection of the mundane and the sacred: the meditation travel experience »). 旅游论坛, vol. 12, no. 2: 14-19.

Jing Jun. (2000). *Feeding China's Little Emperors: Food, Children, and Social Change*. Stanford University Press.

Krotkov, N. N. (1912). Kratkie zametki o sovremennom sostoianii shamanstva u sibo, zhivushchikh v iliiskoi oblasti I Tarbagatae. *Zapiski vostochnogo otdelniia imp. Russkogo arkheologicheskogo obshchestva, 21*, 2–3.

Lai Lili. (2004). The Local Intimacies of China's Rural-Urban Divide. *Positions: Asia Critique, 22*(3), 543–550.

Lai Lili. (2016). 中医科学化的人类学考察 (*An Anthropological Investigation of the Scientificization of Traditional Chinese Medicine*). 中国人类学评论.

Li Anshan. (2011). *Chinese Medical Cooperation in Africa*. Nordiska Afirikainstitutet.

Li Xingxing. (2008). "李星星论藏彝走廊" (on Tibetan Corridor). 北京:民族出版.

Li Yiyuan. (2003). Environment, ethnic groups and culture. *Journal of Guangxi University for Nationalities, 2*, 77–89.

Li Zhang. 2004a. "Intersecting Space, Class, and Consumption: A Cultural Inquiry of the Middle-Class Making in Reform China". Paper presented at the Annual Meeting of the Association for Asian Studies, San Diego, March 2004.

Li Zhang. (2004b). Forced from Home: Property Rights, Civic Activism, and the Politics of Relocation in China. *Urban Anthropology, 33*(2–4), 247–281.

Liang Yongjia. (2018). *Religious and Ethnic Revival a Chinese Minority: The Bai people of Southwest China*. Routledge.

Lin Yaohua. (1948). *The Golden Wing: A Sociological Study of Chinese Familism*. Kegan Paul.

Liu Mingxin. (2014). L'antropologia cinese tra passato, presente e futuro. In R. Malighetti (Ed.), *Antropologie dalla Cina* (pp. 25–37). Seid.

Liu Shipei. (1903). 中国民族志(*Chinese Ethnography*). 中国青年会.

Liu Xin. (2000). *In One's Own Shadow: An Ethnographic Account of the Condition of Post-reform Rural China*. University of California Press.

Liu Xin. (2002). Urban Anthropology and the 'Urban Question' in China. *Critique of Anthropology, 22*(2), 109–132.

Liu Xin. (2004). *New Reflections on Anthropological Studies of (greater) China*. China Research Monograph Series, the Institute of East Asian Studies. University of California Press.

Liu Xin. (2010). China's oversea studies. *Open Times, 1*(1), 5–65.

Ma Changshou. (1947). Anthropology in border governance of China. *Public Opinions on Border Governance, 3*, 7–21.

20 CHINESE PERSPECTIVES ON ANTHROPOLOGY AND ETHNOLOGY 613

Ma Guoqing. (2017). 记忆的多层性 与 中华民族共同体认同 ("The multi-layered nature of memory and the identity of the Chinese nation"). 民族研究, 玻璃 vol. 6: 47-57.

Ma Guoqing. (2020a). 费孝 民族研究理 与" 合之又合" 的 中华民族共同性 ("Cohesion and integration. The Commonality of Chinese Nation and Fei Xiaotong's Ethnic Researches"). 中央民族大学学报 哲学社会科学版, vol. 4 no. 4: 13-23.

Ma Guoqing. (2020b). 社会与人民: 中国人类学的学术 格 ("Society and People: The Academic Style of Chinese Anthropology"). *China Academic Journal Electronic Publishing House*: 174-245

Ma Laurence, & Wu Fulong. (2005). *Restructuring the Chinese City: Changing Society, Economy, and Space*. Routledge.

Ma Rong. (2004). A New Perspective to Examine Ethnic Relations: Depoliticization of Ethnic Minority Issues. *Journal of Peking University: Philosophy and Social Science, 6*, 122–133.

Ma Rong. (2017). Reconstructing 'nation' (minzu) Discourses in China. *International Journal of Anthropology and Ethnology, 1*(1), 60–74.

Malighetti, R. (2014). *Antropologie dalla Cina*. Seid.

Malighetti, R. (马力罗), (2018). 民族学与人类学方法 研究 (Research Methods in Ethnology and Anthropology). 北京: 知 产权出版社。

Malighetti, R. (2021a). *Antropologia Applicata. Problemi e prospettive*. Scholè, Morcelliana.

Malighetti, R. (2021b). *Anthropology and Ethnography. Science, Method, Writing*. Brescia: Scholè, Morcelliana (ebook).

Malighetti, R., & Wang, M. (2014). Dal punto di vista cinese. Dialogo sulle antropologie. *Etnoantropologia, 2*(2), 11–25.

Malighetti, R., & Yang Shengmin. (2017). The Contributions of Chinese Anthropology. *ANUAC, 6*(1), 15–28.

Malinowski, B. (1939). Introduction. In F. Xiaotong (Ed.), *Peasant Life in China: A Field Study of Country Life in the Yangtze Valley* (pp. 5–21). Routledge.

Manganaro, M. (1990). *Modernist Anthropology*. Princeton.

Mei Fangquan. (2002). 21世纪 市可持续发展暨中国人类学百年国际学术研 会 在我校召 开(*International Symposium on the International Conference on Sustainable Urban Development in the 21st Century and Commemoration of the Centenary of Chinese Anthropology*). 中山大学学报(社会 科学版.

Morgan, L. H. (1877). *Ancient Society*. Charles H. Kerr & Co..

National Bureau of Statistics of PRC, 2013, 北京: 人口普查公报。

Niu Zhongguang. (2016). China's Development and Its Aid Presence in Africa: A Critical Reflection from the Perspective of Development Anthropology. *African and Asian Studies, 2016, 51*(2), 199–221.

Pan Tianshu. (2005). Historical Memory, Community-Building and Place-Making in Neighborhood Shanghai. In M. Laurence & W. Fulong (Eds.), *Restructuring the Chinese City: Changing Society, Economy, and Space* (pp. 122–137). Routledge.

Pan Tianshu. (2019). 全球化和地方转型时代的都市商业人类学. 田野凝视焦点的变移和学科想象 ("Anthropology of Urban Business in the Era of Globalization and Local Transformation. Shifting Perspectives and Disciplinary Imagination"). 华东师范大学(哲学社会科学版, vol 51, no. 2: 103-109.

Ping Song. (2017). Anthropology in China today. *Asian Anthropology, 16*(3), 228–241.

Pozdneev, A. M. (1896-1898). *Mongolia and the Mongols. Results of the trip to Mongolia in 1892-1893.* Imperial Academy of Sciences, St. Petersburg.

Pun Ngai. (2003). Subsumption or Consumption? The Phantom Consumer Revolution in Globalizing' China. *Cultural Anthropology, 18*(4), 469–492.

Qiao Jian. (2008). Tentative Analysis of Historical Functionalism of Fei Xiaotong. In S. Yang (Ed.), *Selected Works on Chinese Anthropology and Ethnology in the Century* (pp. 37–71). Intellectual Property Publishing House.

Ren Hai. (2013). *The Middle Class in Neoliberal China: Governing Risk, Life-Building, and Themed Spaces.* Routledge.

Rosaldo, R. (1989). *Culture and Truth.* Beacon Press.

Ryuzo Torii. (1903). 人种志 *(Ethnography).* 闽学会印.

Shi Jin. (1964). Question Ethnology: Talking with Yang Kun. *Academic Research, 2,* 3–47.

Shi Lin. (2021). 非洲民族研究的"中国视角 (*A Chinese Perspective in African Ethnic Studies*).世界民族. Vol. 1:115-126.

Shirokogoroff, S. M. (1924). *Ethnic Unit and Milieu.* Esdward Evans Sons LTD..

Song Shuhua. (2004). *Five Decades of Chinese ethnology.* People's Publishing House.

Spencer, H. (1872). *The Principles of Sociology.* Williams and Norgate.

Sun Xuewu. (1916). 人類學之槪略 ("An Introduction to Anthropology"). 科学杂志, vol. 4:429-435.

Sun Yat-Sen (Sun Zhongshan). (1921). *Complete Works of Sun Zhongshan.*北京: 民出版社.

Wang Chao. (2013). *跨国民族文化适应与传承研究:以中亚东干人为例 (Research on the cultural adaptation and inheritance of transnational ethnic groups: A case study of Donggan people in Central Asia)* 北京:中国社会科学出版社.

Wang Linzhu. (2015). The Identification of Minorities in China. *Asian-Pacific Law & Policy Journal, 16*(2), 1–21.

Wang Mingming. (2008). 中间圈:"藏彝走廊"与人类学的再构思 (*The intermediaries: "Tibetan-Yi corridor" and the reformation of anthropology*).北京: 社会科学文献出版.

20 CHINESE PERSPECTIVES ON ANTHROPOLOGY AND ETHNOLOGY 615

Wang Mingming. (2012). All Under Heaven (tianxia). Cosmological Perspectives and Political Ontologies in Pre-modern China. *Journal of Ethnographic Theory*, *2*(1), 337–383.

Wang Mingming. (2014). Nuove vie per la storia dell'antropologia moderna. In R. Malighetti (Ed.), *Antropologie dalla Cina* (pp. 13–30). Seid.

Wang Mingming. (2018). Afterwords: A View from a Relationist Standpoint. *Cargo, Revue Internationale de Anthropologie Culturelle & Sociale (The New Chinese Anthropology)*, 8, 149–166.

Wang Shuling. (1993). 中国 市人类学会第一届全国学术会综 (*Summary of the First National Symposium of the Chinese Urban Anthropology Association*). 民族研究, 5 (5), 102–106.

Wang Shunan. (1902). 欧洲族类源流略 (*A Brief Summary of the Origin of the European Ethnic Groups*). 中卫县署刊印.

Wang Yanzhong. (2014). Lo sviluppo socioeconomico delle aree etniche. In R. Malighetti (Ed.), *Antropologie dalla Cina* (pp. 41–66). Seid Editore.

Wu Wenzao. (1926a). "民族与国家" (Nation and State). In吴文藻社会学人类学研究文集 (*Sociological and Anthropological Writings by Wu Wenzao*), 19-36. 北京, 民族出版社.

Wu Wenzao. (1926b). 留美学生季报 (Quarterly Report of Students Studying in America), 11 (3), 19-36.

Wu Wenzao. (1942). Introduction to Border Politics. *Public Opinions on Border Governance, 1*, 5–6.

Wu Wenzao. (1990). 吴文藻人类学社会学研究文集 (Wu Wenzao on Anthropology and Sociology). 北京: 民族出版社.

Xiang Biao. (2002). "跨越边界的社区-北京"浙江村"的生活史" (Communities Across Boundaries. The Life History of the "Zhejiang Village, Beijing*)*. 北京: 新知联书瓜.

Xie Lizhong. (2014). *De-politicization of Ethnic Questions in China*. World Scientific Publishing Co..

Xiongzhi Wang, & Chaozhi Zhang. (2020). Contingent Effects of Social Norms on Tourists' Pro-Environmental Behaviors: The Role of Chinese Traditionality. *Journal of Sustainable Tourism, 281*(10), 1646–1664.

Xu Xinjian, Wang Mingming, & Zhou Daming. (2008). 人类学的中国话语 (The Chinese Discourse of Anthropology). *第六届人类学高级论坛圆桌会议纪实 (*Records of the Roundtable Conference of the Sixth Advanced Forum on Anthropology*), 广西民族大学学报30 (2), 86-93.

Yang Qingmei. (2017). 车里摆夷之生命环 陶云奎历史人类学文选 (Selected Works of Tao Yunkui's Historical Anthropology). 生活.读书.新知三联书店.

Yang Shengmin (2003a). Ethnic Relations in Chinese History. In Yang Shengmin (Ed.), *Chinese Ethnography*. : Minzu University Press 12-33.

Yang Shengmin. (2003b). Characteristics of social Organization in Arid Environment. *Environment, Development and Culture in Asia-Pacific Societies, 6,* 120–129.

Yang Shengmin. (2014). La via dell'etnologia cinese. Tra passato e contemporaneità. In R. Malighetti (Ed.), *Antropologie dalla Cina* (pp. 39–57). Seid Editore.

Yang Shengmin. (2017). A Review of Chinese Ethnology in the Past Hundred Years and Its Summary in the New Era. *International Journal of Anthropology and Ethnology, 1*(1), 32–59.

Ye Jinhzhong. (2011). Development as a Western Discourse: Preface of the Chinese Version of Encountering Development. *Journal of China Agricultural University, 28*(2), 10–11.

Yu Bromley. (1974). *Soviet Ethnology and Anthropology Today.* Mouton.

Yu Dan Smyer. (2020). A Sino-Tibetan Buddhist Modernism: Religious Marketplace, Constellative Networking, and Urbanism. In T. Brox & E. Oerberg (Eds.), *Buddhism and Business: Merit, Material Wealth and Morality in the Global Market Economy* (pp. 40–58). University of Hawai'i Press.

Zhang Chaozhi, Zhou Xiaofeng, & Song Xiaofei. (2018). 我国世界文化遗产旅游发展现状分析报告 (Report on the current situation of the development of my country's world cultural heritage tourism). 中国文化遗产, 6, 35-39.

Zhang Chaozhi, & Zhou Minmin. (2020). 民宿业背景下乡村绅士化的特征与驱动机制:莫干山镇案例研究 (The characteristics and driving mechanism of rural gentrification in the context of homestay industry. A case study: Moganshan Town). 旅游论坛, 13 (2), 33-45.

Zhang Jijiao, & Wu, Yue. (2021). Seventy Years of Chinese Anthropology. *International Journal of Anthropology and Ethnology, 5*(7), 1. https://doi.org/10.1186/s41257-021-00048-3.

Zhang Shichao. (2018). 媒介化 与新媒体语境下少数民族传播研究 (Research on communication among ethnic minorities and new media). 文化产业, 15, 38-40.

Zhang Shuyun. (1990). 第一届 市人类学国际会 在北京召开 (The First International Conference on Urban Anthropology Held in Beijing), 北京: 城市问题。

Zhao Chunming, Ma Long, & Xiong Zhenqin. (2021). 中国对非洲国家直接投资的影响效应研究 (A study on the impact of China's direct investment in African countries). 亚太经济, 2, 73-95.

Zhao Suisheng. (2014). A Neo-colonialist Predator or Development Partner? China's Engagement and Rebalance in Africa. *Journal of Contemporary China, 23*(90), 1033–1052.

Zhao Yongjun. (2013). China-Africa Development Cooperation in the Rural Sector. *Environment, Development and Sustainability, 15*(2), 355–366.

Zheng Tiantian. (2004). From Peasant Women to Bar Hostesses: Gender and Modernity in Post-Mao Dalian. In A. M. G. Tamara Jacka (Ed.), *On the Move:*

Women in Rural-to-Urban Migration in Contemporary China (pp. 80–108). Columbia University Press.

Zhou Daming. (2005). 渴望 生存 中国农名工.流动的人类学研究 (To survive: an anthropological study of rural labour migrant mobility). 广州. 中山大学出版社.

Zhou Daming. (2012). 怀念梁 先生 ("Reflections on the Orientation of Anthropology"). 广西民族 大学学报(哲学社会科学版), 1, 79-83.

Zhou Xing. (1995). 社会 文化人类学 级研 班 得初步成功 (The Initial Success of the Advanced Seminar on Social and Cultural Anthropology of Peking University). 民俗研 究, 3 (3), 103-104.

Zhou Yongming. (2005). Living in the Cyber Border: 'Minjian' Online Writers in China. *Current Anthropology, 46*(5), 779–804.

Zhu Tan. (2010). Reflections on Researches on China's "development" and "development intervention". *Sociological Studies, 4*(1), 175–197.

Zhu Xing. (2004). New Strategy of Poverty Alleviation: From "impossible mission" to Managing the Poor. *Sociological Studies, 2*(1), 98–102.

CHAPTER 21

The Birth and Development of Anthropology in Arab Countries: A still Controversial and Marginalised Knowledge?

Irene Maffi

The fact that colonial governments made use of Anthropology does not mean that Anthropology was constituted perforce to serve colonialism.
This fact should not detract from Anthropology, just as the atomic explosion in Hiroshima should not detract from Nuclear Physics.
(Abou Zeid, 1997, *Alif: Journal of Comparative Poetics, 17,* pp. 260–261)

I. Maffi (✉)
University of Lausanne, Lausanne, Switzerland
e-mail: irene.maffi@unil.ch

© The Author(s), under exclusive license to Springer Nature
Switzerland AG 2023
G. D'Agostino, V. Matera (eds.), *Histories of Anthropology,*
https://doi.org/10.1007/978-3-031-21258-1_21

619

620   I. MAFFI

INTRODUCTION

This chapter is the result of a synthesis of the existing written sources[1] on the historical itinerary of anthropology in Arab countries[2] in the postcolonial period, practised by researchers from that region and based in local institutions. For some countries, such as Egypt or Algeria, there are sources through which it is possible to reconstruct the history of anthropology in local research institutions. For many other countries, however, no written sources exist—or at least, none are available except by physically going to their university libraries. To address these gaps and silences, I turned to colleagues who work or have worked in those countries as researchers and teachers, and conducted a series of interviews.[3] Much of the literature consulted does not relate directly to anthropology, but more broadly to the social sciences in the Arab world. Compared to sociology, political science, economics or social psychology, anthropological knowledge still occupies a marginal place in academic institutions—when it is

[1] Unfortunately, I was unable to consult any Arabic sources published locally and inaccessible to Europe.

[2] The terms "Arab countries" or "the Arab world" should be used with caution in light of the historical specificities of the various units that make up this region of the world. However, in addition to constituting a common linguistic area (despite differences in local dialects), most of the countries of the Arab world were under the aegis of the Ottoman Empire for several centuries (1516–1918). Many of them therefore shared a common political and administrative centre and were exposed to the religious and cultural repertoires that circulated within the empire. More recently, the creation of the Arab League (1945), ALECSO—its branch dedicated to education, culture and science—and especially the circulation of ideas, cultural products and common religious repertoires—thanks to new technologies and the media—have all helped reinforce the existence of a common Arab-speaking area. The policies of the Arabisation of education in the last third of the twentieth century in many countries that still used European languages, as well as numerous wars, have also caused a wide circulation of people within the Arab world: teachers, researchers, professionals and refugees. For all these reasons, although the term *Arab world* does not allow us to account for the differences that characterise the countries within it, it seems to me that it has historical, linguistic and cultural relevance.

[3] The generosity of many colleagues has been crucial to the writing of this chapter. I would like to thank (in alphabetical order): Abdallah Alajmi, Laure Assaf, Sebastien Boulay, Abaher al-Sakka, Marion Breteau, Pellegrino Luciano, Frank Mermier and Maho Sebiane. My thanks also to Anna Baldinetti, Hassen Boubakri, Marion Breteau, Abdel Wedoud Ould Cheikh, Federico Cresti, Linda Herrera, Abdelhakim al-Husban, Sulayman Khalaf, Imed Melliti, Antonio Morone, Betty Rouland, Neïla Saadi, Zina Sawaf and Valentina Zagaria.

21 THE BIRTH AND DEVELOPMENT OF ANTHROPOLOGY IN ARAB... 621

not completely absent.[4] The few reviews of anthropological literature in the Arab world are written in English and include only works in this language, leaving aside not only works written in other European languages but also those written in Arabic (Abu Lughod, 1989; Deeb & Winegar, 2012). Whereas production in Arabic is limited for now and consists in many cases of university manuals for student use (al-Zuabi, 2019; Hanafi, 2011; Hanafi & Arvanitis, 2014; Roussillon, 2002; Shami, 1989), Anglo-Saxon anthropologists' lack of consideration for French-language ethnological literature seems problematic. Indeed, one must consider not only the rich historical corpus of works in French (e.g., Berque, 1956; Rachik, 2012), but also the lively and prolific scholarly activity that French research centres based in Arab countries nurture mostly in this language (Hanafi, 2010). Two recent works written by researchers based in the region that take stock of anthropological production in Arabic should be noted because they are an exception. The first is the review of anthropological literature produced in Arab countries by Ali al-Zuabi (2019), a Kuwaiti researcher. This is an interesting attempt by an academic from the region to review anthropological works in Arabic, although the scholarly quality of the article is mediocre. The second is the 2012 book *Al-antropolojia fi al-watan al-'arabi* (*Anthropology in the Arab World*), written jointly by a Moroccan anthropologist, Hassan Rachik, and a Saudi anthropologist, Abu Baker Bagader. The book is an unprecedented attempt by two academics from two areas of the Arab world—that do not usually collaborate—to produce a history of anthropology in the region that includes many researchers from this area who also or only write in Arabic. Although the book focuses mainly on Saudi Arabia and Morocco, it is a work that bears witness to an interesting attempt at synthesis.

It is important to point out that the studies written by Arab anthropologists working in the region are mainly in English and French rather than Arabic. Arabic itself remains marginal for various reasons related to the history of educational policies and academic institutions in each country, the need to join international networks, and the influence of the NGOs and international institutions that fund a large part of social science research in the region (Currie-Alder et al., 2018; Hanafi, 2011; Hanafi &

---

[4] For example, the volume coordinated by Eberhardt Kienle (2010) on the itinerary of social sciences in Arab countries, *Les sciences sociales en voyage. L'Afrique du Nord et le Moyen-Orient vus d'Europe, d'Amérique et de l'intérieur*, includes four sections on history, sociology, political science and economics, but none on anthropology.

Arvanitis, 2016). In fact, the contemporary Arab world can be divided into three different areas in terms of the organisation of academic institutions, the links maintained with the Global North and the languages used in teaching and scholarly publication (Arvanitis et al., 2010; el-Kenz, 2008; Hanafi, 2011).[5] North Africa is characterised by public universities and state research centres that are inspired by European models, particularly the French model. The state is the main actor on the academic scene and the funder of research. The Near East, on the other hand, is characterised by the existence of a private university system modelled on the Anglo-Saxon one;[6] there are few public universities, and they often lack sufficient funding to become centres of scientific excellence (Arvanitis et al., 2010). In Lebanon, for example, the famous American University of Beirut produces half of the country's internationally visible scientific publications (Hanafi, 2010). Especially since the 1990s, there has been a proliferation of private research centres producing commissioned reports on topics that are often imposed by the international agencies that fund them and are not necessarily related to the interests of local researchers (Bamyeh, 2015; Hanafi, 2010). The states of the Arabian Peninsula established their first public universities after independence in the 1960s and are now experiencing the explosion of a vast number of private universities inspired by the North American model. After Arabising higher education by mobilising mainly teachers and researchers from the Mashrek and North Africa, the states of the Arabian Peninsula have changed course by Westernising secondary and university education since the 2000s. This development has been stimulated by the international policies of the so-called knowledge economy (Cantini, 2019; Eickelman & Mustafa Abusharaf, 2017). English has become the dominant language in high schools and private universities created over the past two decades, which are often branches of North American universities.

In the remainder of this chapter, I intend to first highlight some general characteristics of anthropology in Arab countries and then briefly examine the situation of the discipline in those countries for which I have been able to gather documentation.

---

[5] French is still the main language in which many social science researchers in North Africa publish, whereas English is dominant in the Near East and the Arabian Peninsula.

[6] Seventy per cent of universities in the Arab world were founded after 1991 (Bamyeh, 2015).

The Weakness of Anthropology in the Arab World

Social sciences in the Arab world are considered to be of mediocre quality (Abdul-Jabar, 2014; Lamine, 2009; Shami, 1989). Their weakness is attributed to structural problems in academic institutions; a lack of public funding; censorship imposed by many authoritarian states; the absence of a scientific community, resulting in limited exchanges between researchers within and among countries and a lack of dialogue with civil society (Arvanitis et al., 2010; Hanafi, 2010; Hopkins, 2014; Shami, 1989). Arab societies' disconnection from their past, the absence of pan-Arab scientific associations and the lack of policies to support the development of social sciences are other factors that explain their marginality in the Arab world (Shami, 2017). Moreover, since the 1980s, the Arabisation and Islamisation of social sciences, the former linked to the contestation of the colonial legacy and relations of political and economic dependence (Morsy et al., 1991), the latter to the "Petro Islam" policies (Abaza, 2000) promoted by Saudi Arabia, have contributed to disconnecting the social sciences in Arab nations from the knowledge produced in the countries in the Global North (Abaza, 2000; Shami, 1989). However, the "radical perspective" on Euro-American knowledge adopted by some Arab intellectuals (Morsy et al., 1991, p. 84) has nurtured a critical understanding of Western social sciences and their application to the Arab world that is still relevant today. Abdelkebir Khatibi's (1975) critique of colonial sociology sums up this perspective well:

> The essential task of the sociology of the Arab world consists in doing a double critical work: (a) a deconstruction of the concepts coming from the sociological knowledge and discourses that have spoken in the place of the Arab world and that are marked by Western dominance and an ethnocentric ideology; (b) and at the same time a critique of the knowledge and discourses elaborated by the different Arab societies for themselves. (As cited in Roussillon, 2002, p. 209)

Although radical intellectuals have not rejected dialogue with the social sciences of colonial origin, the Islamisation and the "neo-traditionalist perspective" (Morsy et al., 1991, p. 84) of the social sciences have produced an impoverishment—an emptying and a "communatarisation" of the work of Arab and Muslim researchers who have joined this movement (Melliti, 2006; Roussillon, 2002). In a few countries, anthropology has been taught at university and practised in the field, often by student groups trained by resident Western anthropologists or local researchers trained in Europe or the United States. For example, Sudan (Ahmed, 2003), Egypt (Fahim, 1977; Hopkins, 2014), Morocco (Roussillon, 2002) and Tunisia (Mahfoudh & Melliti, 2009) have had such programmes. Apart from these, the discipline has little presence in Arab universities (Bamyeh, 2015; Shami & Herrera, 1999).[7] In some countries (Libya, Syria, Mauritania and Yemen), anthropology has never been present in academic institutions born after independence, or it has only recently become present (Tunisia, Arabian Gulf countries). An episode recounted by Seteney Shami, a pioneer of cultural anthropology in Jordan, reveals the discipline's marginal status in the Arab world. Shami (1989) explained that when the anthropology department was created at Yarmouk University in 1984, they decided to send questionnaires to all Arab universities to get information on anthropology teaching, propose student exchanges and organise joint workshops. Only the American University in Cairo, one of the oldest and most prestigious foreign universities in the region, responded (Shami, 1989). At the end of the 1980s (and still today), anthropology departments and specific courses of study in anthropology were rare in the Arab world; anthropology is often taught in social science or sociology departments, where other disciplines dominate. With few exceptions, it is not possible to continue anthropology studies at the Master's or doctoral level, although there are some Bachelor's degrees with an anthropological orientation. In general, economics, social psychology, political science, sociology, history and geography all enjoy greater legitimacy in universities in the Arab world. The figure of the professional researcher in anthropology or the social sciences has only recently, and with difficulty, been considered legitimate, and is mainly linked to private research centres that produce commissioned reports for international agencies. However, these centres do not allow the accumulation of knowledge nor the training of young researchers, let alone nurture academic publications and the development of critical knowledge (Hanafi, 2010). With few exceptions, outside private universities, existing anthropology courses are usually in Arabic and oriented towards a theoretical approach that does not allow students to apply knowledge to field research (Shami, 1989). Although this was

---

[7] As Bamyeh (2015) pointed out, "A look into the disciplinary composition of social sciences in Arab universities reveals that economics is the frontrunner, comprising 26% of social science faculties, while anthropology does not exceed 2% of these faculties" (p. 20).

true in the late 1980s, the review of literature by al-Zuabi (2019) and Bagader and Rachik's (2012) handbook seems to confirm this trend even at the beginning of the twenty-first century. Monographic studies in Arabic are rare, as are translations of works written in other languages (Ben Salem, 2009; Hanafi & Arvanitis, 2014; Salhi, 2002). This makes anthropology a purely theoretical discipline in the eyes of students in many Arab universities (Shami, 1989).[8] Prior to the Arabisation of education, which took place in many Arab countries in the 1970s and 1980s, most students of anthropology or other social sciences were able to read and write in at least one European language, allowing them to access a large body of texts and publish their work in Euro-American journals or books. The disconnection from the international anthropological landscape, which is still largely dominated by the countries in the Global North, has resulted in the provincialisation of anthropology written in Arabic. This reinforces its peripheral nature, to which the lack of an academic community in this discipline within the Arab world contributes (el-Kenz, 2008).[9] Although this view is shared by many observers, Colonna (2010) pointed out that the Arabisation of social sciences in Algeria has also produced positive effects, as the new generation of researchers trained in Arabic has been able to "conceive new research themes from Arabic or Berber sources ... which their previous 'academic Francophonie' did not allow them to access" (p. 105).

The rejection or marginalisation of anthropology after independence, especially in North Africa, is due to the discipline's links with the colonial enterprise (Ahmed, 2003; Boëtsch & Ferrié, 1998; el-Kenz, 2005; Lucas & Vatin, 1982; Mahfoudh & Melliti, 2009; Rachik, 2012). This situation has produced an effect highlighted by Melliti (2006) for Tunisia (but also present in other countries). Melliti (2006) pointed out that in his country,

> Most anthropologists cannot fully claim to belong to the discipline, because they are used to circulating on the margins, on the border between disciplines such as history and anthropology, or sociology and anthropology. Their work is the result of an obligatory interdisciplinarity. (p. 176)

[8] A few exceptions are mentioned below in the sections discussing specific countries.

[9] For example, according to a report by the French Insitut de Recherche sur le Développement, scientific cooperation between North African countries "does not exceed 3%" of relations between them (cited in el-Kenz, 2008, p. 53). The absence of inter-Arab or even national academic associations or their low activity is also denounced by Bamyeh in his report on the state of social sciences in the Arab world (2015).

A different fate befell sociology, which could be more easily adopted in Arab countries; it was not directly compromised by colonial administrations as a knowledge long confined to the study of "civilised societies." Although it is a science elaborated by former colonisers (Ben Salem, 2009; Madoui, 2015), its link with European societies—which symbolised modernity—meant that sociology was put at the service of the development policies that many Arab states adopted in the first decades after independence (1950–1980). Algeria, Tunisia, Morocco and Egypt, for instance, created research centres including disciplines such as sociology, economics, demography and geography; or employed researchers in social sciences in their state administrations to promote social, economic and technological transformations (urbanisation, industrialisation, mass schooling, changes in family structures, etc.) and solve associated problems. To cite just a few cases, we can mention the National Centre for Social and Criminological Research (1956) in Egypt, which was designed specifically to study "social destructuring and cultural underdevelopment" (Roussillon, 2002, p. 213). In Tunisia, the National Office for Family and Population was formed in 1973. Over several decades, it has funded research in the fields of demography and sociology linked to birth limitation policies (Maffi, 2020).

To conclude the first part of the chapter, I feel it is important to point out that many anthropologists from Arab countries occupy important positions in the Euro-American academic world and have made major contributions to the development of the anthropology of Arab majority societies and beyond. These researchers have studied and made careers in the academic system of the Global North and have rarely returned to their countries of origin or their parents' countries to teach and train new generations of researchers. Or, they have returned but have taught in private English-language universities reserved for elites that appear to have minimal influence on anthropology in the countries where they are located (Shami, 1989). Such institutions, such as the American University in Cairo, the American University of Beirut, the Université Saint Joseph (also located in the Lebanese capital) or the more recent New York University and Université Sorbonne in Abu Dhabi, do not seem to participate in creating a national anthropological tradition, remaining rather connected to a Euro-American academic space. Thus, despite the importance of their work, such researchers from the Arab diaspora have not been considered in this chapter; I have decided to focus on the development of anthropology in Arab countries and the university institutions that shape the discipline locally.[10]

TEACHING AND PRACTICE OF ANTHROPOLOGY IN ARAB COUNTRIES

In light of these general considerations about anthropology in the Arab world, in the second part of the chapter, I briefly examine the situation of the discipline in the countries where it is taught and practised. The boundary between anthropology and sociology is not always clear-cut when looking at the research practices of scholars in different Arab countries. However, from an institutional point of view, sociology has been clearly distinguished from anthropology because of the latter's ties with European colonialism. My analysis is limited to examining the scientific production of those who claim affiliation with anthropology, leaving aside sociologists who use ethnography and are partly inspired by anthropological theories.

For the sake of convenience, my analysis is divided into three sections that correspond to the three geographical areas into which the sources I consulted divide the region on the basis of historical, institutional and linguistic characteristics. The first section is devoted to the countries in North Africa, the second to those in the Near East and the third to the countries in the Arabian Peninsula or the Gulf.

ANTHROPOLOGY IN NORTH AFRICA (THE MAGHREB)

With the exception of Libya, Morocco, Algeria, Tunisia and Mauritania were colonised by France and share the fact that they still have strong links with French academic institutions and still partly use the language of their former colonisers. The influence of the French anthropological and sociological tradition has been fundamental to constructing the discipline in each of these states, and intellectual exchanges with France continue to be intense. Many Maghrebi students take their doctoral studies in France or in a French-speaking country. Local researchers and teachers collaborate with French research centres and universities, write and read in French and Arabic, and contribute to the construction of French-speaking anthropology in the Arab world.

[10] The academic itinerary of Arab anthropologists of the diaspora could be the subject of another chapter.

628   I. MAFFI

Algeria

The occupation of Algeria,[11] the first North African country colonised by France in 1830, generated a large body of ethnographic and ethnological texts from the mid-nineteenth century onwards (Berque, 1956; Lucas & Vatin, 1982). A few years after the end of Algeria's war of liberation (1962), anthropology was condemned by its institutions as a colonial science. From 1971 on, the teaching of anthropology disappeared from Algerian universities (Salhi, 2008); and during the International Congress of Sociology held in Algiers in 1974, the Minister of Education peremptorily condemned ethnology as opposed to sociology, which was considered an ally of postindependence Algerian nationalism (Bourdieu et al., 2003). During the 1970s and 1980s, however, anthropology continued to be practised on the fringes of the academic world, particularly by researchers linked to the Centre national des recherches anthropologiques, préhistoriques et ethnologiques in Algiers under the leadership of Mouloud Mammeri (1991). The "thaw" towards the discipline began towards the end of the 1980s: in 1992, the Centre de recherche en anthropologie sociale et culturelle (CRASC) was founded at the University of Oran (Salhi, 2008). A few years earlier, departments of Amazigh language and culture had been created at the universities of Tizi Ouzou (in 1990) and Béjaïa (in 1991; see Assam, 2013). Despite the continuing controversy surrounding the reintroduction of anthropology in Algerian universities (Assam, 2013; Salhi, 2008), two Master's degree programmes in cultural and social anthropology were created in the universities of Constantine and Oran. Anthropology courses were also introduced at the Institut des cultures populaires in Tlemcen (created in 1981). The discipline thus seems to have found an academic space as knowledge linked to the preservation of heritage and popular traditions, particularly in the Berber-speaking world. The anthropological Master's theses of students studying the Berber language and culture are detailed village monographs written very often in the Amazigh language (Assam, 2013). At the same time, a decline in sociology has been linked to the nationalist ideology and development policies that had triumphed in previous decades (Akli, 2015; Chachoua, 2010). Interestingly, anthropology made its appearance in Algerian universities during the black decade of the civil war, at a time

---

[11] On the postcolonial development of anthropology in Algeria, see Benghabrit-Remaoun and Haddab (2008) and Marouf et al. (2002).

when social science researchers and journalists were often victims of attacks or forced to leave the country (Beaud, 1998; Chaulet, 2008).

Of a different orientation is CRASC (http://www.crasc.dz), a centre that brings together 69 permanent researchers and 309 associate researchers and that has been coordinating and guiding anthropological research in Algeria for several years. The CRASC, which comprises 4 research units (2 located in Oran, 1 in Constantine and 1 in Algiers), created a national PhD in anthropology in 2006 in which 6 universities participate, and has played a fundamental role in training researchers in anthropology for 15 years (Bengharbit-Remaoune & Haddab, 2008). The CRASC regularly organises conferences and seminars attended by researchers from other Maghreb countries and publishes one of the main regional journals in the social sciences: *Insaniyat* (https://journals.openedition.org/insaniyat). The journal aims to give visibility to research carried out in Algeria as well as to open a space for meetings with researchers from other countries (Soufi, 2008). CRASC also regularly publishes collective and monographic works on various historical, anthropological, linguistic and literary themes in French and Arabic. Today, CRASC plays a key role in the consolidation of anthropology in Algeria in light of the fact that in 2008, the discipline was considered "a field of study not yet established" (Salhi, 2008, p. 79) and that some researchers (Haddab, 2008) complained about the poor quality of locally published works. Finally, I would like to mention a few of the topics dealt with by *Insaniyat* journal over the last ten years: young people and everyday life, the family and social challenges, spaces and funeral rites, migration from the south, women in Arab countries, reforms in Algeria, health in Arab countries, graffiti in North Africa and the *Hirak* movement.

Tunisia

Anthropology in Tunisia in many ways shares the fate of the discipline in Algeria. It was born as a colonial science practised first by military officers, doctors and administrators (1881–1930), then by civil servants and a few university researchers (1930–1945) and finally by "indigénophiles" missionaries (1945–1959) (Mahfoudh, 1988–1989, p. 251). Characterised by stereotypes similar to those found in the ethnographic corpus produced in Algeria such as on the conflicts between Berbers and Arabs, nomads and sedentary, the works on Tunisia are imbued with colonial ideology. Therefore, it is not surprising that after independence, ethnology and

630   I. MAFFI

anthropology were excluded from the Institut des hautes études (ISST), the first academic institution created under the pressure of the Tunisian elite at the end of World War I. This institution depended on the Sorbonne, and the teachers were French (Ben Salem, 2009). The three disciplines in which it was possible to obtain certification in Tunis out of the four required were general sociology, social psychology, and political and social economy. Those who wanted to study ethnology had to go to Paris; the others could choose the human geography option offered locally (Ben Salem, 2009). Although there were figures such as Jacques Berque and Georges Balandier among the teachers and directors of the doctoral theses, anthropology did not become part of the teaching of the nascent Tunisian academy during the 1950s and 1960s. When the Centre d'études et de recherches économiques et sociales (CERES), which would play a central role in the development of the social sciences in Tunisia, was created in 1962 at the initiative of the Secretariat of National Education (Mahfoudh & Melliti, 2009; Melliti, 2014), anthropology would be "kicked out" because of its links to colonialism and would "take refuge in heritage" (Melliti, 2006, p. 173). CERES researchers adhered for several years to the ideology and development policies the independent Tunisian state promoted, and they dealt with ongoing social transformations with a Marxist and functionalist approach promoted in particular by Paul Sebag,[12] who at the time was teaching at ISST (Ben Salem, 2009; Mahfoudh & Melliti, 2009; Pouessel, 2013).

Anthropology often ended up being practised by historians or specialists in popular traditions who conceived of it as knowledge aimed purely at documenting archaic cultural forms or "traditional culture." Especially from the 1970s onwards, a movement aimed at the valorisation of local identity and the preservation of popular traditions presided over ethnological studies in Tunisia. These were relegated to the sphere of the institutions responsible for preserving cultural heritage, such as the Institut d'archéologie et d'arts and the Centre des arts et traditions populaires (Melliti, 2006, p. 174). The paradox is that the absence of anthropology

---

[12] It is interesting to note that in North Africa, after independence, despite the negative reactions of Maghrebi intellectuals to the social sciences the colonisers developed, French researchers critical of colonialism trained the first generations of local sociologists and anthropologists: Paul Pascon in Morocco, Pierre Bourdieu and Claudine Chaulet in Algeria, and Paul Sebag and Jean Duvignaud in Tunisia. Jacques Berque directed most of the doctoral theses of Maghrebi sociologists who completed their studies in the first years after independence (between the end of the 1950s and the 1960s).

from academic institutions meant that most historians working in the heritage institutions mentioned "were ignorant of all the ethnology that was to become their discipline" (Gargouri-Sethom, 1987, as cited in Melliti, 2006, p. 174). The rebirth of anthropology that was applied to less stale objects and with a critical approach took place thanks to a group of historians interested in minorities (the poor, Jewish people and Black people) of which Jocelyne Dakhlia was one of the first representatives. Later, an interest in popular religious traditions such as the cult of saints or Sufi brotherhoods developed. During the 1990s, studies on young people, nutrition, sexuality and the use of the veil contributed to recreating a relationship between the anthropology practised in Tunisia and "the experience around the objects of everyday life" (Pouessel, 2013, p. 2). However, during the years of Ben Ali's authoritarian regime, it was difficult for Tunisian researchers to deal with contemporary subjects without incurring the repression that a critical orientation could induce.

After the introduction of a course in historical anthropology at the Faculté des lettres, arts et humanités at the University of Manouba in Tunis, a Master's degree in anthropology was created at the Faculty of Law and Political Science at the University al-Manar in Tunis, but it was abolished shortly afterwards (Pouessel, 2013). In 2005, a Master's degree in social and cultural anthropology was created at the Institut supérieur des sciences humaines in Tunis, but it disappeared four years later. In 2007, the Tunisian Association of Cultural and Social Anthropology (ATASC) was created (https://www.facebook.com/Association-Tunisienne-dAnthropologie-Sociale-et-Culturelle-ATASC-758819427551235/), proving the existence of a group of researchers of various generations interested in the institutional recognition of the discipline. Only after the revolution of 2011 were the first attempts to institutionalise anthropology crowned with success through the creation of a 3-year degree at the Institut supérieur des sciences humaines in Tunis, coordinated by Sihem Najar and at the same time, the creation of the Institut d'anthropologie at the University of Sousse, thanks to the support of Pierre-Noël Denieuil, previously director of the French Institut de recherches sur le Maghreb contemporain (IRMC). Often, young researchers who completed their doctorates at universities in the Global North work alongside teachers from previous generations who, despite employing an anthropological approach, had not hitherto been able to declare their disciplinary affiliation openly. Two examples are Khaoula Matri, who completed her doctorate in 2014 at the Université Paris 5 in conjunction with the Université de

632   I. MAFFI

Tunis 1 with a thesis on the use of the veil and the representations and practices of the female body in Tunisia, and Ramzi Ben Amara, who completed a doctorate in 2011 at the University of Bayreuth with a thesis on the Izala Islamic movement active in Northern Nigeria.

The 2011 revolution and the democratisation of Tunisian society seem to have enabled a new departure even in the field of anthropology by offering it an institutional re-legitimisation.

Morocco

Anthropology and social sciences in Morocco share similar destinies to those of Algeria and Tunisia, although direct colonisation was shorter in Morocco than in the other two countries. At the time of independence, anthropology, "suspected of being a 'science' in the service of colonialism" (Madoui, 2015, p. 105), disappeared from the Moroccan academy under construction. During this period, sociology took on a fundamental role among young Moroccan researchers in the social sciences, a large proportion of whom trained with Paul Pascon, a French administrator and scholar who had taken a very critical stance on colonialism (Roussillon, 2002). The sociology that developed in the 1960s at the Institut de sociologie at the University of Rabat made a fundamental contribution to the institutionalisation of the social sciences in Morocco, a country where the colonisers had not created any academic institutions (Rachik & Bourquia, 2011; Roussillon, 2002). Critical, committed and Marxist-inspired, early Moroccan sociology would be condemned by the monarchy in 1970 and would remain in universities as marginal knowledge until the late 1990s (Madoui, 2015). Its marginalisation coincides with the opening of a space for anthropology, which came about as Moroccan sociologists' response to the dialogue initiated by Anglo-Saxon anthropologists conducting research in Morocco in the 1970s and 1980s, such as Clifford Geertz, Ernest Gellner and David Hart (Madoui, 2015; Rachik & Bourquia, 2011). These anthropologists renewed studies on Morocco and allowed Moroccan researchers to distance themselves from the French ethnographic corpus and approach the study of their own society from a new perspective. Some local researchers could thus complete their training in England or the United States, for example, the sociologists Fatima Mernissi and Fatma Bourquia (Madoui, 2015; Rachik & Bourquia, 2011). Others, such as Abdallah Hammoudi, left Morocco permanently to become professors in the United States. Moroccan anthropology has developed classic themes of anthropology, including colonial anthropology, but with innovative approaches such as religious rituals, brotherhoods, the cult of saints, segmental organisation and rural societies (Rachik & Bourquia, 2011). Although the institutionalisation of this discipline remains weak and there are no undergraduate or doctoral courses in anthropology, its teaching has been initiated in several universities and research centres over the last few decades, such as in the Centre marocain des sciences sociales at Hassan II University and the Institut universitare de la recherche scientifique, both in Rabat, and the Moulay Ismail University in Meknes. A new generation of very dynamic researchers is fuelling anthropology education in Morocco by introducing novel themes such as kif consumption (Khalid Mouna), critical reflection on anthropological tradition (Hassan Rachik) and medical anthropology (Zakaria Rhani and Saadia Radi) (Baylocq, 2013; Planeix, 2014). A more "rational and dispassionate" (Planeix, 2014, p. 400) attitude towards the Western anthropological tradition on Morocco and a critical distancing of the indigenisation of the discipline now seem to have been acquired. However, as several North African anthropologists pointed out during the 2014 Antropologie du Maroc et du Maghreb conference organised by the Jaques Berque Centre in Rabat, anthropology continues to have a precarious status in their countries. In many cases, the discipline is still banned or censored by the authorities, precarious within academic institutions, not completely legitimate in the eyes of social sciences professionals, and difficult to distinguish from the history or sociology in which it has often taken refuge to continue to exist (Planeix, 2014).

Libya

Libya, first an Italian and then a British colony, does not seem to have developed a local anthropological tradition. The Italian occupation (1911–1947) was at the origin of several expeditions of an anthropological nature oriented mainly towards a physical anthropology imbued with racial ideology, due to Italian ethnologists' generalised adherence to fascism (Di Bella, 1998; Dore, 1980). Italian anthropological studies on Libya are rare because the populations that inhabited the country did not correspond to the category of "primitive peoples" in which the discipline was interested in the first decades of the twentieth century (Grottanelli et al., 1977). However, some studies dedicated to the popular and linguistic traditions and to the history of the Berber populations were published

(Bruzzi, 2020; Cresti, 2016; Dore, 1980). Some expeditions were organised to collect objects and artefacts from Libyan populations to enrich the collections of museums in Italy and Libya. Some of them, such as the Museum of Anthropology and Ethnology in Florence, were centres of production of ethnographic knowledge about Libya (Dionisio et al., 2020; Falcucci, 2017, 2019). During colonisation, ethnography was usually conceived as a part of knowledge about the country alongside geology, botany, zoology and so on. This is illustrated, for example, by the Museum of Natural History in Tripoli, which, in 1937, was "built to provide an all-encompassing view of natural history" (Falcucci, 2017, p. 89) and included an ethnographic section highlighting knowledge of local populations. The link between colonial conquest and scientific knowledge, understood simultaneously as an instrument of domination and propaganda, was also present in the speech of the governor-general of Libya, Italo Balbo, at the museum's opening (Falcucci, 2017). After independence (1951), a university was created in Tripoli in 1955 that later split into two universities, one in Benghazi and one in Tripoli (1973). In 1956, sociology was introduced among the disciplines taught at the university (A. Baldinetti, personal communication, August 27, 2021). In the 1950s and 1960s, university teachers were recruited mainly from Egypt and other Arab countries and often subsidised by them (Clark, 2004). In 1995, there were 13 public universities in the country, but in 2021, anthropology did not appear in the degree courses of the universities whose websites I consulted. However, according to my Italian colleague Anna Baldinetti, who is a specialist of Libya, anthropology is now taught in several sociology departments, although it is not clear whether this is cultural or physical anthropology (A. Baldinetti, personal communication, August 27, 2021, and October 11, 2021). In any case, it is likely to be theoretical rather than research-oriented teaching in the field because doing research, even before the beginning of the civil war, seems to have been almost impossible. Extracts from the field diary of a French anthropologist, Xavier Thyssen (1987), indicated that in the 1980s, it was not possible to carry out field research because of the capillary control Gaddafi's regime had established. Thyssen (1987) denounced "a daily climate of tension imbued with suspicion" (p. 102) and the necessity for each researcher to sign a contract according to which "no secret information that could be obtained during the stay should be divulged" (p. 99). It was impossible to use a tape recorder, camera or typewriter (Thyssen, 1987). Despite my efforts to contact social science researchers in Libya through colleagues living and working in North Africa, I was unable to obtain any names or responses from those to whom I wrote.

Of note, however, is the recent creation of a social science journal hosted by the University of California, Berkeley: *Lamma: A Journal of Libyan Studies* (https://escholarship.org/uc/lamma), the first issue of which came out in 2020. Among the members of its editorial board are numerous Libyan researchers and intellectuals residing in the United States or Europe and only one Libyan scholar, Amal Sulayman al-Oweis, who obtained a doctorate in political science in Britain and teaches at the Faculty of Economics and Political Science at the University of Benghazi. Although there are important works on the history of Libya and Italian colonisation in Libya such as those by Libyan–American political scientist Ali Ahmida (1995, 2000), anthropological works written by Libyan researchers trained and active in academic institutions in Libya are not known.

Mauritania

In Mauritania, there is no anthropology teaching at the University of Nouakchott, the only public university in the country. However, some professors have doctorates in this discipline, including Yahya Ould-al-Bara, who in 2001 completed his doctorate under the direction of the well-known French anthropologist Pierre Bonte on the attitudes of specialists in religious law in Mauritania between the seventeenth and twentieth centuries. A French anthropologist specialising in the country, Bonte, has greatly contributed to making the discipline known and training researchers in Mauritania (Ben Hounet et al., 2020). Also noteworthy is his collaboration with Abdel Wedoud Ould Cheikh, a central figure in Mauritanian anthropology, who, with Bonte, contributed to raising the profile of the discipline in the country. Ould Cheikh began his career as a researcher at the Institut mauritanien de la recherche scientifique (IMRS), where he eventually became director (1970s and 1980s); he later became a professor at the University of Nouakchott and ended his career in the French Academy. He published his research mainly in French, placing himself more in the context of French anthropology than that of Mauritania, which has no scientific community in this discipline. Ould Cheikh (1988, 2014) has published many important works on Mauritania dealing with different aspects of the local society: from the history of tribes to the formation and functioning of the independent state, from Islamic finance to religious brotherhoods and from cultural heritage to slavery.

Ould Cheikh trained, among others, Mohamed Fall Ould Bah, who is among the founders of the Centre d'étude et de recherche sur l'Ouest saharien (CEROS, created in 2008), which has played an important role in building a scientific community in social sciences in Mauritania. Ould Bah (2010) completed a doctoral thesis on Islamic finance at Metz University, which led to several publications in French-speaking social science journals on an original topic little treated by anthropologists (Ould Bah & Ould Cheick, 2009).

Supported by Ould Cheikh and Bonte, among others, CEROS has organised conferences and seminars to bring together local and foreign researchers working in the Western Sahara region, welcoming foreign and local students and promoting scientific publications on the region. Some young Mauritanian anthropologists are now working in American universities or doing research in the country as part of international research projects or providing expertise for foreign organisations such as Mariem Baba Ahmed (S. Boulay, personal communication, August 12, 2021).

Anthropology in the Near East (The Mashrek)

Having examined the situation of anthropology in the Maghreb countries that colonisation has linked to the French ethnological tradition, next I highlight the history of anthropology in the countries of the Near East. France and Great Britain colonised the latter after World War I at the time of the dissolution of the Ottoman Empire, and these countries are thus part of the Anglo-Saxon academic tradition.

Egypt

Although in Egypt,[13] a country Britain first colonised in 1882,[14] "anthropology is not yet 'naturalised', integrated into the academy" (Hopkins, 2014, p. 120), it has enjoyed greater legitimacy than in the Maghreb countries. This is partly due to the fact that anthropology never became an

---

[13] Although Egypt is located in North Africa, for historical, political and linguistic reasons, it is considered part of the Mashrek.

[14] Following Napoleon's expedition to Egypt (1798–1801), France exerted great influence on Egypt during the nineteenth century, although the country was not directly colonised.

instrument of power for the Egyptian colonial authorities as it did in other African countries. At the Egyptian University (founded in 1908), now Cairo University, Edward Evans-Pritchard and Maurice Hocart, two of the major figures in British anthropology at the time, taught successively, the first during the academic years 1932–1934 and 1936–1937 and the second from 1934 to 1939. In 1946, Reginald Radcliffe-Brown taught for a year at the University of Alexandria, where he founded the Institute of Social Sciences "to train social workers by allying the methods of functionalist micro-anthropology and the reformist optimism of Anglo-Saxon-inspired social services" (Roussillon, 2002, p. 211). At Alexandria University, the only anthropology department present in the country was created in 1974 by Ahmed Abou Zeid, the most eminent Egyptian anthropologist of the twentieth century (Hopkins, 2014). Abou Zeid trained with Radcliffe-Brown during the latter's stay in Alexandria and in later years completed his training at Oxford under Evans-Pritchard. Therefore, his work is part of a structural-functionalist perspective, as was clearly illustrated by his research in the oasis of Kharga on the changes in the local social structure following the migration of some of the area's inhabitants. A follower of Jamal Abdel Nasser's ideology, Abou Zeid's work was geared towards fostering an understanding of the social changes linked to the development projects the regime promoted.

Abou Zeid is one of the few local anthropologists to have trained a generation of students, many of whom went on to careers in the United States, such as Safia Mohsen and Abdul-Hamid el-Zein (Hopkins, 2014). Mohsen worked with the Awlad Ali Bedouins, taking an interest in their legal system and ways of resolving conflicts and taking into account changes due to the intervention of the Egyptian central state. El-Sayyed el-Aswad has taught in the United States and Gulf countries,[15] whereas Iman al-Bastawasi made her career at the Institute of African Studies at Cairo University (Hopkins, 2014). Although some early anthropologists such as Mohammad Galal[16] trained in France at the school of Durkheim and Mauss, British functionalist anthropology dominated the country in

---

[15] Many social science researchers from North Africa and the Mashrek have migrated to universities in the Gulf countries over the last three decades due to the explosion in the number of universities in this area, the lack of qualified local teachers, and high salaries (al-Husban & Na'amneh, 2010; Bamyeh, 2015; Roussillon, 2002).

[16] Galal (1905–1943) was mentored by Marcel Mauss and the famous orientalist Louis Massignon. He studied and published his work in Paris. He did not hold any position in the Egyptian academy (Hopkins, 2014).

the 1950s and 1960s. Anthropology was also present in the aforementioned National Centre for Social and Criminological Sciences and put in the service of the economic and social development of the country, which under Nasser, had undergone important reforms (Roussillon, 2002). The other institution that played a key role in the training of many Egyptian anthropologists was the Centre for Social Sciences hosted by the American University in Cairo (AUC), one of the oldest and most prestigious universities in the country.[17] The Centre for Social Studies played a central role during the Nubian Project (1961–1964) (Fahim, 1977; Hopkins & Mehanna, 2010), a large-scale research project designed to study the resettlement of a population of approximately 100,000 people due to the construction of the Aswan Dam. This project, led by the AUC and funded by the Ford Foundation, included many young Egyptian, American and European researchers, including Hussein Fahim (1982), famous for fuelling the debate on "indigenous anthropology" in colonised countries, and Laila al-Hamamsy, who contributed much to women's studies and to the scientific organisation of anthropology in Egypt and other Arab countries (Hopkins, 2014, p. 100).[18] Since the period of optimism linked to the development policies in the 1960s and 1970s, Egypt has seen no real development of anthropology in the academy nor the construction of a scientific debate in this discipline (Sholkamy, 1999). The absence of a national scientific community, the difficulties of doing research due to censorship by local authorities and the lack of funding are major obstacles to the development of the discipline in the country (Fahim, 1977; Shami & Herrera, 1999). Many brilliant Egyptian researchers, often trained at AUC, where several anthropology courses are offered, have thus left the country after completing a PhD in the United States or Europe to pursue an international career. Although Egypt is their field of research, they do not contribute to the building of a scientific community of anthropologists in the country, prevented by political, structural and economic conditions.

---

[17] This university was founded in 1919 by a group of Americans interested in furthering higher education in the Middle East (https://www.aucegypt.edu/about/history).

[18] In particular, al-Hamamsi took over as director of the Organisation for the Promotion of Social Sciences in the Middle East (Hopkins, 2014, p. 100).

Sudan

During British colonisation, Sudan played a key role in the history of anthropology because it was the focus of studies by such well-known anthropologists as Charles and Brenda Seligman, Edward Evans-Pritchard, Siegfried Nadel, Godfrey Lienhardt and many others (Assal, 2018). The British colonial government equipped itself in the 1930s with both an Anthropology Board and the post of government anthropologist in order to secure, through the studies carried out in the field, control over the country's rebel groups. British influence was very strong in Sudanese academic institutions and in the training of the first local anthropologists. In 1958, Ian Cunnison founded the Department of Anthropology and Sociology at the University of Khartoum, where until the late 1970s, the teaching staff were mainly British anthropologists (Ahmed, 2003). Despite the hostility of the Sudanese elite towards anthropology, which had been an instrument of colonial domination, local and foreign anthropologists teaching in Sudan managed—at least in part—to revive it by putting it in the service of the development policies of independent Sudan. Anthropology courses were thus also created at the Universities of Juba and Gezira. Starting in the 1970s, thanks to Fredrik Barth's presence in Sudan and the agreements he established between the University of Khartoum and the University of Bergen, close ties were forged between Sudanese anthropology and European academia. During the 1970s and 1980s, despite the civil war, Sudanese students were able to obtain doctorates in Britain, Norway and the United States. Thus, since the end of the 1970s, the teaching staff of almost exclusively Europeans has been replaced by Sudanese anthropologists, although European researchers have continued to make regular visits to the Department of Anthropology and Sociology at the University of Khartoum (Ahmed, 2003). The advent of the Islamist government (1989), the war in Darfur and the Arabisation of higher education caused a weakening of Sudanese anthropology (Assal, 2018). Here, as in other Arab countries since the 1990s, the lack of research funding and low salaries prompted many university teachers to work full-time for international agencies and NGOs, producing reports on the humanitarian situation and conflicts between different groups in the country (Ahmed, 2003). Despite the discipline's weakening in recent decades, Sudanese anthropologists have acted as reference sources in the field of anthropology for many Arab countries. Some of them have contributed to the circulation and institutionalisation of anthropology in the

640   I. MAFFI

academic institutions of the Gulf countries, even creating a department of anthropology at Addis Ababa University in Ethiopia (Ahmed, 2003). Among the issues Sudanese anthropologists have addressed are nomadism, the relationship between state and tribe, sedentarisation and the impact of development projects on the populations concerned (Ahmed, 2003).

Jordan

In Jordan, a former British colony, the country's first and only anthropology department was created in 1984 at Yarmouk University in Irbid, a city in the country's north. Founded as a research unit by a group of anthropologists and archaeologists at the encouragement of European, American and Turkish researchers (Al-Husban & Na'amneh, 2010), the department offered only Master's-level courses until 2002, when a Bachelor's degree in anthropology was created. Since then, the department has reinforced its teaching vocation by relegating research to a secondary activity (Al-Husban & Na'amneh, 2010). Since 1991, researchers in physical anthropology and bioarchaeology have also joined the department, which today has a dual vocation (Abu Dalou et al., 2014). In its early days, the department had very dynamic teachers such as the aforementioned Seteney Shami, a Jordanian anthropologist trained at the American University of Beirut and the University of California, Berkeley, who is among the founders and president of the Arab Council for the Social Sciences, "an independent regional non-profit organisation that aims to strengthen social science research and knowledge production in the Arab world" (https://arab-foundationsforum.org/author/ACSS/). Founded in 2010, the Council for the Social Sciences encourages quality research in Arab countries through grants and subsidies to academic institutions, organises scientific meetings and congresses that bring together researchers from different Arab countries and publishes their work. For several decades, Shami has been involved in organising and coordinating social science research in the Arab world, convinced of its importance and aware of the difficulties it faces at regional and national levels (Shami, 2017). Whereas Shami completed her studies in the United States, even today most of the professors in Yarmouk's anthropology department earned their doctorates in Europe or the United States. Several former students of the department have made academic careers in Jordan or in the Arab world, including Abdelhakim al-Husban, Mohammed Tarawneh, Mohammed Tabishat and Mahmoud Na'amneh. Their research interests are manifold and include relations between state and tribe, cultural heritage (al-Husban & Na'amneh, 2010); collective memory, poverty, the impact of capitalism on rural populations (Tarawneh, 2014); organ transplantation, popular representation of illness (Tabishat, 2014); the construction and circulation of scientific knowledge, love and marriage (Alibeli & Na'amneh, 2018) and representations of local society in cinema.

Despite the existence of the anthropology department at Yarmouk University, published research on Jordan by Jordanian researchers is still a minority compared to that published by Western researchers (Al-Husban & Na'amneh, 2010), and it is mainly Euro-American universities or research centres that fund research projects, international academic meetings and publications on Jordan. The proliferation of private research centres and the practice of carrying out short-term research commissioned by international organisations have spread in Jordan since the 1990s. Several anthropologists working at the university supplement their teaching activities with research activities determined by the interests of international organisations. This is also because field research is undervalued in local Acadaemia and poorly funded (Al-Husban & Na'amneh, 2010).

Syria

Syria, which was under French mandate between 1920 and 1946, after a period of great political instability characterised by coups d'état and army interventions, experienced a very harsh authoritarian regime that left little room for the development of the social sciences and anthropology in particular. Dominated by the Assad family since 1970, the country, due to strong censorship and political repression, could not create a local academic community capable of producing critical knowledge, although sociology was taught at university (F. Mermier, personal communication, July 6, 2021). As Sari Hanafi (2010) effectively summarised, in Syria, "the government continues to control production in the social sciences and humanities. These sciences are highly apologetic, limited in their approach to research, controlled by single-party authorities and used for ideological propaganda and political manipulation" (p. 7). Some anthropologists of Syrian origin have trained and taught in universities in other countries of the Arab world. Among them is Sulayman Khalaf, who, after training in anthropology at the American University of Beirut and in the United States, spent most of his career at universities in Gulf countries (University of Kuwait, University of the United Arab Emirates, University of Sharja and University of Bahrain). Khalaf has worked on the construction of tangible and intangible cultural heritage in the Gulf countries, writing numerous works on popular culture and practices considered traditional, such as camel racing and falcon training. Khalaf (2020) is also one of the few Arab anthropologists to have published works on Syria, such as the very recent *Social Change in Syria: Family, Village and Political Party*. Another example is Zouhair Ghazzal, who, although not strictly trained in anthropology, studied at the American University of Beirut and then completed his doctoral thesis at the Haute Ecole en Sciences Sociales in Paris in the field of social studies on Arab-Islamic societies; he is presently a history professor at Loyola University in the United States. Interested in the modern history of the Near East at the turn of the nineteenth and twentieth centuries, Ghazzal (2007) is well-known for his book *Grammars of Adjudication: The Economics of Judicial Decision Making in Fin-de-Siècle Ottoman Beirut and Damascus.*

Lebanon

In Lebanon, a country colonised by France in the period between the two world wars, the region's first Western-style universities were founded in the second half of the nineteenth century: the American University of Beirut (AUB; 1866) and the Université Saint Joseph (USJ; 1875). Both founded by clerics, these institutions made Lebanon a locus of higher education and culture in the Near East (Kabbanji, 2012). Even after independence (1946) and the explosion of private universities in the country (since the 1990s), anthropology remained "on the margins of both the academe and the wider society" (Sawaf, 2021, p. 241) and is still a secondary discipline for those enrolled in Bachelor's and Master's degree programmes in social sciences where sociology is dominant (King & Scheid, 2006). The civil war, which ravaged the country between 1975 and 1990, caused the closure of the only Bachelor's and Master's degree programmes in anthropology that AUB offered. Only in 2005 was a Master's degree in anthropology re-established, allowing students to specialise in this discipline. The enhancement of anthropology at the AUB was strongly advocated by Fuad Khouri, one of Lebanon's leading anthropologists, along with Selim Abou and Chawki Douaihy (King & Scheid, 2006). Khouri has worked on various issues related to political power and the role of the army in Arab countries and conceptions of the body and bodily expressions in Arab-Islamic societies. His autobiography humorously traced his career as an anthropologist in the Arab world (Khouri, 2007). Abou, who did his university studies in France, played a major role in promoting the social sciences and anthropology in particular at the USJ, of which he was also a rector. A writer, philosopher and anthropologist, Abou has studied identity conflicts, intercultural dialogue, acculturation processes and multiculturalism by doing research in Argentina, Canada and Lebanon. Douaihy has worked on issues related to urban and political anthropology in Lebanon and on the organisation of the Maronite community. Annie Tohme Tabet, a Lebanese anthropologist teaching at the USJ, studies urban and political anthropology and the anthropology of war and violence. One of her recent works is on Syrian refugees in Lebanon (Boissière & Tohme Tabet, 2018).

Although there are anthropology teachings at the AUB, the USJ and the Lebanese University,[19] Tohme Tabet believes anthropology remains an individual initiative of some researchers and a sensibility rather than an autonomous discipline (Boissière & Tohme Tabet, 2018). Lebanese anthropologists who teach and do research in Lebanon, with a few exceptions, do some or all of their training in Europe or the United States. Famous diaspora anthropologists such as Suad Joseph and Ghassan Hage have not succeeded in making anthropology visible in Lebanon or in creating important training centres. In recent years, initiatives by young researchers, such as the creation of the Anthropology Society in Lebanon, seem to indicate a new dynamism. One of the difficulties encountered in the institutionalisation of anthropology in Lebanon is related to multilingualism: the few Lebanese anthropologists who exist publish mainly in French and English and much less in Arabic (King & Scheid, 2006), making it difficult to create a "unified Lebanese anthropology" (Puig & Tabet, 2021, p. 227) and thus a community of local researchers.

Palestine

In Palestine, universities offering training in the social sciences are concentrated in the occupied territories and particularly on the Ramallah-Jerusalem axis (Romani, 2003). No university has an anthropology

---

[19] The Lebanese University offers an applied Master's degree in urban socioanthropology and a research Master's degree in anthropology (https://www.ul.edu.lb/faculte/branches.aspx?facultyId=8).

department, and anthropologists often teach sociology (Romani, 2010). The only institution where anthropology has a visible presence is Bir Zeit University in Ramallah, the seat of the Palestinian Authority. A Department of Sociology and Anthropology was founded there in the early 1970s at the behest of one of the first anthropologists to teach there: Sharif Kanaana. Like Khalil Nakhleh and Ismail Nashif, two other anthropologists who taught in the department, Kanaana was born into a Palestinian family living in Israel. These three anthropologists completed their studies in the United States and arrived at Bir Zeit with disciplinary backgrounds influenced by the North American anthropological tradition. Kanaana, a folklorist and anthropologist, launched a project in 1984 to collect the oral traditions of the inhabitants of Palestinian villages destroyed by the Israeli occupation (Van Teeffelen, 1997). Although his work has a critical slant, he is part of a local anthropological tradition initiated in the early decades of the twentieth century by Palestinian physician and scholar Tawfiq Canaan and his circle (Nashef, 2002; Tamari, 2008). Oral history, folkloric studies and anthropology intersected and determined the interests of several anthropologists in the 1970s and 1980s. In recent decades, new themes have emerged in relation to the social transformations that occurred following the Oslo Accords, the increasing colonisation of the West Bank, the fragmentation of the Palestinian people and the interest in the status of women. The Institute for Women Studies at Bir Zeit, one of the first research centres for gender studies in the region (founded in 1984), employs a number of anthropologists who helped create the first Master's degree in gender studies and the first doctorate in social sciences in Palestine. Although Bir Zeit does not offer any degrees in anthropology, some anthropologists teach in the social sciences curriculum, but their courses are often thematic or methodological rather than disciplinary. Examples include Ala Alazzeh, who conducts research on resistance to Israeli colonisation in the West Bank, and Rema Hammami, whose work focuses on gender studies, nationalism, religion, humanitarian interventions and civil society in the Palestinian territories.

The Israeli military occupation, the first and second intifadas, the censorship exercised by the Israelis and even the Palestinian Authority make it difficult to do research and sometimes to maintain a critical approach that is nevertheless considered proper in the social sciences (al-Sakka, 2018, 2020; Hammami & Tamari, 1997; Romani, 2010). The proliferation of private research centres and the scarce resources available to universities combined with professors' very long teaching hours (A. al-Sakka, personal communication, August 16, 2021) mean that research, practised mainly on the mandate of international organisations, is uncritical and often unpublished (Tamari, 1994). Therefore, the construction of a dynamic scientific community in the field of anthropology and more generally in the social sciences seems yet to be achieved (A. al-Sakka, personal communication, August 16, 2021). However, in 2016, the Palestinian Association of Sociology, which brings together anthropologists, and the Insaniyat Association, which brings together only anthropologists residing in the occupied territories and Israel, were created (A. al-Sakka, personal communication, August 16, 2021).

Iraq

I was able to assemble little information about anthropology in Iraq. The pioneer of the discipline is Shakir Mustapha Salim (1919–1985), who obtained a doctorate from University College London in 1955. His doctoral research, carried out in southern Iraq, was published first in Arabic (1956–1957) and then in English as *Marsh Dwellers of the Euphrates* (Salim, 1962) and was reviewed in several Anglo-Saxon scientific journals. He has taught in the Department of Sociology at Baghdad University and is the author of an English-Arabic anthropology dictionary. The censorship imposed by Saddam Hussein first and the massive destruction related to the American occupation of the country later almost annihilated the possibility of doing social science research in the country (Ahram, 2013).

However, in the 1980s and 1990s, numerous studies on folk traditions were published and several folklore museums, which Hussein's regime supported for nationalistic purposes, were established (Baram, 1991). Finally, Omar Dewachi, although he has made his career abroad, is one of the very few known Iraqi anthropologists. A medical doctor by training, he converted to anthropology after escaping from Iraq and completed a thesis in medical anthropology at Harvard, later becoming an associate professor at Rutgers School of Arts and Science. Dewachi (2017) authored *Ungovernable Life: Mandatory Medicine and Statecraft in Iraq*, a highly original study on the role of medicine in the history of independent Iraqi state-building, and other works on therapeutic geography and toxic legacies related to Near Eastern conflicts.

Anthropology in the Arabian Peninsula

The Arabian Peninsula is one of the regions where Western-style universities have emerged later than in other Arab states—mostly during the last three decades. Having shifted from the British to the American aegis, most countries on the Arabian Peninsula either did not develop a local anthropological tradition or gave it only a certain legitimacy as a discipline serving nation-states. In their attempts to create a national identity based on a common tangible and intangible cultural heritage (Davis & Gavrielides, 1991), the Gulf States employed anthropologists to collect and document local traditions that could create a sense of authenticity and historical depth. Anthropology addressing more contemporary issues and understood as a critical discipline is very recent and has been developed mainly by private universities, which are often branches of American universities. For Saudi Arabia, I was unable to get in touch with the only anthropologist about whose work I was able to learn: Abu Baker Bagader. Bagader obtained his doctorate in the United States and taught sociology at King Abdul Aziz University in Jeddah over several years. He was interested in youth in Saudi Arabia (Bagader, 2010), environmental issues in relation to Islam and Saudi literature.

In the 50 or so Saudi universities whose websites I examined, I could not find any anthropology courses, although I do not rule out the possibility of anthropologists practising in the country. Two well-known anthropologists of Saudi origin who have made careers in other countries are Soraya Altorki, who taught for many years at the American University in Cairo in the Department of Sociology, Egyptology and Anthropology, and Madawi al-Rasheed, who enjoyed a brilliant career in Great Britain. Mai Yamani, an independent researcher known for her media appearances and affiliated with various international bodies, also has an anthropological background and has published work on Saudi Arabia. Yamani taught at King Abdul Aziz University in Jeddah for a few years at the beginning of her career, as did Altorki, who was a visiting professor at the same university (1974–1976) and then a visiting professor at King Saud University (1982–1984). The three anthropologists conducted research in Saudi Arabia and published their work in English. Their work was concerned with the condition of women and the family in Saudi Arabia (Altorki, 1986); the construction of the Saudi state (al-Rasheed, 2002); the relationship between tribes and the central state, young people (Yamani, 2000); political opposition to the Saud regime (al-Rasheed, 2007);

feminism in the Arab-Islamic world, relations between the Arab Gulf states, Iraqi opponents exiled in England and changes in Egyptian society (Altorki & Cole, 1998). Though I was not able to contact Saudi anthropologists based in the Kingdom, according to Kuwaiti anthropologist Abdallah Alajmi (personal communication, June 30, 2021), there is a group of historians in Saudi Arabia who publish good quality work in the field of ethnohistory.

In Yemen, anthropology has never been taught, and research in the social sciences has been driven mainly by sociologists, the pioneer of whom is Hammoud al-Audi (F. Mermier, personal communication, July 5, 2021). In South Yemen, research in the field was impossible before unification, whereas in North Yemen, the ideology of development allowed the emergence of social sciences applied to government projects (F. Mermier, personal communication, July 5, 2021). The devastation of the country since 2011 has also destroyed university life, and today, academic activities seem to be reduced to a minimum (F. Mermier, personal communication, July 5, 2021).

Sociology is taught in Bahrain, but anthropology plays a marginal role. For example, the University of Bahrain offers a Bachelor's degree in sociology and a Bachelor's degree in history, both of which include anthropology courses. The teachers in the social studies department are all Arabs and have studied in Bahrain, Jordan, Egypt and England.

Al-Ayn University in the United Arab Emirates has an applied sociology course in the College of Education, Humanities and Social Sciences, but anthropology is absent today, although an Egyptian-born American anthropologist, El-Sayyed el-Aswad, taught the discipline for a decade (2008–2018). El-Aswad also taught at the University of Bahrain and established the Folk Studies Unit at UAE University (1994–1996). This university includes a unit dedicated to training in "Tourism and Heritage," areas the Gulf States also strongly supported in relation to the creation of branches of the Louvre, British Museum and Guggenheim Museum in the Emirates. In general, universities in the Gulf States offer courses in engineering, medicine, biology, nursing sciences, economics, information technology and education sciences, with the aim of producing professionals to fill posts in public administration, the health system and schools. Social sciences are considered of little value and are at the bottom of the university hierarchy (A. Alajmi, personal communication, June 30, 2021).

In Abu Dhabi, there are two recently founded universities that are branches of prestigious institutions in the Global North: Sorbonne Abu

Dhabi and New York University Abu Dhabi (NYUAD). NYUAD has many anthropologists (European and American) dispersed among its various departments, and anthropology is a minor available within the Bachelor of Social Sciences and Humanities. Anthropologists teach general introductory courses, courses on the Arab world and Gulf societies, and other thematic courses related to their research (youth, musical traditions, environmental issues and migration). One of the minors in the Bachelor's degree programme in which anthropologists teach is called Arab Cross-Road Studies, and it covers societies in the Arab world. In 2021, there was still no Master's degree in anthropology. Zayed University has a College of Humanities and Social Sciences oriented towards political science, from which anthropology is absent.

In Kuwait, at the American University of Kuwait, it is possible to follow a Bachelor's degree programme with an anthropology orientation, although there are few teachers and they are not all in the same department. The Department of Social and Behavioural Sciences brings together several sociologists and political scientists and only two anthropologists. Three anthropologists I interviewed who are active in universities in the Gulf noted that there is almost no dialogue between anthropologists who teach in universities in the Arabian Peninsula or even within the same state (A. Alajmi, personal communication, July 30, 2021; L. Assaf, personal communication, July 6, 2021; P. Luciano, personal communication, June 27, 2021). Alajmi, an anthropologist trained in the United States and England, teaches at Kuwait's Arab Open University in the field of social sciences but does not conduct any anthropology courses. He continues his anthropological research without access to university funds or other grants, except when they come from foreign institutions. Alajmi is interested in the migration of native workers from Hadhramaut to Kuwait and studies the links between migrant communities and communities of origin and the relations between Kuwaitis and foreign workers (Alajmi, 2012, 2019). The Kuwaiti anthropologist is equally interested in the construction of social sciences in the Gulf countries and their role in the legitimation of political power.

In Oman, anthropology is absent from the universities, even in social science departments, although there are teachers with doctorates in anthropology from countries in the Global North (M. Sebiane, personal communication, August 18, 2021). Mainly European and American researchers have conducted anthropological research on Oman, which is still quite limited. Omani universities, however, have institutionalised sociology, which is understood more in a quantitative sense as a tool of government than as critical knowledge aimed at analysing social phenomena (M. Sebiane, personal communication, August 18, 2021). As in the other Gulf States, anthropology is generally understood as the study of folklore and is used as a tool to establish collections of material objects and oral traditions that can form the basis of a national identity (M. Sebiane, personal communication, August 18, 2021).

In conclusion, anthropology in the Arab world still appears to be knowledge that is primarily related to the Euro-American world. Poorly institutionalised, marginalised, perceived as an instrument of colonial domination and censored because it is too critical, anthropology still seems little known or appreciated in the Arab countries considered in this chapter. American or French universities are the main institutions that teach and practise the discipline, although there are a few departments in Arab universities where the term "anthropology" appears in the name. A new local interest in the discipline has arisen in some North African countries such as Algeria and Tunisia, but the overall balance is poor; even countries where anthropology seemed to have more solid and ancient roots, such as Egypt and Sudan, have failed to create local traditions, and the best-known researchers have often had solitary trajectories, which have taken them abroad.

REFERENCES

Abaza, M. (2000). The Islamization of knowledge between particularism and globalization: Malaysia and Egypt. In C. Nelson & S. Rouse (Eds.), *Situating globalization: Views from Egypt* (pp. 53–95). Transcript Verlag.

Abdul-Jabar, F. (2014). Reflections on Arabs and sociology. *Contemporary Arab Affairs, 7*(4), 499–509.

Abou Zeid, A. (1997). Anthropology as vocation. *Alif: Journal of Comparative Poetics, 17*, 259–261.

Abu Dalou, A. Y., Alrousan, M. F., & Khwaileh, A. M. (2014). Thirty years of the Department of Anthropology at Yarmouk University, Jordan (1984–2014): The overview of bioarchaeological research. *Bioarchaeology of the Middle East, 8*, 109–118.

Abu Lughod, L. (1989). Zones of theory in the anthropology of the Arab world. *Annual Review of Anthropology, 18*, 267–306.

Ahmed, A. C. (2003). The state of anthropology in the Sudan. In A. C. Ahmed, M. A. Assal, M. A. Salih, & I. S. El Hassan (Eds.), *Anthropology in the Sudan: Reflections by a Sudanese anthropologist international* (pp. 25–42). Nooks, OSSREA.

650 I. MAFFI

Ahmida, A. (1995). *The making of modern Libya: State formation, colonization, and resistance 1830–1932*. The Center for Arab Unity Studies.

Ahmida, A. (2000). *Beyond colonialism and nationalism in North Africa: History, culture and politics*. Palgrave Press.

Ahram, A. (2013). Iraq in the social sciences: Testing the limits of research. *Journal of the Middle East and Africa, 4*, 251–266.

Akli, F. M. (2015). Sociological research in Algeria: Between theoretical language and social reality. *Procedia Social and Behavioral Sciences, 185*, 352–356.

Alajmi, A. (2012). House-to-house migration: The Hadrami experience in Kuwait. *Journal of Arabian Studies: Arabia, the Gulf, and the Red Sea, 2*(1), 1–17.

Alajmi, A. (2019). The birth and death of a *Siby*: Life of a Hadrami immigrant in Kuwait. *Journal of Anthropological Research, 75*(2), 183–205.

Al-Husban, A.-H., & Na'amneh, M. (2010). Internationalization of the humanities and social sciences: Realities and challenges in Jordan. In M. Kuhn & D. Weidmann (Eds.), *Internationalization of the social sciences: Asia—Latin America—Middle East—Eurasia* (pp. 191–212). Transcript Verlag.

Alibeli, M., & Na'amneh, M. (2018). Marital happiness in marriage in time of change: The case of the United Arab Emirates (UAE). *Perspectives on Global Development and Technology, 18*, 229–248.

Al-Rasheed, M. (2002). *A history of Saudi Arabia*. Cambridge University Press.

Al-Rasheed, M. (2007). *Contesting the Saudi state: Islamic voices from a new generation*. Cambridge University Press.

Al-Sakka, A. (2018). Les universités palestiniennes: entre hiérarchisations académiques et attente sociale. *Hérodote, 68*(1), 141–150.

Al-Sakka, A. (2020). Palestinian sociology: Divergent practices and approaches. In S. Hanafi & C.-C. Yi (Eds.), *Sociologies in dialogue* (pp. 223–239). Sage.

Altorki, S. (1986). *Women in Saudi Arabia: Ideology and behavior among the elite*. Columbia University Press.

Altorki, S., & Cole, D. P. (1998). *Bedouins, settlers, and holiday-makers: Egypt's changing northwest coast*. American University in Cairo Press.

Al-Zuabi, A. Z. (2019). History and development of anthropology in the Arab world. *International Journal of Humanities and Social Science, 9*(6). https://doi.org/10.30845/ijhss.v9n6p17

Arvanitis, R., Waast, R., & al-Husban, A.-H. (2010). Social sciences in the Arab world. In *World social science report* (pp. 68–72). UNESCO.

Assal, M. A. (2018). Sudan, anthropology. In *The international encyclopaedia of anthropology.* Wiley and Sons. https://doi.org/10.1002/9781118924396.wbiea2101

21 THE BIRTH AND DEVELOPMENT OF ANTHROPOLOGY IN ARAB... 651

Assam, M. (2013). Le développement d'une "ethnologie de l'intérieur" en langue berbère: l'exemple des monographies villageoises (mémoires de licence) des Départements de Langue et Culture Amazigh (DLCA) de Tizi-Ouzou et Bejaia. *Revue des Etudes berbères, 9*, 119–151.

Bagader, A. (2010). *La jeunesse saoudienne: identité, mutations, défis, enjeux et perspectives à l'aube du XXI siècle*. L'Harmattan.

Bagader, A., & Rachik, H. (2012). *Al-antropoloja fi al-watan al-'arabi [Anthropology in the arab world]*. Dar al-Fikr.

Bamyeh, M. (2015). *Social sciences in the Arab world: Forms of presence*. Arab Council for the Social Sciences.

Baram, A. (1991). *Culture, history and ideology in the formation of Ba'athist Iraq, 1968–1989*. Palgrave Macmillan.

Baylocq, C. (2013). *Le Maroc, terre d'élection de l'anthropologie*. Centre Jacques Berque. http://cjb.ma/123-edito/le-maroc-terre-d-election-de-l-anthropologie-2371.html

Beaud, S. (1998). Regards sur la sociologie en Algérie et dans le monde arabe. Entretien avec Ali EI-Kenz [Translation]. *Genèses, 32*, 127–139.

Ben Hounet, Y., Brisbarre, A.-M., Casciarri, B., & Ould Cheikh, A. W. (2020). *L'anthropologie en partage. Autour de l'œuvre de Pierre Bonte*. Karthala.

Ben Salem, L. (2009). Lilia ben Salem, Propos sur la sociologie en Tunisie. Entretien avec Sylvie Mazzella. *Genèse, 2*, 125–142.

Benghabrit-Remaoune, N., & Haddab, M. (2008). *L'Algérie 50 ans après. Etat des savoirs en sciences humaines et sociales 1954–2004*. Oran, Editions du CRASC.

Berque, J. (1956). Cent vingt-cinq ans de sociologie maghrébine. *Annales. Economies, sociétés, civilisations, 3*, 296–324.

Boëtsch, G., & Ferrié, J.-N. (1998). *L'anthropologie coloniale du Nord de l'Afrique: Science académique et savants locaux. Les usages de l'anthropologie. Discours et pratiques en France (1860–1940)*. https://hal.archives-ouvertes.fr/hal-02558504/document

Boissière, T., & Tohme Tabet, A. (2018). Une économie de la survie au plus près de la guerre. Stratégies quotidiennes des réfugiés syriens à Nabaa. *Critique internationale, 80*, 89–109.

Bourdieu, P., Mammmeri, M., & Tassadit, Y. (2003). Du bon usage de l'ethnologie. *Actes de la recherche en sciences sociales, 150*, 9–18.

Bruzzi, E. (2020). Per una storia incrociata tra l'Italia e la Libia: Il percorso dell'etnologa e arabista Ester Panetta (1894–1983). *Studi maghrebini North African Studies, 18*, 18–42.

Cantini, D. (2019). Reforming universities in the Middle East: Trends and contestations from Egypt and Jordan. *Learning and Teaching, 2*(1), 74–92.

Chachoua, K. (2010). La sociologie en Algérie. L'histoire d'une discipline sans histoire. In H. Kienle (Ed.), *Les sciences sociales en voyage. L'Afrique du Nord et le Moyen Orient vus d'Europe, d'Amérique et de l'intérieur* (pp. 135–155). Karthala.

Chaulet, C. (2008). Anthropologie et/ou sociologie? Retour en arrière sur nos pratiques. In N. Benghabrit-Remaoun & M. Haddab (Eds.), *L'Algérie 50 ans après. Etat des savoirs en sciences sociales et humaines. 1954–2004* (pp. 75–78). Editions du CRASC.

Clark, N. (2004). *Education in Libya.* WENR. https://wenr.wes.org/2004/07/wenr-julyaugust-2004-education-in-libya/print.

Colonna, F. (2010). Sociologie et anthropologie au Maghreb: la circulation régionale des disciplines. Vers une mise en commun des ressources au Sud? In E. Kienle (Ed.), *Les sciences sociales en voyage: l'Afrique du nord et le Moyen-Orient vus d'Europe, d'Amérique et de l'intérieur* (pp. 95–112). Karthala.

Cresti, F. (2016). Conoscenza scientifica e politica coloniale: Francesco Beguinot, l'impresa di Tripoli ed un progetto incompiuto di "Storia dei Berberi" (1911–1923). In A. M. Di Tolla (Ed.), *La lingua nella vita e a vita della lingua* (pp. 171–189). UNIOR.

Currie-Alder, B., Arvanitis, R., & Hanafi, S. (2018). Research in Arabic-speaking countries: Funding competitions, international collaboration, and career incentives. *Science and Public Policies, 45*(1), 74–82.

Davis, E., & Gavrielides, N. (Eds.). (1991). *Statecraft in the Middle East: Oil, historical memory and popular culture.* University Press of Florida.

Deeb, L., & Winegar, J. (2012). Anthropologies of Arab-majority societies. *Annual Review of Anthropology, 41*, 337–358.

Dewachi, O. (2017). *Ungovernable life: Mandatory medicine and statecraft in Iraq.* Stanford University Press.

Di Bella, M.-P. (1998). Ethnologie et fascisme: quelques exemples. *Ethnologie française, 18*(2), 131–136.

Dionisio, G., Bigoni, F., Mori, T., & Moggi Cecchi, J. (2020). La collezione di maschere facciali del Museo di Antropologia e Etnologia di Firenze. *Museologia scientifica, 14*, 12–28.

Dore, G. (1980). Antropologia e colonialismo italiano. Rassegna di studi di questo dopoguerra. *La Ricerca folklorica, 1*, 129–132.

Eickelman, D., & Mustafa Abusharaf, R. (Eds.). (2017). *Higher education investment in the Arab states of the Gulf: Strategies for excellence and diversity.* Gerlach Press.

21 THE BIRTH AND DEVELOPMENT OF ANTHROPOLOGY IN ARAB... 653

el-Kenz, A. (2005). Les sciences humaines et sociales dans les pays arabes de la Méditerranée. *Insaniyat, 27*, 19–28.

el-Kenz, A. (2008). Les sciences sociales dans les pays arabes: cadre pour une recherche. In N. Benghabrit-Remaoun & M. Haddab (Eds.), *L'Algérie 50 ans après. Etat des savoirs en sciences sociales et humaines. 1954–2004* (pp. 53–74). Editions du CRASC.

Fahim, H. (Ed.). (1982). *Indigenous anthropology in non-Western countries.* Caroline Academic Press.

Falcucci, B. (2017). Il museo di storia naturale di Tripoli, realtà contemporanea di un museo coloniale. *Museologia scientifica, 11*, 87–96.

Falcucci, B. (2019). Sources for colonial historiography: Museums and colonial collections, a mapping and memory project on the Italian national territory. *Cahiers d'histoire, 37*(1). https://doi.org/10.7202/1067955ar

Ghazzal, Z. (2007). *Grammars of adjudication: The economics of judicial decision making in fin-de-siècle Ottoman Beirut and Damascus.* Institut Français du Proche Orient.

Grottanelli, V., et al. (1977). Ethnology and/or cultural anthropology in Italy: Traditions and developments. *Current Anthropology, 18*(4), 593–601.

Haddab, M. (2008). Les sciences sociales en Algérie; sont-elles en progrès?. In N. Benghabrit-Remaoun & M. Haddab (Eds.), *L'Algérie 50 ans après. Etat des savoirs en sciences sociales et humaines. 1954–2004* (pp. 125–130). Editions du CRASC.

Hammami, R., & Tamari, S. (1997). Populist paradigms: Palestinian sociology. *Contemporary Sociology, 26*, 275–279.

Hanafi, S. (2010). Donor community and the market of research production: Framing and deframing the social sciences. In M. Burawoy (Ed.), *Facing an unequal world: Challenges from sociology* (Vol. 3, pp. 3–35). Internet Association of Sociology.

Hanafi, S. (2011). University systems in the Arab East: Publish globally and perish locally vs publish locally and perish globally. *Current Sociology, 59*(3), 291–309.

Hanafi, S., & Arvanitis, R. (2014). The marginalization of the Arab language in social science: Structural constraints and dependency choice. *Current Sociology, 62*(5), 723–242.

Hanafi, S., & Arvanitis, R. (2016). *Knowledge production in the Arab world: The impossible promise.* Routledge.

Hopkins, N. (2014). *Anthropology in Egypt 1900–67: Culture, function, and reform.* American University in Cairo Press.

Hopkins, N., & Mehanna, S. R. (2010). *Nubian encounters: The story of the Nubian Ethnological Survey 1961–1964.* American University in Cairo Press.

654 I. MAFFI

Kabbanji, J. (2012). Heurs et malheurs du système universitaire libanais à l'heure de l'homogénéisation et de la marchandisation de l'enseignement supérieur [Translation]. *Revue des mondes musulmans et de la Méditerranée, 131*, 127–145.

Khalaf, S. (2020). *Social change in Syria: Family, village and political.* Routledge.

Khouri, F. (2007). *An invitation to laughter: A Lebanese anthropologist in the Arab world.* Chicago University Press.

Kienle, H. (ed). (2010). *Les sciences sociales en voyage. L'Afrique du Nord et le Moyen Orient vus d'Europe, d'Amérique et de l'intérieur.* Karthala, Paris.

King, D. E., & Scheid, K. (2006). Anthropology in Beirut. *Anthropology News, 47*(6), 40.

Lamine, B. (Ed.). (2009, May 31–June 2). *Towards an Arab higher education space: International challenges and societal responsibilities.* Arab Regional Conference on Higher Education, Cairo, Egypt.

Lucas, P., & Vatin, J. C. (Eds.). (1982). *L'Algérie des anthropologues.* La Découverte.

Madoui, M. (2015). La sociologie marocaine: du déni à la réhabilitation. *Sociologies pratiques, 30*, 99–113.

Maffi, I. (2020). *Abortion in post-revolutionary Tunisia: Politics, medicine and morality.* Berghahn Books.

Mahfoudh, D. (1988–1989). Essai d'analyse critique des recherches sociologiques pendant la période coloniale. *Hésperis Tamouda, 26–27*, 249–264.

Mahfoudh, D., & Melliti, I. (2009). Les sciences sociales en Tunisie. Histoire et enjeux actuels. *Sociologies pratiques, 19*(2), 125–140.

Mammeri, M. (1991). *Une expérience de recherche anthropologique en Algérie. Culture savante, culture vécue (études 1936–1989).* Tala.

Marouf, N., Faouzi, A., & Faouzi, K. (Eds.). (2002). *Quel avenir pour l'anthropolgie en Algérie?* Éditions du CRASC.

Melliti, I. (2006). Une anthropologie "indigène" est-elle possible? Réflexions sur le statut de l'anthropologie en Tunisie. *Arabica, 53*, 163–176.

Melliti, I. (2014). Sociologie et francophonie en Tunisie. *Sociologies pratiques, 3*(HS1), 167–170.

Morsy, S., Nelson, C., Saad, R., & Sholkamy, H. (1991). Anthropology and the call for indigenization of social sciences in the Arab world. In E. L. Sullivan & J. S. Ismael (Eds.), *The contemporary study of the Arab world* (pp. 81–114). The University of Alberta Press.

Nashef, K. (2002). Tawfiq Canaan: His life and works. *Jerusalem Quarterly, 16*, 12–26.

Ould Bah, M. F. (2010). Les réseaux de la finance Islamique en Afrique. *Politique étrangère, 4*, 805–817.

Ould Bah, M. F., & Ould Cheikh, A. W. (2009). Entrepreneurs moraux et réseaux financiers islamique en Mauritanie. *Afrique contemporaine, 3*(231), 99–117.

Ould Cheikh, A. W. (1988). *Eléments d'histoire de la Mauritanie*. Centre Culturel Français.

Ould Cheikh, A. W. (2014). *Etat et société en Mauritanie. Cinquante ans après l'indépendance*. Karthala.

Planeix, A. (2014). Compte rendu du colloque: "Anthropologie du Maroc et du Maghreb". *Journal des anthropologues, 136–137*, 399–405.

Pouessel. S. (2013). D'ici et d'ailleurs. L'anthropologie en Tunisie. *Lettres de l'IRMC, 11*. http://irmc.hypotheses.org/1293

Puig, N., & Tabet, M. (2021). Introduction: Anthropologies et temps d'incertitudes, Anthropologies libanaises. *Ethnologie française, 51*, 227–238.

Rachik, H. (2012). *Le proche et le lointain. Un siècle d'anthropologie au Maroc*. Éditions Parenthèses, Éditions MMSH.

Rachik, H., & Bourquia, R. (2011). La sociologie au Maroc. Grandes étapes et jalons thématiques. *Sociologies*. https://doi.org/10.4000/sociologies.3719

Romani, V. (2003). Sociologues et sociologies en Cisjordanie occupée: engagements et hétéronomies. *Revue des mondes musulmans et de la Méditerranée, 101–102*, 107–125.

Romani, V. (2010). Sciences sociales entre nationalisme et mondialisation. Le cas des Territoires occupés palestiniens. *Sociétés contemporaines, 78*, 137–156.

Roussillon, A. (2002). Sociologie et identité en Égypte et au Maroc. Le travail de deuil de la colonisation. *Revue d'histoire des sciences humaines, 7*, 193–221.

Salhi, F. (2002). Réflexion froide sur des questions chaudes: quelle anthropologie du religieux en Algérie? Quelques éléments pour un débat. In N. Marouf, A. Faouzi, & K. Faouzi (Eds.), *Quel avenir pour l'anthropolgie en Algérie?* (pp. 87–94). Éditions du CRASC.

Salhi, F. (2008). L'anthropologie et les sciences sociales en Algérie: éléments pour un bilan. In N. Benghabrit-Remaoun & M. Haddab (Eds.), *L'Algérie 50 ans après. Etat des savoirs en sciences sociales et humaines 1954–2004* (pp. 79–89). Editions du CRASC.

Salim, S. M. (1962). *Marsh dwellers of the Euphrates*. University of London, The Athlone Press.

Sawaf, Z. (2021). Anthropology in Lebanon: At the margins of academe. In C. Raymond, M. Catusse, & S. Hanafi (Eds.), *Un miroir libanais des sciences sociales. Acteurs, pratiques, disciplines* (pp. 214–241). Diacritiques éditions.

Shami, S. (1989). Socio-cultural anthropology in Arab universities. *Current Anthropology, 30*(5), 649–654.

656   I. MAFFI

Shami, S. (2017). *The social sciences in the Arab region: Gaps, elisions and glosses* [Video]. Conference at the Central European University. https://www.youtube.com/watch?v=0tW_OhxUftA

Shami, S., & Herrera, L. (Eds.). (1999). *Between field and text: Emerging voices in Egyptian social sciences.* American University in Cairo Press.

Sholkamy, H. (1999). Why is anthropology so hard in Egypt? In S. Shami & L. Herrera (Eds.), *Between field and text: Emerging voices in Egyptian social sciences* (pp. 119–138). American University in Cairo Press.

Soufi, F. (2008). Le CRASC et Insaniyat. Une pratique éditoriale au service de la recherche en sciences sociales et humaines. In N. Benghabrit-Remaoun & M. Haddab (Eds.), *L'Algérie 50 ans après. État des savoirs en sciences sociales et humaines 1954–2004* (pp. 47–50). Editions du CRASC.

Tabishat, M. (2014). *The moral discourse of health in modern Cairo, persons, bodies and organs.* Lexington Books.

Tamari, S. (1994). Problems of social science research in Palestine: An overview. *Current Sociology, 42*(2), 67–86.

Tamari, S. (2008). Lepers, lunatics and saintes: The nativist ethnography of Tawfiq Canaan and his Jerusalem circle. In S. Tamari (Ed.), *Mountain against the sea: Essays on a Palestinian society and culture* (pp. 93–112). University of California Press.

Tarawneh, M. (2014). *Rural capitalist development in the Jordan Valley: The case of Deir Alla: The rise and demise of social groups.* Sidestone Press.

Thyssen, X. (1987). Lybie [Lybia]. *Bulletin de l'Association française des anthropologues, 29–30,* 93–103.

Van Teeffelen, T. (1997). *Sharif Kanaana, anthropologist and folklorist.* Palestine-Family.net. https://palestine-family.net/sharif-kanaana-anthropologist-and-folklorist/

Yamani, M. (2000). *Changed identities: Challenge of the new generation in Saudi Arabia.* Royal Institute for International Affairs/Chatham House.

Index[1]

A

Abade, Augusto, 246
Abashin, Sergei, 261–264
Abbagnano, Nicola, 171
Abdelkebir Khatibi, Mohammed, 623
Abèlés, Marc, 78, 85, 86, 92, 104
Aboites, Luis, 449
Abou, Selim, 642, 643
Abu-Lughod, Lila, 357, 358, 361, 365, 621
Abu Zeid, Ahmed, 637
Adandé, Alexandre, 279, 280
Adelung, Johann Christoph, 134, 135
Adorno, Theodor W., 169
Afonso, Ana Isabel, 245
Agassiz, Louis, 137
Agier, Michel, 91
Aguilar Criado, Encarnación, 182, 186, 186n5, 192, 194, 197, 198, 204n27

Aguirre Beltrán, Gonzalo, 441, 443–445, 449–455, 454n3, 457, 460
Agustín, Lara, 445
Ahmed, Abdel Ghaffar M., 20n23
Ahmed, Mariem Baba, 636
Ahmida, Ali, 635
Alcina Franch, José, 187, 199n19, 200, 201n22
Alekseeva, Ljudmila, 258
Alazzeh, Ala, 644
Alliegro, Enzo V., 159, 161, 162, 321, 322
Althabe, Gérard, 76, 91, 105–107
Althusser, Louis, 169
Altorki, Soraya, 646, 647
Alves Costa, Catarina, 246
Alves Moreira, Adriano José, 234
Amante, Fátima, 245
Amara, Ramzi Ben, 632

---

[1] Note: Page numbers followed by 'n' refer to notes.

© The Author(s), under exclusive license to Springer Nature
Switzerland AG 2023
G. D'Agostino, V. Matera (eds.), *Histories of Anthropology*,
https://doi.org/10.1007/978-3-031-21258-1

658 INDEX

Ambedkar, Bhimrao Ramji, 474, 477, 478, 486, 506
Amin, Samir, 285n14
Amin, Shahid, 500
Amselle, Jean-Loup, 4, 76, 85, 91, 92n24, 286, 606
Anderson, Benedict, 231, 261, 551
Anderson, John, 586
Angioni, Giulio, 167
Ankermann, Bernhard, 140–142, 144
Anta Félez, José Luís, 186
Antón y Ferrándiz, Manuel, 194n11, 195
Appadurai, Arjun, 15, 108, 237, 352, 367, 374, 510, 606
Arabía y Solanas, Ramón, 194
Aragón Andrade, Orlando, 462
Aranzadi, Telesforo de, 194n11, 196, 197
Araújo, Daniela, 246
Archer, William George, 484
Archetti, Eduardo, 24
Arcila, Graciliano, 413
Ardener, Edwin, 56, 57, 500, 606
Ardener, Shirley, 56, 57
Areia, Manuel, 245
Aritiunov, Sergei Aleksandrovich, 533
Arocha, Jaime, 405, 424, 425
Asad, Talal, 49, 56, 58n3, 62, 65, 66, 71, 302, 352, 370, 562
Assad, Family, 641
Assier-Andrieu, Louis, 95n29
Astuti, Rita, 56
Attias-Donfute, Claudine, 110
Al-Audi, Hammoud, 647
Augé, Marc, 7, 76, 84, 85n15, 91, 92, 104
Azevedo, Thales de, 389, 393

B
Bachelard, Gaston, 183
Bachofen, Johann Jakob, 136

Baer, Hans, 374
Bagader, Abu Baker, 621, 625, 646
Baiburin, Albert, 259, 262–264
Balandier, Georges, 54, 75, 84, 91, 273, 280–284, 280n10, 287, 290, 456, 561, 630
Balbo, Italo, 634
Ballesteros Gaibros, Manuel, 192, 199n19, 200
Bamyeh, Mohammed, 622, 624, 624n7, 625n9, 637n15
Bank, Leslie, 305, 307n6
Barandiarán, José Miguel de, 196
Barbe, Noël, 98n35, 112
Barbichon, Guy, 76, 99, 100, 105, 111
Barker, John, 555, 561
Barnard, Alan, 150, 319
Barnard, Frederick Mechner, 130–134, 135n2
Barnard, Thomas Theodore, 302, 304
Barnes, John A., 150, 319
Barth, Fredrik, 16n15, 48, 49, 52, 55, 57, 58, 62, 66–68, 70, 71, 146, 204, 302, 365, 639
Barthes, Roland, 502
Bartov, Pavel Evgenevic, 258
Basaglia, Franco, 364
Basauri, Carlos, 450
Al-Bastawasi, Iman, 637
Bastian, Adolf, 50, 137–139, 150
Bastide, Roger, 107n51, 392n6, 393
Bastos, Cristiana, 228, 230, 234, 235, 235n11, 239, 242, 244n22, 245, 246
Bastos, Susana, 245
Bataille, George, 90
Batalha, Luís, 245
Bateson, Gregory, 53, 553
Battaglia, Debbora, 351n6
Bausinger, Hermann, 169
Baviskar, Baburao Shravan, 491
Bayart, Jean-François, 86, 92n24

INDEX 659

Beattie, John H.M., 3n2
Beckett, Jeremy, 558
Beemer, Hilda, 52
Bell hooks (Gloria Jean Watkins), 228
Bellagamba, Alice, 9, 34, 281,
 282, 587
Bellier, Irène, 106
Belmont, Nicole, 94, 94n27, 94n28
Ben Ali, 631
Benedict, Ruth, 138, 139, 311, 326
Beneduce, Roberto, 170
Benfey, Theodor, 232n7
Benjamin, Walter, 352
Bensa, Alban, 84
Benveniste, Émile, 502
Berglund, Eeva, 23n26
Berkhofer, Robert, 18
Bernardi, Bernardo, 66–68, 136, 139,
 141n6, 150n14, 170
Berndt, Ronald M., 558
Bernot, Luciene, 94n28
Berque, Jacques, 621, 628, 630,
 630n12, 633
Bertho-Lavenir, Chaterine, 99n37
Bertrand, Régis, 99n37
Besserer, Federico, 440–442
Best, Elsdon, 581, 583
Bestard, Joan, 190
Béteille, Andre, 470, 491
Bế Viết Đăng, 534
Bhabha, Homi K., 504
Bhaduri, Bhuvaneswari, 503
Bieder, Robert, 18
Bierschenk, Thomas, 85, 85n14
Biko, Steve, 307, 314
Bismarck, Otto von, 129
Blanchard de la Brosse, Paul-Marie,
 525, 525n5
Bloch, Maurice, 56, 62, 66, 68–70,
 339, 354
Boas, Franz, 32, 36, 50, 128, 132,
 134, 137–139, 145, 149, 150,

254, 257, 311, 322–328, 390,
 391, 440, 446–448, 478, 582,
 583, 598
Boggiani, Guido, 159
Bogoraz, Vladimir G., 253–255
Bohannan, Laura, 49, 58–60
Bohannan, Paul, 49, 60
Boilat, Pierre-David, 275, 289
Bolsonaro, Jair, 388, 396n14, 398n19
Boltanski, Luc, 90
Bonfil Batalla, Guillermo, 421,
 453, 455–457
Bonfil, Guillermo, 442, 444,
 453–459, 457n4
Bonifacy, Auguste, 524–525
Bonte, Pierre, 635, 636
Bordonaro, Lorenzo, 231n4, 245
Borutti, Silvana, 171
Bosch Gimpera, Pedro, 196
Bose, Nirmal Kumar, 480, 484, 486,
 493, 494, 496
Bosio, Gianni, 166
Bott, Elizabeth, 54
Bourdieu, Pierre, 98, 105, 106,
 349n4, 354, 355, 628, 630n12
Bourquia, Fatma, 632, 633
Braga, Teófilo, 232, 232n8, 233
Branco, Jorge Freitas, 238, 241
Brand, Donald, 452
Braudel, Fernand, 68
Bretell, Caroline, 241
Briceño, Jacquelin Clarac de, 28
Briggs, John, 483
Brito, Joaquim Pais de, 241
Brocklesby Davis, Edith Lucy, 60
Bromberger, Christian, 76, 93, 94n27,
 97, 104, 104n43, 108, 110
Brown, Elizabeth, 52
Brudnij, Vladimir Ivanovic, 258
Brutti, Lorenzo, 80n9, 81, 81n11
Buck, Peter, 573, 581–583
Bueno, Carmen, 444

660 INDEX

Burguière, André, 104n44
Burszta, Józef, 20n23
Butler, Christopher, 2n1
Buttitta, Antonino, 167

C
Cadena, Marisol de la, 23n26
Cadière, Leopold, 524
Caetano, Marcelo, 238
Cai Yuanpei, 596, 597
Caillé, Alain, 90
Caillié, René, 272
Caldas, Francisco José, 412
Caldeira, Teresa, 28n35
Callan, Hilary, 26, 27, 27n34
Callier-Boisvert, Collette, 241
Calvert, James, 571
Câmara Cascudo, Luis de, 392
Campos, Álvaro, 238
Canaan, Tawfiq, 644
Canclini, Néstor García, 440, 441, 599, 606
Cantoni, Remo, 171
Caplan, Pat, 56
Carby, Hazel, 11
Cardeira da Silva, Maria, 242, 243n19, 245
Cárdenas, Lázaro, 450
Cardona, Giorgio, 7
Cardoso de Oliveira, Roberto, 27, 390, 391, 392n6, 393
Carneiro, Robert, 337, 392, 392n7
Carniero, Edson, 391
Caro Baroja, Julio, 186n5, 187, 197, 197n15, 197n17, 200
Carrère, Frederic, 275, 289
Carrier, James, 365, 371n11, 372, 561
Carsten, Janet, 56, 303, 303n4, 304
Carstens, Peter, 303, 303n4, 304
Carvajal Contreras, Miguel ángel, 186n4
Carvalho, Clara, 242, 245, 396

Casal, Yáñes, 239, 245
Casanova, Catarina, 246
Casarrubias, Vicente, 450
Caso, Alfonso, 450, 457
Castro Faria, Luís, 391
Cátedra, María, 187n6, 192, 200n20
Caviedes, Mauricio, 404, 422, 423
Certeau, Michel de, 98, 99, 106, 109, 349, 350
Cerulli, Ernesta, 170
Césaire, Aimé, 92
Chakrabarty, Dipesh, 500
Chalvon-Demersay, Sabine, 106
Chan van-Thuan, 532
Charuty, Giordana, 100, 105n47
Chatterjee, Partha, 486, 500, 505
Chattopadhyay, Kshitish Prasad, 479, 484
Chatty, Dawn, 56
Chaube, Ram Gharib, 473
Chaulet, Claudine, 629, 630n12
Chauliac, Marina, 98n35
Chavenau, Jean Pierre, 84–85
Chávez, Carlos, 445
Chávez, Milciades, 413
Checa Olmos, Francisco, 187
Cheikh Moussa Kamara, 276n5
Chen Yinghuang, 596
Chevalier, Sophie, 76–79, 77n2, 82, 89–91, 96, 98, 101, 102, 109, 109n57
Chiang Kai-Shek, 597
Chirac, Jacques, 81n10
Chiva, Isac, 93, 94, 94n28, 96, 100, 104n44
Cirese, Alberto Mario, 30, 32, 160, 165, 167
Clarke, Edith, 52
Clastres, Pierre, 62
Claverie, Élisabeth, 95n29
Clemente, Pietro, 81n11, 162n1, 165, 167, 174
Clenninden, Inga, 560n11

Clifford, James, 2n1, 3, 76, 343, 344, 347, 573, 588, 606
Clozel, Marie Françis Joseph, 276
Cocchiara, Giuseppe, 167
Cochrane, Glynn, 559
Codazzi, Agustín, 412
Codrington, Robert Henry, 572
Coedès, George, 528
Coelho, Adolfo, 232
Coertze, Pieter J., 311, 312
Cohen, Abner, 54, 62, 64, 65
Cohen, Anthony, 351n6
Cohn, Bernard, 480, 500, 560
Cole, Douglas, 149, 340, 647
Cole, Sally, 391n5
Collier, John, 329
Colonna, Fanny, 625
Comaroff, Jean, 5, 11n7, 302, 351, 354, 355, 371, 606
Comaroff, John, 11n7, 302, 309, 351, 354, 357, 371, 375, 606
Comas, Juan, 440n1, 445, 446, 449
Comte, Auguste, 188n7
Condominas, George, 529
Confucius, 537
Conklin, Harold, 325
Consiglieri Pedroso, Zófimo, 232, 232n6
Contreras, Jesús, 190
Copans, Jean, 85, 274, 283, 291, 292
Coquery-Vidrovitch, Catherine, 272n2, 283, 284
Corbin, Alain, 99
Cordeiro, Graça, 242
Corrêa, Mariza, 389–393, 391n5, 392n8, 395
Correia, Vergílio, 234
Corso, Raffaele, 160
Costa Pinto, Luiz de Aguiar, 393
Costa Teixeira, Carla, 246
Cowlishaw, Gillian Kier, 554, 558, 558n8, 559, 562
Crehan, Kate, 164, 349

Crespo, Jorge, 239
Croce, Benedetto, 32, 159, 165, 171
Crocombe, Ron, 578–580
Crooke, William, 472, 473
Cruise, Fritz, 144
Csordas, Thomas, 351n7
Cuisenier, Jean, 93, 94, 94n28, 112
Cunha, Eugénia, 246
Cunha, Luís, 245
Cunha, Manuela Ivone, 243, 245
Cunnison, Ian, 639
Cushing, Frank Hamilton, 322
Cushman, David, 343
Cutileiro, José, 241

D

Da Furna, Vilarinho, 236n13
D'Agostino, Gabriella, 16, 51, 157, 163, 225n1
Dakhlia, Jocelyne, 631
Dalton, George, 60
DaMatta, Roberto, 395
Đặng Nghiêm Vạn, 534
Darnell, Regna, 16, 18, 18n20
Das, Veena, 63n4, 362
Dassié, Véronique, 108
Davenport, Charles B., 323
Davidson, James Wightman, 560
Davis, Bradley Campo, 537, 538
De Arana, Vicente, 194
De Gaulle, Charles-André-Joseph-Marie, 413
De Heusch, Luc, 239
De la Fuente, Julio, 450, 451, 454
de la Peña, Guillermo, 448
de La Pradelle, Michèle, 101, 101n40, 107
De la Soudière, Martin, 104n44
De L'Estoile, Benoît, 80–82, 86, 86n17, 87, 87n18, 272, 281, 284
De Madariaga, Jiménez C., 186

662 INDEX

De Martino, Ernesto, 6, 30n38, 32, 48, 160, 164–167, 171–173, 175
De Oliveira, Manoel, 238
De Onor, Rio, 236n13, 241
De Sousa, Claudia, 246
De Sousa, Ernesto, 238
de Sousa Santos, Boaventura, 460, 462
De Teresa, Ana Paula, 442–443
Deale Hurston, Zora, 326
Debonneville, Julien, 92n25
Declich, Francesca, 68
Del Pino Díaz, Fermín, 183, 185, 186, 187n6, 191, 191n9, 192
Delafosse, Maurice, 272, 272n2, 276, 276n5, 289
Delavignette, Robert, 272, 272n2
Deleuze, Gilles, 349, 374
Delgado, Noémia, 241
Delgado Rosa, Frederico, 23n27
Deloria, Ella, 326
Denby, David, 130, 132–134
Deng Xiaoping, 602
Denieuil, Pierre-Noël, 631
Dening, Greg, 560
Derrida, Jacques, 56, 90, 92, 349, 503
Desai, Akshay Ramanlal, 485
Desai, Morarji, 507
Desai, Neera, 497, 499
Descola, Philippe, 2, 12, 70, 76, 78, 87, 87n19, 89–91, 89n22, 419
Desvallées, André, 94n28
Desveaux, Emmanuel, 89, 90
Devereux, Georges, 100n38
Dewachi, Omar, 645
Diallo, Ousman Poréko, 279, 279n8
Diamond, Stanley, 339
Dias, António Jorge, 235
Dias, Jill, 243n19
Dias, Margot, 230, 236
Dias, Nélia, 245, 525, 528
Díaz, Porfirio, 444, 454
Dillingham, William P., 328

Dimpflmeier, Fabiana, 159, 160, 574
Di Nola, Alfonso M., 166
Dole, Christopher, 374
Domingos, Nuno, 246
Domínguez Gregorio, Ignacio, de, 186n4
Dorsey, J. Owen, 322
Douaihy, Chawki, 642, 643
Douglas, Bronwen, 555, 560, 561
Douglas, Mary, 55, 58n3, 59, 108
Doumer, Paul, 522, 523n4
Dozon, Jean Pierre, 85, 284
Dreyfus, Dina, 392n6
Driberg, Jack H., 51, 305
Dube, Leela, 488, 499, 500
Dube, Shyama Charan, 487, 488
Dullo, Eduardo, 23n27
Dumont, Louis, 63, 94n28, 494, 495, 606
Duque Gómez, Luis, 413
Durand, Jean-Yves, 245
Durão, Susana, 245
Duret, Evelyne, 99n37, 105
Durkheim, Émile, 53, 68, 70, 75, 82, 83, 87, 87n18, 90, 93, 94n26, 111, 276, 303, 495, 532, 550, 596, 637
Dussán, Alicia, 413, 417
Dussart, François, 562
Duvignaud, Jean, 630n12
Dyao, Yoro, 275, 276, 289

E

Edward VII, 309n8
Eickstedt, Egon von, 144
Eiselen, Werner Max, 311
El-Aswad, El-Sayyed, 637, 647
Elfimov, Alexei, 257, 260, 268
Elias, Norbert, 68, 128, 129, 134
Elkin, Adolphus P., 553, 553n3, 554
Ellen, Roy, 56

INDEX 663

Eltsin, Boris Nikolaevič, 268
Elwin, Verrier, 484, 485, 491–493
El-Zein, Abdul-Hamid, 637
Engelbrecht, Johannes Anthonie, 310
Engels, Friedrich, 255, 321, 601
Epstein, Arnold Leonard, 556
Epstein, Trude Scarlett, 556
Eriksen, Thomas H., 50, 226
Ernst, Thomas M., 559
Escobar, Arturo, 22–25, 85, 422, 427, 460, 462
Escobar, Pablo, 408
Esteva Fábregat, Claudio, 187, 200, 201n22, 202n26
Estévez González, Fernando, 186
Evans-Pritchard, Edward E., 51–53, 55, 57, 59, 63, 191, 197, 200, 261, 299, 300, 309, 309n8, 489, 555, 637, 639

F
Fabian, Johannes, 3, 605
Fabietti, Ugo, 6n3, 7, 49, 170, 171, 320
Fabre, Daniel, 76, 94n27, 96, 97n33, 100, 105, 105n47, 112
Fabre-Vassas, Claudine, 105n47
Fahim, Hussein, 28n35, 624, 638
Faidherbe, Louis, 275
Fairhead, James, 56
Falk Moore, Sally, 3, 4
Fals Borda, Orlando, 421, 422, 462
Fanon, Frantz, 9, 10, 92, 113, 455
Fassin, Didier, 83, 84, 100n38
Faubion, James, 348, 374
Favole, Adriano, 8, 39, 174
Favret-Saada, Jeanne, 93, 95n29
Fei Xiaotong, 39, 593, 594, 598–600, 603, 607
Feldman-Branco, Bela, 244n22
Ferguson, James, 24, 85, 365

Fernandes, Florestan, 393, 394n12
Fernandes, Margarida, 246
Fernández de Rota, José Antonio, 192, 200n20
Ferraz de Matos, Patrícia, 23n27
Ferro, António, 234
Fforde, Cressida, 12n11
Fialho Feliciano, José, 245
Finot, Luis, 522
Firth, Raymond, 51–53, 55, 67, 69, 553, 554, 575, 577, 582, 583, 594, 598
Firth, Rosemary, 52
Fischer, Michael, 144
Fisher, Eugen, 144
Fisher, Melissa, 336, 343, 348
Fison, Lorimer, 550
Flecther, Alice, 322
Florêncio, Fernando, 245
Forde, Daryl, 452
Fortes, Meyer, 49, 50, 52, 53, 55, 59, 67, 68, 301, 305, 309, 555
Fortune, Reo, 552, 553, 562
Foster, George, 197n17, 329
Foucault, Michel, 56, 70, 92, 113, 349, 349n3, 356, 364, 370, 427
Fournier, Laurent-Sébastien, 99n37
Foustel de Coulanges, Numa Denis, 232n7
Fradique, Teresa, 242, 246
Frake, Charles, 325
Frankenberg, Ronald, 56, 58n3
Frazão-Moreira, Amélia, 245
Frazer, James George, 50, 51, 232n7, 256, 540
Freedman, Maurice, 20, 55, 594, 609
Freyre, Gilberto, 233, 237, 390, 391n3, 392
Friede, Juan, 413, 416
Friedman, Jonathan, 352
Friedrich, P., 345n2
Frigolé, Joan, 200n21

664 INDEX

Frobenius, Leo, 140, 142, 143, 150
Fróis, Catarina, 245
Fu Sinian, 597
Fürer-Haimendorf, Christoph von, 55

G

Gaboriau, Patrick, 107
Gaddafi, Muammar, 634
Gaden, Henri, 272, 272n2, 275, 276, 276n5, 289
Gait, Edward, 476
Galal, Mohammad, 637, 637n16
Galera Gòmez, Andrés, 187
Galhano, Fernando, 236
Gallini, Clara, 167
Galván, Alberto, 200n20
Gamio, Manuel, 440, 441, 444–451, 454, 455, 457, 460
Gandhi, Mohandas Karamchand, 486, 501
Ganti, Tejaswini, 371, 371n11
García, Antonio, 414
García Gavidia, Nelly, 28
García Mora, Carlos, 441
García Villareal, Cesáreo, 450
Garma, Carlos, 442
Garralda Benajes, María Dolores, 187
Gaugin, Paul, 572
Geddes, Patrick, 479
Geertz, Clifford, 6, 9, 12, 61, 99, 149, 170, 261, 336–339, 342–344, 349, 350, 560, 632
Gellner, Ernest, 55, 56, 632
Gerholm, Tomas, 19
Gérome, Noëlle, 106n50
Ghazzal, Zouhair, 642
Ghurye, Govind Sadavish, 63, 479, 480, 482, 484, 485, 489, 491, 494
Giacometti, Michel, 238
Giddens, Anthony, 365, 366
Giglia, Angela, 174, 442

Gillen, Francis James, 550
Gilroy, Paul, 11
Gingrich, Andre, 16n15, 129, 133–138, 142, 144–146, 144n8, 149, 150
Girke, Felix, 147, 148
Glass, Philip, 225
Gleach, Frederic W., 16n16
Gledhill, John, 55
Glissant, Édouard, 11
Gluckman, Max, 53–55, 59, 64, 65, 304, 308–310, 312, 357, 556
Gobineau, Joseph Arthur de, 137
Godbout, Jacques T., 90
Godelier, Maurice, 75, 78, 90, 190, 263, 339
Godinho, Paula, 230, 234, 238, 240, 241, 245
Goffman, Erving, 111
Gold, Gerald L., 20n23
Goldenweizer, Alexander, 477
Golovnin, Vasilij Michajlovič, 252
Gomes Cardoso, Eduardo, 238
Gomes da Silva, José Carlos, 239n17, 240
Gómez García, Pedro, 187
Gómez-Pellón, Eloy, 187, 200
Gondola, Charles Didier, 284, 291n19
González Alcantud, José Antonio, 212n44
González Casanova, Pablo, 453, 454, 454n3
González Gamio, Ángeles, 447
Gonzalez, Lélia, 397
González Montero de Espinosa, Marisa, 187
González Velasco, Pedro, 194, 195
Goodenough, Ward, 325, 337
Goody, Jack, 55, 56, 66–68
Gordon, Robert, 54, 300–302, 301n3, 310, 311
Gouldner, Alvin Ward, 189
Gourou, Pierre, 526, 527

INDEX   665

Goy, Joseph, 104n44
Graeber, David, 58, 62, 104
Graebner, Fritz, 140–142
Gramsci, Antonio, 32, 70, 160, 164–167, 169, 349, 349n4, 355, 358, 364, 370, 500, 501
Granet, Marcel, 595
Granjo, Paulo, 245
Greenough, Paul, 506, 508
Gregory, Herbert, 582
Griaule, Marcel, 76, 281
Grignon, Claude, 106
Grimm, Jacob, 256
Grimm, Wilhelm, 256
Grottanelli, Vinigi L., 150n14, 159, 161, 170
Gruzinski, Serge, 102
Gu Jiegang, 597
Guattari, Félix, 349, 374
Gudeman, Stephen, 147
Gueusquin, Marie-France, 99n37, 105
Guggino, Elsa, 167
Guha, Biraja Sankar, 480
Guha, Ranajit, 485, 491, 493, 500–502, 504
Guha Thakurta, Tapati, 473
Guhl, Ernest, 413
Guiart, Jean, 575
Guidieri, Remo, 574
Guiteras, Calixta, 450
Guo Yaogen, 596
Guolo, Renzo, 79n6, 79n7, 84
Gupta, Akhil, 24, 351, 360, 365
Gupta, Dipankar, 506, 507
Gusman, Alessandro, 271
Gutiérrez, Virginia, 413
Gutwirth, Jacques, 107, 107n51
Guzmán, Antonio, 418–419

H
Haberland, Eike, 143, 145
Haberland, Michael, 596

Haddab, Mustapha, 628n11
Haddab, Mustaphas, 629
Haddon, Alfred Cort, 50, 192, 300–303, 550, 552, 573, 574
Hage, Ghassan, 643
Hale, Charles R., 457, 462
Hale, Horatio, 322
Hall, Stuart, 11, 109, 169
Hallowell, Irving, 13, 185, 449
Hama, Bobou, 277, 278, 280
Al-Hamamsy, Laila, 638
Hammami, Rima, 644
Hammoudi, Abdallah, 632
Hanafi, Sari, 621–625, 641
Handler, Richard, 351, 365
Hann, Chris, 146
Hannerz, Ulf, 2, 3, 14, 15, 19, 20, 146, 404, 599, 606
Haraway, Donna, 463
Hardiman, David, 500
Hardy, Georges, 276
Harré, John, 577
Harris, Marvin, 183, 185n2, 189, 327, 337
Harrison, Rodney, 12
Hart, David, 632
Hartman, Saidiya, 11
Hassoun, Jean-Pierre, 106, 107
Hau'ofa, Epeli, 570, 578, 579, 583–586, 588
Hays, Terrence, 555n5
Heaton Nicholls, George, 309n8
Heaton Nicholls, Ioma, 309
Heine-Geldern, Robert, 137, 138, 141, 142, 145, 150
Helepololei, Justin, 356n8
Hellman, Ellen, 304
Helu, Futa, 586
Helu Thaman, Konai, 579
Henry, William, 581
Herder, Johann Gottfried, 127–151, 537
Hereniko, Vilsoni, 579

666 INDEX

Héritier, Françoise, 75, 89, 90, 110
Hernández de Alba,
  Gregorio, 412–416
Herskovits, Melville, 150, 311, 323,
  391n5, 449–451
Herzfeld, Michael, 7n5, 348, 350,
  351, 354, 358–360, 365, 371
Hewitt, Cynthia, 449
Hilgers, Mathieu, 371n11
Hirsch, Eric, 371n11
Hitler, Adolf, 144
Ho Chi Minh, 518, 519n2, 525n5,
  529, 530n10, 532n14
Hoàng Xuân Hãn, 537
Hocart, Maurice, 550, 637
Hodson, Thomas, 305
Hoernlé, Agnes Winifred, 53, 54,
  303–305, 303n4
Hoernlé, Alfred, 303
Hogbin, Ian, 52
Holle, Paul, 275, 289
Holmes, Douglas, 365, 367
Hottin, Christian, 76, 97
Hountondji, Paulin, 284, 285, 292
Houphouët-Boigny, Félix, 287n17
Howard, Michael, 573–575, 577
Howitt, Alfred, 550
Hoyos Sainz, Luis de, 196
Huffer, Elise, 579
Humboldt, Wilhelm von, 135, 138,
  148n13, 149, 412
Humphrey, Caroline, 56
Hunter Wilson, Monica, 305, 307
Hussein, Saddam, 645
Husserl, Edmund, 537
Hutton, John H., 475, 479, 484
Huxley, Thomas H., 595
Huỳnh Tịnh Của, Paulus, 521
Hymes, Dell, 6, 13, 17, 17n19, 18,
  28n35, 336, 337

I

Ibbetson, Denzil, 472
Iglesias Ponce de León, María
  Josefa, 187
Inglis, Gordon, 20n23
Ingold, Tim, 55, 56, 70
Isaac, Rhys, 560
Isaacs, Jorge, 412
Isherwood, Baron, 108
Iyer, Ananthakrishna, 474, 475
Izard, Michel, 69, 87n20

J

Jabavu, David (son Don Tengo), 302
Jabavu, John Tengo, 302
Jacobson, Roman, 502
Jaramillo, Enrique, 404, 406,
  426, 427
Jeggle, Utz, 100
Jensen, Adolf, 143
Jézéquel, Jean-Hervé, 277n6,
  279, 281
Jiménez, Celeste, 211n34
Jones, Gaynor, 64
Jones, William, 199, 473
Joseph, Suad, 643
Julien, Marie-Pierre, 109
Junod, Henri-Alexandre, 300n2

K

Kaberry, Phyllis, 52
Kamenskii, Aleksandr
  Vladimirovic, 253
Kanaana, Sharif, 644
Kane, Abdoulaye, 276
Kane, Yahia, 276
Kant, Immanuel, 130, 132
Kardiner, Abraham, 150, 326

K

Karnoouh, Claude, 84
Karve, Irawati, 482, 483, 499
Kasarhérou, Emmanuel, 82
Keesing, Felix, 582
Keesing, Roger M., 337, 338, 561, 587
Keita, Madeira, 281, 282, 290
Kenyatta, Jomo, 304, 455
Kerchache, Jacques, 81n10
Kerney, Michael, 366
Kessler, Kim Andreas, 576, 577
Khlebnikov, Kirill, 252
Khouri, Fuad, 642, 643
Kialo, Paulin, 286
Kienle, Eberhardt, 621n4
Kilani, Mondher, 3n2
King, Charles, 311, 324, 326, 327
King, Martin Luther, 508, 509
Klemm, Gustav, 136, 149, 189
Kluckhohn, Clyde, 149, 150, 261
Knauft, Bruce, 555
Koch-Grünberg, Theodor, 412
Kopczyńska-Jaworska, Bronislawa, 20n23
Köpping, Klaus-Peter, 138
Kopytoff, Igor, 108
Korsbaek, Leif, 461, 461n8
Kouroma, Ahmadou, 11
Kramer, Jennifer, 12n9
Krige, Eileen, 303, 304
Kroeber, Alfred, 50, 149, 150, 192, 323, 325, 414, 452, 598
Kropotkin, Pëtr Alekseevič, 53
Krotkov, Nicolai N., 596
Krotz, Esteban, 27, 28, 404, 442, 443, 445n2, 447, 458, 459
Kryukov, Mikhail, 533
Kucklick, Henrika, 49
Kuper, Adam, 49, 52, 54, 57, 62, 65, 66, 70, 185, 289, 300, 301, 301n3, 305, 309, 312, 313
Kuper, Hilda, 66, 304, 308
Kuwayama, Takami, 25

L

Labouret, Henri, 272, 272n2, 276
La Fontaine, Jean, 55, 303
Laidlaw, James, 55, 56
Lallament, Emmanuelle, 77
Lamaison, Pierre, 84, 103, 105
Lambert, Helen, 56
Lameiras, José, 440
Landes, Ruth, 391, 391n5, 392n7
Lang, Andrew, 141n5, 256
Lanternari, Vittorio, 166
Lara, Agustín, 445
Latouche, Serge, 83
Latour, Bruno, 12, 13, 70, 83, 84, 91, 101, 108, 111
Lavigerie, Charles Martial Allemand, 273n4
Layard, John, 573
Lazarus, Moritz, 149
Le Breton, David, 104n44, 110
Le Meur, Pierre-Yves, 86n16
Le Wita, Béatrix, 106, 106n49
Leach, Edmund, 51–53, 55, 62, 67, 70, 261, 312, 365, 488
Leacock, Eleanor, 339, 500
Leal, João, 229, 231–233, 233n9, 237–241, 238n16, 243, 245
Lechner, Elsa, 246
Leenhardt, Maurice, 572, 573
Leiris, Michel, 76
Lelivai, Petelo, 579
Lenclud, Gérard, 76, 84, 99
León, Nicolás, 445–447
Lepoutre, David, 107
Leroi-Gourhan, André, 109
Leroy, Alexandre, 273n4
Lévi-Strauss, Claude, 6, 79n8, 83–85, 84n13, 87, 89–90, 89n21, 89n22, 92, 93, 96, 96n31, 103, 110, 189, 255, 256, 272n1, 338, 353, 391, 392n6, 419, 495, 532
Lévy-Bruhl, Lucien, 79, 261, 276, 583
Lévy, Paul, 526, 529

668 INDEX

Lewis, Ioan M., 67
Leyva, Xóchitl, 462
Li Anzhai, 598
Li Ji, 597
Liang Zhaotao, 602
Lienhardt, Ronald Godfrey, 639
Lima, Antónia, 242, 245
Lin Kaiqing, 596
Lin Shu, 596
Lin Yaohua, 598, 600
Ling Chunsheng, 597
Linton, Ralph, 326, 451
Lisón Tolosana, Carmelo, 187,
    200, 201n22
Lissouba, Pascal, 287
Llera Blanes, Ruy, 245
Llobera, Josep Romón, 183–185,
    185n3, 187–189, 188n7,
    188n8, 198
Lock, Margaret, 351n7
Löfgren, Orvar, 169
Lombard, Jacques, 280, 280n10
Lombardi Satriani, Luigi M.,
    166, 357n9
Lomnitz, Claudio, 371n11, 440, 443
London, Jack, 572
Lopes, Raimundo, 391
Loria, Lamberto, 159, 574
Lorimer, Frank, 452
Lounsbury, Floyd, 325
Lourenço, Eduardo, 233
Lowie, Robert, 49, 136, 150, 189,
    192, 323, 325, 414, 598
Loyo, Engracia, 449
Lydall, Jean, 147

M
M'ba, Léon, 274
Macdonald, Charles, 76, 77n2, 86–88
Mac-Duong, 532, 533
MacFarlane, Alan, 56

Machado Álvarez, Antonio, 194, 195
Machado Núñez, Antonio, 194
Maconi, Vittorio, 170
Madan, Triloki Nath, 481, 482, 495
Mafeje, Archibald, 284, 289, 307, 308
Magalhães Godinho, Vitorino, 240
Magubane, Bernard, 308
Maher, Vanessa, 68
Māhina, 'Okustino, 586
Mahmood, Saba, 368, 368n10, 369
Maine, Henry J.S., 49
Mair, Lucy, 51, 52, 304
Majumdar, Dhirendra Nath, 470n1,
    480, 481, 484
Malighetti, Roberto, 39, 40, 171, 599,
    605, 606
Malinowski, Bronislaw, 2, 3, 39,
    50–53, 55, 66, 71, 149, 236,
    261, 299n1, 304, 305, 311,
    311n9, 312, 327, 421, 550–552,
    574, 575, 577, 582, 584, 593,
    594, 598, 601, 609
Malleret, Luis, 525
Mammeri, Mouloud, 628
Manchuelle, François, 274
Mandal, Bindeshwari Prasad, 507
Mandela, Nelson, 302, 306, 307, 314
Mantegazza, Paolo, 159
Mapril, José, 245
Marcus, George, 336, 343–346,
    348, 367
Mariner, William, 571
Marouf, Nadir, 628n11
Marques Alves, Vera, 245
Marques, Emília M., 245
Marrett, Robert Ranulph, 552
Marriot, McKim, 487
Martial, Charles, 273n4
Martins, Humberto, 243, 245
Marwick, Max, 58n3
Marx, Karl, 255, 321
Massignon, Louis, 637n16

INDEX 669

Matera, Vincenzo, 3, 13, 16n15, 149, 170, 171, 174, 225n1
Mathew, Gordon, 27n34
Matínez Veiga, Ubaldo, 185, 187
Matos Viegas, Susana, 230, 245
Matri, Khaoula, 631
Matthews, Zachariah Keodirelang, 304, 306, 307
Mauss, Marcel, 62, 68, 75, 79, 79n7, 82, 83, 90, 93, 94n28, 109, 111, 540, 637, 637n16
Mawyer, Alexander, 570n2
Mayer, Iona, 307, 308, 315n11
Mayer, Philip, 307, 308, 315n11
Mazumdar, Vina, 499
Mbeki, Govan, 307
Mbeki, Thabo, 314
Mbembe, Achille, 2, 9–11, 11n8, 272, 285n15, 286, 291, 291n19
Mbot, Jean-Émile, 286n16
McCall, Grant, 578
Mead, Margaret, 53, 326, 553, 577
Mechthild, Rutsch, 445
Medeiros, António, 187n6, 245
Medina San Román, María del Carmen, 187
Medina, Andrés, 441, 458, 459
Meillassoux, Claude, 75, 263, 339
Meiners, Christoph, 189
Melnikova, Ekaterina, 262
Melville, Herman, 572
Memmi, Albert, 455
Mencius (Meng-Tzu), 537
Mendes Correia, António Augusto, 235, 235n11, 237
Mendes, Paulo, 246
Meneses, Inês, 246
Menon, Achuta, 474
Mercier, Paul, 192, 280, 280n10
Merleau-Ponty, Maurice, 90
Mernissi, Fatima, 632
Mesquitela Lima, Augusto, 239

Meyer, Christian, 147, 147n11, 148
Miani, Giovanni, 159
Michaud, Jean, 535, 536n21
Miller Macmillan, William, 306
Miller, Daniel, 70, 109
Mills, David, 49, 58, 64
Mintz, Sidney, 338–340, 352
Mitchell, J. Clyde, 54, 65
Mitra, Ramesh Chandra, 473
Modi, Jivanji Jamshedji, 473
Modigliani, Elio, 159
Mohsen, Safia, 637
Molina Enríquez, Andrés, 445, 446, 448, 451
Mommsem, Theodor, 232n7
Monod, Theodore, 279, 280, 280n10
Montagu, Ashley, 51
Monteil, Charles, 272, 272n2
Mooney, James, 322
Moore, Henrietta, 55–57
Mora, Carlos García, 441
Morant, Geoffrey, 481
Moreno, Isidoro, 198, 200n20, 200n21, 201n22
Morgan, Lewis Henry, 49, 50, 136, 192, 255, 289, 320, 321, 446, 550, 596, 601
Mosonyi, Esteban Emilio, 28
Mosse, David, 56
Mota Santos, Paula, 245
Mouna, Khalid, 633
Mudimbe, Valentin Y., 273, 273n3, 285n15
Muehlebach, Andrea, 374
Mukerji, Dhurjati Prasad, 481, 482
Mukherjee, Radhakamal, 480
Mukherjee, Ramkrishna, 470n1
Mukhlinov, Anatolij I., 534–536, 538
Muller, Max, 256
Murdock, George, 575
Murguía, Manuel, 194
Murray, Gilbert, 552n2

670 INDEX

Murray, Hubert, 550–553
Mussolini, Benito, 160
Mutis, José Celestino, 412

N

Na'amneh, Mahmoud, 637n15, 640, 641
Nadel, Siegfried, 51, 145, 639
Nagao, Ariga, 596
Nagpur, Chota, 475–477, 480, 493
Najar, Sihem, 631
Nakhleh, Khalil, 644
Napoleon Bonaparte, 273n4
Napoleon III, 521
Narotsky, Susana, 23n26
Nash, June, 339, 340
Nashif, Ismail, 644
Nassau, Robert Hamill, 274
Nasser, Jamal Abdel, 637, 638
Natrajan, Balmurli, 506, 508
Nayacakalou, Rusiate, 575, 584
Needham, Rodney, 55, 57, 312
Nehru, Jawaharlal, 486, 491–493, 501
Nencel, Lorraine, 345n2
Ner, Marcel, 529
Ngarongo-ki-tua, 581
Ngata, Apirana, 581–583
Ngô Đình Diệm, 532n14
Ngubane, Harriet, 308, 313
Nguyễn Phuong Ngoc, 520, 521, 537, 538
Nguyễn Thiệu Lâu, 526
Nguyen Van Chinh, 521, 531, 533, 534, 534n17, 541
Nguyen Van Huy, 541
Nguyễn Văn Huyên, 526, 529, 541
Nguyễn Văn Khoan, 526
Nguyen Van Ngoc, 527, 529
Nguyen Van Nguyen, 529
Nguyễn Văn Tố, 526
Nguyễn Văn Vĩnh, 526
Nielsen, Finn S., 50
Nimuendaju, Curt, 390

Nina Rodrigues, Raymundo, 389, 391
Nkwi, Nchoji Paul, 23n26, 282, 282n11, 284
Nogueira, Oracy, 391n4
Nolasco, Margarita, 454
Nora, Pierre, 112
Norton, William Alfred, 300, 301n3
Nyamongo, Isaac, 23n27

O

Ochoa, Blanca, 413
Oliveira Martins, Joaquim Pedro de, 235
Oliver, Douglas, 575
Olivera, Mercedes, 454
O'Neill, Brian, 241
Oneto Nunes, Francisco, 246
Ong, Aihwa, 351
Opler, Morris, 488
Orozco, José Clemente, 444
Ortiz García, Carmen, 182, 186, 186n5, 187, 192, 197n16
Ortner, Sherry, 336, 349, 350, 351n6, 352, 358, 360, 372, 373
Osella, Filippo, 68
Ouattara, Fatoumata, 290
Ould Bah, Mohamed Fall, 636
Ould-al-Bara, Yahya, 635
Ouologuem, Yambo, 11

P

Pacheco de Oliveira, João, 394, 397, 398
Paci, Enzo, 171
Padez, Cristina, 246
Pais de Brito, Joanna, 241
Palerm, Ángel, 192, 204n27, 442
Palmeira, Moacir, 395
Palmeirim, Manuela, 245
Palumbo, Berardino, 22n25, 29, 30n38, 36, 161, 173, 345, 347, 372n12

INDEX 671

Palvadre, M. Iu., 258
Pan Guangdan, 600
Pandey, Gyanendra, 500
Pardo, Mauricio, 426, 427
Parkin, Robert, 16n15, 75n1
Pascon, Paul, 630n12, 632
Passeron, Jean-Claude, 106
Patel, Sujata, 496, 498, 499
Patterson, Thomas, 335, 336, 338,
  339, 344, 347
Paulme, Denise, 281
Peirano, Mariza, 390n1, 391n4, 393
Peixoto da Rocha, António
  Augusto, 234
Pels, Peter, 345n2, 528, 540
Penda, Fara, 275
Pennacini, Cecilia, 170
Peralta, Elsa, 245
Pereira Bastos, José Gabriel, 239
Pereira, Benjamin Enes, 236, 237, 241
Pereira, Pedro, 245
Pereira, Rui, 235, 235n12, 242, 245
Pereiro, Xerardo, 245
Pérez, Andrea, 418, 429, 430
Perez, Rosa, 239–241, 245
Perrot, Martine, 104n44, 109n57
Peters, Emrys, 55
Pétonnet, Colette, 93, 107, 107n51
Pettazzoni, Raffaele, 160
Phan Bội Châu, 530n9, 537, 537n23
Phan Châu Trinh, 537, 537n23
Phan Hữu Dật, 534
Piaggia, Carlo, 159
Pignatelli, Marina, 230, 241, 245
Pina-Cabral, João de, 24, 225n1,
  228–230, 237, 241, 244n22,
  245, 247
Pinçon-Charlot, Monique, 106n49
Pinçon, Michel, 106n49
Pineda Giraldo, Roberto, 413, 414
Pinelli, Barbara, 344, 368n10
Pinto, Ambrose, 506
Pitrè, Giuseppe, 159, 167
Pitt-Rivers, George, 552

Pitt-Rivers, Julian, 197n17, 198,
  198n18, 552
Pizza, Giovanni, 30n38, 164, 351n7
Pocock, David, 494, 495
Polanyi, Karl, 60, 62
Poppi, Cesare, 68
Portal, María Ana, 459
Porto, Nuno, 235, 242, 245
Pouillon, Jean, 96n31, 99
Povinelli, Elizabeth, 13, 14, 375
Powdermaker, Hortense, 51, 52
Powell, John Wesley, 321, 322, 327
Pozdneev, Alexaner, 596
Prat Carós, Joan, 182, 186, 186n5,
  187, 187n6, 192, 194, 197
Preuss, Konrad T., 412
Primo de Rivera, José
  Antonio, 193n10
Prista, Pedro, 245
Propp, Vladimir, 34, 255, 256
Puccini, Sandra, 159, 574
Puig-Samper Mulero, Miguel
  Ángel, 186n4
Pujol i Sanmartín, J.M., 187

Q
Quintais, Luís, 245
Quintela, M. Manuel, 246

R
Rachik, Hassan, 621, 625, 632, 633
Radcliffe-Brown, Alfred Reginald, 3,
  4, 35, 49, 52–54, 63, 67, 70,
  300–306, 309, 311, 311n9,
  315n11, 327, 392n6, 489, 553,
  554, 574, 575, 602, 637
Radi, Saadia, 633
Radin, Paul, 583
Ramírez, Xóchitl, 459
Ramos, Arthur, 389, 391n5
Ramos, Manuel J., 245
Ramos, Samuel, 444

672 INDEX

Ramphele, Mamphela, 313, 314, 315n11
Raposo, Paulo, 246
Rappaport, Roy, 337, 421, 422
Al-Rasheed, Madawi, 646
Ratzel, Friedrich, 138n3, 139, 139n4, 140, 142
Reche, Otto, 144
Redfield, Robert, 160, 241, 451, 452, 487
Reichel-Dolmatoff, Gerardo, 413, 417–420, 420n2
Remotti, Francesco, 3, 50, 128, 130, 149, 170, 171, 570
Renan, Joseph-Ernest, 232n7
Rendón Monzón, Juan José, 461n8
Reshetov, Leonid, 262
Restrepo, Eduardo, 27, 28, 28n35, 404, 415, 426–428, 430
Reygadas, Luis, 440, 442, 443, 459
Reynolds, Henry, 559
Rezanov, Nikolaij Pavlovic, 252
Rhani, Zakaria, 633
Ribeiro, Darcy, 394
Ribeiro, Gustavo Lins, 22–25, 23n26, 23n27, 404
Ribeiro, Orlando, 236, 238n16
Ribeiro, René, 389
Ricci, Antonello, 166n2
Riccio, Bruno, 68, 174n5
Richards, Audrey, 51, 52, 304
Ridington, Robin, 13n13
Risley, Herbert, 472, 474, 478, 480
Rival, Lara, 70
Rivera, Diego, 444
Rivers, William H. R., 49, 50, 52, 63, 302, 303, 479, 550, 551, 573, 574
Rivet, Paul, 80, 87, 94n28, 413, 415, 525, 527, 528
Rivière, George-Henri, 80, 93, 94n28, 96

Robbins, Joel, 373, 561
Robinson, Kathryn, 557
Robinson-Pant, Anna, 27n34
Rodney, Walter, 285n13
Rodríguez Becerra, S., 187
Rogers, Susan Carol, 76, 93, 101n39, 102, 103
Rojas, Axel, 404, 426–428
Roosevelt, Theodore, 328
Roquette-Pinto, Edgar, 389
Rorty, Richard, 349
Rosa, Frederico, 245
Rosaldo, Renato, 2n1, 366, 606
Rosales, Marta, 245, 246
Rose, Frederick, 556
Roseberry, William, 339, 345n2
Rosselin, Céline, 109
Rossi, Annabella, 166, 173
Rossi, Pietro, 128, 130, 149, 171
Rousseau, Jean-Jacques, 537
Rousseau, Raymond, 275
Rowley, Charles Dunford, 559
Roy, Rai Bahadur Sarat Chandra, 474–477, 480
Ruggles Gates, Reginald, 481
Ruiz Trejo, Marisa, 463
Rumsey, Alan, 559n10
Rushefort, Scott, 13n13
Rutsch, Mechthild, 445, 446

S
Saberwal, Satish, 20n23
Sahlins, Marshall, 62, 352, 353, 355, 370–372, 388, 561, 584
Said, Edward, 2n1, 8, 500, 502
Salazar, António de Oliveira, 33, 235n11, 247
Salim, Shakir Mustapha, 645
San Román, Teresa, 200n20
Sánchez Montañés, Emma, 187
Sanchez, Iñigo, 245

Sánchez-Gómez, Luis Ángel, 182, 186, 186n5, 192, 195n12
Sanchis, Pierre, 241
Sandoval, Prudencio de, 412
Sanga, Glauco, 174
Sangari, Kumkum, 498, 499
Sangreen, Paul Steven, 345n2
Sanjek, Roger, 345n2, 348
Sanmartín, Ricardo, 200n20, 201
Santos, Gonçalo D., 245
Saouter, Anne, 110
Sapir, Edward, 150, 323, 598
Saraiva, Clara, 232n5, 237, 242, 245
Sarana, Gopala, 471, 481
Sardan, Jean Pierre Oliver de, 85, 85n14, 85n15, 86n16, 283, 284, 290, 291
Sardo, Susana, 246
Sarkar, Sumit, 504
Sarkozy, Nicolas, 82
Sariego, Juan Luis, 442, 458
Sarr, Felwine, 11
Sarr, Jean-Pierre, 276n5
Sarraut, Albert, 524
Sarró, Ramon, 245
Sassou Nguesso, Denis, 287
Saunders, George R., 159, 161, 167
Schapera, Isaac, 51–54, 67, 302–305, 308, 309
Scheper-Hughes, Nancy, 11n6, 351n7, 362–364
Schirripa, Pino, 171
Schlee, Günter, 146
Schmidt, Wilhelm, 141, 141n6, 145, 273n4, 283
Schneider, David, 337
Schneider, Jane, 339, 340
Schneider, Peter, 339, 340
Schoeman, Pieter J., 311
Schumaker, Lyn, 290, 309n7
Schurtz, Heinrich, 143
Schwartz, Olivier, 107

Schweitzer, Albert, 261
Scoditti, Giancarlo, 574
Scollon, Ronald, 13n13
Scott, James, 356–360
Seabra, Daniel, 245, 246
Sebag, Paul, 630, 630n12
Sedas Nunes, Adérito, 238, 239
Segalen, Martine, 93, 94, 94n28, 95n29, 95n30, 100, 103, 107, 108, 110–112
Segalen, Victor, 572
Seixas, Paulo C., 246
Seler, Eduard, 446, 448
Seligman, Brenda, 639
Seligman, Charles George, 50, 51, 300, 550, 552, 639
Seppilli, Tullio, 162, 168, 172, 173n4
Sharp, John, 310, 312
Shah, Arvind M., 473, 491
Shami, Seteney, 621, 623–626, 638, 640
Shapera, Isaac, 303
Shirokogorov, Sergei M., 254
Shryock, Andrew, 348, 361
Sibeud, Emanuelle, 272n1, 272n2
Sidibé, Mamby, 277–280
Sigaud, Lygia, 395
Signorelli, Amalia, 168, 174
Signorini, Italo, 170
Silva, Luís, 245
Silva Pereira, Luís, 246
Silvano, Filomena, 246
Silverman, Sydel, 323, 334n1, 336
Simonicca, Alessandro, 171, 173, 174
Singh, Manmohan, 508
Sinha, Dharni P., 471, 479
Sinha, Surajiit, 470n1
Siqueiros, David Alfaro, 444
Sire-Abbas-Soh, 276
Skinner, Henry, 574
Smart, Josephine, 23n26
Smith Bowen, Eleonore, 59

674 INDEX

Smith, Percy, 581
Smuts, Jan, 300, 301, 305
Sobhuza II, 304
Sobral, José, 229, 230, 234, 235, 237, 245, 246
Sobrero, Alberto, 170, 174
Sobukwe, Robert, 306
Soeiro de Brito, Raquel, 239
Solinas, Pier Giorgio, 167
Sorrenson, Maurice P. K., 581–583
Spate, Oskar H.K., 571
Speed, Shannon, 462
Spencer, Baldwin, 550
Spencer, Herbert, 596
Spencer, Jonathan, 49, 56, 71, 345n2
Spiegel, Mugsy, 312
Spiro, Melford E., 2n1
Spivak, Gayatri Chakravorty, 500–504
Spradley, James, 337
Srinivas, Mysore Narasimhachar, 62, 63, 65, 471, 474, 485, 487–491
Stalin, Josif Vissarionovič, 601
Starobinski, Jean, 90
Stavenhagen, Rodolfo, 199, 453, 454
Steiner, George, 149
Steinthal, Heymann, 149
Sternberg, Lev Y., 253–255
Stevenson, Robert Louis, 572
Steward, Julian, 339, 413
Stocking, George W., 14, 17, 17n18, 18, 18n20, 19n21, 20, 21, 24, 50, 138, 149, 183, 191, 233, 404, 440
Stolcke, Verena, 184, 187, 188n7, 189, 365
Strathern, Marilyn, 55, 56, 70, 111, 555
Strecker, Ivo, 127–151
Stuart Mill, John, 188n7
Subramani, 579
Suharto, Haji Mohammad, 557
Sukarno, Akmed, 557
Sulayman al-Oweis, Amal, 635

Sun Xuewu, 596
Sun Zhongshan, see Sun Yat-sen

T
Tabishat, Mohammed, 640, 641
Tamagnini, Eusébio, 235n11
Tambiah, Stanley Jeyaraja, 58n3
Tambo, Olivier, 306, 307
Tarawneh, Mohammed, 640, 641
Taussig, Michael, 348, 352, 362
Tawney, Richard, 602
Teissonnières, Gilles, 108n55
Teixeira, Vasco V., 246
Tengan, Ty Kāwika, 587–589
Tentori, Tullio, 160, 168
Terray, Emmanuel, 69, 339
Terrolle, Daniel, 107
Thomas, Nicholas, 561, 571
Thoresen, Timothy, 18
Thurnwald, Richard, 451
Thyssen, Xavier, 634
Tishkov, Valerii A., 261, 262, 264–266
Tohme Tabet, Annie, 643
Tonda, Joseph, 286–288, 286n16, 290
Tonkinson, Robert, 559, 561
Torii, Ryuzo, 596
Tornatore, Jean-Louis, 98n35, 112
Torres, Alberto, 392n8
Torres, Camillo, 421
Torres, Heloísa Alberto, 391, 392, 392n8
Toschi, Paolo, 160
Toussaint, Sandy, 23n26
Trần Văn Giáp, 526, 527, 529
Traoré, Dominique, 278–280
Tréfaut, Sérgio, 237n14
Tremblay, Marc-Adélard, 20n23
Trilles, Henri, 274
Trouillot, Michel-Ralph, 28n35, 288
Truong Huyen Chi, 540
Trương Vĩnh Ký, Pétrus, 521

INDEX 675

Tsing, Ana, 346, 367
Tumiña, Francisco, 416
Turner, Victor, 58, 60–62, 64, 65, 111
Tutu, Desmond, 306
Tyler, Stephen, 147, 337
Tylor, Edward B., 50, 50n2, 52, 128,
  148, 149, 192, 194, 232n7

U

Uberoi, Patricia, 470, 483
Ulin, Robert, 342, 345n2
Uribe, Maria Victoria, 404, 426
Urla, Jacqueline, 356n8
Utekhin, Ilya, 261

V

Vaid, Sudesh, 498, 499
Vakhtin, Nikolai, 23n26
Vale de Almeida, Miguel, 228, 242,
  243, 244n22
Valencia, Enrique, 454
Valeri, Valerio, 574
Valladares, Laura, 462
Valsecchi, Pierluigi, 271
Van Eeden, Bernardus Isak
  Christiaan, 310
Van Gennep, Arnold, 93, 94n28, 111
Van Warmelo, Nicholas, 310
Vansina, Jan, 67
Varagnac, André, 93
Vasco Uribe, Luis Guillermo, 422
Vasconcelos, João, 242, 245
Vasconcelos, José, 444
Vasconcelos, José Leite de, 232
Vasconcelos, Luís, 242
Vayda, Andrew, 337
Vaz da Silva, Francisco, 245
Vázquez León, Luis, 442, 443, 446,
  447, 457n4, 458
Veiga de Oliveira, Ernesto, 229,
  236, 241

Velasco Maíllo, Honorio Manuel, 187
Velho, Otávio Guilherme,
  20n23, 23n26
Verde, Filipe, 245
Verdier, Yvonne, 105n47
Verret, Michel, 106
Vespeira de Almeida, Sónia, 246
Viazzo, Pier Paolo, 68, 158, 159, 161,
  163, 172
Vidal, Frédéric, 245
Vidyarthi, Lalita Prasad, 470n1,
  480, 486
Viellard, Gilbert, 272
Vilakasi, Absolom, 308
Visvanathan, Shiv, 23n26
Viqueira, Carmen, 204n27
Virchow, Rudolf, 138, 139, 150
Viveiros de Castro, Eduardo, 12
Võ Nguyên Giáp, 527, 527n6, 530n9

W

Wagley, Charles, 391, 391n5
Wagner, Roy, 555
Waitz, Theodor, 136, 149, 150
Wallerstein, Immanuel, 340, 365
Wang, Shunan, 595
Warman, Arturo, 441, 454,
  457, 457n4
Warman, Enrique Valencia, 454
Warnier, Jean-Pierre, 101, 108, 109
Weber, Florence, 84, 94n26, 94n27,
  103, 106, 111
Weber, Max, 338, 349, 478, 602
Webster, David, 313
Wei Yi, 596
Weiner, James, 559, 559n10
Wendt, Albert, 579
Werbner, Pnina, 70
West, Martin, 307n5, 312
West, Robert, 452
Westermarck, Edward
  Alexander, 51, 300

676 INDEX

White, Geoffrey M., 586, 588, 589
Whitehouse, Harvey, 56
Wild, Stephen A., 272
William I (Wilhelm I), King of
Prussia, 129
Williams, Francis Edgar, 552, 562
Williams, Raymond, 109
Williams, Thomas, 571
Wilson, Godfrey, 306, 308
Wiser, William Henricks, 487
Wissler, Clark, 150
Wittgenstein, Ludwig, 349
Wolf, Eric, 145, 336, 338–343, 345,
351–353, 356, 365
Worsley, Peter, 58n3, 556, 575
Wu Wenzao, 593, 594, 598–600, 607
Wu Zelin, 600
Wundt, Wilhelm, 137

X
Xavier Inda, Jonathan, 366

Y
Yamani, Mai, 646
Yamashita, Shinji, 23n26
Yang Chengzhi, 600
Yeltsin, Boris Nikolaevič, 267

Z
Zagoskin, Lavrenty A., 253
Zeleza, Paul, 283–286, 292
Zerilli, Filippo, 19n21, 87n18
Ziervogel, Dirk, 310
Zolotarev, David A., 254
Al-Zuabi, Ali, 621, 625

Printed in the United States
by Baker & Taylor Publisher Services